# A Brief History of Photography

*From the Very Beginning
to the Age of Digital*

David S. Young

rockynook

**A Brief History of Photography**
David Young
https://furnfeather.ca/Stories.html

Project editor: Maggie Yates
Project manager: Lisa Brazieal
Marketing manager: Koryn Olage
Proofreader: Michelle Drown
Interior design and layout: Kim Scott/Bumpy Design
Cover design: Amy Degrote

ISBN: 979-8-88814-306-3
1st Edition (1st printing, February 2025)
© 2025 David Young

Rocky Nook Inc.
1010 B Street, Suite 350
San Rafael, CA 94901
USA

www.rockynook.com

Distributed in the U.K. and Europe by Publishers Group UK
Distributed in the U.S. and all other territories by Publishers Group West

Library of Congress Control Number: 2024942835

**Dedicated to the memories of**
**Ted Grant**
**and**
**Tom Abrahamsson**

*Both giants in their fields . . . and friends.*

# Contents

# Preface

This *Brief History of Photography*, at over 360 pages, doesn't seem particularly brief. The name comes from the brief nature of the entries, for they must be short to cover virtually every aspect of photography in the last 400+ years.

I began this project in 2004, intended as a three-to-four-page appendix for a book that was never written. It then took on a life of its own and the research consumed much of the next 16 years of my life. My journey ended in 2020, as it must end somewhere. Still, a few minor additions were made during the editing process, to keep it as "up to date" as possible.

The goal was not to compile an encyclopedia of every camera ever made, though it sometimes feels like that, but to include the seminal cameras . . . those that were first to have a certain feature which then went on to influence the development of cameras in general; or those, like the Pentax Spotmatic or the Nikon F, neither of which were first with anything, but both of which influenced camera development forever after. Likewise, significant inventors, lenses, and their designers, as well as a few of the major magazines and photographers, have been included to give a clear, overall picture of how photography has developed.

Please note that prices, unless otherwise indicated, are in U.S. dollars and not all are exact today, as many were converted during different years of the research. Thus, allowances must be made for differing exchange rates over nearly two decades. But I think you will find they are all "close enough for government work."

Dates of birth and death of the various persons referred to in the book (where known) are noted only in the first mention of that person.

Last, but by no means least, this book would simply not have been possible were it not for the incredible and unwavering support of David Scollard and his dear wife, Rose. David's extensive skills as an editor are very much appreciated.

I want also to acknowledge the patience and understanding of my own wife, also a Rose, without whose ongoing love and support I'd not manage anything.

David Young
Logan Lake, Canada 2024

# Introduction

I'd like to tell you about one of the truly great innovators of our time.

He was a college dropout yet had the ability to foresee products that the public did not even know they wanted. He built a massively successful technology firm that employed tens of thousands, which was fuelled by remarkable innovations. By the time of his death, he had collected over 500 patents. He was a driven man who worked hard, drove his employees hard and seldom listened to advice from others.

He was famous for nearly always wearing the same clothes and for his marathon work sessions. He was obsessed by innovation, and designed products that were as beautiful as they were useful.

Not only was he a great innovator, but he also understood his market and how to promote his products so that they became "must have" items. He was the first to release new creations in major magazines rather than to the specialist or trade press. He was a master of publicity, sometimes appearing on the covers of those same magazines.

He wasn't afraid to fail . . . but his board of directors were not so forgiving and eventually they fired him from the company he'd created.

By now you are probably thinking that I'm talking about Apple's legendary CEO, Steve Jobs (1955–2011), and I could be. After all, much, if not most, of what I have written is true of Jobs.

But the man I'm talking about is Edwin Land (1909–1991), the creator of both the first practical polarizing films for sunglasses and the revolutionary Picture-in-a-Minute cameras that bore his name.

And Jobs so admired Land that he once described meeting his hero being "like visiting a shrine."

The history of photography is filled with many such people. Some of them invented films and developers, while others designed cameras, lenses, and accessories. Some made fortunes, while others lost them. These people—and their inventions—make a fascinating and remarkable story.

# The Early Years

*There are many contenders for the title of "first" or "inventor" in photography. Many of these "photo-alchemists" were working, in separate places, on similar or even identical ideas or methods at the same time. Similarly, many talented designers and inventors are responsible for the cameras, lenses, films, and chemistry that make modern photography possible. They all stood on the shoulders of those who came before them. The history of photography is the story of how all these people and their inventions came together to make photography what it is today.*

"If pictures of an illuminated object enter a dark room through a small hole, they may be captured on white paper, at a specific distance from the hole. They permit identification of the objects in their true colours and shape." So wrote Leonardo da Vinci (1452–1519) about the camera obscura.

The camera obscura, first mentioned by Aristotle in 330 BC as an aid in observing solar eclipses, is first fully described by Italian Giovanni Battista della Porta (1535–1615) in 1558. In his book *Magiae Naturalis* (*Natural Magic*), della Porta specifies that a round hole be installed in the shutter of a darkened room and that the image be shown on a white screen. He tells how the image would appear upside down and reversed from left to right and would be proportional in size to the distance from the hole to the viewing screen. All these observations are true for today's cameras as well.

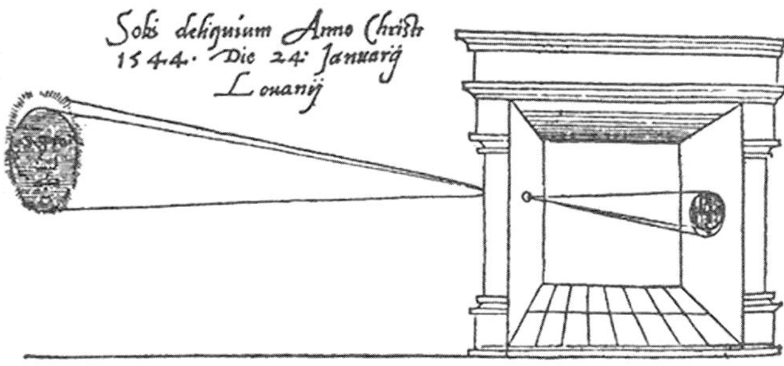

*The first published picture of a Camera Obscura, from Gemma Frisius' 1545 book,* De Radio Astronomica et Geometrica.

Della Porta suggests that the image can be used as a guide for drawing and goes on to invent a method for producing an erect image using simple lenses and curved mirrors. With this apparatus, he astonishes friends with images of elaborate theatrical productions staged outside—and is accused of sorcery for his troubles!

In his 1567 work *La Pratica della Perspettiva*, a Venetian nobleman, Daniele Barbaro (1514–1570), describes using a camera obscura with a biconvex lens as a drawing aid, and points out that the picture is more vivid if the lens "is covered as much as possible to leave a circumference in the middle." It is the first known use of an aperture or diaphragm to control aberrations in lenses. Though few Renaissance artists will admit they use a camera obscura as a drawing aid, it is thought that many if not most of them probably do. Their reasons for not openly admitting it are either the fear of being charged, like della Porta, with sorcery or witchcraft; or simply not wanting to admit to what many artists see as "cheating."

The oldest known optic is the Nimrud lens, from Assyria, dating between 750 and 710 BC. It is made from a polished crystal, most likely quartz. The lens is slightly oval and is roughly ground. It has a focal point about 11 centimetres (4.5 inches) from the flat side and a focal length of about 12 centimetres, making it the rough equivalent of a 3× magnifying glass. The lens apparently can focus sunlight, although the focus is far from perfect. If you're interested, you can find the lens on display in the British Museum, London.

The manufacture of glass is known to the Egyptians by about 3,000 BC and is further perfected by the Phoenicians, who are credited with the invention of the glass blowpipe. During Roman times, glassmaking is elevated to an art form. Yet even in the 16th century, glass, even window glass, is a huge luxury. However, glass lenses are not created until the Middle Ages (500–1500). It is thought that they are used either as magnifying glasses or as a burning-glass to start fires by concentrating sunlight. By the 13th century, simple biconvex lenses are known, and eventually used in camera obscuras.

Camera evolution proves to be rapid. In the 15th century, the brightness and clarity of the camera obscura is improved by enlarging the hole and inserting a lens. Smaller models are designed, which allow the operator to view or trace the image from outside the main enclosure. Finally, completely portable cameras appear. In 1676, a reflex version, in which the image is reflected onto a top-mounted viewing screen by a polished metal mirror inclined at 45°, is built (they are replaced with better, silvered glass mirrors soon after their invention in 1835). A ball and socket mount (similar to modern tripod heads) appears in 1680 and even a "long-focus" (telephoto) lens is fitted to a camera obscura in 1685. The camera is ready, but for what?

The discoveries in chemistry will take a wee bit longer . . .

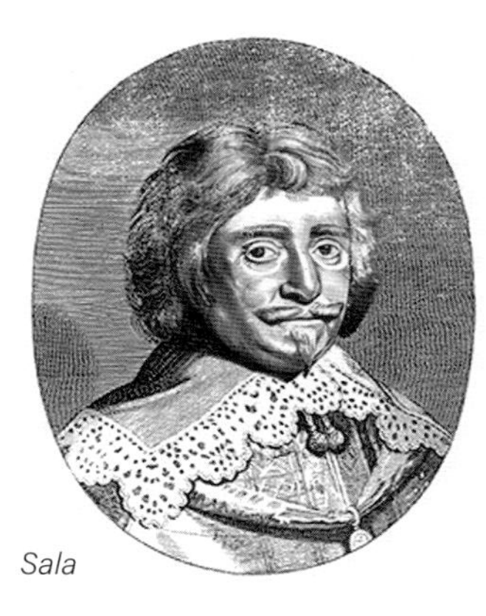

*Sala*

**1614:** A self-educated Italian doctor, Angelo Sala (1576–1637), publishes a paper noting that silver nitrate salts turn black when exposed to the sun, but attributes the effect to the heat rather than the light of the sun. Some time later, the same observation is made by Englishman Robert Boyle (1627–1691), who erroneously attributes the reaction to contact with air, not sunlight. In the late 1600s, William Homberg (1652–1715) will observe the same reaction, but, like Sala, attributes it to the heat of the sun.

**1664–66:** Sir Isaac Newton (1643–1727) discovers that sunlight is composed of different colours when he refracts white light with a prism, resolving it into its component colours: red, orange, yellow, green, blue, indigo, and violet.

**1676:** Johann Sturm (1636–1703) of Germany describes the first known use of a reflex mirror in a camera obscura.

**1685:** Johann Zahn (1641–1707) of Karlstadt am Main, Germany, develops a portable camera obscura with a focusing lens, an adjustable aperture and a translucent viewing screen which shows an image reflected by a mirror—all the core elements of a modern SLR camera except, of course, the shutter and film or, these days, a digital sensor.

**1727:** An absent-minded German doctor, Johann Heinrich Schulze (1687–1744), leaves a flask filled with a mixture of chalk, silver, and nitric acid by his laboratory window and finds that it turns deep purple. Coating some paper with the mixture gives the same result. He cuts a stencil and produces photographic lettering for the amusement of his friends. Sadly, the image disappears after a short while and he never learns why it appears or fades. However, by using the stencil, he does create the first form of non-permanent photography.

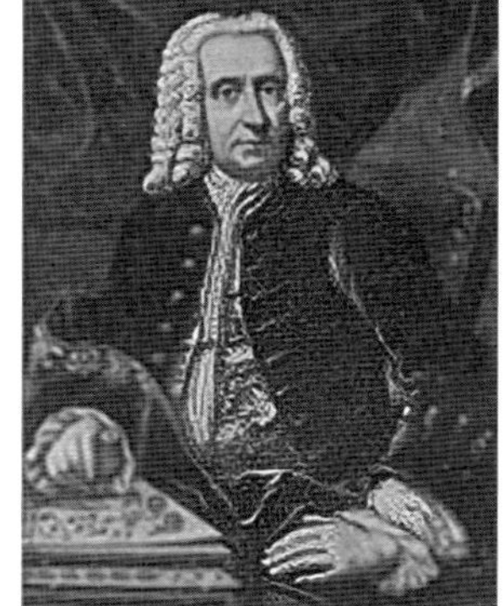

*Schulze*

**1756:** Johann Christoph Voigtländer (1732–1797) starts his firm in Vienna, Austria, making compasses and quadrants.

**1758:** Crown glass (sand, soda, and lime) has been known for nearly 4,000 years, but in 1758, flint glass, which contains lead oxide, and which is denser and disperses light more strongly into a spectrum, becomes available. This will have a huge effect on lens design.

---

**TRIVIA**

The term "flint" derives from the flint nodules found in the chalk deposits of southeast England that were used as a source of silica in glass making. Traditionally, flint glasses contain around 4% to 60% lead oxide. However, the disposal of flint glasses is a source of pollution. In many modern flint glasses, the lead oxides are replaced with other metal oxides such as titanium dioxide and zirconium dioxide without significantly altering the optical properties of the glass.

---

**1758:** An English barrister and amateur optician named Chester Moore Hall (1703–1771) invents the first achromatic doublet lens sometime between 1729 and 1733 (nobody is sure). He devises a composite lens composed of two individual lenses made from glasses with different degrees of dispersion. The result is that both the red and blue rays of light come into the same plane of focus, making for a sharper lens. He uses his achromatic lens to build the first refracting telescope free of significant chromatic aberration.

> **TRIVIA**
>
> Hall wanted to keep his invention a secret and so contracted the manufacture of the crown and flint lenses to two different opticians, Edward Scarlett (1688–1743) and James Mann (1706–1743). They then sub-contracted their work to another optician, George Bass. Bass (1700–1770) realized the two components were for the same client and, after fitting the two parts together, noted the achromatic properties. Unfortunately, Bass failed to appreciate the importance of this invention and it remained known to only a few opticians.
>
> In the late 1750s, Bass mentioned Hall's lenses to John Dollond (1706–1761), who understood their potential and was able to reproduce their design. Dollond was granted a patent on the technology in 1758 . . . hence the date of the entry above.

**1763:** John Dollond's son Peter (1731-1820) invents the apochromat, an improvement on the achromat, which brings all three primary colours of light (red, blue and green) into a common point of focus, making for an even sharper lens.

> **TRIVIA**
>
> Dollond's telescopes for astronomical or terrestrial use were among the most popular in both Great Britain and abroad for over one and one-half centuries. Admiral Lord Nelson (1758–1805) himself owned one. Another sailed with Captain Cook (1728–1779) in 1769 to observe the transit of Venus on the island of Tahiti.

**1764:** The Arsenal factory is established in Kyiv, Ukraine, as a producer of armaments for the Imperial Russian Army and, later, the Soviet Union. During the Cold War (1947-1991) Arsenal will produce optical components for the Soviet military and space programs.

> **TRIVIA**
>
> Of all the companies that will go on to produce cameras and/or lenses, Arsenal is the first. Though no longer producing either, Arsenal is still going strong after 266 years.

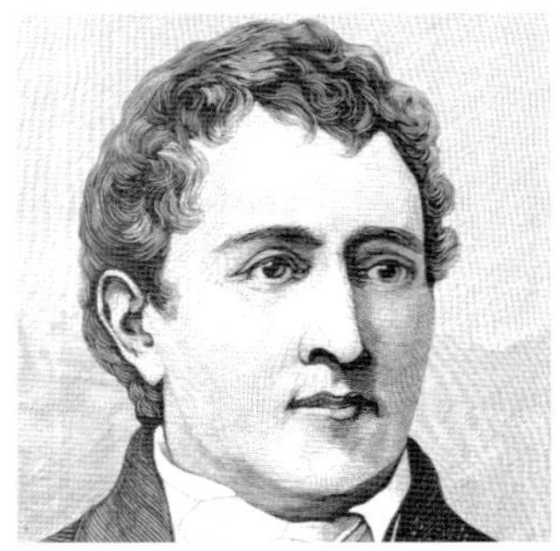

*Scheele*

**1777:** A Swedish apothecary, Carl W. Scheele (1742–1786), experiments with nitrate and chloride salts of silver and finds they turn brown when exposed to light (this is because they have been converted to metallic silver). He notes that ammonia, which is known to dissolve silver chloride, does not dissolve the blackened silver, giving a way to "fix" silver chloride images permanently. Had Scheele realized the importance of this last discovery, he might have become the inventor of photography for, by this time, the other essential processes are known.

Scheele dies young, after years of working with toxic chemicals. This is not surprising, particularly when you consider that his work includes descriptions of the smell of chlorine gas and what hydrogen cyanide tastes like.

**1795:** Thomas Wedgwood (1771–1805), the son of Wedgwood Pottery's founder and uncle to Charles Darwin (1809–1882), working with Sir Humphrey Davy (1778–1829) of safety lamp fame, makes negative prints he calls "photograms" or "sun pictures" by bathing paper in a silver nitrate solution and then exposing it to light. He is able to record halftones as well as pure black and white, but the image is not permanent and fades rapidly if displayed under any light stronger than candlelight.

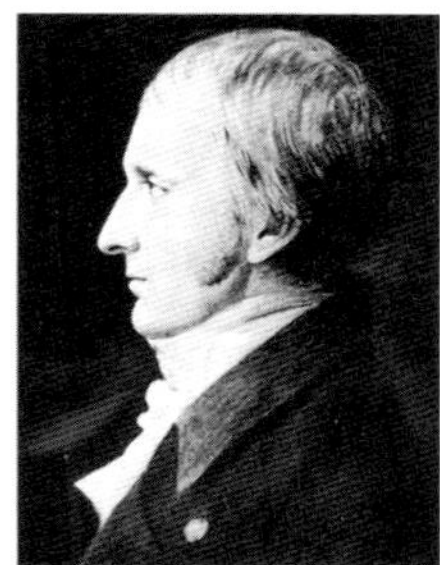

*Wedgwood*

# 1800 to 1849

*The early 1800s see a huge expansion in the chemistry of photography. From the very first permanent photograph in 1827 to the first modern photograph, the Daguerreotype, which arrives a mere decade later, developments are rapid. Lens development, as you can see from the diagrams, also takes tremendous strides forward.*

**1802:** The Scovill Manufacturing Company starts in Waterbury, Connecticut, as a maker of brass buttons, sewing hardware, and other brass and copper items. The factory, housed in a former grist mill on the Mad River, will go on—in 1839—to become the first maker of silvered photographic plates in the USA.

**1804:** William Hyde Wollaston (1766–1826) invents a modern positive meniscus lens for eyeglasses.

**1812:** Wollaston adapts his meniscus lens for the camera obscura by mounting it with the concave side facing out to receive the incoming light and putting an aperture stop in front of it, making the image both brighter and reasonably sharp over a wide field.

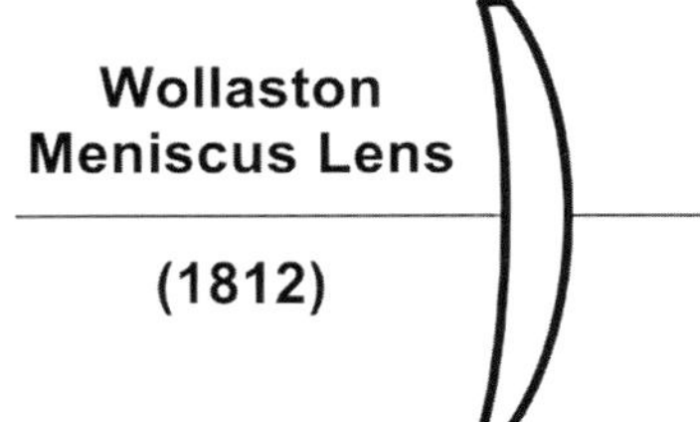


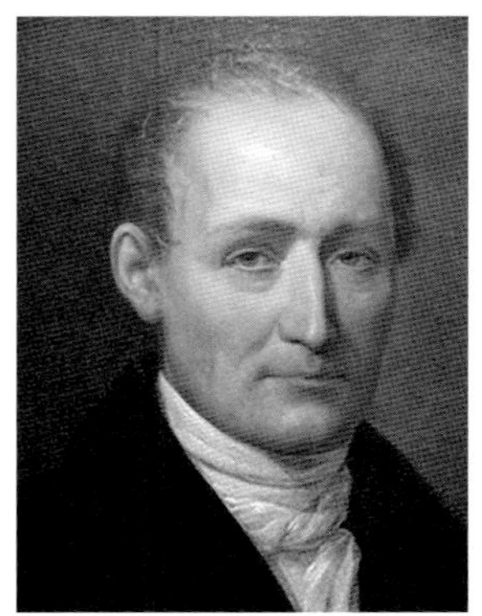
*Joseph Nicéphore Niépce*

**1816:** In France, Joseph Nicéphore Niépce (1765–1883) uses a locally made camera obscura and paper sensitized with silver chloride to record the view from his attic window. It never occurs to him to take the next step and print the negative onto another sheet of sensitized paper. He has photography in his hands, but lets it slip through his fingers. "We don't lack patience," he writes to his brother, "and with patience anything can be done." He will have success 11 years later using a different method.

**1817:** C. F. Gauss (1777–1855), a German mathematician, improves the telescope objectives of the day by adding a meniscus lens to make a simple convex and concave lens design. This "Gauss type" design, or more particularly the "Double Gauss," will become the basis of many modern large aperture "standard" photographic lenses by makers in both Europe and Asia.

**1819:** The Kern Company is founded in the town of Aarau, Switzerland, by Jakob Kern (1790–1867) for the purpose of manufacturing and selling drawing instruments and, later, all types of scientific equipment. They will go on to produce fine lenses including the superb Kern Macro-Switar for Alpa in 1958.

**1819:** Sir John Herschel (1792–1871), an accomplished chemist, discovers that hyposulphite of soda will dissolve otherwise insoluble silver salts. This discovery will eventually lead to the use of "hypo" as a fixing agent in photography for making images permanent, a method that is still in use today.

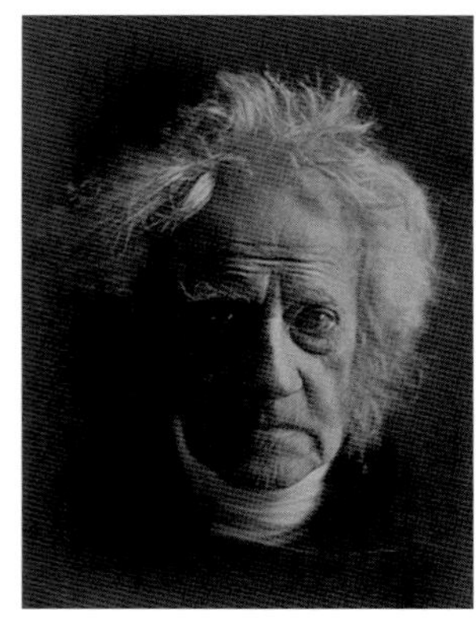

*Sir John Herschel*

---

### TRIVIA

Hyposulphite of soda ($Na_2S_2O_3$) is known today as sodium thiosulphate. When mixed with water it dissolves silver salts, making it an excellent "fixer" for photographs. It is also used in medicine as a treatment for cyanide poisoning!

---

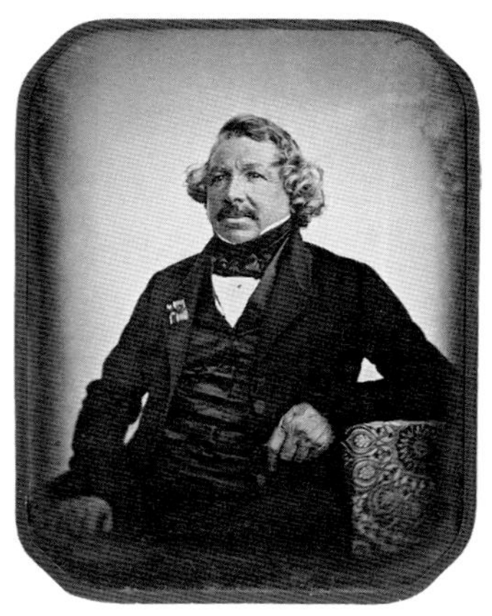

*Louis Daguerre*

**1822:** Louis Daguerre (1787–1851) opens his diorama theatre in Paris. It is a giant multimedia show in the tradition of the panoramas popular in the early 19th century, to which he adds a blend of natural and artificial light. The audience sits in a darkened room, facing a huge painting which shows a scene or interior in lifelike detail. The painting is 45 x 69 feet (14 x 21 metres) and is illuminated from both front and back, creating effects which hold the audience spellbound. Monsieur Daguerre quickly becomes *the Celebrated Monsieur Daguerre.* In another 15 years he will go on to invent the first practical method of photography.

**1822:** French physicist Augustin Fresnel (1788–1827) invents the lens that will make his name commonplace along the seacoasts of Europe and North America. Designed for lighthouses, it is a compact, stepped-element design that allows the construction of lenses of large aperture and short focal length without the mass and volume of material that would be required by a lens of conventional design. Popular as a condenser lens in SLR and dSLR viewfinders, in the early 21st century some makers will adapt its principles to photographic lenses.

**1827:** Joseph Nicéphore Niépce produces his "heliograph" by coating a highly polished pewter plate with Bitumen of Judea dissolved in oil of lavender. The Bitumen of Judea is a variety of asphalt that hardens when exposed to light.

He makes an eight-hour exposure from the same attic window at Le Gras that he used 11 years before, and then washes away the softer unexposed and unhardened portions of the plate with turpentine to produce the first permanent positive photographic image. Photography is born, although in modern terms Niépce's plate has an ISO sensitivity of just 0.000035!

Because of the inordinately long exposure times, the process is quite impractical for photography but, in a modified form, is later used for the production of printing plates, his original goal.

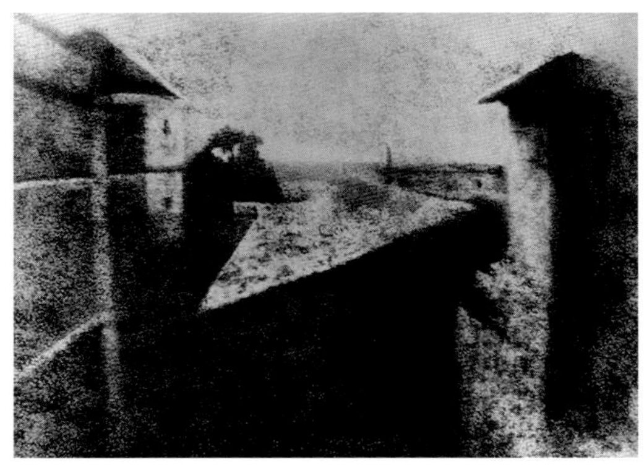

*The first permanent photograph.*

**TRIVIA**

Joseph and his brother, Claude, also invent a somewhat cranky internal combustion engine that runs on a mixture of powdered lampblack and ground resin for fuel. It is arguably the first internal combustion engine and is powerful enough to drive a boat up the Seine, but it is never a commercial success.

**1828:** Working independently of the British and French, James Wattles of Indiana, USA, invents a method of photography but withholds any announcement for "want of encouragement and fear of ridicule." This is reported in the "History and Practice of the Art of Photography" when it is published in 1849.

**1830:** Around this time (nobody is exactly sure), Joseph Plateau (in Belgium) and Simon Stampfer (in Austria) independently develop the phenakistoscope, a device with a spinning disc with slots through which a series of drawings can be viewed, creating the effect of a single moving image. It is the precursor to the modern cinema.

**1832:** With the help of a pharmacist friend, Joaquim Correa de Mello (1816–1877), Hercules Florence (1804–1879), a French ex-patriot living in Brazil, begins to study ways of permanently fixing camera obscura images, which he calls *photographia*. In 1833, they settle on silver nitrate on paper, a combination that had been the subject of experiments by Thomas Wedgwood around 1800. Unlike Wedgwood, who was unable to make photographs of real-world scenes with his camera or render the photograms that he did produce light-fast, Florence's notebooks indicate that in 1834 he succeeds in doing both, three years before Daguerre (but six years after Nicéphore Niépce), using the negative/positive process that is universally used today.

Unfortunately, in part because he never publishes his invention adequately and partly because he is an obscure inventor living in a remote and undeveloped part of the world, Hércules Florence is never recognized internationally as one of the inventors of photography. It is rumoured that in 1834 he uses the French form of "photography," the word *photographie*, in private notes, though this remains unconfirmed.

**1833:** Sir Charles Wheatstone (1802–1875) comes up with the idea of presenting slightly different images to the two eyes using a device he called a reflecting mirror stereoscope. When viewed stereoscopically, he showed that the two images are combined in the brain to produce 3D depth perception. His idea won't become truly popular until 1849.

---

**TRIVIA**

Wheatstone is best known for contributions in the development of the Wheatstone bridge, originally invented by Samuel Hunter Christie (1784–1865), which is used to measure an unknown electrical resistance. His circuit is first used, photographically, in the Yashica Lynx 500E (see **1968**).

---

**1833:** An English mathematician and physicist Peter Barlow (1776–1862) develops his "Barlow lens"—a negative achromat magnifier for use with astronomical telescope eyepieces—to increase magnification while narrowing the field of view. Such lenses, which are still sold today, work by magnifying the central part of the image, so that effective focal length is increased, although resolution is decreased.

---

**TRIVIA**

The Barlow lens was introduced to photographers in the early 1960s by the American entrepreneur Fred Spira (1924–2007) of Spiratone Incorporated, as a low-cost way to increase the effective focal length of a lens. The teleconverter (or teleXtender, as Spira called it) is the photographic equivalent of the Barlow lens (see **1941**).

---

**1834:** Henry Fox Talbot (1800–1877) creates permanent negative images using fine writing paper coated with salt and brushed with a solution of silver nitrate, then fixed with a strong salt solution. He uses this discovery to make precise tracings of botanical specimens by pressing a leaf or plant on a piece of sensitized paper, covering it with glass and setting it in the sun. Wherever the light strikes the paper it is darkened, but wherever the plant blocks the light it remains white. He calls his new discovery "the art of photogenic drawing." Because the images are fuzzy, due to the use of paper as a base, he tells no one.

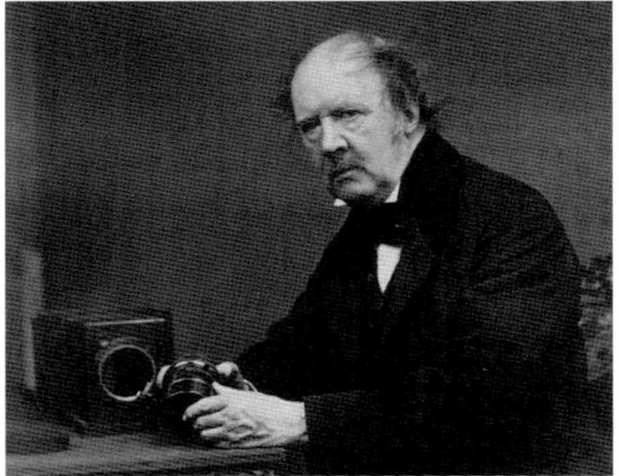

*Henry Fox Talbot*

**1835:** As his understanding of chemistry improves, Talbot returns to his original idea of photographic images made in a camera. During the summer, he places pieces of sensitized photogenic drawing paper in miniature cameras, which his wife calls "mouse traps," and sets them around the grounds. Talbot writes that the pictures "without great stretch of the imagination might be supposed to be the work of some Lilliputian artist."

**1837:** Quite by accident, Louis Daguerre discovers his Daguerreotype process. He finds that a plate that had its exposure ruined by clouds is somehow "developed" when left in his chemical cabinet overnight. By painstakingly repeating the process, removing one chemical per day, he discovers that the "developer" is an open bottle of mercury.

His method is simple. A copper plate is coated with silver, pumice powder, and sweet oil, and then washed in diluted nitric acid and gently heated over a flame. The plate is then placed over a tray of evaporating iodine in a darkened box or room. A layer of light-sensitive silver iodine then forms on the plate, making it ready for exposure in the camera. The exposure takes just 45 minutes rather than the several hours previously required, and the image is fixed by developing the plate in mercury vapour. Practical photography is born!

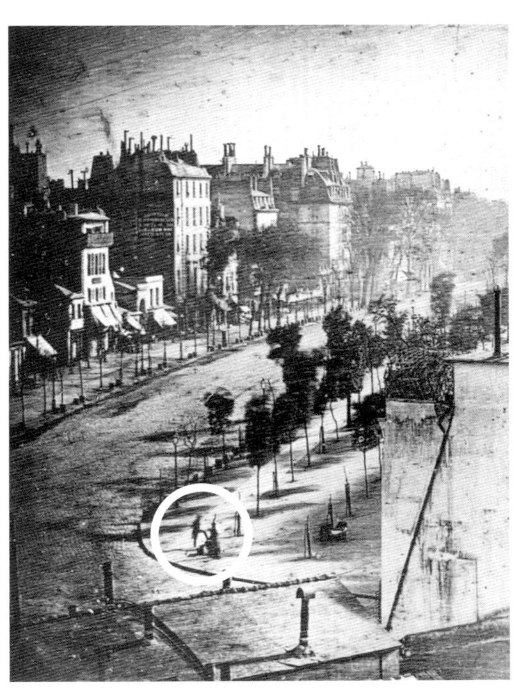

*View of the Boulevard du Temple in Paris.*

**1838:** Louis Daguerre makes the first photograph showing living people. The long exposure times register buildings and other stationary objects, but moving objects, such as horse carts, walking people and such, all disappear. By coincidence, the gentleman, and the bootblack (highlighted in the circle in the photograph at right), stayed still long enough to put a shine on his shoes and register on the plate—thus creating the first image with people in it. It is also one of the earliest surviving Daguerreotypes.

---

### TRIVIA

Some say the photo (above right) was a happy coincidence. Others say that Daguerre paid the two to hold their pose. Nobody knows for sure, but Daguerre . . . and he's not talking.

---

**1839:** On 6 January, the Paris newspaper *Gazette de France* prints the following notice: "This discovery . . . upsets all scientific theories of light and optics, and it will revolutionize the art of drawing. M. Daguerre has found the way to fix the images which paint themselves within a camera obscura so that these images are no longer transient reflections of the objects, but are fixed and everlasting impressions which, like a painting or engraving, can be taken away from the objects."

**1839:** Prompted by the announcement of Daguerre's invention, on 25 January, Fox Talbot shows his three-and-a-half-year-old pictures at England's Royal Institution. Within a fortnight Talbot gives the details of his *photogenic drawing* process (see **1834**) to the Royal Society, whereas Daguerre does not reveal the details of his process until mid-August.

---

### TRIVIA

Early photographs are mostly identified as Daguerreotypes, but variations on Talbot's "salted prints" became commonplace in both Europe and America until roughly 1860, specifically because they could be produced as multiple prints. In 2018, The Yale Center for British Art (New Haven, CT) mounted an extensive exhibition (*Salt & Silver—1840–1860*) of early non-Daguerreotype photography.

---

**1839:** It is said that German astronomer Johann von Maedler (1794–1874) uses the word "photography" in an article published on 25 February in the Berlin newspaper *Vossische Zeitung*. However, no copies of the article survive, and this remains unconfirmed.

**1839:** Constance Talbot (1811–1880), wife of William Henry Fox Talbot, experiments with her husband's process and becomes the first woman ever to take a photograph.

**1839:** Sir John Herschel, the only son of the distinguished British astronomer William Herschel, realizes his earlier discovery (see **1819**) that sodium thiosulphate (then called hyposulphite of soda and still referred to as "hypo" by photographers today) will dissolve previously insoluble silver salts, makes it a perfect way to "fix" (or make permanent) a photographic image. He writes to Talbot (some say to Daguerre as well) with this suggestion, but because the process also reduces Talbot's rather weak "photogenic drawings," Talbot decides not to use it, preferring to stay with the less efficient method of strong salt solutions.

---

### TRIVIA

The first confirmed use of the word "photography" (from the Greek φωτός (phōtos) [light] and γραφή [graph - drawing or writing]) is recorded in a private correspondence by Sir John Herschel, dated 19 February 1839, and in his well-documented use of the term in a Royal Society lecture, which he presents on 4 March 1839. Thus, Herschel is credited with coining the word. Herschel is also commonly credited with coining the terms "positive" and "negative" as well as "snapshot," though there is some debate that "snapshot" might have already been in use.

Later, Herschel makes the first glass negative, but his process is difficult and goes nowhere.

---

**1839:** Working independently, Parisian Hippolyte Bayard (1808–1887) works out a method of making positive photographic images on paper.

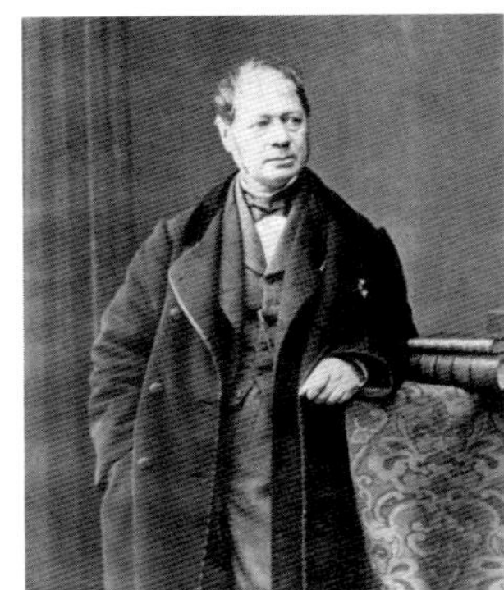

*Hippolyte Bayard*

In June, Bayard hangs the world's first photographic exhibition: 30 photographs of architecture, sculpture, and still life, to raise money for earthquake victims in Martinique. It is two months prior to Daguerre's public announcement and although Bayard's photographs are duly noted in the press, they make little impression on the public. For reasons of his own (some say he was persuaded by the influential François Arago, a friend of Daguerre's), Bayard does not divulge his method until 1840—when it is too late to gain any credit as an inventor of photography.

His process is relatively straightforward. A sheet of paper is treated with sodium chloride. After drying, the paper is submerged in silver nitrate to create silver chloride, which is sensitive to light. The paper is then exposed to light until it turns black, is then washed and dried, and eventually is stored in a portfolio until needed. Before the paper can be used, it has to be saturated in potassium iodide, placed into the camera, and exposed. Then it is soaked with sodium thiosulphate and placed in a bath of ammonia and water until a positive photographic image appears. Though pin-sharp, each one is unique and cannot be duplicated.

Bayard's process is good for architecture and landscapes, but when people are photographed, they are told to close their eyes, to avoid a "dead look," caused by wandering eyes and blinking during the 12-to-14-minute exposures.

**1839:** In February, American artist and entrepreneur Samuel Morse (1791–1872) travels to Paris to secure a patent on his telegraphic apparatus. While there he writes Daguerre requesting to view some actual Daguerreotypes before they are shown to the public at large, offering to show Daguerre his telegraph in return. Thus, Morse learns the Daguerreotype process firsthand. When Morse returns to America, he and his brothers Sidney and Richard convert their home to a studio where, in April of the year, they create the first photographs taken in North America. Morse's photographic career lasts only two years, until he sells his first telegraph system, but the impact he makes announcing the photographic process in America and then teaching the profession to the first wave of pioneering photographers is monumental.

**1839:** Monday, 19 August, is a hot sunny day in Paris. The official public unveiling of the Daguerreotype process is held under the joint auspices of the Academy of Arts and the Academy of Sciences, in recognition of photography's roots. Scheduled for 3:00 p.m., every seat is taken by 1:00 p.m. and an overflow crowd of some 200 mills about outside. Curiously, Daguerre is not in attendance and the crowd reacts bitterly when no demonstration of this "mirror with a memory" is given.

Daguerre is awarded a state pension of 6,000 francs per annum by the French government in exchange for publication of his methods and the rights by other French citizens to freely use the Daguerreotype process. In the end, free use of Daguerre's process is allowed everywhere except in France's age-old enemy, Britain. There, Daguerre patents his process, just days before revealing it to the world. The Brits have to pay a royalty on every Daguerreotype made!

**1839:** A Frenchman, Charles Louis Chevalier (1804–1859), creates an achromatic version of the meniscus lens that combines field flattening and chromatic aberration control. The lens has a reverse concave flint glass side facing the subject and an $f$16 aperture stop at its radius of curvature, making it reasonably sharp over a wide field of about 50°. Reversing the lens

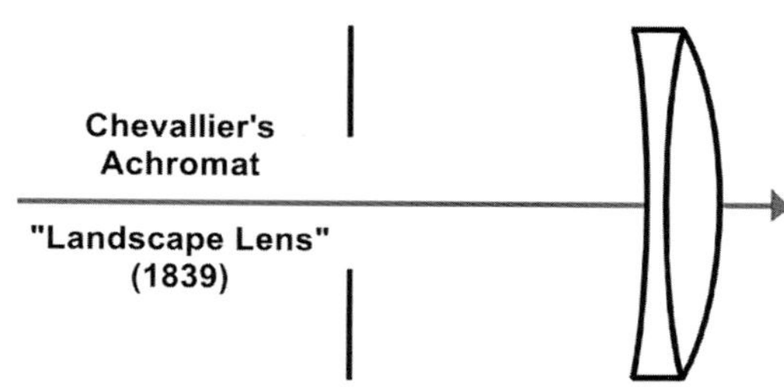


does increase chromatic aberration, but this is somewhat corrected by adjusting the achromat to bring colours at the blue end of the spectrum into focus to match the blue-sensitive nature of the photographic emulsions of the day. This design was quickly copied by other lens makers. Because of its large flat field over a wide angle of view, and its "slow" $f$16 aperture (requiring 20 to 30 minutes for outdoor Daguerreotype exposures), this lens becomes known as the "French landscape lens" or simply the "landscape lens."

**1839:** Daguerre contracts with his brother-in-law, Alphonse Giroux (1776–1848), to produce a wooden camera with a Chevalier lens and a full set of chemicals for his process. Each bore on its side a metal label: "No apparatus is guaranteed unless it bears the signature of M. Daguerre and the seal of M. Giroux." Giroux and Daguerre had already been mass-producing these before the official announcement and were selling them minutes after the announcement was made.

---

### AUCTION MADNESS

In May of 2010, a Giroux Daguerreotype camera was sold at the Westlicht Auction, not for the expected €200,000 but a modest €732,000 ($827,450).

---

**1839:** The Scovill Company in Waterbury, Connecticut, starts limited production of Daguerreotype plates.

---

### TRIVIA

In December 1839, J. M. L. Scovill was quoted as saying, "The Frenchman here says the plates cannot be made here and calculates to make a fortune by importing them from France. We will try to disappoint him." By 1840, after implementing improvements (such as importing better quality copper from England), the Scovill-produced plates are of equal quality to plates shipped from Paris.

---

**1840:** An English science teacher, John Goddard (1795–1866), discovers that treating Daguerre's plates with bromine vapour greatly increases their sensitivity to light. Exposure times are reduced to 30 to 40 seconds in bright daylight.

**1840:** Disappointed in his lack of recognition, Hippolyte Bayard creates the world's first photographic joke (pictured right). He makes a macabre image of himself as a corpse, half naked and with eyes closed. On the back he writes, "The body you see is that of Monsieur Bayard . . . The government which gave Daguerre too much said it could do nothing for Monsieur Bayard at all and the poor wretch drowned himself." In fact, he lives a good long life, becomes a fine photographer, and goes on to create the Société Française de Photographie.

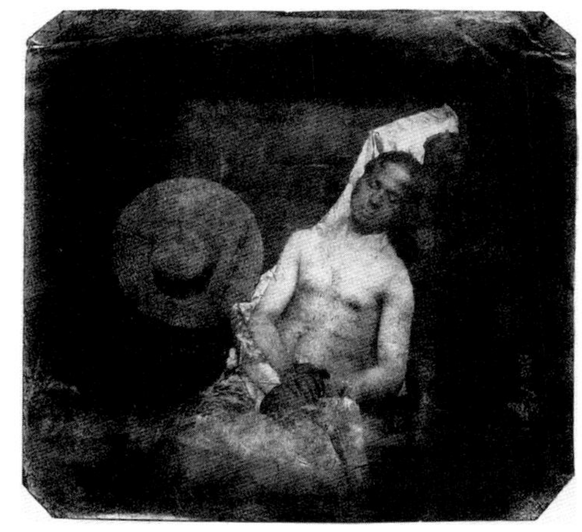

**1840:** On 23 September, Henry Fox Talbot discovers that an exposure of mere seconds, while leaving no visible trace on chemically treated paper, nonetheless leaves a latent image that can be brought out by applying an "exciting liquid" (essentially a gallic acid solution). In February 1841, he patents his method and calls it the "calotype" process (from the Greek *kalos*, meaning beautiful). This gives a much stronger image, so that fixing it in Herschel's "hypo" becomes practical.

---

### TRIVIA

Gallic acid is found naturally in gallnuts (hence its name), sumac, witch hazel, tea leaves, oak bark, and grape seeds, among other plants. Its chemical formula is $C_6H_2(OH)_3CO_2H$. Originally used for tanning hides, it was also a prime component of iron gall ink, the standard European writing and drawing ink from the 12th to 19th century, with a history extending to the Romans.

---

**1840:** Hungarian-born mathematician Józeph Petzval (1807–1891) develops his "portrait lens" at the request of the Austrian Imperial Court. Petzval's $f$ 3.6 design (four elements in three groups) is the first lens specifically designed for photography and gathers 16 times more light than the more common meniscus lenses of the day, thereby reducing the amount of time that subjects had to remain motionless.

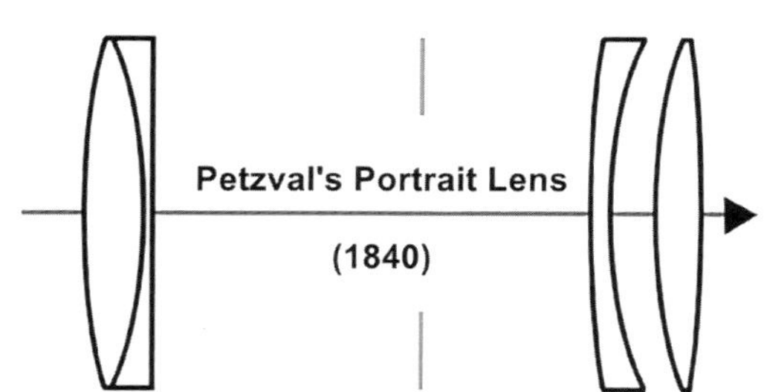


Petzval patents his lens and, at the encouragement of the Austrian Court, sells the Voigtländer family the rights to produce 600 copies. But Voigtländer builds thousands of copies. When Petzval sues, in 1849, they abscond to Braunschweig (now part of Germany, but then an independent state, where Petzval's patent is not recognized) to escape the Austrian courts. Over time, Voigtländer builds some 60,000 Petzval lenses without paying royalties and makes a fortune. Petzval makes next to nothing.

---

### TRIVIA

Petzval's design is the first camera lens made based on scientific calculation rather than trial and error. When the 32-year-old Petzval accepts the challenge to make a flat field lens fast enough for portraiture, he approaches the Archduke Ludwig, the Director General of Artillery in the Austrian Army. Ludwig orders three corporals and eight gunners "skilled in computing" to be placed at his disposal.

With this rather unusual help, within six months Petzval designs two lenses: a portrait lens of *f* 3.6 and a wide-angle objective of *f* 8.7. By 1850, some 8,000 of Petzval's portrait lens are made.

Petzval's second lens, the Dialyte, is a landscape lens of a smaller aperture (*f* 8.7) but with excellent edge-to-edge sharpness.

In 1859, Petzval's house is robbed of his lens designs and his optical manuscripts. Almost immediately, Voigtländer starts making their Orthoskop, an almost perfect copy of the Dialyte. A coincidence? Perhaps. But Petzval is adamant that Voigtländer had burglarized his home, though he cannot prove it. Petzval abandons optics completely and lives as a recluse until his death in 1891.

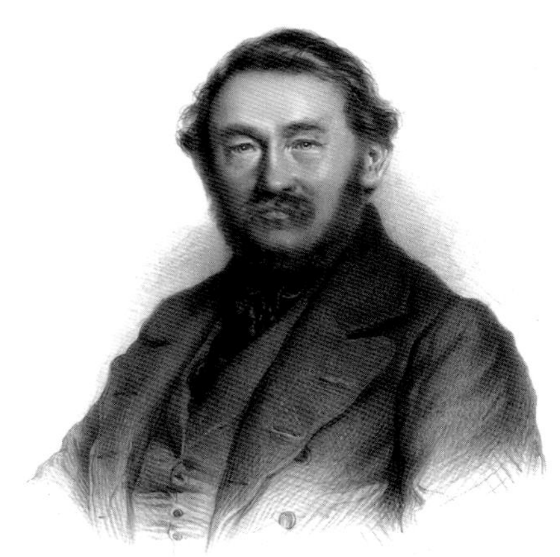

*Józeph Petzval. 1854 drawing by Adolf Duathage.*

---

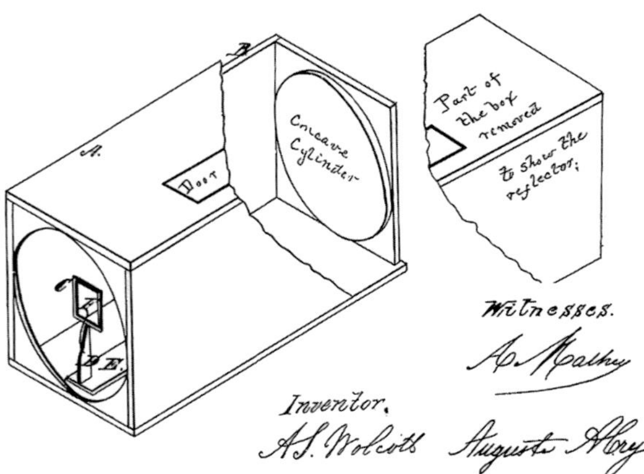


**1840:** An American, Alexander Wolcott (1804–1844), patents a Daguerreotype camera that uses a concave mirror to focus the light on the plate, which is positioned at the front of the camera. The advantage is that the image produced is not reversed, as in all other Daguerreotype cameras. The drawback is that the mirror requires longer exposure times; as a result, the camera is never particularly popular. Still, Wolcott's is the first patent issued in the USA for any photographic item or process.

**1840:** Hippolyte Fizeau (1819–1896) discovers that treating the incredibly fragile Daguerreotype image with a heated solution containing gold chloride not only improves the tone of the image but makes it remarkably more resistant to physical damage. Soon, gold toning is standard Daguerreotype practice.

**1840:** William Lewis and his son, William H. Lewis, of New York City, produce the first cameras, coating boxes, mercury baths, and head rests for photographers in America. They are used by Alexander Wolcott and John Johnson (1813–1871) in the first "Daguerreotype room" in the city of New York.

**1841:** In France, Antoine Claudet (1797–1867) shows that chlorine has a similar accelerating affect to the bromine vapours John Goddard had used. Chlorine vapours are highly toxic and dangerous, however, as will be proved by their use in the Great War of 1914–1918.

**1841:** William Henry Fox Talbot publicly introduces his "calotype." It is an improvement of his earlier photogenic drawing process. The calotype, or Talbotype (the honorific term is bestowed by friends; today, both terms are used interchangeably), is the first real competition for the Daguerreotype. The translucent calotype negative makes it possible to produce as many positive prints as desired by simply making a contact print on a similar piece of sensitized paper. However, despite waxing of the negative to make the image clearer, the prints are still not pin sharp like the metallic Daguerreotype, as the paper fibres degrade the image produced. However, it is the first negative-to-positive process, a method that forms the basis of all modern film photography.

---

### TRIVIA

Because the Talbotype is a patented process, all who wish to use it must pay Talbot a royalty. This rather slows the adoption of the method.

---

**1841:** Fritz Viktor Hasselblad starts his trading firm, F. V. Hasselblad & Company, in Gothenburg, Sweden. The founder's son, Arvid Viktor Hasselblad, is interested in photography and starts the photographic division of the company.

---

### TRIVIA

Arvid Hasselblad has been quoted as saying, "I certainly don't think that we will earn much money on this, but at least it will allow us to take pictures for free."

---

**1841:** An American jeweller from upstate New York, Jeremiah Gurney (1812–1891), moves his shop to New York City. Shortly thereafter he turns his attention to photography, having learned the skill from Samuel Morse. Gurney becomes the first of many to suffer the dangers of the new process. He is confined to his bed for a protracted period, with great pain and swelling of his limbs, after inhaling the fumes of the mercury used to develop the plates.

**1841:** A Mrs. John Fletcher becomes the first woman Daguerreotypist to work in Canada, and possibly in North America. She describes herself as a "professor and teacher of the photogenic art," in an ad in the local newspaper of Pictou, Nova Scotia. Within months she starts studios in Quebec City and Montreal. Sadly, while her ads remain, none of her Daguerreotypes are known to survive.

**1842:** Edward Anthony (1819–1888) starts a Daguerreotype gallery in New York, which rapidly expands as a photographic supplier in 1847. In 1852, his brother, Henry T. Anthony (1814–1884), joins the firm and by 1870 the company starts making cameras. In 1902 they will merge with Scovill into Anthony & Scovill and, in 1907, the name will be shortened to Ansco.

**1842:** The cyanotype process is invented by Sir John Herschel. It is a crisp, clear, and long-lasting process if protected from alkalis, but the blue image it produces never becomes popular. However, the process survives today as the basis of modern-day blueprints.

---

### TRIVIA

Currently, the world's largest cyanotype was created on 19 September 2015 in Johnson City, Texas. The cyanotype-making was organized by Shootapalooza, a photographic art collective, and was 30 x 90 feet in size. Many people lay on the cloth, which was exposed to the sun for 10 minutes to make the image, and a fire truck was used to hose the work with water to fix it.

---

**1843:** One of the first photographically illustrated books is published by Anna Atkins (1799–1871) with Herschel's cyanotypes. The first part of Atkins's *Photographs of British Algae: Cyanotype Impressions* contains what we now call photograms. (For the first 100 or so years of photography this word was used interchangeably with "photograph.") The cyanotypes are made by placing pressed, dried pieces of seaweed and other specimens on cyanotype paper.

**1843:** The Reverend Levi Hill (1816–1865) of upstate New York claims to have invented a colour Daguerreotype process. Experts still debate the validity of this claim, as few records of his process, and no such images, are ever found. (Still, researchers have recently found that his very difficult process does have a limited ability to reproduce colours.)

**1843:** Henry Fox Talbot travels to Paris in May to negotiate a licensing agreement for the French rights to his patented calotype process and to give firsthand instruction in its use. The trip is a failure.

**1843:** The Edinburgh Calotype Club in Scotland is the first photographic club in the world and runs until roughly 1855. Its members consist of pioneering photographers, primarily from the Edinburgh and St. Andrews areas. The efforts of the club's members result in the production of two of the world's earliest assembled photographic albums, consisting of more than 300 images in total.

---

**TRIVIA**

By the early to mid-1840s Daguerreotypes were beginning to replace miniature portraits among the well-to-do. While they produce a far more faithful likeness, they lack a portrait's colour. Thus, from the very early years, photographers tried to add colour by hand. The simplest way was to apply pigments directly to the fragile surface of the Daguerreotype, often with mixed success. Because of this difficulty, colour was added sparingly, usually a slight touch of pink to the cheeks and gold to the jewellery. Only rarely was colour added to backgrounds or clothing, and only to dresses or uniforms.

---

**1844:** Friedrich von Martens (1809–1875) builds the first panoramic camera. It is a pivoting-lens design that moves in an arc of 150°, exposing a curved Daguerreotype plate. His camera, the Megaskop, features a set of gears which ensures a relatively steady panning speed, thus preventing uneven exposure as the lens turns. Because of the high cost of materials and the technical difficulty of properly exposing the photographs, few Daguerreotype panoramas are made, and surviving ones are exceedingly rare.

**1844:** John Whipple (1812–1891) of England begins to experiment with an albumen (egg white) emulsion on glass to avoid the texture of paper appearing in his photographs.

**1844-1846:** Henry Fox Talbot publicizes his calotype process in a six-part publication illustrated with 24 original calotypes.

**1845:** The first known shutter, a "drop" or "guillotine" design consisting of a board with a hole in it moving past the lens opening, is used by the French physicists Hippolyte Fizeau and Léon Foucault (1809–1868) for photographing the sun. Although this shutter is powered simply by gravity, later versions will be powered by springs or rubber bands to achieve shorter exposure times.

---

**TRIVIA**

Because gravity causes the "dropped" component to be constantly accelerating, the longer the piece of board over which it travels, the faster the shutter speed. It does, of course, require a different shutter for each speed. Exposure can also be varied by changing the height of the hole.

---

**1846:** Two Frenchmen, Nicolas Ménard (1822–1901) and Flores Domonte, create a mixture they call "Collodion" by dissolving gun cotton in either sulphuric ether, or acetone, or a mixture of both. The result is a colourless, gelatinous mass which, when spread on a smooth surface, solidifies quickly by evaporation, and leaves a transparent membrane which adheres with surprising tenacity and is insoluble in water. Although they are primarily interested in creating bandages for surgeons, the significance of their discovery is not lost on the photographic community.

**1846:** German Carl Zeiss (1816–1888) opens his workshop, making high-quality magnifying glasses for the faculty of Jena University. From this grows the Carl Zeiss Works, one of the largest and most prestigious optical houses in the world.

**1847:** Frenchman Abel Niépce de Saint Victor (1805–1870) makes a successful dry plate by coating a sheet of glass with a mixture of albumen, potassium iodine, and acidified silver nitrate solution. When dried, sensitivity is low and, given the "slow" lenses of the day, exposure times are about a half hour in bright sunlight.

---

### TRIVIA

In the 1850s, Niépce de Saint-Victor tried to develop colour photography, using light-sensitive metal salts, including uranium salts. In 1857, long before Henri Becquerel's famous discovery of radioactivity in 1896, Niépce de Saint-Victor observed that, even in complete darkness, certain salts could expose photographic emulsions. He soon realized that uranium salts were responsible for the phenomenon. Other photographers soon confirmed his findings.

---

**1847:** A Berlin entrepreneur, Theodor Teichgräber, starts offering chemicals for the development of collodion plates through his wholesale pharmacy. In 1910 he will trademark the "Tetenal" brand as the company diversifies into both X-ray and print chemistry. The company will become famous for its Neofin Blue and Red liquid developers and, more importantly, will become a major supplier of chemicals to both Ilford and Kodak, especially in Europe.

**1849:** Karl Kellner (1826–1855) invents the first modern achromatic eyepiece for telescopes that is free from the spherical and chromatic aberrations that are usual in other optical instruments of the day (see **1758**, **1833** and **1839**.) He then starts his Optical Institute in Wetzlar, Germany, to make telescopes and, later, microscopes that use his eyepiece. By 1851, the company employs 12 people and is successful. Kellner dies

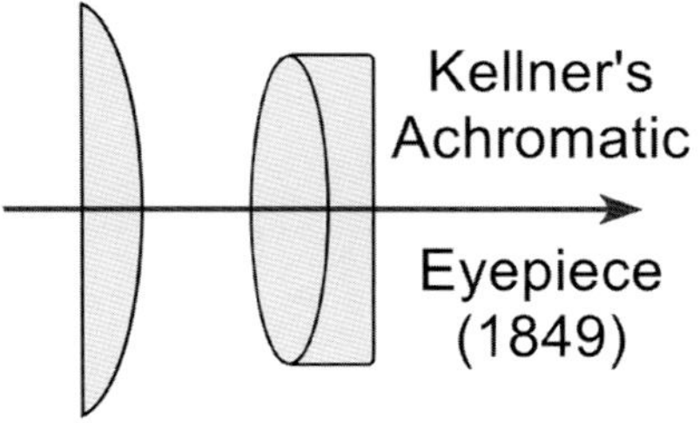


just four years later from the great scourge of the day—tuberculosis—at just 29 years of age. His eyepiece is still being made by many telescope makers and is well-known as the Kellner eyepiece.

**1849:** A Scotsman, Sir David Brewster (1781–1868), improves on the stereoscope design of a man he identifies as "Mr. Elliot, a 'Teacher of Mathematics' from Edinburgh." According to Brewster, Elliot conceived the idea as early as 1823 and, in 1839, constructed "a simple stereoscope without lenses or mirrors" used for viewing drawn landscape transparencies, since photography had not yet become widespread. Brewster's contribution was the use of lenses for uniting the dissimilar photographs. Thus, the lens-based (or lenticular) stereoscope is born.

This in turn stimulates the mass production of stereo photography, which flourishes alongside regular photography. It gets a real boost in 1855 from Queen Victoria (1819–1901) and remains popular until the turn of the century. Stereo photography slowly goes out of fashion as movies increase in popularity.

### TRIVIA

In 1861 Oliver Wendell Holmes (1841–1935), with the help of American photographer Joseph L. Bates, will create—and deliberately not patent—a much more economical stereoscope than the existing version, which dates from the 1850s and consists of two prismatic lenses and a wooden stand to hold the stereo card. The Holmes Stereoscope becomes the most popular type and remains in production for a half century. There are still companies making them, in limited production, today.

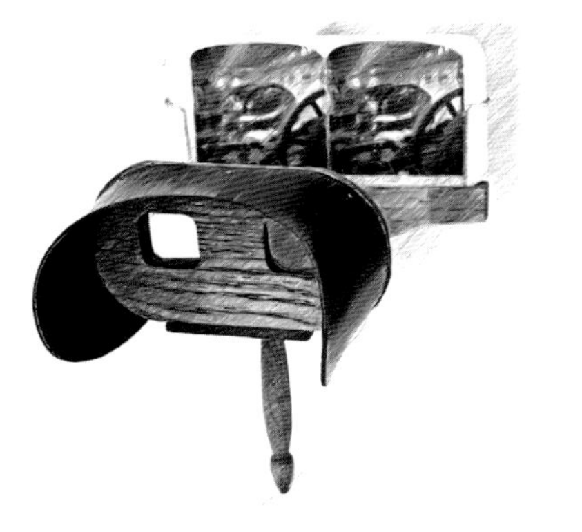

# 1850 to 1899

*The latter half of the 19th century sees the advent of the first colour photographs, though, curiously, these early colour plates appear well before panchromatic emulsions (which are sensitive to all three primary colours) are produced. For that, we will have to wait until the next century. Lens development, as you can see from the diagrams, becomes more complex, achieving faster apertures and sharper results.*

**1850:** John Whipple and William B. Jones introduce their dry plate, which they call the "Crystallotype." But, like Abel Niépce de Saint Victor's version, it is not very sensitive to light, and neither is widely used.

**1851:** Gustave Le Gray (1820–1884) finds that waxing the paper before sensitizing it greatly improves the keeping properties of the negative paper. While "normal" calotypes need to be exposed soon after sensitizing, preferably while still wet, the waxed negative paper can be kept for weeks without loss of sensitivity. This pre-waxed paper is capable of capturing very fine detail but proves much less sensitive than plain calotype paper.

**1851:** On 1 March, an issue of *The Chemist* describes a technique invented by Frederick Scott Archer (1813–1857), a London sculptor, for sensitizing plates using a syrupy substance called collodion, which had been invented in 1846. This becomes known as the wet plate process. A glass plate is coated with a mixture of gun cotton (nitrocellulose) and potassium iodide, then sensitized with silver nitrate. The plate must be exposed while still damp (if allowed to dry, the sensitivity to light is greatly diminished) and returned immediately to the darkroom for processing.

Wet plate collodion photography proves much cheaper than Daguerreotypes, the negative-positive process permits unlimited reproductions, and the use of a glass plate results in much greater clarity in the images as compared to earlier systems using paper. The process is published but not patented, which leads to its rise in popularity as there are no fees to pay. Once dried, the plate is used to make positive prints on calotype or albumen papers.

**1851:** Louis Daguerre dies of a heart attack on 19 July, at the age of 64.

**1851:** Hiram W. Hayden (1819–1904), a Daguerreian photographer and maker of photographic accessories who also holds numerous patents, claims to be the first to successfully take direct positive photographs on paper. *The Waterbury American* newspaper reports the event as

"Mr. Hiram Hayden, ingenious artist of this village, has shown three landscape views taken by the unusual Daguerreian apparatus upon a white paper surface, all at one operation."

**1851:** Queen Victoria visits the "Great Exhibition" (commonly referred to as the first World's Fair) in London's Crystal Palace. She is so enthralled by the stereoscopes on display that she precipitates an enthusiasm for three-dimensional photography that spreads worldwide; the fad lasts for nearly 50 years.

**1851:** Henry Fox Talbot attaches a page of the London *Times* newspaper to a rotating wheel, placed in front of his wet plate camera, in a darkened room. As the wheel rotates, Talbot exposes a few square inches of the newspaper page for about 1/2000 of a second by using spark illumination from Leyden jars, a container that stores high-voltage electrical charges. This experiment results in a readable image and the world of high-speed photography is born.

**1851:** In the United States, W. Lewis (~d. 1876) and his son, W. H. Lewis (see **1840**) introduce what is believed to be the first commercial camera to incorporate a folding bellows (U.S. patent #8513). The camera is half the usual size when collapsed and sells well.

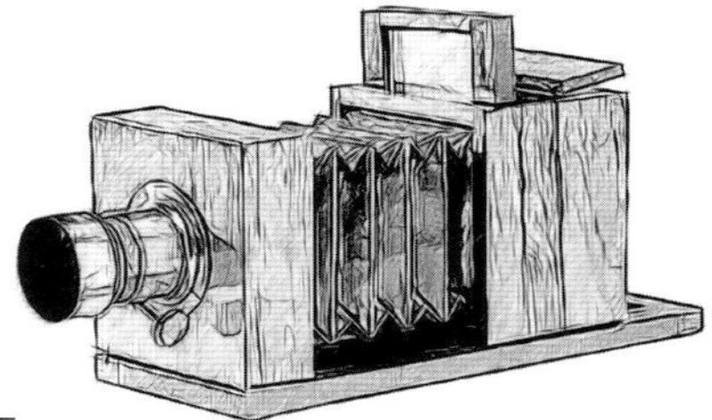

---

**TRIVIA**

The bellows for the prototype was reputed to have been made from Mrs. Lewis's good black taffeta dress, much to her distress.

---

**1852:** Bowing to public pressure, Henry Fox Talbot releases his patented calotype process for all to use, without charge, other than for professional portrait photographers, who still have to pay a royalty.

**1853:** The optical shop of Bausch & Lomb opens in Rochester. Started by two German immigrants, John Jacob Bausch (1830–1926) and Henry Lomb (1829–1908), they first produce pince-nez spectacles, but when Bausch's son Edward (1854–1941) finishes his engineering studies in 1875, he convinces them to start making microscopes. In 1883, the company starts making camera lenses and, in 1888, the firm produces the lenses for the Kodak Number 1, the pioneering roll-film camera by George Eastman. Camera lenses continue to be made until well into the 1930s, especially for Kodak.

---

**TRIVIA**

Bausch & Lomb continue to produce specialized optics, movie camera and projector lenses today. For example, they make the special lenses for the widescreen "cinemascope" films as well as the lenses for the cameras aboard the 1965 "Surveyor" lunar probes.

---

**1853:** Nadar, the professional pseudonym of Felix Toumachon (1820–1910), opens his portrait studio in Paris. Nadar is a French photographer, caricaturist, journalist, novelist, balloonist, and proponent of heavier-than-air flight. He will go on to perform many photographic firsts. Photographic portraits by Nadar are held by many of the great national collections of photographs.

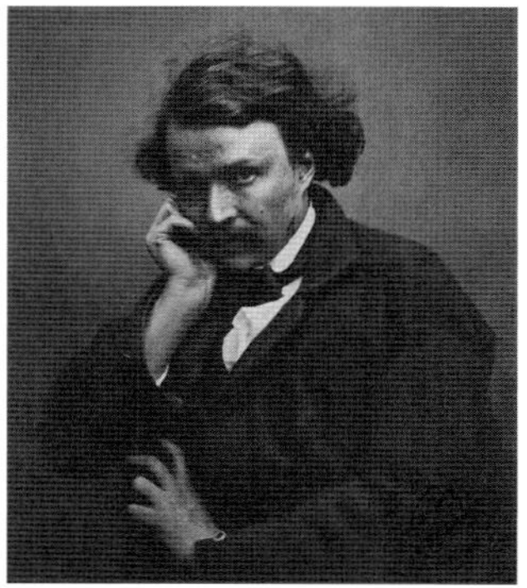
Nadar

> ### TRIVIA
> Nadar was a good friend of Jules Verne (1828–1905) and is said to be the inspiration for the Michael Ardan character in Verne's novel *From the Earth to the Moon.*

**1853:** Adolphe Martin (1824–1896), a Frenchman, describes a variation of the collodion positive process, the ambrotype, using a black enamelled tin plate instead of glass. These become popular around 1860 as the ferrotype or (in America) the tintype. Though ferrotypes are rarely of good quality, they are the cheapest form of photograph at the time.

> ### TRIVIA
> While regular wet-plate exposures vary from 10 to 90 seconds for landscapes, the exposures for the thin (underexposed) ambrotypes are in the order of just two to 20 seconds, making indoor portraits possible providing the windows are large and the day bright.

**1853:** The first English language photo magazine, *The Journal of the Photographic Society* (later the Royal Photographic Society), is published in the U.K. It will remain in continuous publication to this day.

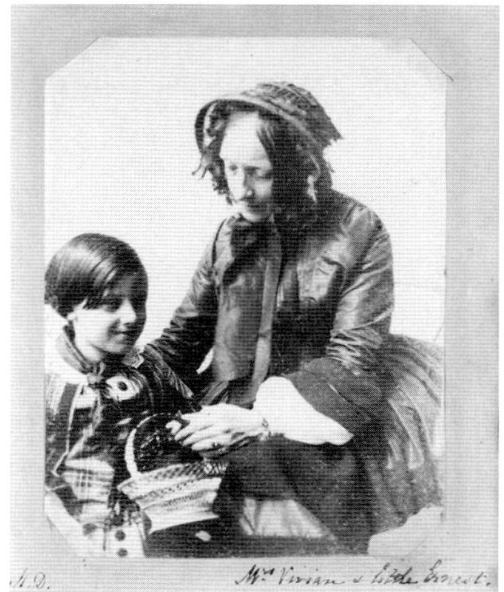
*"Mrs Vivian and little Ernest" (Photo by Mary Dillwyn)*

**1853:** Mary Dillwyn (1816–1906) of Wales becomes one of the earliest female photographers and is the first to capture a smile "on film." She is both a family friend of Fox Talbot and the younger sister of John Dillwyn Llewelyn (1810–1882), who will invent the oxymel process in 1856.

Starting in the late 1840s, she favours small cameras which allow shorter exposures and thus the opportunity to take more spontaneous photographs that capture the intimate moments of her family and friends. Her work appears more natural than that of other photographers of the period and she pushes the boundaries of what could be considered worthy subjects to photograph. Her interest in photography appears to end in 1857, when she marries the Reverend M. E. Welby.

> **TRIVIA**
>
> Mary Dillwyn's photographs have been preserved in two albums: one containing 42 salt prints and one albumen print, while the other contains 72 salt prints from the calotype process. Should you wish to see them, both are in the National Library of Wales, Aberystwykth.

**1853–1854:** Henry Fox Talbot sees that the collodion wet-plate process is cutting into his royalties from his patented calotype process. He threatens a number of prominent photographers with lawsuits if they do not pay him a royalty. His reasoning is that Archer's un-patented collodion process is covered by his calotype patent. In December of 1853, he obtains an injunction against a French-Canadian, William Silvester Laroche (1840–1889), who has a studio on Oxford Street, London. But Laroche resists and the case goes to trial in December of 1853. After three days in court, and after only an hour's deliberations, the jury finds that while Talbot is the true inventor of the calotype, Laroche is not guilty of infringing on that process by taking collodion portraits.

> **TRIVIA**
>
> Talbot is not happy with the verdict but realizing that there is no future in royalties for the calotype process, he fails to renew his patent. With the Daguerreotype patent having run its course by 1853, the calotype no longer patented, and Archer's collodion method having never been patented, all the known photographic processes are now free to all.

**1854:** George Eastman (1854–1932) is born in Waterville, New York.

**1854:** In Paris, Adolphe Disdéri  (1819–1889) patents a method for taking multiple images on a single glass plate, using either a camera with multiple lenses or with a single lens camera where the plate is rotated between exposures. This means several prints can be made at once, greatly lowering costs. The print is cut up and mounted on cards, each roughly 2.5 x 4 inches, become known as the carte-de-visite.

They fail to gain much popularity until May of 1859, when Napoleon III (1808–1873) drops by Disdéri's studio and has his portrait taken. This leads to a worldwide boom in portrait studios. A craze soon develops for collecting carte photographs of celebrities as well as one's friends. Some photographs run into editions of thousands, especially photos of the English Royal Family. Disdéri earns millions. While the fad peaks in the 1860s, it ends as fast as it had started and by 1870 Disdéri is bankrupt.

**1854:** A Bostonian, James A. Cutting (1914–1867), and Isaac Rehn (1815–1883) of Philadelphia start promoting the ambrotype.

If a thin (underexposed) glass plate is viewed against a black background it appears as a positive. Depending on the price and quality of the image, this backing can be fabric, cardboard, or a metal sheet. Sometimes the back of the glass is simply painted. It is also possible to use a dark red piece of glass, obviating the need for any sort of backing. Such photographs are called ambrotypes and are promoted as "Daguerreotypes on glass." They become quite popular, particularly for portraits. Being transparencies, they can be turned over before mounting, thus both protecting the emulsion and correcting the lateral reversal of the camera that plagues the Daguerreotype.

Ambrotypes have a short life. They become quite popular in America, less so in Britain, and fail to achieve great popularity elsewhere in the world. Their popularity begins to fade within two to three years, as they are replaced by the cheaper-to-produce ferrotype.

---

**TRIVIA**

The name "ambrotype" was coined by Marcus Root (1808–1888), from *ambrotos*, the Greek word for "imperishable."

---

**1854:** England's second photographic magazine starts as the *Liverpool Photographic Journal*. It becomes *The British Journal of Photography* in 1860. The magazine is published monthly until 1864, then weekly until March 2010, when it reverts back to being a monthly. Still in print, it is now also available as an electronic magazine.

**1854:** Arthur Melhuish (1829–1895) and J. B. Spencer produce the first roll-film holder, a special back that can be attached to a camera. It uses sensitized waxed paper, prepared using Talbot's formula. Its drawback is that to be developed, the roll must be cut into pieces, and it never proves popular.

This is followed by other attempts at roll-film adapters and backs that attempt to solve various problems such as how to advance the film without overlapping frames yet without wasting valuable film.

**1855:** On 13 May, Carl Kellner dies, at the age of 29, from tuberculosis. The management of the Optical Institute is assumed by Kellner's widow and an apprentice, Friedrich Belthle, who marries her the following year and subsequently manages the company. In 1865, Belthle will take on a new partner, Ernst Leitz (1843–1920).

**1855:** During the Crimean War, *The Illustrated London News* pioneers photojournalism when they print pictures of the war taken by Roger Fenton. Fenton is the first official war photographer; his work, which documents the effects of war on the troops, lays the groundwork for modern photojournalism.

**1855:** Carl August von Steinheil (1801–1870), a German physicist and astronomer, starts the Steinheil Optical Institute in Munich (München), Bavaria. The company makes many of the astronomical telescopes for German observatories as well as camera lenses. In the 1860s Carl's son, Hugo (1832–1893) buys out his father and will go on to develop the Steinheil Aplanat (see **1866**).

**1856:** Alexander Parkes (1813–1890) invents celluloid. It will become the basis of all modern films until "safety film" is developed in 1951.

**1856:** William Thompson takes the first underwater pictures, in the waters of Dorset in the U.K. He puts a 4 x 5 inch dry-collodion plate camera in a watertight box and lowers it to a depth of 18 feet. After a 10-minute exposure, he brings it up and develops the plate. Although water pressure causes the box to leak, a weak but discernible image is obtained, showing the underwater plant growth of the shallow sea bottom.

**1856:** Dr. Richard Norris (1830–1916) markets his dry plates. Previously, attempts had been made to produce dry plates, but all efforts result in very low sensitivity and a short shelf life. Norris's method, made by coating wet-collodion emulsions with gelatin, results in a plate that, once dry, can be stored for up to six months. It is the first commercially successful dry plate, though it fails to gain significant traction against the more light-sensitive wet-collodion plates.

**1856:** An American, Hamilton Smith (1809–1903), is issued a patent for "photographic pictures on Japanned surfaces." Utilizing a collodion emulsion like that used in ambrotypes, and applying it on black-lacquered metal plates, positive photographs can be made less expensively than by using glass and without the need for a black backing. Ferrotypes, or "tintypes," as they become known, quickly supplant the ambrotype because of their lower cost.

### TRIVIA

To work outdoors in the 1850s, a photographer had to bring along his camera and plates, a darkroom tent, all its equipment and chemicals, and water for washing the plates. In all it weighed as much as 75 pounds, assuming he used the common smaller-sized plates, not the larger and heavier 20 x 24-inch glass plates favoured by top-flight landscape photographers.

Because good quality flat-surfaced glass was both uncommon and expensive in the mid-1800s, unsatisfactory negatives, and those no longer needed, were often stripped of their emulsions and the glass re-used.

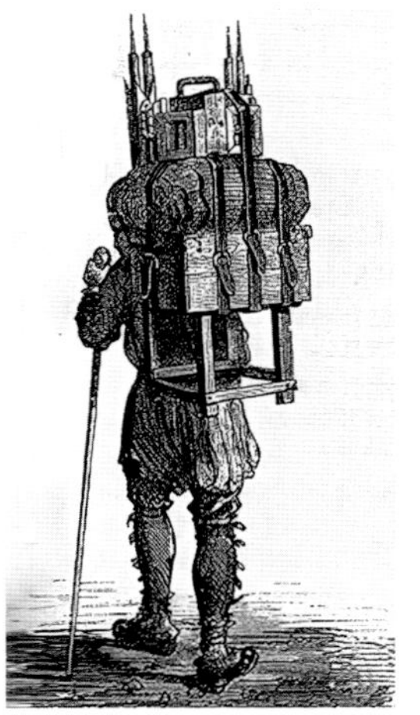

*1874*

**1856:** John B. Dancer (1812–1887), an English optical instrument maker, patents a camera that takes two pictures simultaneously through two lenses set slightly apart, making stereo photography practical as well as popular.

**1856:** Invented by J. D. Llewelyn, the oxymel process is one of the first "dry" processes and is immediately hailed by the *Illustrated Evening News* as a considerable advance. It is a variation on the collodion process, but it differs in that it is given further treatment in a bath of oxymel, a honey/vinegar solution. The resulting plate is roughly one-fifth as sensitive as a standard wet-collodion plate but allows negatives to be prepared in advance and later developed at leisure.

**1857:** Frederick Scott Archer, inventor of the wet-plate (collodion) process, dies at the age of 44, "worn out with the struggle for his bare existence, and having spent all his money and energy on various improvements to photography." His collodion process provides thousands with a fascinating hobby or a rewarding career. Yet he is almost forgotten among the various inventors in photography, with only the Manchester Photographic Society publishing a tribute. He dies a broke and broken man. Yet it is almost certain that had he patented the use of collodion, his profits would have been enormous.

**1858:** Gustave Guilleminot (1830–1895), of Paris, starts selling supplies for collodion photographers. He will go on to make pre-sensitized plates (also known as dry plates) and, eventually, photo films and paper. The company enjoys a 116-year run but closes in 1994.

---

### TRIVIA

In 1995, Guy Gerard, a chemical engineer at Guilleminot for 30 years, will go on to start a new film company, Bergger, in its stead. His film is good, his firm successful, and Bergger continues today.

---

**1858:** Near the end of the Daguerreotype era, some three million Daguerreotypes a year are being made in the United States alone. Some photographers are turning out inferior quality Daguerreotypes at a cost of just 25 cents . . . for two!

**1858:** Nadar becomes the first aerial photographer by taking photographs from a hot air balloon.

**1858:** Charles Harrison and Joseph Schnitzer invent the adjustable iris. Their iris diaphragm is capable of rapid open and close cycles, an absolute necessity for modern auto-aperture control. However, it will not find popular use as an adjustable stop in cameras until the 1880s.

---

### TRIVIA

The earliest lenses did not have adjustable stops because their small working apertures and the lack of sensitivity of the Daguerreotype process meant that exposure times were measured in many minutes. A photographer would not want to limit the light passing through the lens and further lengthen the exposure time. When the increased sensitivity of the wet collodion process came along, in 1851, exposure times shortened dramatically, and adjustable stops became necessary.

---

**1858:** John Waterhouse (1806–1879) creates the first selectable stops or aperture plates. Called "stops" because the small aperture "stopped" excess light from getting in, they consist of a series of brass plates with variously sized holes in them and are mounted between the lens elements by way of a slot in the top or side of the lens barrel. The term was so useful that aperture openings are still referred to as "stops" to this day.

**1859:** William Crookes (1832–1919), then editor of *The Photographic News*, is the first to suggest using artificial light for taking photographs. In October he writes: "A still more brilliant light but a terribly expensive one, can be obtained by burning the new metal, magnesium, in oxygen. A piece of magnesium wire held by one end in the hand, may be lighted at the other extremity by holding it to a candle. It then burns away of its own accord evolving a light insupportably brilliant to the unprotected eye."

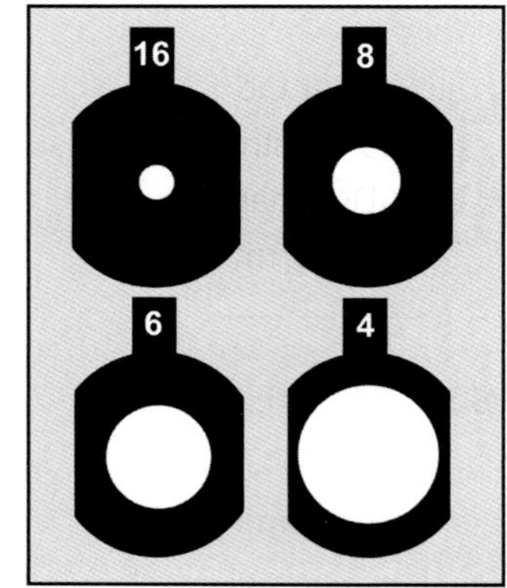


*Waterhouse stops*

---

### TRIVIA

Magnesium is indeed expensive. In 1859 it costs £6 per pound, or roughly £650 per pound today. This means that magnesium wire costs around 12½ pence per foot at the time, and the equal of £5½ per foot today. And a photographer might need several feet of wire to expose a photograph.

---

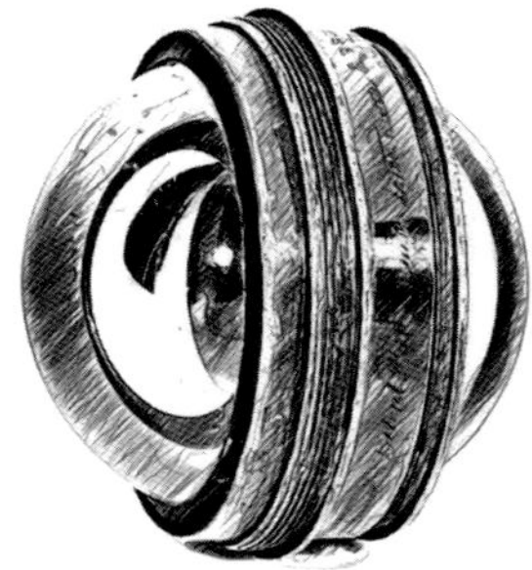

**1860:** Thomas Sutton (1819–1875) produces the "Patent Panoramic Water Lens," the first wide-angle lens. Patented the year before, it consists of two thick flint glass lenses with concentric surfaces that enclose a hollow space filled with crystal clear water. The result is a lens with a field of view of 100° to 120°, depending on plate size, and an aperture of *f* 12. Very few are made, and today it is probably the rarest photographic lens ever produced.

**1860:** The Daguerreotype, ferrotype, ambrotype, and calotype processes are all virtually obsolete and are rapidly being replaced by the wet collodion plate.

**1860:** In Germany, Dr. C. Schleussner Fotowerke GmbH start producing photographic materials under the ADOX name. The Schleussner company will make film until 1972, when their new owner, DuPont, will sell off the film-making machines to the Yugoslavian company Fotokemika, along with the rights to use the ADOX name.

---

**TRIVIA**

Fotokemika's rights to the ADOX name expired in the early 1990s. After that they sold their film under the Efke brand. Fotokemika ceased all production in June 2012 but continue to this day as a distributor of medical films and materials made by other manufacturers. In 2009, the ADOX name and original formulas are re-introduced by ADOX Fotowerke GmbH, in Bad Saarow, Germany.

---

**1860–61:** Using physicist Thomas Young's new theory of primary colours, James Clerk-Maxwell (1831–1879), with the help of photographer Thomas Sutton, produces the first colour image. The subject is a tartan ribbon, and the photograph is comprised of three black-and-white positives, each photographed and then projected through a different primary colour filter onto a screen. (This is the "colour separation" method.)

Although his experiment is a success, it is more by good luck than good management. The films of the day are not yet sensitive to red light, so the negative recorded through the red filter is actually recording ultra-violet light reflecting off the red areas of the subject. Still, it works.

---

**TRIVIA**

Colour photography is difficult for the early inventors, for while it was long known that all colours could be created from red, yellow and blue pigments, the primary colours of the light spectrum are red, green, and blue. It took some time for photographers and scientists to discover this.

---

**1861:** Nadar makes the first photographs with artificial light, descending into the catacombs below Paris with magnesium flares.

**1861:** C. P. Smyth (1819–1900), Astronomer Royal for Scotland, builds the first true miniature camera. The negative is a wet collodion plate, just one inch square. It features a well-corrected 44mm lens with an aperture of $f4.5$ and a focal-plane shutter.

**1861:** Thomas Sutton patents the first single-lens reflex camera using glass plates. He describes the instrument this way: "The ground glass lies horizontally, beneath your eye, and you look down upon it and see the picture erect, thus obtaining a very perfect idea of the composition." The manually levered reflex mirror also serves as the camera's shutter. A small number are hand-built, but none are known to survive.

**1861–65:** Washington photographer Mathew B. Brady (c.1822/24–1896) and staff (mostly staff) cover the American Civil War, exposing 7,000 wet-plate negatives. Brady records not only the soldiers and their battles, but also the consequence of war: battlefield corpses. Sales are good during the war, but after 1865 the public has little interest in such gruesome reminders, and Brady becomes bankrupt.

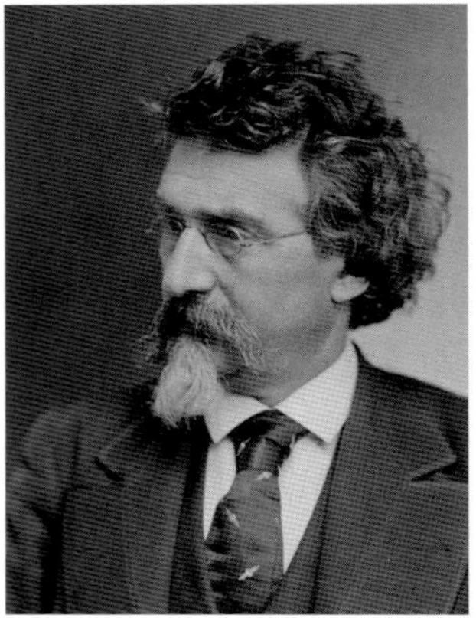

*Mathew Brady, 1875*

---

### TRIVIA

In 1875, the U.S. congress purchases Brady's entire archive of Civil War negatives for $25,000 (or almost $545,000 today). This not only saves him financially but cements his reputation as the preeminent photographer of the war.

---

**1862:** The Achromat Landscape lens (see **1839**) is afflicted with rectilinear distortion (straight lines appear as curved). This is a pressing problem—since buildings do not move (to state the obvious) they are an ideal subject for photographers of the era, who are limited to using the existing slow processes. The distortion gets progressively worse as the field of view is increased, which means the Achromat Landscape cannot be used as a wide-angle lens.

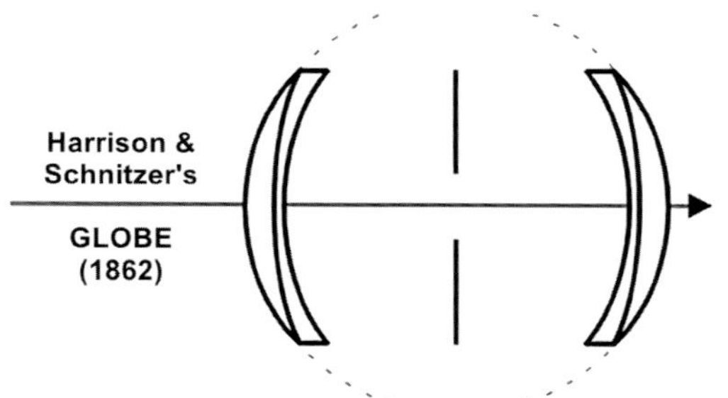


**1862:** The first successful wide-angle lens (a 92° maximum field of view is claimed, with 80° being more realistic) is the Harrison & Schnitzer Globe (USA), with an $f$16 maximum aperture ($f$30 was more realistic). It uses a symmetric four element formula—the name refers to the fact that if the two outer surfaces were continued and joined, they would form a sphere.

The Globe's symmetric formula directly influences the design of the Dallmeyer Rapid-Rectilinear in 1866.

**1862:** Louis Ducos du Hauron (1837–1920) discovers a way to make colour prints. He makes three negatives, each with a different primary-colour filter. From these, positive prints are made using semi-transparent paper coated in pigments of colours complementary to the original filters used. When they are carefully laid atop each other, a coloured print emerges. It is a complex process, but it works, and he gets his patent in 1868.

**1863:** Hippolyte Bayard's photographic innovations are finally officially acknowledged when he receives the prestigious cross of the French Legion of Honour (see **1839**).

**1863:** Magnesium, discovered in 1807 by Sir Humphrey Davy, finds little immediate practical application, but after two years of intensive experimentation, an Englishman, Edward Sonstadt, patents a method to prepare magnesium on a commercial basis, and magnesium wire is placed on sale. It is expensive, but will find many uses in photography, particularly after Sonstadt successfully takes a photograph in a darkened room in just 50 seconds by burning magnesium wire as the only light source.

**1864:** Invented by Walter B. Woodbury (1834–1885), the Woodburytype is the first successful photo-mechanical process, meaning that sensitivity to light plays no role in the actual printing. The process is able to reproduce beautiful continuous tone images from photographs on a printing press without the use of screens. It is used for books, magazines, and special-edition printings between 1864 and 1910. Although attempts are made to adapt Woodburytype to rotary printing, the process cannot compete with the quickly developing halftone photo-mechanical processes, and the Woodburytype is soon gone.

**1864:** C. Piazzi Smyth (1819–1900) successfully uses magnesium wire to illuminate a photograph of the interior of Egypt's Great Pyramid.

**1866:** John Henry Dallmeyer (1830–1883) of the U.K. introduces his Rapid Rectilinear lens. Composed of two matching doublet lenses symmetrically placed around the focal aperture, it removes many of the aberrations present in more simple constructions.

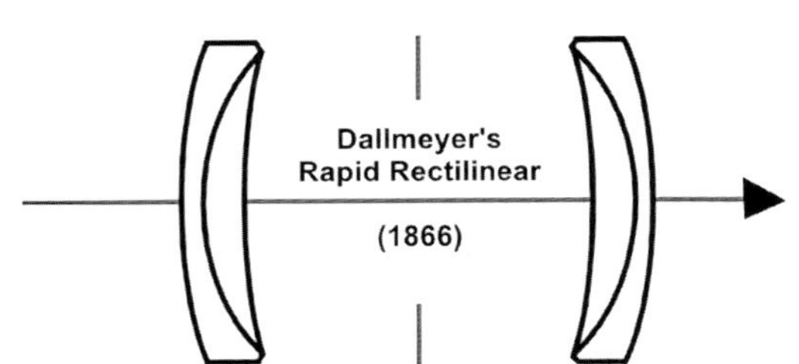


> **TRIVIA**
>
> At this time, the Landscape lens, Petzval's Portrait lens, the wide-angle Globe and the Rapid Rectilinear constitute the photographer's entire lens arsenal.

**1866:** Almost simultaneously with Dallmeyer's Rapid Rectilinear, Steinheil brings its Aplanat to market. Although developed independently of each other, John Dallmeyer's Rapid-Rectilinear and Hugo Steinheil's Aplanat have virtually identical symmetric, four-element formulas and arrive on the market almost simultaneously. Both correct most optical aberrations, except for spherical and field curvature, all the way to $f$ 8!

**1866:** Barium glass is introduced. Until now, only crown glass (a soda-lime-silica composite) and flint glasses (containing 45–65% lead oxide) were available to lens designers. Barium glass uses barium oxide rather than lead oxide, and has a refractive index comparable to flint glass, but lower dispersion. Now designers have three weapons with which to tackle aberrations. This breakthrough in glass technology will eventually result in the anastigmat lens, but this will have to wait another 20-plus years.

**1866:** German Ernst Abbe (1840–1905), a mathematician at the University of Jena, is approached by Carl Zeiss regarding various optical problems. This turns his attention towards optics. In addition to his university posts, Abbe becomes research director of the Zeiss optical works. Abbe then develops the scientific basis for the design and construction of optical instruments. The missing factor is the availability of standardized types of glass with constant and planned properties. This bottleneck will be solved when Otto Schott (1851–1935) joins Zeiss in 1882.

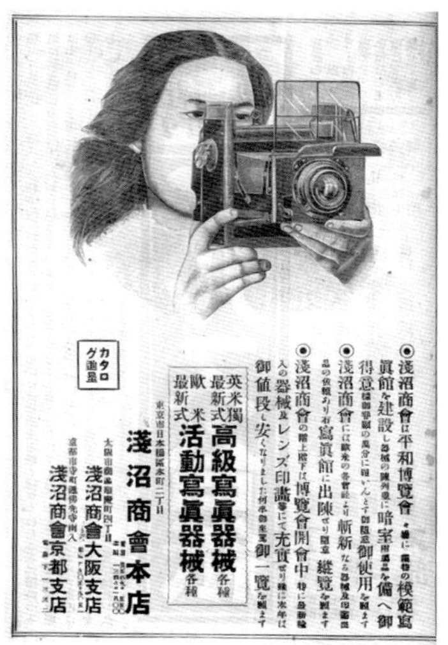


**1867:** Aktien Gesellschaft für Anilin Fabrikation, or Agfa, is started, but the Agfa name will not appear on cameras until 1925.

**1867:** Asanuma Shōkai (in English, Asanuma & Co.) is established by Asanuma Tōkichi to distribute photographic equipment. In the 1910s and 1920s, they will manufacture their own large-format studio and field cameras. Some time in the 1930s the "KING" brand name is used for various accessories, such as an exposure table, an accessory rangefinder, and tripods. In the 1970s and 1980s, Asanuma distributes manual focus lenses in mounts for a variety of camera brands, under their own name as well as that of Vivitar and others. It is unclear if they actually manufacture the lenses, but these arrangements end with the appearance of auto-focus lenses in the late 1980s. Today Asanuma continues to sell accessories under the KING brand.

---

**TRIVIA**

Starting around 1933, Asanuma distributes the Happy and various Minolta models from the Molta company (later Chiyoda Kōgaku Seikō). The company apparently had the exclusive right to sell these cameras, at least in Japan, until the end of the Second World War. After the war, it still appeared as an authorized dealer of the Minolta cameras until at least 1952.

---

**1867:** The American Optical Company becomes a division of the Scovill Company. American Optical manufacture box cameras, stereoscopes, and accessories, and develop an international reputation due to their high-quality products and the low cost of American wood craftsmanship.

**1868:** In Bordeaux, France, Ducos du Hauron publishes a book proposing a variety of methods for colour photography.

**1869:** In Paris, du Hauron and a fellow Frenchman, Charles Cross, introduce an alternative method of creating a colour photograph. They make photographs through red, green, and blue filters, which are then converted to positives. However, rather than converting them into transparencies for projection as Maxwell had done, they dye each positive with the complementary colour of its original filter. Precisely overlapped on white paper, the three films fuse into a full colour image of the original.

**1869:** Kuichi Uchida (1844–1875) opens Japan's first photographic studio in Tokyo, using a wet-plate camera of his own manufacture. Among the Japanese public there is a strong superstition that being photographed shortens one's life. To counteract this, he calls his studio "Kuichido Manju"—*The Kuichi Studio of Everlasting Life*.

---

**TRIVIA**

Little is known about photography in Japan prior to 1869. Daguerreotype cameras had been imported, though only five Daguerreotypes and none of the cameras are known to have survived. As well, there are records of wet-plate cameras in the country by 1857. Photography was practised by a small group of "Dutch Scholars"—so called because they pursued "western" sciences imported by Dutch merchant ships, the only ones allowed into Nagasaki harbour during the Tokugawa isolation of 1615–1868.

---

**1869:** Precision mechanic Ernst Leitz, having joined Kellner's Optical Institute in 1864 and become a partner with C. F. Belthle in 1865, becomes sole owner of the company when Belthle suddenly dies. Leitz keeps the Wetzlar Optical Institute name temporarily, but in 1870 the company introduces a new achromatic microscope that bears the name Ernst Leitz Company. The company expands rapidly, and a newly developed binocular microscope is a huge market success. The Ernst Leitz Company goes on to become the only effective competitor to Zeiss and, in 1924, will start the 35mm revolution by introducing the Leica camera.

**1870–1878:** A Scottish expat, J. R. Black (1826–1880), publishes an illustrated English news magazine called *The Far East*, which appears first in Japan and later in China. As the technology of the day does not allow photographic reproductions in magazines or newspapers, Black has staff paste original photographic prints on to the pages to illustrate the stories. Each issue has a press run of just 500 to 1,000 copies.

---

**TRIVIA**

These original photos are what make surviving copies of *The Far East* so valuable today. In 2009, Sotheby's auctioned 18 issues for £30,000 (about $52,000). In 2017, a Vancouver homeless man found 24 issues, bound in Moroccan leather, in a dumpster. Their value has yet to be determined.

**1871:** Richard Leach Maddox (1816–1902), an English doctor, proposes using an emulsion of gelatin and silver bromide on a glass plate, creating the modern "dry plate." Although he publishes his process in September, health problems prevent him from perfecting the details.

**1872:** In the U.S., Eadweard Muybridge (1830–1904), born in England as Edward Muggeridge, settles a "Do a horse's four hooves ever leave the ground all at once?" bet among wealthy San Franciscans. He photographs a galloping horse using a dozen cameras triggered one after another by a set of strings and proves conclusively that they do. He later copies the photos on to a rotating disc and invents a device to make it appear as if the horse is moving, long before flexible film cinematography exists.

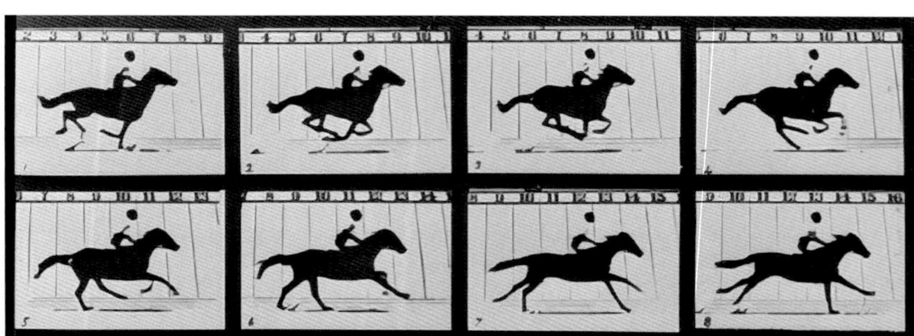

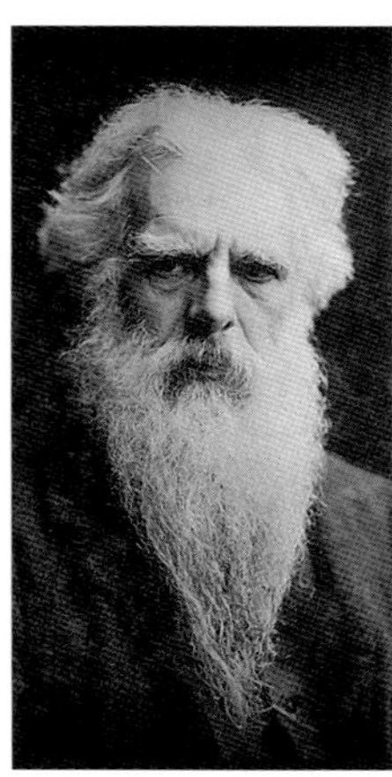

*Eadweard Muybridge*

### TRIVIA

In 1871, the 41 year old Muybridge married a 21 year old divorcee, Flora Stone, who, almost three years later, gives birth to a son. Because of his frequent absences, the photographer suspected his young wife of being unfaithful and became convinced that the child was fathered by her friend, Major Harry Larkyns. On 17 October 1874, Muybridge tracked down and shot his supposed rival to death. The sensational trial that followed featured an insanity defence, in which his attorney argued his client suffered a serious head injury after an 1850 stagecoach accident. The jury was not convinced, but acquitted Muybridge on the grounds of "justifiable homicide." Though the scandal did not ruin his career, it irreparably damaged his marriage. Ironically, photographs of his son as a young man reveal a striking resemblance to Muybridge.

Today, the court case and transcripts are important to historians and forensic neurologists, because of the sworn testimony from multiple witnesses about Muybridge's state of mind and past behaviour.

In 1982, the American composer, Philip Glass, premiered his opera (sometimes called a "chamber opera") *The Photographer*, with a libretto based, in part, on court transcripts from the case.

**1872:** While not what he is most famous for, Charles Darwin's third book, *The Expression of Emotions in Man and Animals*, is the first scientific text to include photographs.

**1873:** Until now, all emulsions have been "colour blind," sensitive only to blue, violet, and ultra-violet light. In Berlin, Hermann Vogel (1834–1898) discovers the process of dye sensitizing, which greatly extends the sensitivity of silver halide emulsions into the green and yellow regions of the spectrum. By 1884, he has discovered how to extend the sensitivity to orange light. Such emulsions are called "orthochromatic." However, the achievement of a fully panchromatic response (with sensitivity into the red) has to wait for German E. König's discovery of sensitizing cyanine-dyes in 1904.

**1873:** A young pharmacist, Rokusaburo Sugiura, has his photograph taken at a photography studio when he is just 25. The experience impresses him greatly. In 1887, he leaves his family's business and launches his own shop, Konishi Honten (Konishi Main Shop), in Tokyo, to deal in imported photographic materials and medicines. It is the start of what will become Konishiroku Photo Industry and, later, Konica. It is Japan's oldest photo company.

By 1882, Konishi has three established factories for manufacturing lithographic materials and equipment as well as matte paper for picture mounting, and has begun to produce box cameras. In 1890, Konishi expands camera manufacturing from an on-order basis to planned production and, four years later, is producing a variety of studio, field, and folding cameras. In 1903, Konishi will sell the "Cherry Portable Camera," the first Japanese, mass-produced, end-user-oriented camera. In 1921, Sugiura's elder son takes over the company and the name is changed from Konishi Honten to Konishiroku Honten.

**1873:** John Joly (1857–1933) devises a screen made of microscopic transparent strips arranged in alternating patterns of red, green, and blue. This screen is positioned in front of the emulsion of a conventional black-and-white plate. Once exposed, developed, and converted to a positive and finally projected through the original screen, it provides a colour image from a single plate with just a single projector. It is a forerunner of the Bayer filter that is at the heart of most digital cameras today.

**1873:** Ernst Abbe releases a scientific paper describing the mathematics behind optical design. For the first time, aberration, diffraction, and coma are described and understood. Abbe describes the optical process so well that this paper becomes the foundation upon which much of our understanding of optical science rests today. In 1876, as a reward for his efforts, Carl Zeiss makes Abbe a partner in his burgeoning business.

**1873:** In July, John Burgess, a resident of London, begins selling a gelatin emulsion that photographers can use to make their own dry plates. It is not a success, perhaps because to achieve adequate sensitivity the emulsion

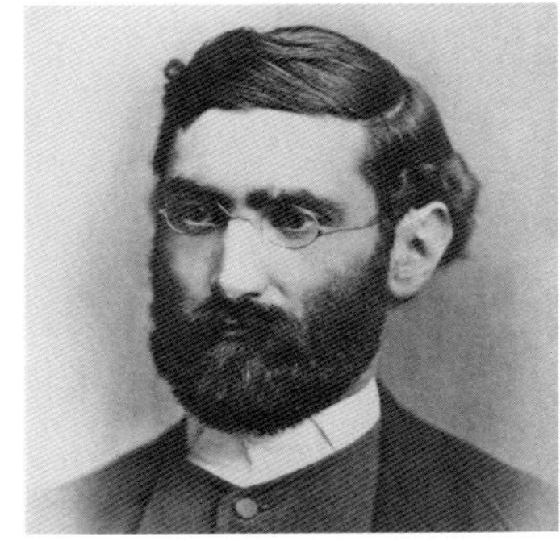

*Ernst Abbe*

requires fermentation above 70° Fahrenheit, which he does not realize. Burgess starts selling prepared plates in August and does better, but not by a lot.

**1874:** Amateur photographer Richard Kennett puts on sale a dried gelatin emulsion which, like Burgess's reconstituted product, is intended for coating onto glass plates by the photographer. Kennett's preparation is dried by heat and, unknown to Kennett, the heat is responsible for a huge increase in sensitivity, which is soon observed in the coated plates. But again, the emulsion is not a market success.

**1875:** John Arthur Roebuck Rudge (1807–1903), a British instrument maker and inventor, creates his Biophantic Lantern, which displays seven slides in rapid succession, giving the illusion of movement.

**1875:** Ferdinand Hurter (1844–1898) and Vero Driffield (1848–1915) begin their investigations into photographic sensitometry, a method to measure accurately the intensity of light and its effects on dry plates. These measurements will lead to discovering the optimal exposure and developing times given certain brightness ratios, developers, and temperatures. Their results are published in 1890 and, for the first time, make it possible to develop plates in total darkness with predictable results.

### TRIVIA

Hurter and Driffield proposed the first standardized exposure method, the "H & D Speed System" in 1890. Eventually, Hurter and Driffield's work leads to other standardized sensitivity rating programs, such as the DIN, ASA, GOST, and ISO, among others.

**1876:** D. H. Cussons & Company of Leeds publishes *The Photographers Almanac*, which becomes a popular reference book, the first of its kind.

**1877:** Leon Warnerke (1837–1900), a Russian living in England, offers a roll-film back which uses "stripping film." A light-sensitive emulsion blended into transparent gelatin or collodion is coated on an opaque roll of paper. Once the exposures are developed and fixed, the transparent layer is separated (or "stripped") from the paper backing by soaking the film in warm water. The delicate negatives are then mounted on a sheet of glass and printed. While mechanically sound, the process is complex and does not fare well in the market. Other roll films of the day all have design flaws that prevent widespread use.

**1877:** In preparation for a trip to Santo Domingo, a young American bank clerk, George Eastman, buys a wet-collodion outfit and takes photography lessons from a local photographer. He never does make the trip to Santo Domingo, but soon becomes dissatisfied with the messy, cumbersome process and begins to search for a better way.

**TRIVIA**

The source of George Eastman's dissatisfaction with wet-plate photography is a little-known story. While on a short trip with his camera, he discovered that most of the clothes packed in his trunk had been ruined by a leaking bottle of silver nitrate. Whether working in a studio or in the field, it was impossible for photographers to avoid silver nitrate. It stained your hands, your clothes, everything it touched. No wonder photographers were quick to adopt dry-plates and film when they became practical.

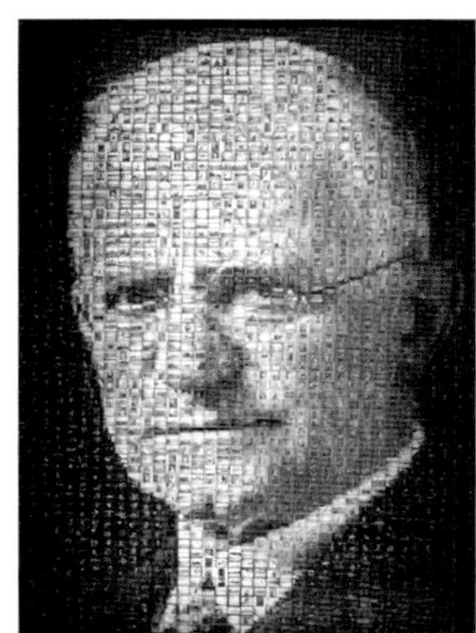

*George Eastman*

**1878:** Emil Suter (1875–1944) forms the Optical Institute of Emil Suter (*Optische Anstalt E. Suter*) in Basel, Switzerland. The company produces high-quality lenses and parts, which it sells wholesale to various camera manufacturers in France, Germany, and Italy. The company grows into a large photographic manufacturer, the first of its kind in Switzerland, and survives for over 125 years, only ceasing operations in 2005.

**1878:** Charles Bennett (1840–1927) of London investigates the effect of heat on Kennett's dried emulsion and, in March, publishes a paper in the *British Journal of Photography*. Now, dry plates can be easily manufactured, and exposure times reduced to a fraction of a second. Within months, over a dozen firms are producing dry plates.

**TRIVIA**

While Bennett advocated a drying temperature of 90º Fahrenheit for two to seven days (depending on the sensitivity desired), others found that raising the temperature to near boiling (about 200º F) for 10 minutes worked just as well, saving considerable time and effort.

**1879:** John Carbutt (1830–1905) sells his Keystone dry plates, the first to be made in the USA, while the E. & H. T. Anthony & Company soon follows with its Defiance dry plates in 1880.

**TRIVIA**

Dry plates supplanted wet plates more quickly in Britain than on the Continent but took longer in America. Professionals were concerned about the cost, both of the new dry plates and because with wet plates they could re-use the glass from failed or unwanted exposures, something not possible with prepared plates. Amateurs, on the other hand, were quick to pick up on the convenience.

**1879:** The Britannia Works are founded in Ilford, U.K. by Alfred Hugh Harman (1841–1913). The company begins making dry photographic plates and in 1902 takes the name of the town to become Ilford Limited, despite the objections of the local council.

**1879:** Oskar Barnack (1879–1936) is born on 1 November, in Linow, Germany. He will go on to design the Leica camera and become the most influential camera designer in history.

**1880:** Bausch & Lomb of Rochester, New York, begin the manufacture of photographic lenses, selling most of their production to the Rochester Optical Company, who start making cameras the same year.

**1880:** Otto Perutz (1847–1922) develops a method for the industrial production of eosin-silver plates, which had been invented by Hermann Vogel and Johann Obernetter (1840–1887). This will prove crucial in the later development of colour photography. Perutz sells his firm in 1897 and Perutz-Photowerke becomes part of Agfa in 1964. Agfa will continue to make the original Perutz film until 1983, when it becomes Agfa film sold under the Perutz label. The Perutz brand will be discontinued in the late 1990s.

---

### ODDITIES

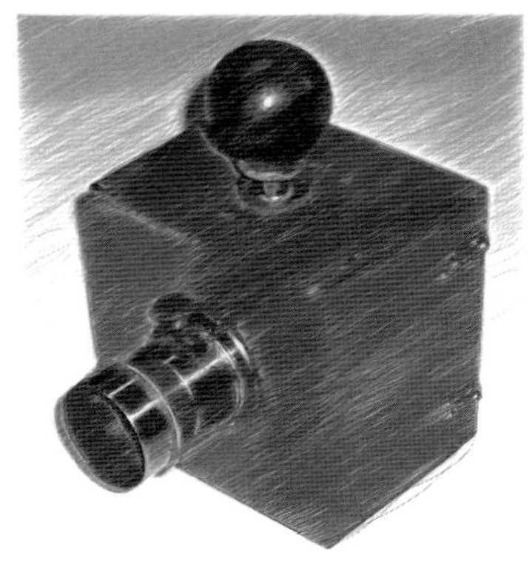

The 1880 Dubroni was the first "instant camera," beating the Polaroid by almost 70 years. It was made of wood, with an internal ceramic lining. After the exposure, the processing chemicals were inserted through a light-sealed hole in the camera's top by means of a large rubber syringe called a "pear." The camera was then tilted and agitated, to allow the developer (and later the fixing bath) to coat the plate. The camera back had a rubber seal and a strong spring system, making it leak-proof.

This basic idea will be seen again in the Speed-o-Matic (see **1948**), the Pinsta, in 2021, and the InstaBox in 2023.

---

**1880:** George Eastman invents an emulsion-coating machine that enables him to mass-produce photographic dry plates. His first commercial plates are sold in 1880, though these early plates tend to quickly lose their sensitivity to light. The problem is a missing sulphur-bearing compound in the gelatin. This compound is necessary for the "ripening" or "curing" process.

**1880:** The first known twin-lens reflex (TLR) camera is a one-of-a-kind model made by R. & J. Beck, London. It has the advantage, like all TLRs, that you can view the subject while the photograph is being made.

**1880:** The William H. Walker Company sets up shop in Rochester, New York, to build cameras and, in 1881, manufactures Walker's Pocket Camera. Its design is so precise that all of its parts are fully interchangeable from one camera to the next—a remarkable accomplishment for a camera made of wood!

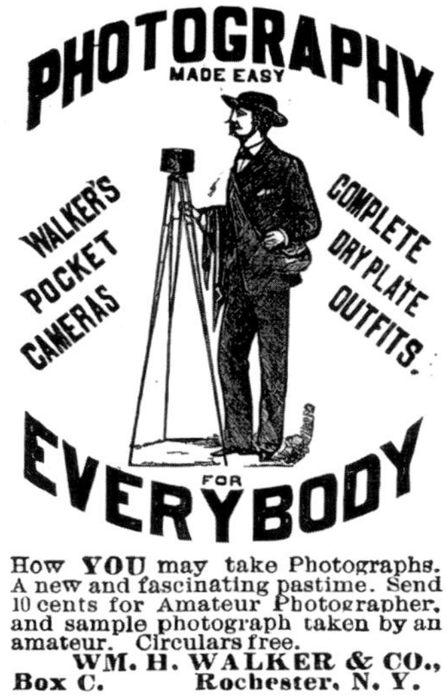

**1881:** At age 24, George Eastman expands his operation, setting up the Eastman Dry Plate Company in Rochester in partnership with Henry Strong (a family friend and buggy-whip manufacturer). To fix the dropping-sensitivity problem, Eastman goes to England, where he purchases a formula for a top-quality dry-plate emulsion and the machines to make the plates. He returns to Rochester, installs the new equipment and re-starts production.

**1881:** In North Dakota, David Henderson Houston patents a camera design which uses roll film, just as we use it today. His genius is that while roll film will not be created for almost another decade, he can see that film is coming and how it might be used. Eventually he will license his patent to Kodak, for $5,750—a considerable sum for a 19th-century farmer. He proves to be a prolific inventor and will go on to license other patents to Kodak, including ones for folding, panoramic, and magazine-loading cameras.

---

### TRIVIA

It is said that Houston may have contributed to George Eastman's choosing the Kodak name. Eastman said, "A trademark should be short . . . vigorous . . . incapable of being misspelled . . . " and "it must mean absolutely nothing." Eastman felt the letter "K" was a strong letter and wanted his brand name to start with it. He claimed the rest was a "purely arbitrary collection of letters." But, according to a book by Houston's niece-in-law, Mina V. Hammer, the rest of the name came at Houston's suggestion, from a common shorthand of the time, for Houston's home state of North Dakota, even though it would not gain statehood for another eight years: Nodak.

True or not, it's a great story.

---

**1881:** Walter Bentley Woodbury (1834–1885) patents his automatic balloon camera (see **1864**). This 12-pound camera holds four plates and has an electromagnetically actuated spring mechanism which brings each successive plate into place for exposure. The shutter is also electromagnetic and is controlled by wires running along the rope tethering the balloon to the ground. Watching through a telescope, the operator fires the camera by pressing one button to put the plate in position and a second to fire the shutter.

**1881:** The first halftone photograph appears in a daily newspaper, the *New York Graphic*.

**1882:** Explosives manufacturer SIPE (*Società Italiana Prodotti Esplodenti*, or "Italian Society of Explosives Products") is founded in Ferrania, Italy. Since the manufacturing processes for explosives and early film-backing materials are very similar, they will start production of Ferrania film in 1923.

**1882:** Otto Schott sets up his glass laboratory in the Zeiss works and systematically determines the dependence of optical properties on the composition of glass. Schott develops numerous new types of optical glass with hitherto unknown properties. Remarkably, within six months he is able to issue a catalogue with 44 different types of glass and is thus seen as the founder of modern glass technology.

**1882:** Étienne-Jules de Marey (1830–1904) produces pictures of birds in flight with his "gun camera." A forerunner of motion-picture cameras, it looks like a machine gun and employs a clock mechanism to make 12 photos on successive portions of a rotating glass plate.

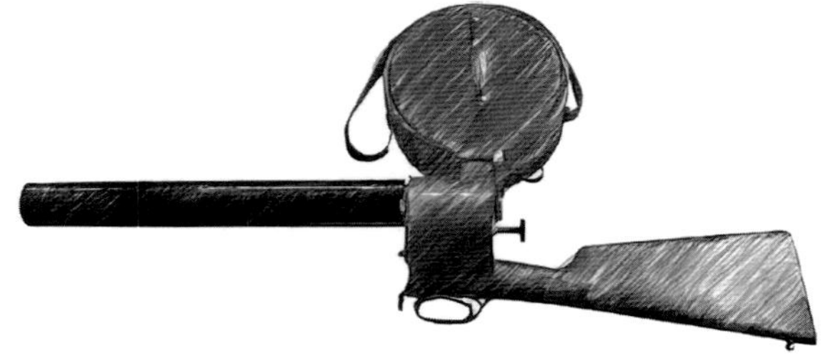

**1883:** The Schmidt Patent Detective Camera comes to market. Using box-in-box construction, the inner box can be moved for focusing. A focusing scale is mounted atop the camera and a rotary shutter sits between the camera's front and the lens. The shutter spring's tension is adjustable to allow several shutter speeds, and there is a small reflecting finder in the upper corner of the body, which means that the user can shoot from waist level, looking less conspicuous. It is the camera's relatively small size and this ability to shoot inconspicuously that led to the "detective" label. It is the first commercially made camera designed to be hand-held, and it brings on a revolution.

---

### TRIVIA
While the term "detective camera" was rapidly replaced by the term "hand camera" in both Britain and the USA, it persisted much longer in France, referring to any small box-like camera.

---

**1883:** To lighten the photographer's load, Eastman experiments with waxing paper as in the earlier calotype process but coating it with "modern" emulsions. This paper proves quite sensitive and (with a suitable adapter) is used in standard plate holders, but it is not a huge success.

**1884:** W. H. Walker (1846–1917) leaves his firm to join the Eastman Dry Plate Company, but his business continues as part of the Rochester Optical Company.

**1884:** Otto Schott, along with Ernst Abbe and Carl Zeiss, found Jenaer Glaswerke, later called the Jenaer Glaswerke-Schott & Genossen.

**1884:** William H. Walker, a camera maker, joins Eastman's firm and together they develop a roll holder suitable for use with any standard plate camera (see **1880**). It holds a roll of negative paper sufficient for 24 exposures. This paper is developed and then soaked in warm water. Soon the emulsion can be stripped off the paper and, in a series of tricky operations, transferred to glass or gelatin sheets for subsequent printing. As well, their roll-film holder has a mechanical exposure counter . . . a first.

Unlike the many earlier efforts at roll film, the Eastman & Walker unit is well-made, reliable, and holds paper of consistent quality, so it becomes immediately successful. The name of the firm is changed to the Eastman Dry Plate & Film Company.

**1884:** Calvin Rae Smith (1847–1918) builds his Monocular Duplex. It is the first SLR to be made in the USA, and Smith's overly enthusiastic advertisements quickly make it the world's first commercially viable SLR.

The Monocular Duplex uses glass plates (originally quarter plate and later 4 x 5 inches), although many will subsequently be adapted to use the latest technical advance, Eastman's roll film holders. Large-format SLRs are the dominant SLR type until around 1915, though SLRs of any type will not be commonplace until the 1930s.

**THE PATENT MONOCULAR DUPLEX,**
Or, **ARTIST CAMERA.**
C. R. Smith's Patent, 1884, England, France, & United States.

THIS CAMERA is invaluable for Instantaneous Exposures. Enables the Operator to see the picture non-inverted, and the full size of the plate the very instant of making the exposure. Dispenses with Tripod, Focusing-cloth, and Carrying-case. The Camera is leather-covered, and presents the appearance of a small portmanteau when carried. No metal work exposed to sight. Focused by means of Rack and Pinion. Time-exposure Attachment. Carries Eight Plates when in use.

Price, with Rectilinear Lens and three Double Holders for Plates $6\frac{1}{2} \times 4\frac{1}{4}$, £16.

Fitted with Eastman Roll-Holder, $4\frac{3}{4} \times 6\frac{1}{2}$, £19.

Forwarded to any address on receipt of price. *Send for Circular.*

**E. W. SMITH & CO.**
**42 JOHN STREET, NEW YORK, U.S.**

**1885:** The London Stereoscopic Company produces its "Carlton" TLR, the first known series-produced TLR, which is offered in quarter plate (3¼ x 4¼ inches), 4 x 5 inches, and full plate sizes. The Carlton is a magazine camera, holding 12 glass plates. After an exposure a lever is pushed, causing the plate to fall down flat in the bottom of the camera while springs push a fresh plate to the focal plane.

### TRIVIA

Twin-lens reflex cameras were created when someone realized that having a second lens alongside the taking lens meant that the photographer could focus and make the shot without having to keep swapping a ground glass screen for the plate, thus dramatically reducing the time between imagining and making the shot.

**1886:** Carl Paul Goerz (1854–1923) starts his company in Berlin, making geometrical drawing instruments for students. In 1888, Goerz discontinues manufacturing instruments in favour of producing his famous Dagor lenses as well as the Goerz-Anschütz folding press camera. Designed by Ottomar Anschütz (1846–1907), this is the first camera equipped with a focal plane shutter and is capable of 1/1000 second exposures. In 1895, Goerz will open a branch in New York that becomes the C. P. Goerz American Optical Company in 1905.

In 1926, Goerz will merge with ICA, Contessa-Nettel and Ernemann to form Zeiss Ikon. The Carl Zeiss company holds a majority stake in the new Zeiss Ikon and demands that the other member firms stop their lens production, bringing the famed Dagor lenses to an end, at least in Europe. However, Dagor production continues in the USA until 1972, when the C. P. Goerz American Optical Company merges with Germany's Schneider Optics.

**1886:** In January, a Vermont farmer named Wilson A. Bentley (1865–1931) combines a bellows camera and a microscope and becomes the first to photograph the beauty of snowflakes with what will become known as photomicrography. His method is to catch the snowflakes on black velvet and quickly photograph them before they disappear. Regarding the project he famously said: "Under the microscope, I found that 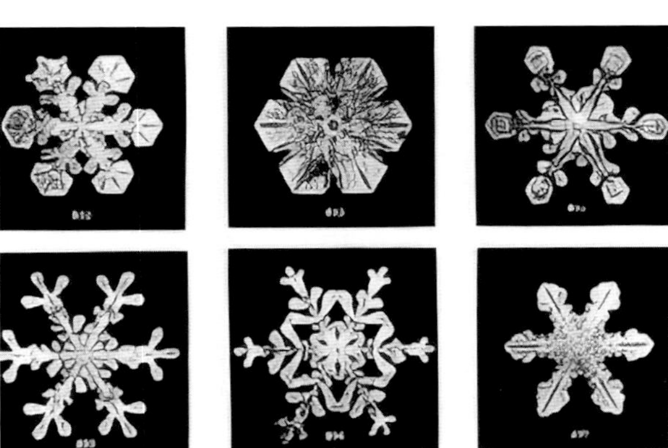 snowflakes were miracles of beauty; and it seemed a shame that this beauty should not be seen and appreciated by others. Every crystal was a masterpiece of design, and no one design was ever repeated. When a snowflake melted, that design was forever lost." In 1931, Bentley will publish a book, *Snow Crystals*, which features 2,500 different snowflake photos.

> **TRIVIA**
>
> In 2020, 10 of Bentley's original prints sell in New York for $4,800 each.

**1886:** On 5 September, *Le Journal Illustré* (Paris) publishes *L'Art de vivre cent ans: Trois entretiens avec Monsieur Chevreul*. Besides the portrait of Chevreul on the cover, the article includes halftone reproductions of a series of 12 unposed photographs taken on 18 August 1886 by photographer Paul Nadar (1856–1939) of his father, the photographer Félix Nadar, interviewing the chemist Michel Eugène Chevreul (1786–1889) on Chevreul's 100th birthday. This is the first photographically illustrated interview and is sometimes called the first media interview.

> **TRIVIA**
>
> In front of the camera, Nadar and Chevreul discuss photography, colour theory, Molière and Pasteur, the scientific method, the crazy ideas of balloonists, and, of course, how to live for 100 years. It is a lively and interesting conversation between two legends of the 19th century: one born before the French Revolution, the other destined to see the marvels of the airplane and motion pictures. When Felix Nadar dies, in 1910, son Paul continues with the studio.

**1886:** The Eastman Dry Plate and Film Company introduces a photofinishing service aimed at professional photographers. Negatives can be sent in and enlargements as big as 25 x 30 inches can be produced. Before long, this service is opened to all users with any camera, and thus it can be fairly said that the photofinishing industry is started by Kodak.

> **TRIVIA**
>
> Just five years apart in age, George Eastman and Frank Brownell (1859–1939), owner of the Brownell Manufacturing Company (makers of professional and studio cameras), are forever experimenting with camera designs that they hope will be both trend-setting and profitable. In October 1887, Eastman proposes a camera concept that will become the Kodak when it is introduced in 1888. Brownell's firm makes the wooden parts, which are then assembled at Yawman & Erbe.
>
> In 1889, Brownell becomes the principal designer of the first folding Kodak camera. Two years later he designs Eastman's daylight-loading camera. However, in April of 1892, his uninsured factory is seriously damaged by fire. George Eastman constructs a new factory for his chief designer and in return, Brownell signs an exclusive contract with his benefactor. Within four years, the Brownell Camera Works employs 700 people.

**1886:** The Berne Convention is developed at the instigation of Victor Hugo (1802–1885) of the *Association Littéraire et Artistique Internationale*. The convention establishes copyright for artists, writers, and photographers in all signatory territories, regardless of where the work is originally created. This is of huge importance to photographers.

---

**FURTHER DETAILS**

Before the Berne Convention, national copyright laws usually only applied to works created within each country. (For example, a work published in the United Kingdom would be covered by copyright there, but could be copied and sold by anyone in, say, Canada or the USA.) Under the Berne Convention, copyrights are automatically in force upon creation of the work. As soon as a work is written or recorded on some physical medium, its author is automatically entitled to all copyrights in the work, unless and until the author explicitly disclaims them or until the copyright expires.

The length of a copyright varies country to country, but for photographs, the Berne Convention sets a minimum term of 25 years from the year the photograph was created, and for cinematography, 50 years after first showing. In the USA and some other countries, photographic and cinemagraphic works created before 1923 are now considered in the public domain.

---

**1887:** The Folmer & Schwing Manufacturing Company is founded as a maker of crown glass lighting fixtures and Sterling bicycles. It will become the Folmer & Schwing Bicycle and Camera Company in 1896.

**1887:** *Blitzlichtpulver*, or flash powder, is invented in Germany by Adolf Miethe (1862–1927) and Johannes Gaedicke (1853–1916). They mix potassium chlorate and antimony sulphide with the magnesium powder to make a more stable flash powder out of the volatile and very dangerous magnesium (see **1864**).

---

**TRIVIA**

Being the explosive that it is, flash powder accidents were inevitable. Simply grinding the components was dangerous enough, and a number of photographers died while preparing the flash powder or setting it off. Around the start of the 20th century, several improvements made the process simpler and safer. The flashes now lasted for just 10 milliseconds, so subjects no longer automatically closed their eyes during the exposure, which helped portrait photographers immensely!

---

**1887:** The Reverend Hannibal Goodwin (1822–1900) of New Jersey invents a method for making transparent flexible film and applies for a patent, but the patent is not granted until 13 September 1889.

**1888:** The Kodak name is trademarked, and in June, the first Kodak box camera is mass marketed. It is the first easy-to-use camera and contains a 20-foot roll of stripping film, enough for one hundred 2½-inch-diameter circular pictures. The body is made by Frank Brownell, and the 57mm *f* 9 lens is from Bausch & Lomb. When the last picture is taken, the entire camera is sent back to Kodak, where the film is developed and printed and the camera is reloaded with a fresh roll of 100 exposures, for $10.

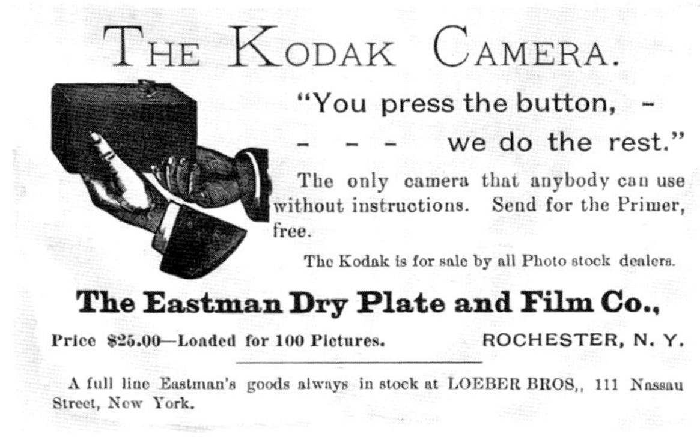


It is an uncomplicated box but costs $25—a significant amount of money when the average annual wage is just $1,200 ($25 is the equivalent of over $850 today). The camera is not yet a product for the masses, but that will change in 12 years time.

---

**TRIVIA**

Eastman advertised his new Kodak camera, using the "Kodak Girl" theme. By the mid-1890s, Kodak had become a household word and the "Kodak Girl" a symbol of the "modern" photographer.

A film shot in 1889 with a Kodak No. 1 camera was developed in 2023 with considerable success!

---

**1888:** Agfa introduce Rodinal, a concentrated liquid developer with an exceptionally long shelf life. Rodinal is diluted with water for use, typically at 1:25, 1:50, or 1:100. Working solutions can only be used once and will not keep even if unused. Rodinal remains available today from ADOX Fotowerke, Germany, under the name Adonal.

**1888:** John Carbutt, a dry-plate pioneer in Philadelphia, persuades a celluloid manufacturer to produce sheets which he then coats with gelatin emulsion using equipment borrowed from George Eastman, thus producing the first modern film. He supplies Thomas Edison (1847–1931) with strips of his film, which Edison uses in early prototypes of one of his inventions, which he calls a *kinetoscope*. The main drawback is that Carbutt's film is thick, stiff, and not truly suitable for motion picture use.

**1888:** While on his honeymoon, Arvid Hasselblad meets George Eastman and, as a result, Hasselblad becomes the sole Swedish distributor of Eastman's products. The business is so successful that in 1908 the photographic operations are spun off into their own corporation, Fotografiska AB, which includes a nationwide network of shops and photo labs. Management of the company eventually passes to Karl Erik Hasselblad (1874–1942), Arvid's son, and then, when Karl dies, in 1942, to his son, Victor Hasselblad (1906–1978).

**1888:** Hurter and Driffield, pioneers in the science of sensitometry, build the first exposure calculator, the Actinograph. This device is a light-tight case that, when opened, exposes a small piece of "printing out" paper to the light. By measuring the time it takes to darken to match a standard tint and applying this knowledge to a chart or calculator wheel, the required exposure can be determined.

**1888:** Louis Aimé Augustin Le Prince (1841–1890), a Frenchman who also works in the United Kingdom and the United States, shoots the first moving pictures, using a camera of his own design, at a rate of about 12 pictures per second—near the 16 frames per second speed of modern silent films.

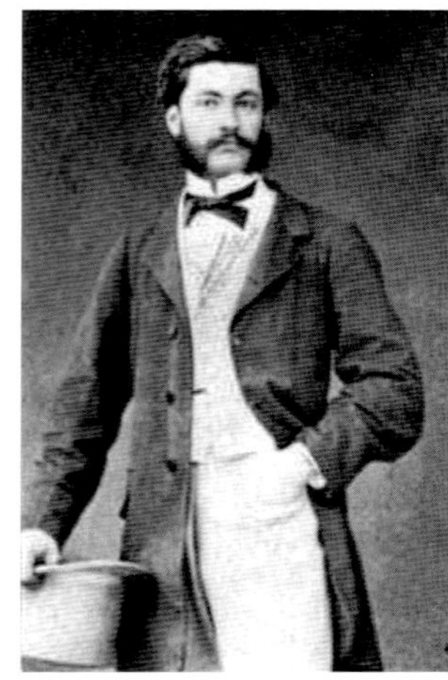

*Louis Aimé Augustin Le Prince*

During October of 1888, Le Prince uses his single-lens camera and Eastman's paper film to photograph two moving-picture sequences in Leeds, England: one in Roundhay Garden and a second of the traffic on the Leeds Bridge. This is several years before the work of competing inventors such as William Friese-Greene, Auguste and Louis Lumière, and Thomas Edison, thus securing his place as "the father of cinematography." Both La Prince's cameras and copies of his clips still exist, although without definite proof of their date.

Le Prince experiments with projection techniques and schedules his first public screening, to be held in New York in the late fall of 1890. It is a screening he will not attend.

---

### TRIVIA

Both of Le Prince's film clips can be found on the Internet by simply searching for "Roundhay Garden Leeds" on Yahoo, Google, or a similar search engine.

---

**1888:** Étienne-Jules de Marey invents his "chronophotograph" that achieves 60 images per second on George Eastman's paper roll film. Some point to de Marey, rather than the Lumière brothers, as the true father of motion pictures, though de Marey's equipment has neither transparent film, perforation in the film stock, nor a claw to move the film along.

**1888:** Edward Weston (1850–1936) starts Weston Electrical Instruments and begins designing and manufacturing electrical measuring devices. The firm will go on to manufacture what will become the gold standard in exposure meters, in 1932. (Note that this is *not* the famous photographer of the same name.)

> **TRIVIA**
>
> Around 1880, photographers began to realize that aperture size affects depth of field. Aperture control gained much more significance, and adjustable stops became a standard lens feature. The iris diaphragm (invented in 1858) made its appearance as an adjustable lens stop in the 1880s and will become the standard adjustable stop around 1900.

**1889:** Wordsworth Donisthorpe (1847–1914), a pioneer of cinematography, patents a camera that he calls the "kinesigraph," together with the necessary projector. In 1890, he produces a moving picture of London's Trafalgar Square. Ten frames of this ground-breaking film still exist today.

**1888:** Zeiss founder Carl Zeiss dies following a stroke.

**1889:** After Carl Zeiss's passing, Ernst Abbe establishes the Carl-Zeiss-Stiftung (loosely translated as Carl Zeiss Foundation), essentially a holding company, which manages the various Zeiss concerns and research activities, including the Carl Zeiss Optische Werkstätte (Jena) and the Jenaer Glaswerke Schott & Genossen. Between 1891 and 1919, the foundation will become the sole owner of all things Zeiss.

**1889:** Late in the year, Kodak introduces the first gelatin emulsion on a roll of celluloid film. The new film is so widely preferred over stripping film that production of the firm's stripping film is discontinued in 1891. The availability of this thinner, more flexible film also makes possible the development of Thomas Edison's motion picture camera in 1891. A new firm is formed, called "The Eastman Company."

**1889:** On 21 June 1889, William Edward Friese-Greene (1855–1921) is issued patent number 10131 for his "chronophotographic" camera. It is capable of taking up to 10 photographs per second using perforated celluloid film. Friese-Greene gives a public demonstration in 1890 but the low frame rate combined with the device's apparent unreliability make for an unfavourable impression.

Friese-Greene's experiments in the field of motion pictures are at the expense of his other business interests and in 1891 he is declared bankrupt. To cover his debts, he sells the rights to the chronophotographic camera patent for £500. The renewal fee is never paid, and the patent eventually lapses.

**1889:** Hannibal Goodwin files suit against Eastman, claiming infringements of his patent for making transparent, flexible film (see **1887**). Eastman promptly released a statement saying, "We do not think Goodwin ever had any workable process for making a transparent film. If he had, we never heard of his using it or anyone else making any use of it." The suit will drag through the courts (see **1914**).

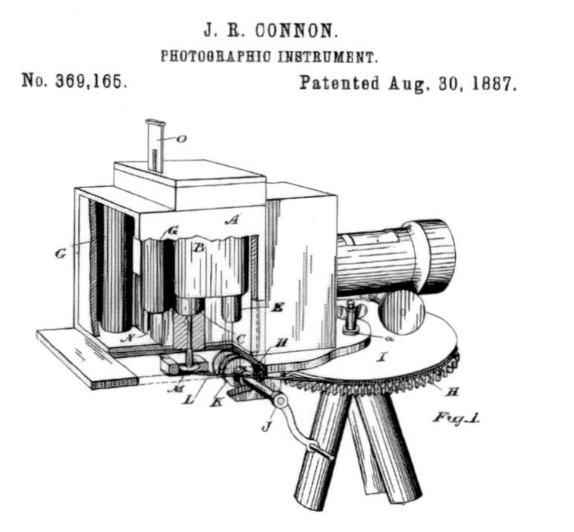


### ODDITIES

The Connon Panoramic Camera uses a hand-crank that is rotated above a tripod to take photographs over a 360° angle of view, rather like the better-known Cirkut Camera (see **1904**). Invented by John R. Connon (1862–1931) and patented 1887 in the U.K. and the USA and in 1888 in Canada, it may have been Canada's most significant contribution to early photography. Connon's is the first panoramic camera to use flexible (waxed paper) film, which was spooled through the camera and synchronized to its rotation on the tripod.

Connon's son is said to have credited his father with inventing a device in 1881 for putting gelatin emulsion onto a strip of plastic film, although plastic film was first commercially manufactured by Eastman Kodak in 1889.

**1889:** Henry Reichenbach, a chemist working for George Eastman, discovers that by dissolving cellulose nitrate (celluloid) in alcohol, he is able to make thin sheets by pouring the "dope" onto glass-topped tables and letting them dry. However, as the sheets dry, the film's surface becomes wavy and wrinkled. He finds that by adding a camphor solution to which a solution of amyl acetate and fusel oil has already been added, he can create perfectly clear, flexible film suitable for photographic use. Although Goodwin was first, two years earlier, and was granted his patent in September, Eastman has better patent attorneys, and Reichenbach is granted his patent in December of the year.

### TRIVIA

George Eastman fired Reichenbach in early 1892, accusing him and two others of seeking to start a competing company. And that's exactly what they did. Twice. Both firms failed in short order.

**1889:** The Scovill & Adams Company is established as a separate subsidiary of the Scovill Company to make photographic supplies and cameras.

**1890:** While working at Carl Zeiss, German physicist Paul Rudolph (1858–1935) designs the first anastigmatic lens, the Protar. An anastigmat or anastigmatic lens is "completely corrected" (at least by the standards of its day) for spherical aberration, coma, and astigmatism. It is scalable from $f\,4.5$ portrait to $f\,18$ superwide angle. All modern photographic lenses are close to being anastigmatic.

> **TRIVIA**
>
> Early lenses often included the word anastigmat in their name to advertise this new feature (Doppel-Anastigmat, Voigtländer Anastigmat Skopar, etc.). Originally, the Protar was simply called the Anastigmat, but that descriptive term quickly became generic, and the lens was given its trade name in 1900.

**1890:** Louis Le Prince disappears under suspicious circumstances. On 16 September 1890, just after patenting his invention and before he is to go to New York to publicly demonstrate his motion picture system, he boards a train from Dijon to Paris and is never seen again (see **1888**).

> **TRIVIA**
>
> Theories abound as to why Le Prince disappeared. Some say Edison or the Lumière brothers had him killed, but it is more likely that Le Prince was robbed after his late evening arrival in Paris and his body dumped in the Seine. But no one knows for sure.
>
> Not long after Le Prince's disappearance, Thomas Edison tried to take credit for Le Prince's invention. But his widow, Elizabeth, and son, Adolphe, were keen to defend Le Prince's status as "the inventor of the cinematograph." In 1898, Adolphe was a witness for the defense in a court case brought by Edison against the American Mutoscope Company. (The suit claimed that Edison was the first and sole inventor of cinematography and thus entitled to royalties for the use of the process.)
>
> Adolphe Le Prince was not allowed to present his father's two cameras as evidence (and so establish Le Prince's prior claim as inventor) and the court ruled in favour of Edison. However, in 1902, that ruling was overturned, allowing all to use Edison's patents without a fee.

**1891:** George Eastman introduces an improved version of his camera, now called the Kodak #1. The camera features a modified shutter and darkroom-loaded roll of celluloid film. The price is still $25.

**1891:** Thomas Edison patents the Kinetoscope, a 35mm motion picture projector in a small cabinet with a peephole, suitable for solitary viewing. The first "nickelodeon parlour," a storefront with 10 Kinetoscopes with each viewing costing a nickel, opens on 14 April 1894, at 1155 Broadway in New York. It is soon followed by others in major cities in the U.S. and Europe.

**1891:** The son of John Henry Dallmeyer (see **1866**), Thomas R. Dallmeyer (1859–1906), and Adolph Miethe simultaneously attempt to patent new lens designs with nearly identical formulas, creating the first photographic telephoto lenses.

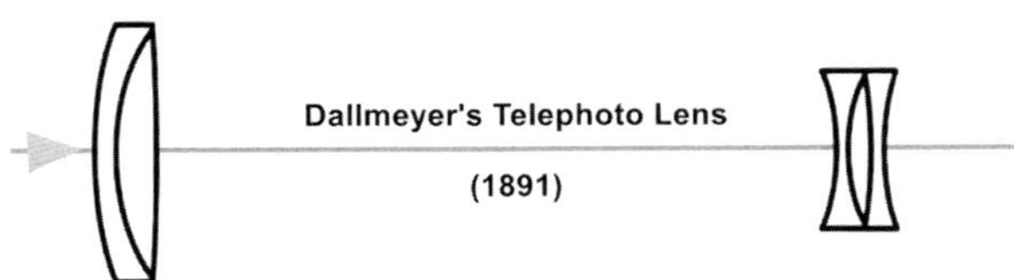

Primacy was never established, and no patents are ever granted. The front and rear cells of these early telephotos were not matched to one another, and the rear cell also magnifies any aberrations, as well as the image. For a truly corrected telephoto lens, we will have to wait until 1905.

---

**TRIVIA**

In 1896, for his contributions in the field of tele-photography, the Royal Photographic Society will award Thomas R. Dallmeyer their prestigious Progress Medal.

---

**1891:** On 2 February, Professor Gabriel Lippmann (1845–1921) announces to the Academy of Sciences: "I have succeeded in obtaining the image of the spectrum with its colours on a photographic plate whereby the image remains fixed and can remain in daylight without deterioration." In his process, light first passes through an almost transparent emulsion layer and is then reflected by a layer of mercury that acts as a mirror. The interference between reflected and incident light produces a latent image in the emulsion, which is then processed in conventional black-and-white chemistry; when backed with a mirror, however, it appears in colours similar to the original scene. The technique has very low sensitivity due to the emulsions of the time and never comes into general use. Still, this discovery will win Lippmann the Nobel Prize in Physics in 1908.

---

**TRIVIA**

"Lippmann process" techniques are being developed today to produce images which can easily be viewed—but not copied—for security purposes.

---

**1891:** In the Netherlands, the Loman Reflex Camera is the first focal-plane-shutter SLR. The mirror rise is synchronized with the release of a roller blind shutter, which is internally mounted in front of the plate, as opposed to the previously normal arrangement as an un-synchronized external accessory placed in front of the lens. Speeds are from 1/2 to 1/250 second.

---

**TRIVIA**

The main advantage of an internally mounted travelling-slit focal-plane shutter is the ability to use a very narrow slit to offer shutter speeds up to an action-stopping 1/1000 second. Unfortunately, the available emulsions of the day offer sensitivities equivalent to between ISO 1 and 3, which rather limits the opportunities to use such high speeds.

---

**1892:** W. K. L. Dickson (1860–1935) is working at Thomas Edison's Menlo Park facility when he takes 70mm film supplied by Eastman Kodak (and later the Blair Camera Company), cuts it in half lengthwise and perforates it down both edges. The result is the now standard 35mm (actually 34.925mm) motion picture film.

---

**TRIVIA**

Edison's image size is defined as single frame of film exactly four perforations high. For still photography use, it is standardized at eight perforations wide, thanks to Oskar Barnak's experimenting with 35mm film between 1905 and 1913. Edison claims exclusive patent rights to his design for 35mm motion picture film, but he neglects to file for a European patent and his American patent is invalidated by the U.S. courts in 1902.

---

**1892:** Samuel Turner's Boston Camera Manufacturing Company markets the "Bull's-Eye" camera, in which a length of celluloid film is attached to one end of a longer length of black paper and then wound on a spool. Numbers are printed on the outside of the paper backing in white ink, which can be read through a red or yellow translucent window in the back. By winding the film from number to number, the film can be advanced with great precision. Turner applies for a patent for this film, including the red window, in 1892; it is granted in 1895.

**1892:** Based on the success of their Kodak camera, "The Eastman Company" is renamed "The Eastman Kodak Company" (see **1888**).

**1892:** Bausch & Lomb of Rochester become the sole American company licensed to make the Zeiss "Anastigmat" and other lenses. The production of Zeiss products in the USA enables Zeiss to bypass costly import tariffs. This agreement continues until the start of the First World War in 1914.

**1893:** A Frenchman, Louis Boutan, is the first to take underwater pictures while diving using "hard hat" diving gear. He also develops an underwater flash and a remote control for deep waters using an electromagnet. As a professor of marine biology at the University of Paris's marine biology lab at Banyuls-sur-Mer, he develops a variety of underwater cameras and writes a substantial book on underwater photography, which will inspire generations to come.

**1893:** H. Dennis Taylor (1862–1943) designs the Cooke Triplet lens (British patent GB 22,607). The lens consists of three basic elements and has a maximum aperture of $f6.3$. It is the quintessential 20th-century photographic lens, a deceptively simple looking, asymmetric, three-element anastigmat formula created by re-examining lens design from first principles to take maximum advantage of the advances in the

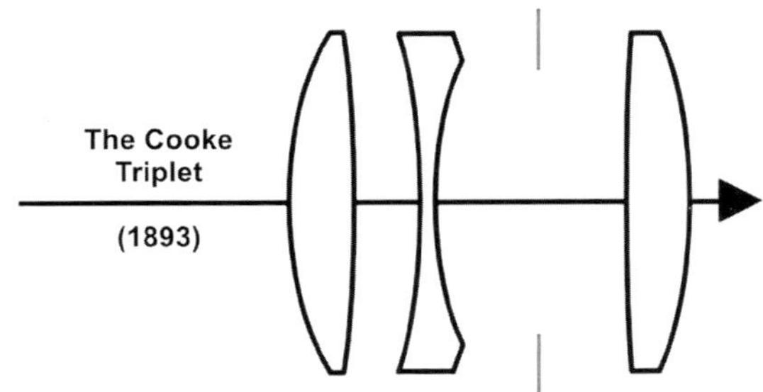


new Schott optical glasses. The elements were all of such strong power that they are highly sensitive to misalignment and require very tight manufacturing tolerances for the era.

> **TRIVIA**
>
> The Triplet is adequate for contact prints from medium-format roll-film cameras and small enlargements from 35mm "miniature" format cameras, but not for big enlargements. The films of the first half of the 20th century do not have much resolving power, however, so that is not a problem.

**1893:** After two years of development, Leo Baekeland (1863–1944) produces the first photographic paper, which allows enlargements to be printed using artificial light. He calls it "Velox" and in 1899 will sell his patent and firm to George Eastman of the Eastman Kodak Co. for $750,000. (See **1907**.)

**1894:** Etienne-Jules Marey invents the first true slow-motion camera (see **1882** and **1888**), which takes 700 images per second.

**1894:** George Eastman arranges to license Turner's roll film (called "cartridge film" because of its resemblance to a shotgun cartridge).

**1894:** Capitalizing on the relative speed with which tintypes can be produced, the National Photograph Machine Company advertises its Automatic Photo Machines in the October 1894 issue of *Scientific American* with the slogan: "A nickel dropped in the slot produces a photograph . . . in 35 seconds." These photos are made on ferrotype cardboard but over the next decade there is a transition to machines that make strips of photographs on regular photo paper.

**1894:** Lieven Gevaert (1868–1935) starts his first coating plant for photographic emulsions in Antwerp, Belgium.

**1895:** Louis Ducos du Hauron is the first to describe a technique for producing modern colour films. As described, he would position four separate emulsions, one atop the other, so that a true "one shot" colour photo might be taken. With this technique, however, he would have to separate the layers for processing, which he is unable to do. His film is never produced.

**1895:** Eastman introduces the Pocket Kodak, a small, mass-produced box camera accepting a 12-exposure roll of paper-backed film. The camera becomes wildly popular and between July and December, 100,000 are made. By comparison, production of the original Kodak reached just 5,200. Later in the year, Eastman buys Turner's roll-film invention and his company outright for $22,000 (or just over $615,000 today) and introduces more models, including an updated version of the Bull's-Eye, now called the "Kodak Bull's-Eye," of course. The Kodak Bull's-Eye name will continue to be used until 1913.

> **TRIVIA**
>
> A critical element of George Eastman's success was his standard practice of controlling all patents related to photography. He realized the competitive advantage of the Bulls-Eye's daylight loading and David Houston's front roll holder (as used in the Bull's-Eye). However, the rights to Houston's system were held by Thomas Blair's American Camera Manufacturing Company. So, in 1898, Eastman bought American Camera, giving him control over the most significant patents for roll film as well as the clout to stifle competition.

**1895:** Two Germans, Max Skladanowsky (1863–1939) and his brother, Emil (1866 –), invent the Bioskop, an early movie projector. Inspired by magic-lantern technology, the Bioskop uses two loops of 44.5mm-wide unperforated film, one frame being projected alternately from each. This makes it possible for the Bioskop to project at 16 frames per second, a speed sufficient to create the illusion of movement. The Skladanowsky brothers display the first moving picture show to a paying audience on 1 November 1895, almost two months before the public debut of the Lumière brothers' technically superior Cinématographe in Paris.

**1895:** Auguste (1862–1954) and Louis (1864–1948) Lumière invent the Cinématographe (motion picture) camera, which uses a claw movement derived from the mechanism used in sewing machines to advance the film—a principle that still applies in motion photography today. The Cinématographe can be both a camera and a projector. The Lumière brothers have their first public showing on 28 December that year.

**1895:** Wilhelm Roentgen (1845–1923) of Germany invents the X-ray photograph.

**1896:** The Folmer & Schwing Bicycle and Camera Company first offers its "Cycle Graphic," a 4 x 5 sheet film camera with a Victor Shutter and Rapid Rectilinear lens for $25. By 1912, it will evolve into the famous "Speed Graphic" camera.

**1896:** Dr. Rudolph of Carl Zeiss develops the legendary Planar, a photographic lens still on the cutting edge of optical performance today. The Planar solves the problems of spherical aberration and astigmatism by employing a symmetrical optical configuration. The Planar becomes one of the most copied lens formulas in the world.

**1896:** The Multiscope & Film Company of Burlington, Wisconsin produces the Al Vista camera. Introduced to the public in 1897, it features a rotating lens that exposes roll film stretched on a 180° arc. The Al Vista camera proves to be the first successful series-produced panoramic camera.

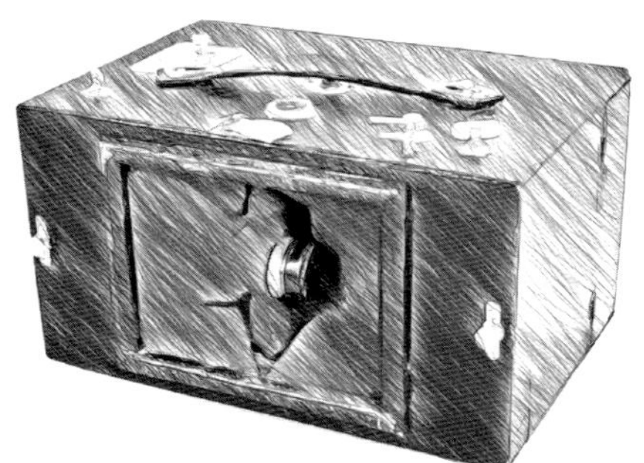

**1896:** Dennis Taylor (designer of the Cooke Triplet lens) notices that some lenses with glass tarnished by age produce brighter images. Investigation reveals that the oxidation layer suppresses surface reflections by destructive interference. This is the basis of modern lens coating, but it will be 1940 before a practical system of lens coating is developed.

**1896:** The firm of Meyer Optik is formed in Görlitz, Germany, by optician Hugo Meyer (1863–1905) and businessman Heinrich Schätze. By 1936, Meyer is producing 100,000 lenses per year.

### TRIVIA

After the Second World War, under the Soviet occupation of East Germany, Meyer Optik were absorbed into the VEB Zeiss Ikon collective and, after 1971, the Meyer-Optik name was no longer used. However, after the reunification of Germany, Meyer Optik is reconstituted as a private company (GmbH) but go bankrupt in 1991. In 2014, a new firm, Globell Deutschland (part of Net SE-Koblenz), acquires the brand and introduces lenses under the Meyer Optic brand once again. However, it goes under in 2018 and the brand is taken over that December when OPC Optical Precision Components Europe GmbH, based in Bad Kreuznach, acquire the trademark rights to the Meyer Optik Görlitz name. As of 2020, the Meyer brand is once again going strong.

In 2020, a Meyer Primoplan 5cm $f$ 1.9 lens in collapsible Leica (M39) mount will sell at a South African flea market for the equivalent of $10. Months later it sells in a private sale for $50,000.

**1896:** The Zar, also called the "Pocket Zar," is made by the Zar Camera Company of Chicago and uses special 2 x 2-inch glass plates. The camera is constructed of cardboard covered in leatherette. Despite its Spartan details and extremely low price, it is surprisingly well-made, and sells well through major outlets, including Sears Roebuck.

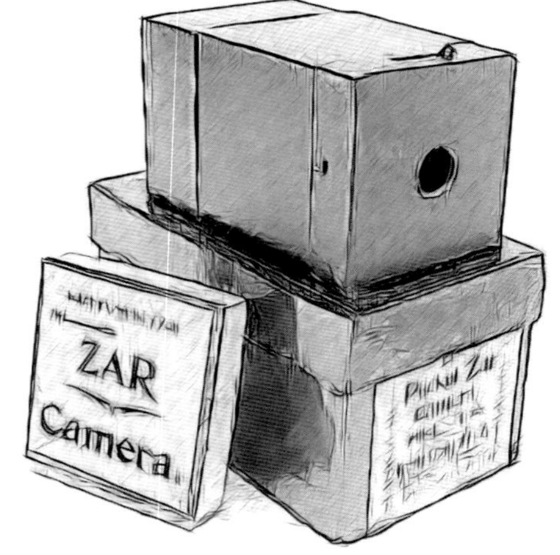


The real genius of the Pocket Zar is in its price and presentation. While Eastman Kodak will charge just $1 for their 1900 Brownie, four years earlier the Pocket Zar sells for just 85 cents. A six-shot roll of film for the Brownie is 15 cents (2½ cents per shot), but a box of one dozen glass plates for the Pocket Zar is just 20 cents (or just over 1½ cents per shot). For an additional dollar you can buy an entire developing outfit for the Zar including a ruby darkroom lamp, two trays, a bottle of developer, a package of fixing powder, a printing frame, two dozen sheets of printing paper, and a dozen pieces of photographic card stock. The idea of an affordable camera for the masses is taken to a level never before seen. However, due to its cardboard construction, very few survive.

The Zar Camera Co. was used for the assembly of various low-cost cameras such as the Zar, the Yale, the Vive, and the Cyclone. In 1899, the company merged with several other manufacturers to create the Rochester Optical and Camera Company, intended to compete with George Eastman's Kodak. But Eastman purchased the Rochester consortium outright in 1903, making it a subsidiary manufacturer for Kodak. The Cyclone, Vive, Zar, and the rest were immediately discontinued.

**1897:** The first U.S. camera magazine, *The Camera*, starts publishing. Early issues through to the 1930s are the regular magazine size, but then they shrink to digest size (think *Reader's Digest*, *TV Guide*, et al). The magazine has a good run, ending in 1953.

**1898:** Heinz Kilfitt (1898–1980) is born in Hörntrop-Wattenscheid, Germany. The son of a watchmaker, he will become known for the spring-driven 35mm Robot cameras, Macro-Kilar lenses, the Voigtländer Zoomar (designed by Frank Back), and the Mecaflex and Kowa 2¼ SLRs.

**1898:** W. F. Folmer builds his first Graflex camera with a complicated variable-aperture focal plane shutter. The shutter gives so much trouble that in 1904 it is changed to a simple cloth curtain with a series of apertures of different widths, leaving the user to select the required one. It is now so reliable that it is manufactured for over 60 years. The firm is bought by George Eastman in 1905 and resold, as the Folmer Graflex Company, in 1926.

**1898:** Started in 1896, the Monroe Camera Company of Rochester produces some 22 different cameras. However, they become famous for their #2 pocket camera. Designed for portability by Silas French and patented in 1897, it incorporates a unique compact design that is extended by simply pulling out the front. The front and the back are connected by brass bearers in what they call a "lazy tongs" pattern. The half-plate camera when closed measures just 4.5 x 4.5 x 1.5 inches and easily fits into a pocket. It is most likely the first of the compact dry-plate pocket cameras incorporating the lazy tongs bed extension design and sells for just $7.50. In 1899, the Monroe Camera Company will merge with the Rochester Optical Co. and disappear.

**1899:** On 22 March, film pioneer Edward Raymond Turner (1873–1903), with the backing of financier F. Marshall Lee, patents a sequential three-colour motion picture system. It is based on James Clerk Maxwell's discovery in the mid-19th century that virtually all colours can be produced by a combination of the three primary colours (red, green, and blue). Turner shoots some test films in 1902 but this pioneering work ends abruptly when he dies suddenly of a heart attack in 1903.

Development is passed to George Albert Smith (1864–1959) in the hope of creating a commercially viable product. Smith, however, finds the process unworkable and instead develops

Kinemacolor in 1906, a greatly simplified two-colour version that enjoys moderate commercial success for several years. Turner's three-colour process never sees the light of day.

**1899:** Kodak introduces their Panorama cameras, using a design patented by Kodak Brownie designer Frank Brownell. The cameras have a swinging lens in a leather tube and have a pronounced curve to the film plane. The swinging mechanism forms the shutter. Various models are sold through 1928.

**1899:** Andrew (1862–) and John Wollensak, with financial backing from Stephen Rauber, a former president of the Union Brewing Company, form Rauber & Wollensak to manufacture high-quality low-cost camera shutters. In 1901, Rauber dies, and his name is dropped. In 1902, the Wollensak Optical Company starts the manufacture of photographic lenses as well. At its peak in 1950, Wollensak employs over 1,000 people, but will cease operations in 1972.

**1899:** The electric flashlamp is invented in France by Joshua Lionel Cowen (1877–1965), of Lionel toy train fame, and Paul Boyer (1861–1952). Earlier flash powder trays had to be ignited manually; Cowen and Boyer's invention uses an electric current to ignite the flash powder, making it much safer, though photographers' hands can still get burned. While Cowen and Boyer's invention, which utilized a small electrically powered detonator to ignite flash powder, one of its first practical applications was as a detonator for underwater mines. In 1899, the year the invention was patented, the U.S. government awarded Cowen a $12,000 contract for 24,000 detonators. That $12,000 equates to roughly $360,000 today.

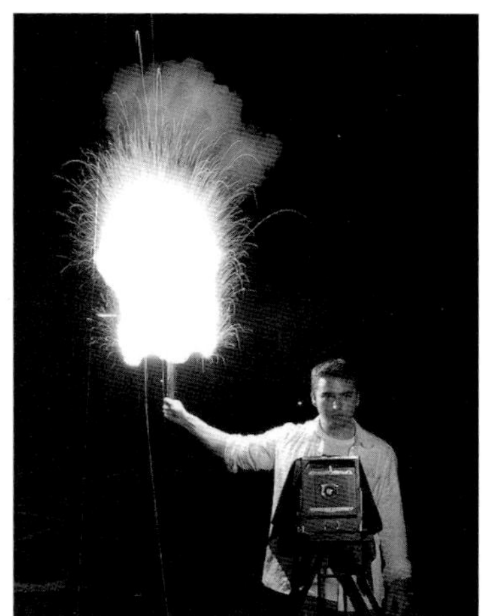

*Photo Courtesy of Race Gentry (CC-by SA, 2.0)*

# 1900 to 1949

*The early 1900s are a time of great camera development. The modern colour tri-pack film is first proposed in 1905 and becomes a practical reality in 1935. But the hallmark of this period is the rapid development of highly functional rangefinder "miniature" cameras and the early SLRs such as the Kine Exakta, in 1936. It is also the time when cameras become affordable, and thus accessible to the public at large, making photography a feature of everyday life.*

**1900:** After the Reverend Hannibal Goodwin's death from a heart attack at age 78, his widow, Rachel, forms the Goodwin Film and Camera Company, which, along with his patent, is sold to the E. & H.T. Anthony Company in 1901.

**1900:** Kodak introduce a new low-cost box camera named after Eastman's camera maker, Frank Brownell. The fixed-focus Brownie is sold for the princely sum of $1.00 (equivalent to $30 in 2018). Two dollars will get you the camera, a film, and the film's processing. The Brownie looks similar to the original Kodak, but the film can be taken out of the camera after shooting and developed by a Kodak dealer, your local drug store, or even at home. Photography has suddenly become not only portable and affordable but immensely popular and, for George Eastman, immensely profitable.

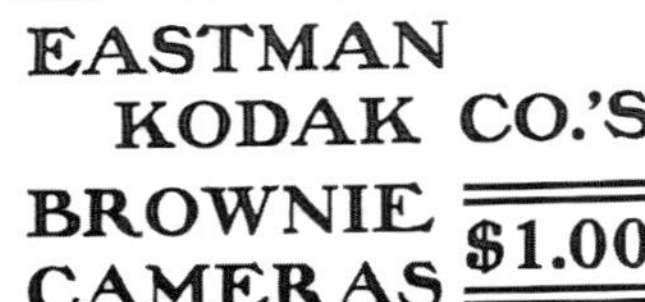
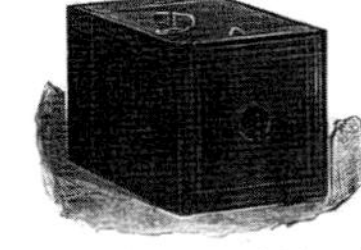


The Brownie has a single-speed ever-set shutter with a fixed aperture. It truly is the first "point-and-shoot" camera. These early Brownies don't even have a viewfinder. Marks on the top of the camera provide a rough guide as to what might be in the frame. You shoot . . . and you hope.

Also introduced is the Kodak Number 3 Folding Pocket Camera with a fold-down front and a pull-out lens on a bellows. It will be produced until 1914 in several versions, all making twelve 3¼ x 4¼ inch exposures on 118 roll film. These two designs set the style of cameras for the next 30 years.

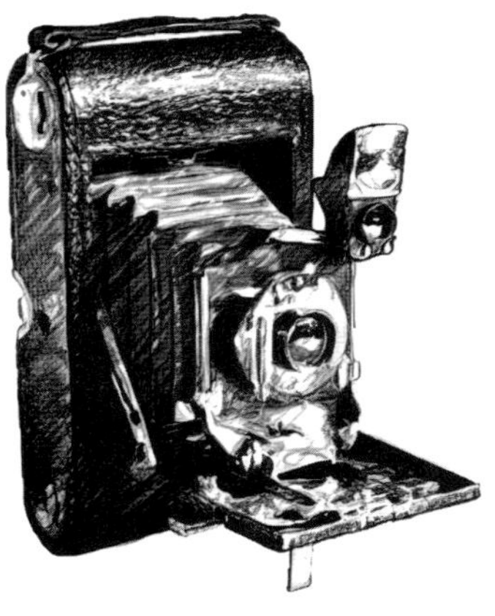

**TRIVIA**

The Kodak Brownie's price was kept low in order to promote sales of Kodak's 117 roll films, which took 2¼-inch square pictures. Essentially, this is the same business model used by inkjet-style computer printers of today. The first Rolleiflex twin-lens reflex used the same film (see **1929**).

In a trade circular, Eastman Kodak Company tells dealers to "Plant the Brownie acorn and the Kodak oak will grow."

**1900:** The Chicago & Alton Railway commissions Jonas Anderson (1842–1911) of Chicago to build the largest camera ever made in order to promote a new train at the 1900 "Exposition Universelle" in Paris. The camera weighs 900 pounds and takes 15 men to move. Each glass plate measures 8 x 4½ feet, costs $500, and, until 2006, holds the record for the largest photo ever shot. Three enormous contact prints are displayed, at a total cost of $5,000 (equivalent to more than $150,000 today)—significantly less than the cost of shipping the actual train.

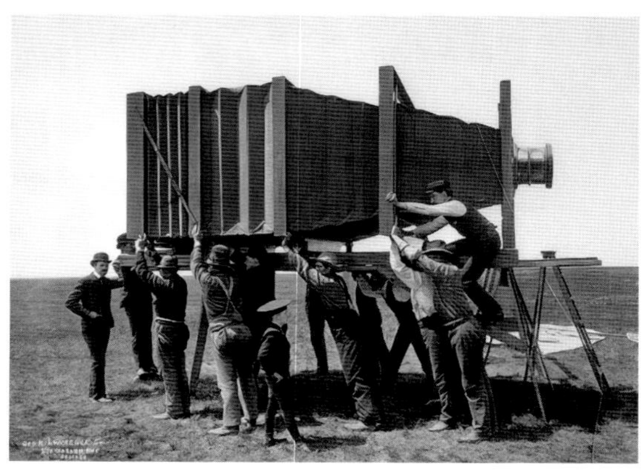

**1901:** At Carl Zeiss (Jena), Dr. Von Rohr (1868–1940) produces the world's first aspherical lens. Incredibly difficult to make, it is not put into production.

**1901:** Kodak introduces 120 size roll film. It is 60mm wide and is held in an open spool originally made of wood with metal flanges, later all metal and, finally, all-plastic. The length of film is typically 30 inches (760mm) attached to a piece of backing paper that is longer and slightly wider than the film. The backing paper protects the film while it is wound on the spool, with enough extra length for loading and unloading the roll in daylight without exposing any of the film. Frame number markings for the four standard image formats (6 x 4½ , 6 x 6, 6 x 7, and 6 x 9cm) are printed on the backing paper. Today, 120 roll films remain readily available in both professional and amateur emulsions.

**1901:** The #2 Brownie is released, just 18 months after the original. It uses a slightly different film format, taking 2¼ x 3¼-inch photos on the new 120 roll film (see previous entry). Many millions of #2 Brownies roll off the production lines, the last of them in 1935. It is a remarkable run!

### TRIVIA

There were five models of the #2 Brownie, "A" through "F," each with minor variations (usually made with a view to lowering manufacturing costs).

Unlike the original Brownie, the #2 also came with a viewfinder and a handle and was made in a choice of three materials: cardboard, costing $2.00; a colour model, which cost $2.50; and an aluminum one, costing $2.75.

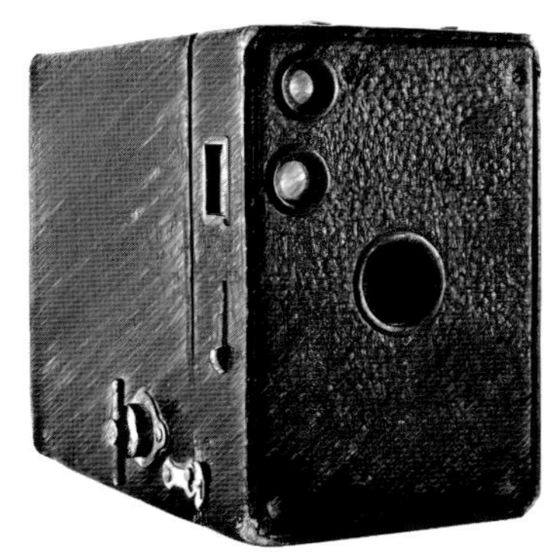

**1902:** U.S. courts invalidate one of Edison's key patent claims, allowing any and all producers or distributors to use Edison's 35mm film format without license. Filmmakers are already doing so in Britain and Europe, where Edison has failed to file patents.

### ODDITIES

Manufactured by various makers between 1885 and 1920 were the Multiple Cameras or, as they were more popularly known, "Penny Picture Cameras." These were cameras with backs that slid horizontally and vertically, allowing anywhere from two to 24 small images per plate or sheet of film, thus greatly reducing the cost per picture. Such cameras were made by Gennent, Century, Folmer & Schwing and even Kodak, among others.

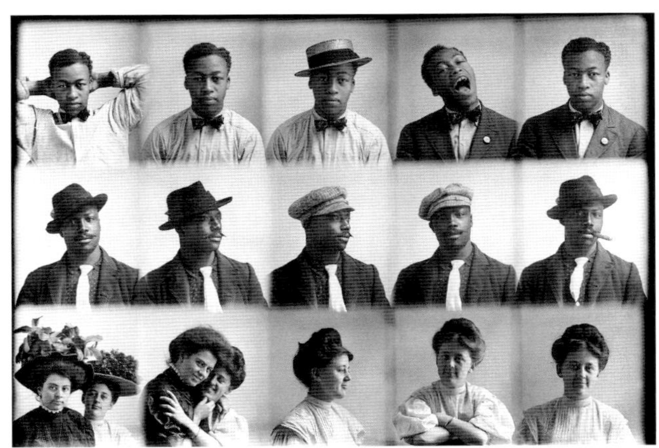

Multiple cameras were usually supplied with a Packard shutter and a portrait lens with a graceful fall-off to the edges that was greatly cherished by 19th-century portraitists. The image fall-off (or vignetting, in modern terms) was quite desirable because it drew a viewer's attention to the centre of the portrait by softening the background. Photographers would encourage sitters to have several poses taken, at a cost as little as a penny per pose (hence the name).

Today, such cameras are quite rare, as it seems each maker produced only a few hundred cameras, over many years, to fill a particular niche market.

**1902:** Arthur Korn (1870–1945) devises a practical photo-telegraphy technology: the reduction of photographic images to data bits which can be transmitted by wire to other locations. Wirephotos are in wide use in Europe by 1910 and are transmitted intercontinentally by 1922.

**1902:** Carl Zeiss begins making cameras.

**1902:** Precision mechanic Oskar Barnack goes to work for Carl Zeiss. He will stay until 1911, when he jumps ship and moves to Leitz, in Wetzlar. There he becomes head of the construction department of what is, at the time, an optical factory specializing in microscopes.

**1902:** Friedrich Deckel (1903–1994) develops the first mechanical leaf shutter, called the "Compound" shutter. Unlike later mechanical shutters such as the Compur, which use a clockwork mechanism, shutter timing is achieved by releasing air from a small cylinder mounted horizontally at the top of the shutter through a small hole. When the shutter opens, air in the cylinder is gradually released, letting the piston move, which closes the shutter when it reaches the end of its travel. This shutter opens and closes in as little as 1/100 second.

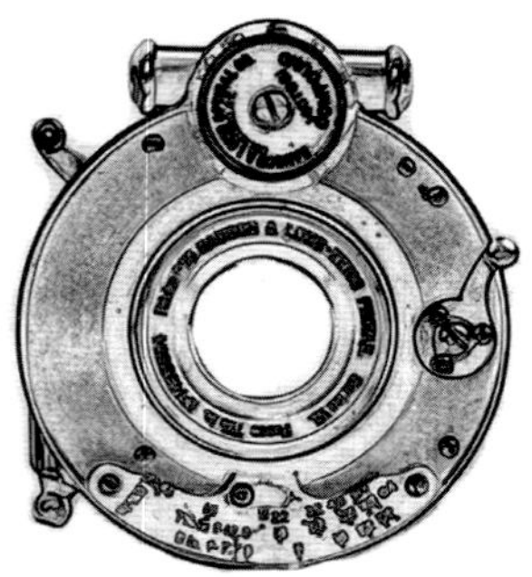

**1902:** While working at Bausch & Lomb in Rochester, William Bausch, the son of the founder, develops a process to create a desired lens shape directly by casting molten glass. Previously, the glass parts for the lenses had to be ground and polished from cast glass blocks, a complicated process. Bausch's innovation brings significant savings in both time and materials to lens manufacturing.

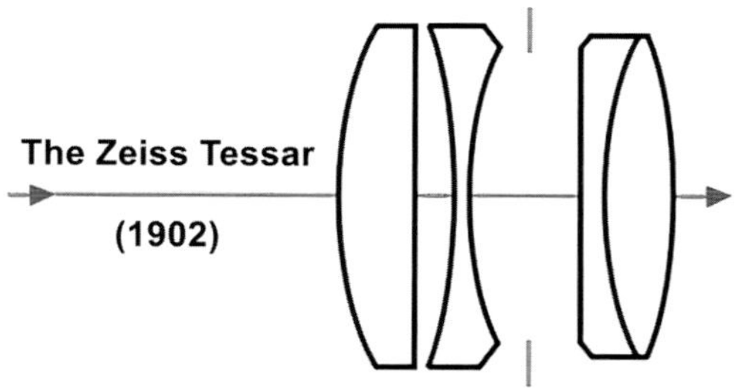


**1902:** The Tessar lens is designed under the tutelage of Paul Rudolph at Carl Zeiss. Much of the original work and almost all of the subsequent work is conducted by his assistant and successor, Ernst Wandersleb (1879–1963). Over time, the original $f$6.3 lens is gradually opened to $f$4.5, then to $f$3.5, and finally to $f$2.8. It earns the nickname "The Eagle Eye" for its high resolution and excellent contrast. The Tessar combines the glued rear doublet of the Protar with the front group of the Unar (a never- produced developmental lens). This relatively simple lens design of four elements in three groups allows good contrast even without modern lens coatings (see **1935**) and is copied by virtually every other lens manufacturer in the world.

---

**TRIVIA**

The Tessar name is from the Greek word *téssera*, four, to indicate a design of four elements.

---

**1902:** The Minnesota Mining & Manufacturing company (later, simply 3M) is started. Best known today for "Scotch Tape," the firm will go on to be a major maker of film, most of which is "private labelled" for other companies. Though it no longer makes photographic film, the company continues to manufacture various materials involved in filmmaking, photo processing, and printing.

**1902:** Folmer & Schwing introduce the single-lens reflex camera that will dominate the American SLR market for the next 30 years. The Graflex accepts holders for 4 x 5-inch glass plates or sheet film and proves to be a durable, high-performance camera.

---

**TRIVIA**

In 1903, Folmer & Schwing will introduce their Stereo Graflex, which becomes the first (and only) stereo SLR. Strictly speaking, the Stereo Graflex is not a "single" lens reflex camera because it has two imaging lenses. However, it has a reflex mirror and, typical for the era, a leather "chimney" which shields a waist level finder. It takes 5 x 7-inch glass dry plates.

---

**1902:** Plaubel & Company are founded in Frankfurt, Germany, by Hugo Schrade as a lens manufacturer and distributor. They will become known for their Makina series of press cameras, introduced as early as 1911 and made until 1960. (The price in 1941 is $249!) After the Second World War, they will become famous for their monorail studio cameras. However, they will cease both manufacturing and repairs in May, of 2017.

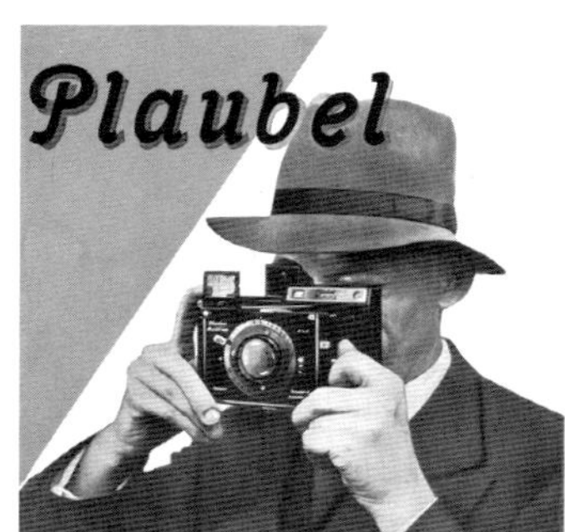


---

**TRIVIA**

Doi Camera, a well-established camera retailer in Japan, purchased rights to the Plaubel brand in 1970. Doi set out to use the best Japanese technology to create a new version of a classic German press camera. The result was the Plaubel 67 with its superb *f* 2.8 Nikkor lens and its classic compact lazy-tongs design. While the new Makina's design would have a strong German influence, its engineering and production were handled by Konica. However, quality control issues hampered production so much in the early days that production was moved to Mamiya. Unfortunately, this sealed its fate. The updated models, the Makina 670 and the wide-angle Makina W67, were made at Mamiya's plant until Mamiya's bankruptcy meant Makina production would never restart (see **1986**).

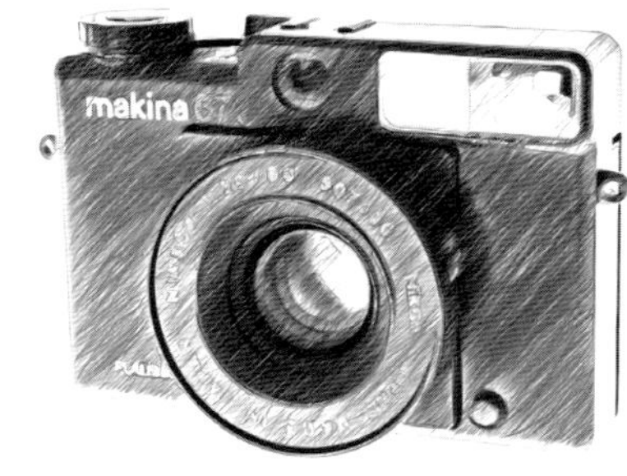


Today, Plaubel 67s command $2,500+ on the used market—far, far, more than they cost when new!

**1902:** The inaugural issue of *Camera Work* is published. The magazine is dated January 1903 but mailed 15 December 1902. It becomes known for its high-quality rotogravure printing of photos by some of the most important photographers in the world. Its editorial purpose is to establish photography as a fine art and is called "by far, the most beautiful of all photographic magazines." Published by Arthur Stieglitz (1864–1946), it will run until 1917.

---

### TRIVIA

In addition to photography, Stieglitz was well known for his passion for all aspects of the avant-garde. He was of course a photographer himself, but he also owned several New York art galleries, where he introduced many European avant-garde artists to the American public. Stieglitz was among the first to show photographs as art and set up various exhibitions where photos were judged by photographers. Until then, photos had been mainly judged by painters, since photographers were usually seen as "scientists." Stieglitz also promoted photography through newly established journals such *Camera Notes* and his own *Camera Work*.

Many believe it was Stieglitz who made photography, as art, what it is today.

---

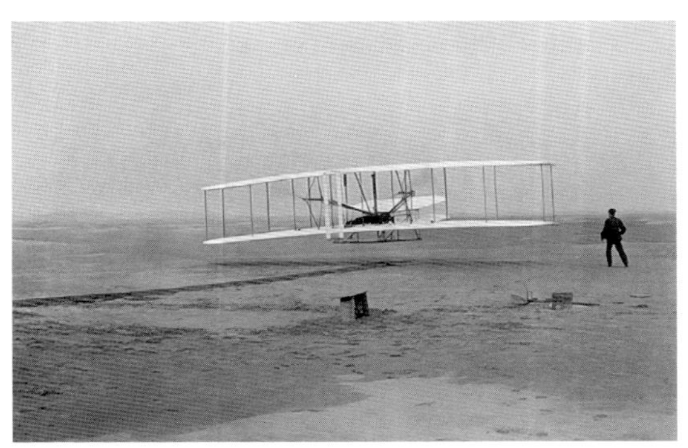

**1902:** Wilbur (1867–1912) and Orville (1871–1948) Wright of Dayton, Ohio, purchase a Rochester-made Gundlach "Korona V" 5 x 7 glass plate camera for the sum of $55.55 (or roughly $1,450 today). The next year, at precisely 10:35 a.m. on 17 December, John T. Daniels (1873–1948) of the Kitty Hawk Life-Saving Station, who has never taken a photograph before, uses the Korona V to capture the image of Orville Wright making the world's first powered flight at Kill Devil Hills, four miles south of Kitty Hawk, North Carolina.

---

### TRIVIA

The Gundlach Korona V was originally the "Milburn Korona." Founded in 1894 in Rochester by Gustav Milburn, a former camera constructor for George Eastman, the Milburn Company was bought by Gundlach in 1896. Gundlach itself survived many incarnations, under many different names, until 1972.

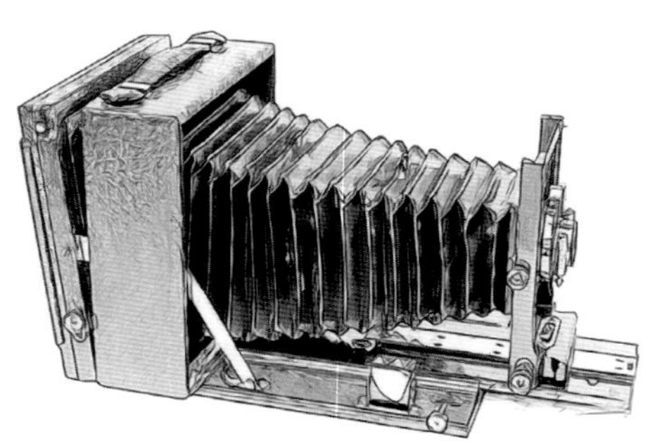

In 1927, Ansel Adams will make his most famous photograph, "Monolith, the Face of Half Dome," as well as many others, with a Korona camera.

**1903:** H. Dennis Taylor is awarded the first patent for lens coating. In 1896, he'd observed that old lenses that have become tarnished by long exposure to air transmit more light than newly polished lenses. He postulates that the layer of tarnish has a lower refractive index than the glass and therefore reflects less light and transmits more. However, his method of chemical or acid fuming proves highly unreliable, and the components are very caustic. A viable method of coating lenses will not be developed for another 30 years.

**1903:** The Lumière brothers in France patent their Autochrome plates for colour transparencies. The plates are coated with potato starch that has been dyed in orange-red, green, and cyan. These starch particles have a diameter of only 15/1000 millimetre and thus function as *dots* in an additive screen colour process. When dry, these coloured powders are applied to a sticky glass plate to obtain a single layer of the starch particles. The resulting open spaces between these particles are then closed with pulverized charcoal. After three years of further research, they are able to devise a commercially feasible process to produce these plates, and they will go to market in 1907.

**1903:** Konishiroku build a new factory to make the Cherry Hand Camera (Japan's first series-produced brand-name camera) and Japan's first photographic paper, Sakura Hakkin.

**1904:** The German firm of Gauthier starts building its Prontor shutters in Calmbach, in the Enz Valley of the Black Forest.

---

### TRIVIA

Carl Zeiss buys Gauthier in 1932. By that time, Zeiss owns Deckel's Compur works as well. In 1957, over 3,000 workers produce up to 10,000 shutters daily, and in 1970 Gauthier takes over the production of Compur shutters. The Gauthier works, in Calmbach, Germany, is still in limited production today.

---

**1904:** E. König, a chemist at Hoechst, Germany, produces a series of sensitizing cyanine dyes that, in various combinations, are sensitive to all colours, thereby paving the way for true panchromatic plates and films.

**1904:** William Johnston patents his rather unique rotating "Cirkut Camera" that captures a panoramic image by pivoting horizontally along a vertical axis while a roll of film moves across the film plane. There are several models: No. 5, No. 6, No. 8, No. 10, and No. 16, named according to the maximum length of the film accepted, measured in feet. The various models of Cirkut Camera can produce 360° photographs measuring up to 20 feet long. Both the camera and the film rotate on a special tripod during the exposure. Manufacture of the camera continues through 1949.

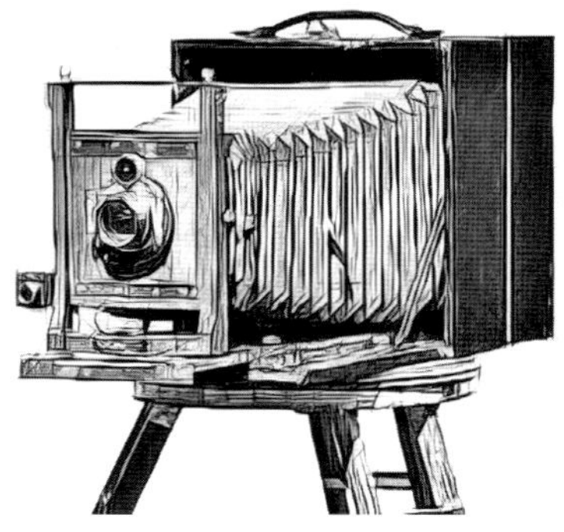

**TRIVIA**

The original Cirkut catalogue describes the camera's operation this way:

"The Cirkut Panoramic Outfit is in itself a most complete affair, being made up of a camera which can be used in the ordinary manner for plates when desired and a Panoramic Attachment which is easily and quickly attached to the camera, thus converting it into a Panoramic Outfit. The Attachment in itself is much like an ordinary Cartridge Roll Holder in that it is made to use Eastman Daylight-loading Cartridge Film. In addition, it contains the mechanism which, when the outfit is in operation, unwinds the film past a slot on a roller and in so doing exposes it and at the same time revolves the camera about on an axis, a special tripod and top being furnished. A pressure on the release is all that is necessary to start the motor—another pressure stops it, thus negatives of any desired length up to six feet with the No. 6 and 7 feet with the No. 8 may be made. A complete circle of 360° may thus be photographed if desired. There is an indicator on the top of the Film Holder showing the exact quantity of film exposed and that remaining unexposed. By another very ingenious arrangement one is enabled to determine before exposure is made how long a photograph the view decided on will be."

**1904:** Austrian army Captain Theodor Scheimpflug (1865–1911) devises and patents a method of tilting a lens to correct perspective distortion in aerial photographs. This becomes known as the Scheimpflug Principle and today his swings and tilts are found on most large format cameras.

**1905:** Karl Schnizel of Austria proposes the first tri-pack colour film in which no separation of the layers is needed. This is the true predecessor to modern colour films, but he too is unable to produce such a film. Seven years later, Rudolph Fisher (1881–1957) of Germany will patent a process along the same lines, but with the same disappointing level of practical success.

**1905:** Eugen Bauer (1879–1958) opens a small factory to repair and manufacture fine mechanical and optical instruments and, in 1907, is among the first to produce a projector with a take-up reel. In 1928, Bauer introduces carbon arc lighting and introduces projectors synchronized to gramophones. In 1930, the company produces one of the first projectors with optical sound. By 1938, Bauer is producing an 8mm camera with five speeds and six different lenses. In 1965, Bauer buys the Italian projector maker Silma; as a result, many Bauer products bear "Made in Italy" markings. Bauer and Silma produce projectors and cameras such as the Bolex SM8, the Eumig 933-Series, and all Rollei Super-8 projectors for chain-stores and other companies. Cinema Bauer, as it is known, becomes part of Bosch in 1932 and expands into the world's biggest producer of movie projectors and Super-8 cameras in the 1960s. But all production of 8 and 16mm products stops in 1985 and the company is dissolved in 1992.

**1905:** Emil Busch AG, of Rathenow, Germany, produces the first optically corrected telephoto lens system: the *f*9 Busch Bis-Telar, designed by K. Martin of Germany. Two series are produced. The first, for general use, has an aperture of *f*9, giving it a one and two-thirds magnification in focal lengths from seven to 14 inches for half-plate cameras. A second series will be produced around 1908 at *f*7 in lengths of eight to 22 inches for camera sizes up to a whole plate.

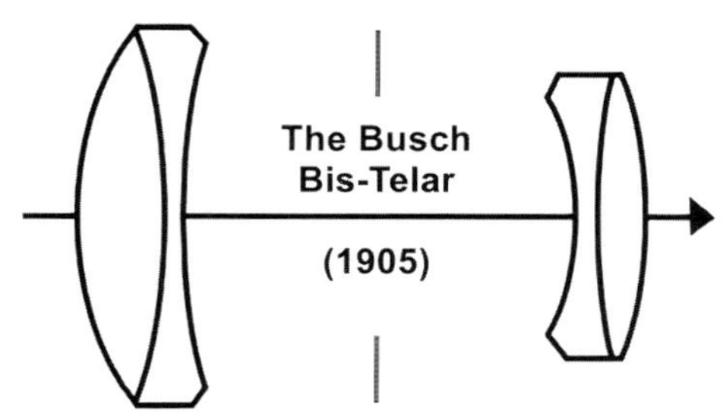


---

**TRIVIA**

A telephoto lens is made physically shorter than its nominal focal length by pairing a front positive imaging cell with a rear magnifying negative cell. The powerful front group forms the image while the rear restores the focal plane, thereby greatly shortening the physical length of the lens.

---

**1905–1910:** An unknown maker builds a prototype all-metal camera equipped with a focal plane shutter that uses 35mm film in a 24 x 32mm format. While the exact production date is unclear, the maker is thought to be Goerz, as the camera has a Goerz lens and the rangefinder is marked "C.P. Goerz, Berlin." The camera is never produced but is the forerunner of all 35mm still cameras.

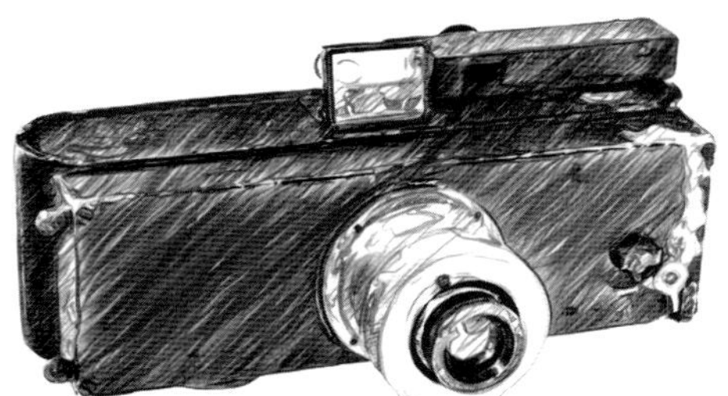

**1906:** Frederick Wratten (1840–1926) incorporates a company along with his son S. H. Wratten and Kenneth Mees (1882–1960) as owners, and with Mees in charge of product development. To make it possible to take photographs using specific wavelengths of light, Mees develops dyed gelatin filters which are placed between the plate or lens and the subject matter. These coloured filters become known as Wratten filters. George Eastman will purchase the Wratten Company in 1912 and both Wratten father and sons continue working at Kodak's branch in Harrow, while Mees moves to Rochester to start Eastman Kodak's Research Laboratories.

---

**TRIVIA**

Kodak's filters still carry the Wratten brand name. They remain in production and are now sold through the Tiffen Corporation.

---

**1906:** Frederick Wratten forms a partnership with Henry Wainright (1877~) and the first panchromatic plates are marketed by Wratten and Wainwright (London). They make high-quality colour separation colour photography possible.

**1906:** Canadian entrepreneur Léo-Ernest Ouimet (1877–1972) opens the world's first cinema, on Montreal's St-Catherine Street.

---

### TRIVIA

In 1957, another Canadian, Ottawa cinema owner Nat Taylor (1906–2004), will add a second screen to his movie-house. Et voilà! The multiplex is born!

---

**1907:** Patented by the brothers Auguste and Louis Lumière in 1903, Autochrome is the first commercially available colour "film." It is interesting to note that the emulsions of these glass plates are only about twice as thick as those of modern colour films. However, Autochrome is relatively insensitive, with a sensitivity equivalent to ISO 0.2, and requires 50 times more exposure than straight black-and-white emulsions of the day. When Autochrome is used, the photographer must put a yellow filter over the lens to compensate for the film's relatively high sensitivity to blue light. Despite these drawbacks, not to mention many later competitors, Autochrome becomes the dominant format for colour transparencies until the advent of sub-tractive colour film in the mid-1930s.

**1907:** Leo Hendrick Baekeland, a Belgian chemist working in New York, invents the first entirely synthetic plastic. It is a thermosetting phenolic resin he calls Bakelite that is made by combining phenol and formaldehyde using heat and pressure. Once the resin hardens, it cannot be re-melted by the application of heat. This discovery not only gives birth to the modern plastics industry, but camera makers will soon realize that Bakelite is ideal for making inexpensive camera parts and entire cameras, as it is opaque, sturdy, durable, and can be moulded to any shape. (See **1934**.)

**1907:** Two former projectionists, Donald J. Bell (1869–1934) and Albert S. Howell (1879–1951), form Bell & Howell, in Wheeling, Illinois, to manufacture motion picture cameras and projectors.

**1907:** Folmer & Schwing's Graflex No. 1A is the first medium-format roll-film SLR, taking eight exposures of 2½ x 4½ inches each on 116 roll film. The Graflex 1A features a folding waist-level finder and a focal-plane shutter. A sister camera, the Graflex No. 3A, is released at about the same time and makes six 3¼ x 5½ inch "postcard" frames on 122 roll film.

---

### TRIVIA

In 1908, the first patent for a still camera using 35mm movie film is issued to Leo, Audobard and Baradat in England. Nothing more is ever heard from them, and their camera is never produced.

---

**1908:** The Multi-Speed Shutter Company is established by Gustav Dietz in Long Island, New York. The firm initially designs and patents shutter mechanisms with amazing speeds of up to 1/2000 second, bettering focal-plane shutters of the day. In 1912, it will go on to build a series of cameras under the Simplex name until the company folds in the 1920s.

**1908:** The Motion Picture Patents Company (also known as the Edison Trust) groups together all the major American film companies, the leading film distributor, and the biggest supplier of raw film stock (Eastman Kodak). The MPPC ends the domination of foreign films on American screens, standardizes the way films are distributed and exhibited in America, and improves the quality of American motion pictures by internal competition. But it also discourages its members' entry into feature film production and the use of outside financing, to its members' eventual detriment. The group disbands in 1915.

**1908:** Kinemacolor movies in "natural colour"—as opposed to those coloured by hand-tinting or toning—are shown publicly for the first time.

Kinemacolor is developed in England by George Smith (1864–1959) and American ex-pat Charles Urban (1867–1942). The roots of the system date back to the work of Edward R. Turner, who had received a patent for a three-colour motion picture system in 1889. Turner enlisted the aid of Urban in 1901, and research to produce a workable three-colour system continued until 1903, when Turner suddenly died in his laboratory.

Urban buys the rights and he and Smith spend several more years trying to put three colours on the screen, but without acceptable results. A major impediment was that existing film stocks were orthochromatic—that is, insensitive to red light—so that frames exposed through the red filter are all too light, making colour balance impossible. Mechanical alignment of the frames also proved difficult.

Ultimately, a simpler system using two colours was developed in 1906 and the results were deemed workable. The Kinemacolor system is born.

**TRIVIA**

How Kinemacolor works: The camera is fitted with a rotating wheel with red and green filters, so that alternate frames are exposed through either the red or the green but resulting in a black-and-white positive. Both the camera and projector run at 32 frames per second (double the normal rate). This is then projected through the Kinemacolor projector, which itself has a rotating red-green filter wheel. If the film is loaded so the frames are in the correct red-green sequence, the results are remarkably good. The chief defect of the system is colour "fringing" (fringes of red or green) that is apparent when objects are filmed in motion, since the two colour images are not recorded at the same time.

**1909:** German camera maker C. P. Goerz begins making a special camera for wildlife and similar photography. They build two versions of an SLR camera with an Ottomar Anschütz focal-plane shutter with speeds to 1/1000 second. The first version uses glass plates up to 13 x 18cm and has a 600mm *f*7 Special Lynkeioskop lens in a square lens-tube. A second model will follow in 1912, taking 9 x 12cm plates and equipped with a 480mm Special Lynkeioskop lens in a tapered round tube.

### AUCTION MADNESS

In 2020, a Goerz wildlife camera along with five plate holders and a custom-fitted case will be offered at auction for a mere $3,500.

**1909:** Four small camera makers, Hüttig AG in Dresden, Kamerawerk Doktor Krügener in Frankfurt, M. Wünsche AG (Reick-Dresden) and Carl Zeiss Palmos AG in Jena, join forces to combat growing competition, and become International Camera AG (ICA), based in Dresden. In 1912, Zulauf & Company of Zurich will join the firm.

**1910:** A paper called Utocolor is produced by J. H. Smith in Zurich. Smith's paper uses the direct bleaching action of light on dye layers. It is a difficult process to control and the material is not successful. The problem is that the bleaching process never stops, and so the prints gradually faded away. However, his work will point J. H. Christiansen in the right direction in 1918.

**1910:** Two former Bausch & Lomb employees, Rudolph Klein and Theodore Brueck, invent and patent a shutter-delay mechanism that uses a rotating gear and a rocking pallet. For the first time, shutters are accurate despite temperature and other atmospheric concerns. They set up "Ilex Manufacturing Company" in Rochester to build the shutter. Later, during the Second World War, an Ilex employee, Alfred Schwartz, invents the first practical internal flash synchronization. This is rapidly copied by all other shutter makers.

**1910:** Kodak establish a colour laboratory at Kodak Park lead by Emerson Packard. He instructs Packard to develop a colour film without infringing on the Lumière patents. Their efforts result in a process using red and green filters which transforms negatives directly into positives. Dubbed Kodachrome, it is prevented from going to market by the outbreak of the First World War. Later, Eastman's Kodachrome prints receive poor reviews at a 1915 demonstration before the Royal Photographic Society, and Eastman scraps the project.

**1910:** An American, Robert R. Wood (1868–1955), develops the first infrared film. Unfortunately, his experimental film requires very long exposures. Practical infrared film will have to wait until the 1930s.

**1910:** C. P. Goerz introduces their spectacular Hypergon ultrawide-angle lenses for view cameras, covering between 110° and 135°. The Hypergon is one of a small number of extreme wide-angle lenses based on nearly symmetrical, sharply curved meniscus elements positioned around a central stop. This design reduces distortions while providing a flat field across a very wide angle of coverage. (Harrison's Globe lens of 1860 was also based on this concept.) These lenses are made through the late 1920s and will form the base designs for numerous other ultrawide-angle lenses, including the incredible Zeiss Hologon of 1966.

---

**TRIVIA**

Goerz cameras and lenses are part of every major photographic development from the 1890s through the First World War. Goerz himself is not a scientist of any kind, but a superb entrepreneur who realizes he owes his workers a huge debt for his success. Goerz gains further fame by introducing social benefits for employees: a regulated 48-hour work week (in 1894) and an annual two-week paid vacation (in 1897).

---

**1911:** Friedrich Deckel licenses the clockwork escapement from Ilex and adds it to his shutter, now called the "Compur" shutter. The name is a combination of the words "Compound" from the original shutter and the German word "uhr" for clock.

**1911:** Henry Gaisman (1869–1974) invents Autographic film. Gaisman is a prolific inventor and founder of the AutoStrop Company, a safety razor manufacturer. The purpose of Autographic film is to allow a photographer to make notes about a photograph and have those notes appear in the margin of the processed print. The back of an Autographic camera has a narrow slot that is covered by a light-tight door. To write a note, the door is lifted, giving access to the film's paper backing. Autographic cameras were provided with a metal stylus to scribe the notation onto the paper backing. To capture the handwriting, the door is left open for a few seconds, exposing the marked area to the light.

**1912:** A Dutchman living in Dresden, Germany, Johan Steenberg, starts Industrie und Handelsgesellschaft, which builds cameras under the IHAGEE brand name. (IHAGEE is the pronunciation of the abbreviation of the company's name, IHG (*eehagáy*). The company is successful but will not become widely known outside Europe until 1936, when it will bring the world its first 35mm mirror reflex camera, the Kine Exakta.

**1912:** The Folmer & Schwing Company (now a division of Eastman Kodak) brings out its "Speed Graphic" camera, which takes 4 x 5-inch sheet film. In the United States, it becomes the dominant "press" camera for decades.

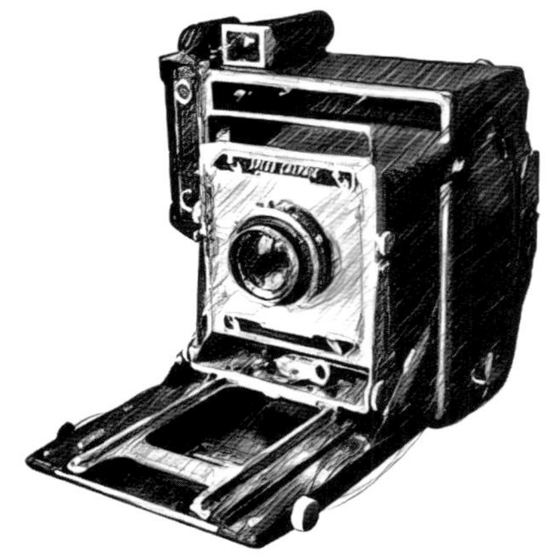

In 1941, the Speed Graphic sells, without lens, for $49.50. It will be produced, in various versions, until 1973.

**TRIVIA**

During the 1930s, 40s, and 50s, Arthur Fellig (professionally known as Weegee), prowled the dark streets of New York with his Speed Graphic, becoming the preeminent crime photographer of his day. He writes in his 1945 monograph *Naked City*: "The only camera I use is a 4 x 5 Speed Graphic with a Kodak Ektar lens in a Supermatic Shutter. All-American made. The film I use is Kodak Super-Panchro Press B. I always use a flashbulb for my pictures which are mostly taken at night. If you are puzzled about the kind of camera to buy, get a Speed Graphic—for two reasons. It is a good camera, and moreover, with a camera like that the cops will assume that you belong on the scene and will let you get behind police lines." (See **1935**.)

**1912:** The Vest Pocket Kodak introduces 127 roll film for still photography. The film itself is 46mm wide, placing it between 35mm and 120 "medium format" films in terms of size. The image format normally used is a square 4 x 4cm. However, rectangular 4 x 3cm and 4 x 6cm versions are also used. The 127 format enjoys mainstream popularity until its usage declines in the 1960s in the face of newer cartridge-based films. However, as of 2020, it survives as a niche format, though very hard to find.

**1912:** Max Berek (1886–1949) joins the Ernst Leitz Company and will go on to compute the first Leica lens for 35mm photography.

**1912:** Two German chemists, Hans Siegrist and Rudolph Fisher, discover the "colour coupling" process, which will eventually become the basis for Kodachrome. They describe the process and patent it but are unable to make the process reliable enough to start film production.

**1912-1913:** Henry Herbert, an American importer of movie equipment, observes that leftover lengths of 35mm film can be had for one-third of the usual price. He asks his technician, Paul Dietz, to design a camera to use these roll ends, and Dietz creates the "Tourist Multiple."

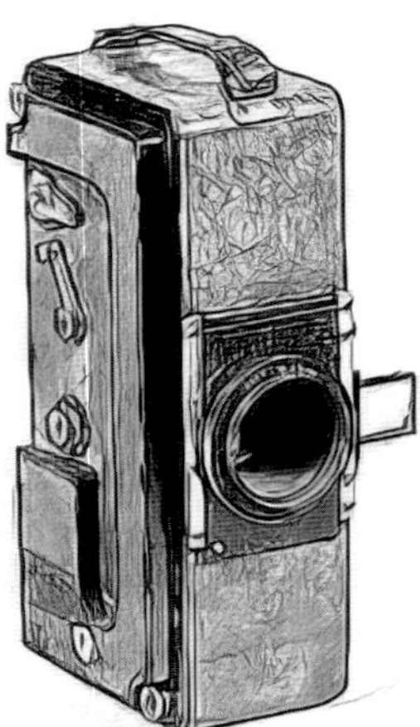

The camera is introduced in 1913 and becomes the first publicly sold still camera to use 35mm film. It takes seven hundred and fifty 18 x 24mm exposures (the standard movie frame, today called "half-frame" in still cameras) on a 50-foot length. The body can also be used as a projector, but an anticipated enlarging accessory is never produced. Roughly 1,000 cameras are built before the outbreak of the First World War in 1914, which sharply limits demand. Production is suspended, never to be resumed.

---

**TRIVIA**

Although several 35mm still cameras follow, the format will not become popular until the introduction of the Leica in 1925.

---

**1913:** Kodak introduce Eastman Portrait Film, which begins the transition to the use of sheet film instead of glass plates for professional photographers.

**1913:** The first 35mm stereo camera in series production is the Homeoscope, produced in France by Jules Richard from 1913 to 1920. The camera takes stereo pairs, 18 x 24mm, with two Tessar lenses.

**1913:** Joseph Schneider (1855–1933) starts Schneider Optik in Bad Kreuznach, Germany, creating a company that will grow into, and remains today, a world leader in high-performance lenses for photography, cinematography, cinema projection, television, and various industrial applications.

---

**TRIVIA**

Joseph Schneider had no background in optics—he was a brewer of beer in Springfield, Illinois, in the late 1800s. When he saw prohibition coming, he returned to his native Rhineland and grew grapes, eventually becoming vintner to the Russian Tsar. His son, Joseph August Schneider, studied optics at Frankfurt University, and Joseph, ever the entrepreneur, saw an opportunity. So, in 1913, Joseph sold his vineyards and started Schneider Optik with his son. They made their first Xenar *f* 4.5 lens in 1919 and their one-millionth lens in 1936.

---

**1913:** The prototype Ur-Leica is invented by Oskar Barnack at Ernst Leitz, in Wetzlar. Oscar is asthmatic and finds lifting the heavy cameras of his day exceedingly difficult. As early as 1905 he has the idea of reducing the format of negatives and then enlarging the photographs after they had been exposed. This *"small negative—large print"* idea has never been tried before. As development manager at Leitz, he can put his theory into practice. He turns 35mm motion picture film sideways and doubles the image size to the now-standard 24 x 36mm, creating a camera that will lead to a revolution in camera design.

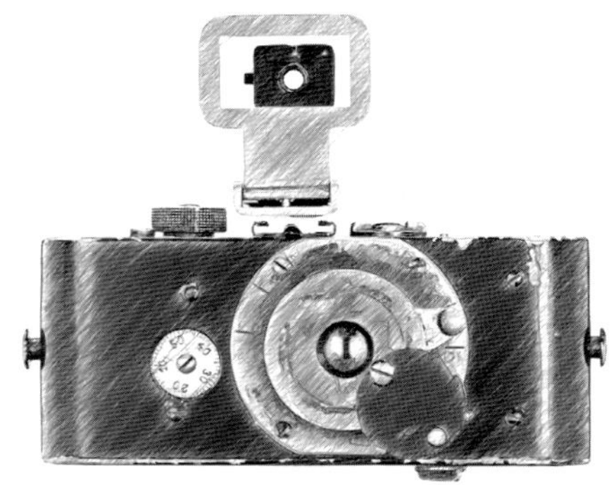

---

**TRIVIA**

UR is the Leitz code name for experimental models and is a German prefix meaning "original or primitive." Today, in English, we'd use the term "prototype."

---

**1914:** George Eastman purchases the rights to Gaisman's Autographic film (see **1911**) for $300,000, and Kodak introduce the Autographic cameras and film later in the year. Kodak make a series of Autographic cameras and even replacement backs to adapt older cameras to use this feature. Kodak also produces Autographic film for eight different negative sizes. The smallest is A127 (1½ x 2½ inches) and the largest A126 (4½ x 6½ inches). The film is never very popular and the manufacture of both Autographic cameras and film ceases in 1937.

**1914:** Sawyer's, Inc. is started as a photofinisher, in Portland, Oregon. In 1939 it will go on, to develop the View-Master stereo viewer, and in the 1950s will start manufacturing projectors. In 1966, it will become part of the GAF Corporation, eventually disappearing in 1977.

**1914:** In Germany, Agfa introduces Agfacolor, a substantial improvement over Autochrome. Agfa replaces Autochrome's starch particles with coloured particles made of a resin. These screens can be made without the necessity of pulverized charcoal since the resin particles fit together without leaving any spaces. Sensitivity and granularity are also greatly improved, although exposure times are still eight times more than with black and white.

**1914:** A court rules the Eastman Kodak Company has infringed Goodwin's patent for making transparent flexible film, and Kodak is ordered to pay $5 million (or $104,750,000 in 2014 dollars) to the Ansco Company, now the holders of the Goodwin patent.

**1915:** Herbert Kalmus (1881–1963) starts his Technicolor Corp. The "Tech" in Technicolor comes from the company's association with MIT. That, and the name "has a nice *ring* to it."

**1915:** Sixty-eight aerial photographs are taken of the Gallipoli battlefield, the first use of wartime aerial photographic reconnaissance.

**1915:** Karl Braun KG, Fabrik optischer Geräte und Metallwaren (for the fabrication of optical goods and metalware) starts operations in Nuremberg, Germany. In 1948, the company will begin producing box cameras, in both roll film and 35mm format, and change its name to Carl Braun Camera-Werke.

**1916:** With Britain at war, a "large number" of Konishi Honten's "Lilly II" cameras are exported to war-ravaged England. The Lilly-II has a leather-covered wood body with a leather bellows and uses the Tefuda format (quarter-plate or 3¼ x 4¼ inch). It is the first time a Japanese-produced camera is exported.

---

### TRIVIA

It is ironic that the first Japanese camera to be exported should go to the U.K., which had supplied highly regarded (and often copied) cameras to Japan for decades.

**1916:** The Haloid Photographic Company is started in Rochester to manufacture photographic paper and equipment. It will go on to become the XeroX Corporation.

**1916:** The Kodak No. 3A Autographic Special becomes the first camera with a coupled range-finder. Depending on the lens and shutter, the price varies between $49 and $110. Considering that a teacher's annual salary is $970, it is an expensive camera. Variations will be made until 1937.

**1917:** Nippon Kogaku (literally "Japan Optical")—which will eventually become Nikon—is established in Tokyo as a general optical company by the merger of two optical firms with military connections.

**1917:** Arsène Gitzhoven starts the French firm Gitzo, initially producing cameras, shutters, and cable releases. In the early 1950s, Gitzhoven retires, and his daughter Yvonne Plieger takes over the firm. She and her husband are dedicated to creating the range of high-quality photographic tripods for which Gitzo is renowned today. After more than 40 years in the business, they will sell Gitzo to the U.K.'s Vitec Group (which also owns Italy's tripod maker, Manfrotto).

**1917:** Arri is founded in Munich as Arnold & Richter Cine Technik Gmbh. They eventually become one of the leading makers of cinema cameras and will continue until the current day.

---

### TRIVIA

In 1924, Arnold & Richter developed their first film camera, the small and portable Kinarri 35. In 1937, Arri introduced the world's first reflex mirror shutter in the Arriflex 35 camera, an invention of engineer Erich Kästner. This technology employs a rotating mirror that allows a continuous motor to operate the camera while providing parallax-free reflex viewing to the operator and the ability to focus the image by eye through the viewfinder, much like an SLR camera for still photography. This reflex design was subsequently used in almost every professional motion picture film camera and is still used in the Arri Alexa Studio digital camera.

---

**1917:** Technicolor introduce their System 1, an additive colour process for motion pictures. Unlike Kinemacolor, it records the red and blue-green images simultaneously through a single lens, using a beam splitter and colour filters to record the images stacked one on top of the other. No rotating colour wheel is involved on either the camera or projector. Because the projector uses an adjustable prism to align the two images on the screen, the system is plagued by fringing and fuzziness.

**1918:** J. H. Christiansen describes the principle of dye destruction and patents a method of bleaching the dye layers with a sodium hydrosulphite catalyst bath. In this process, the image dyes are incorporated in the emulsion during manufacture. The dyes are selectively bleached as the silver image is removed during processing. This has the advantage of using very stable AZO dyes and producing exceptional sharpness.

While no films are ever made using this process, it is well known today as the Cibachrome or Ilfochrome papers that make high-quality prints directly from slides.

---

**TRIVIA**

Sadly, Cibachrome and/or Ilfochrome are no more. The last manufacturing run was in 2012, a result of the rise of digital photography.

---

**1918:** Pignons SA are founded in the village of Ballaigues, Switzerland, to supply parts (pignons) for the Swiss watch industry. They will later go on to produce the famous Alpa cameras.

**1918:** Japanese camera maker Sone Shunsuidō starts selling the Adam (アダム), a cardboard box camera with no viewfinder and no shutter (the exposure time is controlled by the lens cap). It uses 4 x 5cm plates that must be inserted into the camera one by one, in a darkroom. Inconvenient, but the Adam is the first Japanese camera to sell for ¥1 (roughly 50 cents at that time, or about $19 today).

**1919:** The company that will become Pentax is founded as Asahi Kōgaku Kōgyō G.K. (Asahi Optical Company) and begins by making eyeglasses under the Aoco brand (presumably the acronym of Asahi Optical COmpany). By 1933, Asahi are making lenses under the "Optor" brand for a variety of camera makers.

**1919:** In October, Takeshi Yamashita starts Takachiho Seisakusho, a maker of microscopes and thermometers under the "Tokiwa" brand. They first use the "Olympus" brand name in 1921 and in 1936 they introduce their first camera, the Semi-Olympus equipped with the Zuiko 75mm $f$4.5 lens (see **1936**). In 1949, Takachiho Seisakusho will become Olympus Optical Company, Ltd.

---

**TRIVIA**

Takeshi Yamashita, a lawyer and the founder of Olympus, wanted to start up a microscope manufacturing business in Japan. At that time Japan lacked the necessary technology, yet they produce their first microscope under the "Asahi" brand after just six months, in March 1920. The Asahi was priced at 125 yen (about 1.25 million yen today) and was the only model made of gunmetal, a bronze alloy made from copper and tin that is used for cannon barrels.

---

**1919:** Paul Friedrich Karl Gossen (1872–1942) and Otto Cohn start Paul Gossen Company, Fabrik elektrischer Messgeräte, in Baiersdorff. Within a few years, the company moves to Erlangen, grows, sees Cohn leave and Rita Gossen join, goes into, and emerges from bankruptcy, and successfully sells ammeters and similar devices along the way. Gossen will begin producing photographic exposure meters in 1933.

> **TRIVIA**
>
> In 1950, Gossen started production of the Gossen "Tippa" portable typewriter. Soon Gossen was churning out a typewriter every eight minutes. In 1956, after making about 100,000 units, the Tippa was sold to Adler. In the early 1970s, production was moved to Japan, quality fell, and the brand soon disappeared.

**1919:** Kamera-Werkstätten Guthe & Thorsch (KW-G&T) is established in Dresden by Paul Guthe and Benno Thorsch (1898–) to manufacture the Patent Etui plate camera. The company prospers and in 1939 will launch the 35mm SLR Praktiflex camera with a waist-level finder.

**1919:** Engineers Evžen Schier (1876–1958) and J. Bárta start a company in Nusle (later, to become part of Prague) to produce photographic plates, which are sold under the "Ibis" brand. In 1921, the company will move to Hradec Králové and change its name to Fotochema, marketing its films and chemicals under the Foma brand. In 1930, they will start making black-and-white papers and, in 1933, the production of roll films.

> **TRIVIA**
>
> In 1995, the company, by then state-owned, was re-privatized as Foma Bohemia Ltd., and remains one of the last traditional producers of panchromatic black-and-white photographic film and related materials.

**1920:** Reinhold Heidecke (1881–1960) and Paul Franke start "Franke und Heidecke Werkstatt fur Feinmechanik und Optic" in Braunschweig, Germany, and one year later introduce their first product, a stereo camera called the "Heidoscop," which is followed in 1927 by the "Rolleidoskop." Production of their classic vertical style twin-lens reflex will not start until 1928.

**1920:** Enna Werk (Munich) start making lenses under their Enna brand. They go on to make lenses for a variety of camera manufacturers and retailers, most notably Alpa, Balda, and Porst.

Siegfried Schäfer, the primary design engineer at Enna Werk, is responsible for many of the Enna lens designs. Some of his designs are based on drafts by Ludwig Bertele (1900–1985), designer of the Ernostar and its more famous offspring, the Sonnar.

In the 1950s and 1960s, Enna are quite innovative. In 1953, they are the first company in West Germany to produce a wide-angle lens with retrofocus design for 35mm SLR cameras, the 35mm $f$4.5 Lithagon. It is followed by what was then the world's fastest 35mm wide-angle, the 35mm $f$1.9 Super-Lithagon, in 1958. In 1961, the first German-designed telephoto zoom lens, the very impressive 85–250mm $f$4, was introduced.

---

**TRIVIA**

The Enna Werk still exists today but stopped producing lenses in 1992. They are now based in Wegscheid, where they manufacture plastic injection moulding equipment.

---

**1920:** The Bartlane Facsimile (fax) machine is developed in Great Britain. It is one of the first applications of digital technology and is used to send newspaper photos between London and New York, via submarine cable.

---

**ODDITIES**

An interesting forerunner of the Leica is the 1921 "Argus" from Francesco Morsolin of Turin, Italy. The only known surviving example has serial number 289. Depending on where they started numbering (probably 100) it would seem that only a few hundred were made. The Argus features a Meyer lens marked "Helioplan 6/53" (probably meaning a 53mm *f* 6 lens) and a Prontor shutter and uses unperforated 35mm film.

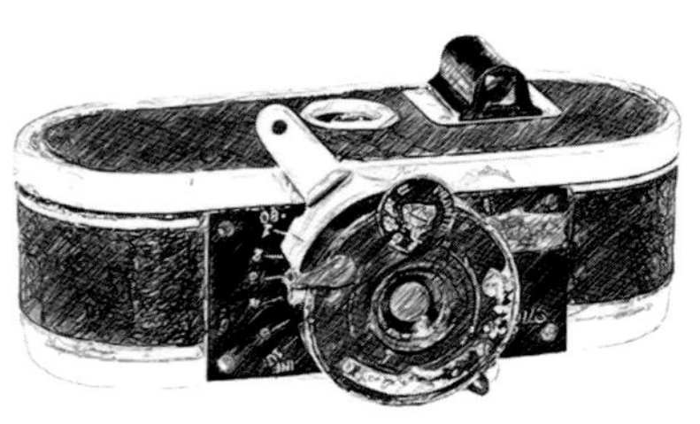

---

**1921:** Konishi Honten changes its name, becoming Konisiroku Photo Industries. It will later become Konica.

**1922:** Technicolor introduces its subtractive System 2 motion picture process. As with System 1, a beam splitter produces the red and blue-green record of the original scene on black-and-white film, with the images alternating and inverted from each other.

Two separate prints are made on half-thickness film and printed as mirror images that will be placed back-to-back after the application of the colour dyes. After these prints are developed, the silver halide is removed, and the gelatin remains as a "contour map" of the colour. This gelatin is then dyed a colour that is complementary to the original colour record. The prints are then cemented back-to-back to form the final release print. Registration problems are gone, image sharpness is vastly improved, and standard projectors can run the prints.

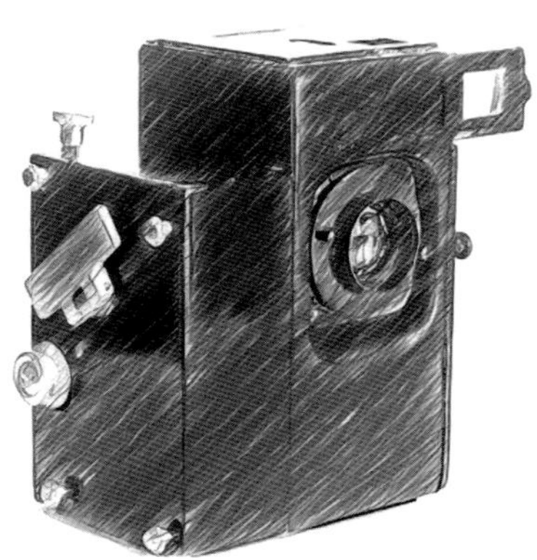

**1922:** At the end of the First World War, Giuseppe Giovanni Battista Tartara's firm F.A.C.T. in Turin, begins producing his Autocinephot—a 35mm camera that can take stills, sequence shots, or movies. (In movie-use, it exposes a five-metre-long roll of film in 17 seconds.) No more than 100 units are produced. The design is then sold to the Paris firm of André Debrie (1891–1967) and produced, in slightly modified form using French lenses, as the "Debrie Sept," between 1922 and 1927. Two versions are made; the first version has a square front for housing a single spring motor. The second version has a rounded front for housing a double spring motor. If a lamp house had been added to the back, the camera could also have served as a projector or an enlarger, but unfortunately that accessory was never produced.

**1922:** Kodak introduce infrared film for scientific use.

**1923:** The Beck "Sky" is introduced for taking meteorological images of cloud cover. Designed by Robin (Robert) Hill, it is sometimes known as the "Hill Cloud Camera." The first true "fisheye" lens, it sees 180° in both vertical and horizontal planes, resulting in a circular image. It will later become the basis of Nikon's series of fisheye Nikkors, the 8mm $f$8 (1962–1965), 7.5mm $f$5.6 (1966–1970), and 8mm $f$2.8 (1970–1997).

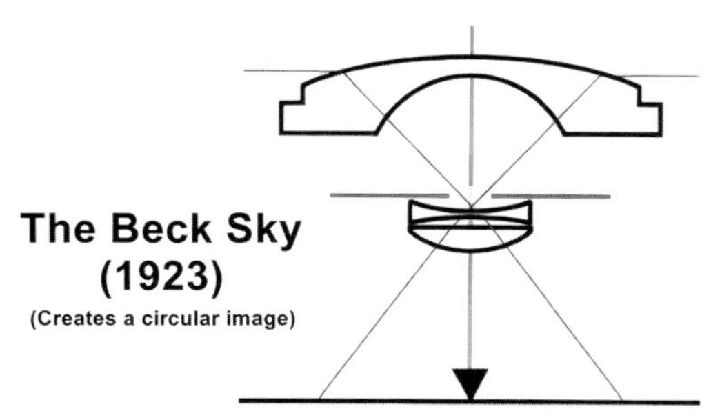


**1923:** FILM (*Fabbrica Italiana Lamine Milano*, or "Italian Lamination Factory, Milan"), co-owned by the French Pathé Brothers and SIPE, is founded as a maker of photographic film, papers and photographic equipment, including cameras under the Ferrania brand (see **1882**).

**1923:** The Ernst Leitz Company produce between 21 and 23 (the records are not clear) handmade cameras for the factory and outside photographers to test. Though the prototypes receive mixed reviews, Ernst Leitz II decides in 1924 to produce the camera. A decision that will change photography forever.

These cameras become known as the Leica O-series and serve as a prototype run for the Leica Standard, which will be released two years later. The camera sports a fixed 50mm $f$3.5 lens called the Leitz Anastigmat and based on the design of the Cooke Triplet. (Leica will later drop "Anastigmat" when the Standard is released, calling the lens the Leitz Elmar instead.)

---

### AUCTION MADNESS

Of the 12 to 16 O-series cameras believed to still exist, only three are in original condition. In 2018, one of these three sold at auction for a whopping $2.97 million, breaking its own record from 2012 of $2.79 million, making it the most expensive camera ever sold, to that time. Then, in 2023, O-Series No.121 sold at auction for €3.5 million ($3,700,000). But, not a record, for in 2022, Leica O-Series No.105, which had been owned by Leica inventor Oskar Barnack, became the most expensive camera ever sold with a hammer price of €14.4, or just north of $15 million!

**1923:** Bell & Howell's Filmo 70 is the first spring motor-driven 16mm camera. It is based on the company's brilliantly designed 1917 prototype for a 17.5mm camera. When, in 1920, Kodak announce their intention to make 16mm film, the company is quick to redesign the prototype for the new 16mm film. The design is so successful that many models are built on the same basic design for over half a century.

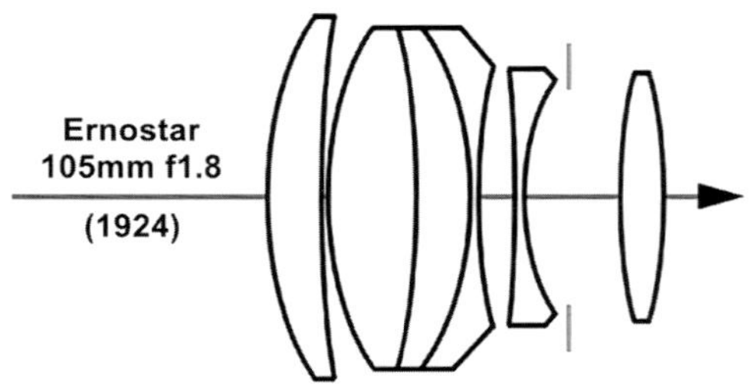


**1923:** The first commonly available very-wide-aperture lens suitable for "available light" photography is the Ernemann Ernostar, made in Germany. Ludwig Bertele's formula is originally a 10cm $f$2 lens, but he improves it, creating the 85mm $f$1.8 lenses in 1924 and, later, a 105mm $f$1.8 version. Bertele continues the Ernostar's development after Ernemann is absorbed into Zeiss Ikon in 1926, but under the Sonnar name.

---

### TRIVIA

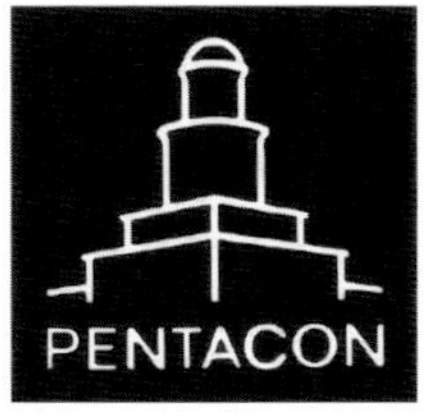


In 1923, Ernemann's camera division moved to a new, highly advanced factory in Dresden-Striesen, still known today as "The Ernemann Tower." The building survived the 1945 Dresden fire bombing because of its suburban location, although the interior was badly damaged. After the war, it became the symbol for VEB Pentacon.

---

**1923:** Kodak introduce 16mm file as a less-expensive alternative to 35mm and was intended for amateur use. Sixteen millimetre is one of the first formats to use acetate safety film as its base.

**1923:** The Kern Company (formed in 1819 by Jakob Kern to produce scientific equipment) begins to make and sell cameras in limited production. This lasts until 1935. It also makes top-quality lenses for other cameras including, in 1958, the renowned Kern 50mm $f$1.8 Macro-Switar for the Alpa. Because of high production costs, and after several changes of ownership, the company ceases operation in 1991 after just 175 years.

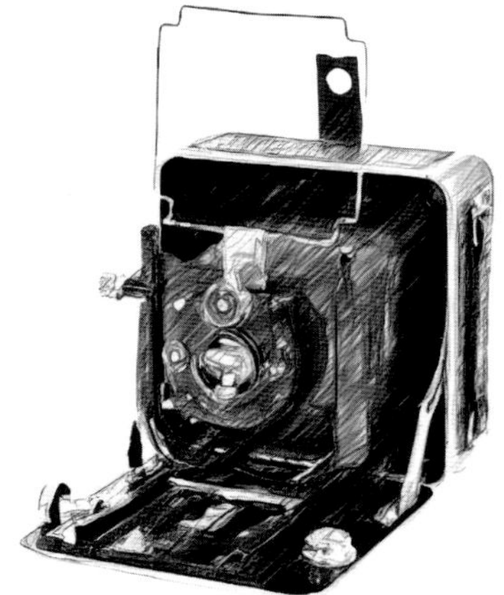

**1923:** Nippon Kogaku takes over the glass research department of Japan's Aeronautical Research Institute and soon afterwards successfully anneals a 350kg crucible of glass, its first venture into this aspect of optical production. This unit becomes the Nikon Optical Materials unit, making Nippon Kogaku/Nikon the only camera maker to manufacture its own optical glass. This tradition continues to this day.

**1924:** E. Krauss, Paris, markets his EKA camera. The EKA features a dial-set Compur shutter and holds enough film for 100 exposures, each 30 x 44mm. Because it uses unperforated 35mm film with paper backing, its negative size is somewhat larger than that of the Leica Standard.

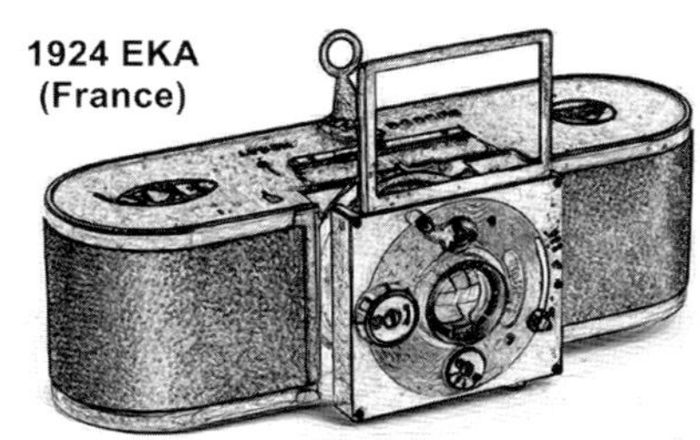


**1924:** The Ermanox is the first camera to sport Bertele's 85mm *f* 1.8 Ernostar, a lens that makes available-light photography practical for the first time (see **1923**). Made by Ernemann in Dresden, it uses 6 x 4.5cm glass plates and has a focal plane shutter with speeds from 1/20 to 1/1000 second. The Ermanox is discontinued in 1931 with the advent of the Leica and the Zeiss Contax.

---

**TRIVIA**

The original production run is called the "Ernox," but this is soon changed to Ermanox. Some examples of the Ermanox are also seen with a 100mm *f* 2 Ernostar and one (just one) was produced with a 165mm *f* 1.8 Ernostar. By 2002, Ermanox cameras sell for €1,200. By 2019, they are being offered on Ebay for $5,200!

---

**1924:** Jacques Bolsky (1895–1962), born in the Ukraine as Jacques Bogopolsky, but also known by the names by Boolsky or Bolsey, starts Bol SA, in Switzerland, to market his 35mm combination movie/still camera, the Cinématographe Bol. Later, in 1927, he will produce his 16mm Bolec camera, which becomes the famous 16mm Bolex. Paillard SA of St-Croix will take over Bol SA in 1930, acquiring the rights to the Bolex in the process. Even today, Bolex remains a world-famous name in 8 and 16mm motion picture cameras.

**1925:** In 1924, Ernst Leitz II decides to produce Oskar Barnack's 35mm camera as the "Leica," the first high-quality modern 35mm camera. The name "Leica" is derived from Leitz and Camera. The Leica is introduced at the Leipzig Trade Fair, with an initial run of 1,000 cameras. It is a success and virtually all 35mm cameras for the next 60+ years will follow its basic design. It is so successful, in fact, that a number of camera companies build models based on the Leica rangefinder design, including the Leotax, Nicca, and early Canon models in Japan; the Kardon in USA; the Reid in England; and the FED and Zorki in the USSR.

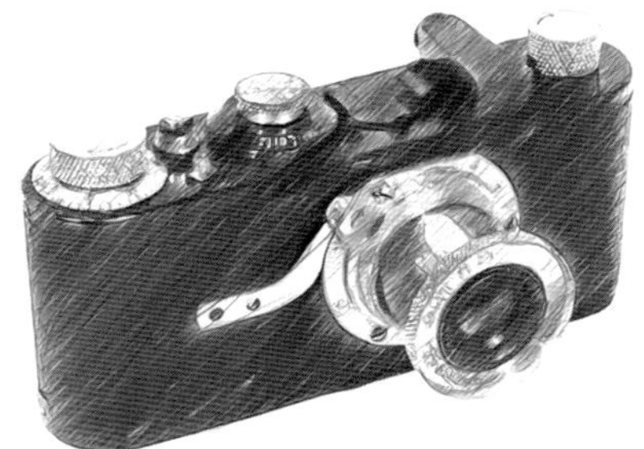

## TRIVIA

Leitz considered many names for their new camera. "Lilliput", suggested by Oscar Barnack himself, was discarded as it had already registered by a competitor, Ernemann (see **1924**). They settled on "Leca" (the first two letters of Leitz and camera) but, just before the camera was introduced, someone noticed that the name of the French Eka camera (see **1924**) would commonly be pronounced "L'Eka", uncomfortably close to Leca. So, they included the "i" from Leitz, to create the now-familiar Leica brand-name.

## TRIVIA

The early Leitz lenses have a story of their own. Oskar Barnack tried a Zeiss Tessar on his early prototype camera, but because the Tessar was designed for the 18 x 24mm movie format, it did not adequately cover the Leica's 24 x 36mm negative. Barnack resorted to a Leitz Mikro-Summar $f$ 4.5 42mm lens for the prototype, but to achieve the resolution necessary for making satisfactory enlargements, the 24 x 36mm format needed a lens designed specially for it. The first Leica lens was a 50mm $f$ 3.5 design based on the Cooke triplet of 1893, adapted by Max Berek at Leitz. The lens has five elements in three groups and was initially named the Leitz Anastigmat. When the Leica was first sold, this lens was renamed the Elmax, for **E L**eitz and **Max** Berek.

By 1925, newer glass types were developed with improved optical properties, and Professor Berek designed an improved version of the Elmax, named the Elmar, that had four elements in three groups. The third group was simplified to two cemented elements, which was easier and cheaper to make. Fewer than 150 cameras were made with the 50mm $f$ 3.5 anastigmat lens, followed by a short run of cameras with an Elmax lens before production settled down to use a 50mm $f$ 3.5 Elmar, the lens which you'll see today on the vast majority of early Leicas.

The chief lens designer at Leica, Max Berek, had two dogs, Hektor and Rex. The first of these, Hektor, gave his name to a series of Leica lenses, starting with the 50mm $f$ 2.5 Hektor, and later a series of short telephoto lenses. Berek's second dog appeared in the Summarex line of lenses.

## TERMINOLOGY

The dominant still picture film formats of the day are 4 x 5 inch and larger sheet films. With the advent of cameras using 35mm film came the term "miniature" cameras. Though that term has now largely disappeared, cameras using film smaller in size than 35mm film, such as 16mm, 9.5mm, 17mm, or 17.5mm are still referred to as "sub-miniature" cameras.

**1925:** The first modern photo-flash bulb or flashbulb is invented by an Austrian, Paul Vierkotter. He uses magnesium-coated wire in a glass globe. In 1927, he will sell his patent to the General Electric Company. The magnesium is soon replaced by zirconium, which gives a brighter light.

**1925:** In Tokyo, the Kobori Manufacturing Company, Ltd. is formed to manufacture watch components. They expand into aeronautical instruments for the military and, after the end of the Second World War, begin to focus on optical equipment and camera lenses. Most of the lenses will be made for other companies, including Minolta, Sony, Nikon, and Vivitar. They continue today, making everything from assembly jigs to lens parts to finished lenses for other camera brands.

---

**TRIVIA**

The company also sold lenses under its own Koboron brand and previously under the Tefnon, Teknon and Technon brands, though these trademarks are no longer in use.

---

**1925:** Schering, a German maker of film and other photographic materials, acquires Voigtländer. Film is now sold under the Voigtländer name.

**1926:** Charles Martin (1877–1977), the chief of the National Geographic Photo Lab; a botanist, W. H. Longley (1881–1937); and an unknown National Geographic chemist concoct a "hyper-sensitizing" solution. When the solution is used to coat Autochrome glass plates, exposure times are reduced from one second of daylight to 1/20 second. With this breakthrough, and an ingenious flash, they take the first colour undersea photographs, in the Dry Tortugas archipelago west of Key West, Florida.

Using flash underwater had not been done before. Magnesium powder is the material of choice and normally a small pinch of powder is all that was needed to create enough light for a flash. Underwater, it was a different story. So, Longley and Martin build a raft which contains a battery, a reflecting hood and one pound of magnesium powder. The shutter of the camera is wired to the battery on the raft, and when Longley clicks the shutter it completes the circuit, igniting an enormous explosion that illuminates the seabed down to 15 feet. This entire process was repeated for every single autochrome.

---

**TRIVIA**

In the experimental stages an ounce of magnesium powder flashed prematurely and burned Longley's hands. He was laid up for six days but had one pound been used, Longley probably would not have survived.

---

**1926:** *Asahi Camera* is first published and, along with *Camera*, becomes one of Japan's two dominant photo magazines, much as *Modern* and *Popular* will dominate in the United States. Other than a hiatus during the Second World War, *Asahi Camera* continues to publish until July 2020—a remarkable 93-year run.

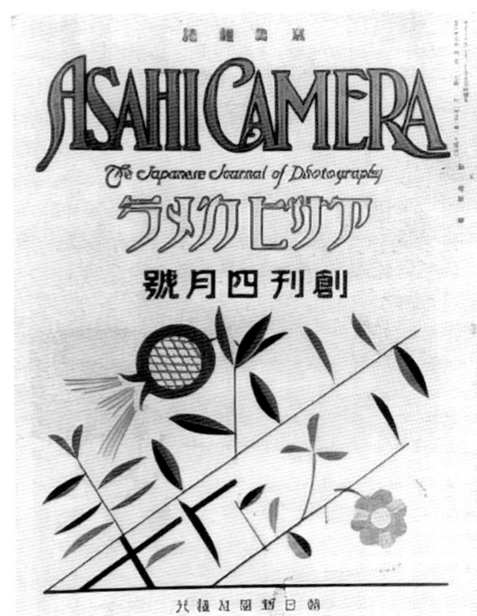

**1926:** Zeiss Ikon AG is formed out of the merger of four companies: ICA, Erneman, Goerz, and Contessa-Nettel, along with a huge injection of capital from Carl Zeiss (Jena). Though largely owned by Carl Zeiss, it is a fully independent company.

Zeiss Ikon becomes a huge corporation with offices in five cities in Germany and offers a wide variety of cameras. Unfortunately, that is also its downfall. The various divisions compete against each other aggressively and there was much duplication of effort. Zeiss Ikon never really takes advantage of its size, and eventually folds, in 1972.

**1926–1927:** Early Bell & Howell Filmo cameras (see **1923**) use different lens mounts, known as the "A" mount and "B" mount. Filmos with serial numbers 54090 and higher, probably from late 1926 or very early 1927, use the "C" mount. Soon after, other camera manufacturers adopt the "C" mount, which becomes a de facto standard for 16mm cine cameras.

---

### TRIVIA

The term "C-mount" says very little about its intended use. C-mount lenses have been made for 8mm and 16mm film formats and for the one-third, one-half, two-thirds, one inch, and four-thirds inch video (TV) formats. Image circles vary from 5mm to 22mm in diameter. Some TV lenses lack provision to focus or vary the aperture, while others have components that protrude behind the mount far enough to interfere with the shutter or reflex-finder mechanisms of a film camera.

---

**1927:** The company founded in 1920 by the brothers Heinrich (d. 1989), Max, and Josef Wirgin, introduce their first camera, the Edinex, which is also produced for ADOX as the Adrette. In 1934, the company brings to market a very small viewfinder camera for 127 film, the Gewirette. From the mid-1930s they also make Edinex 35mm viewfinder cameras. In 1938, Nazi persecution compels Jews to escape to America, and the Wirgin factory in Wiesbaden becomes part of the ADOX company.

**TRIVIA**

After the war, Heinrich Wirgin (by then known as Henry Wirgin) returned to Germany to restart the family business (see **1951**). Max Wirgin remained in America, becoming the U.S. importer of Exakta cameras, and selling other photo products through his Camera Specialty Company. Little is known of Josef's fate.

**1927:** The Ansco Memo is released, with its vertical wooden leather-covered body and tubular optical finder on top. The Memo makes fifty 18 x 32mm exposures (very close to today's half-frame cameras) on 35mm film in special cassettes, which are initially made of wood. (The 35mm film format will not be standardized for another seven years; see **1934**.) Film advance is by a sliding button on the back; the Memo also has an automatic exposure counter. Versions are made with both $f$3.5 and $f$6.3 lenses in focusing and non-focusing mounts, a choice of beautifully finished wood bodies or leather-covered bodies, and even a wood "Boy Scout" model, painted olive-drab. Lenses are provided by Wollensak, Bausch & Lomb, Ilex and Agfa, among others. Production probably ends in 1931, as the Memo does not appear in any catalogues or other promotional material after that year.

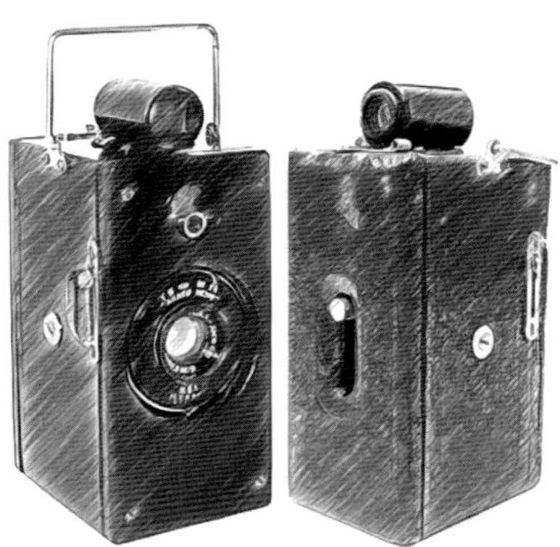

**TRIVIA**

The Ansco Memo was one of the first American-made 35mm cameras to receive widespread popularity. Production numbers on the Memo are not known, but must have been considerable, at least prior to the Great Depression, for Ansco was selling the Memo's special cassettes with film loads as late as 1954.

**1927:** Started in 1921 as Sakaki Shōkai by Hidenobu Sakaki, the first ELMO 16mm projector (the model A) is released. It is the first such device manufactured in Japan. From the late 1940s through the late 1950s, they will also build the Elmoflex series of 6 x 6 TLR cameras. Elmo will go on to become one of the best-regarded makers of cine equipment. At their peak, the Elmo factory, in Nagoya, has 1,000 employees, 30% of whom are responsible for inspection and quality control!

**UPDATE**

Elmo will abandon making cine equipment with the advent of digital video cameras and, in 1984, moves into manufacturing CCTV cameras. The firm still exists, making document cameras (the digital equivalent of the overhead projector) and other technical equipment for schools, government, and business.

**1927:** Technicolor unveil their System 3 for commercial (i.e., Hollywood) movies. The new process overcomes the cupping that plagued the earlier system by eliminating the cementing of film prints. Instead, it uses the matrices to transfer the dye to a specially prepared clear film base.

Technicolor goes far beyond supplying film and their special cameras to movie producers, however—now their consultants advise on numerous production aspects in addition to colour. Set and costume design, props, make-up, and lighting (including the camera work) are all controlled by Technicolor. Specially trained cameramen handle the numerous difficult processes involved, as particular care has to be given to shadows and highlights (otherwise, bright white image segments tend to produce obtrusive blotches of white, while blacks are sometimes reproduced with unwanted colour hues). The emulsions are very slow, meaning that high levels of illumination are required, which must also be adjusted to the colour temperature of daylight. Both these requirements lead to the use of brilliant carbon-arc lamps.

Given the complexity of these problems and the need for technical advice, the company dominates the market for colour films from the mid-1930s to the 1950s.

**1928:** Edward Weston (not the famous photographer by the same name) patents his "Illumination Meter." Not really an exposure meter as we think of one, it is a meter to measure light in foot candles.

**1928:** Kodak's first use of the "Kodacolor" name is given to a lenticular colour film made only for 16mm movies. The system uses tiny, embossed lenses pressed into the film base of a panchromatic black-and-white film and requires a special striped filter on both the camera and projector. Filming requires the camera's lens to be used only at $f$ 1.9, so that the striped filter works correctly. Exposure is about a 1/30 second in bright sunlight, representing a film speed (sensitivity), in modern terms, of about 0.5 ISO. Kodacolor is retired after Kodachrome film makes it obsolete in 1935.

---

**TRIVIA**

In 1928, the Ernst Leitz company introduced their now-famous product codewords. Indecipherable to many, they were a shorthand ordering code. A film cassette was a FILCA (later IXMOO) and a spring-wound motor-drive was a MOOLY, while the early reflex finder was a PLOOT. The company's reasoning was pure genius. At the time, most orders were sent to head office by telegraph, which had to be paid for by the word. So, ordering "qty 3 spring drive motors for Leica IIIc" would cost eight times as much to send as "MOOLY3."

**1928:** Agfa (Germany) merges with Ansco (USA) to become Agfa-Ansco, in order to compete globally with competitors such as Kodak and Zeiss. The new firm, Agfa-Ansco, added many Agfa cameras and accessories to its sales in the USA as a result. Eventually it will become part of the GAF Corp.

**1928:** August Nagel (1882–1943), founder of Contessa and co-founder of Zeiss Ikon, splits off to start his own camera factory in his hometown of Stuttgart. The company becomes famous for its small format camera, the Nagel-Pupille. In 1931, the company becomes Kodak's German branch, Kodak AG. After that, the model range continues under the Kodak name.

**1928:** Kazuo Tashima (1899–1985) starts Nichidoku Shashinki Shōten (meaning Japan-German Camera Company), and releases the Nifcarette, a 4 x 6.5 folding camera. The firm becomes a leading camera manufacturer and in 1931, the company adopts its brand-name, Minolta, an acronym for "Mechanism, Instruments, Optics, and Lenses by TAshima."

**1929:** Meant to appeal to women, the Kodak Petites are the first cameras with pastel-coloured coverings.

**1929:** Edwin Land (1909–1991) patents the first synthetic polarizing material.

**1929:** Konishiroku (which will become Konica) launches the Sakura (meaning Cherry Blossom) brand of black-and-white film. In 1987, the Sakura brand will be replaced worldwide with Konica.

**1929:** Franke & Heidecke introduce the Rolleiflex twin-lens reflex producing a 6 x 6cm image on Kodak's 117 (also known as B1) roll film. (The Rolleiflex "Standard" of 1932, and all later Rolleiflex and Rolleicord cameras, would use the B2 or Kodak 120 film.) This camera becomes the standard bearer for 6 x 6 (2¼ square) twin-lens reflex cameras.

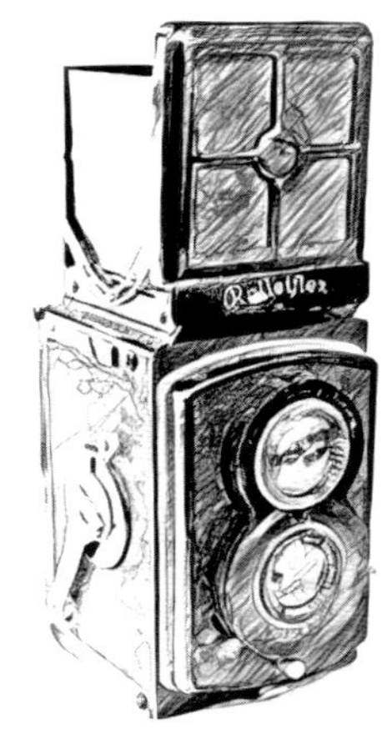

### TRIVIA

Reinhold Heidecke didn't invent the Twin Lens Reflex format. As a long-time professional camera designer, he'd undoubtedly have been aware of the earlier large-format designs (see **1885**). What sparked his interest, however, was the realization that in the trenches of The Great War (now known as World War I), photography over the parapet was an extremely hazardous business. His idea was to use an upside-down TLR, of compact dimensions, which the photographer could fasten to a pole and hold above his head (sort of like a periscope), and then take the photograph by using a long cable release to activate the shutter. Used in this fashion, the photographer's life would be not only easier but also rather longer.

**1929:** In February, a Paramount cinematographer, Joseph B. Walker (1892–1985), applies for a patent for his "Traveling Telephoto" lens, an early form of zoom lens that stays in focus when moved from wide angle to telephoto.

In the 1950s, Walker will adapt an electric motor to his zoom lens and rename it the Electra-Zoom. Marketed by RCA, this new version allows the operator to zoom in or out smoothly and becomes very popular in the early days of postwar television.

**1929:** A German photographer, Alfred Eisenstaedt (1898–1995), joins the Associated Press office in Germany, and within a year is described as a *photographer extraordinaire*. Four years later, he photographs the famous first meeting between Adolf Hitler and Benito Mussolini, in Italy. In 1935, he shoots some 3,500 images of Italy's invasion of Ethiopia, before fleeing Nazi Germany and emigrating to the United States (see **1936**).

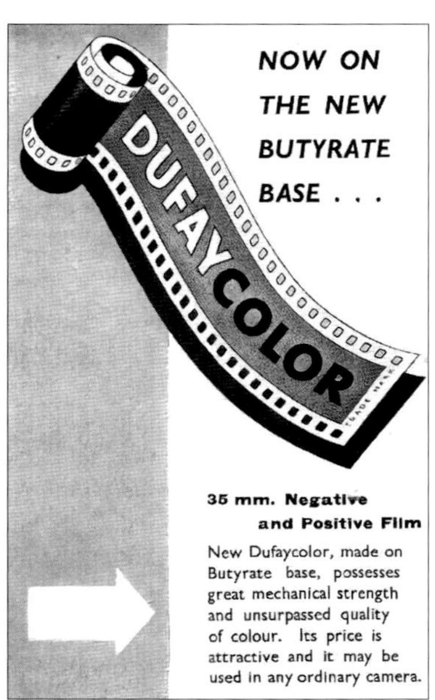


**1930:** Dufaycolor is based on Autochrome but replaces the starch particles with a screen of lines ruled at 20 lines per millimetre. Experience has shown that the screen (or *reseau*) becomes invisible at some 60 feet from a 25-foot-wide screen. Dufaycolor is one of the most successful early colour films, with an ASA (later: ISO) speed of 16; it remains available as both still and movie camera stock until the early 1940s. Although many additive processes are developed for still photography (Autochrome, Agfacolor, Omnicolor, and Paget and Finby, for example) and motion-picture photography (Multicolor, Sennett Color, Harriscolor, Fox Color, Vitacolor, and others), Dufaycolor is the only truly successful colour motion picture film of the era.

**1930:** The Vacublitz, the first commercially available photo-flash bulb, is patented by a German, Johannes Ostermeier. It is rapidly followed by the Sashalite from the General Electric Company in the USA. (Some say the GE bulb was marketed first.) Both use aluminum foil in a low-pressure oxygen atmosphere, as the aluminum is safer than magnesium and the low pressure keeps the bulbs from exploding.

**1930:** The Leica I Schraubgewinde (screw thread) is produced, with an interchangeable lens system based on a 39mm-diameter screw thread, often referred to as the Leica Thread Mount (or LTM for short). In addition to the 50mm normal lens, a 35mm wide-angle and a 135mm telephoto lens are also available. Unfortunately, the distance from the lens mount to

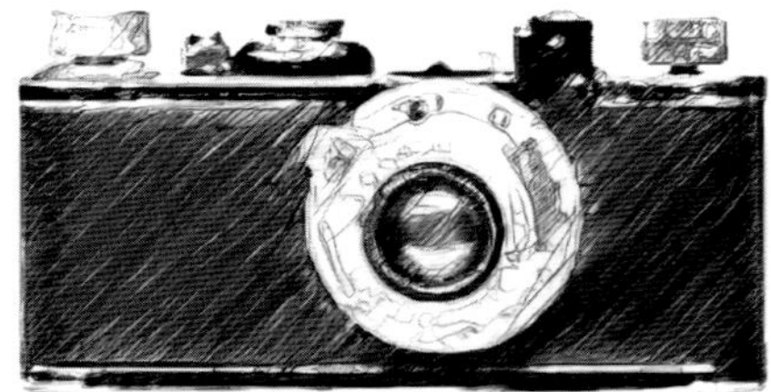

the film plane is not yet standardized, so each lens is fitted to a specific camera and the last few digits of the camera's serial number are marked on the inside of the lens barrels.

The distance from the lens flange to film plane (often called the "registration") will be standardized at 28.8mm the next year. This means that for the first time, lenses are truly interchangeable. The two types of Leica I cameras are differentiated by a small "0" engraved on the lens and body mounts of the standardized cameras and lenses.

---

**TRIVIA**

Competitors find the Leica lens mount difficult to copy, as it is a mixture of both metric (a 39mm diameter thread) and Imperial (with 26 turns, or threads, per inch). This comes about because Leitz is at the time a major maker of microscopes, and the English Whitworth threads are then the norm in microscope manufacture. Thus, the tooling at the plant is already set up to produce Whitworth threads.

The mount is developed by Oskar Barnack to provide a system that allows for the exchange of lenses on their Leica cameras. However, the early lenses must be matched to a specific camera and usually have the last three digits of the body's serial number scratched inside their lens barrels. The need for a standardized version of the mount is spurred on by Zeiss Ikon, who had indicated that their forthcoming Contax rangefinder cameras would have interchangeable lenses. The flange-to-focal-plane distance is set at 28.8mm and this standardized LTM system is first used in 1931, on a small batch of lenses manufactured by Hugo Meyer in Germany and test marketed with a run of standardized Leitz cameras by their London distributor, A. O. Roth. The program is a success, and regular production with standardized Leica camera bodies and lenses is introduced with the Leica II, starting in 1932, with serial numbers engraved on the lenses, at either the 10 or 7 o'clock position.

The high cost of quality lenses leads to the use of camera lenses on enlargers, hence the fact that nearly all film enlargers, to this day, accept LTM lenses.

---

**1930:** Nippon Kogaku manufacture a small number of Tessar style lenses under the "Anytar" name (see **1917**). The first Anytar, a 12cm *f* 4.5 lens, is completed in 1929, while improvements in design and manufacture continue through 1931. In all, seven designs are developed, in 7.5, 10.5, 10.7, 12, 15, 18 and 36cm focal lengths, but only the 12cm Anytar lens reaches pre-production level. The company buys 20 of Konishi Honten's "Lilly II" folding plate cameras (see **1916**) and equips them with the Anytar lenses and dial-set Compur shutters, for experimental purpose. None are sold to the public and the remaining Anytar lenses are sold to company employees for ¥20 in 1937. Only three are known to still exist.

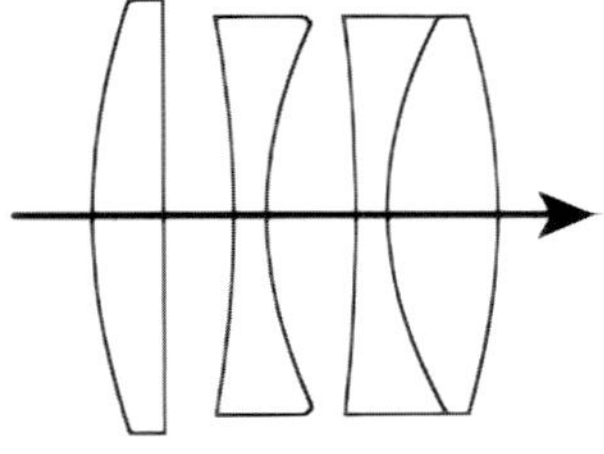

**105mm f4.5 ANYTAR lens.**

**TRIVIA**

In July of 1931, Nippon Kogaku applies for the "Nikkor" brand name, combining "Nikko," the common abbreviation for Nippon Kogaku at the time, with the letter "R," often used as a suffix for photographic lens names. This name is registered as a trademark in 1932. The first two Nikkor branded lenses are 50cm *f* 4.8 and 70cm *f* 5 Aero-Nikkors, in 1933. In 1934, Nippon Kogaku will supply Nikkor lenses for the new Canon cameras.

**1931:** Strobe (electronic flash) photography is developed by Harold ("Doc") Edgerton (1903–1990) at MIT. An electronic flash contains a tube filled with xenon gas. When a high voltage current is discharged through the tube, a bright but very short flash of light is generated. However, it takes a good amount of improvement and decreased costs before electronic flashes finally become popular in the second half of the 20th century.

**1931:** Nichidoku make the "Lidex," the first all-Japanese between-the-lens shutters. The Lidex is a two-blade shutter #0 shutter with speeds of T, B, and 1 through 1/200 second.

**1931:** Konishiroku Photo (later Konica) produce the first Japanese photographic lens (albeit with German-made glass), the Hexar 105mm *f* 4.5 in a four-element "Tessar" configuration.

**TRIVIA**

The race is close, as Nippon Kogaku soon completes a 120mm Anytar lens for the 6.5 x 9cm format, though it is never commercially produced. Later still, Asahi Optical produce a three-element triplet, the Coronar 105mm *f* 4.5, which is sold by Molta Goshi Kaisha (later Minolta) with their "Eaton" and "Happy" hand cameras.

**1931:** The Shostka Chemical Plant, located in Shostka, Sumy Oblast, Ukraine, starts producing film under the "Svema" brand and becomes a major photographic film manufacturer in the USSR. Later, colour film is made with equipment dismantled from the Agfa-Wolfen factory at the end of the Second World War. However, Svema loses market share to imported products after the dismantling of the Soviet Union in 1991, and the factory closes in 2000.

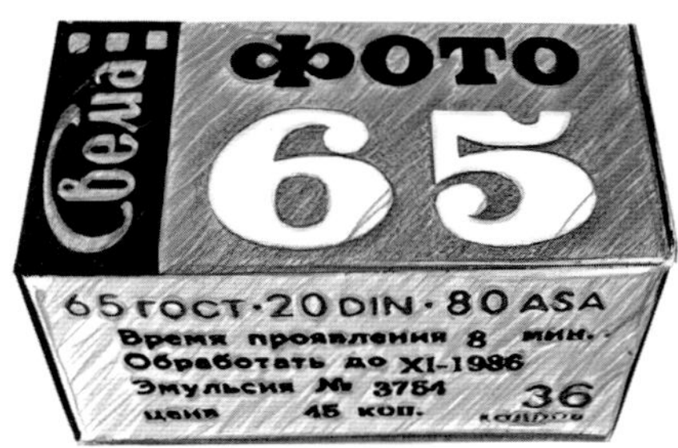


**1932:** The Leica II is introduced, with a built-in rangefinder. It is viewed in a window separate from the viewfinder and coupled automatically to lenses from 35mm to 135mm focal lengths. More importantly, it is the first Leica with standardized interchangeable lenses.

**1932:** The Weston Universal 617 is the first dedicated photographic exposure meter with a selenium photovoltaic cell and a galvanometer to measure the current. The Type 1 has two big selenium cells and a meter in the middle; it is about the width of a set of binoculars and nearly as heavy. Almost immediately it is replaced by the 617 Type 2, which is a little less than half the size and has one cell. But even though it's still heavy, it's easily held in one hand (sideways, as shown) and is a hit. Weston continues to set the gold standard in exposure meters, particularly in the U.S., for the next 30 years.

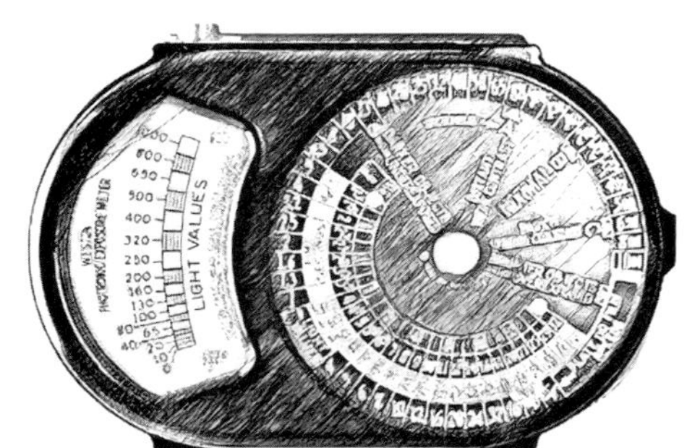

---

**TRIVIA**

A couple of years later, Weston will further slim down the Universal 617 to become the 650 Senior, which shows just how fast the state of the art was moving at the time.

---

**1932:** On 14 March, after two years of very poor health and in great pain (caused by a spinal condition), George Eastman takes his own life, at his Rochester home. He leaves a note which reads, *My work is done. Why wait? GE.* He is 78 years old and is buried on the grounds of the company he founded, at Kodak Park, in Rochester.

**1932:** Zeiss Ikon launch their new Contax rangefinder camera, to compete with Leica. Sadly, it has an unreliable shutter. It goes through six major upgrades to improve features and reliability in just four years, and many early units are recalled by the factory. It will be made until the Contax II is introduced in 1936.

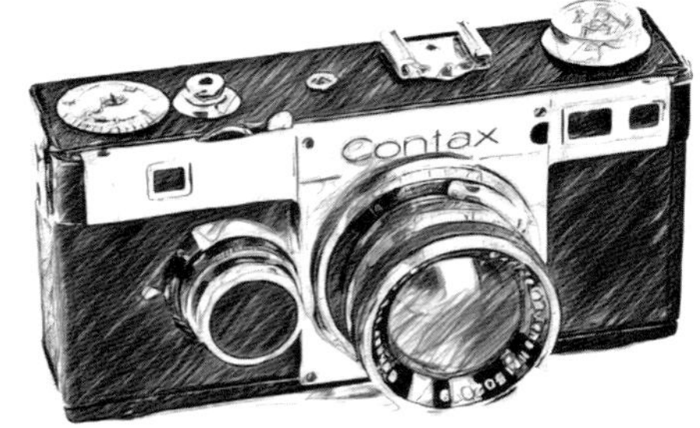

**1932:** On 26 October, the first three Soviet copies of the Leica 'A' are completed at the F. E. Dzerzhinsky Labour Commune in Kharkov, then the capital of the Ukraine. The commune devotes 1933 to the planning of production—with over 300 parts, fine tolerances, and exacting optics, it is a daunting task for the relatively unskilled "inmates" of the commune. Thus, the first 10 production cameras are not built until January of 1934, although the target is 30,000 cameras per year. (They manage only 4,000 in their first year, and do not reach 30,000 units annually until 1939.) They are given the FED brand-name, after the commune. The Soviet government newspaper *Izvestiya* reports the quality of these new

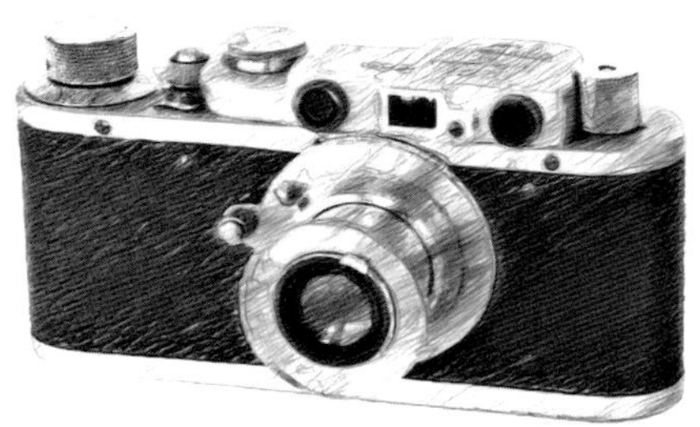

"commune-produced Leicas" and their lenses "are of higher quality in comparison with similar foreign-made lenses." History will not be so kind.

**TRIVIA**

The FED Commune was a colony for "the rehabilitation of youth," run by the Soviet Secret Police (OGPU) of the time and named for Felix Edmundovich Dzerzhinsky (1877–1926), founder of the secret police. Of the 340 members, about 50 were girls and virtually all were under 20 years of age.

Before the commune produced cameras, they built furniture and then electric drills. In late 1932, they started building copies of the German Leica cameras, lenses, and accessories, continuing until the factory was destroyed by the Nazis.

**1932:** Agfa introduce Agfacolor, a film-based version of their Agfa-Farbenplatte color plate, a "screened plate" similar to the French Autochrome (see **1903**).

**1932:** Tokyo Kogaku Kikai K.K. (Topcon) are established in September to manufacture surveying instruments, binoculars, cameras, and other optical instruments for the Japanese Army.

The company's first camera is the Lord, released in 1937, which was not a big success, but is followed by the Minion 4 x 5cm folders in 1938. The company starts making 35mm cameras in 1948 with the Minion 35 and 6 x 6 TLR cameras in 1950, sold as the Topcoflex, Primoflex, and Laurelflex. The Topcon brand name will appear in 1953 on the Topcon 35, successor of the Minion 35 series, and the Topcor lens name appears in 1954, soon replacing all the previous lens names. The company will finally hit success with its Topcon 35mm SLRs (see **1957**).

**1932:** Eight millimetre film is introduced by the Eastman Kodak company during the Great Depression to create a home movie format that is less expensive than 16mm. The film spools contain a 16mm film with twice as many perforations along each edge as normal. On its first pass through the camera, the film is exposed along only half of its width. When the first pass is complete, the operator opens the camera and flips and swaps the spools (the design of the spool hole ensures that the operator does this properly) and the same film is subsequently exposed along its other edge (i.e., the edge left unexposed on the first pass). After the film is developed, the processor splits it down the middle, resulting in two lengths of 8mm film, each with a single row of perforations along one edge. Each frame is half the width and half the height of a 16mm frame, so there are four times the number of frames in a given film area, which is why it costs less. The film will become known as "Regular 8mm" with the introduction of Super-8 film (see **1965**).

Common-length film spools allow filming times ranging from about three minutes to 4.5 minutes at 12, 15, 16, and 18 frames per second, though the normal speed is 16 frames per second.

---

**TRIVIA**

Kodak will quit selling standard 8mm film under its own brand in the early 1990s, but continues to manufacture the film, which is sold through independent film stores.

---

**1932:** Kinoptik starts lens production in Paris. In 1944 they will concentrate their efforts on cinema lenses and viewfinders for 35mm cine cameras and are known in the film industry for their robust build and the high quality of their optics. Kinoptik S.A. will close their doors in 2003.

**1932:** Technicolor introduce their System 4. It is similar to the earlier System 3 but uses three synchronized spools of black-and-white film without coloured filters. The blue-sensitive and red-sensitive films are run through one gate with their emulsion surfaces in contact, while the red-sensitive film is run at 90° to the other two. A beam splitter directs some of the light to each film gate. The blue-sensitive film is coated with an orange dye to prevent any red light from contaminating the image. These images are then optically printed (a process known as "optically flipping the red record") onto matrix films, which are dyed and printed on a special base, as in System 3. It is the first practical colour process that does away with the fringing and other artifacts of earlier systems.

System 4 is first used by the Disney Studio for their animated *Silly Symphony* film, "Flowers and Trees." The film is a hit with critics and the public alike. Walt Disney (1901–1966) sees potential in full-colour Technicolor and agrees to use it for filming all *Silly Symphony* cartoons in return for the exclusive use of the process for animated films until 1935.

**1932:** Ludwig Bertele continues development of his Ernostar design at Zeiss Ikon, but under the more famous Sonnar name. He reaches $f$ 1.5 in 1932 with the 50mm Zeiss Sonnar.



The Sonnar is always at least slightly telephoto because of its powerful front elements. The Zeiss Olympia Sonnar 180mm $f$ 2.8 (produced for the 1936 Berlin Olympics) is a classic, if not mythic, example and remains in production to this day.

**1932:** Already famous for their Cooke Triplet (see **1893**), this year sees Taylor-Hobson introduce their first zoom lens for cine applications. By 1939, Taylor-Hobson claim to have produced over 80% of lenses for film studios across the world. Like much of the British photographic industry, the company becomes part of the Rank organization at some time in the 1940s. The company exists today, making lenses and lens measurement equipment, and medical replacement joints, among other precision items.

---

**TRIVIA**

William Taylor (1865–1937), one of the founders of Taylor-Hobson, was also responsible, in 1905, for testing golf balls in an early wind tunnel and developing today's dimpled golf ball design.

---

**1932:** Henri Cartier-Bresson (1908–2004), a French photographer who will become known as "the Father of Photojournalism," has his passion for photography affirmed when he acquires a 35mm Leica. Cartier-Bresson has his first exhibition at New York's Julien Levy Gallery. His use of the 35mm camera makes the format the standard and does much to cement the brand's reputation. And it was Cartier-Bresson who coined the now-universal term for the peak of any action: *The Decisive Moment*.

---

**TRIVIA**

Despite all the fame and glory, there are very few photographs of the man. Cartier-Bresson hated being photographed, almost as much as he was embarrassed by his fame.

---

**1932:** Konishiroku add a Hexar 75mm *f* 6.3 lens to a Japanese-made Pegasus shutter and put it into a 1929 Pearlette, creating the first entirely Japanese-made camera.

**1932:** After a failed tie-up with the Pathé Brothers (see **1923**), Italian film-maker FILM-Ferrania acquires Milan-based Cappelli, and its products are briefly marketed and sold as FILM Cappelli-Ferrania. In 1936, camera production begins in Cappelli's Milan factory, which continues for many years. However, Ferrania's connection with Cappelli is dissolved in 1938.

**1932:** Edwin H. Land is researching the polarization of light when he realizes that instead of attempting to grow a large single crystal of a polarizing substance, he can manufacture a film with millions of micron-sized polarizing crystals that are coaxed into perfect alignment with each other. With his physics instructor, he establishes Land-Wheelwright Laboratories to commercialize his polarizing technology. Five years later, they will change the name to the Polaroid Corporation, where he continues to develop and produce his sheet polarizing films, which quickly find applications in scientific work and in the manufacture of sunglasses.

---

**TRIVIA**

Edwin Land is a driven, somewhat eccentric, but brilliant inventor. Once Land could see the solution to a problem in his head, he would lose all motivation to write it down or prove his vision to others.

Land was notorious for his marathon research sessions. When he conceived an idea, he would experiment and brainstorm until the problem was solved, taking virtually no breaks. He needed to have food brought to him and be reminded to eat. It is reported that he once wore the same clothes for 18 consecutive days while solving problems with the commercial production of polarizing film. As the Polaroid company grew, Land had teams of assistants working in shifts. As one team wore out, the next team was brought in to continue the work.

Land often made technical and management decisions based on what he felt was right as both a scientist and a humanist, much to the chagrin of Wall Street and his investors. From the beginning, he hired women and trained them to be research scientists. Following the assassination of Martin Luther King, Jr. in 1968, he led Polaroid to the forefront of the affirmative action movement.

After developing his polarizing film, Land returned to Harvard University, but did not complete his degree. In 1957, Harvard University finally awarded him an honorary doctorate.

---

**1932:** Edward Weston (1886–1958), his son Brett (1911–1993), Ansel Adams (1902–1984), Imogen Cunningham (1883–1976), and other San Francisco-area photographers form a group of like-minded realists called Group $f$64, for the aperture setting giving the sharpest focus with the large-format cameras the members were using at the time. Along with Ansel Adams, Weston will pioneer a modernist style using large-format cameras to create sharply focused and richly detailed black-and-white photographs. The two will be among the 20th century's most influential art photographers.

---

**TRIVIA**

Weston left Chicago in the spring of 1906 and moved to Tropico, California (now a neighbourhood in Glendale). There, he decided to pursue a career in photography, but soon realized he needed more professional training. A year later, he enrolled in the Illinois College of Photography. Weston finished their nine-month course in six months, but school refused to give him a diploma unless he paid for the full nine months. Weston refused and returned to California.

---

**1933:** Jacques Bolsky, designer of the Bolex movie cameras, convinces Pignons SA to expand into manufacturing still cameras. Through to the 1940s, prototypes and experimental cameras are developed, under a variety of brands, including Bolca, Teleflex, and Viteflex.

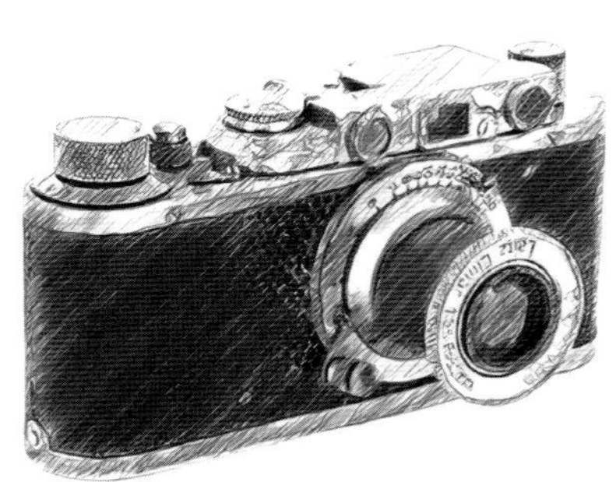

## AUCTION MADNESS

In 1932, Leica manufactured a "special edition" of their Leica II. Called the Luxus II, it was a standard Leica II under the hood, but had a gold-plated body and a lizard-skin covering. It was usually paired with a gold plated 50mm *f* 3.5 Leitz Elmar lens and delivered in a crocodile-skin camera case. Just four were made and only one is known to survive. It first went to auction in 2013, after the death of the original owner and sold for a mere $620,000 . . . well below expectations!

**1933:** A Hungarian, Béla Gaspar (1898–1973), introduces his Gasparcolor, a dye-destruction colour movie film which uses the process first described by Christiansen in 1918. It is not particularly successful in the marketplace.

**1933:** Fujimoto is a Japanese company that produces photographic equipment. Started in 1913, the Fujimoto Mfg. Co. begins the production of cameras in 1934 and the production of enlargers in 1935. After the Pacific War (as the Second World War is known in Japan) the firm is revived as Fujimoto Camera Mfg. Co., but it soon drops camera production to concentrate on enlargers and slide projectors. It becomes Fujimoto Photo Industries Co. Ltd. in 1966 and in 2008 becomes part of Kenko.

**1933:** Founded in 1919 as a maker of ammeters and similar devices, Gossen (now a renowned maker of exposure meters in Nuremberg, Germany) builds its first photographic meter, the Photolux.

## ODDITIES

The Eder camera is the only well-known camera manufactured by the Eder Prazisionskamera GmbH of Munich, Germany. It had a very unusual design with twin side-by-side bellows, making it the first, and perhaps only, horizontal twin-lens camera.

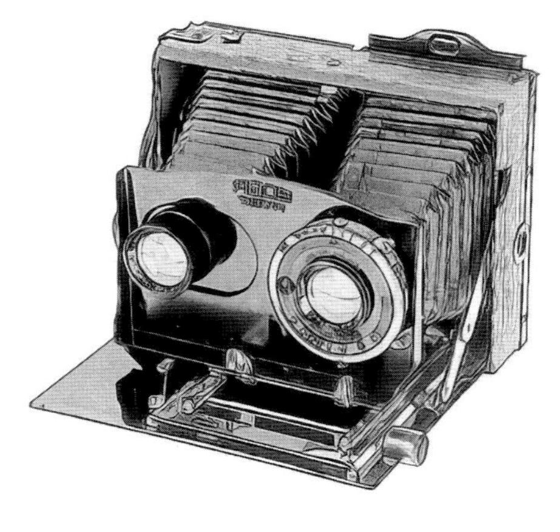

It was made in 4.5 x 6cm, 6 x 6cm, and 6 x 9cm sizes, and in roll film and plate versions. It was delivered with either a Tessar, Schneider Radionar, or Xenar *f*4.5 lens in a Compur shutter as the taking lens and with an Edar Anastigmat or Radionar *f*4.5 as the finder.

**1933:** Tasma is started in the Russian city of Kazan as "Film Factory #8" to manufacture black-and-white film as well as x-ray and aerial products. Colour films will be added in 1950. The Tasma name is derived from the Russian phrase for "TAtar Sensitized Materials," and will be adopted in 1974.

---

**TRIVIA**

Today, the company manufactures black-and-white negative films (KN-1, KN-2, and KN-3), which are popular with photographers in Russia, as well as motion-picture films in 16, 35, and 70mm formats. At one time, the company offered an array of colour photographic products, but these were discontinued following the fall of the Iron Curtain as they could not compete with the newly available Kodak, Agfa, and Fuji colour films.

---

**1933:** Ihagee introduce the first truly compact roll-film SLR, the Exakta VP (for Vest Pocket). It takes eight exposures of 4 x 6.5cm (1⅝ x 2½ inch) on 127 "Vest Pocket" roll film and features both a folding waist-level finder and a focal-plane shutter. The 1935 version is the first camera to have built-in flash synchronization to automatically synchronize the shutter with the recently invented flashbulb.

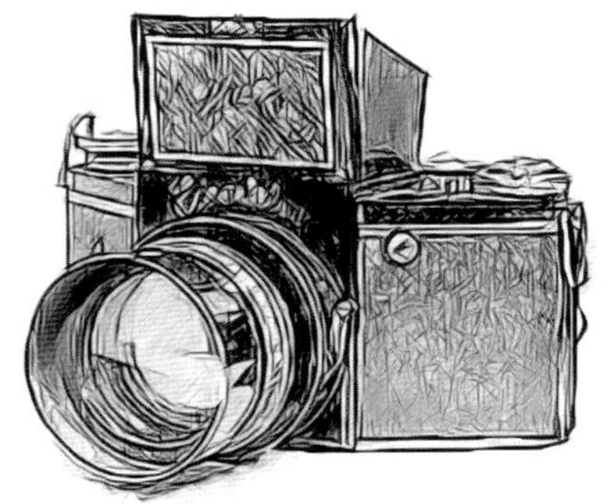

**1933:** Ansel Adams makes a pilgrimage to meet Arthur Stieglitz at Stieglitz's New York gallery, "An American Place." Although Adams is initially rebuffed, at their second meeting Stieglitz carefully views, and then views again, the prints Adams has brought, before saying, "These are some of the finest photographs I have ever seen."

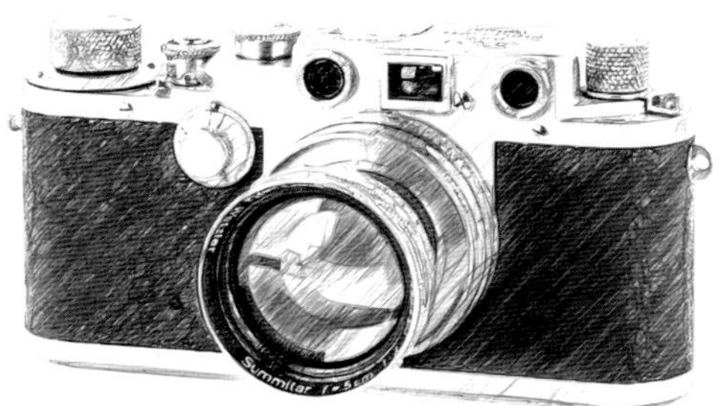

**1933:** Third time's a charm. The Leica III is introduced with a separate slow speed dial, taking shutter speeds down to one second; and in 1935, the top speed was changed from 1/500 to 1/1000 second with the launch of the Leica IIIa. This is the camera that brings Leitz true success and sets the standard for decades to come.

**1933:** Established in 1924 as a designer of optical instruments for the Japanese military, Tomioka Kogaku (Tomioka Optical) starts manufacturing lenses on an OEM basis for a variety of small Japanese camera makers. But high costs and low volumes make it difficult to compete with low-cost German imports. In 1949, they will become the exclusive lens supplier for Yashica and will eventually be bought out, becoming part of Yashica in 1968.

---

## TRIVIA

It is interesting to note that most of the Japanese lens manufacturers started by copying the Carl Zeiss "Tessar" formula as their first high-quality lens. After Yashica was taken over by Kyocera in 1983, many modern Carl Zeiss lenses were manufactured under contract in Kyocera's Tomioka plant until Kyocera left the lens-manufacturing business in 2005.

---

## ODDITIES

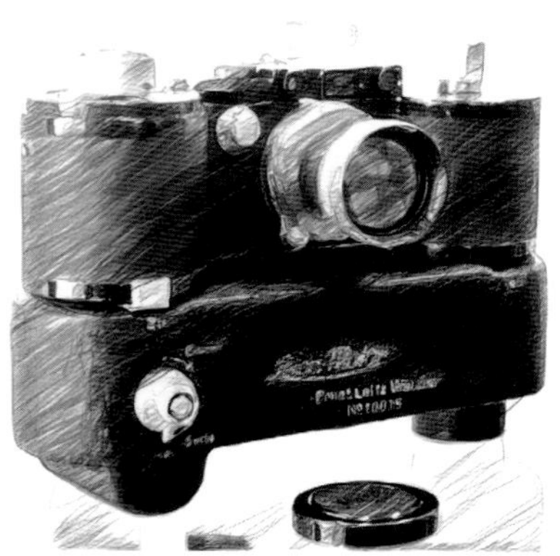

In 1933, Leitz introduced the Reporter model, based on the Leica III, with speeds to 1/500 and a later version, based on the IIIa, with speeds to 1/1000 second. The ends of the camera were modified to accept 10 metres of film, enough for 250 exposures. Under the wind knob is a counter that runs up to 250. Production officially ceased in 1942, but Reporters were built and sold as late as 1953. In total, however, just 983 Reporters were made. The majority were finished in black, but a few were produced in chrome for the American market. Some were also built to accept an electric motor drive, but there are far fewer motors available than motor-capable cameras.

In the 1950s, the East German firm VEB Kamera-Werkstätten Niedersedlitz produced a 450-exposure interchangeable back that held 17 metres of film for the then-current Praktina models that featured a spring-wound clockwork motor drive.

Leica's 250-exposure Reporter inspired Nikon to make a 250-exposure back for their F2 and F3 cameras, and even a massive 750-exposure back for their F2, in 1971.

---

**1933:** A shortage of soft leather in the wake of Japan's military expedition to Manchuria forces Minolta to introduce their "Vest" camera with a collapsing three-part Bakelite bellows. Bakelite had been used in camera bodies (see **1907**), and a few lens barrels, but until now, never for a camera's bellows.

**1934:** Kodak's Baby Brownie, designed by Walter Teague (1883–1960), will be the first all-Bakelite camera. It is a huge success and is made well into the 1950s (see **1907**).

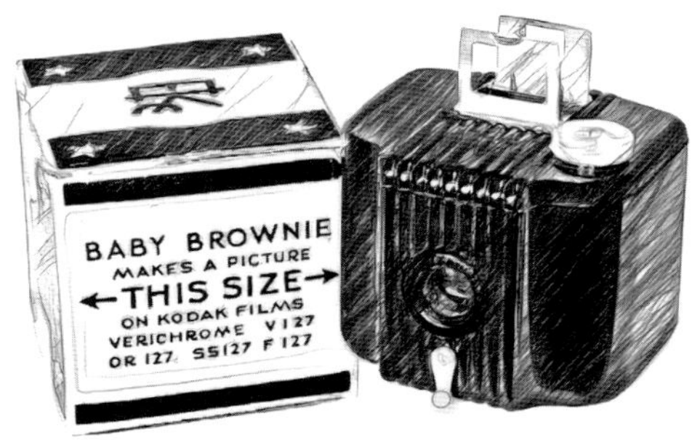


---

## TRIVIA

In Argentina, Kodak's Baby Brownie, pictured at right, is sold as the "Kodalinda."

**1934:** Kodak purchase polarizing materials from Edwin Land's Land-Wheelwright Inc. for use in photographic filters.

**1934:** In February, MGM releases *The Cat and the Fiddle*, a romantic comedy. The Depression-era movie is filmed in black-and-white to save money, but the last reel is shot using Technicolor's "Process 4" (see **1932**). It is the first time that Technicolor's System 4 is used in live action film and is so successful that it becomes the standard process used by the major Hollywood studios until the mid-1950s.

**1934:** Dr. Nagel of Kodak AG devises a 35mm film cassette that will fit both the Leica and Contax rangefinder cameras. *This is critical*—Contax and Leica cassettes are incompatible with one another, and only Kodak's introduction of a cassette that could be used in both cameras allows standardization. *Also important*, this innovation saves photographers from having to load their cassettes from bulk rolls of film, in the dark. In the USA, Kodak promotes this new film packaging as its 135 format, which soon becomes the 35mm standard that is universal today. Nagel also shrinks his earlier Vollenda camera to fit this new, smaller film, thereby creating the Kodak Retina—which of course can use the new standardized cassettes.

---

### TRIVIA

There remains one problem, which Kodak never manage to solve: the flocked-felt light traps at the film gate forever remain the most expensive part of Dr. Nagel's cassette, costing more than the metal canister, its printing, the cardboard box or even the film itself.

---

**1934:** Molta Gosi Kaisha releases its first camera bearing the "Minolta" name—a folding camera with a die-cast body and a moving lens-board on struts and clearly inspired by the by the Plaubel Makina (see **1902**).

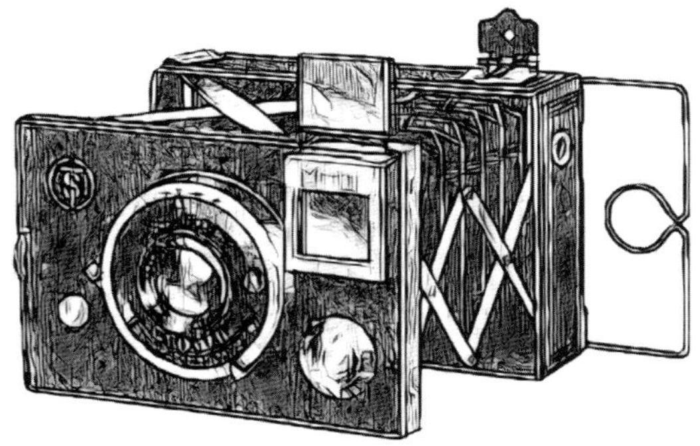

**1934:** Fuji Photo Film Company, Ltd. is established, based on a Japanese government plan to create a domestic photographic film-manufacturing industry. By February, Fuji is producing photographic film, photographic printing paper and dry plates. By 1938, Fuji is making cameras and lenses in addition to film.

**1935:** At Carl Zeiss, a Ukrainian physicist, Dr. Alexander Smakula (1900–1983), invents the first successful lens coating process, which is used on lenses for aerial photography for the German Luftwaffe. Lens elements are coated by vacuum deposition of a very thin layer (approximately 130–140 nanometres) of magnesium or calcium fluoride, which suppresses surface reflections by two-thirds.

The process is held secret by the Nazis, and application on camera lenses doesn't start until 1943, when a shipment of coated lenses is sent to Sweden; the only shipment of coated lenses until after the war.

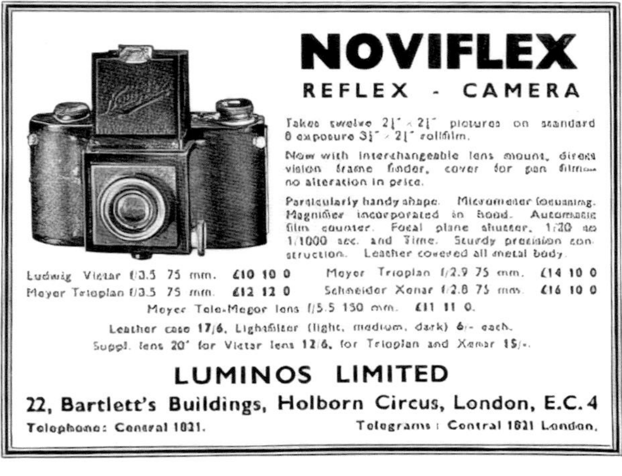



**1935:** Germany's Eichapfel "Noviflex" becomes the first 6 x 6cm medium-format roll-film SLR. It takes 12 exposures on 120 roll film, has a focal-plane shutter with speeds from 1/20 to 1/1000 second, and is fitted with either an $f$3.5 7.5cm Victar lens from Ludwig (Dresden) or a Meyer Görlitz 7.5cm $f$2.9 Trioplan. Focusing is unusual, since the lens is not in a helical mount—instead, its box-in-box construction is focused by a large, knurled wheel on the side of the mirror housing. The Noviflex has a fixed waist-level finder, the front of which is made of metal, while the other three sides are cloth on a wire frame. As is common practice in 1937, the Noviflex II will feature interchangeable lenses. The Noviflex is not a commercial success.

**1935:** The first camera with a built-in (albeit uncoupled) exposure meter is the Zeiss Ikon Contaflex, a 35mm twin-lens reflex (TLR) camera. The Contaflex has a selenium meter cell above the taking lens and requires the user to read the meter and manually transfer the shutter and lens settings to the camera.

**1935:** The Russian Gomz Sport is rumoured to be the first 35mm film SLR prototype. It is designed in 1934 and 1935, but it takes the company until late 1937 to bring it to market, thus losing the title to the 1936 Kine Exakta. The camera is ugly and lacks good lenses. It would have failed in an open marketplace, but the Soviet Union has government-controlled production, so an estimated 16,000 to 19,000 cameras are made. It is not widely available within the Soviet Union and totally unavailable outside the country, so the Sport has no influence on later SLRs. Which is probably just as well.

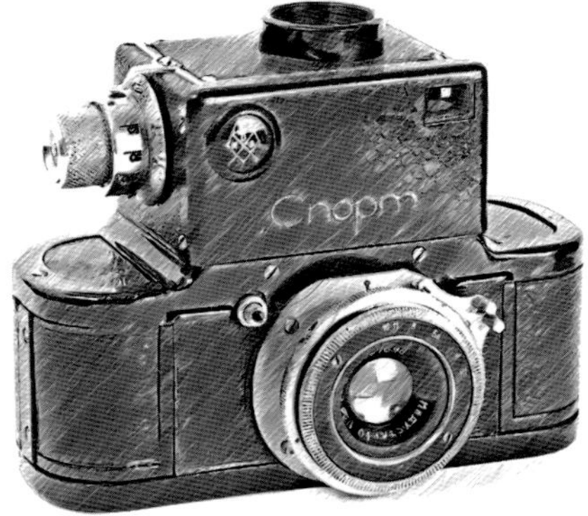

> **TRIVIA**
>
> It is interesting that no wide-angle lenses were available for the 6 × 6 SLR format before the
> 1950s. One of the first was the 65mm *f* 2.8 Flektogon from Carl Zeiss (Jena). Two prototypes
> of this lens were produced in the Meister Korelle mount in March 1952, and a further two
> prototypes, in another mount, in May 1953. But the Flektogons were not commercially pro-
> duced until September of 1956, after the 60mm *f* 5.6 Distagon by Carl Zeiss (Oberkochen), for
> Hasselblad, in early 1954.

**1935:** The Dresden camera manufacturer Franz Kochmann (1921–1952) shows his Reflex Korelle 6 x 6 at the Leipziger Messe (Trade Fair). The camera proves reliable and is gradually improved in various models over the subsequent years until just before the beginning of the Second World War. Several German lens manufacturers make lenses for it (75 to 500mm— or 7.5 to 50cm, in the nomenclature of the day), and it is a commercial success. As with the Noviflex (see **1934**), the mirror is gradually raised by pressure on a lever to the right of the throat. Pressing it to the end of its travel releases the shutter, after which the mirror returns as the lever is released. Both the Noviflex and the Reflex Korelle are considered the grandparents of the modern Pentacon Six.

> **TRIVIA**
>
> In 1938, Herr Kochmann was threatened by the Nazi regime because of his Jewish faith and
> fled Germany. The Nazis did not like to nationalize firms, a practice they considered com-
> munist, so the Kochmann Fabrik was seized and renamed Korellewerke KG in 1939. Precise
> details are unclear but the ownership of the Korellewerke was transferred to G. H. Brandtman
> & Co. and production of the high-quality Reflex Korelle continued. In mid-1940, Hitler's gov-
> ernment required the new owner to cease building cameras and instead produce materials for
> the armaments industry. The factory was destroyed in the bombing of Dresden, in February
> of 1945.
>
> Several firms built copies of Kochmann's Reflex Korelle. During the Second World War, a
> British firm, Aeronautical and General Instruments, produced cameras based on the Reflex
> Korelle for the RAF and the Royal Navy. After the war, in 1946, they produced a version for the
> general public, called the Agiflex. It proved to be cosmetically and even mechanically very
> similar to the Reflex Korelle, but both heavier and less reliable. In 1948, another copy of the
> Reflex Korelle, the Reflex Beauty, was made by the Japanese firm of Taiyōdō Kōki K.K.—the
> same firm that distributed the Beauty Six (see **1950**).

**1935:** Leopold Mannes (1899–1964) and Leopold Godowsky, Jr. (1900–1983) are professional musicians and passionate amateur photographers who have been attempting to develop a colour transparency film in Godowsky's mother's kitchen. After years of intermittent experimentation, they are introduced to George Eastman, who, surprisingly, does not recognize their potential.

But in 1929, they meet Kenneth Mees, the founder of the Kodak Research Laboratories, who offers them the use of the facilities if they will agree to come to Rochester. And he gives them three years to come up with a viable, commercial product. They accept an offer of $5,000 a year and a 2.5% royalty on Kodachrome sales.

Mannes and Godowsky (affectionately nicknamed "Man" and "God" by their colleagues) experience problems with dye migration and finally give up on the idea of confining the dye couplers to specific emulsion layers. Instead, they research the possibility of using colouring agents contained in the developing solutions. This simplifies the problem of isolating the colours to specific emulsion layers and is the first integral tri-pack film using subtractive processes and colour formers in its developer. By early in 1935, they have the viable commercial product that Kenneth Mees was looking for.

Mannes and Godowsky are the primary inventors of colour photography as we know it today. The original Kodachrome, Ektachrome, Kodacolor, and Ektacolor films are all the result of their genius.

**1935:** Always carrying his Speed Graphic camera, he works nights and sometimes arrives at a crime scene or accident before the police, which greatly helps him sell his photographs to tabloids and photographic agencies. His *nom de guerre*, Weegee, comes from a nickname his competitors give him: he was nearly always first on the scene, as if he'd gotten a tip from a "ouija board" that foretold the future. Specializing in crime and catastrophe, Weegee's best work was done between 1935 and 1946 when, if he didn't sell, he didn't eat. His work is regarded as some of the most powerful imagery of the 20th century.

---

### IN HIS OWN WORDS

The story told above about how Weegee got his nickname is the generally accepted account as found in many books and on the Internet. However, in a 1978 article in *Pop Photo*, Weegee told a different story: "I got job at Acme News Service. I learned a lot there. That's where I was first called Squeegee. I used to dry glossy prints on ferrotype tins, see, and after the darkroom guy made a batch of prints, he'd yell *'Squeegee!'* It sounded like Weegee and the name stuck to me like glue." Which story is true? A bit of each? You decide.

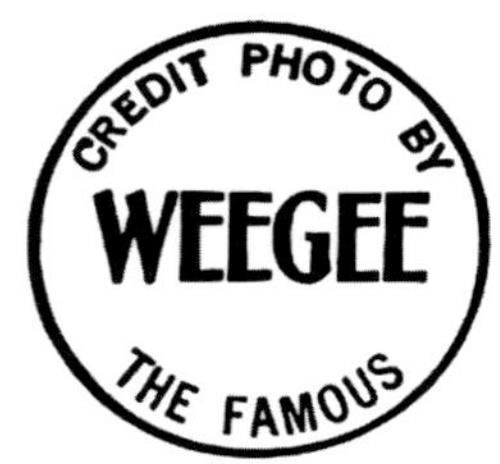


When asked about his photo technique, Weegee famously answered *"f 8 and be there"*, a phrase that has gone on to become one of the greatest clichés in the photographic world. He is said to have always carried a jug of water with him which, if he had the chance, he would splash around a body, as it looked like blood in his black and white photos. He was famous for developing his photos in the back of an old ambulance, which had been kitted-out with a darkroom as it raced through the streets, siren wailing.

**1935:** Kodachrome film is introduced, becoming the first commercially successful amateur colour film. Initially available only in 16mm for motion pictures, 35mm slide film and 8mm home movie film will follow in 1936. Popularity of the 16mm format is boosted by the switch to a single set of perforations, allowing an optical soundtrack to be added.

---

### TRIVIA

The techniques for developing Kodachrome remain so involved that even today it requires complicated machinery to develop the film. Thus, developing Kodachrome is done exclusively by Kodak until 1954, when the U.S. government sues them to allow independent processors, at least in the USA. Kodak continued to monopolize Kodachrome processing in the rest of the world until the closure of Kodak's plant in Lausanne, Switzerland, in 2006. Dwayne's Photo, in the U.S., continues Kodachrome processing until January 2011, when the last rolls are developed.

That statement about Kodachrome being difficult to develop is the common wisdom . . . and Kodak's official line. But, not quite true. It is possible to develop Kodachrome at home. In the late 1960s, your scribe and a friend interviewed a gentleman based in Nanaimo, B.C., Canada, who regularly developed his 16mm Kodachrome movies at home. The chap (who's name is, sadly, on notes now long lost) said his main problem, aside from having to build all his processing equipment out of wood, was getting the required chemicals in small quantities. Some, for which a few dozen grams would last him a lifetime, were only readily available in 45-gallon drums. Sourcing them all, in small quantities, took him almost five years.

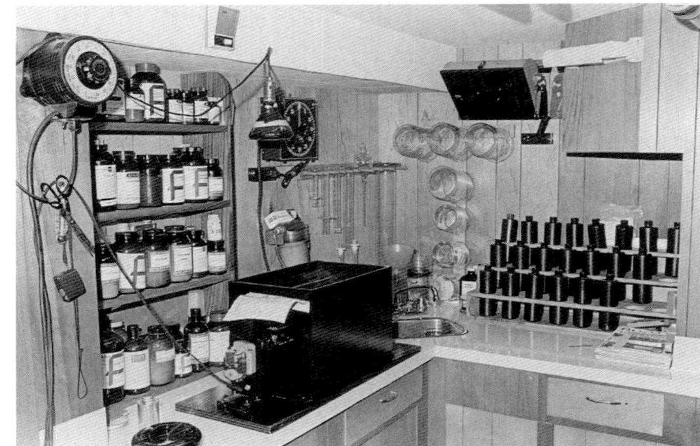

*The Nanaimo (Canada) darkroom where Kodachrome 16mm home movies were developed in the late 1960s.*

He also told your writer that because the film took a couple of hours to process, he found it very useful when friends of his wife's, of whom he was not particularly fond, would come to visit. He'd take movies of them arriving, then disappear into the basement. He'd later emerge, to show them the movies of their arrival, just before they left!

**1935:** Two women and eight men are sent out by the Farm Security Administration to document America in a time of great poverty. Among them are Walker Evans (1903–1975), Dorothea Lange (1895–1965), and Marion Post Wollcott (1910–1990), who become some of the best-known photographers of their era. Between them, they captured some of the most powerful images of the Great Depression.

**1935:** Otto Berning & Company of Schwelm, Westphalia, launch their Robot cameras. Designed by Heinz Kilfitt, they have two remarkable features: a modern type of film advance, with double-exposure lock and coupled shutter cocking; and a multi-speed, rotating, all-metal shutter from Gauthier. The cameras are equipped with fine Zeiss or Schneider lenses, but the Robot 2's special feature (found in all subsequent models) is a strong spring motor for film advance, produced by the Black Forest clockmaker Baeuerle & Söhne,

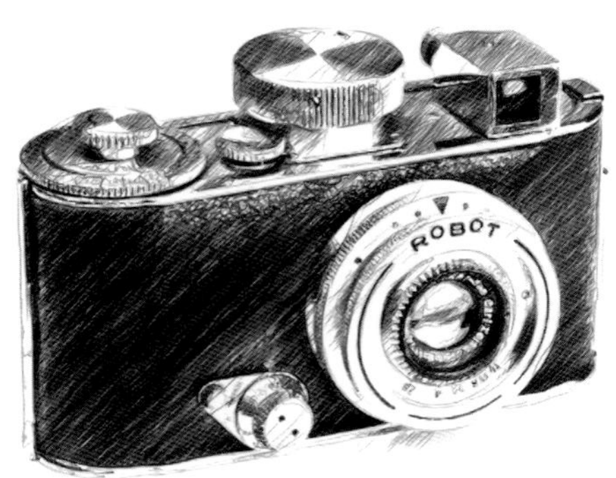

which allows a series of images to be made in just a few seconds. It is this feature and the camera's legendary sturdiness that, in the late 1960s, brings them into the market for photo-radar speed-control cameras. Production will end with a special limited edition collector's model, the "Star Classic," in 1996.

**1935:** Seiki Kogaku ("Precision Optical") designs a prototype of a 35mm rangefinder camera closely based upon the Leica II, which it calls the "Kwanon" (after the Buddhist *bodhisattva* of mercy). The next year they will adopt the Canon name (see **1936**).

**1936:** The Simmon brothers, Rudolph and Frederick, establish their business in Long Island City, New York, manufacturing Omega photographic enlargers. Their brother, Alfred, does most of the original design work for the enlargers in his spare time, while keeping his day job until the company "gets on its feet."

**TRIVIA**

At their peak, Simmon Omega enlargers became the best-selling enlargers in the world. The firm remains in business today under the Omega-Satter name, manufacturing and distributing photographic lighting and darkroom equipment, but no longer making enlargers.

**1936:** Argus evolves from the International Radio Corporation, an innovative maker of radios in inexpensive Bakelite cabinets, to a manufacturer of inexpensive Bakelite cameras. The Argus "A" is possibly the most important American-made camera of its day, for it is largely responsible for popularizing the 35mm (135) format in the United States. The camera features a collapsible

50mm *f* 4.5 lens and is the first low-cost, easy-to-use 35mm camera. Thirty thousand copies are sold in the first week, for just $12.50 each. The Argus "A" will be made in Ann Arbor, Michigan, until 1941.

**1936:** The "Hansa Canon" appears, though "Hansa" is the name of its distributor, not Seiki Kogaku, and the cameras come equipped with Nikkor lenses (see **1935**).

**TRIVIA**

In 1932, Japanese camera designer Goro Yoshida (1900–1993) dismantles a Leica for inspiration. He writes: *"I just disassembled the camera without any specific plan, but simply to look at each part. I found that there were no special items like diamonds inside the camera. The parts were made from brass, aluminum, iron and rubber. I was surprised that when these inexpensive materials were put together into a camera, it demanded an exorbitant price. This made me angry."*

In 1933, with financial backing from his brother, Yoshida starts Seiki Kogaku with the intention of building and selling his camera. The Kwanon is advertised in Asahi Camera (see **1926**), starting with the June 1934 issue, although the photos in each issue differ as they are all of wooden mock-ups since the camera is still under development. However, Yoshida is unable to circumvent Leica's rangefinder-coupling patents and he leaves the company in 1934. Development of the Kwanon is continued by Tomitaru Kaneko.

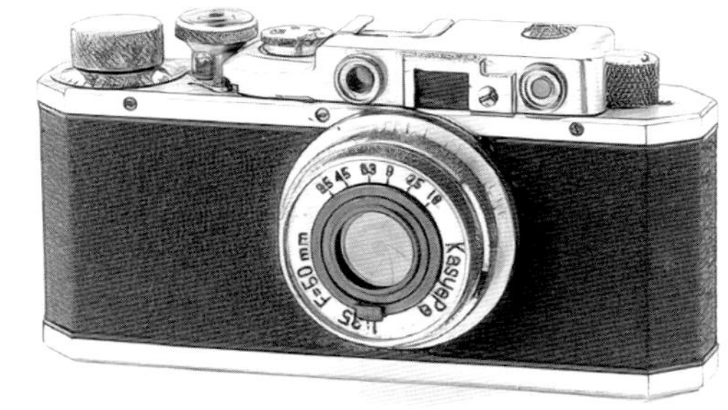

Only one actual Kwanon camera is thought to have ever been sold. The incorporation of a folding viewfinder on the top plate, the advance/rewind knob (which does not appear in the advertised cameras) and the spindle-disengagement were the penultimate modifications of the Kwanon's body design and suggest that the prototype shown above probably dates from late 1934 or early 1935. The number "2" stamped into the inner surface of the base plate raises the possibility that this is a second operable Kwanon, though only one is known to have survived.

**1936:** At Agfa, Gustav Wilmanns (1881–1965) and Wilhelm Schneider (1900–1980) research emulsions incorporating dye couplers. They finally solve the problem by formulating dye couplers where the molecules of the resulting (fat-tailed) dyes were so large that they cannot migrate within the much smaller molecules of the emulsion layers. Virtually all colour films today are based on this Agfa technology, the only exception being Mannes and Godowsky's Kodachrome.

**1936:** Oscar Barnack, designer of the Leica camera, dies.

**1936:** Zeiss introduce their Contax II, the first camera with a rangefinder and the viewfinder combined in a single window. The Contax II is a strong competitor to Leica. In some ways, it betters Leica and is often considered *the* Professional 35 system.

**1936:** Ansel Adams is offered a huge honour: a one-man show at Arthur Stieglitz's top New York gallery, An American Place. Adams will go on to produce photographs such as "Moonrise, Hernandez, New Mexico" and "Moon and Half Dome, Yosemite National Park" that will one day hang in museums around the world. Adams says his photographs are "images and not just records" of the world.

**1936:** Ihagee introduces the Kine Exakta, generally agreed to be the first 35mm single-lens reflex (SLR) camera. It is first shown at the Leipzig Spring Fair in March and is in production by April. It is called the "kine" Exakta because of the 35mm cine film it uses; it features a folding waist-level finder, a left-handed shutter release and rapid film-wind thumb lever, a 1/2 to 1/1000 second focal-plane shutter, and sports an array of high-quality interchangeable lenses. Fewer than 30,000 Kine Exaktas are made before the Second World War stops production in 1940.

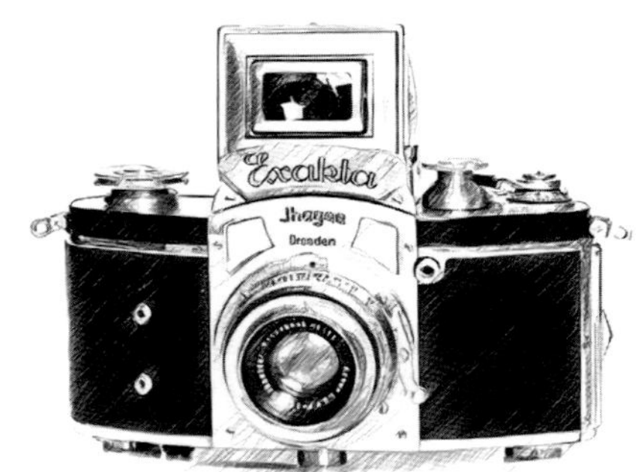

Production of improved models will restart after the war and, until the arrival of the Japanese SLRs in the mid-1950s, Exakta dominates the 35 SLR field, with a market share of more than 95 percent.

---

### TRIVIA

Collectors frequently debate if the Russian Sport (see **1935**) was the first 35mm SLR. Information provided by the Polytechnical Museum in Moscow says that a prototype Sport was made in 1934, and it was "perfected and put in production" at the end of 1937. The Kine Exakta was exhibited at the Leipzig Spring Fair in March 1936 and was in production from April 1936.

The designer of the Kine Exakta, Karl Nüchterlein (1904–1945), patents a TTL (through-the-lens) metering version in 1943. This camera is never built, as Nüchterlein is drafted into the German Army during the Second World War and is later declared "missing in action."

---

**1936:** In an effort to make cameras more convenient, Agfa introduce their "Karat" cassette. It uses standard 35mm film and takes 12 exposures, held in separate feed and take-up cassettes. The film is advanced by the sprocket holes but is held loose in the cassettes rather than being wound onto a spool.

When the film is finished, the empty feed cassette is moved over and becomes the next take-up cassette. It is not a huge success, but will be given a second chance, as the Agfa "Rapid" cassette, in 1964. The Karat cassette was also used in a few non-Agfa cameras.

**1936:** *TIME* magazine's founder, Henry Luce, buys *LIFE* magazine. *LIFE* had been started in 1893 as a humour and general interest publication; Luce does not care about the magazine but wants the title. He transforms it into America's first all-photographic news magazine, and it dominates the market for almost 40 years.

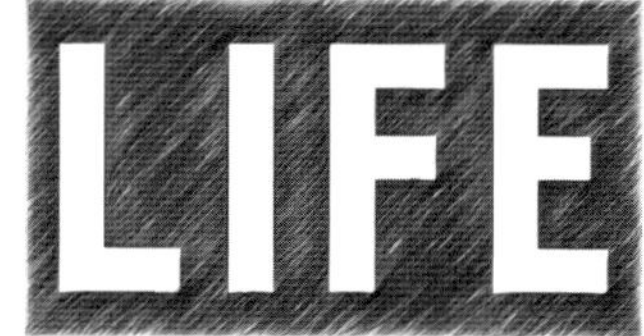

---

**TRIVIA**

*LIFE* will remain a weekly until 1972, then a monthly until 2002. The name is still used by TIME Inc. for special editions, and the quality of the photography remains high.

---

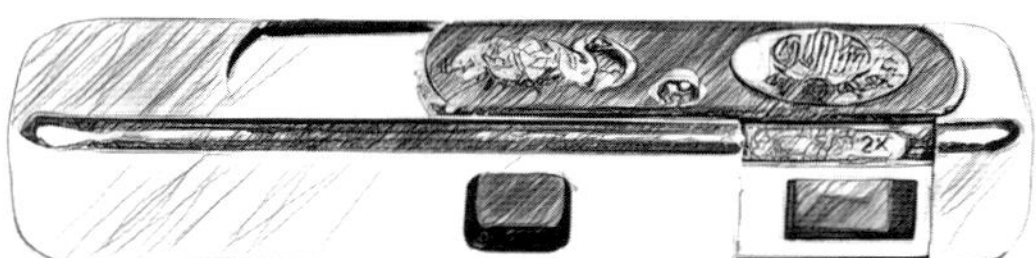

**1936:** From an idea conceived in 1922, Walter Zapp (1905–2004) produces the prototype Minox, a camera that can be hidden in a closed hand. He begins making them in 1937 in Riga, Latvia, in conjunction with VEF (Valst Elektrotechniska Fabrika), a large manufacturer firm in that country. The first camera is sold to a diplomat, who probably used it for spying, an application Zapp had never considered, but which was pivotal in establishing the Minox reputation as a precision camera for document photography and secret snapshots. A total of about 17,000 subminiature cameras of the "VEF-Minox brand" were sold before the outbreak of the Second World War. Zapp flees to Germany in 1943 when the Baltic States are occupied by the Soviet Union. After the war, Zapp, working with his friend Richard Jürgens, starts Minox GMBH in Wetzlar and the Minox goes on to become the camera of espionage legends.

---

**TRIVIA**

After the USSR invaded Latvia in July of 1940, production continued under Soviet management in 1940-41. Thus, somewhat fewer than 2,000 Minox cameras came to be "Made in USSR."

---

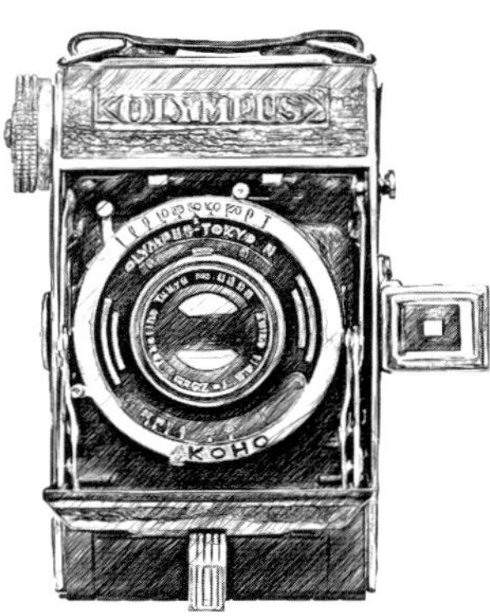

**1936:** The Semi-Olympus I is the first Olympus camera and is fitted with the newly developed Zuiko lens, which is mounted on a Semi-Proud body (supplied by Proud—an early Japanese camera maker of which little is known). It is a high-quality camera priced at 103 Japanese yen in an era when a typical starting wage was 75¥ a month.

**TRIVIA**

"Zuiko" is the brand name used by Olympus for their top-line lenses. It is taken from Japanese kanji characters and means "Light of the Gods." Fans of Olympus lenses often refer to themselves as "Zuikoholics."

**1936:** Margaret Bourke-White (1904–1971) becomes one of the first four staff photographers at the new *LIFE* magazine, and the only woman in the group. Bourke-White's photos of the building of the Peck Dam are featured in the magazine's first issue, including the cover. She will remain at *LIFE* until 1940, returning in 1941 and 1942 and again in 1945, staying this time until her retirement in 1957.

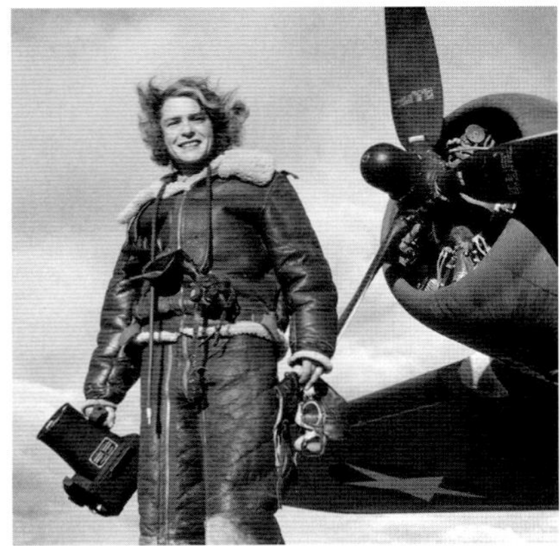

*Margaret Bourke-White*

**1936:** Although available a year earlier as 16mm motion picture film, in September, Kodak introduces Kodachrome, the first modern three-emulsion-layer colour film, in both 8mm movie and (more importantly) in their standardized 135 pre-loaded cassettes. The film is rated at ASA 10 (now called "ISO" 10—see **1974**). This spurs explosive growth in the popularity of all types of "miniature format" 35mm cameras, mostly as basic amateur models.

**TRIVIA**

The original 135 Kodachrome films gave 18 exposures and cost $3.50 with processing and postage.

**1936:** Robert Capa and Gerda Taro photograph the Spanish Civil War. In September, Capa takes what many consider his most famous photograph, "Death of a Loyalist Militiaman."

**TRIVIA**

Perhaps the best-known picture printed in *LIFE* is Alfred Eisenstaedt's photograph of a woman in a sailor's arms, snapped on 14 August 1945, as they celebrated Victory over Japan Day, in New York City. The couple did not know each other. The kiss was spontaneous between George Mendonsa (1923–2019) and Greta Zimmer (1924–2016). Widely identified at the time as a nurse, Zimmer was actually a dental assistant.

After retirement and until shortly before his death, in 1995, Eisenstaedt would walk daily from his home in Queens, to his *LIFE* office on the Avenue of the Americas at 51st Street.

**1936:** Renowned German-born photographer Alfred Eisenstaedt settles in New York after fleeing Nazi Germany. Shortly thereafter, he joins *LIFE* magazine. He leaves *LIFE* in 1972, leaving a legacy of nearly 2,500 published photo essays and having had more than 90 of his photos on the cover.

**1936:** Noted war photographer Robert Capa (born Endre Friedmann, 1913–1954) and Bernard Hoffman (1913–1979) join *LIFE* magazine, rounding out the four founding photographers.

---

### TRIVIA

Never as well known as some *LIFE* photographers, Hoffman was the first American photographer on the ground at Hiroshima and Nagasaki after the atomic bomb was dropped in 1945, providing some harrowing glimpses into the destructive power of the atom bomb.

---

**1936:** The firm of E. Leitz introduces the PLOOT, the first reflex housing for 35mm rangefinder cameras. Intended for use with a Leica IIIa, the PLOOT allows Leica rangefinder cameras to use long lenses such as the Leitz 20cm $f$4.5 Telyt or 40cm $f$5 Telyt.

---

### TRIVIA

Long focus (and telephoto) lenses have very shallow depth of field, and the short-baseline rangefinders built into Leica (and other) rangefinder cameras cannot triangulate the subject distance accurately enough for acceptably sharp focusing. Reflex housings such as the PLOOT converted rangefinder cameras into SLRs by inserting a reflex mirror and focusing screen between the lens and camera, a solution that also solved the rangefinder camera's parallax-error problem in macro-photography. The "solution" was a very awkward one, and for this reason, single-lens reflex cameras mostly supplanted rangefinder models during the 1960s. The last reflex housing for a film camera, Leica's Visoflex III, was discontinued in 1984.

---

**1936:** Pierre Angénieux (1907–1998) starts his lens-making firm in Paris. Within a year he expands, making a second workshop in his home village of Saint-Héand. Mechanical parts are manufactured in Paris and optical parts in Saint-Héand. During the Second World War he will be forced to close his Paris operations, but he makes lenses for 35mm cameras, in very limited quantities, in Saint-Héand. He takes advantage of Switzerland's neutrality, and early Alpa Reflex cameras (circa 1942) come equipped with 50mm $f$2.9 Angénieux lenses.

**1936:** Late in the year, Agfa introduce Agfacolor Neu (New Agfacolor), a modern tri-pack film reversal film with three differently colour-sensitized emulsion layers. Unlike Kodachrome, the colour-forming dye couplers are built into each layer of the reversal film. In 1939, it will be adapted into a negative film and a print film for use by the German motion picture industry.

After the Second World War, the Agfacolor brand is applied to several varieties of color negative film for still photography, in which the negatives are used to make colour prints on paper. The reversal film is then marketed as Agfachrome.

**1937:** The very first photographic spot-meter is built by Arthur Dalladay (1894–1989), who describes his construction method in the 1937 Almanac of the *British Journal of Photography* (of which he is the editor). However, it is a Do-It-Yourself project and never commercially available.

---

### ODDITIES

The 1936 Mikut (Dresden) uses beam-splitters, mirrors and red, green and blue filters to make three, 4 x 4 cm, colour separation positive images on a 15 x 5cm glass plate. The images are viewed using the Mikut Projector which uses three lamps, each with a color filter. Mirrors bring the three images together and project them onto a screen.

The camera has a Mikut "Mikutar" 130 mm lens and a Compur shutter (1-1/200, B, T).

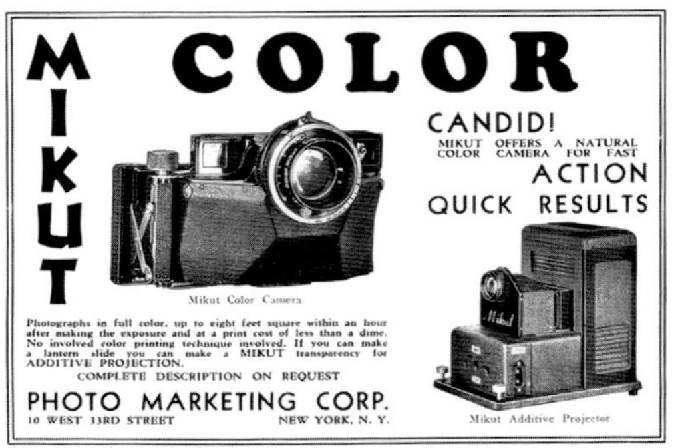


---

**1937:** War photographer (and Robert Capa's lover), Gerda Taro (1910–1937) dies while covering the Spanish Civil War, becoming the first female photojournalist to die while covering the front-line in a war, although the circumstances of her death remain in doubt. Capa continues to cover the war.

**1937:** In May, the U.S. magazine *Popular Photography* (commonly referred to as *Pop Photo*) starts as a monthly. It will grow to become America's biggest photographic monthly, enjoying an 80-year run.

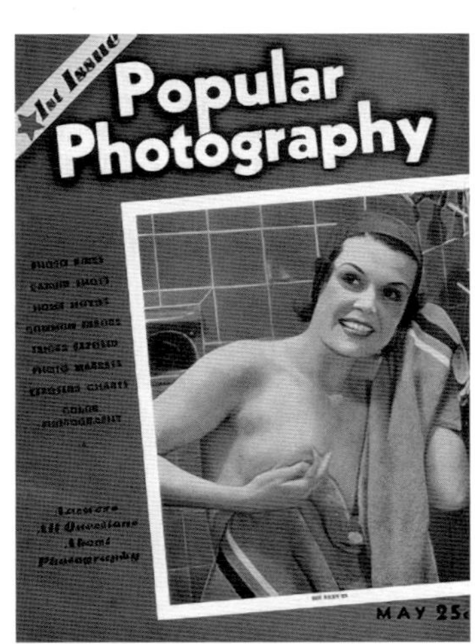


---

### TRIVIA

The colour photograph on the cover of the first issue is made with a custom-designed camera that uses colour filters to capture the image on three black and white negatives. The camera sells for $1,200 in 1937 (equivalent to just over $20,000 today).

**1937:** The influential American magazine *US Camera* starts with a Fall edition. By 1940, it goes from quarterly to bi-monthly and then to monthly issues. The magazine is the work of Thomas J. Maloney (1904–1988), an advertising executive, poet, and photographer, who will later start another popular camera magazine, *Camera 35*. At its peak, *US Camera* sells 300,000 copies per month, but finally ceases operations in 1969.

**1937:** Photos by photographer W. Eugene Smith (1918–1978) are published in two Wichita newspapers by the time he is 15 years old. In 1937, Smith joins *News-Week* (later *Newsweek*), but he is soon fired for refusing to use medium-format cameras rather than his 35mm Contax.

Smith will go on to become one of the best war photographers in the Pacific theatre, working for *LIFE* magazine and following the island-hopping American offensive against Japan. He continues at *LIFE* until 1954 and, in 1955, becomes a Magnum photographer (see **1947**). There he is commissioned to produce a photographic profile of the city of Pittsburgh. The project is initially expected to take a month and to produce 100 images; it ends up taking more than two years and producing 13,000 photographs (see **1948** and **1971**).

**1937:** Franke & Heidecke unveil their Rolleiflex Automat, which features the first automatic film loading and frame counting system for roll film, doing away with the need for a red window.

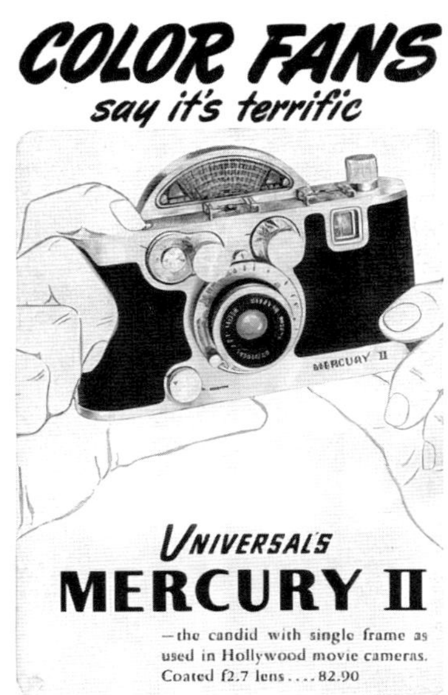



**1938:** Argus introduce their "C" model (with non-coupled rangefinder) and "C2" (with coupled rangefinder) cameras. Neither is particularly successful, but they lead the way to the "C3 model" the next year.

**1938:** The first camera with any kind of hot-shoe connector is the Univex Mercury half-frame 35mm camera. The Mercury also features a rotary shutter that runs though a huge "hump" on the top of the camera. With German-made cameras from Leitz and Zeiss selling for hundreds of dollars, the American-made Mercury, at a mere $25, is a very appealing alternative, and some 45,000 of them are sold, but Universal goes broke in the 1950s.

---

**TRIVIA**

When the Contax II claimed a shutter speed of 1/1250 second, Univex responded in 1947 with the Mercury II, with a top shutter speed of 1/1500. The model II is hard to find today, as fewer than 3,000 were manufactured.

**1938:** After 15 years of development, Chester Carlson (USA), a physicist working independently, invents "electron photography," a process for printing images using an electrically charged drum and dry powder toner.

**1938:** Kodak's Super Six-20 is the first still camera with auto-exposure. Pressing the shutter release first locks the selenium meter's needle and then moves a lever controlling the aperture up to the needle before firing the shutter. At $225, it is very expensive (roughly $3,800 in 2015 dollars). The Super Six-20 takes 620 film and between 1938 and 1944 just over 700 are made.

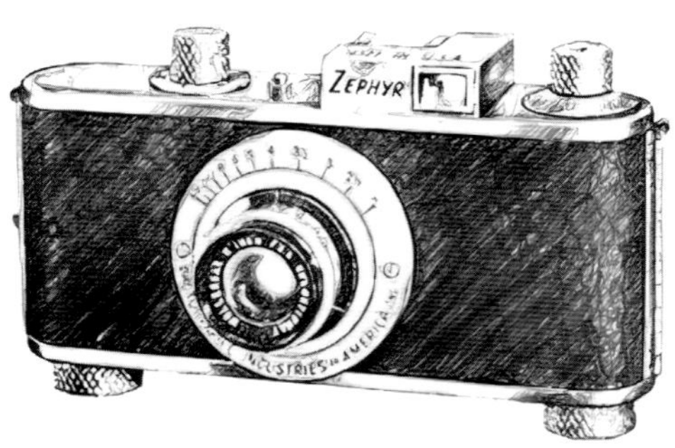

**1938:** *Minicam* magazine starts as a digest-sized (similar to *Reader's Digest* today) guide to photography. In 1949, they will go to a full-size magazine format and change the name to *Modern Photography*. Under this name they have a good 40-year run, with their last issue in July of 1989.

**1938:** The Zephyr Candid Camera is manufactured by Photographic Industries of America (New York). It's the first American-made 35mm camera to incorporate a focal-plane shutter. It accepts interchangeable lenses in a proprietary helical thread mount. Other features include an automatic film counter, built-in rangefinder attachment, an adaptable flash synchronization, and a Wollensak telescopic viewfinder. The camera can capture 36 exposures on Kodachrome or Dufaycolor 35mm film. It is priced at $22.50 with an $f$ 3.5 lens and $29.50 with an $f$ 2.9 lens (about $400 or $500 respectively today). The leather carrying case is an extra $4.95.

**1938:** Amster Spiro, city editor of the *New York Evening Journal*, buys 60 carrier pigeons and builds a pigeon coop on the newspaper's roof. He sends staff photographers and trained pigeon handlers aboard the quarantine inspector's boat to meet incoming Atlantic liners and photograph any celebrities aboard. The photographer then sends his 35mm film, with captions and notes, by means of a carrier pigeon. The photos are often in the newspaper and on the streets before the ship docks! The pigeons are also used for sports and special events. The system is adopted by newspapers across the USA and is used into the 1950s.

**HOW IT'S DONE**

The photographer shoots no more than four or five frames and then a blank frame (Contax) or two (Leica). Then, in a film changing bag, he cuts the film from the camera, clips off the leader and rolls what's left in black paper, to prevent scratching. It is put in small light-tight tubes of very thin (0.08mm) aluminum, which are then attached to the pigeon's back or leg. Copy and/or captions are written on ultra-lightweight rice paper in "cablese" and sent in a second canister on the bird's other leg. When the bird lands on the newspaper's roof, it triggers an alarm in the newsroom. The canister can be dropped, via a wire, to a box outside a window on the darkroom floor, where it is retrieved and developed. The copy can be set in type within 10 minutes of arrival and it's all in the next edition.

In 1987, President Reagan visited Florida to attend a memorial for sailors killed on the *USS Stark*. When told the base would be locked down until after Reagan flew out, a local newspaper smuggled a pigeon in to deliver the photos. Later, the scheme was widely reported as something new and ingenious. Ingenious, yes. But new? No.

**1938–1939:** To help his Jewish workers, Ernst Leitz II (a Christian), quietly establishes what becomes known among historians of the Holocaust as the *Leica Freedom Train*, a covert means of allowing Jews to leave Germany in the guise of Leitz employees being assigned overseas. Employees, retailers, family members, even friends of family members were "assigned" to Leitz sales offices in France, Britain, China, and the United States.

Most of these new "employees" arrive in New York with a brand-new Leica around their neck. They go to the E. Leitz office, where they are helped to find jobs. Each new arrival is paid a small stipend until they can find work. Out of this migration come the designers, repair technicians, salespeople, marketers, and writers for the American photographic industry. The "Leica Freedom Train" is at its height in 1938 and early 1939, delivering groups of refugees to New York every few weeks until the invasion of Poland on 1 September 1939, when Germany closes its borders.

Members of the Leitz family and firm suffer for their good works. A top executive, Alfred Turk, is jailed for working to help Jews and freed only after the payment of a large bribe. Leitz's daughter, Elsie Kuhn-Leitz (1903–1985), is imprisoned by the Gestapo after she is caught at the border helping Jewish women cross into Switzerland. She is eventually freed but endures rough treatment during questioning. She later falls under suspicion when she attempts to improve the living conditions of more than 700 Ukrainian slave labourers, all of them women, who are assigned to work in the plant during the war.

The Leitz family makes no mention of its heroic efforts, and it is only after the last member of the Leitz family has died that the story finally comes to light, in the book *The Greatest Invention of the Leitz Family: The Leica Freedom Train* by Frank Dabba Smith (b. 1955).

To this day, many large New York photo dealers are staunch supporters of the Leica company and their products. This may have to do with the fact that many of their founders and their families came to America via the Leica Freedom Train.

**1939:** Originally introduced in 1936 as a colour reversal film, Agfa modifies Agfacolor to make Agfacolor Neu, the first dye-coupler-incorporated negative movie film. It is not intended for paper prints but for movie film production, where it will be printed onto a second film stock to make colour prints for release in theatres.

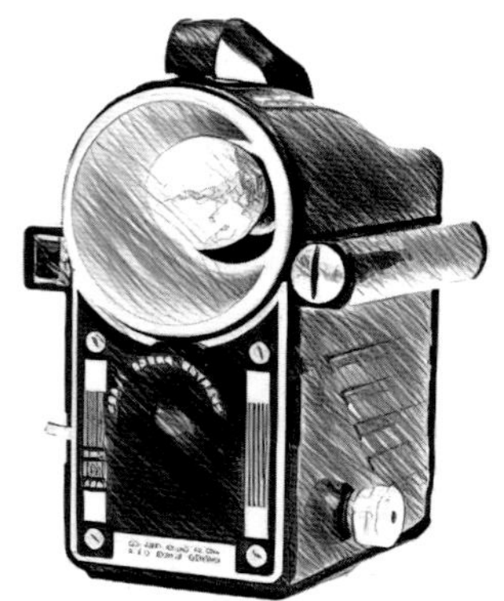

**1939:** Spartus Corp. (USA) introduces the Spartus Press Flash, the first camera to have a built-in unit for flash bulbs. The camera also appears under the names the Falcon Press Flash, Galter Press Flash, and the Regal Flash Master.

**1939:** The Kamera-Werkstätten Guthe & Thorsch (KW-G&T) Camera factory (see **1919**) introduces its Praktiflex, which features a "returnable" mirror system, which raises the mirror as the photographer presses the shutter release and returns it to the viewing position when her finger is removed from the shutter release. However, it is not a true "instant return" mirror. That will not occur until Asahi release their Asahiflex IIb (see **1954**). Still, it makes the Praktiflex more convenient than other SLRs of the day. Sadly, this feature is not found on later Praktiflex models. Production is limited by the Second World War, but they manage to make 60,000 of them between 1939 and 1945. After the war, KW-G&T is seized by the Soviets (see **1946**).

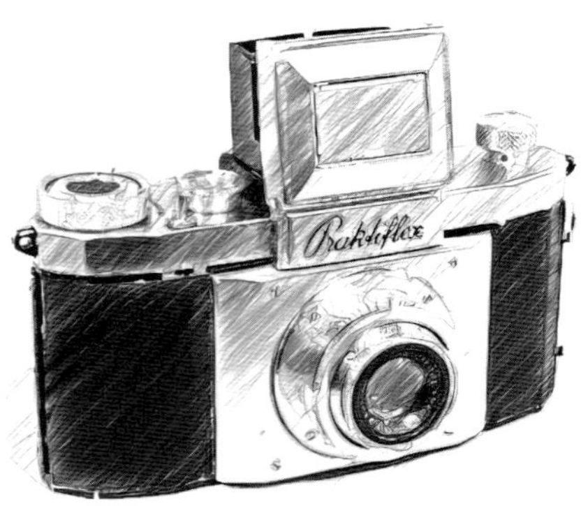

The Praktiflex is the world's third 35mm SLR (after the Kine Exakta in 1936 and the Russian GOMZ Sport in 1937). Besides being the first one with a returnable mirror, it also features a screw mount for interchangeable lenses. However, this is not the so-called "Universal" M42 thread-mount—that will not arrive until the Zeiss Contax S is introduced in 1949. But the concept proves successful. After the Second World War, VEB Zeiss Ikon (Dresden) continue the camera's development. Late in 1949, Praktica abandon their original 40mm thread mount, adopt the Zeiss M42 lens mount, and become one of the most popular 35mm SLR brands for several decades.

---

### TRIVIA

The Praktiflex FX name was used in the 1950s in the USA for a version of the Praktica FX. It was also sold under several other brand names, such as "Columbia 35" and "Rival Reflex" in other markets.

**1939:** Edwin Eugene Mayer (1896–1956) develops Sawyer's View-Master system. It is premiered at the 1939 World's Fair in New York and is an instant success, partially due to its use of Kodachrome slide film for vivid colour images. The system is comprised of special-format stereoscopes and corresponding View-Master "reels," which are thin cardboard disks containing seven stereoscopic 3D pairs of small colour photographs. Tourist attractions and travel views dominate during View-Master's early years, but after Sawyer's acquisition by GAF in 1966, children's titles will dominate. GAF also changes to cheaper E-6 slide films to replace Kodachrome. Thus, many reels of the 1970s now have faded colours, unlike the original Kodachrome reels.

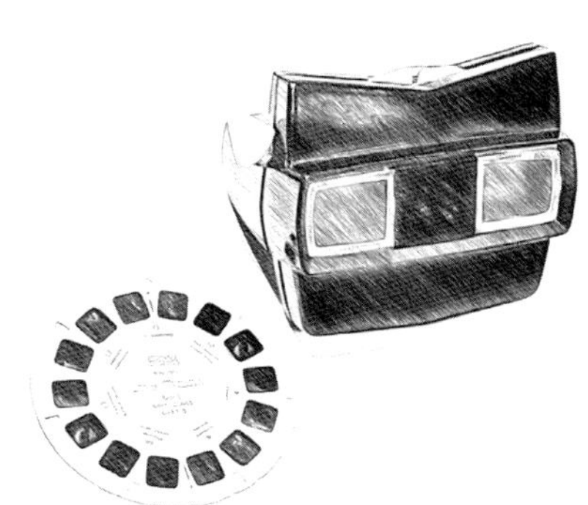

Some 25 viewer models, thousands of titles, and 1.5 billion copies of reels are made. Despite its long history and many changes in models, materials and ownership, the same basic mechanism remains, ensuring that every reel will work in every View-Master (see **2009**).

**1939:** Dutch lens maker Oude Delft starts producing optical and related fine mechanical products for the photographic, medical, and military markets. From the late 1940s through the 1960s they make an excellent series of lenses for many brands, but primarily for Alpa and Exakta, as well as lenses for large format cameras, all in limited quantities.

**1939:** As tensions rise just prior to the start of war, Agfa-Ansco is renamed GAF (General Aniline & Film Corporation), essentially to disguise its German connections.

---

### TRIVIA

In the months after the bombing of Pearl Harbor (7 December 1941), the U.S. government seizes GAF. The business, now government-run, continues to survive as a "hostile alien property," making versions of Agfa films in the USA. It remains under government control until 1965. Throughout the postwar period GAF sells re-branded cameras made by other manufacturers, including Agfa, Ricoh, Chinon, and Minolta, under either the Ansco, GAF, or GAF-Ansco brands. A Minolta-made Ansco was the first 35mm camera in space (see **1962**).

When GAF made an ill-fated purchase of Ruberoid, it acquired not only a product line containing considerable quantities of asbestos, but also ownership of Ruberoid's asbestos mine in Vermont. In 1975, GAF ceased mining activities, selling (virtually giving) the business to the mine workers, who continued operations until 1993. GAF filed for bankruptcy in 2001 and, after settling 50,000 lawsuits, was reorganized as a maker of asbestos-free shingles.

---

**1939:** Kajiro Kōgaku Kenkyūjo start selling lenses under the K.O.L name. The name changes to Gojō Kōki in 1941, but that firm ceases to exist in 1945. It is soon revived as Sun Kōki, selling lenses under the Sun name with "Sun Opt" or "Sun Optical" appearing on some lenses, with others being made for distributors like Soligor and Spiratone. Sometime in the late 1970s or early 1980s, the firm is renamed to Gotō Sun and continues to sell lenses until some time in the late 1980s, when they appear to have been absorbed by Goyō Kōgaku Shōji, also known as Goyo Optical, and the Sun name disappears, forever.

> **TRIVIA**
>
> Today, Goyo Optical is a maker of CCTV lenses, and is also the maker of the NOKTOR 50mm *f* 0.95 lens currently being offered for micro-FourThirds (mFT).

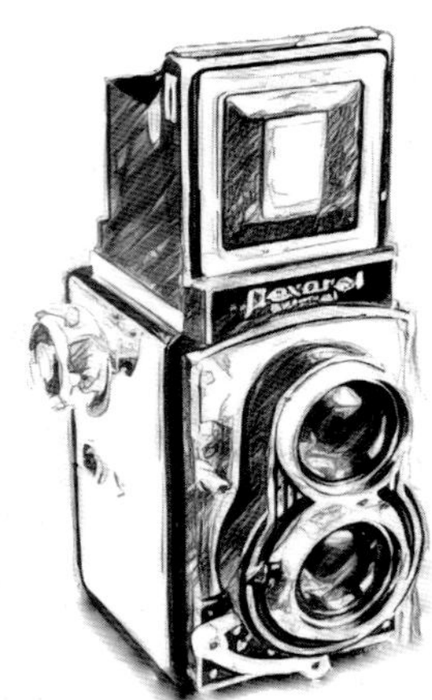

**1939:** A Czechoslovakian firm, Optikotechna, introduces its first camera, the Flexarette, a 6 x 6 TLR. It is the start of what will become a long line of TLRs little seen outside Europe. In 1946, the company is nationalized, renamed Meopta, and becomes famous world-wide for top-quality enlargers. After the fall of communism, the firm is privatized, making binoculars and OEM optical products, but, sadly, no longer makes enlargers.

**1939:** Katharine Blodgett (1898–1979), working at General Electric, experiments on glare and reflected light and discovers that glass can be made almost invisible and glare-proof by applying a thin coating of soap, just one-quarter of a wavelength of light in thickness. Most lenses lose 25% to 30% of their light due to reflections. While she is not the originator of the idea, she shows that reflections are reduced to just 2% to 4% for each lens element, paving the way for Dr. Hawley Cartwright in 1940.

**1939:** Kenneth Becker (1931–2000) starts the Calumet Manufacturing Company in Chicago. In the beginning, its main business is sporting goods, but it begins to sell cameras and eventually to manufacture darkroom equipment. In 1955, Calumet buys the rights from Kodak to the Master View 4 x 5 camera and starts to develop innovations for view cameras like the Caltar large-format lens line and the C-2 roll-film holder. By 1980, Calumet is a full-line supplier of professional photographic products, selling cameras by the Dutch manufacturer Cambo and eventually taking over the company.

> **UPDATE**
>
> Calumet goes bankrupt in 2014, but C&A Marketing Inc. of New Jersey will buy the assets and reopen the chain, only to close its U.S. stores and website in 2016. In 2017, the U.K. Calumet division was merged into Britain's Wex Photo/Video.

**1939:** The Argus C3 rangefinder camera is put on the market. It is a minor revision of C2, having added flash sync sockets to the side of the camera. However, this model strikes a chord with the American public and some two million units are built through 1966, making it one of the best-selling cameras in history. Fondly known as "the Brick," and priced at just $35, it makes 35mm rangefinder photography affordable.

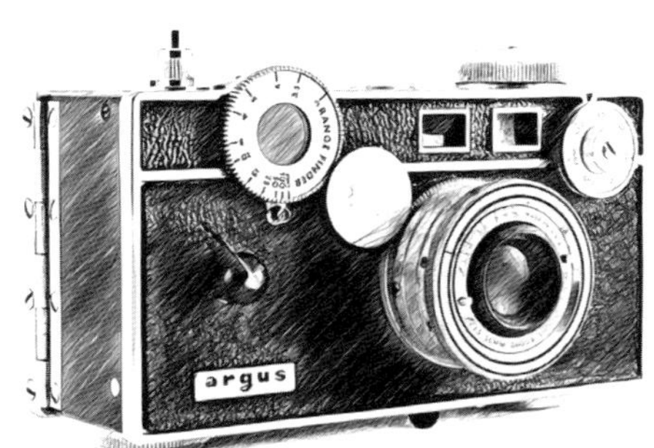

**1940:** Hawley Cartwright, a young physics professor at MIT, coats a lens, not with Blodgett's soap, but with a hard, durable coating of evaporated calcium, magnesium, or other metallic fluoride, about four one-millionths of an inch thick. Although similar to the 1935 Zeiss process, Cartwright's is a more practical method, and becomes the basis of all modern lens coatings.

**1940:** Rowland Potter, working at DuPont, invents a multi-layer enlarging paper that can yield multiple contrast grades from a negative. The gradations between soft and hard are produced by printing through blue, yellow, or other special filters. Such variable-contrast papers were produced by DuPont, Ilford, Kodak, Ansco, and Haloid. Today, only Ilford "Multigrade" remains available.

---

### ODDITIES

"Not a Toy!" At least, that's what the ad said. In 1940, the American Advertising and Research Corporation of Chicago creates the CUB, a small plastic camera with an ever-set shutter that takes bigger than 35mm negatives on 828 film. The price is 15 cents and a box from any Pepsodent product . . . postpaid!

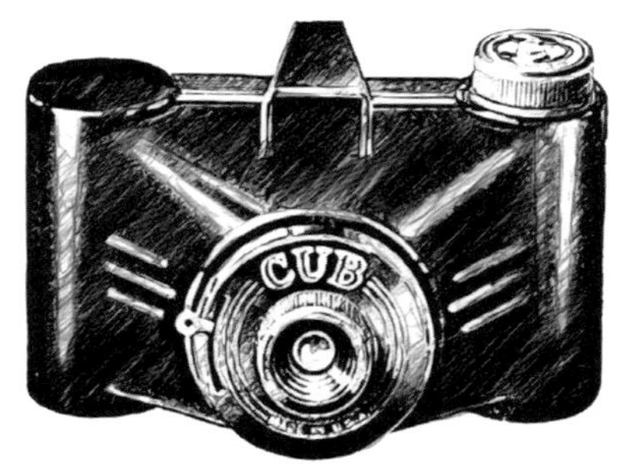

The Cub was also made with a white film-wind knob under the "Scenex" brand by Earl Products, also of Chicago. Its retail price is unknown.

---

**1940:** Jaques Bolsky leaves Europe for the USA and has success with movie and still cameras made by his Bolsey Corporation of America. The first Bolsey cameras are manufactured by Pignons SA, but soon newer designs appear, manufactured by the Obex Corporation of Long Island, NY. In 1956, Obex will take over Bolsey.

**1940:** Donald W. Norwood is a cinematographer interested in exposure meters. Incident meters with flat diffusion panels are useful for photographing flat objects or copying documents but are less effective for three-dimensional objects. He comes up with the idea that a hemispherical diffuser which covers the photocell will provide a much better reading. He is right. For this, Norwood receives U.S. Patent #2,214,283.

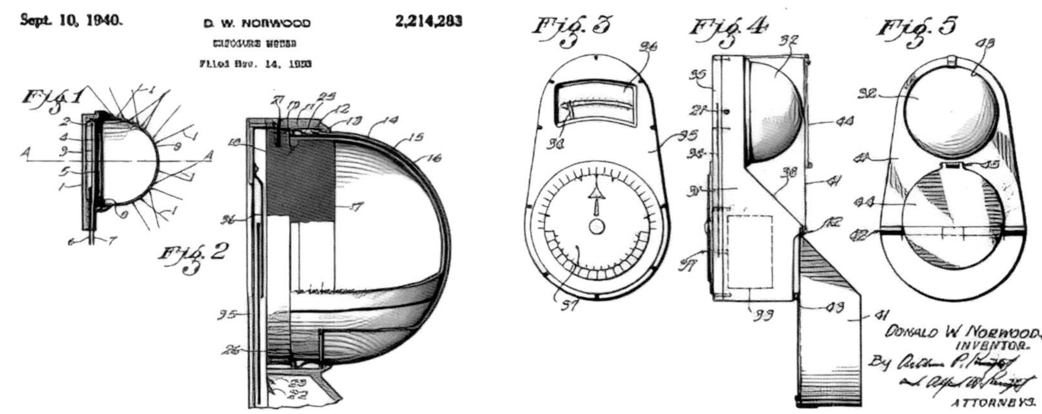

**1940:** Victor Hasselblad establishes a camera workshop, Ross AB, in a shed behind an automobile repair shop near a junkyard. Along with his brother and a mechanic from the repair shop, he designs the HK-17 aerial camera for the Swedish government. The next year they will build another camera for the Swedish Air Force, the SKa4. Between 1941 and 1945, Hasselblad will deliver 345 aerial cameras to the Swedish military. But all the while, Hasselblad views the production of military cameras as merely a first step towards the development of a civilian camera.

**1940:** The Mamiya Camera Company (Mamiya Koki Seisakusho) is started in May by camera designer Seichi Mamiya and financial backer Tsunejiro Sugawara. They soon introduce their Mamiya Six, a 6 x 6cm folder with a coupled rangefinder. It has a unique focusing mechanism that moves the film plane instead of the lens. The Six goes through several models over the next 10 years, each with fixed lenses made by various Japanese manufacturers.

**1940:** Having previously relied on lenses from other suppliers, Minolta start producing some of their own optics, and the Rokkor brand is born. By 1949, Minolta will be in a position to start making lenses for other camera companies.

**1940:** Konishiroku introduce the first made-in-Japan colour film . . . Sakura Natural Color.

**1941:** Wilmanns's and Schneider's research makes possible the production of the first full-length colour motion picture film (by UFA in Berlin) that did not require the more cumbersome and more expensive Technicolor process (see **1936**).

**1941:** Karl Freund (1890–1969), an ex-pat Czech cinematographer living in Hollywood, starts a company called Photo Research, with the goal of developing the perfect exposure meter, both for himself and to sell to colleagues. Freund becomes aware of a patent held by Donald Norwood (see **1940**). He contacts Norwood and offers to make a "real" product out of the idea.

**1941:** Hoya are founded as manufacturers of optical glass under the name Tōyō Kōgaku Garasu Seizōsho (meaning Oriental Optical Glass Manufacture). They are perhaps best known for their photographic filters, but in fact are among the leading manufacturers of optical glass for all lens makers. Today, Hoya also provide precision moulded glass elements (regular and aspherical) to various lens makers around the world. Hoya also produce glass for semiconductor blanks and hard disk substrates as well as eyeglass lenses and various medical optics.

---

### ODDITIES

The Detrola 400 had the looks of a great camera, even if it wasn't. It was an American-made, Leica-inspired design equipped with a coupled rangefinder and a Wollensak Velostigmat 50mm *f* 2.8 lens. The Detrola had excellent specifications for the era, but at a selling price of $69.50 was too expensive to compete with the Argus C3 (see **1939**) and not good enough to compete with the Leica and Contax models. 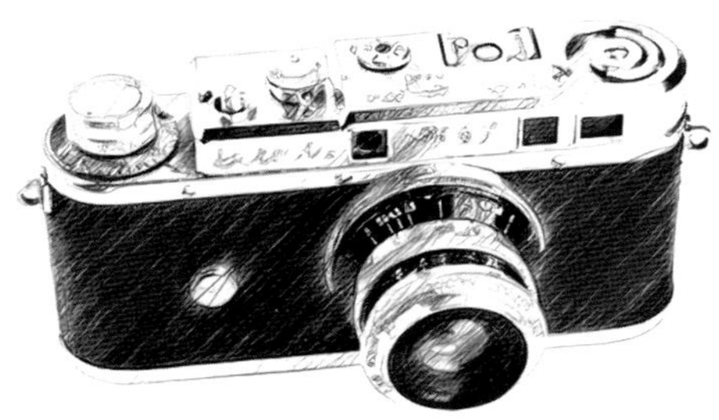

Among its chief deficiencies were inconsistent film advance and a shutter which gave uneven exposures. Its top speed of 1/500 was, well, optimistic. The body parts were stamped sheet steel, riveted together; and the 38mm threaded lens mount was not compatible with LTM lenses. Production ran from 1940 to 1941, when the factory went bankrupt. Few survive today.

---

**1941:** Margaret Bourke-White becomes the first female war correspondent. She is sent to Moscow after Germany attacks the USSR, and later is attached to U.S. forces in North Africa, Italy, and Germany.

---

### TRIVIA

Bourke-White was torpedoed in the Mediterranean, strafed by the Luftwaffe, stranded on an arctic island, bombarded in Moscow, and pulled out of the Chesapeake when her chopper crashed. *LIFE* staffers simply called her "Maggie the Indestructible."

---

**1941:** Prior to the Second World War, GAF (the previously named Agfa-Ansco—see **1939**) markets the German-made Agfacolor film in America. After the war begins, however, at the request of the War Department, Ansco engineers a colour film similar to Agfacolor, which it produces in Binghamton, New York. After the war, "Ansco Color" (and later Anscochrome) is widely distributed but meets with limited commercial success in competition with Kodak products, finally ceasing production in 1969.

**1941:** After Pearl Harbor, David Douglas Duncan (1916–2018) joins the U.S. Marine Corps, earns an officer's commission, trains as a photographer, and becomes famous for his dramatic combat photos of the Second World War (see **1946** and **1950**).

**1941:** The Ektra is Kodak's (and America's) first and only attempt to outshine the contemporary Leica and Contax cameras in terms of features. Production is soon interrupted when America enters the Second World War in December of 1941. Still, the Ektra's firsts and features are way ahead of their time. It has removable magazine backs, a lever film-advance, and a very long-base rangefinder. There are six lenses: 35mm *f* 3.3, 50mm *f* 3.5, 50mm *f* 1.9, 90mm *f* 3.5, 135mm

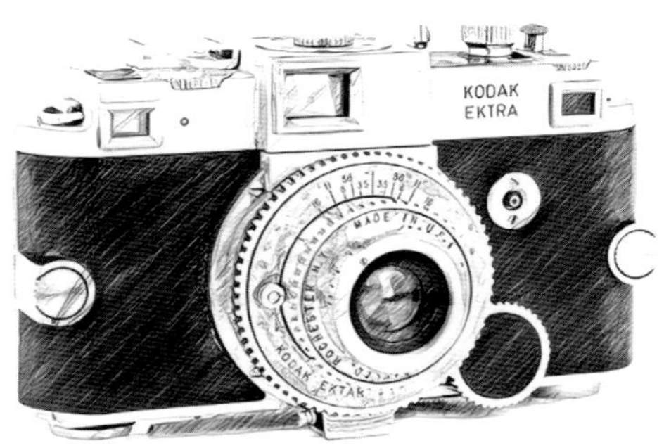

*f* 3.8, and a 153mm *f* 4.5, all of which are coated—a feature not even the best lenses from Leica or Contax can match. There is a zoom viewfinder with parallax adjustment for all six focal lengths plus 254mm (for a lens that is planned but never produced).

Unfortunately, most photographers found the Ektra's left-side shutter release inconvenient, its lens mounting difficult and its shutter speed setting awkward. Worse, the shutter proves to be quite unreliable. These factors, plus its incredibly high price of $373.50 with a 50mm *f* 1.9 coated Ektar lens (equivalent to $6,615 today) means the camera finds almost no market, and only 2,000 are made. There is work done on an Ektra II, which features a spring-wind motor back, but it is never produced.

**1941:** Willard D. Morgan (1900–1967) publishes *The Complete Photographer* magazine three times per month at just 35 cents per issue. The articles and images are by the likes of Ansel Adams, Mathew Brady, Robert Capa, Andreas Feininger (1906–1999), Laura Gilpin (1891–1979), Lewis Hine (1874–1940), Barbara Morgan (1900–1992), Edward Weston, and many others. At 35 cents per issue, it costs $12.60 per year, equivalent to $200 per year today, a princely sum at the tail end of the Great Depression. Still, it manages a 55-issue run over 18 months.

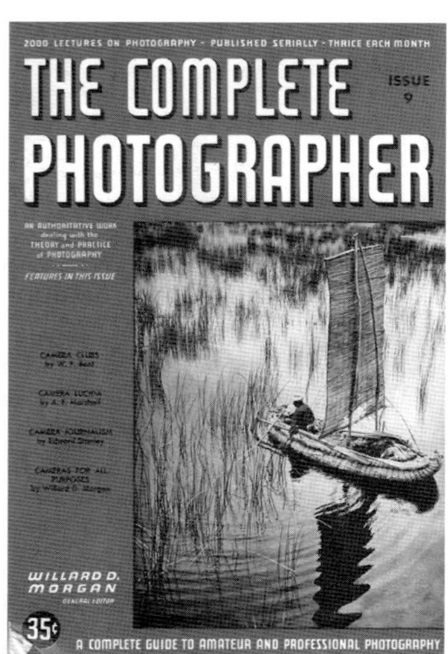

**1941:** Fred Spira (1924–2007) starts offering developing services as "Spiratone Fine Grain Labs," operating out of his mother's New York City apartment until the venture is closed by the NYC fire department. After opening a New York retail store in 1946, Spiratone quickly expands into distributing lenses and all sorts of photo and darkroom accessories, but never sells cameras.

The company becomes famous for locating and importing quirky photographic items: impossibly cheap 400mm lenses and accessories such as the "Barlow lenses" (see **1833**) made in mounts for various cameras, which Spira calls "TelXtenders." All are sold by mail through visually overstuffed ads on the back pages of photo magazines. Spiratone has its heyday in the late 1960s and 1970s, finally closing its doors in 1990.

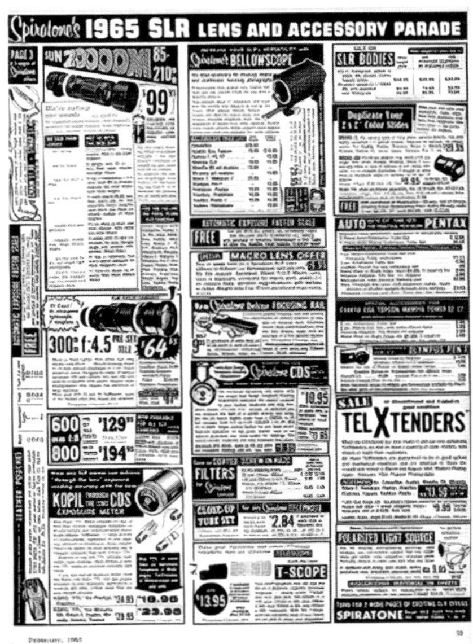

---

### TRIVIA

Over his lifetime, Fred Spira amassed one of the world's finest collections of photography-related items. The collection included some 20,000 objects relating to the history of photography, including many rarities not found in any museum. An excellent illustrated history, initially written by Fred and completed by his son after his father's death, is called *The History of Photography as seen through the Spira Collection*. It's out of print but readily available, used. Well recommended.

In 2002, the majority of the Spira Collection was sold to the State of Qatar, which planned a purpose-built photography museum in Doha. The remainder was sold at auction in 2006. But in 2014, Qatar scrapped plans for the museum and the current fate of the Spira Collection is unknown.

---

### TRIVIA

During the Second World War, Japanese camera production was limited to cameras for military use. However, makers were allowed to assemble consumer cameras from materials already on hand, so limited production was possible.

Photography itself became prohibited in increasing portions of the country. Photographs with sweeping views, taken from places higher than 20 metres, were totally forbidden, even in the cities. Photographers, anxious not to be identified as such, would carry their cameras in brief cases or "furoshiki" (Japanese wrapping cloths).

**1941:** Kodak's Kodacolor brand is again used, this time claiming Kodacolor as the "world's first true colour negative film." More accurately, it was the first colour negative film intended for making paper prints (in 1939, Agfa had introduced a 35mm Agfa colour motion picture negative film which was used only for making positive projection prints on 35mm film).

**1942:** While war rages all around neutral Switzerland, Pignons SA produce their first series of Alpa reflex cameras as well as one version, the Alpa Standard, with a non-reflex viewfinder. Although the world has too many problems to take much notice, a few of the new cameras nevertheless make it to the USA under the names "Bolca" and "Bolsey Reflex."

> ### TRIVIA
> The Alpa name was chosen because it was a light, pocket-able camera which might easily be brought along when travelling in the Alps.

**1943:** Jenő Dulovits (1903–1972), both a photographer and a mathematics and physics professor at the University of Budapest, patents the first SLR camera with an eye-level finder. He then designs his Duflex, which uses a system of mirrors to provide a laterally correct upright image in the eye-level viewfinder.

But the war slows things down. Still, with further work by camera designer Jozsef Nemeth (1911–2006), and encouragement from Nandor Baranyl (1889–1977), the technical advisor at Hungary's only camera maker, Gama, the Duflex will go into limited production between 1948 and 1950. It is also the world's first SLR with an instant-return or "auto-return" mirror (see **1947**).

**1943:** In 1941, the U.S. government seizes control of E. Leitz, NY, directing them to manufacture Leica IIIa cameras for the military. They assume that a facility capable of repairing Leicas also can manufacture them. By early 1943, it is apparent that the New York branch is not up to the task.

Peter Kardon's Premier Instrument Corp. takes over and soon produces the first "American-made Leica" from repair parts on hand at E. Leitz. However, the IIIa's design doesn't lend itself to mass manufacture, requiring many adjustments by skilled craftsmen. So, Kardon creates its "Kardon 35," a new Leica IIIa-based camera designed to be mass manufactured and easily repaired. It is supplied with Kodak's Ektar LTM lenses and is very well made. However, just

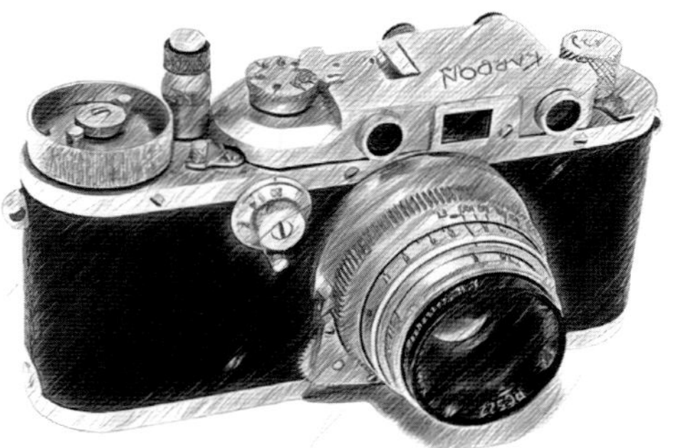

as the first cameras are delivered, the war ends and the government reduces the contract from 6,000 cameras to 2,000, then just 750. Fewer than 2,750 cameras are made, mostly for post-war consumers. They are expensive and their price is undercut by cameras from Japan and Germany, countries that benefit from both lower labour costs and the financial support of the Marshall Plan. The Kardon 35 proves a tough sell. Premier Instrument never recover their investment and are out of business by early 1956.

---

**TRIVIA**

By 1952, the U.S. government was buying foreign cameras, notably German Leicas, but also Japanese-made Leica copies. Premier's executives wrote numerous government departments demanding to know why they were not supporting American manufacturers. They got their answer in a May 1955 meeting at the Pentagon. Apparently, the Kardon 35 was not the camera of choice for American tourists and thus persons carrying one were readily identified as U.S. spies. The military realized that agents carrying Kardon 35s were disappearing and the camera was partly to blame. So, they purchased foreign cameras that served the higher purpose of not compromising agents' lives.

In 1947, the consumer version of the Kardon 35 bore a retail price of $393 (wholesale was $175). Yet, between 2018 and 2020, several Kardon 35s were offered on various auction sites at prices between $1695 and €1899.

---

**1944:** Dmitri Maksutov (1896–1964) develops his MTO (Maksutov Tele-Optic) 500mm $f$ 8 Maksutov-Cassegrain design, the first generally available catadioptric lens for photography. (A diagram of a "Cat" lens can be found under "Catadioptric" in the Glossary.) Catadioptric photographic lens systems fold the light path. A convex secondary acts as a telephoto element, making the focal length even longer than the folded system and extending the light cone to a focal point well behind the primary mirror so it can reach the film plane of the attached camera. In the catadioptric system, a spherical reflector is combined with a lens with the opposite spherical aberration, which corrects the common optical errors of a reflecting telescope, making it suitable for photo-

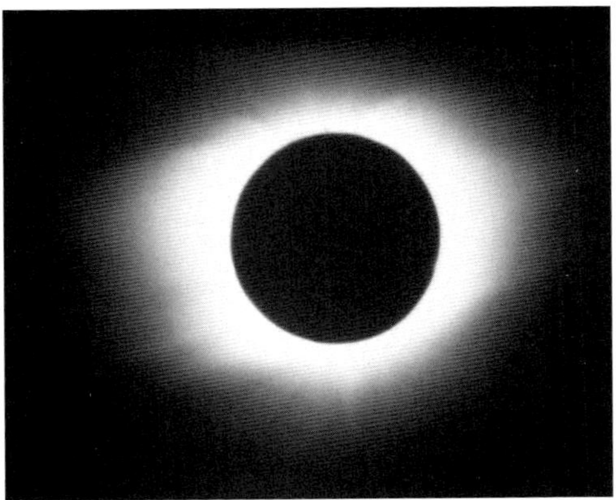

*Solar eclipse photographed off Curacao in 1998 with a Leica R3 and a 500mm Russian-made MTO.*

graphic use. The catadioptric camera lens heyday will come in the 1960s and 1970s. To this day, the Cat is the only reasonable solution for lenses of 1,000mm or more (see **1968**).

**1944:** At Corning Glassworks, chemist Charles F. DeVoe develops a continuous melting process using electric melting and improved stirring techniques to make up to 100 pounds of optical glass an hour. His work results in methods of producing optical and ophthalmic glasses that are still used today.

---

**TRIVIA**

Started in 1851 as the Bay Street Glass Company, Corning is a huge maker of industrial glass of all kinds. Optical glass, used mostly for eyeglasses, is a small part of its production. However, Corning remains an important source of specialty glass for lens makers.

---

**1944:** On 6 June (D-Day), Robert Capa rides with the troops in landing craft in the second assault wave on Omaha Beach. He swims close to shore, taking what shelter he can from the German's beach fortifications. Armed only with two Contax II cameras, equipped with 50mm lenses, and a few spare rolls of film, he shoots 106 photos in the first hours of the invasion before catching a lift back to his ship on another landing craft. However, in a rush to meet deadlines, a staff member at *LIFE*'s London lab sets the film dryer's temperature too high and melts the emulsion on three full rolls of negatives and half of a fourth. Only 11 (some sources say eight) frames are saved. It becomes one of the most famous blunders in photographic history. *LIFE* runs the iconic photos, anyway—for they have nothing else—and the images cement Capa's reputation as the premier war photographer of his time.

---

**TRIVIA**

To make the 1998 movie *Saving Private Ryan* look realistic, director Steven Spielberg and cinematographer Janusz Kamiński base the film's D-Day sequences on the bleached-out, grainy look of the D-Day photographs shot by Capa.

---

**1945:** E. Leitz, makers of the Leica camera, become the first to introduce anti-reflection coatings as standard on consumer (rather than military) lenses, starting with the Summitar 50mm *f* 2 lens, which had been first introduced in 1939.

**1945:** When the Allies break up IG Farben to reduce the size of the German chemical industry, Agfa reappears as an individual business. The Allies claim patent rights to the closely guarded Agfacolor process as "war indemnity," and provide copies to Ilford and Kodak. The Agfa plant, located in Wolfen, East Germany, is dismantled and taken, along with key German personnel, to Russia, where it becomes the basis of the Soviet colour film industry.

**1945:** The Gamma Camera Company of Budapest builds the first working prototypes of what will become the Duflex SLR in 1947.

**1945:** The Carl Zeiss Foundation (Carl Zeiss (Jena) and Zeiss Ikon AG) is split in the aftermath of the Second World War. As the Americans withdraw from what will become East Germany, they relocate 126 skilled technicians to Oberkochen and start Zeiss-Opton Optische Werke (Oberkochen) in the West, while what is left of Carl Zeiss (Jena) becomes VEB Carl Zeiss (Jena) in East Germany. Zeiss Ikon is also split into Zeiss Ikon AG (Stuttgart) in the west and VEB Zeiss Ikon in East Germany.

---

### TRIVIA

The Soviet forces take much of the manufacturing gear from Zeiss (Jena) to Ukraine, installing it in the Arsenal (Kyiv) factory. During the Cold War, Arsenal will produce optical components for the Soviet military and space programs.

The Zeiss trademark was much disputed. The East German Zeiss operation marketed under the Zeiss-Jena and Pentacon names. The West German operation marketed as Carl Zeiss in NATO countries while using the Opton brand in the east. West German camera production ceased in 1972. Lens production continued in Germany, while both camera and some lens production continued in Japan, in cooperation with Yashica, until March 2005. After this, Cosina continued Japanese production of some Carl Zeiss lenses and cameras under the Zeiss Ikon brand, as the Contax name was still owned by Yashica/Kyocera. Camera and lens production ended in Kyiv in 2005.

---

**1945:** As the Shott Glasswerke (Jena) is located in what is to become East Germany, U.S. troops, relocate 41 glass makers to Mainz, West Germany, where they form Glaswerk Schott & Genossen and continue to produce high-quality optical glass to this day.

---

### TRIVIA

After the Second World War, Shott became two firms: VEB Jenaer Glaswerk (Jena) and Jenaer Glaswerk Schott & Genossen in Mainz. After the Soviet Union's collapse, the West German Schott in Mainz acquired the East German company, becoming Schott Glas in 1998. All of Shott's optical glass is now made in Mainz.

---

**1946:** Seiki Kogaku resumes camera production with the Canon S1 and, in 1947, the company begins producing its own lenses and adopts "Canon" as its brand.

---

### TRIVIA

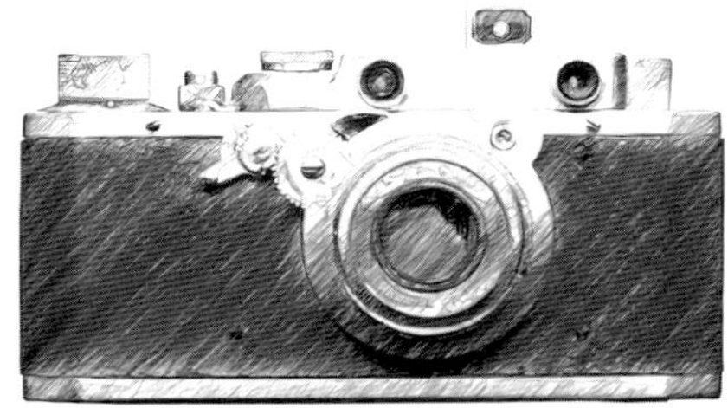

Only about 100 Canon S1 cameras were made, probably from parts made before the war. During that time Seiki Kogaku, a military supplier, was evacuated to the relative safety of Yamanashi Prefecture. After the war ended, the company had no means to transport its factory machinery from Yamanashi back to Tokyo. A camera-loving U.S. commanding officer of a unit stationed in Yokohama heard about this and had U.S. military trucks transport the factory equipment to the company's main factory in Meguro, Tokyo. In appreciation, the company presented him with a Canon S1.

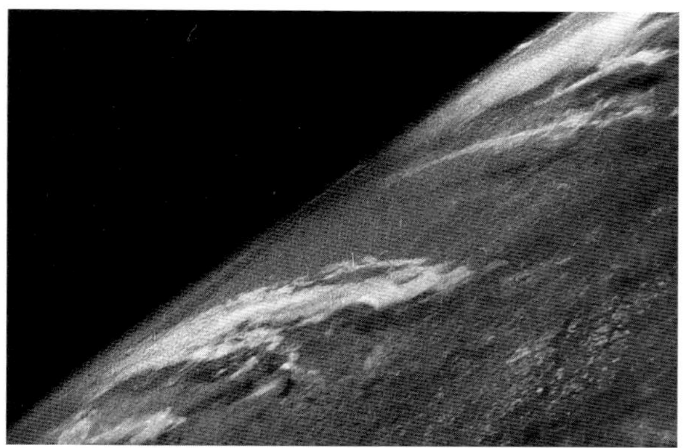

*The first photo taken from space with a V2 rocket in 1946.*

**1946:** On 24 October, a group of soldiers and scientists in the New Mexico desert take the first pictures of Earth as seen from space. The grainy, black-and-white photos are taken from an altitude of 65 miles by a 35mm motion picture camera riding on a V-2 missile launched from the White Sands Missile Range. Snapping a new frame every second and a half, the rocket-borne camera climbs straight up, then falls back to Earth minutes later, slamming into the ground at 500 feet per second. The camera is smashed, but the film is unharmed.

**1946:** An Australian engineer from Sydney, Robert Miller, patents his fluid head for motion picture cameras. In 1954, he will both develop the Miller Viscosity Drag (an invention that greatly improves image quality in films by applying user-variable dampening to the pan and tilt movements of the camera) and start R. E. Miller Pty Ltd. (which now trades as Miller Camera Support Equipment) to manufacture heads and tripods. Miller will go on to become one of the top names in professional tripods and video heads around the world. The firm remains active today.

**1946:** David Douglas Duncan joins *LIFE* magazine.

**1946:** Norwood and Freund finally have an exposure meter in production and ready for sale (see **1941**). The "Norwood Director" is different from anything else being sold at the time, having two sections: a lower half with the meter needle and an upper section with the photo-cell sensor. The upper section has a pivot and can turn 300° so the cell can always be aimed at the camera lens while the meter needle is read at a comfortable angle. The calculator dial is on the rear of the upper section. It is unique and a success.

**TRIVIA**

The "Norwood Director" name was probably adopted at the last minute, as the name moulded into the Bakelite housing was simply "Norwood Exposure Meter."

**1946:** Copal starts business as K.K. Copal Kōki Seisakusho (meaning Copal Optical Works Co. Ltd.), designing a leaf shutter for a 6 x 6cm TLR being developed by Nippon Kōgaku—the "Nikoflex." This Nikoflex is never made. So, the first customer for the Copal shutter is Olympus. Still made today, Copal's high-quality leaf shutters are used on many rangefinder, TLR and view cameras. In 1961, Copal will go on to develop the Copal Square focal plane shutter—the basis of nearly all modern Japanese SLR shutters. They become part of Nihon Denshi in 1998 and continue building shutters to this day.

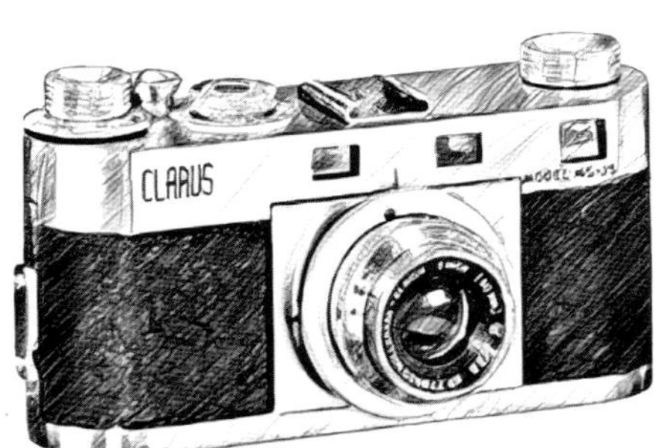

**ODDITIES**

The Clarus was made with typically American die cast moulding instead of pressed parts and had a larger body to allow easier assembly. The Clarus had many good features, including LTM lenses made by Wollensak and Elgeet (a large, Rochester-based, lens manufacturer), but nevertheless suffered an unjustified reputation for poor performance and reliability. Today, surviving examples prove it was the equal or superior to many famous makes of the era. The MS-35 was made by the Clarus Camera Manufacturing Company of Minneapolis between 1946 and 1952 and was the only camera they ever made.

**1946:** The owners of Kamera-Werkstätten, Dresden (see **1919**), which make the Praktina (see **1953**) and Praktiflex (see **1939**) cameras, are forced out and their company expropriated by order of the Soviet military administration. The company is nationalized and re-named VEB Kamera-Werkstätten Niedersedlitz. "VEB" stands for "Volks-Eigener Betrieb," new-speak for "Government-owned" (literally translated as "People's Own Works" or "Publicly Owned Operation"). It is a process that will be repeated with virtually every East German camera company.

**1946:** Frank Back (1902–1980) designs his "Zoomar," the first optically compensated zoom lens. It is a long, narrow 17–53mm *f* 2.9 lens with 22 elements in five sections, including two coupled sliding members. It is designed for use on 16mm cameras, but later a version is designed for 35mm movie cameras.

**TRIVIA**

A prototype Zoomar was used by WCBS-TV (New York) on July 21, 1947, to cover the Brooklyn Dodgers/Cincinnati Reds game. The first commercial version was used by Paramount newsreel photographers to cover the 1947 World Series.

In 1949, WAVE-TV (Louisville) became the first television station in the United States, to present a live telecast of the Kentucky Derby. It was the first use of a Zoomar Lens for television sports.

**1946:** Joseph C. Wilson (1909–1971), president of the Haloid Photographic Company (Rochester), sees the promise of Chester Carlson's "electron photography" invention (see **1938**). He hires Carlson and signs an agreement to develop his invention as a commercial product. Looking for a term to differentiate its new system, Haloid coins the term "Xerography" from two Greek roots meaning "dry writing."

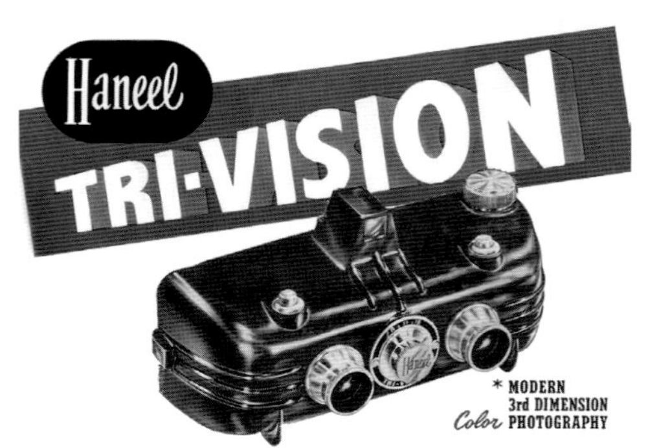


### ODDITIES

This contender for the worst camera ever was originally sold from 1942 as the Kirk Stereo 33. The Haneel Tri-Vision was a Bakelite, 3-D camera camera with a back that nearly closed and a slide-latch that almost held it in place. The film channel (for 828 film) was most often warped, and it seems the two Lestra-Lite *f* 4.5 coated lenses, were single element affairs. The shutter used two buttons. The right one for 1/25th, while the other was (obviously) pulled up, for time exposures. A later version came with an improved metal back. Made from 1946 to 1949 and the firm ceased operations in 1950.

**1947:** Kodak announce Ektachrome, the company's first colour slide film to use the "oily tail" dye couplers earlier used in Agfacolor Neu.

**1946-47:** Two ex-military engineers, Ogihara Akira (1920–1992) and Ōtsuka Shintarō (1921–2005) start Orion Seiki Sangyō Y.K. (meaning Orion Precision Products Industries), a small camera workshop offering repairs and modifications for professional cameras, notably making Leica-mount barrels for older lenses or military camera lenses. Their first product is an ingenious adapter to use Contax or Nikkor lenses on Leica thread mount cameras while keeping the rangefinder coupling. Later products will include the Mirax reflex housings, Supreme lenses, and Focabell bellows. In 1954, they will show their Phoenix SLR, which will be released the next year as the Miranda "T."

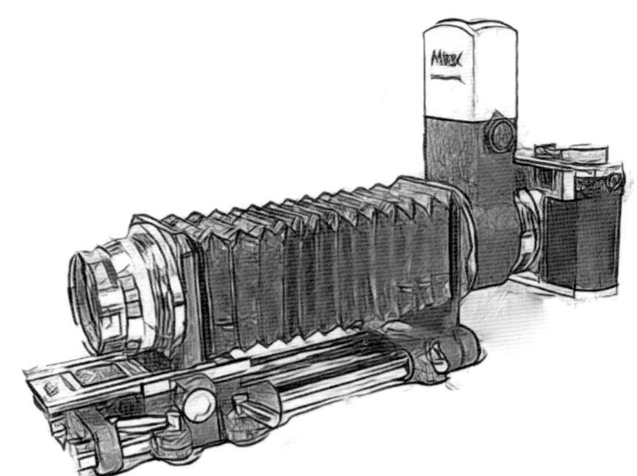

*Focabell bellows with Orian Mirax-B reflex housing.*

**1947:** West Germany's Opton Optische Werke Oberkochen GmbH is renamed "Zeiss-Opton Optische Werke Oberkochen GmbH" and, in 1953, will be renamed again, to "Carl Zeiss AG." The East German division becomes VEB Zeiss (Jena) and, in 1959, becomes part of VEB Pentacon.

> **TRIVIA**
>
> After the split, and until German Reunification in 1990, the West German arm of Zeiss sold its goods under the Opton brand in the Soviet bloc, while VEB Zeiss Ikon (and later Pentacon) marketed its goods as Zeiss Jena or, often, simply Jena.

**1947:** Sometime between 1947 and 1951, Manjiro Komine starts the Komine Co., Ltd., making an all-metal tripod head. They sell their products under the Minec trade name and will go on to make lenses for Vivitar, among others, in the 1970s, before disappearing in bankruptcy in the early 1990s.

> **TRIVIA**
>
> You can often tell the age of many older Japanese cameras since all goods made for export to the USA between 1945 and 1951 were marked "Made in Occupied Japan." However, your scribe's Beauty Six (see **1950**) was made in this period, but is not so marked, as it was exported to Canada.

**1947:** American Bolex (NYC) is the U.S. distributor of Paillard/Bolex movie cameras and accessories like the Horvex line of meters from Germany. Thus, American Bolex acquires the rights to the Norwood Director from Photo Research.

> **TRIVIA**
>
> Nobody knows for sure, but it's probable that American Bolex found out about Bolex/Paillard's plans to set up their own distribution and repair network in the U.S., which would have gutted American Bolex's business. Rumours say this is why American Bolex acquired the rights to the Norwood Director—they needed a new product around which they could build a business. It seems that they acquired the design, the brand and, possibly, the patents. There is no public record of what Photo Research got in return, if anything, though they go on to build variations on the original meter, under the Spectra brand, until the 1980s.

**1947:** Henri Cartier-Bresson, Robert Capa, and David Seymour (1911–1956), also known as "Chim," start the photographer-owned Magnum photo agency. Magnum goes on to be the world's premier photo agency, surviving to this day.

> **TRIVIA**
>
> You cannot join Magnum—you must be "invited" and even then, you must go through a two-year probation period before your membership in the co-op becomes permanent.

**1947:** Dennis Gabor (1900–1979), a Hungarian-British electrical engineer and physicist, invents holography, for which he will receive the 1971 Nobel Prize in Physics.

**1947:** In the post-war period, Japanese copies of the more-expensive German cameras, notably Leicas, are quite popular. The Minolta 35 has a horizontal cloth focal-plane shutter with speeds of 1 to 1/500 plus B & T, with a front dial for setting speeds below 1/35. However, the shutter is a four-post (two pulleys and two rollers) design similar to the Exakta shutter rather than a copy of the Leitz two-post co-axial drum/pulley mechanism. The camera comes with a 45mm $f$2.8 "Super Rokkor" LTM lens, and other lenses are available. Like the early Nikons, it uses an unusual 24 x 32mm format, which is the then-current standard in Japan, as it more closely matches the 8 x 10-inch format for printing paper, and also saves money by getting 40 shots on a 36 exposure roll.

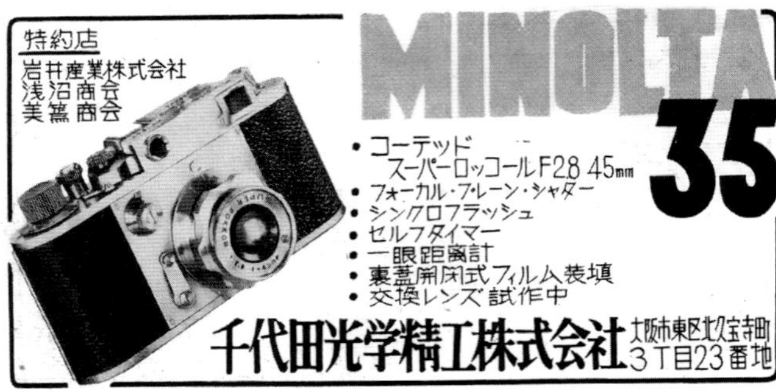


What sets the Minolta 35 (so called because it is Minolta's only 35mm camera at the time) apart from the other Leica copies is a combined viewfinder-rangefinder window and a hinged rear door for easier film loading. It is also the first Japanese camera to be fitted with a hot shoe and self-timer. The camera is a success and Minolta produces some 40,000 units over its 12-year production run.

---

**TRIVIA**

Note that this 32 x 24 format is a 4:3 ratio, identical to the FourThirds digital format of today.

---

**1947:** Fotokemika starts production of black-and-white films in Zagreb, Yugoslavia (now Croatia). Over the years it will produce black-and-white photo paper, photo chemicals, and simple cameras. In the 1970s, Fotokemika will license Dupont's technology for ADOX films, which they market under the Efke brand until they cease manufacturing operations in 2012.

**1947:** Walter Biermann and Johannes Weber start B+W in Berlin, which quickly becomes renowned for high-quality optical filters. B+W will merge with Schneider-Kreuznach in 1985 and continues to this day.

**1947:** The Gamma Camera Company of Budapest introduces the Gamma Duflex, the first SLR with instant return mirror (seven years before the Asahiflex IIb!), a metal focal-plane shutter, bayonet lens mount (although only a 50mm lens is ever produced), and an internal semi-automatic diaphragm.

The Duflex features an unusual Porro-mirror finder and, curiously, also has a standard viewfinder. Fewer than 600 are produced, all by hand, before production ends in 1950. The Duflex is a very ambitious, ultra-modern camera for its day. But the early cameras prove somewhat unreliable, and it will be Gamma's first and last production SLR.

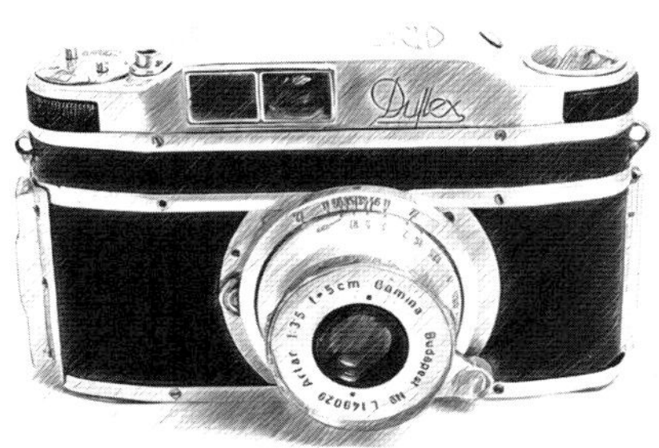

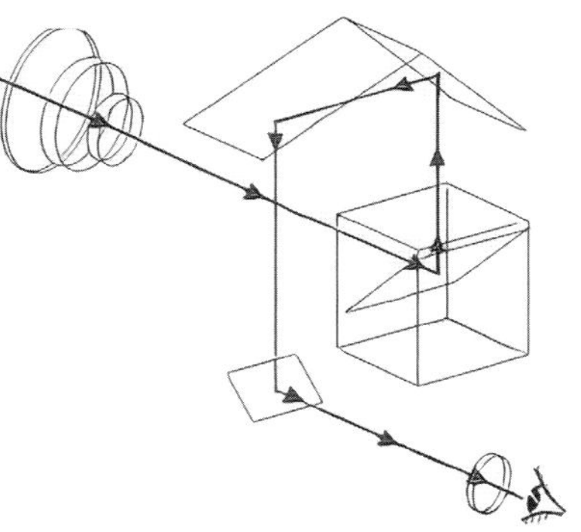

*The Duflex uses a modified Porro-prism viewfinder, with the eyepiece below the optical viewfinder.*

---

**TRIVIA**

Why did the Duflex fail? Ostensibly, it was because it would cost too much to gear up for series production. In reality, the Duflex failed for the same reason that the Mometta, Kinga, Momikon, Hungaretta, and Correcta postwar Hungarian cameras all failed—"instructions" from the Communist bosses in the USSR. In 2004, a Duflex sells for over $3,500 on the collector's market.

---

**1947:** In June, at the Milan Fair, Rectaflex (Italy) shows a partly functional prototype camera designed by Italian engineer Telemaco Corsi. The prototype has a reflex mirror finder which corrects the image inversion, although the image is still laterally reversed. A few months later, a true roof pentaprism is added to the camera, giving a left-right corrected viewfinder. The following year a functioning camera is shown at the Milan Trade Fair in April and the camera is in series production by the fall of 1948, making it the first eye-level roof-prism-equipped SLR, beating the Contax S by a full year.

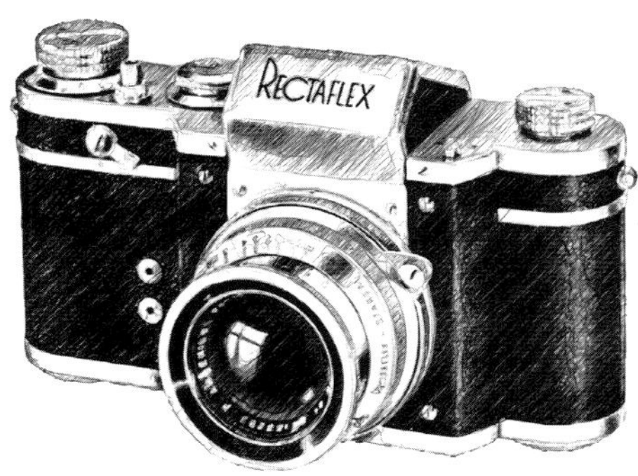

Corsi establishes the Rectaflex enterprise in Rome. Although the cameras are well made, the venture is rather loosely organized and, after some troubled years, the company fails. In 1955, the firm is sold to the Prince of Liechtenstein and production is moved to Lichtenstein, without Corsi. A new Rectaflex 4000 is launched, with a reshaped pentaprism cover, the Liechtenstein coat of arms on the front and other minor changes. The number produced is unknown and the Liechtenstein produced Rectaflexes seem to be plagued by design and/or manufacturing faults. The firm goes out of business for a second time, in 1958, having made fewer than 10,000 cameras in a decade.

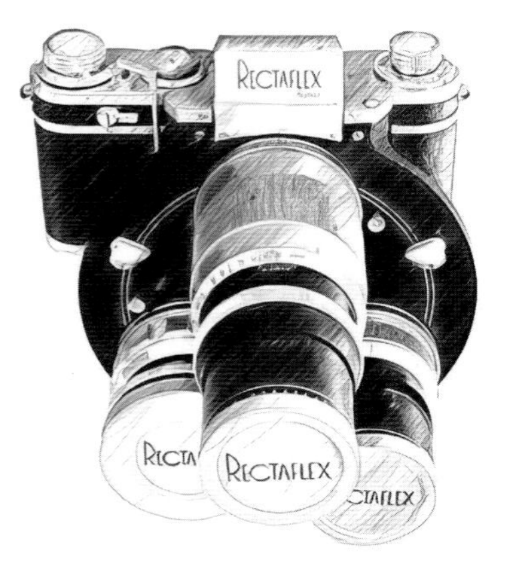

**ODDITIES**

The Rectaflex Rotor was a late model Rectaflex with a three-lens turret that functioned in the same manner as many 8 and 16mm movie cameras of the era. During the 1940s and 1950s, a company called Haber & Fink modified Leica cameras by adding special lens turrets, but Rectaflex is the only camera maker known to build such a feature on a 35mm SLR. It is estimated that between 200 to 300 were made, though some earlier Rectaflex units were independently converted to the Rectaflex Rotor specifications. The way to tell the factory-made Rotors is the word "ROTOR" engraved on the prism housing to the bottom right of the Rectaflex name.

**1947:** In the back rooms of his used-camera store, the son of a wealthy rice-farming family, Zenzaburo Yoshino (1911–1988) sets up a manufacturing workshop with the primary intention to design and manufacture cameras. They fail to do so, but the employees improve their skill and workmanship by making delicate metal fashion accessories such as cigarette cases, brooches, and lighters. This accessory business blossoms and a large proportion of the company's income is re-invested into the development of a camera. Though not a trained camera designer, Yoshino is persistent. It will take eight years to finalize the design and a further four to produce the camera he will call the Zenza Bronica.

**TRIVIA**

The Bronica prototype is called the Yoshinoflex. The final brand name is derived from his first name, Zenzaburo, and the Japanese slang for 120 medium-format-sized film, buroni (Brownie).

**1947:** The David White Company of Milwaukee introduces the Stereo Realist, designed by Seton Rochwite (1904–2000); it is the first commercial stereo camera using 35mm film. Like the Mamiya Six (see **1940**), the focusing knob moves the film plane, rather than the lens or lens elements.

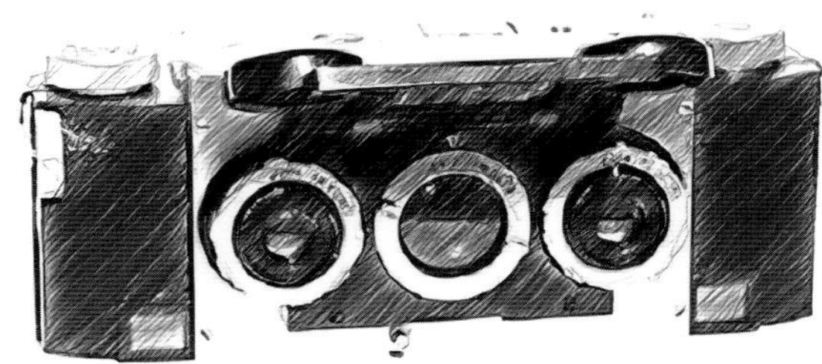

The camera starts the stereo-photography boom of the mid-20th century, and production of various models continues until 1972.

**1947:** On 21 February, Edwin H. Land demonstrates a prototype instant camera and associated film to the Optical Society of America. It will go on sale the following year.

**1947:** Using equipment seized from Zeiss (Jena and Dresden) in 1945, the Arsenal plant in Kyiv starts production of the Kiev II, a virtual copy of the pre-war German Contax II. Many of the early Kievs contained a lot of "liberated" German parts and, perhaps because of this, the Kiev 35mm cameras were considered the "high end" of Soviet rangefinder cameras.

---

### TRIVIA

After the post-war division of Germany, Carl Zeiss, Inc. in New York (which continued to operate throughout the Second World War) imported products from both the Zeiss (Jena) and Zeiss (Oberkochen) factories.

---

**1947:** Roger Cuvillier is hired by the SOM Berthiot Corporation, the maker of "Cinor" lenses for 8 and 16mm cameras. A young filmmaker named Richard Cornu challenges him to design a single lens that can continuously cover all three focal lengths (15, 25, and 75mm) on his Bolex—and thus the famous Pan-Cinor is born. Variations will be manufactured in Dijon, France, until 1970.

**1947:** Ducati (better known today for their motorcycles) had started in 1926 as the Società Scientifica Radio Brevetti Ducati, since Adriano, the youngest of the three Ducati brothers, held patents in the field of radio. After the Second World War, they need to re-enter civilian production and introduce two beautifully made half-frame cameras. The Sogno is a tiny rangefinder-coupled camera which accepts interchangeable lenses, while the Simplex has manual focusing. Both cameras have the shutter release and the film wind knob on the left and take just 15 half-frame images on short lengths of film, which must be wound into special cassettes, in the dark, thus limiting their popularity. In the late 1940s, Ducati purchases a small firm which makes motorcycles, and which quickly proves more profitable than cameras. Camera production ends in 1950 with fewer than 10,000 being made.

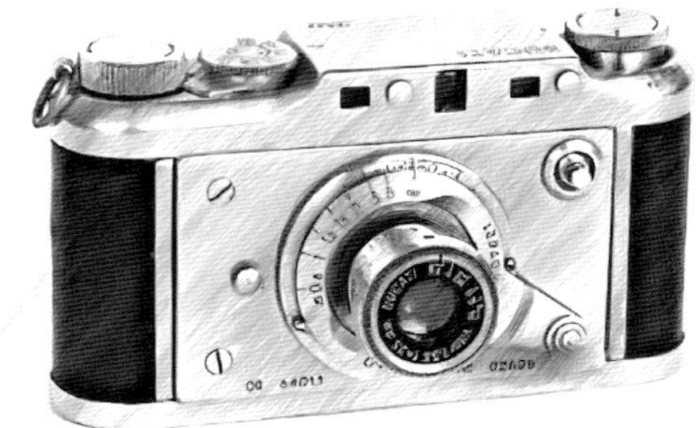

**1947:** Novoflex starts as a German maker of camera accessories. They become renowned for their macro bellows, and also make tripods and tripod heads, flash systems, tilt-shift bellows, lens adapters, and other camera parts. In 1950, they make camera bodies and lenses for Leica cameras, under contract. The company's production is later switched from Leica lenses to their own "Rapid Focus" lenses (called "fast-shot" in Germany) sold under their own name.

**1948:** Having been disbanded at the end of the Second World War, Asahi Optical is allowed to re-form, and resumes manufacturing binoculars and consumer camera lenses for Konishiroku and Chiyoda Kōgaku Seikō (later Konica and Minolta respectively). They will introduce Japan's first SLR, the Asahiflex, in 1952.

**1948:** Edwin H. Land introduces his Polaroid Model 95 camera, the world's first self-developing ("instant") camera. The black-and-white film is loaded on two rolls, although later models will use just one. These peel-apart films use a technology not unlike standard colour films. However, during development, the dyes are allowed to migrate to a receptor sheet, which is the part that is kept as the photograph.

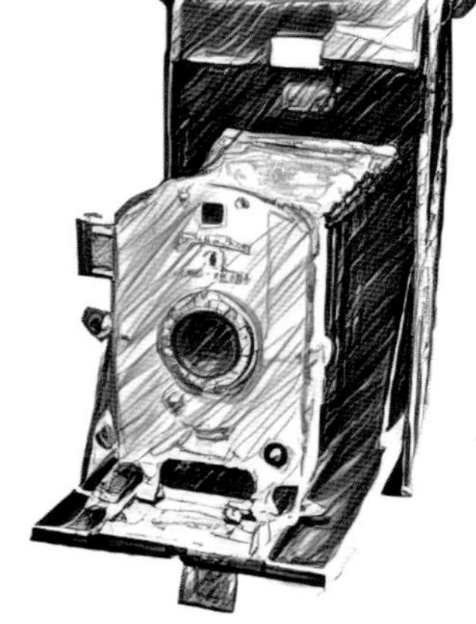

The early instant cameras were called "Polaroid Land Cameras," after the inventor of the instant process, Edwin Land.

---

### TRIVIA

Polaroid's original manufacturing run was 60 cameras. Fifty-seven were put up for sale at the Jordan Marsh (now Macy's) department store in Boston before the 1948 Christmas holiday. Polaroid incorrectly guessed that the camera and film would remain in stock long enough to manufacture a second run, but all 57 cameras and all of the film were sold on the first day of demonstrations.

---

**1948:** Sanshin Seisakusho is established as a maker of camera parts, including lens frames and barrels, in the city of Chino, Japan. It will go on to become one of the larger OEM camera manufacturers, starting with the design and manufacture of 8mm movie camera lenses in 1953. The company will change its name to Chinon in 1973, and it also will manufacture cameras under the names Argus, Alpa, GAF, Revueflex, Tower, and Sears, as well as its own name. It will also produce some of the lower-end models for several of the major camera makers, under contract, in the 1970s and 1980s.

**1948:** In October, Takachiho Optical Industries Co., Ltd. (to become Olympus Optical Co., Ltd. on 1 January 1949) launches what they claim is the first Japanese 35mm viewfinder camera with fixed lens and leaf shutter: their Olympus 35.

Experts generally agree that the Olympus 35 (top) was the first post-war Japanese 35mm viewfinder camera with fixed lens and leaf shutter, but some suggest that the Bakelite bodied Super Olympic Model-D (bottom) of 1935 or 1936 (made by the Olympic Camera Works or the Asahi Optical Works, depending on your source) came first.

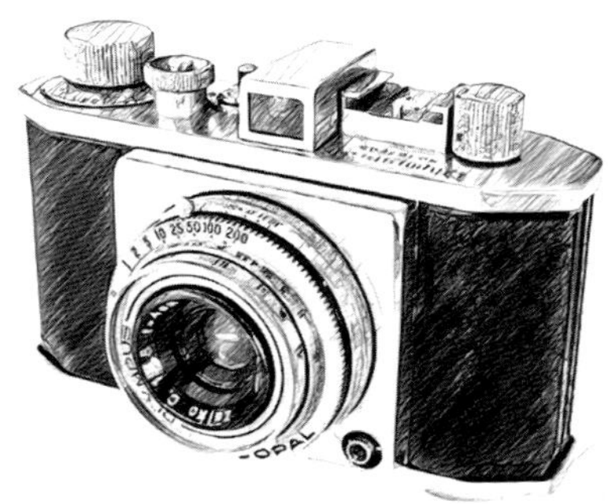

**1948:** After apprenticing as a precision mechanic at Telefunken, Heinz Waaske (1924–1995) becomes a camera designer at Wirgin. He soon becomes the head of the prototype workshop, then their technical designer and, eventually, Wirgin's chief designer. He will be responsible for the design of many cameras but is noted for the Edixa Reflex and its successors (see **1951**).

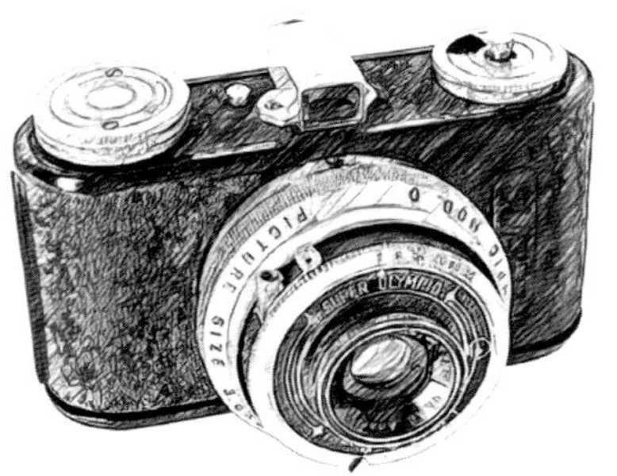

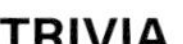

---

**TRIVIA**

Heinz Waaske saw the need for a small 35mm camera and designed and assembled one at home, having the mechanics in the Wirgin prototyping shop make the parts. But when he shows it to Henry Wirgin, he is told that Wirgin will soon leave the camera business. Thus, Waaske leaves Wirgin and, after a time, finds employment at Franke & Heidecke in early 1965, where his prototype will become the Rollei 35 (see **1966**).

---

**1948:** During the Second World War, the Soviet FED camera factory in Kharkov is evacuated in the face of advancing German troops. After the war, the Soviets have problems getting the FED rangefinder cameras (copies of the pre-war German Leica) back into production. Because the Krasnogorsk Mechanical Factory (KMZ) near Moscow has escaped destruction, that company starts making the FED camera under a joint FED-Zorki logo. After FED gets back in operation, KMZ continues to produce the rangefinder cameras under the Zorki (meaning sharp-sighted) trademark. Various improved Zorki models are produced between 1948 and 1978.

---

**TRIVIA**

Both FED and Zorki cameras use the M39 lens mount, also known as the Leica Thread Mount or LTM. In theory, early thread-mount Leica cameras and the FED and Zorki could also use the same lenses, but because the quality control on the Russian cameras and lenses is low, things didn't always fit together as they should.

---

**TOURIST TRIVIA**

In 1975, your scribe had the good fortune to tour the museum in the Kremlin. Each group of tourists had its own guide, provided by the state-run INTOURIST agency. In addition, roving members of the Soviet KGB would wander around, join a group for a few minutes and, seeing nothing untoward, move on to another group. Over the course of our time there, our group enjoyed the company of several of these KGB agents. Each one had a never-used Zorki or FED rangefinder camera hung around his neck and wore a suit reminiscent of the late 1940s or early 1950s, complete with Fedora hat. In the mid-1970s, they stood out like sore thumbs. So much for secrecy!

**1948:** Karl Braun KG (not to be confused with the Braun electrical appliance maker, who also build a series of slide projectors) changes its name to the Carl Braun Camerawerk and begins producing cameras in both roll-film and 35mm formats. Best known for its Paxette series of 35mm rangefinder cameras, most of which are consumer-level models, the company does briefly (1958–1962) produce an interesting 35mm SLR line with leaf shutters, the Paxette Reflex. Their more advanced cameras feature interchangeable lenses.

In 1954, the company will begin making slide projectors, offering one of the first semi-automatic projectors with a tray magazine. Braun will cease camera production in the early 1960s and the production of slide projectors when the firm closes its doors, in 2000. The firm is reorganized in 2001 and introduces the Multimag SlideScan 3600 digital scanner for the consumer market. This scanner is based on the Paximat Multimag series of slide projectors and enables scanning of slides in any of six different types of slide trays. The 3600 and all later models utilize digital ICE (scratch & dust detection) technology. (See **Digital ICE** in the glossary.)

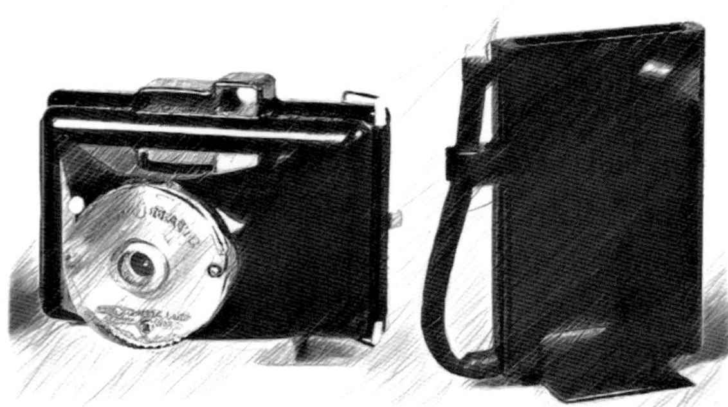

**1948:** According to advertisements, the Speed-O-Matic camera can "Snap, Develop and Print pictures on the spot in only 10 minutes." The camera is constructed of Bakelite with a built-in viewfinder and a metal face plate. Fitted with a meniscus lens and a simple single-speed ever-set shutter, it can capture 2 x 3-inch photos on special film packs. The photo development is not "instant" as with the Polaroid Land Camera—rather, an exposure is taken, and the film pack flipped to take a second exposure. Once taken, the two individual exposed film sheets in the film pack are removed and processed in an external tank. The film is a direct positive, so the full developing operation needs four chemical stages: developing, bleaching, re-developing, and fixing, not to count washing—in all, 11 steps for each picture taken. The mail order price is $12.95 plus $1 for each film pack ordered, which contains 12 sheets. It is not a huge market success.

### TRIVIA

The Speed-O-Matic is nothing new—it uses the same basic process as the Dubroni (see **1880**). The camera is reborn as the Dover, now using conventional 620 film for sixteen 4.5 x 6cm pictures; and the Speed-O-Matic Corporation becomes the Dover Film Corporation.

The Speed-O-Matic's in-camera development process will be revived in the "Instant-Box" view cameras, in 2023. Again, without much success.

**1948:** After stints at Carl Zeiss and Steinheil, Albert Schacht starts his own company, A. Schacht, in 1948 in Munich, making a series of lenses for the Edixa Reflex SLR (see **1951**) as well as for Exakta and Praktina bayonet mounts and M42 and LTM thread-mount cameras. Schacht moves to Ulm in 1954, where the company also produces lenses for the ill-fated Exakta Real (see **1959**). Schact lenses all achieve an enviable reputation for their high manufacturing standards

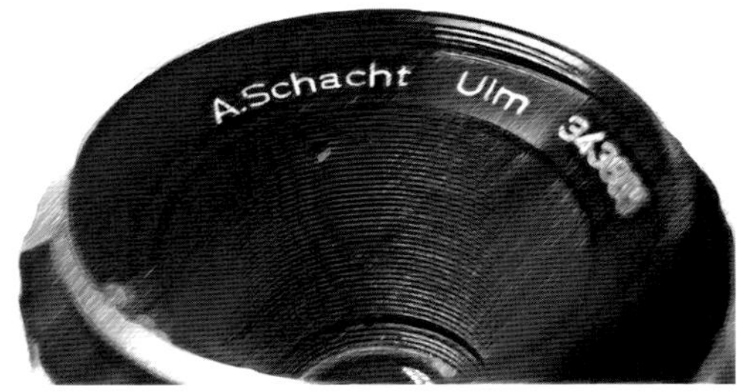


and optical excellence. One interesting feature is their unique mobile red-marking system for indicating depth of field. In 1967, however, Schact is acquired by another firm, and ends all production three years later.

**1948:** Pignons SA show their Alpa "Prisma Reflex," which has a pentaprism viewfinder, but the eyepiece, rather oddly, is angled upward at 45°. The camera does not reach the market until 1949 and production is limited.

**1948:** Takatoshi Shiraishi, a mechanical engineer and photography enthusiast, begins designing his own tripods in Tokyo, Japan, when he is 23 years old. Initially sold as "Alps," he adopts the "Slick" name in the early 1950s and in 1974 drops the letter "c," creating the current "SLIK" brand.

**1948:** The SEI (Salford Electrical Instruments) Photometer is distributed by Ilford in the U.K. and, in the U.S., by Zoomar. It is the first commercially successful spot-meter.

### TRIVIA

An earlier spot-meter, the Ainger Hall Photometer, was patented in June 1939 and manufactured for a short time by the Bowen Instrument Company in England. However, the years 1938 and 1939, just prior to the Second World War, were not the best time to market a photographic exposure photometer that was not particularly suited for use by military photographers. Nevertheless, it seems that some of these instruments were still being hand made on special order into the 1950s by one of the inventors, W. H. Turl.

**1948:** *LIFE* magazine commissions W. Eugene Smith to accompany a Colorado country doctor, Ernest Ceriani (1916–1988) over a 23-day period as he works with his numerous patients. The magazine prints 30 of the 200 photographs chosen by Smith. The resulting selection, *Country Doctor*, becomes the most influential photo essay in history.

---

**TRIVIA**

During his career, Smith used Contax, Leica, Nikon, Miranda, and Minolta cameras, among many others, although he favoured the Minolta SRT-101 after it came out in 1966. He was often broke and would pawn equipment simply to make ends meet. When he got paid, he would buy whatever he thought to be useful at the time.

---

**1948:** Swedish camera maker Victor Hasselblad introduces his Hasselblad 1600F camera. The waist-level 6 x 6 camera is equipped with a Kodak Ektar lens and is well suited to the professional. However, the focal-plane shutter proves unreliable. Roughly 270 units are produced in 1949 and 1950. An improved shutter is introduced and perhaps as many as 3,300 are made from 1950 to 1953. This version proves to be more reliable but is still subject to frequent repairs, with many units being cannibalized or modified by the factory.

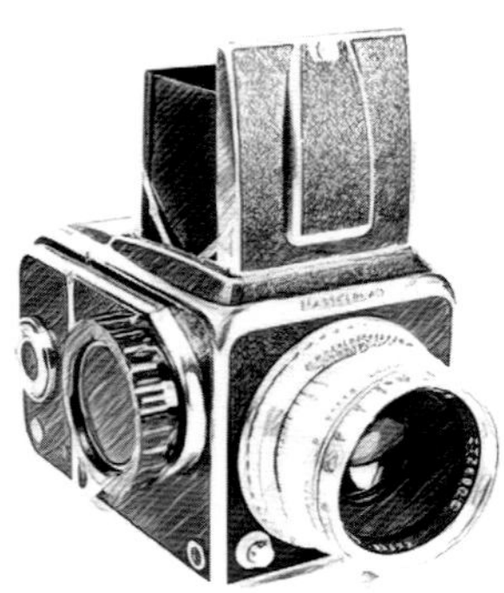

---

**TRIVIA**

During 1945–1946, the first design drawings and wooden models are made for a camera to be called the Rossex. An internal in-house design competition is held, and the classic good looks of the camera can be attributed to one of the winners, Sixten Sason, designer of the bodywork for the original Saab car. The Rossex, of course, becomes the Hasselblad 1600F.

---

**1948:** American Bolex remake the Norwood Director exposure meter. Basic functions are retained, including the swivel head, but the meter changes from a chunky black unit to the rounded, amoeba-shaped design that is still used today. With Bolex now out of their picture, American Bolex will change its name to "Director Products" in 1950 and again, in 1955, to Brockway Director Products. Norwood's meter is sold under all these names.

---

**TRIVIA**

In post-war Japan, shutters remain in short supply, with many makers unable to meet the demand. Some camera manufacturers start building their own. Mamiya buys lenses from Olympus and sells them Koho shutters, which, curiously, Olympus had made and sold to Mamiya before the war.

**1948:** Nippon Kogaku introduce their Nikon camera, which will later be known as the Nikon 1. It is essentially a copy of the Zeiss Contax rangefinder camera but uses a copy of the much superior Leica shutter. It is the company's first camera, and Nikon adopt the philosophy of high-quality, low-friction, close-tolerance mechanisms requiring less lubricant than other cameras. This robust construction will become its key to success.

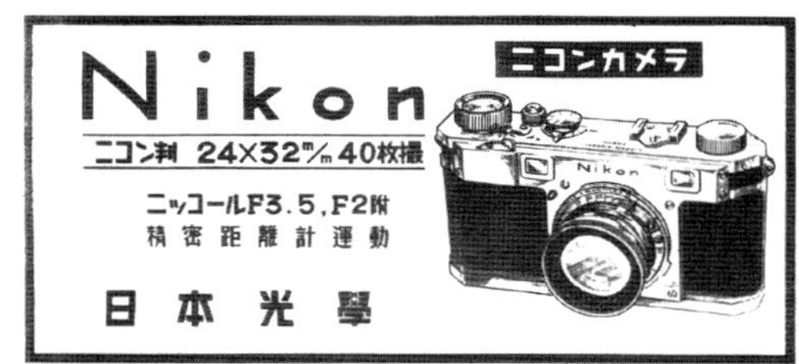

---

**TRIVIA**

In October 1945, Nippon Kogaku had set up a research unit to develop a small camera, to be called the Nikorette (to express "compactness"). Blueprints were complete by September of 1946, with the camera being introduced in 1948. The Nikorette designation was dropped as the firm felt that it was a "weak" name, so they used the Niko base (see **1930**), and added an N to the end, which creates a more masculine impression in the Japanese language—and the Nikon name was born!

Like the Minolta 35, the camera used an unusual 24 x 32mm format (see **1947**). Although the Allied occupation forces had designated Japanese camera manufacturing as a critical export industry, the export of cameras using this 24 x 32mm format was banned, primarily because Kodak had protested that transparencies from such cameras would not fit their standard slide mounts.

---

**1949:** After the Rectaflex (see **1947**) becomes the first 35mm SLR to have a roof-pentaprism, in 1948, the race to be second, third, and fourth is intense. At the 1949 Leipzig Spring Fair, VEB Zeiss Ikon (East Germany) introduce the world's second 35mm SLR camera body with a built-in eye-level roof-pentaprism: the Contax S. Though the design work starts in 1936, development is interrupted by the Second World War. The final prototype is shown in April 1949 and production is started in September, only to be stopped in December due to problems both with the camera and the production line. Production is resumed in March of 1950.

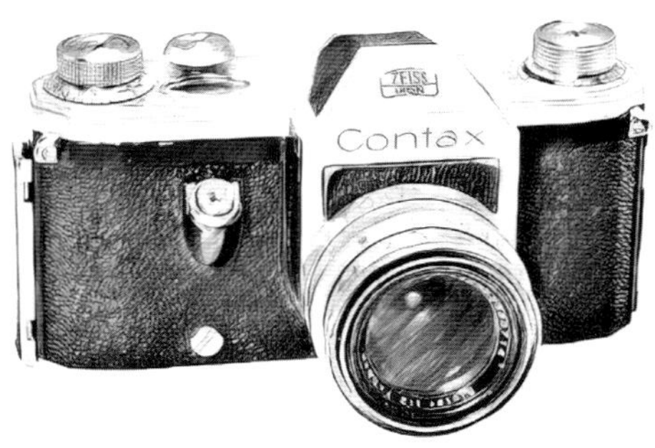

Originally to be called the SYNTAX, the "S" comes from the word Spiegelflex or mirror reflex, though there is no engraved S on the camera. It features a 42mm screw mount for interchangeable lenses. The Contax S also differs from older Carl Zeiss models in that the shutter is a horizontal-travel cloth type to reduce the overall size of the camera.

**1949:** An American, H. M. Stiles, invents a way to enclose 35mm film in an inexpensive cardboard enclosure without the costly precision film-transport mechanism. Produced by the Photo-Pac Camera Mfg. Company of Dallas, the Photo-Pac sells for $1.29 and includes a prepaid mailer for developing and prints. The instructions read: "Aim—Snap—Mail." Though surprisingly like the familiar single-use cameras of today, it is a bit before its time and the Photo-Pac fails to make a permanent impression on the market.

**1949:** Alpa introduces a model with a fixed-roof pentaprism in October the same year, while the Exakta Varex becomes the fourth (third if you do not count the Alpa) to have a roof pentaprism finder, in February of 1950. The Japanese will not follow suit until Miranda introduce their Miranda "T" in 1955.

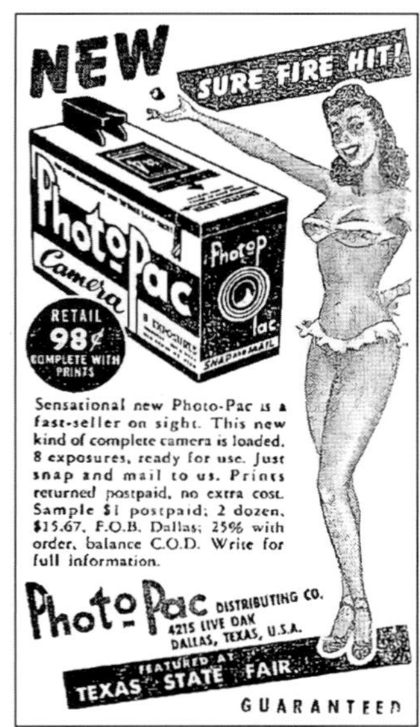


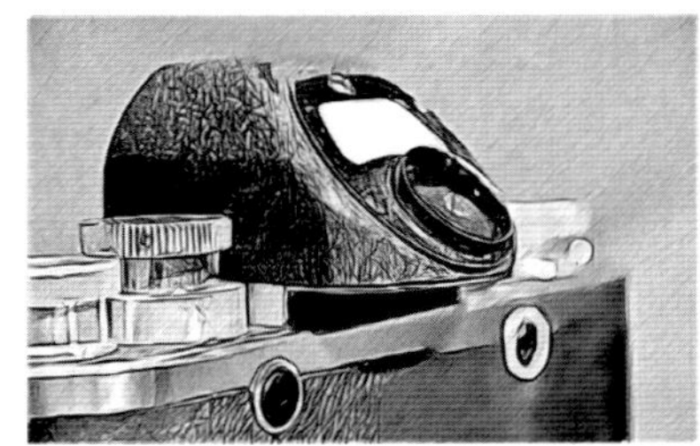

### TRIVIA

Some say that the Alpa does not count, as their finder, though non-inverted and correct left to right, is not a true eye-level finder, as it is set at 45°, requiring the user to peer down into it.

**1949:** VEB Zeiss Ikon bring out their Praktica single-lens reflex camera. It uses the same M42 lens mount that is on the Contax and cements the M42 mount in photographic history. It will go on to be known as the Pentax/Praktica or "Universal" thread-mount.

**1949:** The Mamiyaflex Automat A is introduced, the first Japanese TLR with an automatic film advance. The Automat runs film automatically up to the first frame and through all subsequent frames on the roll. The film counter resets when the back is opened. (Most other Japanese TLRs use a red window through which the film numbers can be seen.) It is successful and goes through a series of evolutionary models.

**1949:** Leica establishes the Leitz Glass Laboratory. Among the new types they develop is LaK9, the first glass with a truly high refractive index. Over the next 40 years, the Laboratory develops 35 new kinds from 50,000 experimental melts, making their Noctilux, Summilux, and other lenses possible.

However, the Leitz Glass Laboratory is a research facility, not a manufacturer, and while glass from the lab is sometimes used in prototype lenses, that used by Leica to manufacture their lenses is usually purchased from Schott (or sometimes Hoya), who produce Leitz proprietary formulas under license, often exclusively for Leica. In 1989, the Leica Glass Laboratory is sold to Schott and absorbed.

---

### BACKSTORY

The advances in glass technology can easily be seen by comparing the index of refraction over the years. The Leitz Elmar 50mm *f* 3.5 (1926) used SK15 glass with a refractive index of 1.625. This increased to 1.694 with the LaK9 used in the Summicron 50mm *f* 2 of 1953. In the 1969 Summicron the refractive index had grown to 1.7479 with LaFN2, and the 900403 glass (used in the 1976 Noctilux 50mm *f* 1) increased the refractive index to 1.9005. This is understood to be the highest refractive index glass ever used for photographic production lenses. Leitz used a proprietary number to avoid divulging its make-up.

Glass types with relatively high refractive indices were available prior to the Second World War, but they were made by adding thorium dioxide, which is radioactive. Besides being both a safety and pollution hazard, thorium dioxide turns glass yellow or even brown over time. However, many of the otherwise suitable replacements turned the glass opaque. The yellow tint of thoriated glass can be reversed by exposure to UV light. Usually, leaving such a lens on a windowsill for several weeks will do the job.

Kodak had some limited success with glass during the war. They were able to make glass that was free of thorium oxide but did have similar properties, although it too was yellowish in colour; Kodak used it to make lenses for aerial cameras and since these were used exclusively with black-and-white films, the "built-in" yellow filter enhanced contrast and was an asset.

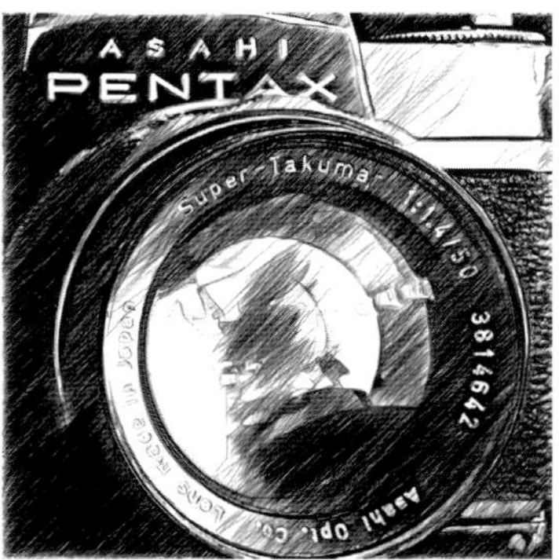

A small number of consumer lenses made with thoriated glass were produced between 1950 and 1980 and their low levels of radiation presented no threat to their users, though they could fog film, if it was left in the camera for an extended period.

The most notable among these lenses were the Leitz collapsible Summicron dating from late 1951 to 1952; the Pentax Super Takumar 50mm *f*/1.4 (left), produced for less than a year, over 1964–1965; and Canon's FL 58mm *f*/1.2, made from 1964 until 1966 or 1967.

Today, lanthanum oxide has replaced thorium dioxide in almost all modern high-index glasses. Both lanthanum and thorium dioxide are radioactive, but the radioactivity from lanthanum is so small that it is not detectable without sensitive lab equipment. The same cannot be said for thorium.

**1949:** Kodak introduce Ektacolor, the first film containing both colour couplers and integral colour masking.

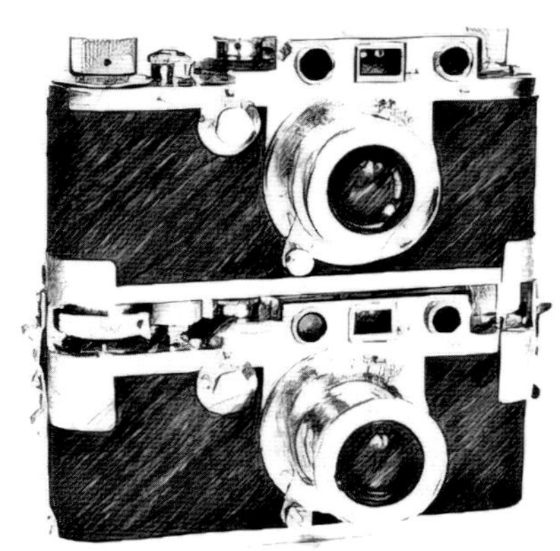

### ODDITIES

In 1949, for just $79 more than the price of two Leica IIIc cameras, Leitz New York offered two coupled in tandem! You wound both cameras using the enlarged wind knob on the lower camera while both shutters trip when the upper shutter release is pressed. However, to set the shutter speed on the lower camera the cameras had to be unclipped, the speed changed, and the cameras clipped together again. It was the same process to change the film. The coupled cameras could be held vertically and used as a stereo camera but could also be used for single shots with two different lenses.

**1949:** In September, Minolta introduce their "Minolta Memo," which has a rapid-wind lever on the bottom—a full five years before a lever wind appears on the Leica M3, which is frequently thought of as the first camera to have one. Unfortunately, like much of the camera, the Memo's wind lever is made of plastic and breaks readily, thus damaging both the reputation and sales of the Memo. This leads to the Memo being the first Minolta widely recalled and makes the Memo one of the rarest of all Minoltas.

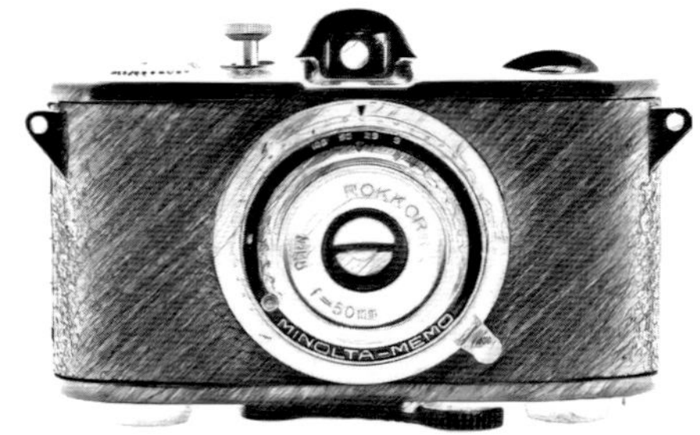

### AUCTION MADNESS

In 2016, the third Nikon 1 built, with its original 50mm *f* 2 Nikkor-H (the 11th one made) sold at auction for a modest $400,000. The camera was in nice condition, but it's unlikely it will ever see another roll of film. At the price, it is not what you'd call a "user."

In October 2020, a prototype of the Nikon "L" rangefinder, with a Leica thread mount, sold at auction for a record-setting €397,000, or roughly $469,000. Made around 1947, it seemed to be an earlier design than the Nikon 1. It did not carry the Nippon Kogaku logo and appeared to have been made as the company was deciding whether to use the Leica thread or the Contax bayonet mount.

**1949:** The Canon IIb is introduced, featuring a viewfinder with a positive and negative lens element in an optical block which rotates to change the viewfinder magnification from 0.67x to 1.5x, so that the view matches that of the interchangeable lens mounted. The price is 60,000 yen (about $166) with a Canon-made Serenar 50mm *f*/1.9 lens.

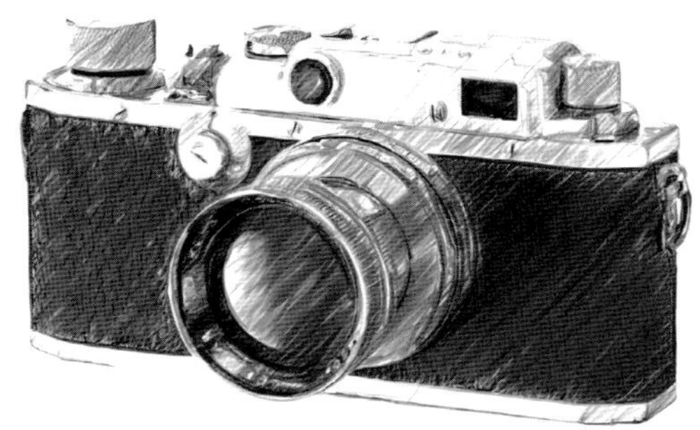

# 1950 to 1974

*The SLR came of age in the 1950s. Early models had a waist-level ground-glass viewfinder and a mirror which remained in the taking position, blacking out the viewfinder after an exposure. Winding the film returned the mirror to the viewing position. The innovations which transformed the SLR were the pentaprism eye-level viewfinder, the instant-return mirror that flips briefly up during exposure and immediately returns to the viewing position, and the introduction of the automatic diaphragm, which allows viewing at maximum brightness, only closing to the taking aperture during the exposure.*

*Introduced in 1959, the Nikon F would become the face of modern photography. By the late 1960s, the transformation of the SLR was complete. With competing models from Canon, Contax, Minolta, Olympus, Pentax, and Topcon, the 1960s starts what will be the "golden age" of film cameras.*

**1950:** The French firm of Pierre Angénieux introduces the first retrofocus (inverted telephoto) lens for SLRs. It is a design that allows fitting a wide-angle lens on an SLR without interfering with the moving mirror. The term "retrofocus" rapidly becomes a generic description of the optical design, and all his life Pierre Angénieux will regret not having registered retrofocus as a trademark.

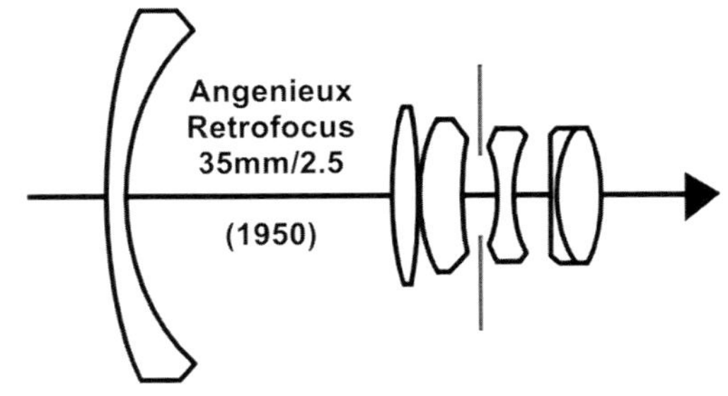


Regular wide-angle lenses (meaning lenses with a focal length shorter than the format's diagonal, that produce a wider field of view) need to be mounted close to the film. However, SLR cameras require that lenses be mounted far enough in front of the film to provide space for the movement of the mirror (the "mirror box"), which was about 40mm for a 35mm SLR, compared to less than 10mm in non-SLR 35mm cameras. This complication required the development of wide field-of-view lenses with more complex ret-rofocus optical designs. Such lenses use very large negative front elements to force back-focus distances great enough to ensure clearance.

**1950:** While working in Japan for *LIFE* magazine, American photographer David Douglas Duncan meets a young Japanese photographer, Jun Miki (1919–1992), who works with the Time-Life bureau in Tokyo. Miki takes a portrait of Duncan, using a Nikkor 85/2 lens, and Duncan is amazed by the sharpness. Thus, a trip to Nippon Kogaku's Ohi plant by Miki, Duncan, and *Fortune* magazine photographer Horace Bristol (1908–1997) is quickly set up.

At the plant, Nikon personnel show them a performance comparison between the Leitz and Zeiss lenses, from their own cameras, and equivalent Nikkor lenses, using a test projector. Both Duncan and Bristol bought the Nikkor lenses on the spot. Duncan then accompanies General MacArthur to Korea, using Nikkor lenses on his beloved Leica cameras, covering the Korean War with great success.

### TRIVIA

Duncan carried two Leica IIIf cameras to Korea, one fitted with a 50mm *f* 1.5 Nikkor (later, with the 1.4), the other with a 135mm *f* 3.5 Nikkor. Jun Miki, in his book *A History of Postwar Japanese Cameras* wrote: "When his first photographs were transmitted to New York, *LIFE* staff members asked us by cable whether the photographs had been taken with a 4 x 5 camera. Their sharpness was outstanding."

In December, *The New York Times* camera editor, Jacob Deschin (1900–1983), wrote an article in which he describes a group of American photojournalists, including *LIFE* magazine photographer David Douglas Duncan, using Nikon cameras and lenses in Korea. The article describes how, on the bitterly cold Korean Peninsula, while other cameras froze and became unusable, the Nikons worked well. *The New York Times* article reported that "NIKKOR lenses are extremely precise . . . and better than German lenses" and "Previous Japanese cameras had only beautiful exteriors, while internal performance was inferior, however, this Nikon camera is intricate and provides beautiful results." This proves to be a very valuable endorsement and ignites a fundamental change in how Japanese cameras, and in fact all Japanese products, were perceived, especially in America.

**1950:** Tōsei Kōki Y.K. (meaning Tosei Optical Instruments), who also build the TKS shutter used by several early Japanese camera makers, introduce their "Beauty Six" 6 x 6cm folding camera. It is made in very limited quantities over roughly a six-month period, and sold through a distributor, Taiyōdō Kōki K.K., who owns the "Beauty" name. Later versions will be sold under the maker's own "Frank" brand.

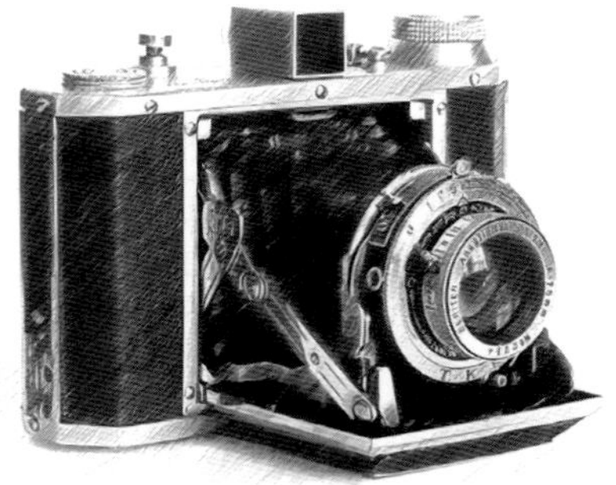

**TRIVIA**

The 1950 Beauty Six was historically insignificant but is mentioned here for two reasons. *First*, only two surviving examples are known to exist in the world. *Second*, your scribe owns one of the two, originally purchased by his father in 1950 or 1951. It is also the only one complete with its original ever-ready case and box. It can also be seen on the front cover of this book.

**1950:** Feinwerk Technik of Lahr, in the Schwarzwald (Black Forest) region of Germany, comes out with the first German subminiature to adopt the 10 x 14mm format on 16mm double-perforated film: the MEC-16. The lens is a 20mm *f* 2.8 colour-Ennit lens that gives a wider angle and greater depth of field than the 23 and 25mm lenses normally found on 16mm cameras; also, the lens is recessed 25mm and surrounded by light baffles to eliminate the 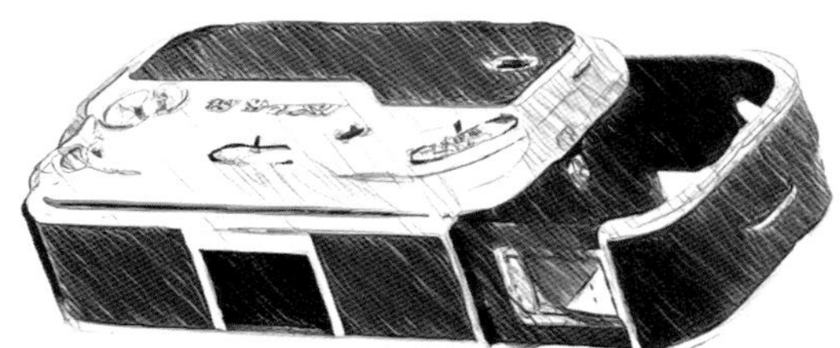 need for a lens hood. The focal-plane shutter has speeds of B, 1/30 (or 1/25), 1/60, 1/125, 1/250, 1/500, and 1/1000 second. The camera is a success, and a later version, the MEC-16 SB, will arrive in 1960, incorporating the first "through-the-lens" (TTL) exposure meter (see **1960**).

**1950:** The Ricohflex III, a 6 x 6 TLR, is introduced. In development since 1947, it has a remarkably simple mechanism, is made entirely of sheet metal, and is designed to be produced inexpensively. Yet, the few moving parts are made with great precision. Principles of manufacturing design not found in earlier Japanese cameras are introduced, with the goal of providing an inexpensive camera while rising above the reputation for *"cheap Japanese goods"*—and it succeeds. When other TLRs sell in the 20,000 yen ($55–$60) range, the Richoflex, equipped with an 80mm *f* 3.5 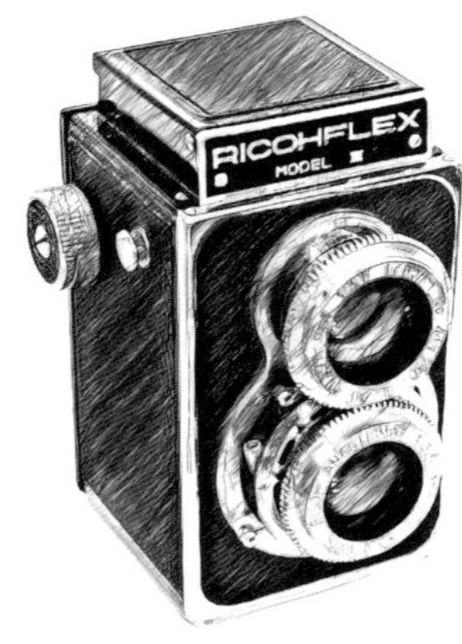 coated Ricoh Anastigmat, sells for just 5,800 yen, just four times the cost of its case! (This price is equivalent to about $16 at the time, or roughly $200 today.)

**1950:** The Ihagee "Exakta Varex" (called the Exakta V in USA) is the first 35mm SLR with an interchangeable viewfinder, the first with interchangeable focusing screens, and the first with a condenser lens in the viewfinder's optical system, for a brighter, more evenly illuminated view. Users have a choice of a waist-level or a pentaprism finder. For the next half-century, interchangeable viewfinder customization is the signal feature of fully professional level SLRs, although this concept has not yet made the transition to digital SLRs.

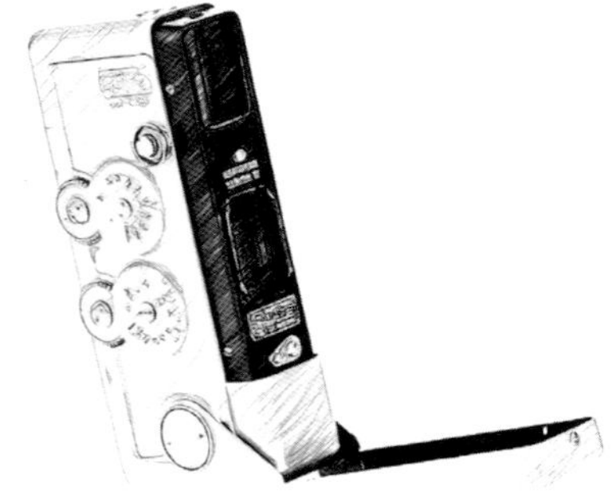

**1950:** Founded in 1862, Officine Galileo builds periscopes and rangefinders for the Italian military. The company starts making cameras in the 1940s but becomes famous in 1950 with the introduction of its superbly crafted 16mm subminiature camera, the GaMi 16, that has the most features and the most available accessories of any subminiature camera.

**1950:** Herbert Keppler (1925–2008), who will go on to become the most influential photo writer in the English-speaking world, joins the new *Modern Photography* magazine. He replaces subjective reviews with scientific testing of cameras and lenses and abolishes the previous pattern of "the bigger the advertiser, the better the review." He establishes the magazine's "Mail Order Code of Ethics" and removes advertisers that engage in shady practices. Over the years, he transforms the former "Minicam" magazine into one of the most respected and financially successful publications of its kind in the world. He will remain at the helm of *Modern* until 1987.

---

### TRIVIA

In the September 1983 issue of *Modern Photography,* Keppler wrote: "I like a camera bag that takes after me . . . sorta lumpy."

---

**1950:** The first Photokina trade fair is held, in Cologne, Germany. It will go on to become the pre-eminent photography exhibition in the world. Held biannually on even numbered years, it will run until 2018. The 2020 edition is cancelled due to the Covid-19 Pandemic. That, combined with the near collapse of the photographic industry in general, leads to its being "suspended indefinitely" at the end of 2020.

**1950:** "Doc" Edgerton of MIT (who invented the electronic flash—see **1931**) develops his Rapatronic Shutter. The Rapatronic (for Rapid Action Electronic) has no moving parts; it basically uses two polarizing filters set at right angles to completely block all light and act as a shutter. An electronic pulse activates a Faraday cell between the two polarizers, changing the polarization and allowing light to pass through for the (very short) duration of the pulse. Exposure times are as short as 10 billionths of a second, which make it possible to photograph nuclear bomb test explosions in 1951.

**1950:** Tokina Co. Ltd. begin lens manufacture as an OEM builder, and also start marketing under the Tokina brand in a range of lens mounts. Along with Sigma and Tamron, they will become one of the few independent lens makers to survive into the next century.

### TRIVIA

In 1999, Tokina will merge with Kenko, another independent or "third-party" lens maker, which also owns the optical glass and filter maker Hoya. They continue today as Kenko-Tokina Co. Ltd.

**1950:** Nittō Kōgaku start manufacturing "Kominar" lenses used in a variety of cameras, as well as enlarging lenses. In 1961, the company begins to manufacture complete cameras, and also make cameras as a subcontractor for other companies, famously making the Fujipet in 1960 and the Olympus Trip 35 in 1967. Today the company continues to manufacture optical equipment, including plastic lenses, CCTV lenses, projection lenses, lens modules for digital still cameras, and more.

**1951:** Pignons SA continue to make the Alpa reflex cameras, but never produce their own lenses. Their suppliers read like a who's-who of top-line lens makers: Angénieux, Asahi, Berthiot, Enna, Kilfitt, Kinoptik, Schneider, Zoomar, and more. While these lenses remain available for the Alpa, in various focal lengths, 1951 sees the introduction of the fabulous Swiss-made 50mm $f$ 1.8 Switar lens, made exclusively for the Alpa by Kern Aarau. In 1958, this lens is replaced by the incredible Kern Macro-Switar.

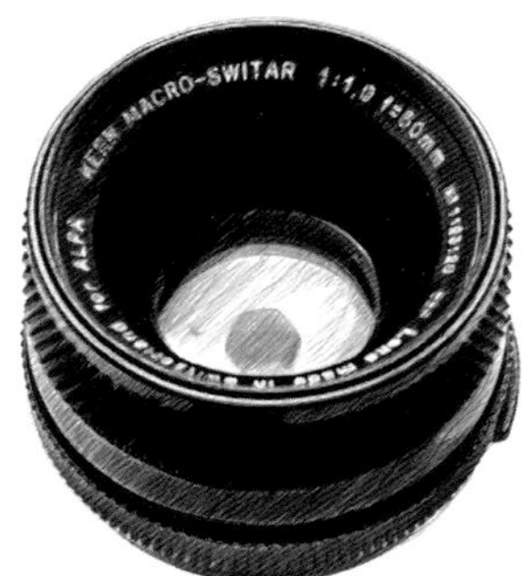

**1951:** Sawyer's purchase Tru-Vue, their main competitor for View-Master. The takeover eliminates a main rival and gains Tru-Vue's licensing rights to Walt Disney Studios. Sawyers capitalize on the opportunity and produce numerous reels featuring Disney characters. The takeover will pay off further in 1955 with reels of the newly opened Disneyland.

**1951:** The Goerz Minicord III is introduced by Goerz, of Vienna, Austria. It is a twin-lens reflex design, with an unbranded viewing lens of about $f$ 2.5 and a 25mm, $f$ 2 Helgor taking lens, and shutter speeds from 1/10 to 1/400 second. Closest focus is about one foot from the front of the lens.

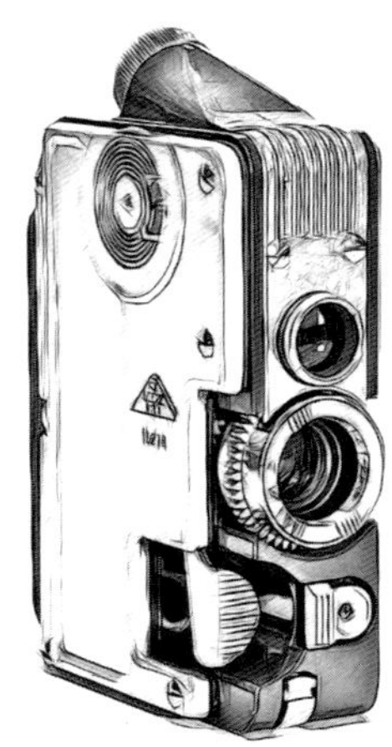

### TRIVIA

Paul Wahl wrote in *Subminiature Technique* magazine, "This is one of the three top subminiature cameras (the others being the Gami 16 and Minox); it is a precision instrument of high optical and mechanical quality, capable of outstanding results."

**1951:** Wray Optical of Bromley, Kent, introduce the only British-designed and built SLR: the Wrayflex. It has a cloth focal-plane shutter with speeds to 1/1000 but shares the 24 x 32mm negative size with Nikon's model 1 rangefinder camera, among others.

Three different models are produced. The first two (1 and 1a) have a low-profile appearance, and use a system of mirrors rather than a pentaprism to provide the reflex viewing image. Unfortunately, the resulting viewfinder image is rather dim compared to their competition and is laterally reversed. The third model, the Wrayflex II, is produced from about 1959 and has a prism, giving it a taller profile. It has the standard 24 x 36mm image format.

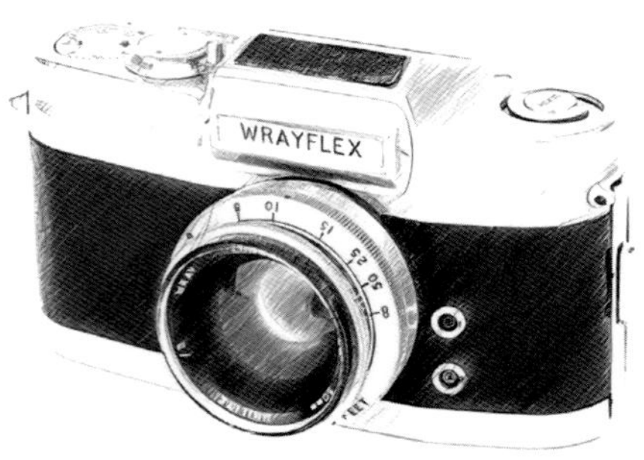

The Wrayflex features a unique reflex mirror, which moves back towards the shutter, then up, allowing the use of deep-seated lenses and obviating the need for retrofocus wide-angle designs. This design is not followed by any other maker, perhaps because it creates significant shutter lag. Only five lenses in four focal lengths (35, 50, 90, and 135mm) are available and, over a 10-year run, just 3,000 are produced.

---

### TRIVIA

Wray's 50mm *f* 2 Unilite lens was a patented design. When Corfield later introduced their 45mm Lumax *f* 1.9 lens for their Periflex camera (see **1953**) they unwittingly infringed the Wray patent and were obliged to acknowledge this fact. The other fascinating feature of the Wrayflex is that it is the only 35mm camera conceived by two women: Katie Studdert and Helena Ruth.

---

**1951:** Bing Crosby Laboratories, which are funded by Crosby (1902–1977) and headed by engineer John Mullin (1913–1999), create an early video tape recorder (VTR) using high-speed tape. It works but is not practical and is never commercially produced. Digital camera technology will evolve from the technology that records television images, although it won't happen until Kodak engineer Steve Sasson develops his digital camera (see **1975**).

---

### TRIVIA

By 1952, Ampex has a design team led by engineers Charles Ginsburgwill (1920–1992) and Ray Dolby (1933–2013), working on a video tape recorder that uses a spinning head and relatively slow-moving tape. Their VR-1000, introduced in 1956, is the first commercially successful video tape recorder, and Ampex will go on to dominate the field.

---

**1951:** The Ilford Witness is a 35mm coupled-rangefinder camera made in the U.K. by Ilford. The camera has a focal-plane shutter with speeds 1 to 1/1000 second plus "B" and "T," with the slow speeds (1 to 1/25 second) controlled by a separate dial. The shutter is synchronized for bulb and electronic flash, with separate sockets on the front of the body. The Witness has a unique lens mount. Based on a standard LTM screw mount but includes an ingenious "interrupted thread" bayonet modification. On both the camera and the lens mounting threads, three grooved channels machined at 90° to the threads enable the lens to be pushed (instead of being screwed) directly into the camera mount. A simple quick twist then engages and secures the "interrupted threads."

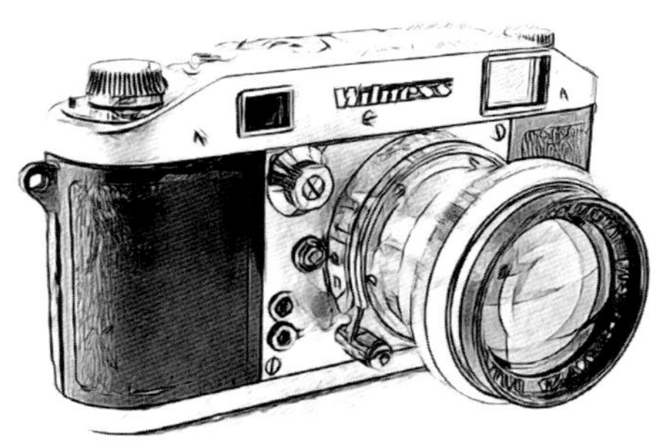

It offers sleeker lines and, some say, a higher level of quality than either the Leica or Contax cameras of the day. But, production difficulties, and management's decision to focus on cheaper models, lead to its being discontinued in 1953. It has been said that the Witness, with its total production of just 350 and few survivors, is rarer than a Stradivarius, of which 512 examples survive.

**AUCTION MADNESS**

In 2013, an Ilford Witness, with collapsible 5cm *f* 2.9 Daron lens, sold for €14,400 (roughly $18,500) at auction. As of late 2020, another Witness is on offer, with a Dallmeyer Super-Six, 2-inch *f* 1.9 lens, for £15,000 (about $19,500).

**1951:** Following the war, the British army contracts with the British aircraft instrument maker Reid & Sigrist (Leicester) to produce a 35mm camera. Reid & Sigrist make the Reid III, a version of the Leica IIIb, using the now-royalty-free patents of Ernst Leitz, Wetzlar. They use the Leica thread mount, while adapting other features according to their assembly needs. The camera features M-sync (for flashbulbs) and, by 1953, X-sync (electronic flash), as well. The cameras are typically fitted with a Taylor-Hobson Anastigmat 50mm *f* 2.0 lens in a collapsible barrel.

The Reid is of high quality and finish, but also of high cost, and is more expensive than an imported Leica IIIf, even with a U.K. import duty of 25%. In 1958, a simpler version, the Reid I, without the slow speeds or rangefinder, is introduced and some 500 units are made, mostly for the British military. By the time production ends, in 1964, between 2,800 and 2,900 Reid cameras are made.

**AUCTION MADNESS**

Because there are more Reids than, say, copies of the Ilford Witness, they are not as sought after by collectors. Still, as of late 2020, a Reid III Body with a Taylor Hobson Anastigmat 2-inch *f* 2 lens was on offer by a London firm for a modest £2,000 (roughly $2,600).

**1951:** Kodak introduces Eastmancolor, a 35 mm color motion picture negative film, followed by a matching print film in early 1952. The first commercial feature film to use Eastmancolor is the National Film Board of Canada's documentary *Royal Journey*, released in December of the year. *Foxfire* (filmed in 1954), becomes the last American-made movie photographed with a Technicolor three-strip camera.

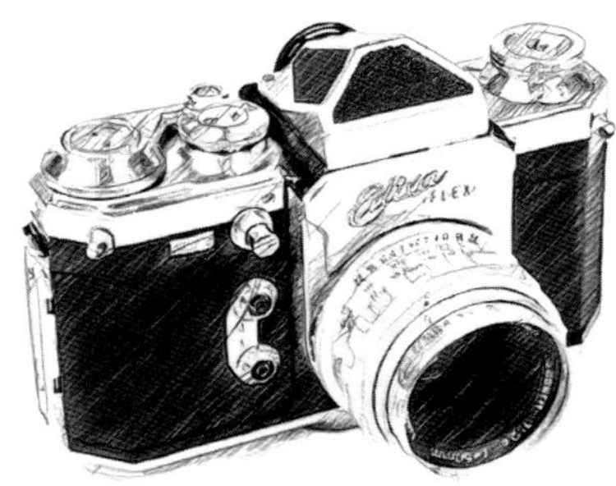

**1951:** After the war, Heinrich Wirgin (now known as Henry Wirgin) leaves America and, with the help of the U.S. government, restarts the Wirgin company in Wiesbaden, West Germany, where he brings a series of viewfinder cameras to market under the Edinex brand (see **1927**). In 1954, he will produce West Germany's first mirror reflex camera for 35mm film, the Edixa Reflex. It is a market success.

Curiously, Wirgin simultaneously made four lines of Edixa cameras. The Type A (shutter speeds up to 1/1000 second), Type B (which has a spring mechanism to close the lens diaphragm at the moment of shutter release), Type C (with uncoupled meter), and the Type D (with exposure times up to nine seconds). In the end, over 60 different variations of Edixa Reflex are made. In 1960, the types B, C, and D will get rapid mirrors and improved shutter mechanics.

---

### TRIVIA

The original name of the first Edixa SLR model was the "Komet," but the Wirgin company had to change the name after complaints from two other companies with identically named products.

---

**1951:** Ihagee (Dresden) brings a lower-cost version of the Exakta to market: the Exa series. The Exas are greatly simplified versions of the Exakta Varex. In place of the focal plane shutter, the mirror doubles as the "opening" shutter blade, and a curved metal guillotine is the "closing" blade. This limits the available shutter speeds to 1/25, 1/50, 1/100, 1/250 second plus B. (Later versions had a top speed of just 1/150.) This in turn limits the usefulness of the camera with long lenses or for sports photography. Use of a smaller mirror (to save cost) means that the

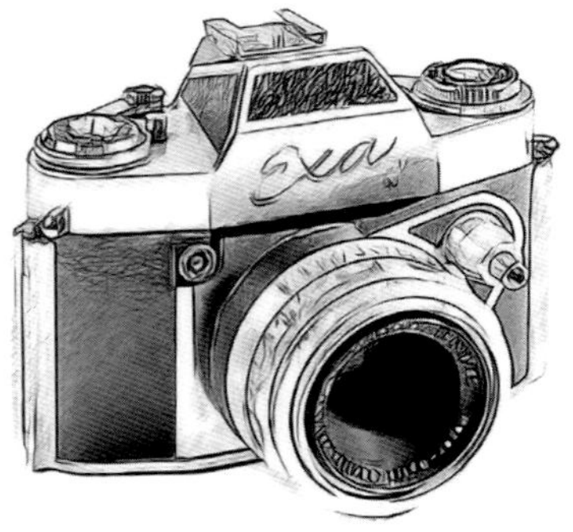

camera suffers from cropping of the top and bottom of the image in the viewfinder when long lenses, extension tubes, or bellows are used. The Exa is manufactured from 1952 through 1970.

In 1959, the Exa II will arrive, a second low-cost version of the Exakta. Called the Exa 500 in some markets, it has a fixed pentaprism and a regular vertical-running focal-plane shutter with expanded, but still limited, speeds from 1/2 second to 1/250 plus B. The Exa II does not replace the Exa series, but co-exists, providing a step-up from the Exa for those who cannot afford the Exakta. They are made until 1977 or so, well after Ihagee is absorbed into VEB Pentacon. Both series accept Exakta lenses.

---

### TRIVIA

From 1977 to 1987, VEB Pentacon build another Exa line: the Exa Ib (later renamed the Ic for no apparent reason), which is basically an Exa which takes Pentax/Practica M42 screw-mount lenses.

---

### ODDITIES

This little discretely unmarked beauty is a Krasnogorsk F-21. As befits a spy camera, it is also known by its aliases: AJAX-12, Ajaks-12, Ayaks-12, and АЯАКС-12.

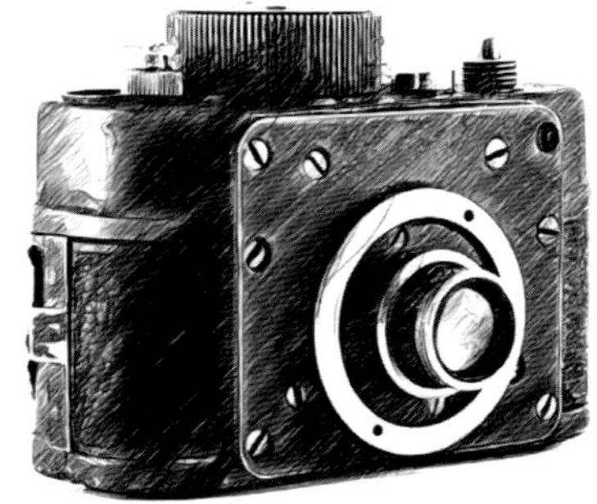

Built in limited numbers by Moscow's KMZ during the Cold War, it was designed to be used with a long cable release, so you could poke it around a corner and shoot, without being seen. The large knob on top winds a spring motor that will power the camera for 22 exposures, though the exposure counter only goes up to 18. A small cassette holds 21mm-wide film, which must be cut from a 35mm roll and then loaded, all in a darkroom, before use. The behind-the-lens shutter has two large blades which, when closed, allow the user to change the lens without fogging the film. Several fixed-focus lenses were produced for the Krasnogorsk, from a 28mm $f$ 2 to tiny lenses (shown) which can poke through a buttonhole of a suit. The shutter speeds are 1/100, 1/30, 1/10, and B. It has neither a viewfinder nor a flash shoe, but it does have two side pins for affixing various articles of camouflage.

---

**1952:** Eastman Kodak start making plastic moulded viewfinder lenses. They work so well for this purpose that Kodak starts using moulded plastic taking lenses in its low-cost cameras just seven years later. As photographic lenses, their use can best be described as "adequate," but comparable to the inexpensive glass lenses used in cameras at similar price points. Unfortunately, these plastic lenses eventually yellow, reducing their ability to transmit light.

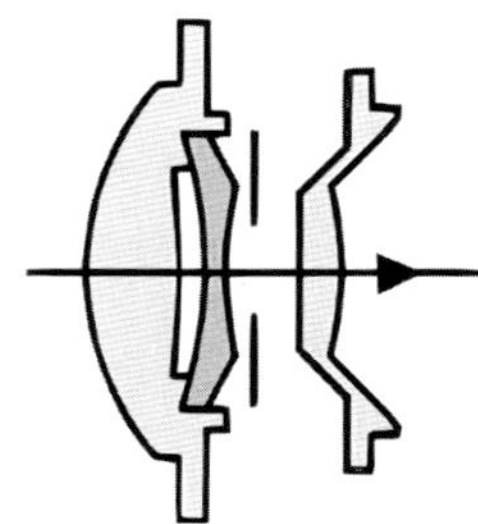

---

### TRIVIA

In the early 1950s, there are only three or four plastics suitable for lens-making, and none with the index of refraction equal to that of barium crown glass, so designers must work with low-index-of-refraction designs. Still, the advantages of cost and ease of assembly (one element can be moulded to fit into another, not to mention that aspherical lenses can be moulded as readily as spherical ones), make them popular in low-cost cameras.

---

**1952:** Kodak bring out their Brownie 127, which proves popular, selling in the millions between 1952 and 1967. It's a Bakelite camera with a simple meniscus lens and a curved film plane to compensate for the deficiencies of the lens.

**1952:** The Aperture Foundation is founded as a non-profit arts institution by Ansel Adams, Minor White (1908–1976), Barbara Morgan, and Dorothea Lange, among others, to create a forum for fine art photography. One of its many endeavours is to publish *Aperture* magazine. The first issue is Spring 1952, and it is still being published today. The Aperture Foundation will go on to publish over 500 fine art photography books, starting with Edward Weston's *The Flame of Recognition*, in 1965.

**1952:** The highly flammable nitrate film base is finally replaced by the acetate "safety film" base in 35mm film stocks.

---

### ODDITIES

The "Look," built in 1952 by Nitto Seiko (see **1938**), somewhat resembles a Contax and uses that camera's double cassette system, with no rewind mechanism (the faux rewind knob was used only the tension the film). The lens is fixed but range-finder coupled, and features a behind-the-lens rotary shutter. The Look was also the first non-Minolta camera to sport a Minolta-made Rokkor lens. It seems the Look "Model A" couldn't com-pete with the other Contax-Leica copies on the market, for a Look "Model B" was never made.

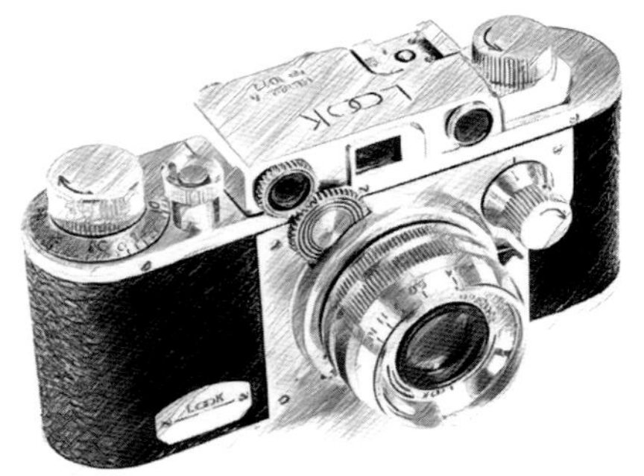


In 1954, the lower-priced Elega 35 is created by removing the rangefinder from the Look and using a cheaper "Eleger" lens. Sales remain poor and both cameras soon disappear.

---

**1952:** The Asahi Optical Company's Asahiflex I is the first Japanese-made 35mm SLR camera. It is fitted with a 50mm *f* 3.5 Takumar lens of the Tessar design and has a cloth curtain focal-plane shutter with shutter speeds ranging from 1/20 to 1/500 second plus Bulb.

---

**TRIVIA**

The lenses were called "Takumar" (later, Super-Takumar or SMC-Takumar), after the great Japanese-born painter and photographer Takuma Kajiwara (1876–1960). Takuma was, it seems, a great friend of the then-president of Asahi Optical, and the name was used until 1975, when Pentax introduced their "K" bayonet-mount lenses under the simpler "Pentax" brand.

---

**1952:** A new division of the Metz company (a maker of radios and TVs) is established in Solms, near Wetzlar, Germany, to make electronic flash units ordered by Braun and Agfa. The units are a great success, and the firm quickly introduces models under its own "Mecablitz" brand. It quickly becomes a world leader in the field, and production passes five million flash units in 1982.

---

**TRIVIA**

With electronic flash comes the infamous "red eye effect." This happens because the light of the flash occurs too fast for the pupil to close and much of the very bright light from the flash passes into the eye through the pupil. The light then reflects off the back of the eyeball and out through the pupil. Since the light goes through the blood in the choroid, which nourishes the back of the eye, the colour of the eye is red, hence this annoying effect everyone is aware of. It occurred less often with flashbulbs, as they burned much longer than an electronic flash and the pupil had time to close, at least partially, thereby reducing the effect.

---

**1952:** With roots going back to 1941, Seikō Denki Kōgyō K.K. (Seiko Electric Industries Co., Ltd.) produce the first exposure meter to be made in Japan—an incident model called the Sekonic P-1. As well as its own Sekonic brand, the company makes meters sold under different names such as Prinz and Hanimex, while others were built into various Japanese cameras. Its meters are of high quality, and the firm remains in business to this day.

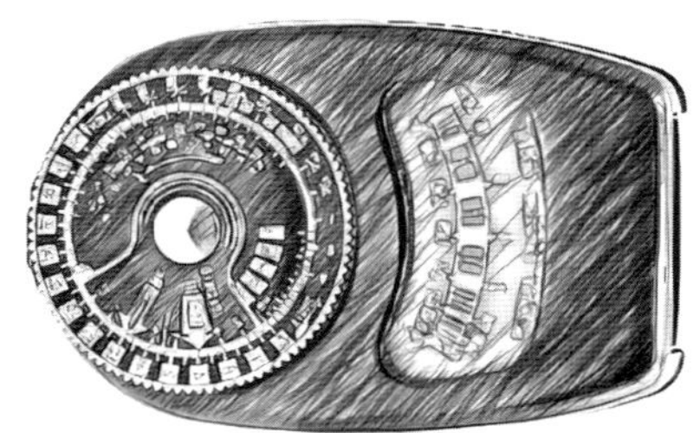

---

**ODDITIES**

Introduced in 1952, the Alsaphot Cyclope (France) is the first camera to use a rotary focal plane shutter, and is capable of synchronizing an electronic flash at 1/1000 second. It uses front surface mirrors to bend the optical path in order to make room for the shutter and is the forerunner of the Olympus Pen-F (see **1963**). For reasons unknown, the cameras also had a Prontor leaf shutter. Versions were made for several years, with a variety of lenses and Prontor shutters.

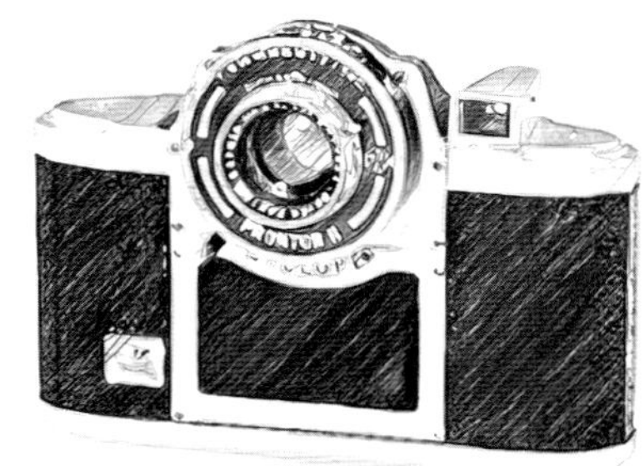

**1952:** The Canon IVb becomes the world's first camera to feature X flash synchronization for electronic flash units (commonly called Speedlites). It also has the regular FP synchronization for flashbulbs.

**1952:** The Russian camera maker KMZ introduces their Zenit (*ЗЕНИТ* in Cyrillic) SLR, based on its earlier Zorki rangefinder models. Many models are produced over the years, and all are inexpensive cameras of robust construction, if somewhat lacking in finesse. Consistent lens quality is a problem and KMZ ceases camera production in 2005.

---

### TRIVIA

The early Zenits used M39 (Leica) thread mount lenses, a mount borrowed from their Zorki, which was a copy of the Leica. But the flange-to-film distance was incompatible, as the mount had to be moved forward to accommodate the mirror. Thus, lenses made to fit the Leica or Zorki would mount on a Zenit but would only focus at extremely close distances. This configuration was often referred to as the ZM-39 mount. Later models would feature the Pentax/ Praktica thread-mount, and later still would use the Pentax "K" mount, both of which were designed for SLR use.

---

### TRIVIA

In the late 1940s and 1950s, these Big Bertha cameras came in a variety of shapes and sizes, sometimes weighing up to 120 pounds (54 kg). All custom-built outside the Graflex factory by various makers, they were nearly all based on the 5 x 7 Home Portrait Graflex, though some were based on various 4 x 5 Graflex bodies (often referred to as "Little Berthas"). Nearly all had 28- or 40-inch (roughly 700 to 1000mm) lenses, but one made for Associated Press had a 60-inch (1500mm) *f* 8 Dallmeyer fitted. Note that the $795 price, circa 1952, would be over $7,000 today.

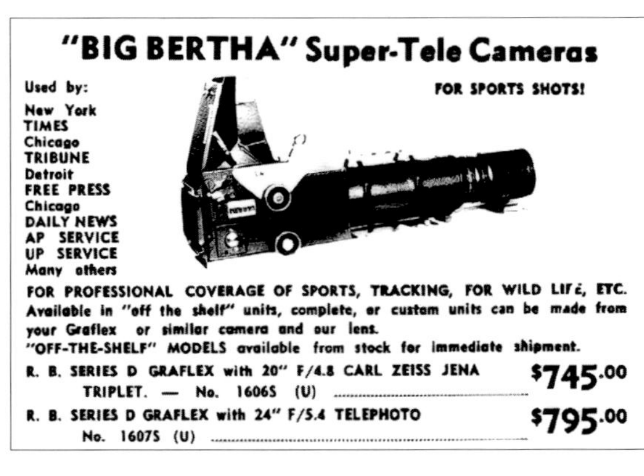


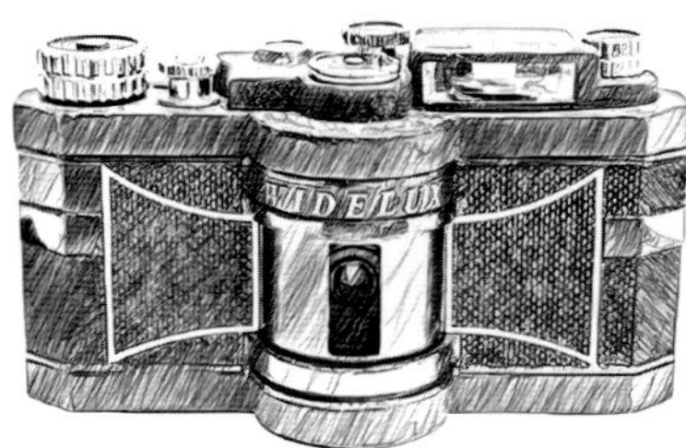

**1952:** The Panon Camera Co., a small-scale camera maker in Tokyo, Japan, introduces its Panon panoramic cameras for 120 film. These will be followed by the better known Widelux (see **1959**) for 35mm film. Instead of a shutter, both cameras have a slit that exposes the film as the lens pivots on a horizontal arc, projecting an image onto a cylindrical film gate. In 1987, Panon again offers a model for 120 film, now called the Widelux 1500, but production ends when the factory suffers a fire in the mid-1990s. The last 35mm model is made in 2000 and the firm shuts its doors around 2005.

**1952:** With the Cold War heating up, Leica start making plans to avoid losing their entire operation once again to war. They open a branch factory, Ernst Leitz Canada Ltd., in Midland, Ontario, Canada. Equipped with the latest, most sophisticated mechanical machines and computers, the plant allows Leitz to leap ahead in both mechanical and optical quality.

A major reason to establish in Canada is that in the USA, the trademark "Leitz" is still under alien property control and Leitz cannot use its own name there. Immigration for German staff is also much easier in Canada, as U.S. immigration is rather tight after the war. Thus, Canada is the best choice.

---

### TRIVIA

It was necessary to establish some quick sales right at the beginning, because Leitz was allowed to bring only $50,000 into the country and they had to make sure that they would not run out of money before new revenues started to come in. Unfortunately, the new facilities were not quite ready for operation when the "Leica people" arrived. To avoid losing precious time, an assembly facility was temporarily set up in the Midland Ice Arena. The first lens components were finished after only one week and the first completed Leica lenses and cameras were ready after only four weeks.

Lens designer Walter Mandler (1922–2005) was sent from Wetzlar to Midland, on a six-month loan. He liked the area so much that he stayed, became a Canadian citizen, and lived in Midland for the rest of his life. His skills establishing Midland as one of the foremost lens design houses in the world. His crowning achievement was the design of the 50mm $f$ 1.0 Noctilux, which was made in Midland from 1976 to 2008. Mandler's Midland lens design team was so successful that most Leica lenses of the day were designed in Midland, even if their manufacture was to be done in Germany (see **1972**).

---

**1953:** The Perriflex is introduced by K. G. Corfield Ltd. in England. It is a 35mm camera that resembles the Leica Standard and has a Leica thread-mount lens and a unique retractable periscope which lowers into the light path for through-the-lens focusing. Pressing the shutter release moves the spring-loaded periscope out of the film path before the focal-plane shutter operates. In 1959, the company moves to Northern Ireland, where several new models are produced until the mid-1960s, when camera production ceases.

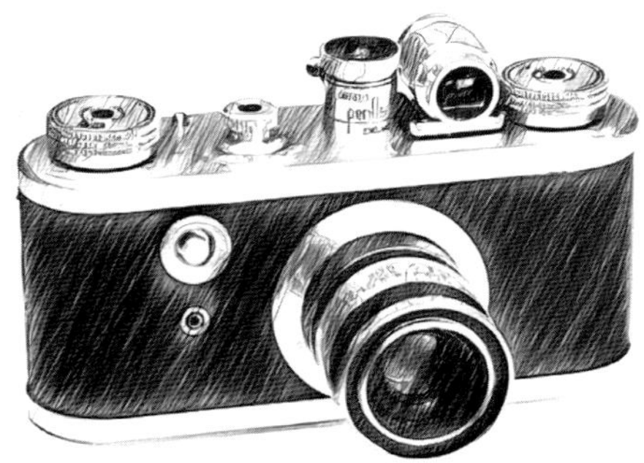

**1953:** Hasselblad introduces its 1000F, with a redesigned shutter and a lower top speed of 1/1000 second, rather than the somewhat over-ambitious 1/1600 of the original model. The company makes a number of internal improvements, including a redesign of the "gear stack" to improve reliability. The camera also now comes with an 80mm *f*2.8 Tessar from Carl Zeiss AG. The 135mm *f*3.5 and 250mm *f*5.6 Zeiss Sonnar lenses are also offered, thus starting a long association with Zeiss. The 1000F shutter proves to be much more reliable than the earlier 1600F but is still somewhat problematic.

**1953:** What remains of the original Agfa plant in Wolfen is restarted by the East German government. A trade agreement settlement gives VEB Film und Chemiefaserwerk Agfa Wolfen the right to sell its products under the Agfa brand in Eastern Europe, while the newly re-established Agfa (West), in West Germany, has the rights to the name in the rest of the world.

**1953:** Zeiss Ikon (Dresden) produce their Contax "E," the first SLR with a built-in light meter. It has an external selenium photoelectric cell mounted behind a door on the pentaprism housing above the lens. The door is a translucent plastic panel, which diffuses the light for daytime use, and the door opens to expose more surface area for metering in dim light. The meter is uncoupled, so the photographer needs to read the meter and then manually set the shutter speed and lens aperture to match the exposure reading.

**1953:** Charles A. Hulcher (1910–1994) develops his "Hulcher 70" while working for the National Advisory Committee for Aeronautics (the predecessor to NASA), because scientists need a way to study rocket launches in slow motion to find out why some of them exploded. The camera becomes so popular, however, that Hulcher can quit his day job and open his own business in 1954. The original Hulcher 70 shoots 70mm film at 50 frames per second (fps). Various models of the camera are built, including one that pushes the speed up to 75 fps with 70mm film. Eventually the company starts producing cameras that shoot 35mm film, and that's when they reach the

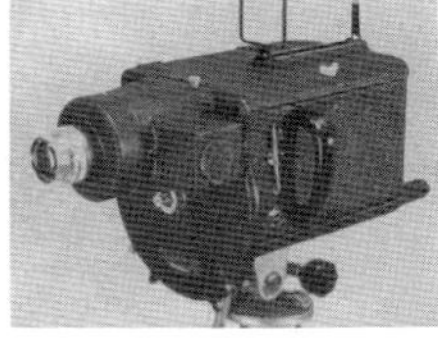



100-fps mark. The cameras achieve this speed by running 100 feet of film between two large spools like a movie camera. But, unlike a movie camera, Hulcher runs the film horizontally instead of vertically, creating a larger image area and in turn a higher-resolution negative. The company also develops panoramic cameras, press cameras and specialized cameras used in aeronautic and military applications.

### TRIVIA

When the Hulcher company started, there were other high-speed cameras already on the market. But the drawback to those cameras was that their frame rates were too high and thus burned through too much film. For sports photographers, the Hulcher was fast enough to capture the action but didn't cost an arm, a leg, and the promise of your first born to operate.

One of the most famous photographers to use the Hulcher was *Sports Illustrated* photographer John Zimmerman, who would often disable the film-advance mechanism, creating vivid multiple exposures that captured the graceful movement of various sports figures.

By 2012, however, the company was down to just four employees, still selling and maintaining the Hulcher 35 (roughly $7,000 at that time) and Hulcherama cameras as well as performing contract machine work for other local companies. As of 2021, the firm's website seems not to exist, but its Facebook page does, and states: "We now specialize in metal finishing and machine work."

**1953:** First shown in Photokina in 1952, the Praktina FX, from VEB Kamera-Werkstätten Niedersedlitz (see **1946**) is the world's first "system camera," beating the much-better-known Nikon F (see **1959**) by six years. Though not very well known in the West, the East German Praktina offers a wide array of lenses from 35 to 500mm, and many unique accessories including motor drives (both spring-driven and electric) and interchangeable finders (even a modified prism with built-in light metering)!

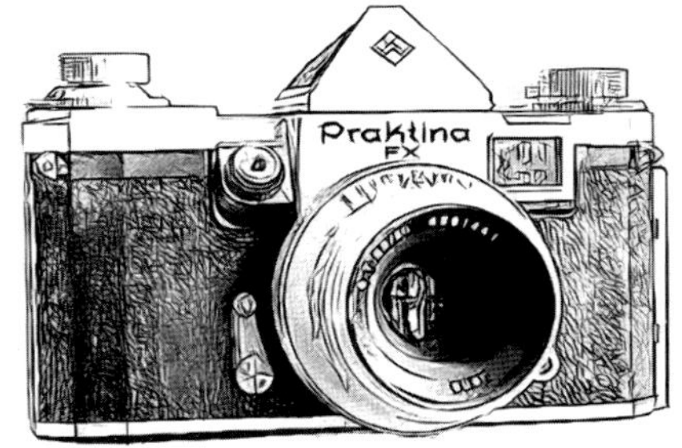


The Praktina features both a straight-through optical viewfinder (to improve usability in low light and for use as a "sports finder" for fast action shots) and a fully interchangeable viewfinder and focus screens for critical work, a first for any 35mm SLR.

The Praktina's firsts include the internal semi-automatic diaphragm in 1954 and a fully automatic one in 1958, despite the fact that the FX never gains an instant return mirror. The price in 1956 for a Praktina FX with a Zeiss Biotar 50mm *f*2 lens was $297.50, or roughly $2,800 today. Development stops in the late 1950s, production ends in 1960 with almost 67,000 cameras made.

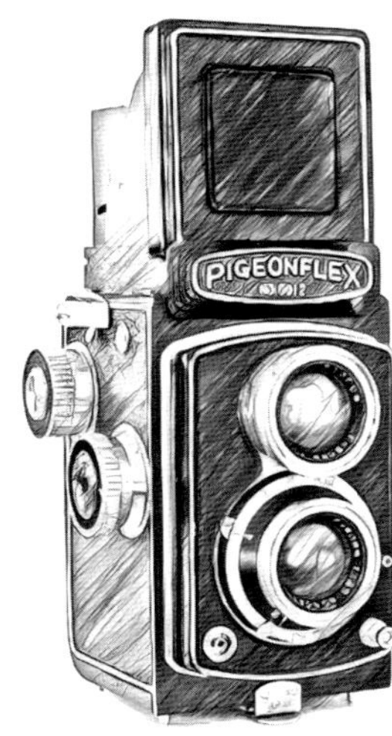


**1953:** Although started in the last months of the Second World War, the Yashima Precision Works produces the Pigeonflex 6 x 6cm TLR for Endō Kamera-ten or Endō Camera Stores. (Later Pigeonflex cameras are produced by a little-known firm, Shinano Kōki.) In June, Yashima changes its name to Yashima Kōgaku Seiki (meaning Yashima Optical Precision Instruments), reflecting its new involvement in the camera business. Later in the year, it introduces its first camera under its own name, the Yashimaflex, another 6 x 6cm TLR. The next year the Yashimaflex is followed by a number of models called Yashicaflex.

---

**TRIVIA**

The Yashica brand is constructed from Yashima and Camera, similar to the way "Leica," "Konica," and many other brands evolved. The "flex" refers to the "reflex" nature of the viewfinder.

---

**1953:** A small Japanese company, Teikoku Kogaku, introduces its 5cm *f* 1.1 Zunow lens in M39 (Leica) and Nikon "S" mounts. It is designed by Michisaburo Hamano (who previously worked at Nippon Kogaku) and features nine elements in five groups. It remains the fastest lens available until Nikon matches the speed with their 50mm *f* 1.1 Nikkor in 1956. Zunow proves to be a highly innovative firm, producing top quality (but expensive to make) lenses, but goes broke shortly after the introduction of their ground-breaking Zunow camera (see **1958**), and is absorbed by Yashica by 1960.

---

**AUCTION MADNESS**

Zunow lenses were made in mounts for Leica, Canon, and Contax, although very few of these super-speed lenses were produced, and 70 years on they fetch upwards of $7,000 at auction.

---

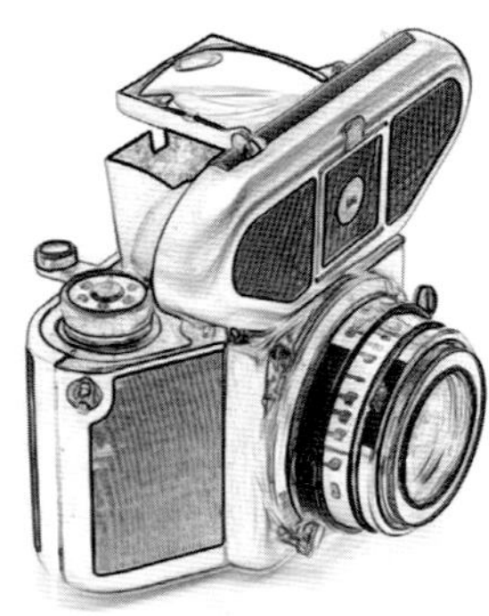

**ODDITIES**

Heinz Kilfitt creates the Metz Mecaflex, which is first presented at the 1951 Photokina and shipped in 1953. It is the first (and only) square format 35mm SLR, which takes up to fifty exposures of 24 × 24mm frames on a 36 exposure 135 film. A behind-the-lens Prontor leaf shutter is used with bayonet mount for interchangeable lenses. In 1958, production was taken over by Kilfitt and moved to Monaco, where it was made for another seven years.

---

**1953:** Zeiss Ikon (Stuttgart, West Germany) offers the first of what will be a long line of Contaflex 35mm leaf-shuttered SLR cameras, utilizing the newly developed Compur reflex shutter. It is the first SLR to employ a between-the-lens shutter and still allow interchangeable lenses. Many models will follow until 1972.

---

**TRIVIA**

When Zeiss Ikon stopped making cameras, they had prototypes in various stages of development. One of them was to be a successor to the Contaflex line with an electronic shutter. The prototype ended in the hands of a firm named Weber, which presented the camera at a Photokina show under the name Weber SL75. However, they could not afford to put it into production and never found a partner to back the project, so the camera was never produced.

The mount for the Weber SL75 was a slightly modified Contarex mount (see **1958**), altered just enough that Contarex lenses would not fit. At one point, Zeiss did advertise seven lenses for the Weber, but only a very small batch, perhaps fewer than 20, of the Carl Zeiss T* 50mm *f* 1.4 Planar were produced for the Weber. Since the camera was never made, the lenses are orphans. This has not stopped one being offered on eBay, in 2020, for an eye-watering $8,900!

---

**1954:** Founded in Nagoya (Japan) in 1894 as a textile shop, Kowa manufactures cameras of modest mechanical quality but with decent optics, from 1954 to 1978. They continue to this day making binoculars, telescopes, and medical optics (among much else), and in 2005 market a "spotting scope" with an integrated digital camera, thereby again becoming a camera manufacturer—of a sort. In 2015, Kowa will return to the consumer market, producing three lenses for the micro-FourThirds (mFT) cameras.

---

**BACKSTORY**

The use a leaf-shutter in their Contaflex cameras was encouraged by the fact that Zeiss already owned the two major leaf-shutter builders, Deckel (Compur) and Gauthier (Prontor). But employing a between-the-lens leaf shutter brought considerable restrictions on lens design.

Later models had a Zeiss Tessar 50mm *f* 2.8 lens with interchangeable front elements. Supplementary lenses in 35mm, 85mm, and 115mm focal lengths, all *f* 4, had to share a common group of rear elements. However, this was not considered a great handicap, as amateur photographers rarely bought additional lenses.

As well, all models could take an 8 x 30B monocular (equivalent to a 400mm lens) which was attached by means of the filter threads. Such an arrangement also requires the shutter to stay open before the picture is taken, in order to see through the reflex finder. This then requires an auxiliary shutter behind the mirror to stay closed. When the shutter-release button is depressed, the camera must close the lens shutter, reduce the lens aperture to the pre-set *f*-stop, raise the reflex mirror, and open the auxiliary shutter. Then the exposure can take place by opening and closing the lens shutter. And this must happen very, very quickly and reliably. The big advantage (for some) is a camera with flash synchronization at all shutter speeds. No Contaflex model ever acquired a rapid return mirror and only a limited range of extra lenses were available. As photography matured and photographers demanded ever more features, these shortcomings would prove fatal for the Contaflex.

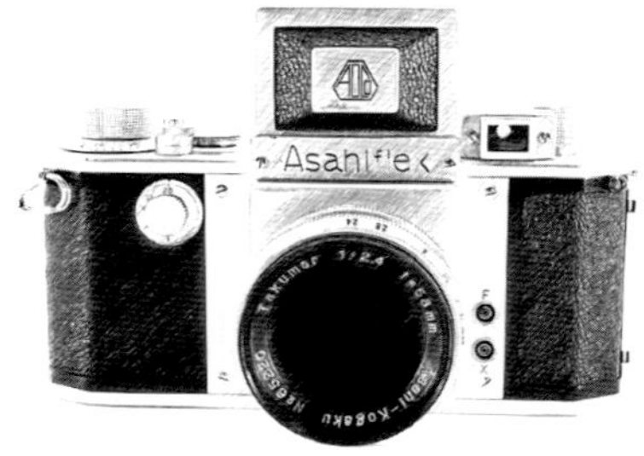

**1954:** The Asahiflex IIB is the world's first series production camera to feature an instant-return mirror. Soon, all Japanese SLR makers use this feature, while the Germans are slow to catch up. But the camera still does not have a pentaprism—it uses a waist-level finder instead.

> **TRIVIA**
>
> The mechanism used in the Asahiflex was invented by Topcon (who called it the "Wink Mirror"), but was first used by Asahi Optical, under license. This was not an unusual state of affairs in the Japanese camera business.

**1954:** The Simmon Brothers, best known for their line of Omega enlargers (see **1936**), release their first and only camera for the civilian market, the Simmon Omega 120 rangefinder, for 6 x 7cm exposures on 120 roll film. The camera comes equipped with a coupled rangefinder and a 90mm *f* 3.5 Omicron lens in a Wollensak Rapax Synchro flash-synchronized shutter with speeds from 1 second to 1/400 second plus B.

> **TRIVIA**
>
> While enlarger production continues in the USA, camera manufacturing is moved to Japan in late 1954, where they are made by Konishiroku (Konica), with the Koni-Omega brand name. In 1961, the brothers sell their company to Kong Photo, which, in the 1970s, becomes Berkey Marketing.

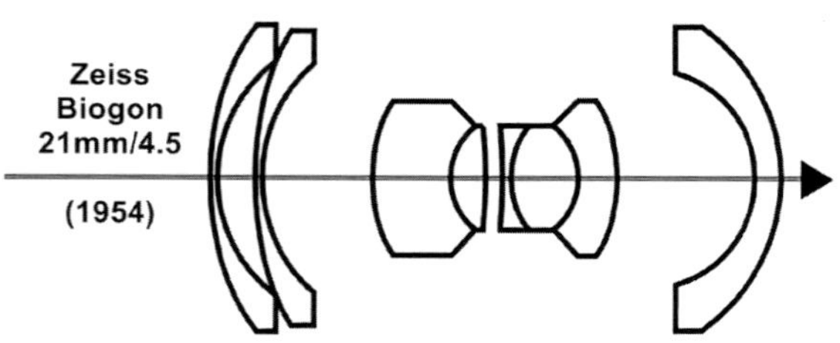


**1954:** Carl Zeiss AG introduce the Biogon 21mm *f* 4.5 for the Contax 35mm rangefinder camera. Both it and its evolutionary successor, the Zeiss Hologon 15mm *f* 8 (see **1966**) are almost symmetrical designs, made possible because they do not need to clear the mirror in an SLR. The Biogon design takes advantage of the large negative elements to limit the light falloff of retrofocus wide-angle lenses.

**1954:** Hasselblad mates the ground-breaking new 38mm Biogon lens for medium-format cameras, designed by Bertele of Zeiss, to a shallow non-reflex body to produce the SWA (super-wide-angle) body employing an external viewfinder. Though a specialty product not intended to sell in large numbers, the SWA is an impressive achievement, and derivatives are sold for decades.

**TRIVIA**

Two things factored in Hasselblad's success. First, Hasselblad took their two products (the 1000F and SWA) to the 1954 Photokina trade show in Germany and word began to spread. Second, in December of 1954, the 1000F camera received a rave review from the influential American photography magazine *Modern Photography*. *Modern* puts over 500 rolls of film through their test unit and then intentionally dropped it, twice. It continued to function.

**1954:** First introduced in 1940 as a sheet film (ASA 200), Kodak sells Tri-X (ASA 400) in both 35mm and 120 formats. It becomes, and remains, the world's most popular black-and-white film.

**1954:** A small group in the back of Kyiv's Arsenal factory starts producing their Salyut, a 6 x 6 SLR. It is the Soviet Union's first effort at a sophisticated medium-format camera, and some 50,000 are made.

**TRIVIA**

The Salyuts are poor copies of the 1948 Hasselblad 1600F. So poor, that adoring fans (yes, there are some!) talk about the wonderful things that can be done with them *"if you are actually able to coax one into working."*

In 2020, the introduction to one web-forum about Kyiv-made cameras summed it up when it said, "Welcome to the best forum about the worst cameras in the world!"

**1954:** In April, at the fourth Photokina, Leica introduces the Leica M3, the first interchangeable-lens bayonet-mount Leica body with an integrated viewfinder/rangefinder. The M3 features a bright, life-size viewfinder with variable frame-lines and automatic parallax correction. The shutter speed dial does not rotate, and film is advanced by a "rapid wind" lever rather than a knob. It has a self-resetting frame counter and an exposure meter that slides into the accessory shoe and couples to the shutter speed dial. Its revolutionary design sets the standard for 35mm rangefinder cameras, both film and digital, for decades to come.

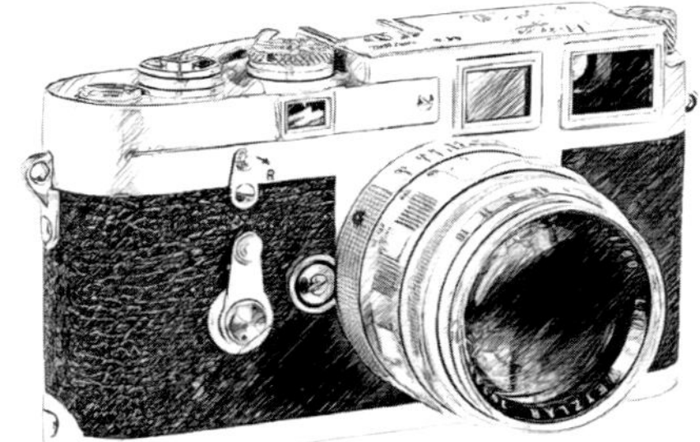

**1954:** Renowned war correspondent, *LIFE* photographer, and Magnum Photo founder Robert Capa dies, 25 May, 1954, in Thai-Binh, Indochina (now Vietnam), when he runs ahead of his group and steps on a land mine.

**1954:** Honeywell acquire Heiland Research Corp. of Denver, Colorado. Heiland manufacture flash synchronizers and both bulb and electronic flash units under the Strobonar brand. They become the photo-importing arm of Honeywell and eventually the U.S. distributor of Asahi Pentax.

**1954:** The Japan Camera Industry Association (JCIA) begins promoting development of a high-quality photographic industry to increase exports as part of Japan's post-Second World War economic recovery. To that end, the Japan Machine Design Center (JMDC) and Japan Camera Inspection Institute (JCII) ban the copying of foreign camera designs (such as the Leica look-alikes of the early 1950s by Tanack, Nicca, Leotax, and others). They also prevent Japanese makers from copying each other's designs.

To raise the image of Japanese cameras abroad, they establish minimum quality levels for exports. This is enforced by a testing program before the issuance of shipping permits and is the start of the famous gold oval "PASSED" stickers found on Japanese cameras.

---

**TRIVIA**

A "passed" sticker did not mean that a particular item had been inspected. It meant that a sample had been tested by the JCII, and that it met or exceeded the minimum quality levels for export. The stickers were then put on all cameras/lenses of the batch from which the sample had been drawn. Like a "Made in Germany" sticker, it was an assertion of quality, but not a guarantee.

---

**1954:** Ihagee introduce lenses for their Exakta and Exa models with an arm that fits in front of their front-mounted shutter release. Thus, pressing the shutter button closes the aperture, while releasing it opens the aperture again, for best viewing. It is a good idea, but it is not made available on all their lenses.

**1955:** Kilfitt (Munich, West Germany) release their Makro-Kilar 40mm $f$3.5 lens for Exakta and Exa 35mm SLRs. It is the first lens to provide continuous focusing from infinity to a mere two inches (50mm) from the front element. The Makro-Kilar is essentially a Tessar design mounted in an extra-long-draw triple-helical mount. It will be followed the next year by the 90/2.8 Macro-Kilar, which offers true 1:1 magnification.

---

**BACKSTORY**

Designing close-up lenses is not really that hard—an image size that is close to object size increases symmetry. It is getting a sharp image continuously from infinity to close up that is difficult—before the Makro-Kilar, lenses generally did not continuously focus to closer than 1:10 ratio. Today, most SLR lens lines include moderate-aperture macro lenses optimized for high magnification. However, their focal lengths tend to be longer than the Makro-Kilar to allow more working distance.

---

**1955:** Germany's Metrawatt A.G. bring their Horvex 2 to market. It is an excellent meter and suits the films of the day, having ASA/DIN settings that range from a maximum of ASA 400/DIN 25 down to ASA 1.5/DIN 7 (see "DIN" in the Glossary). Shutter speeds go no higher than 1/1000. The Horvex 3 will follow, in 1960, and be sold in the U.S. as the Argus L-3. Metrawatt continues to make exposure meters through 1964, when ownership changes. In 1993, after several more changes in ownership, it will be merged with Gossen to form today's Gossen-Metrawatt, which still market exposure meters under the Gossen brand.

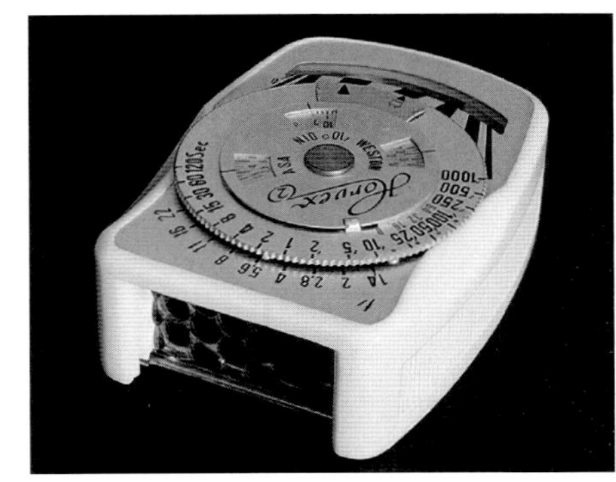

---

**TRIVIA**

The Soviets did not like to spend much on R&D for civilian goods. It would seem they simply copied the Horvex 2 and tweaked the design for Russian consumption, in order to make their "Leningrad" series of exposure meters.

---

**1955:** In August, the Orion Camera Company introduces the Miranda 'T' (for Technology). It is the first Japanese camera with a Pentaprism for eye-level use, which provides an upright and laterally correct image. It is supplied with various standard lenses, including a Zunow 50/1.9. Outside the USA, they are often sold as "Miranda" or "Auto-Miranda" lenses. In the U.S., the Soligor brand is used. The firm will become the Miranda Camera Company in 1957, and Miranda models will be produced until 1976.

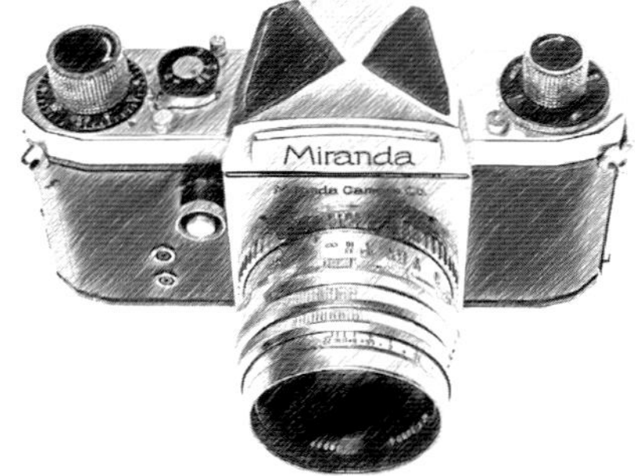

---

**BUSINESS TRIVIA**

As Miranda does not make lenses, all lenses sold for Miranda in the USA (other than the very first few) use AIC's "Soligor" brand. In 1963, using money gained from taking AIC Photo public, Allied will buy a controlling interest in Orion (now called the Miranda Camera Company) and continue until both Allied and AIC Photo go bankrupt in 1976, when both the Miranda and Soligor names disappear.

---

### ODDITIES

The Sputnik is a medium-format twin-lens reflex stereo camera, with a Bakelite body, made by Gomz in Leningrad (now St. Petersburg) and introduced around 1955. Using 120 film, the camera provides six 6 x 6 pairs (or 12 single images). A total of some 86,000 units are produced by Gomz (1955–1961), Loomp (1962–1964), and Lomo (1964–1974), all of which are really the same company under different names at different times. 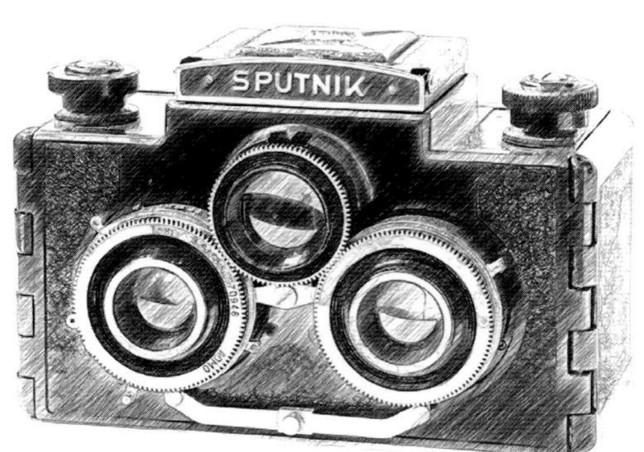

Several versions exist based on shutter speeds, tripod sockets, and lens markings. All have two taking lenses and one viewfinder lens. Most of the cameras are for domestic sale and have their name in Cyrillic letters (for example, Спутник). Those for export have the Sputnik name in Latin characters.

---

**1955:** The Leitz Company builds special versions of their new Leica M3 cameras (see **1954**) for the legendary *LIFE* photographers Alfred Eisenstaedt and David Douglas Duncan. The model numbers are M3E for Eisenstaedt and M3D, for Duncan. The myth is that they were gifts from Leica, but according to Duncan, as he wrote in his 2016 book, *My 20th Century*, "Leica made four M3Ds for me in 1955. They're very silent and had a different type of rapid winder on the bottom. I bought them for $375 [each] in Wetzlar."

All are custom-made black-paint versions with the non-self-resetting frame counter of the M2 and missing the self-timers—modifications necessary to install the gears that connect them to the black Leicavit bottom-mounted rapid-film-advance trigger, previously only available on the screw-mount Leica cameras. Duncan primarily uses the M3D's to cover the Vietnam War. These custom-made cameras will serve as the template for the Leica MP, which will be manufactured in small production runs from 1956.

---

### AUCTION MADNESS

If you have the chance to buy an M3D, don't expect it to be "Minty"—or cheap. Here is the story of Duncan's well-worn M3Ds in his own words: "Cameras 2 and 3, I sold one of them to fellows from Leica in Wetzlar—they still have it—and the other one I sold to a former Marine for about $80,000. He sold it through the WestLicht Photographic Auction in Vienna in 2012 for $2,180,000. The guy who bought it is a very prominent Chinese man living in Hong Kong named Douglas. Unbelievable!"

**1956:** Nippon Kogaku introduce their 50mm *f* 1.1 Nikkor. Its incredible speed, for the day, is matched only by the Zunow (see **1953**). Designed for the Nikon SP rangefinder camera, it is readily available in both inner and outer bayonet styles. A very small number are made in Leica thread mount and are now much sought-after by collectors.

---

### TRIVIA

The *f* 1.1 Nikkor took two years to design. Long before computers, the designers at Nippon Kogaku did all their calculations on an abacus!

---

**1956:** The Zeiss Foundation buys Voigtländer—for their optical design group, most of whom are moved to Oberkochen. In 1965, Zeiss and Voigtländer merge fully, with Zeiss Ikon (Stuttgart) building cameras and Voigtländer producing only the lenses. In 1972, Zeiss Ikon (Stuttgart) ends all operations.

**1956:** Sekonic, rapidly becoming the leading manufacturer of exposure meters in Japan, buys the Norwood Director design in order to gain quick access to the American market with a recognized product. The Norwood Director name is dropped, with the unit becoming first the Sekonic Studio, and then the L-28.

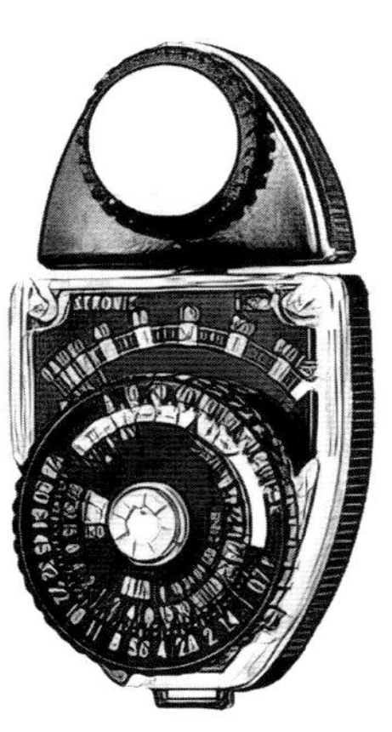

---

### TRIVIA

The L-28 gets a major makeover in 1964, with a redesigned face and calculator dial, a threaded accessories socket, and a needle-lock feature. It gets another facelift in 1970 and again in 1976, becoming the L-398. In 2017, as the L-398A and now with an amorphous silicon metering cell, Sekonic's "Norwood Director" is still being made.

---

**1956:** The world's first commercial, mass-produced aspheric lens element is manufactured by Elgeet for use in the Golden Navitar 12mm *f* 1.2 normal lens for 16mm movie cameras. The lens receives a great deal of industry acclaim.

**1956:** VEB Zeiss Ikon (Jena) release the Praktica FX2. Also marketed as both the Pentacon F and Contax F, these East German cameras are the first to offer fully automatic diaphragm operation by means of an internal pin. It is a huge improvement over Exakta's external system (see **1954**).

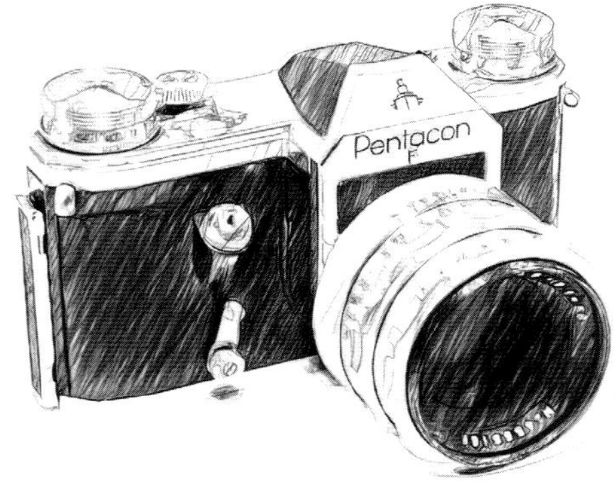

**1956:** Leitz market their "Dual-range" Summicron, a special version with a close-focusing helicoid along with special "eyes" for both the M-3 (see **1954**) and M-2 (see **1957**) cameras, to

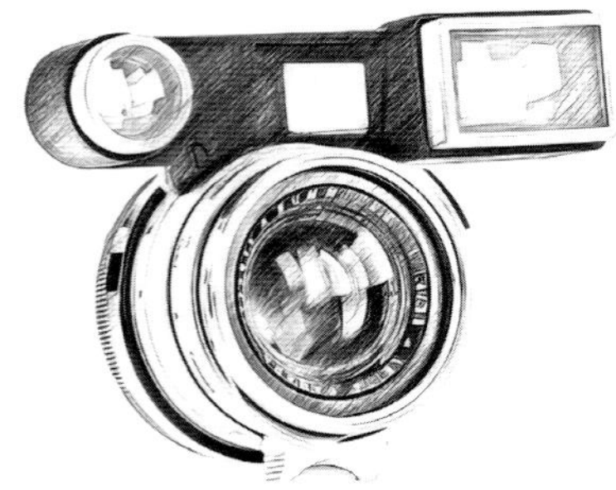

allow parallax-corrected shooting down to 20 or even 19 inches, depending on the camera and version of the "eyes." A 50mm Dual-Range Summicron becomes the highest resolution lens ever tested by the American magazine *Modern Photography*, at over 100 lines per mm. The Dual-Range Summicron will be made until 1968.

Even today, if you wish to shoot closer than 0.7 metres with an M-series Leica, the Dual Range Summicron remains your most convenient choice, though fitting one to a Leica M4, M5, M6, or M7 can be problematic, depending on the camera model and the "eyes." Sadly, they will not fit on the M8 or later digital Leicas. Despite this, the 50mm $f2$ Dual Range Summicron remains unique in the Leica M system and a favourite of users and collectors alike.

**1957:** The original version of Tamron's T-mount, with an M37 x 0.75 thread, is introduced, along with their first T-mount lens, a 135mm $f4.5$ telephoto. It is not a great market success, at least in the USA.

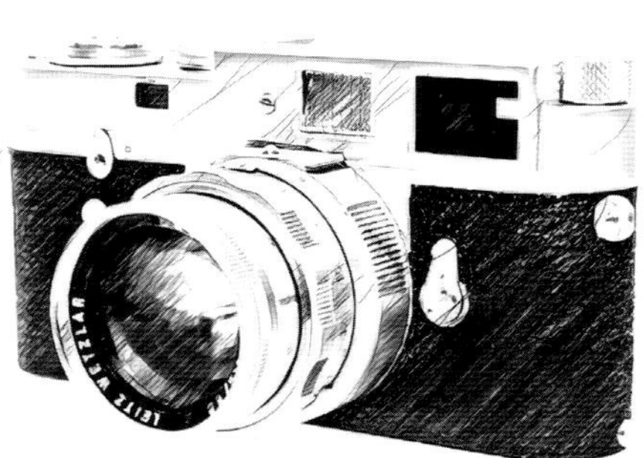

**1957:** Leica bring out their M2 with a viewfinder featuring 35mm, 50mm, and 90mm bright lines, a combination demanded by journalists of the day. It is a simplified, more affordable version of their M3 (see **1954**) without the auto-resetting exposure counter and with a simplified rangefinder (which was a bit more prone to flare). The two models co-exist, setting the design standards for rangefinder cameras.

### ODDITIES

In late 1956 or early 1957, Nippon Kogaku started development of the Nikkorex 8, an 8mm movie camera. The original version was a top-line prototype that was finished in 1959. It featured three interchangeable lenses, on a turret. Film speed could be 16 fps (normal) or 64 fps (slow motion). The direct optical viewfinder changed magnification with each change of lens, and the camera had a selenium-cell match-needle exposure control—in all, a very deluxe machine. However, it was all for naught, as the camera used a film cassette that had to be turned over, halfway through. The cassettes proved expensive to manufacture

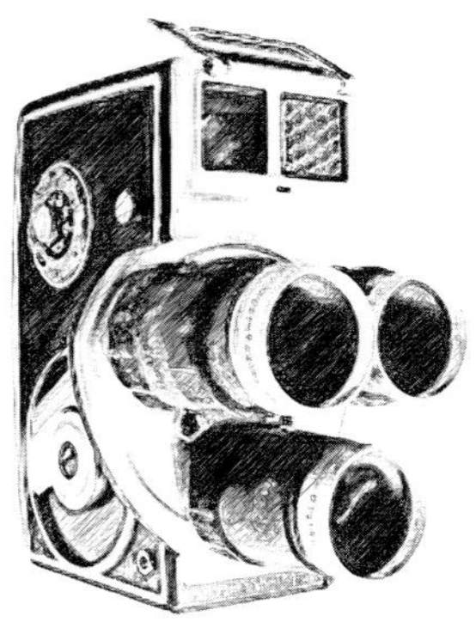

and so the camera was never produced. Later, in 1960, a revised version was released under the Nikkorex name; it was a much simpler camera, although it did boast the world's first CdS (cadmium sulphide) metering system.

**1957:** The Nikon SP is the first rangefinder camera to feature a parallax-corrected viewfinder with automatic frame lines for six different focal lengths.

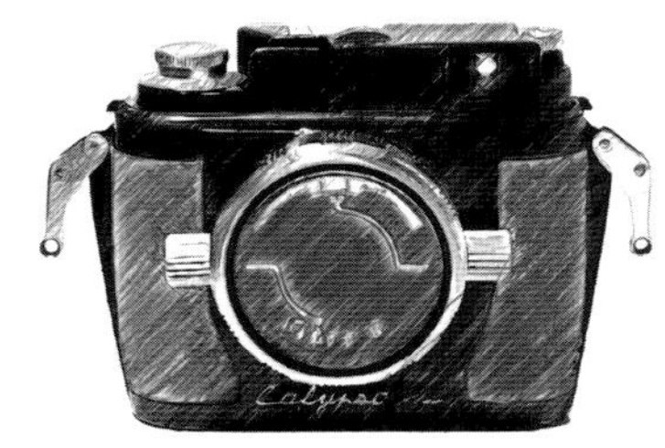

**1957:** Work starts on the Calypso, the first self-contained 35mm film camera designed for underwater use. It is conceived by the famous marine explorer Jacques-Yves Cousteau (1910–1997) and named after his famous research vessel but is designed by Jean De Wouters and built in France by Atoms. The camera operates at depths down to 200 feet or 60m. It is first released in 1960 as the Calypso and features a maximum 1/1000 second shutter speed, though later models will go only to 1/500.

**1957:** Victor Hasselblad ditches the problematic focal-plane shutter and introduces his 500C, which comes with an 80mm $f$2.8 Zeiss Tessar lens. Each lens for the 500C is equipped with a Compur shutter. This is a more expensive and complicated route, but it is well engineered, proves superbly reliable, and has the advantage of having full flash synchronization at all shutter speeds—an essential feature for studio work. It makes Hasselblad the workhorse of professional photographers for decades. It is the turning point for Hasselblad, and variants are produced until 2013.

---

**TRIVIA**

In 1966, John Lennon (1949–1980) met Yoko Ono (b. 1933) at the Indica Gallery, and later she introduced him to Iain Macmillan (1938–2006). In 1969, John invited Macmillan to use his Hasselblad 500C to make the cover photo for what would become one of the best known album covers of all time: the shot of the four Beatles crossing Abbey Road.

---

**1957:** Tessina (Switzerland) introduces the world's smallest 35mm camera. It takes 14 x 21mm pictures on standard 35mm film loaded into a special cassette. It is a very small (2.5 x 2 x 1 inch) twin-lens reflex, with two 25mm $f$2.8 Tessinon lenses, one for taking pic-tures, one for viewing on a tiny ground-glass focusing screen on top of the camera. A 45° mirror is employed to bend incoming light

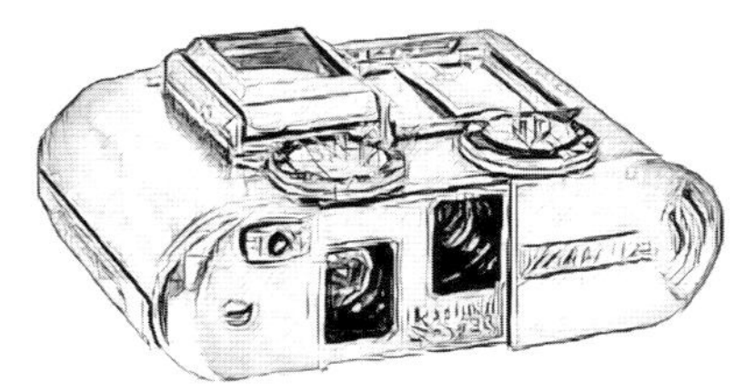

onto the film, which lies along the bottom of the camera rather than on the back, to save space. Apertures are continuously variable down to $f$22, and shutter speeds range from 1/2 to 1/500 of a second and B. The film is advanced by a clockwork master spring built into the take-up spool, with a pullout winder like the crown on a wristwatch. The Tessina remains in limited produc-tion until 1996.

---

**TRIVIA**

In the mid-1960s, your writer worked for a camera shop that carried Tessinas, and sold several of them. The most popular configuration was to wear it on a strap on your wrist, much like a watch. Very convenient.

---

**BUSINESS TRIVIA**

Despite much market success, it was not until 1960 that Hasselblad's cameras became profitable. Prior to that point, the company was supported by the sales of imported photographic supplies, including the distribution of Kodak products, in Sweden.

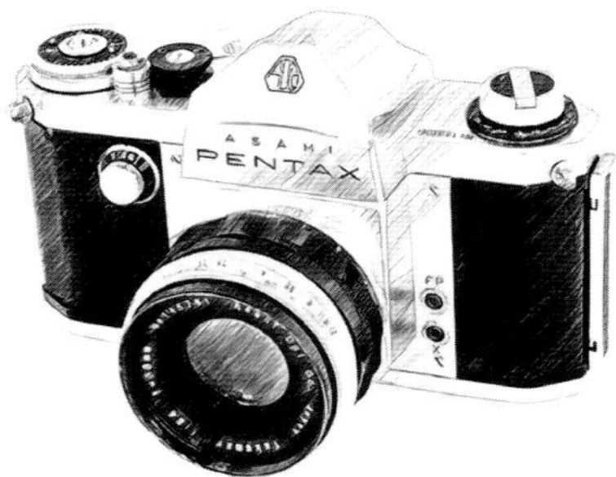

**1957:** The original Asahi-Pentax (sold as both the Honeywell Pentax and the Sears Tower 26 in the USA) is introduced. It is not a revolutionary camera but is the first to combine a pentaprism finder with an internally actuated instant-return mirror, the new fast lever film advance (rather than a winding knob) and an M42 lens mount, not to mention the first fold-out film rewind crank and the first microprism focusing aid. (The Pentax becomes so dominant that the 42mm screw lens mount used on the Pentax and the later Pentax Spotmatic becomes known as the "Pentax universal screw mount," although it had been introduced by Contax in 1949.) Pentax places the controls in locations so convenient to the photographer that they become standard on 35mm SLRs from all manufacturers for decades to come. This combination of modern features and ease of use, in one camera, makes it a best buy at the time and a huge marketing success. Some 19,600 are built in the first year alone—a remarkable achievement for a small firm.

**BUSINESS TRIVIA**

From 1959 through 1974, Asahi-Pentax cameras were branded Honeywell-Pentax in the USA. (Some very early models were marked Heiland Pentax.) People sometimes wonder how Honeywell, a maker of thermostats and industrial controls, could end up marketing cameras. It's quite simple.

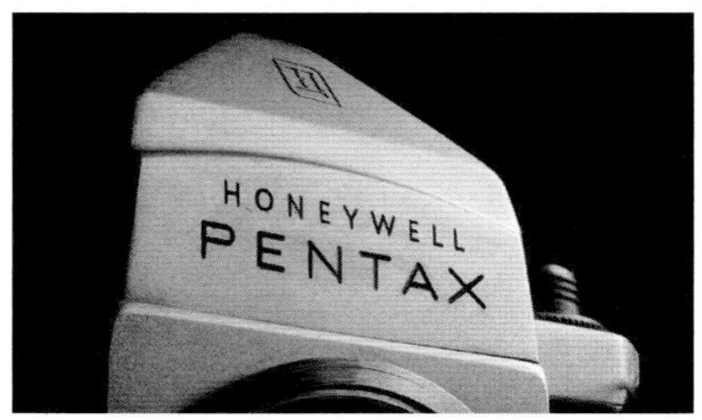

In the aftermath of the Second World War, if you wanted to sell your products in Japan, it could be difficult to get paid, as the yen had almost no value at that time. Therefore, it was common for firms to barter their products for Japanese goods, which they then sold in their home markets to recover their investment. Having bought Heiland Research in 1954, Honeywell had the perfect vehicle for it.

Such arrangements are still common. In an April 1990 article, the *Los Angeles Times* reported, "In 1974, Pepsico began shipping Pepsi concentrate to the Soviet Union, in exchange for Stolichnaya vodka, to be sold on the American market. That reciprocal trade pact has now been broadened and extended until the year 2000." In fact, Pepsico continued this arrangement until 2009. Pepsico has even traded its famous fizzy drink for Soviet tomato paste, which was used by the European arm of Pizza Hut—which Pepsico owned at the time. They have even bartered Pepsi for old Soviet warships, which they then sold for scrap.

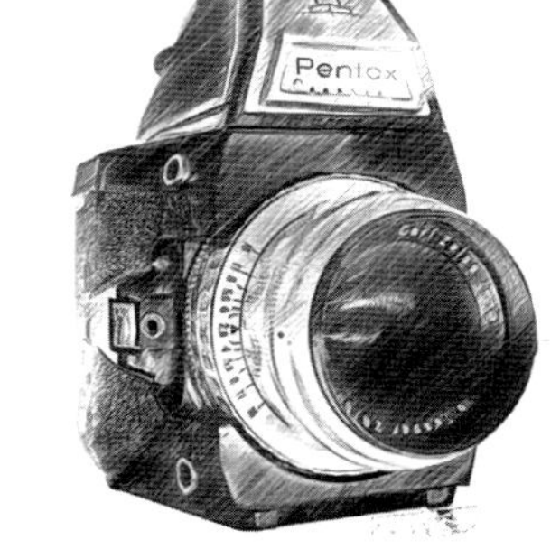

**TRIVIA**

In 1954, VEB Zeiss Ikon (Dresden) made a prototype 35mm camera. It was to be called the Pentax (from "PENtaprism" and "ConTAX"), but Asahi Optical had filed for the Pentax trademark on 22 September 1952. Thus, Asahi Optical had precedence and the Pentax trademark was granted to Asahi in August 1955. Asahi replaced their "Asahiflex'" brand with "Asahi Pentax" in 1957.

However, in 1959 Asahi sold their new Pentax S2 (which now boasted a semi-automatic diaphragm) as the Heiland Pentax H2 in the USA, while in South Africa, to avoid trademark problems with Pentacon, it was sold as the Asahiflex H2, the Asahi Pentar H2, and the Penta Asahiflex H2, though nobody seems to know why three different names were needed. The Asahiflex name was then fully retired. As for the Zeiss "Pentax" prototype—it was never produced and little else is known.

**1957:** Just as Hasselblad is swapping its unreliable focal-plane shutter for the more reliable Compur shutter, the Soviet Salyut is introduced—very similar to, but not an exact copy of, the original Hasselblad 1600. The Salyut has a beryllium copper focal-plane shutter, which is not as reliable as the light titanium foil shutter in the soon-to-be released 1000F and is put together in a series of connected links to make a travelling shutter curtain. This makes the camera noisier and does nothing to improve reliability. Like the Hasselblad, it has its top shutter speed reduced to 1/1000 second, though it retains the Hasselblad 1600F design unaltered in most other respects. It comes equipped with a 90mm $f$2.8 Industar lens that has a semi-automatic diaphragm. After the exposure you press a lever to reset the lens to full aperture.

The Salyut is sold only in the USSR, mostly in Torgsin or Beriozka stores (chains that sell to high party officials and tourists, but only for hard currencies, not rubles) and a few make their way out of the USSR with tourists. The camera is sold as a kit (body, lens with two filters, two 12-exposures backs, and a waist-level finder with magnifier) for about $100—about 20 times the average Soviet workers monthly salary. They are made through 1972.

---

**TRIVIA**

There were at least four versions of the Salyut. The first had a self-timer and shutter speeds up to 1/1500. The second version is the same, but no self-timer, while the third had shutter speeds only to 1/1000. The rarest is an export version of the third iteration, branded as a "Zenith-80" in English.

Wanting to avoid being seen as copying, the Soviets claim that the Hasselblad and the Salyut are both derived from a Nazi prototype. However, none of these supposed forerunners have ever been found, so this story is doubtful—to say the least.

---

**1957:** American computer researcher Russell Kirsch (1929–2020) wonders "What would happen if computers could look at pictures?" and starts a revolution in information technology. Kirsch and his colleagues at the National Bureau of Standards (now the NIST) create a rotating drum scanner and programming that allows images to be fed into their SEAC computer. (The SEAC is America's first stored-program computer to become operational, having entered service in 1950.) The first image, scanned on 20 May, is of Kirsch's three-month-old son, Waldon. It is captured in just 30,976 pixels, a 176 x 176 array, in an area 5 x 5cm. It has a 1-bit depth, so it is in stark black and white, though by combining several scans made using different scanning thresholds, grayscale information can be obtained. It turns out to be the well from which satellite imaging, CAT scans, bar codes, desktop publishing, digital photography, and a host of other imaging technologies will come.

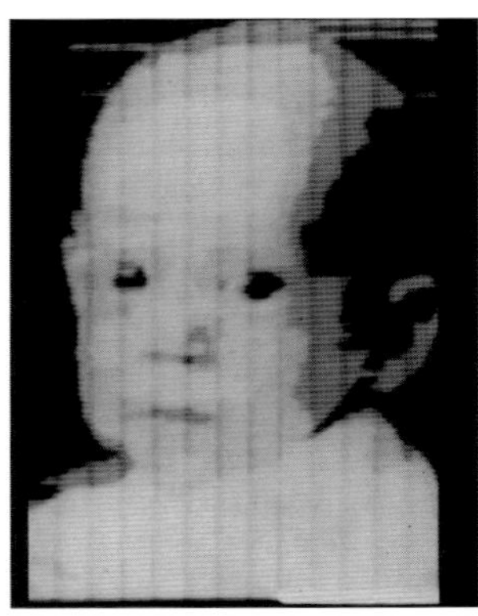

*Photo courtesy: NIST*

---

**TRIVIA**

In the process, Kirsch invents the pixel, or "Picture Element" as he called it. The term "pixel" will not arrive until Fred Billingsley (1921–2002) first uses it (see **1965**). In 2003, *LIFE* magazine will honour Kirsch's image (above) by naming it one of "the 100 photographs that changed the world" due to its importance in the development of digital photography—among other technologies.

---

**1957:** Topcon releases its first SLR camera, the Topcon R (well before either Nikon or Canon produce an SLR). The lens has an externally triggered semi-automatic diaphragm like the Exakta, and the camera boasts an interchangeable finder. It is a success, and the firm soon abandons all other camera production to concentrate on SLRs.

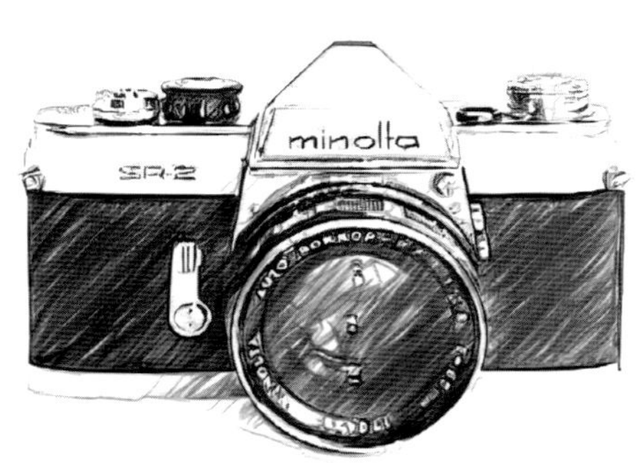

### TRIVIA

The Topcon, like the Miranda and Exakta, has an automatic diaphragm system connected to an appendage on the lens barrel that extends over the shutter release. The 1958 Minolta SR-2 improved on this with an internal tensioned spring which shut down the aperture when the shutter was released. But the diaphragm did not re-open until the film was wound. These and other semi-automatic systems were advertised as "automatic," so when actual automatic apertures were developed, they were called "fully automatic."

**1957:** Franke & Heidecke reintroduce their pre-war 4 x 4 Rolleiflex for 127 films. Commonly called the "Baby Rollei," it and its copies from Yashica, Minolta, Ricoh, Tougodo, Walz, and others start the short-lived 127 film "super-slide" boom.

### TRIVIA

Super-slides use the same 2 x 2 inch slide mounts and projectors as 35mm slides but are considerably larger in image area (approximately 38 x 38mm, compared to approximately 34 x 23mm for 35mm slides). With their larger area of film, the supporting cardboard must be smaller, which makes the slides prone to buckling under the heat of the projector's lamp, thus "popping" out of focus.

**1957:** Mamiya introduce their "C" series TLRs, starting with the Mamiyaflex C. The cameras break away from the traditional 6 x 6 TLR design by offering a variety of interchangeable lenses and an extended bellows range to accommodate them.

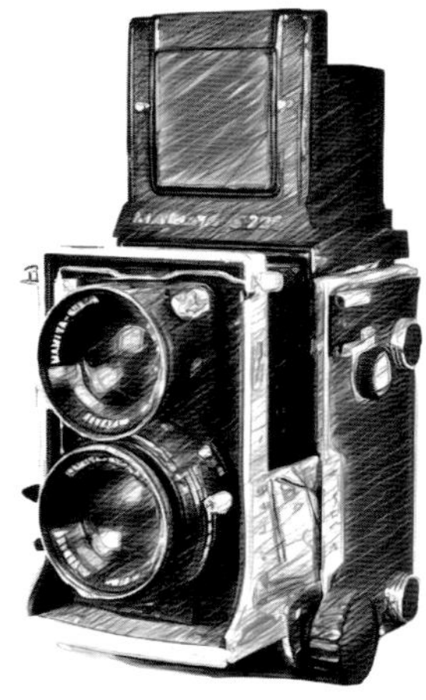

The Mamiyaflex C can use 80, 105, and 135mm lenses. Two more lenses (65 and 180mm) will be added with the introduction of the C2 June of 1958. The "Mamiyaflex" name will be dropped in favour of "Mamiya" when the C3 is introduced in February 1962. The system proves successful, and a series of Mamiya models will follow through 1994.

---

**TRIVIA**

One of the most famous photographers to use the Mamiya TLRs was Diane Arbus (1923–1971). She used them to photograph marginalized people: dwarfs, giants, transgender persons, nudists, circus performers, and others whose normality was perceived as ugly or surreal. In *Newsweek* (22 October 1984), Norman Mailer was famously quoted as saying, "Giving a camera to Diane Arbus is like putting a live grenade in the hands of a child."

---

**1958:** Edward Weston dies at his California home on New Year's Day. Edward Weston's photographs revolutionize both how we see common objects and how we think of the photographic medium itself. For this, he will be posthumously inducted into the International Photography Hall of Fame and Museum, in 1984.

**1958:** The Mamiya ELCA is Japan's first camera with match needle metering. The aperture, shutter and film speeds are connected to the selenium meter by resistors, and the needle is aligned against a fixed pointer when the correct exposure is achieved.

**1958:** Although started in 1955 as a photographic store in Kobe, Japan, the Velbon name is trademarked and the manufacturing of Velbon tripods starts.

**1958:** China's Lucky Film starts making photosensitive products including colour, black-and-white, and x-ray films, as well as magnetic audio and video tape. Lucky's major competitors are America's Eastman Kodak (which holds a 60% market share in China) and Japan's FujiFilm, though Lucky is strong in China's rural markets.

---

**TRIVIA**

In 2003, Eastman Kodak and China Lucky Film will sign a 20-year cooperation agreement, but Kodak will withdraw from the deal in 2007, citing the growth of digital cameras in the Chinese market.

---

**1958:** Canon, Leica, and Nikon rangefinder cameras, among others, suffer an odd problem with wide aperture ("fast," or in the modern parlance, "bright") lenses. If left focused at "infinity" and pointed towards the sun, the sunlight can burn holes in the cloth focal plane shutters. (Your scribe managed to burn a hole in the cloth shutter of his Leica CL this way, during a Caribbean holiday.) Thus, Canon introduce a 0.018mm stainless steel shutter curtain in their Canon VL (see **1958**), while in 1957, Nippon Kogaku swap the fabric and silk shutter in their Nikon SP for the titanium foil one later used in their Nikon F (see **1959**). The original Contax and Contax II cameras do not suffer this problem as badly, as they have brass slat shutters, though the silk ribbons that hold them can be burned by the sun.

**1958:** Around this time (the exact date is unclear), the American portrait and glamour photographer Peter Gowland (1916–2010) creates his twin-lens Gowlandflex camera, which uses 4 x 5- inch film for high-quality images. His cameras are used by Annie Leibovitz (b. 1949) and Yousuf Karsh (1908–2002), among other top-tier photographers. Around 600 of these high-precision, hand-made cameras will be produced, in various configurations.

**1958:** The Shandong Shanghai Photosensitive material factory is established to produce black-and-white film under the "Shanghai" brand. Although relatively unknown outside China, Shanghai film is widely sold domestically.

---

### TRIVIA

Production of Shanghai film stopped in early 2015, while a new factory was built. Production restarted in the summer 2016 and continues today.

---

**1958:** Zunow introduces the first SLR with a removable eye-level pentaprism with full 100% view, an instant return mirror, and fully automatic lens diaphragm. Sold only in Japan, it is an elegant design and particularly small, a size not seen again until the Olympus OM-1, in 1973. The camera is a brilliantly innovative design, but proves to be unreliable and Zunow, already in financial troubles, goes bankrupt in late 1959 and is absorbed by Yashica in early 1960.

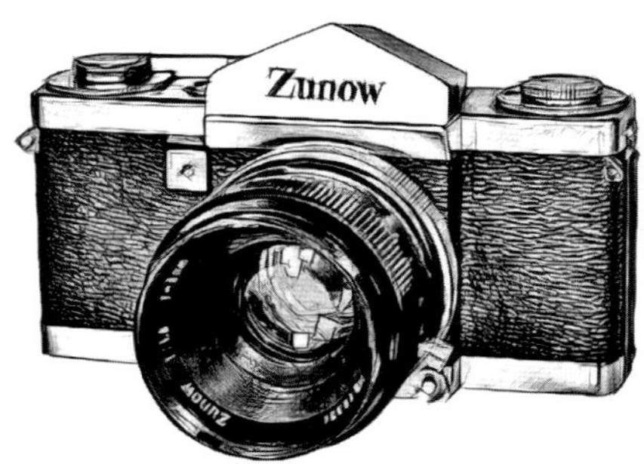

---

### TRIVIA

In a press release, Zunow claimed to make eight hand-built cameras per day. Most sources say fewer than 500 were ever made, but one copy was found with a serial number of 1959552. It was a disassembled body, left in the factory after production ceased. However, the camera seemed to have been used and then disassembled, possibly for repair. So, perhaps, a few more than 500 were made.

---

**1958:** Zunow is ready to introduce their Z16, a 16mm subminiature camera that takes 10 x 14mm images using Minolta 16mm film cassettes. It has a bar-shaped horizontal body, similar to other 16mm subminiature cameras of the 1950s and 1960s. Two wheels, placed above the front plate, control the speed (B, 50, 100, 200) and aperture (from 3.5 to 11). The camera is never released, as Zunow will go out of business in late 1959. Just two surviving examples are known to exist.

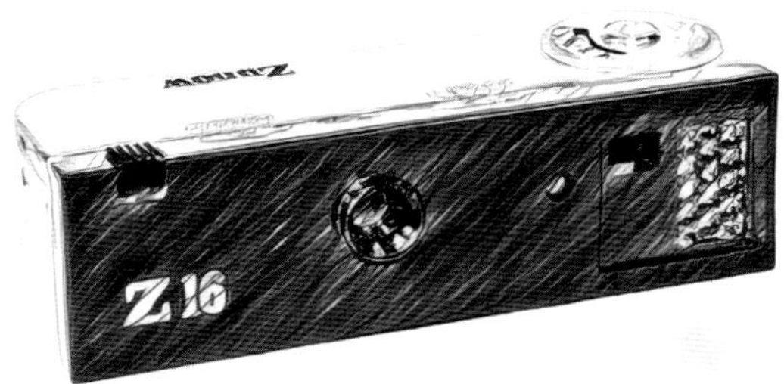

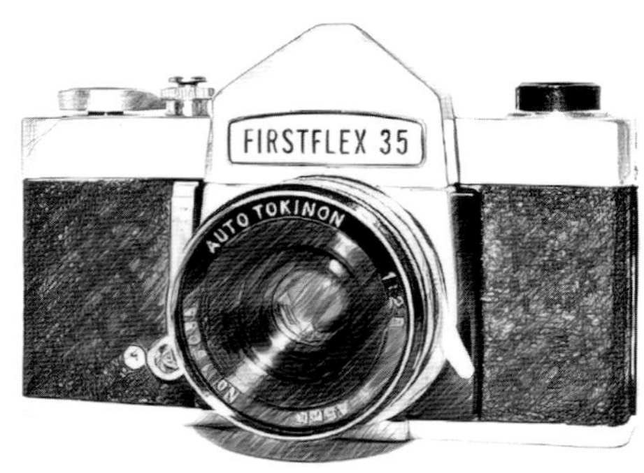


### ODDITIES

In 1958, Tokiwa Seiki (Japan) introduce their Firstflex 35. The Firstflex uses the instant-return mirror as a flash-synchronized shutter (1/125 second + Bulb only), with pentaprism finder and an Exakta bayonet lens mount. It is included here only because it is a strong contender for the title of "Worst 35mm SLR ever made," though it did have a few rivals for the title. In 1966, when your scribe went to work at his first "real" job (selling cameras in Canada's Yukon Territory), the firm still had a by-then eight-year-old Firstflex 35 in stock. When he left their employ, two years later, it was gone, but only because it had been stolen by some less-than-discriminating thieves!

The Firstflex was made only for a short time, being replaced by a version with two shutter speeds, 1/25 and 1/125, bearing the Plusflex name. During the post-war years, various versions of these low-cost mirror/shutter cameras were made, including an earlier (1955) Firstflex; a two-speed Ricoh (1/30 and 1/300) in both 35mm (1966) and 126 cartridge (1967) versions; a Mamiya-made Keystone 126 cartridge version (see **1966**); and Mamiya's own 35mm Autolux of 1965.

**1958:** In its December issue, the American magazine *Photoguide* makes the first known prediction of digital cameras. L. A. Mannheim's article "How Automatic Can You Get?" stated, "For still cameras we want an even simpler system: again, electronic and not photochemical. Such a camera will be small enough to hold in one hand yet will record a permanent and visible electric picture on single plastic discs the moment you expose."

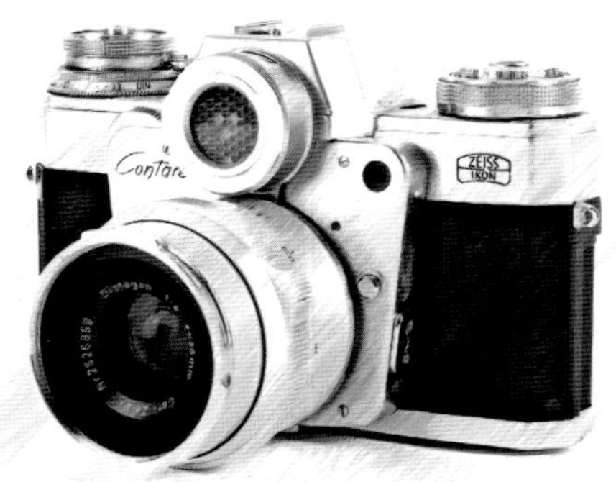

**1958:** The Zeiss Contarex is presented at Photokina in 1958, with deliveries scheduled for the spring of 1959, but it does not become generally available until March 1960. The Contarex is the first 35mm SLR focal-plane-shutter camera providing direct meter coupling to the shutter, aperture, and film-speed settings, which are interconnected by cords. The camera has an aperture simulator *(iris)* in front of the selenium meter cell. The user aligns the meter needle with an index triangle that is visible both in a top plate window and, to the right, in the viewfinder.

It's a wonder of German engineering and manufacture, with a weight and a cost to match. Including the 50mm *f*2 Carl Zeiss Planar standard lens, it sells for 1,450 Deutschemarks, or roughly $450. That's over $100 more than a Nikon F that will be released in 1959. (The equivalent of roughly $4,000 today!) Despite all the superb engineering, including an instant return mirror, the Contarex never does acquire a fully automatic diaphragm. Later variations include the Contarex Special (1960), Contarex Professional (1966), Contarex Super (1967), and Contarex Super Electronic (1968), but with the lack of lenses, lack of features, and high price, the Contarex is never a market success.

---

### TRIVIA

The camera is complex, comprising some 1,100 parts. However, it has proved to be reliable, though it requires a specialist for its repair. Some 43 parts must be removed before you can take off the top plate for internal access!

---

**1959:** The 36~82 *f* 2.8 Zoomar lens is introduced by Voigtländer. Designed by Frank Back of Zoomar Inc., N.Y., and built by Kilfitt of Germany (as are most Zoomar lenses), it is the world's first production zoom for 35mm still cameras. Dr. Back had previously produced zooms for TV and movie cameras and is often credited with coining the term "zoom lens." Although the Zoomar is introduced in May, it does not become generally available until mid-1960. When Heinz Kilfitt retires in 1968, he will sell his factory to Dr. Back, who operates it under the Zoomar name until 1971. In 1986, Zoomar leaves the civilian market to concentrate on military optics.

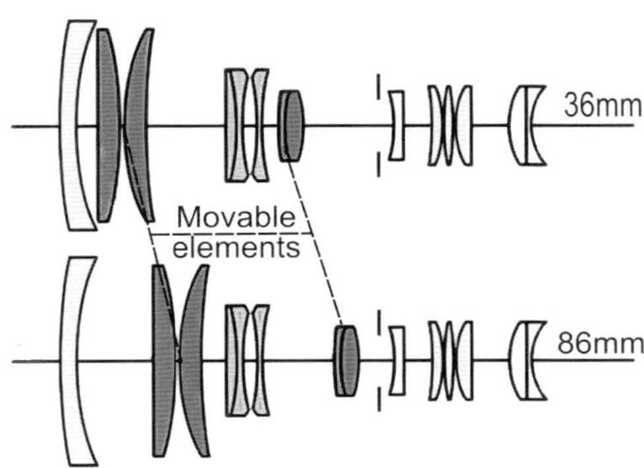


*The Kilfitt made 36~86 mm f 2.8 Zoomar*

---

### TRIVIA

Many people claim that the word "zoom" comes from "Zoomar," though it is more likely it was the other way around. Hollywood filmmakers were using "zoom," in the sense of a variable focal length lens, as early as 1932.

---

**1959:** Yashica introduce their first SLR, the Pentamatic. It is a modern 35mm SLR that features an automatic stop-down diaphragm, an instant-return mirror, a fixed pentaprism, and a mechanically governed focal-plane shutter with speeds to 1/1000 second, along with a proprietary bayonet mount and an array of interchangeable lenses.

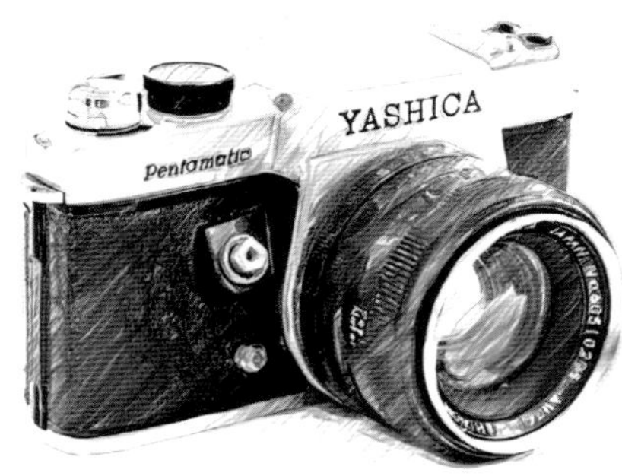

**1959:** American photographer and entrepreneur Lester Bogen (1925–1988) buys a small company that distributes darkroom supplies and renames it Bogen Photo.

**1959:** The Kodak Brownie 44A becomes the world's first camera with a plastic taking lens.

**1959:** Agfa introduce the first camera with automatic exposure: the Optima (sold in Canada as the Agfamatic). Pressing the left-side lever "traps" the exposure meter's needle, giving the camera the correct exposure.

**1959:** The Panon Camera Co. introduces the Widelux, which makes 140° panoramic images on 35mm film by rotating the lens horizontally, while a vertical slit (acting as a shutter and synchronized with the lens) moves across the film. It is the first camera of its type, proves highly reliable and, in various versions, is made until 2000.

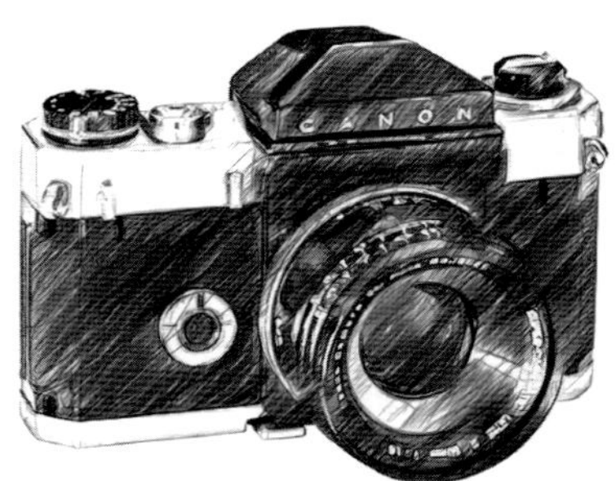

**1959:** Canon's first SLR, the Canonflex, is introduced in May, just one month before the introduction of the legendary Nikon F. It is an innovative camera, with a split image rangefinder with a microprism collar and an exposure meter coupled to the shutter speed dial.

Curiously, the film advance lever is fitted to the base of the camera. Unfortunately for Canon, most photographers do not find the bottom lever advance convenient, especially when the camera is on a tripod. (It is said that the Canonflex is very popular with Edsel owners.) No wide-angle lenses are offered, and only five telephotos, of which only two have automatic diaphragms, an essential feature in any top-line camera of the day. The Canonflex is discontinued after only three to five months (it seems historians cannot agree), and just 17,000 are made.

**1959:** Nippon Kogaku introduce their Nikon F SLR, arguably the most significant SLR in 35mm history. Developed from their Nikon S rangefinder chassis, and with the titanium foil shutter of the later SP, the design is achieved by asking photojournalists (starting with many on R&R breaks from the Korean War) what they want in a camera. Nikon gives them what they ask for, and the F sets the standard for professional SLRs for many years to come. In fact, the F has the longest production run in Japanese camera-making history, ending in 1974 with the production of roughly 862,000 cameras. It is followed by a series of successful F models in subsequent decades, ending with the F6, introduced in 2004.

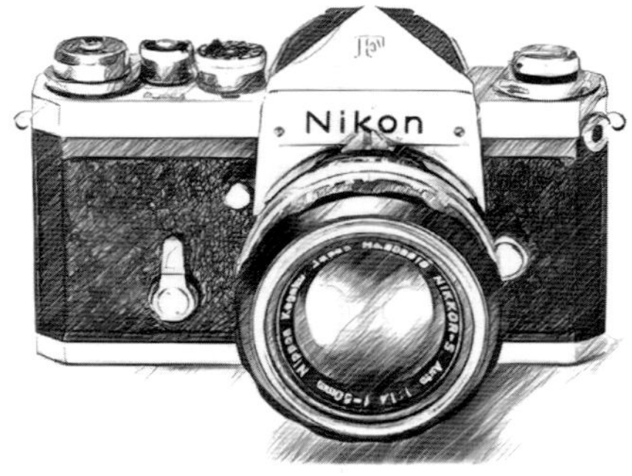

**TRIVIA**

Surprisingly, the Nikon F6 proved a steady, if slow, seller and was reportedly made in the company's Sendai plant by two dedicated and very skilled craftsmen, at the rate of about 50 per month. A remarkable run for a flagship analog camera in the age of digital.

**1959:** The Haloid Company introduces Chester Carlson's "electron photography" to the world, in the form of the Xerox 914. The 914 is the first plain paper photocopier and is generally considered the most successful single product of all time, proving so popular that by the end of 1961, Haloid has almost $60 million in revenues. Haloid will become the Xerox Corporation in 1961.

**1959:** B. Kobayashi starts Nikō (or Nikoh) Co. Ltd., to manufacture lenses. In 1963, filter manufacturing is added and, in 1966, 35mm cameras. The company starts its own glass works in 1968 and, in 1969, starts production of SLRs. In 1973, the company is reformed as Cosina Ltd. and goes on to become the largest OEM camera and lens maker in Japan.

**TRIVIA**

Cosina manufactured the Rollei 35 RF and Zeiss Ikon rangefinder cameras as well as the Epson E-1 digital rangefinder camera. Today, Cosina build Zeiss lenses in Leica mounts for Carl Zeiss AG as well as an extensive range of manual-focus lenses under the Voigtländer name. They have previously manufactured cameras for Canon, Yashica, Nikon, Olympus, and Konica, among many others.

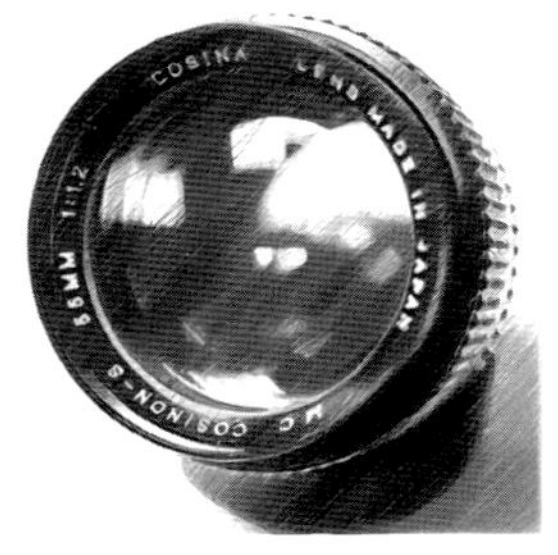

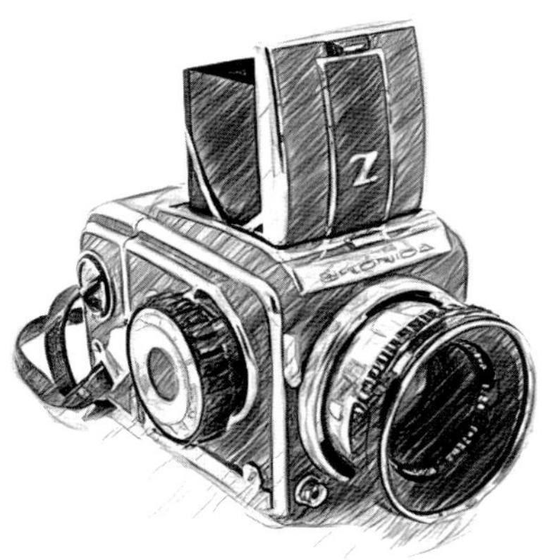

**1959:** In March, Zenzaburo Yoshino finally introduces his Zenza Bronica, at the Philadelphia Camera Show, to rave reviews. It is the Japanese answer to the Hasselblad and in several ways outclasses the Swedish offerings. It is a 6 x 6cm single-lens reflex camera similar to the Hasselblad in design, style, and size, but has several improvements over the original Hasselblad models. It has an instant-return mirror that slides down (rather than flip up) to allow the use of deep-seated wide-angle lenses. Inserting the dark slide detaches the back, preventing missed exposures, and the film can be loaded fully automatically, without lining up start marks. The camera is equipped with high-quality Nikkor lenses. Later models come with Zenzanon lenses which are sourced from a variety of lens makers, including Zeiss (Jena). The camera is an instant success.

---

**TRIVIA**

The early Bronicas have a notorious feature. Just above the strap lug, on the left side of the body, is what appears to be a button. It is a small, slotted screw head . . . the "emergency de-jamming screw." Should your Bronica jam up, you turn it and, in nearly all cases, the camera will be reset to perfect operation. This feature is not found on later, more reliable models.

---

**1959:** Kino Precision is started by Tatsuo Kataoka to manufacture lenses for 8mm movie cameras. In 1965, the company begins making lenses for other manufacturers, including the famous Series One lenses for Vivitar in the 1970s. The success of the Kino-designed Series One lenses prompts Kino to start marketing their own lenses in 1980 in the USA under the Kiron brand. Kino/Kiron quickly become known as one of the very few aftermarket lens manufacturers that can supply products to equal or even exceed the optical and mechanical quality of an original manufacturer. But, citing increasing manufacturing costs, lower-priced competition from camera makers, and the transition to auto-focus lenses—not to mention the auto-focus patent licensing fees demanded by Minolta and Honeywell—Kino/Kiron quits the camera lens business in 1988, to focus on industrial markets.

**1959:** Olympus introduce their PEN. It is Olympus's first and best-known half-frame camera and becomes a huge market success. Gifted with an excellent lens, robust construction, and low cost, over 17 million various PEN series cameras are produced during the 1960s and 1970s.

---

**TRIVIA**

The Olympus PEN is the first product of famed camera designer Yoshihisa Maitani (1933–2009). Upon starting at Olympus, he is sent to the Olympus factory for a period of practical training, where he is rotated to a different department every six months. After two years of this front-line training, he returns to the design department and is given a deceptively simple task: "Try designing something."

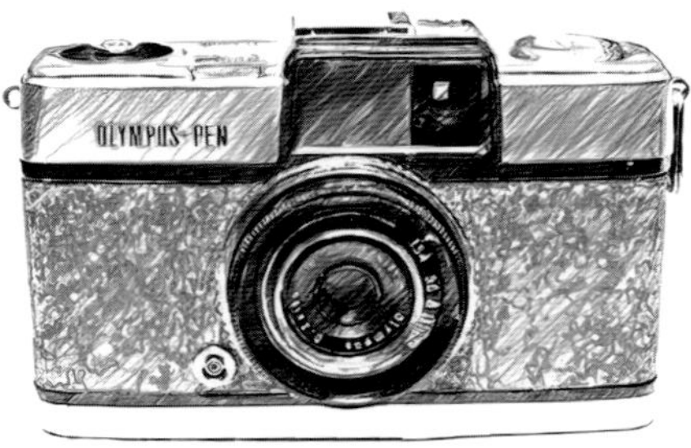

Believing that "the lens is the soul of the camera," he asks his lens designers to "to make a lens as good as his Leica's lens, without any concern for cost." They do, but it consumes his entire budget! Eventually, he comes up with a design both he and his managers think will sell, and the Olympus PEN is born. Maitani will go on to produce the PEN F (1963) and the OM-1 (1972) and the cult-classic XA (1979), among others.

---

**1959:** At the height of the Cold War, VEB Kamera und Kinowerke Dresden are formed by amalgamating the East German Zeiss Ikon (Dresden) with five smaller East German camera makers. Pentacon—the name is derived from the words Pentaprism and Contax—becomes the export brand for the Contax D, since use of the name Contax has been blocked by West Germany's Carl Zeiss AG. In 1964, VEB Kamera und Kinowerke Dresden will be renamed VEB Pentacon (Dresden) and, in 1968, the name will be simplified to VEB Pentacon.

---

### TRIVIA

Throughout the Cold War years, the original owners of Ihagee (Exakta) try to get back their ownership rights. When these efforts prove unsuccessful, they start Ihagee Kamerawerk AG (Ihagee West) in 1959. Ihagee West start numerous lawsuits against Ihagee East, but most of them fail.

In 1966, Ihagee West will produce the Exakta Real. It includes several improvements over the Dresden Exaktas (an instant-return mirror, a right-handed shutter release, and a larger lens mount allowing automatic diaphragm linkage), but the cameras prove unreliable and are not a commercial success. Later they make their own version of the Exakta 66, a high-quality medium-format camera that uses Pentacon Six mount lenses or dedicated Schneider lenses. But the Exakta 66 and their later Exa 35E rangefinder cameras meet with little success and the firm is dissolved in 1976.

---

**1960:** Little is known about Okaya Kōgaku Kikai K.K. (meaning Okaya Optical Works Company, Ltd.), other than they are the producer of "Vista" binoculars and "Lord" cameras during much of the 1950s. Their "Lord Martian" features selenium photocells for its exposure meter placed around the lens—a first, though Canon's much-better-known Canonet will use the same design the following year. Filters covered both the lens and meter cells, providing automatic exposure compensation. An innovative design, but the camera is remembered most for its unusual name. It is also the last camera Okaya Kogaku will make.

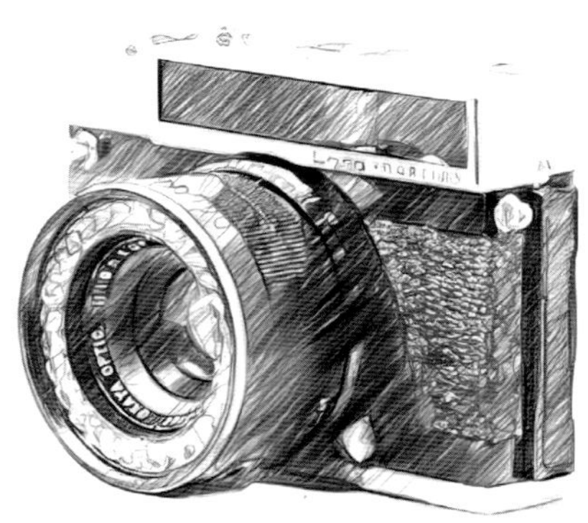

**1960:** Konica's first 35mm SLR, the Konica F, is the first SLR to have a shutter that reaches 1/2000 of a second and a flash sync speed of 1/125—both astounding feats for the time.

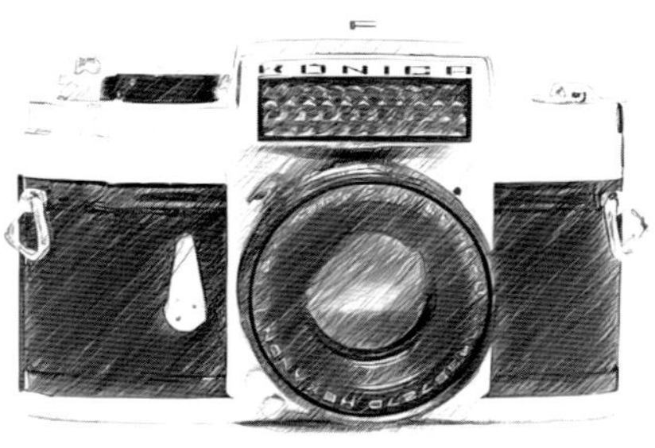

There are no known records on exactly how many are made, but it's believed that the serial numbers are sequential, and numbers up into the 1,400s are known to exist. The big question is: at what number did they start?

---

**TRIVIA**

Konishiroku had been developing a vertical-running metal-bladed shutter since the early 1950s. Later in the decade, they entered a cooperative arrangement with Copal and Mamiya—both of whom were working to develop similar designs—and somewhat later with Pentax (then Asahi Kogaku). The result was the Copal Square Shutter in 1961. Very early Konishiroku shutters tended to be a bit more finicky and delicate, so subsequent Konica shutters and the Copal Square shutters, found in other cameras, were slightly downgraded to 1/1000 top shutter speed for better reliability.

---

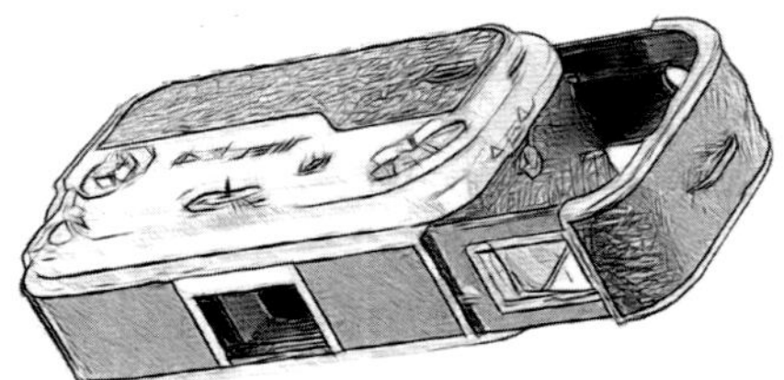

**1960:** Feinwerk Technik in the Black Forest region of Germany update their Mec 16 (see **1950**) to the Mec 16SB, the first production camera of any format with through-the-lens (TTL) metering. A Gossen-made selenium meter is built in, with the meter cell placed behind the lens but in front of the film plane. It swings out of the light path when the shutter release is pressed but before the shutter opens. It is a matched-needle system with aperture scale and exposure needle integrated for ease of setting. (This system will be later used in the Leica M5 (1971) and CL (1973) models, though with more sensitive CdS meter cells.) The lens is a six-element Rodenstock Heligon 22mm $f$2, making it one of the fastest subminiature lenses ever made, not to mention that it was also one of the best quality lenses ever fitted to a subminiature camera.

**1960:** Nippon Kogaku market the Nikkorex 8, their first entry in the home movie market and the first-ever camera, either still or movie, to have a CdS (cadmium sulphide), rather than a selenium meter, built into a camera. The auto-exposure system in the Nikkorex 8 is both novel and simple. Two aperture blades are fixed directly to the axle of the indicator arm of the exposure meter. Thus, the aperture of the taking lens is directly controlled by the swinging arm of the galvanometer. Although the aperture blades are made as light as possible, it was quite a load for any meter; in order to make the system responsive, more power had to be applied to the galvanometer—something that was not possible with the older (but more common) selenium metering cells. By using the battery-powered CdS cell in the metering circuit, this improvement is made possible.

---

**TRIVIA**

Although a thoroughly Nikon design, the Nikkorex movie cameras (and a matching Nikkorex movie projector) were made by Sankyo Inc., while the Nikkorex slide projector, introduced at the same time, was produced by Sawyer's Inc. of Portland, Oregon.

---

**1960:** The honour of being the first SLRs with automatic exposure control is shared by two little-known French-made cameras, the Royer Savoyflex Automatique and the Focaflex Automatic. Both employ selenium-cell exposure meters and the basic "trap-needle" method of aperture control used by previously introduced point-and-shoot cameras. Surprisingly, no other SLR will follow in their footsteps until the Konica Auto-Reflex, in 1966. The Foca is produced until 1962, the Savoyflex until 1963.

### ODDITIES

The Foca SLR camera has a viewfinder like no other. Light from the lens is directed downwards by a semi-silvered mirror to a focusing screen at the bottom of the mirror box. A mirror underneath the screen reflects the light upwards through the semi-silvered mirror to a prism, which sends the image out the eyepiece. During the exposure, the mirror flips downwards and a light cap over the film flips upwards, blocking light from the eyepiece during the exposure. The semi-silvered mirror makes the viewfinder rather dark, so to keep the viewfinder as bright as possible, only a small, central square is used for focusing, and the photographer compares the bright(er), non-focusing area with the focusing spot to determine focus. While this works well outdoors, it makes focusing more difficult indoors. It all seems rather complex, but combined with a leaf shutter, it makes a very quiet, reliable camera. Foca is out of business by 1962.

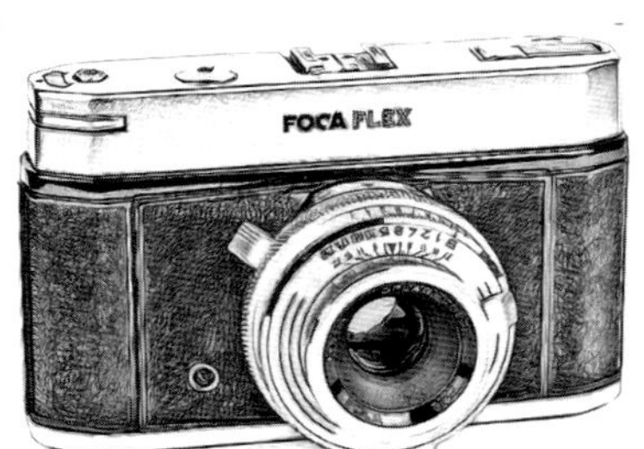


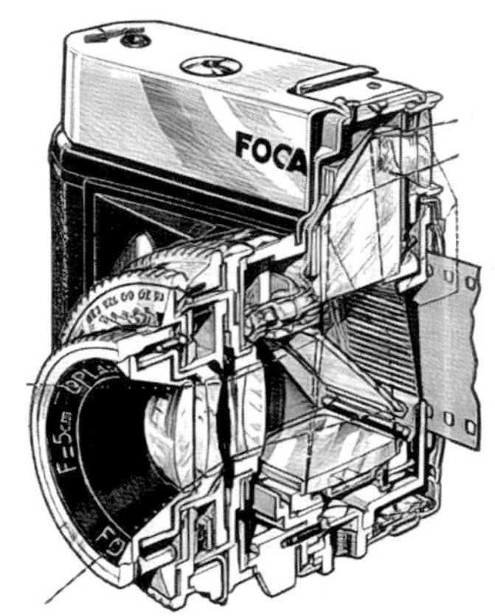


*Diagram from a Foca instruction book*

**1961:** Nippon Kogaku announce their first standard-range zoom lens, the Auto Nikkor Wide-Zoom 35~85m ƒ2.8~4, which they show alongside the Reflex-Nikkor 500mm ƒ5 reflex telephoto and other new lenses. The lens has an eight-group 13-element configuration, with a length of 95mm and a diameter of 90mm. It weighs in at 1.1kg (2.4lbs) and takes an 82mm filter. Within the firm there are concerns about its sheer weight and size, and the lens is never produced.

**1961:** The Kodak Carousel slide projector is introduced, with round, top-mounted 80-slide trays which allow the slides to drop into place by gravity rather than being pushed in by a mechanical arm. This solves most slide jamming problems which have previously plagued all slide projectors. As well, should a slide jam, it may get stuck but is not damaged by a mechanical "pusher" arm. The Carousel soon becomes the "Rolls Royce" of projectors and is made until 2004.

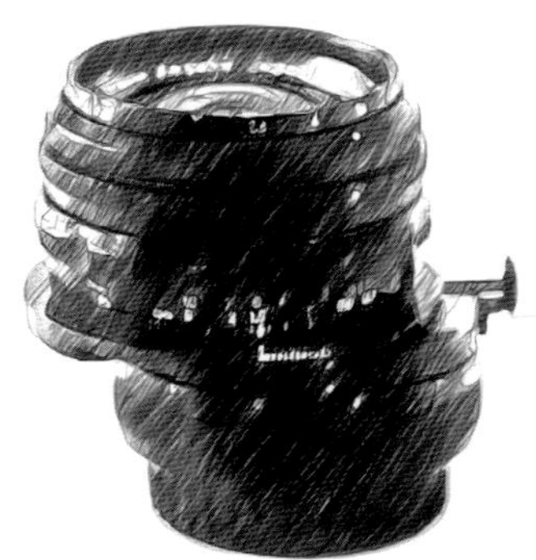

**1961:** Nikon produce their 35mm *f* 3.5 PC Nikkor, the first shift lens for a 35mm camera. The "PC" stands for "Perspective Control" and it is aimed at architectural photographers. By shifting the lens off centre, it can simulate the rise of a view camera to control perspective. Improved versions follow in 1968 and 1980.

**1961:** Zeiss designs their 50mm *f* 0.7 Planar for NASA, to photograph the far side of the moon. Stanley Kubrick makes it famous, using three of them to photograph his movie *Barry Lyndon*.

**1961:** Kodachrome II is born. This new emulsion has better exposure latitude, lower contrast, and a faster speed, being rated at ASA 25.

---

### TRIVIA

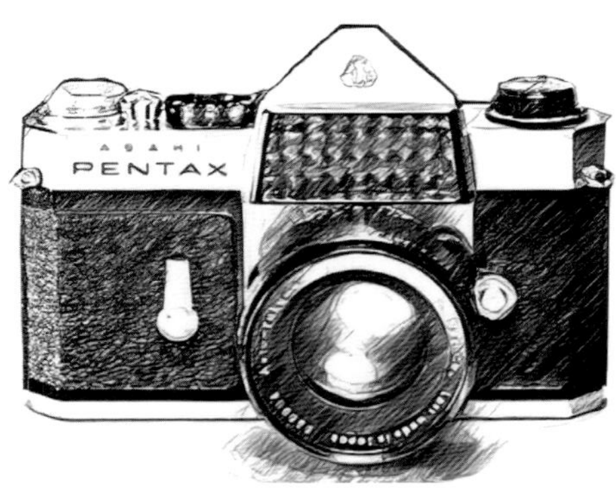

When Asahi Optical showed the prototype of what would become the Pentax Spotmatic at the 1960 Photokina, they also showed a second prototype SLR, called the Metallica. It was a glimpse into the future direction of Pentax cameras. The Metallica featured a prototype bayonet lens mount, a vertical-run metal focal-plane shutter (from which the camera drew its name), and an already-obsolescent coupled selenium exposure meter mounted on the front of the pentaprism. Asahi Optical never put the Metallica into production, but it showed that the ideas of a bayonet lens mount and a metal focal-plane shutter were already being considered by Pentax, among other makers.

In 1966, Asahi Optical showed another prototype, also called Metallica. Gone was the cumbersome selenium exposure meter, replaced with a by-then-standard internal CdS meter. Like the 1960 prototype, the Metallica had a bayonet lens mount, and also featured an improved Copal Square metallic shutter. But the biggest innovation was the fully automatic shutter operation coupled to the TTL meter. The metering system, for the first time in a 35mm SLR, controlled the shutter speed automatically, based on whatever aperture was set. With these innovative developments, the Metallica pioneered features that would not surface on Pentax production cameras until the Electro-Spotmatic (ES) automatic aperture-priority exposure in 1971 and the K2 (vertical metal shutter, bayonet lens mount, automatic aperture-priority exposure) in 1975.

**1961:** The Copal Square all-metal vertical-run shutter is introduced, a joint effort between Copal, Mamiya, Konica, and Asahi Pentax. Top speed is 1/1000 of a second. The Copal Square shutter will form the basis of almost all modern Japanese focal-plane shutters. Its descendants will replace the metal with a light polymer plastic to lower the mass, eventually allowing shutter speeds up 1/8000 second.

**1961:** The history of the digital camera begins with Eugene F. Lally (1934–2014). While working at California's Jet Propulsion Laboratory, he begins to think about using a mosaic photo-sensor to capture digital images. His idea is for astronauts to take pictures of the planets and stars while travelling through space to gather information about their position. Unfortunately, as with Texas Instrument employee Willis Adcock's film-less camera, the technology does not yet match the concept (see **1972**).

---

### ODDITIES

In 1961, Kowa builds the "Graphic 35 Jet" for the U.S. firm Graflex Inc. It is the first (and only!) camera to use gas pressure to advance the film and cock the shutter. A cartridge of $CO_2$ gas, of the type used in soda siphon bottles, drives the film wind mechanism in the camera. (A manual winding lever is provided in case the gas runs out.) It also has an unusual method of focusing: the lens does not move but the film plane is shifted to change the distance to the lens, akin to the Stereo Realist from 1947, and the Contax AX that will follow, in 1996. It is a unique camera but not a market success.

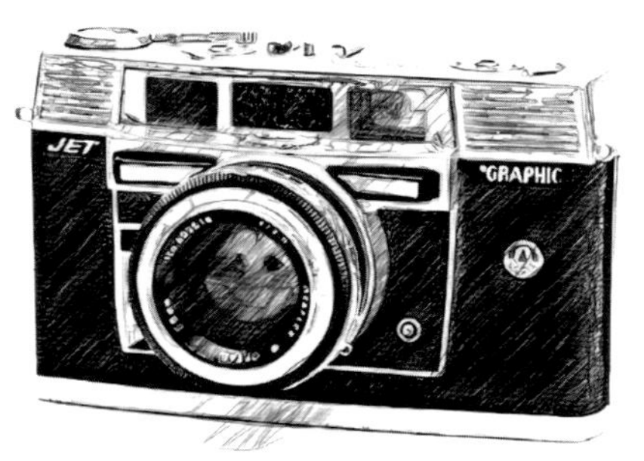


---

**1961:** Sigma is started by Michihiro Yamaki (1934–2012), who will remain Sigma's CEO until his death, as a maker of low-end lenses. It is a family-owned company which will go on to manufacture cameras, flash, and other photographic accessories, as well as lenses. All Sigma products are produced in the company's own Aizu factory in Bandai, Fukushima, Japan. Sigma eventually becomes the world's largest independent lens manufacturer.

**1961:** Gossen introduce their Lunasix exposure meter (called the Luna PRO in the U.S.). The Lunasix is famed for its sensitivity in low light and can give accurate readings by moonlight. Still impressive by today's standards, it quickly replaces the Weston as the gold-standard for exposure meters.

**1961:** Canon introduce their last interchangeable-lens rangefinder camera, the Canon 7. With it is the ultra-fast $f$ 0.95 50mm lens, whose performance is amazing, considering its speed. But the price for camera and lens is high ($800, or just over $6,300 in today's dollars), and lens resolution is found wanting. Lens flare is also a huge problem, and the lens is soon discontinued, along with the camera.

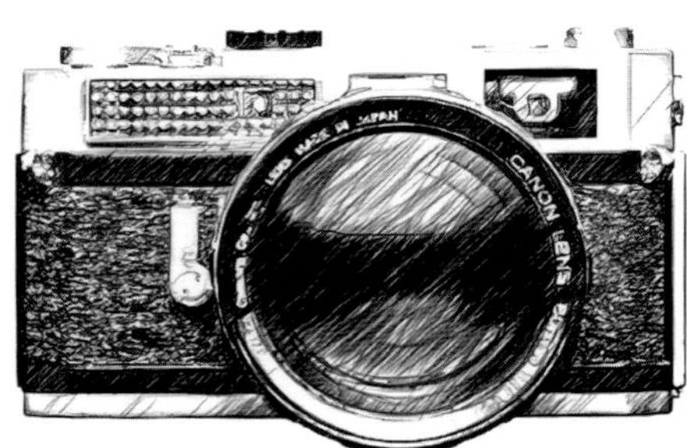

**1962:** Rochester based Elgeet Optical (see **1956**) acquires ownership of Steinheil. The firm goes through several owners until 1995, when the last owner, British Aerospace, dissolves Steinheil and sells off bits and pieces of the subsidiary to various companies. The optical manufacturing facilities and trademarks are acquired by Jenoptik AG. The Steinheil trademark (granted in 1954) expires in December of 1994 and is not renewed.

**1962:** Nippon Kogaku market their Nikkorex 35/2 camera. Designed by Nikon but built by Mamiya, it proves to be a reliable version of the problem plagued Nikkorex 35 of 1960. In 1963, it will be the basis for the Nikkorex Zoom-35, which features Nikon's 43~86 zoom lens that will revolutionize photography and then do it again in 1964, when the lens becomes independently available for the Nikon F. Production of the 35/2 will end in 1965.

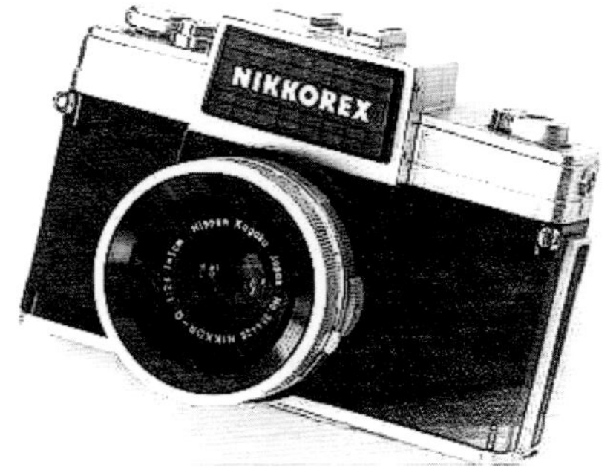

In September 1964, the Nikkorex Auto-35 (a.k.a. Nikon Auto-35 in some markets), will be the last of the Nikkorex fixed-lens cameras. It is fitted with a Nikkor-H 48mm $f$ 2 lens and has both a pentaprism (instead of a Porro-mirror finder) and a quick-return mirror. But it is too little, too late, and is not enough to salvage the marque.

### TRIVIA

For many years, reliable focal-plane shutters were very expensive and SLRs equipped with leaf shutters were strong competitors. But as focal-plane shutters improved and their prices dropped, their faster speeds won out, and by the late 1960s leaf-shutter 35mm SLRs had virtually disappeared.

**1962:** The first camera released with the Copal Square shutter (see **1961**) is the Nikkorex F (called the Nikomat F in Japan). It is Nippon Kogaku's first lower-priced body to accept interchangeable Nikkor lenses and is aimed at amateurs. It is a gamble on Nippon Kogaku's part, as the Copal Square shutter is both new and untested, but the shutter proves reliable, and the camera is a success.

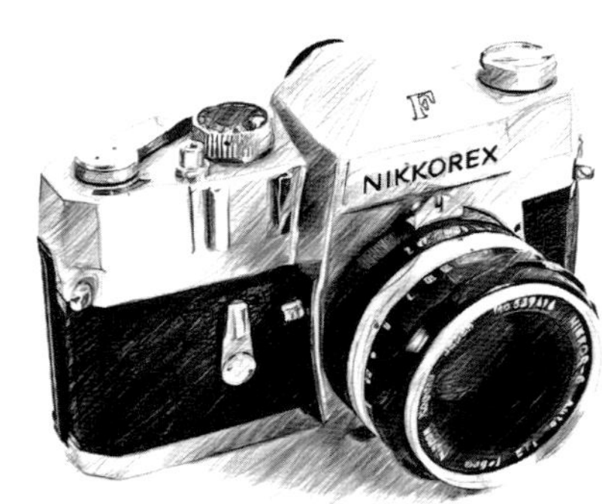

New camera designs do not happen overnight, but when Nippon Kagaku knocks on Mamiya's door, they just happen to have a new design almost ready. It is agreed that Mamiya will modify the camera to use Nikon's F mount and the Nikkorex F is born. It is a good, reliable machine that widens their base of lens customers and gives Nippon Kogaku a toehold in the consumer market until the Nikkormat series, designed and built by Nippon Kogaku, arrives in 1965. Curiously, for reasons unclear to this writer, the Nikkorex F is sold in some markets as the Nikkor "J."

---

### BACKSTORY

The revolutionary Copal Square was developed by Copal, Mamiya, Pentax, and Konica, and only these makers were to receive shipments when it was ready. Nikon was not on the list. But, because the Nikkorex F is built by Mamiya, it receives the unexpected honour of being the first camera to market the new shutter.

Nippon Kogaku wanted to expand their markets but did not have the manufacturing capacity. Their American distributor, Ehrenreich Photo-Optical Industries (EPOI), arranged for Mamiya to produce the camera for Nikon under contract. Simultaneously, with the release of the Nikkorex F, came the release of two Mamiya-Sekor lenses under the Nikkorex brand. The 35mm *f* 2.8 and 135mm *f* 2.8 were the only Nikkorex-branded lenses ever produced.

Production of Nikkorex cameras (and the use of the brand) ended in 1966, and the design was sold to the Riken Optical Co., which introduced it, with minor trim changes, as their first interchangeable lens camera, the Ricoh Singlex (also sold as Sears SL 11), still using the Nikon F lens mount and still made by Mamiya. But by then Nippon Kogaku had introduced their successful Nikkormat series.

---

**1962:** In a second attempt, Tamron introduce their now classic T-mount system. Using a larger M42 x 0.75 thread (see **1957**) provided less vignetting with longer focus and allowed larger aperture lenses to be used. It proves a great market success, as it allows a dealer to stock just one lens along with adapters to fit almost any camera. However, they fall from favour with the advent of lenses with fully automatic diaphragms and autofocus. T-mount rings can still be purchased, but today are essentially restricted to inexpensive, manual-focus long-focal-length lenses (usually 300mm or longer) in both telephoto and catadioptric designs.

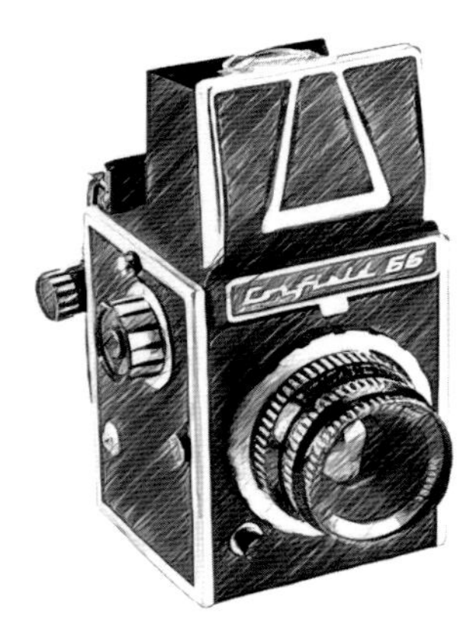

**ODDITIES**

The Corfield 66 was a British-built 6 x 6cm SLR with a focal-plane shutter with speeds from 1/20 to 1/100 second. The camera had a lens mount with a large "throat," which allowed the use of adapters to fit lenses for the Hasselblad 1000, Reflex Korelle, Agiflex, Primarflex, Master Korelle, Praktisix, Exakta 66, as well as Plaubel and Linhof lenses; the adapters, however, were never produced. The only lens made for the Corfield 66 was the Lumax 90mm *f* 3.5 that came with it. The camera top was engineered to accept prism finders from Pentacon Six/Praktisix, Rolleiflex, and Hasselblad. Just 300 cameras were built.

**1962:** The Minolta SR-7 is the first 35mm SLR to be marketed with a built-in (but externally mounted) cadmium sulphide (CdS) exposure meter. The much more sensitive CdS meter relies on a single PX625 battery, stored in the base. Early versions do not have a meter on/off switch, so the owner has to close the ever-ready case to prevent the battery from draining. The SR-7 is built to very high standards and the entire Minolta SR series earns a reputation as being extremely well built and reliable.

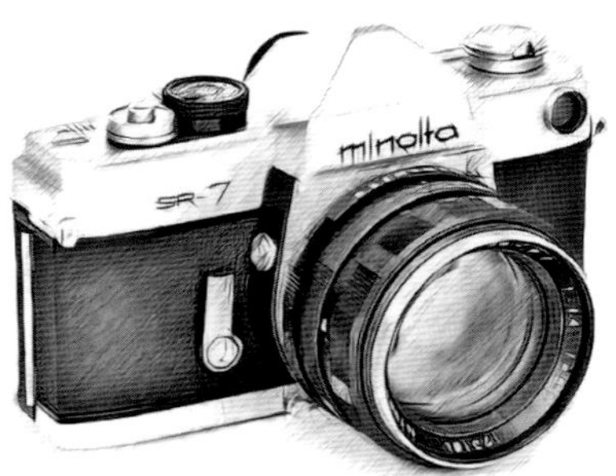

**1963:** Polaroid introduce their first instant colour film.

**1963:** Not widely known and kept well under wraps, Kodak start a six-year run making Polaroid film, for Polaroid, under contract.

**1963:** Nippon Kogaku buy the rights to Cousteau's Calypso underwater camera (see **1957**) which becomes the Nikonos. Lenses in 15, 20, 28, 35, and 80mm focal lengths are offered. It proves popular with both amateur and professional divers alike and remains in production through several models until 2001.

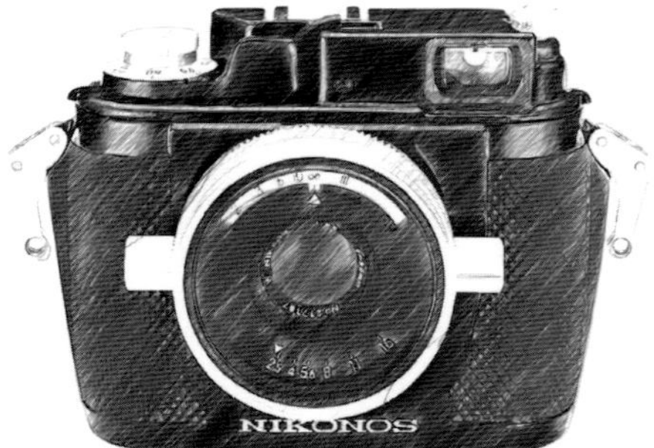

**1963:** Kodak introduce their 126-size cartridge-loading Instamatic cameras, their first of many attempts to solve the problem that some amateur photographers had with loading 135 film. Hugely successful, more than 50 million Instamatics will be produced by 1970. Shown here is the Instamatic S-10, which sells (from 1967 to 1970) for $27.50. The 126-film cassette had many qualities that initially made it extremely popular: it took 12 or 20 frames, each 28 x 28mm in size; the film is 35mm wide on paper backing, and it comes in drop-in loading cartridges. But the quality of the plastic cartridges is uneven, which results in lower quality images, and the 126 format is almost dead by 1972.

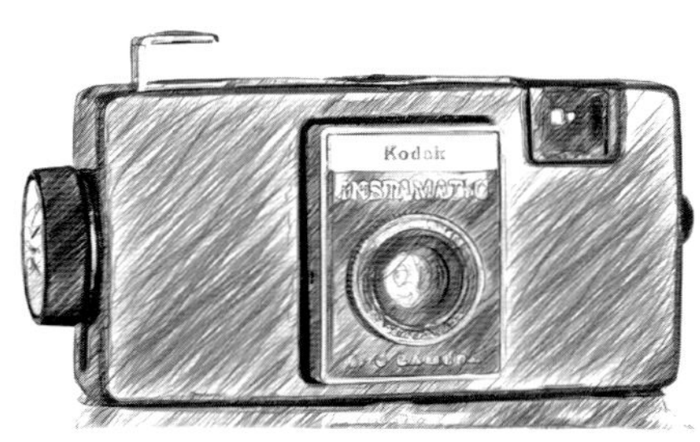

---

## ODDITIES

On 20 February 1962, John Glenn (1921–2016) used a heavily modified Ansco Autoset (actually a re-badged Minolta Hi-Matic) to make the first colour photographs of the Earth during his three-orbit mission. NASA technicians invert the camera and attached a pistol grip handle and trigger to this consumer-grade 35mm camera. Because his helmet prevents Glenn getting his eye close to the built-in viewfinder, the engineers put a larger viewfinder on the bottom, which is now the top. Glenn purchased the Ansco Autoset from a drugstore in Cocoa Beach, Florida, for $40.

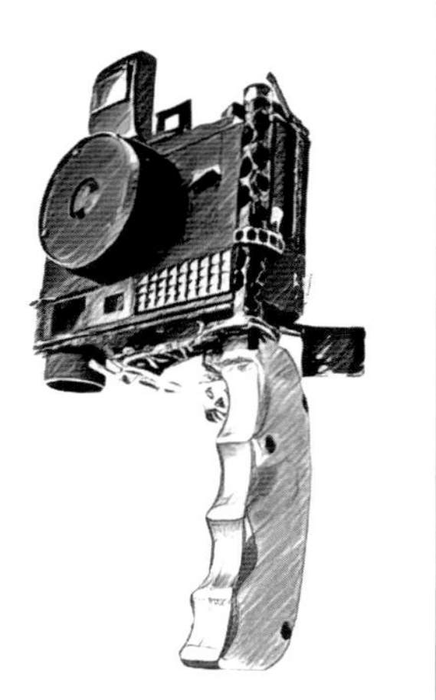

---

**1963:** Olympus introduce the PEN-F, another Yoshihisa Maitani design and the first ultra-compact half-frame (18 x 24mm) SLR accepting interchangeable lenses. The camera and lenses are of very high quality; however, even though the original PEN series of half-frame point-and-shoot cameras sold well, the PEN-F never achieves great success because of the limitations of its half-frame format, together with the fact that SLR users are typically more demanding users.

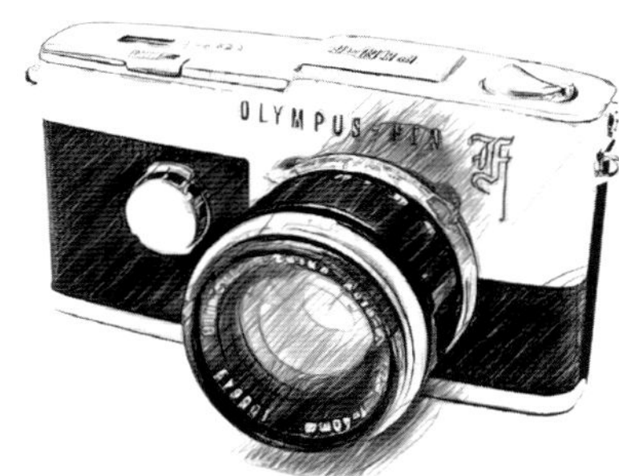

---

## TRIVIA

Although half-frame cameras used standard 135 film, single-frame photofinishing was always a special-order effort, often at extra cost. In fact, your scribe purchased a PEN-F but sold it soon after for that very reason and because it was very difficult to get a decent 11 x 14-inch print from the very small negative. Yashica tried, unsuccessfully, to revive the format, calling it "Double 35," with their Samurai series SLRs in 1988–1989.

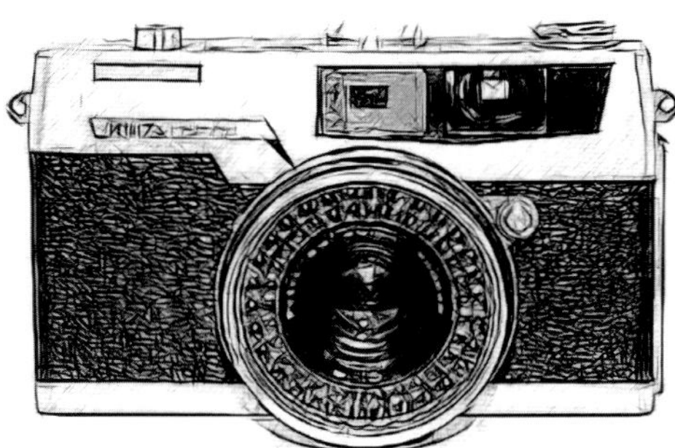

**1963:** Originally founded in 1907 as Kuribayashi Shashin Kōgyō (the company name means "Acorn Grove") as a maker of tripods and accessories, the Petri Camera Co. produce their Petri 7S Circle-Eye System coupled-rangefinder leaf-shuttered model, which is used by some professionals in the 1960s. It proves to be so well built that this model is still used by enthusiasts today and has an almost cult-like following among street photographers. Accounts differ, but Petri declares bankruptcy in either 1977 or 1978.

---

**TRIVIA**

After Petri went bust, the unionized workers purchased the remains and re-organized as Petri Kōgyō K.K. They quickly abandoned camera production and the Petri camera brand was sold to the Dixons Group (U.K.) in the 1980s, though Dixons no longer uses it, and rumour has it that the brand is for sale. Petri Kōgyō K.K. continues to this day as a successful maker of telescopes, in Sugito, Japan.

---

**1963:** Polaroid introduce their model 100, while the Japanese Artronic (made by Yamato Koki Kogyo in Tokyo) is introduced in Japan. They are the first cameras to have electronically controlled shutters. A number of German electronic shutters, including Prontor and Compur models, are introduced shortly after.

---

**TRIVIA**

A small camera maker since the early 1950s, Yamato presented their Artronic F Zoom and Artronic L prototypes at the Photokina in 1963. The company was probably not financially strong enough to manufacture them, and all trace of it is lost after that date, and the Artronic cameras are never heard from again.

---

**1963:** The Cibachrome process of printing from transparencies is introduced by the Ciba-Geigy Corporation of Switzerland. Unlike normal colour prints that have the pigment on the surface of the paper, Cibachrome uses AZO dyes embedded in the paper; the prints are known for their exceptional stability, fade resistance, and colour purity.

---

**TRIVIA**

In 1992, the name is changed to Ilfochrome Classic when Ilford purchases the Cibachrome manufacturing facility, which is then in turn purchased by International Paper. The last manufacturing run of Ilfochrome is in 2012, a result of the rise of digital photography.

**1963:** Topcon introduce their RE-Super (the "Beseler Topcon Super-D" in the USA), the first SLR with full aperture TTL (through-the-lens) match-needle metering. The exposure system is developed in cooperation with Tokyo Shibura Electric (Toshiba) and employs CdS cells on the back of the mirror behind a series of 0.05mm slits in the coating, thus making averaged readings possible at full aperture from just 7% of the light.

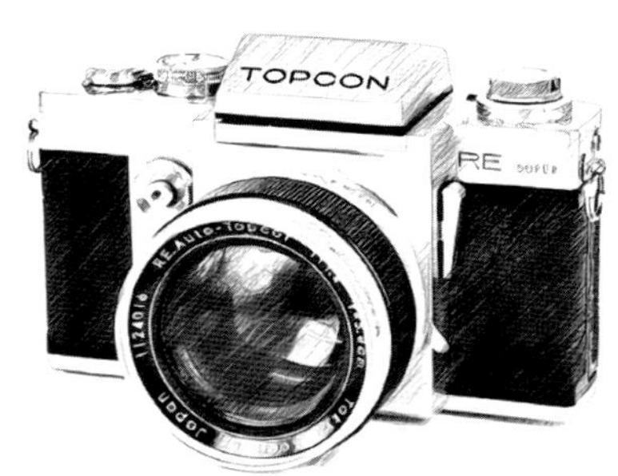

### TRIVIA

About 1965, the U.S. Navy tests cameras from several German and Japanese manufacturers (including the Nikon F, which the Navy is then currently using). The Topcon Super D wins the competition (Miranda comes second) and Topcons are used exclusively by the Navy until the very end of Topcon camera production in 1977. In the U.S., Topcon cameras were distributed by Beseler and the cameras were marked Beseler Topcon. Thus, a popular story at the time was that Topcon got the Navy contract because a Navy purchasing agent thought the Beseler Topcon was an American-made camera. There is no proof of this, but nothing would surprise this writer. The company continues, to this day, making top-quality surveying equipment, opthalmic cameras, and medical instruments.

**1963:** Nippon Kogaku release their mid-priced Nikkorex Zoom 35, the first SLR with a fixed 43~86mm $f$3.5 lens zoom lens. Because of cost constraints, its designer, Takashi Higuchi, reduces the number of elements to the absolute minimum in order to keep both price and size down. This results in, shall we be polite and say, "less than stellar" performance.

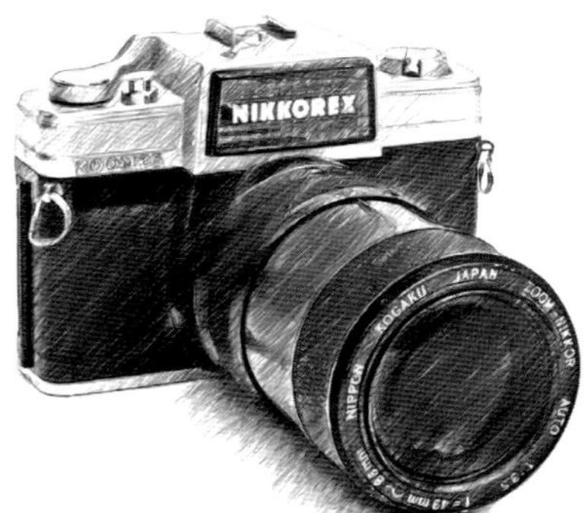

**1964:** Soon after its release, the Pentax Spotmatic becomes the world's most popular camera with through-the-lens (TTL) metering. Originally intended to have spot metering (hence its name), the designers deem that design too difficult, so it uses an averaging (wide field) meter. The user focuses the lens at maximum aperture for a bright view and then pushes a switch on the side of the lens mount to stop down the lens and switch on the metering. The user can then use either the shutter speed dial or the aperture ring to center the meter needle seen at the right of the viewfinder. This stop-down light metering limits the capability of the exposure meter, especially in low light situations. Smaller and lighter than the Topcon RE-Super (see **1963**), and with a combination of excellent performance, reliability, and very convenient controls, the Spotmatic becomes a huge market success. Made from 1964 to 1976, the total production of the Spotmatic family is some four million cameras.

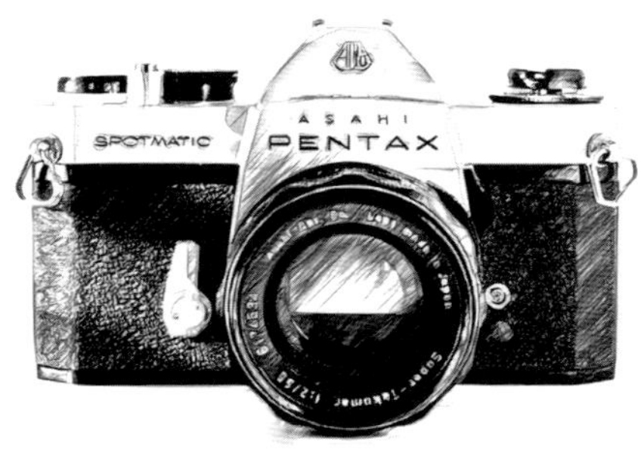

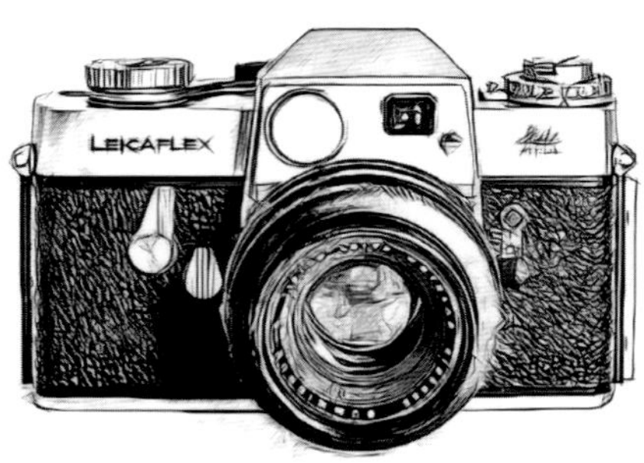

**1964:** The E. Leitz Company introduce their first SLR, the Leicaflex. To have the brightest viewfinder possible, matching their rangefinder models, the camera has a screen with only a small central focusing area, which most people find difficult to use. With an external CdS meter (rather than TTL metering), a limited range of lenses and missing several features present in the competition, the Leicaflex is best described as "a day late and a dollar short." It is an expensive, exquisitely made camera, but not a market success, and production will end in 1968.

---

**TRIVIA**

Leitz was a reluctant entrant into the SLR market. At the beginning of the 1960s, however, rangefinder cameras were being abandoned by professionals and advanced amateurs in favour of SLR designs. Thus, Leica had little choice but to offer an SLR of its own. These days, this first Leicaflex model is generally referred to as the Leicaflex Standard to distinguish it from the models that followed.

---

**1964:** Agfa AG of Germany merges with Gavaert of Belgium, forming Agfa-Gavaert.

**1964:** Kodak's Retina Reflex IV (made in West Germany) is the last of a long line of "quirky" Retina cameras. It is the last SLR that Kodak will build themselves, but the first SLR to feature a standard ISO hot shoe atop the pentaprism housing for direct flash mounting and synchronization.

---

**TRIVIA**

Although the hot shoe had been de facto standardized in the late 1950s, the International Organization for Standardization did not officially set its ISO 518 hot shoe standard until 1977.

The "cold shoe," used to attach a rangefinder, flash, or other accessory, originated with Oskar Barnack and the original UR Leica in 1913. The earliest "hot shoe" is thought to have been on the Univex Mercury, of 1938. After the Second World War, many 35mm cameras featured a Leica-type accessory shoe with a single central electrical contact (the present-day ISO hot shoe). But in this feature, SLRs lagged far behind.

Most 1960s 35mm SLRs used screw-on accessory "cold-shoes" attached to the eyepiece to attach flashes but used a PC cable socket to sync them. The ISO hot shoe only became a standard feature on SLRs in the early 1970s.

---

**1964:** A 1953 trade agreement seriously hampers the ability of VEB Film und Chemiefaserwerk Agfa Wolfen to sell its Agfa-branded film outside the East Bloc countries, so it replaces the Agfa name with the Orwo (for Original Wolfen) trademark and can now sell world-wide.

**1964:** KMZ's Soviet-made Zenit 5 becomes the first SLR with a built-in electric motor drive. It features a Ni-Cd battery-powered motor for automatic single-frame film advance. But it also has a standard film-wind knob—just in case the motor fails. It is not capable of making sequential images.

**1964:** The American firm 3M buys Italy's Ferrania for $55 million and renames the firm Ferrania-3M.

**TRIVIA**

3M quickly replaced the Ferrania name with their own, and eventually dropped even that, becoming the largest supplier of private-label film in the world. In 1995, 3M breaks up Ferrania, spinning off its data-storage and imaging businesses into a new company, Imation. The new company is short-lived and, in 1999, it is sold to an investment firm. The firm is again restructured, breaking it into Ferrania Technologies, focused on pharmaceutical products, and Ferrania Solis, makers of solar panels, both of which remain in business. The film factory brings back the Ferrania brand, but it is too little, too late; and the Ferrania ceases all operations in 2009.

**1964:** Nippon Kogaku take the zoom lens from their earlier Nikkorex Zoom 35 (see **1962** and **1963**) and introduce it as the 43–86mm $f$3.5 Zoom-Nikkor, a separate interchangeable lens for their Nikon F and Nikkorex F cameras. The significance of this lens is not its optical performance (it is a strong contender for the title of "poorest lens ever built") but the fact that it is inexpensive and in plentiful supply makes zoom lenses a force in 35mm photography.

**1964:** Agfa introduces its "Rapid" film system as a rival to Kodak's 126 cartridge film. The Rapid system uses otherwise standard 35mm film in special metal cassettes, which have no central spindle and are shorter in height than standard 135 cassettes. An identical empty cassette is used in the camera's take-up compartment.

The Rapid system is easier to load since the film does not have to be threaded onto a take-up spool as with a 35mm camera. The new full cassette is simply placed in one side of the film chamber with a leader protruding. The camera automatically guides this leader into the velvet light-trap of the take-up cassette, and after shooting one or two blank frames the camera is ready to make its first exposure. The film does not need to be rewound. At the end of the roll, the now-empty cassette is moved to the other side and used as the take-up cassette for the next roll.

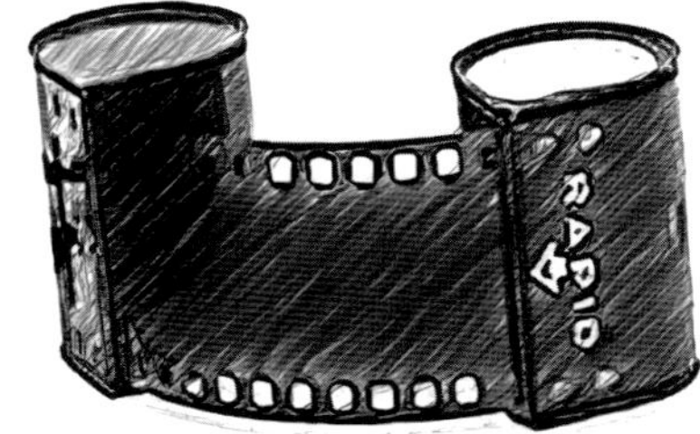

The Rapid system uses the camera's pressure plate, while 126 cartridges rely on the close tolerances of its plastic cartridge to hold the film flat—a less reliable system. Nonetheless, the runaway success of Kodak's Instamatic series pushes the Rapid system off the market. Agfa begins selling 126 cameras and film in 1967 and stops selling Rapid cameras in 1971, although film remains available for few years after that. Cameras accepting Rapid film are also made by Ilford and Minolta and perhaps a few others. None are a huge market success.

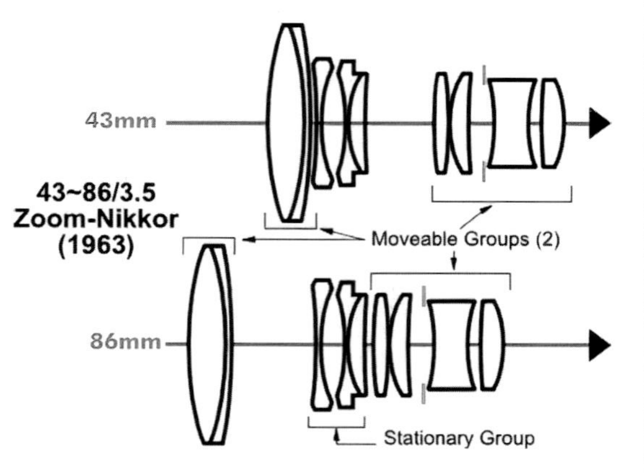


**TRIVIA**

Most early zoom lenses produced mediocre images and the 43~86 Zoom Nikko was typical of the breed. The zoom components are arranged in three groups, the first acting as a convex lens, the second concave, and the third, another convex lens, making this a so-called "three-group mechanical correction" type of zoom lens. The second group is at a fixed distance from the film plane, with the first and third groups moving independently when the subject being photographed is zoomed into. This independent movement of first and third element groups was achieved through the incorporation of a cam, an eccentric curved wheel on a shaft used to transform rotary motion into reciprocating motion. Mass producing such a high-precision mechanism in the mid-1960s was no easy task!

**1965:** The term "pixel," for "picture element" (coined by Russell Kirsch in 1957), is first used publicly in a paper presented by Fred Billingsley of JPL (Jet Propulsion Laboratory, Pasadena) to the Symposium on Electronic Imaging (see **1957**). An alternative term, "pel," is proposed by William F. Schreiber of MIT in the Proceedings of the IEEE two years later but is soon forgotten.

**1965:** Super-8 movie film is released by Eastman Kodak as an improvement of the older "regular" 8mm home movie format. The film is the same as standard 8mm film, but the dimensions of the perforations are smaller than those on the older film, which allows the exposed area to be made larger. The Super-8 standard also specifically allocates the border opposite the perforations for an oxide stripe for magnetically recording sound.

The Super-8 plastic cartridge is the fastest-loading film system ever developed, as it can be loaded into the Super-8 camera in less than two seconds without the need to directly thread or even touch the film. It becomes wildly successful among amateur movie fans and remains popular today.

---

**UPDATE**

In late 2023, Kodak will announce a new, "limited edition" Super-8 film camera with an 11% larger, 14:9 image format, interchangeable C-mount lenses, a 4-inch LCD viewfinder screen, built-in digital sound recorder, filming speeds of 18, 24, 25, 36 FPS, and more. All for just north of $5,000!

---

**1965:** Kodak replace the individual flashbulbs used on early Instamatic cameras with the Flashcube. Developed by Sylvania Electric, a Flashcube contains four AG-1 flashbulbs, each mounted at 90° from the others in its own reflector. Winding the film also rotates the flashcube so that a fresh bulb is ready. Flashcubes will be replaced by the MagiCube in 1970.

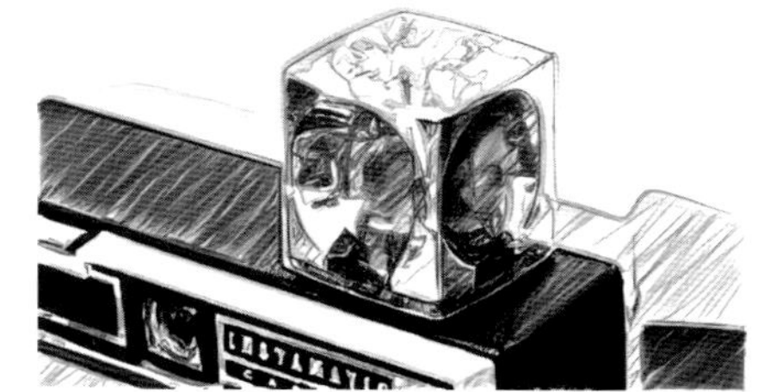

**1965:** The Camera Corporation of America, Hicksville, NY, releases its "Chrislin Insta-camera" to compete with Polaroid's basic "Swinger" model. It is a two-tone blue box camera with a "see-through" handle that doubles as a viewfinder and takes black-and-white 2½ x 3¼-inch positive photos that self-develop in just 60 seconds. With eight photographs per roll, the film is only available by mail. The prints come from the camera coated with a caustic black goo which requires immediate rinsing with cold water. No water? No problem! Each film comes with a package of pre-moistened towelettes. Towelettes or no, it's a messy way to get prints that are not up to Polaroid's quality. Consumer Reports rates the camera "unacceptable" and it fails in the marketplace.

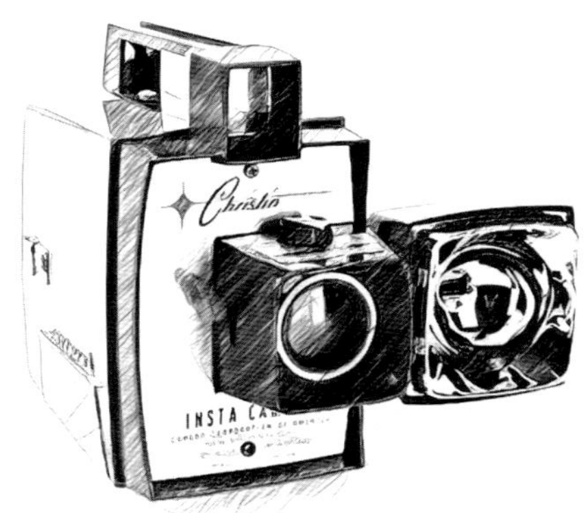

---

**TRIVIA**

Chrislin's instant development method was originally created by Agfa, but never brought to market. After Agfa's patent expired, Chrislin picked up the process and adapted it for their use.

---

**ODDITIES**

The Fotochrome is designed in the USA by Harrison Photochrome Inc., a major Florida photofinisher, and made under contract by Petri for export only. It is loaded with a special cartridge (made by Ansco) containing reversal colour paper, which takes 10 exposures. The process is cumbersome, the colour substandard, and the camera looks like a mantle clock. The auto-exposure system proves unreliable, and the proprietary film type fails to catch on.

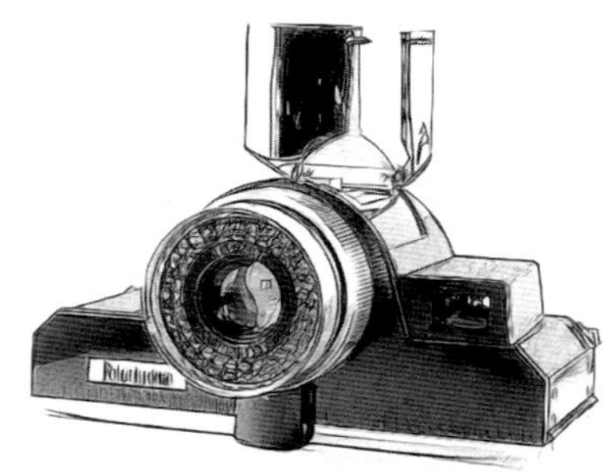

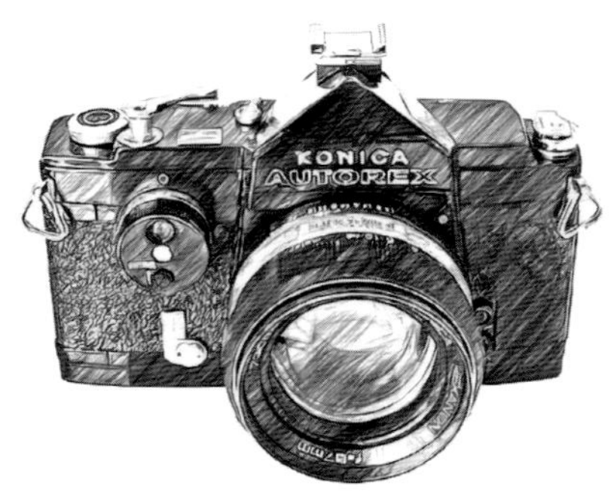

**1965:** Konishiroku introduce their Konica Autorex to the Japanese market; it is the first high-quality SLR with a focal-plane shutter and automatic exposure control. With the shutter speed set, the camera selects the correct aperture, which it indicates by a needle over a scale in the viewfinder. However, the shutter release mechanism requires substantial pressure, as it must also move the mechanism to make the auto-exposure system work.

The dual format Autorex can switch from full to half-frame, even with film in the camera. A lever to the right of the lens moves plates at both sides to reduce the film gate, change the gear ratio of the film advance, and adjust the frame counter.

**1965:** Canon release the Pellix, the first widely sold SLR with a fixed mirror. (The honour of being very first with a fixed semi-transparent mirror goes to the little-known Focaflex—see **1960**.) The mirror is a super-thin, semi-transparent film only 1/50 mm thick, which transmits 65% of the light to the film and reflects 35% to the viewfinder. This results in a camera harder to focus in dim light. It is also Canon's first 35mm SLR camera with TTL metering, using a 12% spot at the viewfinder centre.

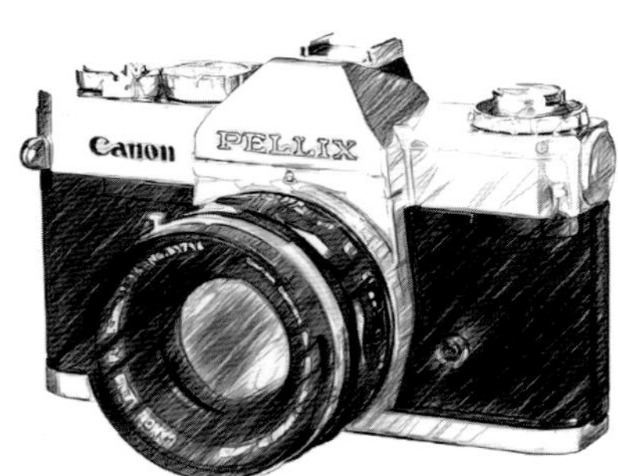

---

### TRIVIA

Pellicle mirrors have several disadvantages. First, they degrade image quality slightly, as the mirror is always in the optical path. Second, they lose roughly one-half an *f*-stop of light, as some light is always directed to the finder. This makes exposure times longer, increasing the chance of camera shake. And it is difficult to keep the mirror clean as pellicle mirrors attract dust like magnets. The last, but perhaps the most important disadvantage, is that over time older pellicle mirrors can (and do) yellow and separate, eventually making them difficult, if not impossible, to use.

In 2010, Sony will introduce cameras with semi-transparent mirrors. They will call them SLTs (Single Lens Translucent) and will claim it is "ground-breaking technology!" (See **2006**.)

---

**1965:** The professional SLR market is small, so Nikon make a second effort in consumer grade cameras and introduce the Nikkormat (Nikomat in Japan) series. Unlike the earlier Nikkorex series, the Nikkormats are produced in-house and prove both reliable and remarkably successful, as they become known as the "poor man's Nikon F." The series will continue, through various models, until 1980.

**1965:** The Soviet maker KMZ introduces its Zenit-E, the first "modern" Soviet SLR. It features a rapid-wind lever and built-in selenium light meter. In 1967, the Zenit E will gain an instant-return mirror. It will be made at the Krasnogorsk Mechanical Plant (KMZ) until 1982 and at the BelOMO factory from 1973 to 1986. Over 12 million of the Zenit-Es are made and exported to 74 countries, sometimes being sold under other brand names, such as the RevueFlex-E.

---

### TRIVIA

KMZ is not the only maker of ZENIT cameras. In 1969, the Vileiskiy-Zenit factory was established in the town of Vilejka, just outside the modern-day Belarusian capital of Minsk. It was a joint effort between the KMZ (Krasnogorsk Mechanical Works) and MMZ (Minsk Mechanical Works), to assist in producing the long-lived line of 35mm SLR cameras. They produced Zenit cameras from 1973 to 1986. The Vileiskiy Zenits are not considered to be as well made as the KMZ models. The two can be told apart by looking at the factory logo on the rear of the camera. The KMZ models have a stylized dove and prism logo, while the Minsk ones have a stylized image of a bird. Now known as Zenit-BelOMO, the Vilejka factory has become the largest producer of spotting scopes in the post-Soviet states. They also produce microscopes and binoculars.

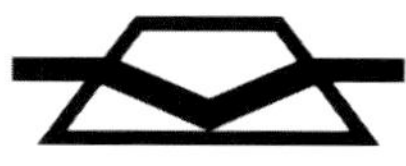

*KMZ logo*

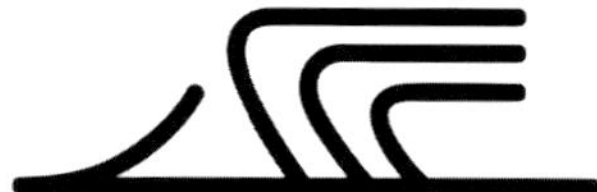

*Vileiskiy-Zenit logo*

---

### TRIVIA

A friend of your scribe purchased a Zenit camera at the Soviet booth at Montreal's Expo 67. The box contained a packing slip which read: "This camera has been inspected and is permitted to be useful."

---

### TRIVIA

Later, quite different cameras, all called Zenit, were produced in China, by the Shanghai General Camera Factory (a.k.a. Seagull), among others, all with a Minolta Rokkor lens mount. Sadly, production dates are unclear. Circa 1995–1997 the Zenit 12XLS and 12 PRO were designed by Belomo (Belarus) but made by BMA Industrial, in Brazil. All of these versions were primarily targeted to the South American markets.

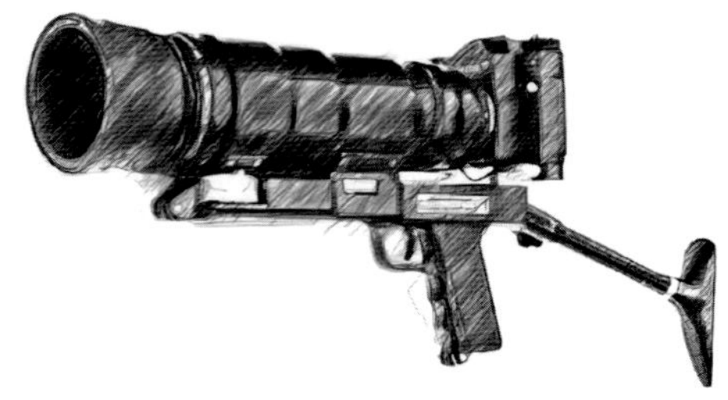

**1965:** Soviet camera-maker KMZ introduces one of the more unusual cameras ever made. Their FS-3 FotoSniper is fitted with a Zenit-ES body (a modified Zenit-E with a second shutter release on the base plate, used by the gun-stock's trigger) and comes complete with a Helios-44 58mm, *f*2 and a Tair-3AS 300mm *f*4.5. The shoulder stock is made of lacquered aluminum. Some 98,000 of them are produced between 1965 and 1982. In 1982, a new, improved FS-12 appears. It is essentially the same as the FS-3 but fitted with the new Zenit 12S body. Roughly 110,000 FS-12's are produced before production ends in 1995.

---

### TRIVIA

The first Fotosniper, called the FS2, was produced between 1937 and 1943 by VOOMP-GOI, a Leningrad plant, with a production run of just under 500. The camera was intended for military use and was available in olive green and black. The lens was a GOI 300mm *f*4.5 while the body was a FED fitted with a special GOI mirror box, making it a rudimentary SLR. The whole thing was mounted on a wooden gunstock.

The second version of the FS2 was produced by KMZ (near Moscow) from 1944 to 1945, after the siege of Leningrad. KMZ produced fewer than 300 outfits with a KMZ Tair-3 300mm *f*4.5. Again, all for the Soviet military.

A single FotoSniper FS2 with an unmarked 600mm *f*4.5 lens was made in 1943, intended for reconnaissance by the Soviet Baltic Fleet. It had its own reflex finder, so a rangefinder camera could be mounted. But such a long lens proved to be unusable at sea, and so was never put into series production. In 2021, this prototype sold at auction, for €144,000, or about $171,000.

---

### BUSINESS TRIVIA

Though East German and Soviet cameras were exported almost everywhere in the 1960s, such cameras were uncommonly common in Italy. At that time, Italy had the biggest and best organized Communist Party outside the USSR, and many Italian firms had commercial relationships with East Germany (DDR) and the Soviet Union. The FIAT automobile company opened a giant production plant in Togliattigrad to make Lada cars, and the Soviet government paid with machinery, and cameras.

Olivetti (the famous maker of typewriting and calculating machines) received most of its payments in cameras and lenses. Some time in the mid-to-late 1960s, Olivetti formed "F.O.S." (Foto Ottica Sovietica, or Soviet Photo Optics), to distribute these Soviet bloc cameras in Italy. These arrangements lasted until the collapse of the Soviet Union at the end of 1991.

**1966:** The Leitz Noctilux 50mm $f$ 1.2 is introduced; it is the first production lens for a 35mm camera that has an aspherical glass lens element. Fewer than 1,700 are produced because Leitz has no way of testing the aspherical version until it is fully assembled—and the success rate for the difficult-to-make aspherical lens is just 50%. In 1976, it is replaced by the much-better-known $f$ 1.0 non-aspheric Noctilux.

**1966:** Richard Avedon (1923–2004) starts work with *Vogue* and becomes one of the first true fashion photographers. He elevates fashion photography to an art form and will remain at *Vogue* until 1988. Avedon becomes well known for his minimalist portrait style. It is said that Avedon often provokes the person depicted to make him or her "look more real."

**1966:** Asahi is the world's first camera manufacturer to produce one million SLRs (after only 14 years of manufacturing).

**1966:** The Praktica Electronic, made in East Germany, becomes the first SLR with an electronically controlled shutter, using electronic circuitry to time its focal-plane shutter instead of spring/gear/lever clockwork mechanisms.

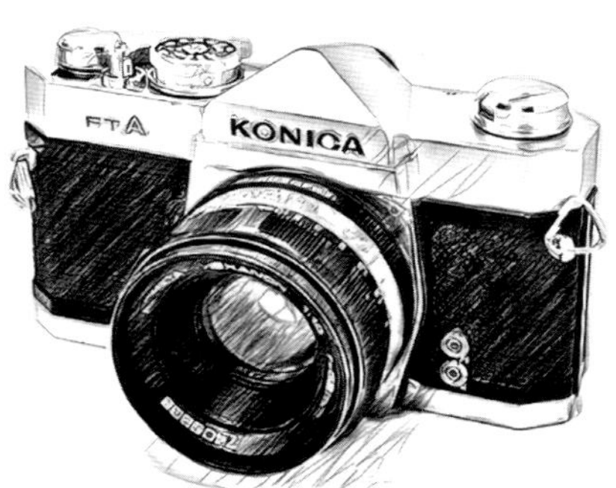

**1966:** Konishiroku introduce the Konica Auto-Reflex (called the Konica FT-A [for Autorex] in Japan and sold as the Revue Auto-Reflex in Germany). It is not the first focal-plane-shutter SLR with automatic (shutter priority) exposure control—that laurel is shared by two rather obscure French-made cameras, the Focaflex and the Savoyflex (see **1960**). However, it is the first widely available SLR with automatic exposure control. Like the 1965 Konica Autorex, it offers a choice of full or half-frame images, changeable at any point, switched by a lever on the camera's top. It proves to be a well-made, reliable camera, with excellent lenses. It starts a revolution in camera design and is followed by a long line of auto-reflex models, all successful in the marketplace.

---

**TRIVIA**

In the March 1966 issue of *Modern Photography*, Herbert Keppler writes: "The inevitable marriage of convenience plus accuracy inherent in automatic exposure systems and the versatility of the interchangeable-lens, focal-plane shutter, single-lens reflex has finally occurred."

---

**1966:** Tamron produce a new series of lenses with the "Adapt-A-Matic" interchangeable mount system which makes it possible to use the automatic diaphragm control on a wide variety of cameras. It succeeds in the marketplace.

**1966:** At Photokina, Carl Zeiss exhibits their "Gigantar," a 40mm *f* 0.33 lens. Zeiss claims it is *"The word's fastest lens."* But is it true? Well . . . no.

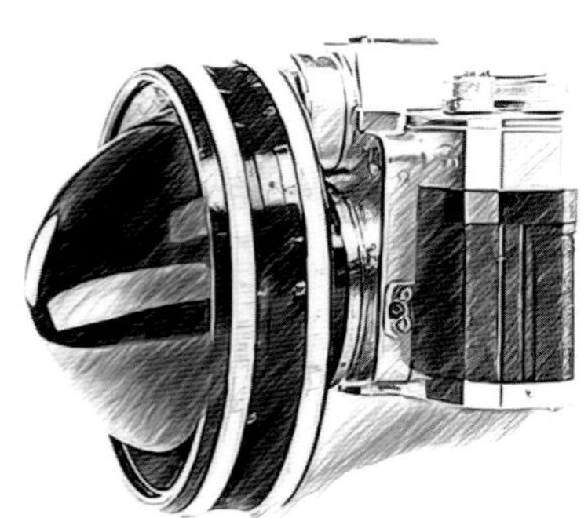

The Gigantar is born at a time when camera companies are aiming for lenses with ever-larger apertures, much as they are going for cameras with more and more megapixels and ever-higher ISO ratings today. Canon has just released their 50mm *f* 0.95 (see **1961**) and photographers are becoming fixated on the speed of lenses, rather than their performance.

Wolf Wehran, head of the Zeiss public relations department, realizes that Zeiss is unable to compete in this area due to the smaller "throat" of its lens mount. So, he decides to poke some fun at this "fast glass fad." In the Zeiss lens design lab, he finds an old condenser lens for an enlarger, and with an engineer's help and a few additional leftover parts, he creates a "Frankenlens" for the Zeiss Contarex. He arbitrarily decides that the lens will have a focal length of 40mm and a maximum aperture of *f* 0.33 and then has it proudly displayed, in a locked glass case, at Photokina.

---

### AUCTION MADNESS

The Gigantar is, of course, a hoax and not capable of actually taking a photograph. This fact does not stop the one-off lens from selling at auction in 2011 for €60,000!

---

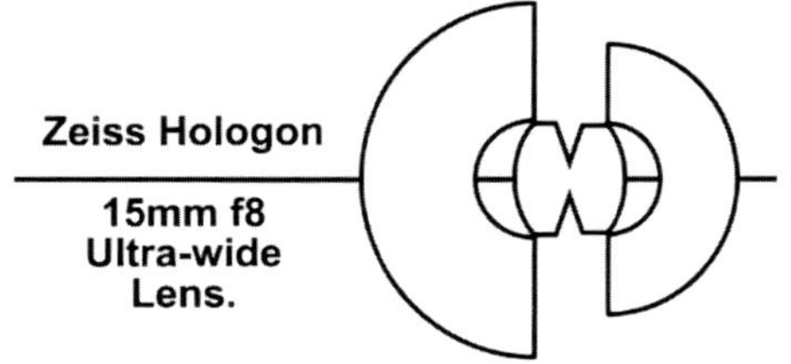


**1966:** Zeiss create their "Hologon Ultrawide," a camera specifically made for one very unusual lens. The 15mm *f* 8 Hologon has a staggering 110° field of view, making it difficult to keep the photographer's fingers out of the photographs! The symmetrical design of the Hologon ensures complete freedom from distortion of straight lines, making it an ideal lens for architectural photography. The camera is not without its problems and requires a graduated neutral density filter to compensate for the extreme light fall-off. Unfortunately, this reduces the effective aperture to *f* 16. Roughly 1,400 Hologon Ultrawide cameras (with integral finder and a special handgrip) are produced.

In 1968 or 1969 (historians seem unable to agree), the Hologon is introduced as a separate lens for the Zeiss Contax camera; then, when Zeiss Ikon fails in 1972, the remaining stock (rumoured to be roughly 400 lenses) of the Hologon is purchased by Leica, who modify them to the Leica "M" mount. The Hologon will have a brief revival in the 1990s, in a modified formulation, as a 16mm *f* 8 version produced for Zeiss, by Kyocera in Japan, to fit the Kyocera-made Contax "G".

**TRIVIA**

The Zeiss Hologon is an amazing beast, but the Zeiss Ikon camera made for it is not. This leads to a thriving cottage industry among some of the very best camera repairmen making modifications to the Zeiss Hologon to fit Leica's M series of cameras. This market evaporates when Leica purchases the remaining Hologons from Zeiss Ikon and puts them in new Leica M mounts.

The original 15mm *f*/8 Hologon was a modification of the Goerz Hypergon, a lens with 110° coverage introduced circa 1910, in six focal lengths, to cover 5 x 7-inch to 24 x 28-inch glass plates. Various Hypergon models ran between $43.50 to $91, the equivalent of $1,000 and $2,119 today. The Goerz Hypergon is considered one of the all-time classic large-format lenses.

**1966:** The first image of the Earth taken from the moon is transmitted from NASA's "Lunar Orbiter 1."

**1966:** NASA chooses the Leica MDa cameras, modified for use in space, for their manned Lunar missions. They have a huge weight advantage over the larger Hasselblad cameras, yet none make it to the moon. While the *Saturn V* rocket has ample horsepower to get to the moon, for the untried lunar liftoff every ounce will

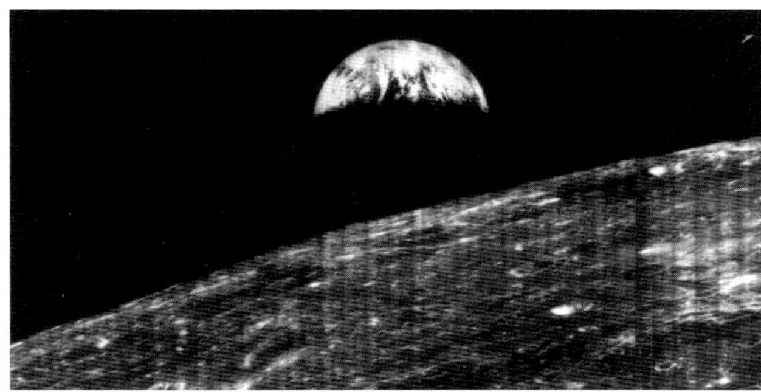

*First photo of Earth from lunar orbit. Courtesy NASA.*

count. Some smart NASA engineer figures out that if they choose the Hasselblad cameras, they could leave the camera bodies behind. Bringing only the film backs with them on their return to Earth, the liftoff weight from the moon will be less than if they'd taken Leicas. (It would seem reasonable to remove the film cartridges and leave the Leicas behind for even less weight, but that proved too difficult for space suited astronauts. Besides, it's likely the engineers really wanted the superior resolution of the 6 x 6cm format.)

**1966:** Introduced in 1966 and produced until 1972, the Rollei 16 (and its successor the 16S) arrive at the end of the 16mm sub-mini camera craze that flourished after the Second World War. The "16" was superbly finished, cleverly engineered, very expensive and arguably one of the best-made sub-miniatures. The lens is a 25mm *f* 2.8 Zeiss Tessar, with beautifully made, and sharp, Zeiss Mutar

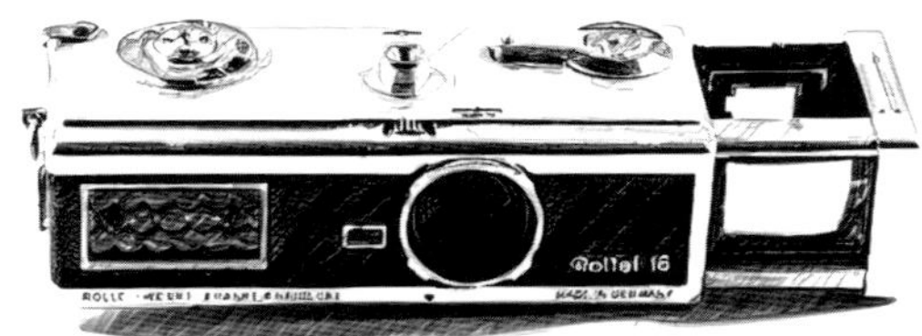

wide and tele auxiliary lens attachments which bayonet over the main Tessar lens. Focusing is by scale, which works just fine with such a short focal length, and the viewfinder is parallax corrected. The 16S offers programmed shutter speeds 1/30 to 1/500 using its selenium meter.

**1966:** Victor Hasselblad sells the distribution company and retailer network "Hasselblad Fotografiska AB" to Kodak, ending their long-term partnership, but not the friendships upon which it was based.

**1966:** General Aniline & Film acquire Sawyer's, a manufacturer of photographic slide projectors as well as the View-Master 3D stereoscopes and reels.

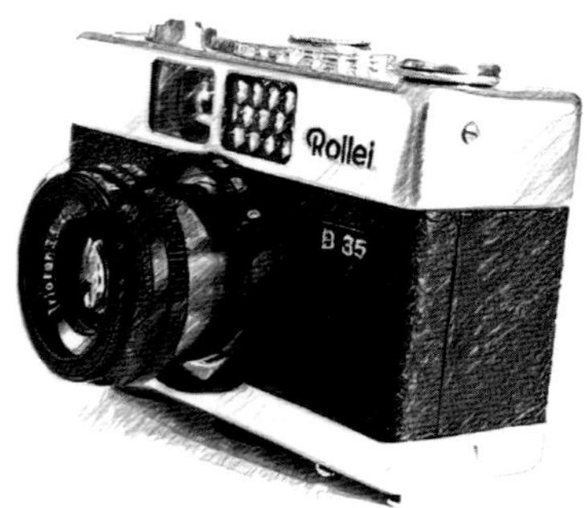

**1966:** The Rollei 35 is designed by Heinz Waaske (see **1948**) to provide a full frame 35mm alternative to Yoshihisa Maitani's half-frame Olympus Pen (see **1959**). Waaske is convinced that buyers of 16mm subminiature and half-frame cameras choose them not because of the small film formats but because of the small size of the cameras. So, he designs a full frame, 35mm camera with a collapsible lens tube barely larger than a pack of cigarettes.

Today, the Rollei 35 series remains one of the smallest 35mm cameras ever made, with only the Minolta TC-1 and Minox 35 being smaller. The lower-cost B35 (later called the 35B), with a non-coupled selenium meter (shown above right), is introduced in 1969. Over 30 years, some two million Rollei 35 series cameras are manufactured, first in Germany and, from 1971, in Singapore, until production ceased in 1981. All are equipped with German-made Schneider S-Xenar or Carl Zeiss Sonnar, Tessar, or Triotar lenses. Despite a perception that German-produced Rollei 35 cameras are better, camera repairmen report that quality control at Rollei Singapore was on a par with Germany and there is no difference.

---

### TRIVIA

Heinz Waaske designed his camera at home while working for Wirgin. When he finally presented the fully functional prototype to his employer, Heinrich Wirgin said: "So you have wasted time on your own construction in my prototyping workshop?" It was not until that moment that Wirgin told his chief engineer that he had already decided to end camera production.

In 1965, Waaske started working for Rollei, in Braunschweig. Their managing director, Heinrich Peesel, accidentally got a glimpse of Waaske's tiny prototype and immediately decided that the camera should be further developed for mass production, but using only parts from Rollei's suppliers.

Waaske's little camera was presented at Photokina in 1966 as the Rollei 35, with a Zeiss Tessar 40mm *f* 3.5 lens, a state-of-the-art Gossen CdS exposure meter and a precision-made diaphragm and shutter assembly made by Compur, using Waaske's patented shutter design.

After 1981, the Rollei 35 continued to be manufactured in Germany by DHW Fototechnik, the successor of Franke & Heidecke, right up to 2015. The last version was the Rollei 35 Classic, an updated Rollei 35 SE.

**1967:** Zeiss Ikon bring out their Contaflex 126, whose only relation to the rest of the Contaflex family is its name. It accepts a Kodak 126 (Instamatic) cartridge, one of very few ambitious cameras to use that film. It has a focal plane shutter and accepts seven dedicated lenses.

---

### TRIVIA

Lenses for the Contaflex 126 are often confused with lenses for other Contaflex cameras. They can only be used on the Contaflex 126 body, that can only take the obsolete 126 cartridge, so the value of these lenses is not very high, despite their famous names.

---

**1967:** The Makina Optical Co., Ltd. (Makina Kogaku K.K.) starts operations in Tokyo as an independent lens maker, manufacturing lenses for other companies' brands (Hamimex, Rexatar, Vivitar, Danbia, Travenar, and others). They start selling lenses under their own brand, Makinon, in 1974. (Note that the Makinon brand had been used by Plaubel prior to the 1970s.) The date of their demise is unclear, but they will go out of business sometime between 1979 and 1985.

---

### TRIVIA

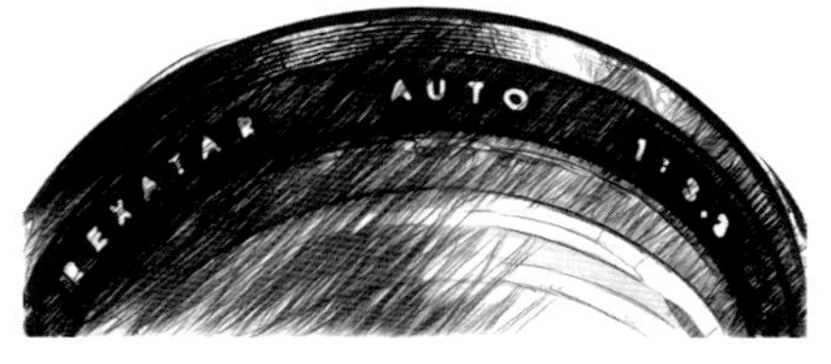


According to various sources, the company started manufacturing in a garage and employed part-time housewives for assembly work. While their lenses were solidly built, they had a reputation for inconsistent quality control and sometimes had alignment issues that affect the image quality or operation of the lens. None of their lenses are considered a match for the quality of lenses by the major camera-makers or even those from the better independent lens makers. In fact, your scribe's 200mm *f* 3.3 Rexatar exhibits the worst chromatic aberration of any lens he has ever seen.

---

**1967:** Kodak produce Technical Pan specifically for photographing the sun. It is introduced to the public in 1977 as the world's finest grain general-purpose film, with an ISO rating of 16 to 25 (depending on how it is developed) and remains on sale until the 2014.

---

### TRIVIA

When the film was discontinued in 2014, Kodak revealed that none had been made since the spring of 2005. Nor could any more be made because the coating line had been shut down and many of the materials used to make it had been discontinued. It was still on the market only because a large roll had been found in frozen storage. The film was created for the military and, as it was no longer required by them, Kodak cut the roll into commercially viable formats and continued to sell it.

**1967:** Olympus introduce the Trip 35, a compact point-and-shoot camera with a stellar 40mm *f* 2.8 lens, programmed auto-exposure and a selenium exposure meter. As the name implies, it is intended for those who want a compact camera for holidays. Though nothing about it is revolutionary, it shapes a generation, ending a lengthy production run in 1984. Over 10 million Trip 35s are sold.

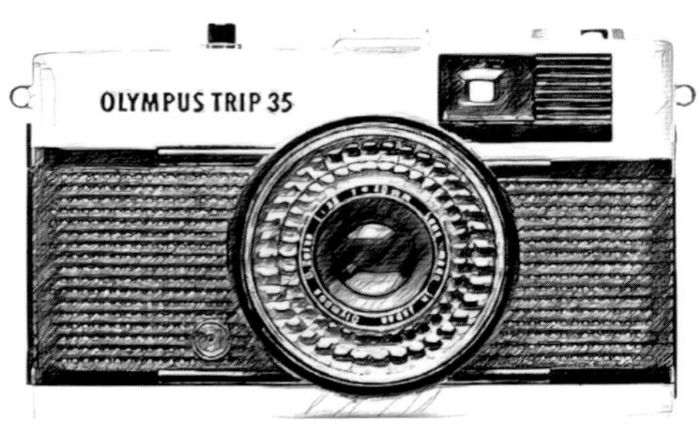


**1968:** VEB Pentacon absorb Mentor, Certo, Ihagee, Meyer, and some smaller specialized optical or camera companies, thus becoming a group comprising nearly the entire East German photography-related industry except film maker Orwo. Production is concentrated on the Praktica SLRs, but also includes the Exakta and Exa lines of SLRs.

---

### ODDITIES

In 1968, Olympus show their MDN (later called the OM-X) prototype. It is the first Olympus SLR designed to be a full-featured, multi-functional system that can be used for a wide range of purposes by assembling different units, each with a single function. It follows Hasselblad's modular design, but for 35mm film. It is never produced, but much of its engineering will go into the OM-1 in 1972.

Curiously, in 2019, FujiFilm will show a prototype of a camera very similar to the MDN/OM-X, but it too is never produced.

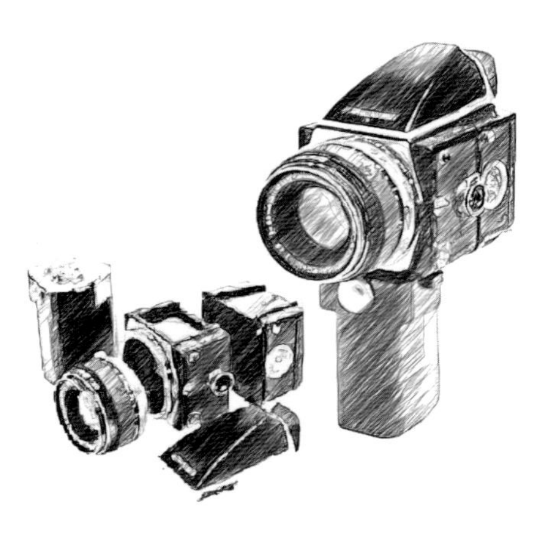

---

**1968:** Mamiya Camera Co. introduces the Mamiya/Sekor 1000DTL, the first camera to offer both spot and averaging TTL metering. Surprisingly, this very desirable feature does not become available on other SLRs for some years.

---

### TRIVIA

A West German court rules that rights to the Exakta brand are to be returned to the heirs of Ihagee's founder. Thus, the East German made "Exakta" cameras are sold, in West Germany, under the Elbaflex brand (named for the Elba River that runs through Dresden). Fifty years on, the Elbaaflex will (almost) rise from the ashes (see **2017**).

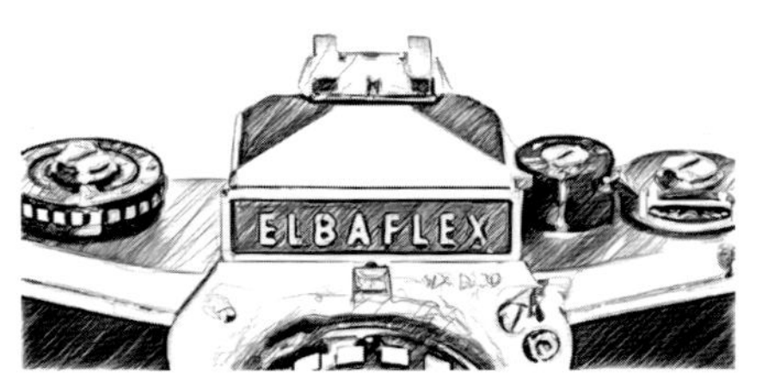

**1968:** The Reflex-Nikkor 500 ƒ8 is introduced and quickly becomes the most sought-after of catadioptric (mirror) lenses. Smaller and lighter than the earlier 500 ƒ5 Reflex Nikkor (1961–1968) and super sharp, it suffers the common CAT deficiencies of low contrast and an odd "donut" bokeh in the out-of-focus areas. It gets multi-coating in 1974 and has a redesign in 1983, when it is replaced by a lighter, more compact version that is made until 2005.

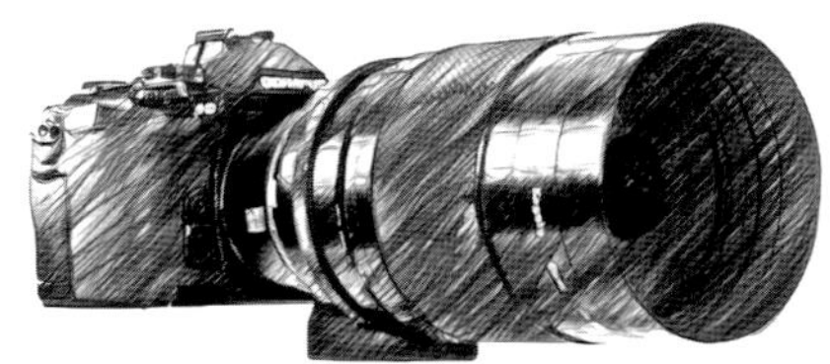

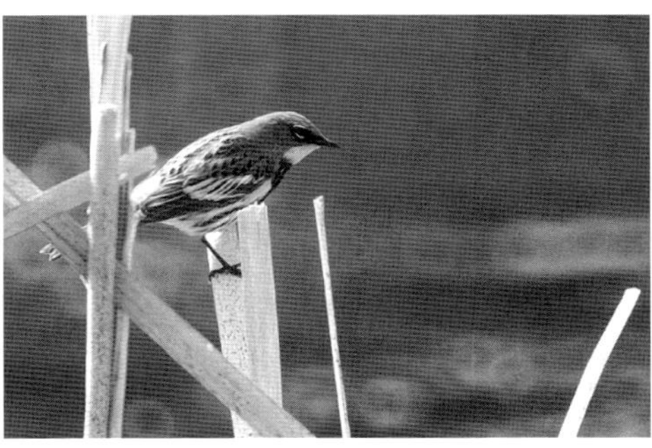

With the high ISO capabilities of modern digital cameras, the ability to manipulate contrast on the computer after the shot is taken, and the new electronic finders of mirrorless cameras which compensate for the dim view of an ƒ8 lens, mirror lenses are becoming more useful and popular than ever before. However, there is still no cure for the odd "donuts" around the highlights in the out-of-focus areas. This problem does not affect all images, showing only when there are strong highlights in the background. The "donuts" are caused by the secondary mirror blocking the centre of the main lens (as can be seen in the diagram with the "Catadioptric" entry in the Glossary).

---

**TRIVIA**

A major advantage of mirror lenses is a total lack of chromatic aberration. Today, various relatively low-cost CAT lenses are produced, primarily in Asia, in focal lengths ranging from 300 to 1000mm. Performance varies.

---

**1968:** Yashica's Lynx 5000E features a bright 50mm ƒ1.8 lens and a Copal between-the-lens shutter capable of 1/1000 second. But its claim to fame is an unusual electronic exposure system. A Wheatstone bridge (see the circuit diagram) is regulated by an integrated chip, which controls the shutter. The aperture ring is turned

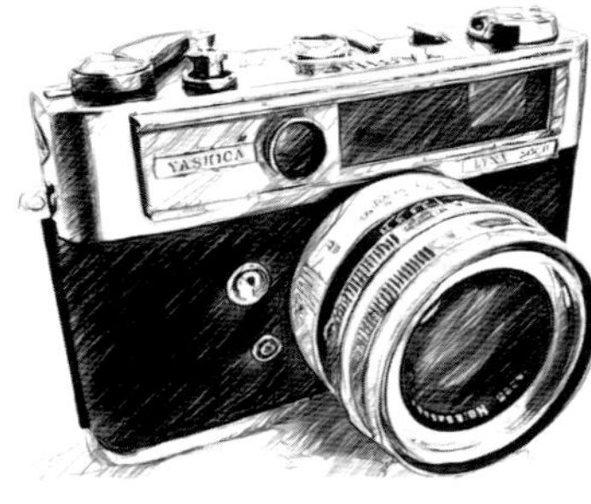

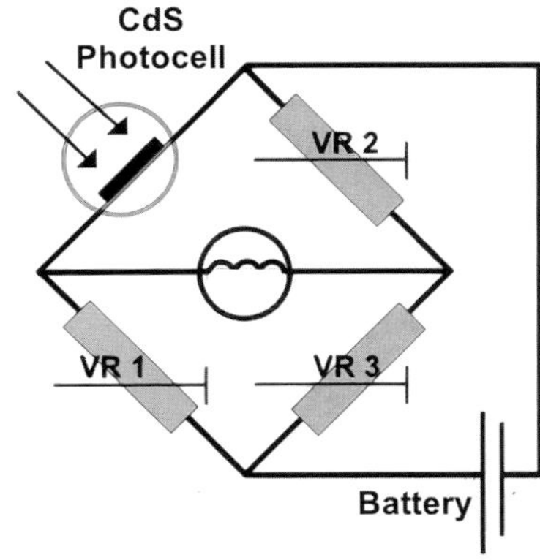


until a small lamp indicates a balanced circuit and thus the correct exposure. It is a simple, sturdy system with virtually no moving parts. It is also the first camera with an electronically controlled shutter.

**1968:** In November, Yashica's "TL Electro-X" SLR is marketed. In addition to using the electronic exposure control that first appeared in the Yashica Lynx (above), it is the first camera with an electronically controlled focal-plane shutter. The Copal Square SE uses a capacitor and transistors as a "governor" and a magnet to control the curtain release. The camera proves noisy, with the shutter, automatic diaphragm, and reflex mirror all disturbingly audible. Still, electronics are starting to make inroads into cameras.

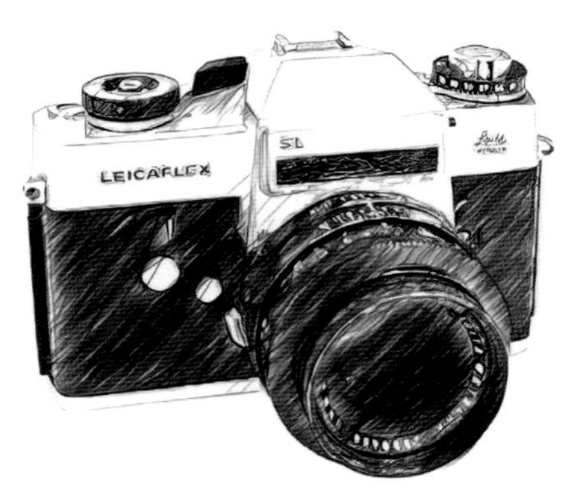

**TRIVIA**

Introduced by Leitz in 1968, the Leicaflex SL is a superbly built camera, but big and clunky, with features somewhat behind the times compared to the competition. Despite retailing for 50% more than the Nikon F, both the SL and the SL-2 (which will follow in 1974) cost so much to produce that Leica has little choice but to sell them below the cost of production, hoping to make up the loss on sales of lenses to go with them. This strategy almost bankrupts the firm.

**1968:** Sedic, a Japanese maker of exposure meters introduces its first meter, the Sedic PR-60, which sells for $9.95.

**TRIVIA**

Sedic will become a maker of inexpensive 110, 126, and 35mm cameras, sold almost entirely under other companies' brands, such as Argus and Hanimex, among others. They also produce dozens of cheap promotional cameras such as cameras built into a can of Coca-Cola. In 1974, they will produce the first 110 camera to accept wide-angle and tele attachment lenses. The last known reference to the firm was in 2006 and it appears it no longer exists.

**1969:** An American, George Smith (b. 1930), and a Canadian, Willard Boyle (1924–2011), both physicists working at Bell Labs, invent the CCD or Charge Coupled Device. CCDs are electronic memory chips that can hold a variable charge that corresponds to the amount of light falling on one section or pixel. This makes them useful as imaging devices for cameras, scanners, and fax machines. For this, they will share the 2009 Nobel Prize in Physics.

**1969:** First debuted in 1965 as a prototype dubbed the Pentax 220, Asahi Optical market their Pentax 6 x 7 SLR for 120 or 220 film. Looking like a 35mm SLR on steroids, it is the first eye-level SLR in the 6 x 7 format—sometimes called the "ideal format," as it closely matches a standard 8 x 10-inch print. The camera features an electronically controlled focal plane shutter, which locks up when the batteries are low. A hit with professional photographers, the Pentax 220 receives several minor engineering updates and cosmetic changes in 1990 and is renamed the Pentax 67. More improvements come in 1999 with the release of the Pentax 67 MkII, which remains on sale until 2009.

---

**TRIVIA**

Released in 1901, 120 film has a backing paper and is around 82 and 85mm (32 to 33 inches) in length. Released in 1965, 220 film has twice the length of film, which is possible as it has only a paper leader and trailer, rather than the full paper backing. Thus, more film can be wound on the same spool. However, 220 can only be used in "professional" cameras able to correctly advance the film without the aid of frame numbers. Today, 220 is no longer being made and is near-impossible to obtain.

---

**1969:** Olympus introduce their Maitani-designed 35-SP. A fixed-lens rangefinder with an incredibly sharp 42mm $f$ 1.7 Zuiko lens, the 35 SP is the first (and even 50 years later, remains the only) 35mm rangefinder with both centre-weighted metering and spot metering in automatic exposure mode.

Introduced at the price of ¥24,800 or $229.95, a recently over-hauled one can command up to $400 on the used market today.

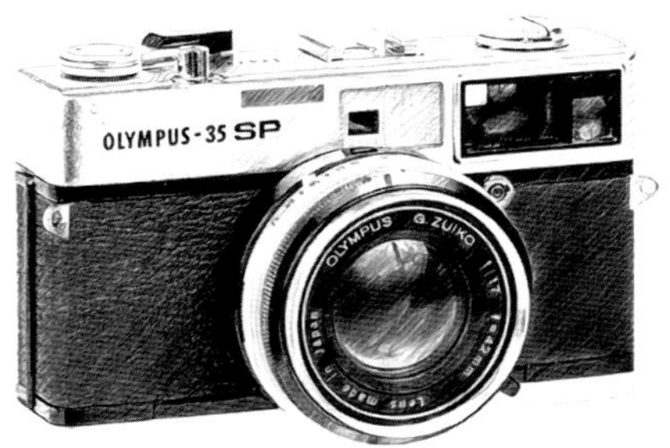

---

**TRIVIA**

The Olympus 35-SP was the point-and-shoot companion of revered large-format landscape photographer Ansel Adams.

---

**1969:** Neil Armstrong (1930–2012) lands on the moon and uses a modified Hasselblad 500EL (equipped with special film magazines for 150–200 exposures) to photograph the scenery. He takes the film but leaves the camera behind to reduce liftoff weight. By the end of the Apollo program, in December of 1972, there are 12 Hasselblad cameras sitting in the lunar dust, just waiting to be picked up . . . each one missing its film back.

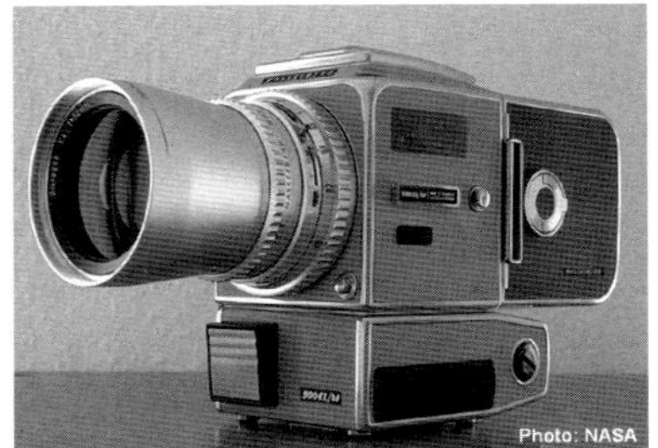

---

**AUCTION MADNESS**

One Hasselblad went to the moon with Apollo 14 in 1971 and was brought back by U.S. astronaut Ed Mitchell, the Lunar Module Pilot on Apollo 14. In May of 2014, it sold at auction to a Japanese collector for a mere $910,000.

---

### TRIVIA

NASA has used cameras by Leica, Hasselblad, Kodak, and Nikon in space, but not Canon. When tested, the Canon bodies perform beautifully, but many Canon telephoto lenses have fluorite elements, which tend to crack or even shatter under the vibrations associated with launch. On one occasion during NASA's testing, a fluorite element completely disintegrated, rendering the lens useless. Fluorite lens elements can even shatter with rapid temperature changes here on earth. Temperature changes in space are far more drastic, varying from 120°C in the sun to –100°C in the shade. Thus, NASA will not consider Canon cameras so long as the company continues to use fluorite elements in required lenses. Today, on the International Space Station, several Canon video cameras are in use, but these cameras have lenses without fluorite elements. Essentially, nothing has changed.

In space, digital sensors are bombarded with all manner of radiation and the sensors quickly get damaged, giving them about a useful life of about six months, no matter what the brand.

---

**1970:** Magicubes (X-Flashcubes) are an improvement on Flashcubes (see **1965**). They look almost identical to the original Flashcubes but are fired mechanically by a small bar striking a pin coated in fulminating material. This eliminates the battery and makes extremely cheap flash cameras possible.

**1970:** Ponder & Best introduce the Vivitar 283 electronic flash (manufactured by the Japanese electrical giant Panasonic). The innovative 283 uses a thyristor to turn off the flash tube when needed, rather than dumping any excess power in to a "quench tube." Thus, the 283 delivers many more flashes on a set of batteries.

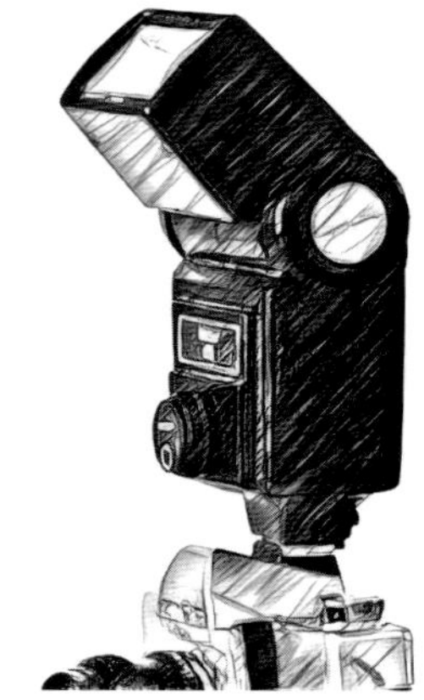

The 283 quickly becomes the number one professional and enthusiast flash unit, outselling all its competitors combined. Some three million units are sold by 1973 and it remains in production for over 30 years. It is twice returned to production after being discontinued, in response to customer demand!

---

### CAUTION!

The early Japanese-made Vivitar 283/285 flashes have a trigger voltage of 250 volts, which will damage the circuits of most digital cameras and some recent film cameras, such as the Canon AE-1 (see **1976**). Use these vintage flashes only with vintage cameras. The newer units, made in China and Korea, have a trigger voltage of five to 12 volts and are safe to use with modern digital cameras. (For more on this, see "Trigger Voltage" in the Glossary.)

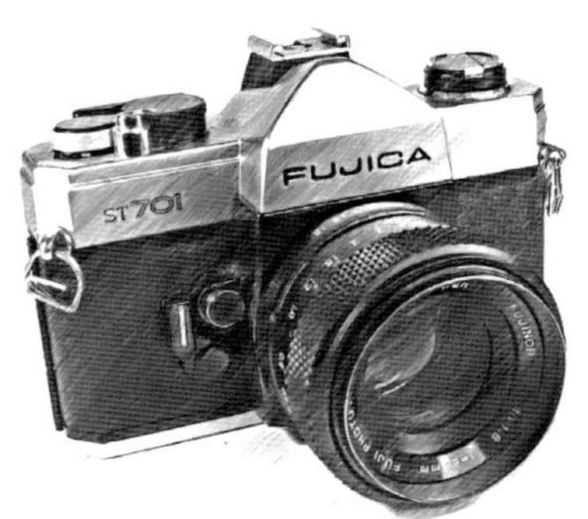

**1970:** Fujica's first 35mm SLR, the ST701, is the first camera to use the new "silicon blue" photocell. It offers up to five stops more sensitivity without the lag of the more common CdS cells. In 1974, the silicon photocell will be incorporated into Canon's EF SLR, and soon after that all makers will use it.

**1970:** The Minolta SRM is the first SLR with built-in electric sequential motor drive and auto film rewind. It is a modified Minolta SRT101 with a permanent bottom-mounted motor drive (using eight AA batteries) with a detachable handgrip. It can shoot a steady three frames per second. Curiously, it has no light meter.

**1970:** Anna-Lou "Annie" Leibovitz starts her career as a staff photographer with *Rolling Stone* magazine just after the magazine is launched. Three years later, she will become its chief photographer and will work there until 1983, creating the look of American culture. She is considered one of the great American portrait photographers and is still working in the field today.

### ODDITIES

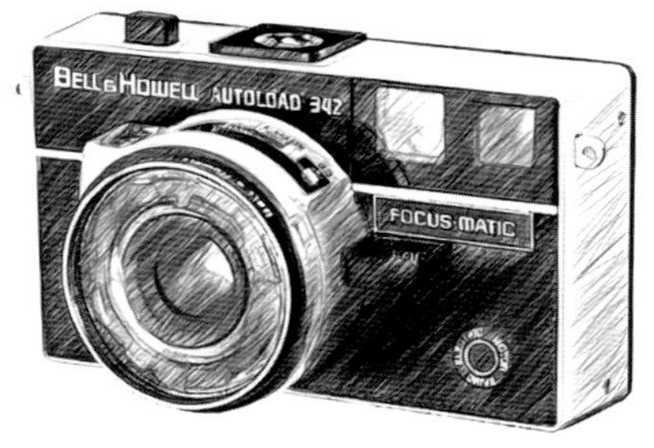

First sold in 1969, the Bell & Howell Autoload 342 is a compact camera (actually made by Canon) for 126 cartridge film that has a single-window rangefinder called "Focusmatic" and a motorized film advance. The Focusmatic lever is pressed down, and the camera is aimed at the base of the object to be photographed. A ball bearing then rolls in a track to measure the angle. When the lever is released, the lens is focused based on the ball bearing's position. It is an inexpensive triangulation system based on the assumption that all photographers are the same height. With sufficient depth of field to cover any errors, it usually works. This early auto-focus system is, thankfully, never seen again.

**1970:** The Mamiya RB67 is the first 6 x 7 medium-format "system" SLR. In other words, the RB67, with its rotatable, interchangeable backs for taking vertical photographs (always a challenge with a format that is basically set up for horizontal photography) and its standard interchangeable waist-level viewfinder, is more like a Hasselblad or Bronica than a Pentax 6 x 7. (In fact, the "RB" in RB67 stands for "rotatable back.")

**1970:** At Photokina, in Cologne, Lester Bogen meets Lino Manfrotto (1937–2017), an Italian photojournalist and entrepreneur who has developed a fine series of lighting stands in conjunction with his friend, Gilberto Battocchio (b. 1941). Bogen recognizes the U.S. sales potential and convinces Manfrotto to develop a separate manufacturing company. (Until that time, Manfrotto had been producing the equipment in a workshop he'd set up in his father's garage in Bassano del Grappa, north of Rome.) It is the start of Lino Manfrotto & Co. SPA. In turn, Bogen gets the U.S. distribution rights, selling Manfrotto's products under the Bogen name. In 1974, Manfrotto add tripods to their product mix. It is for these tripods that the names Bogen (in the U.S.) and Manfrotto (everywhere else) will become famous.

---

### TRIVIA

In 1989, Lino Manfrotto & Co. Spa will be purchased by a U.K. company, the Vitec Group, though manufacturing continues in Italy (Manfrotto) and France (Gitzo). In 2010, Manfrotto will drop the Bogen name in the USA, selling their tripods under the Manfrotto name, as they have since the beginning, in the rest of the world.

---

### ODDITIES

Nikon's 2000mm *f* 11 Reflex-Nikkor holds the distinction of being the longest lens ever made for a 35mm camera, beating out both the 1600mm *f* 5.6 Apo-Telyt for Leica's R-Series and the Zeiss Apo Sonnar T* 1700mm *f* 4 lens (see **2006**), not to mention doing so at a significantly lower price.

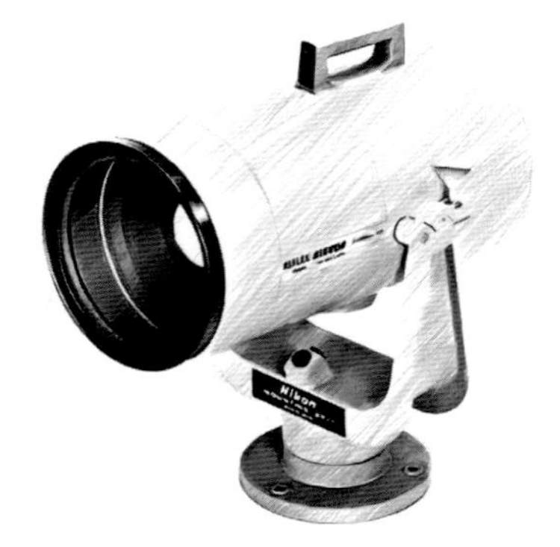

A prototype was shown at the 1968 Photokina and went into production in 1970. It is believed to be handmade and produced only on special order. The number made (probably very small) is known only to Nikon. The closest focusing distance is at 18 metres (60 feet). If the 2000mm focal length is not enough for you, you can always use a 2x converter, for a 4000mm/*f* 22 optic. It has a 1.2° angle of view, and weighs a staggering 17.5 kg or 38.6 lbs.

---

### AUCTION MADNESS

In 2018, two copies of the 2000 *f* 11 Reflex Nikkor were available on eBay. One, from China, was in near pristine condition, complete, and on offer for a mere $32,727. The second one, listed by a seller in the Netherlands, was missing its fitted aluminum case and not in quite so good condition. Thus, it bore a lower asking price of just $20,000.

**ODDITIES**

The Dong Feng (East Wind), Hong Qi (Red Flag), and Heping (Peace) are one and the same camera under different names and were built in Shanghai to commemorate the 20th anniversary of the Chinese Revolution. However, that anniversary was in 1969 and the cameras were not ready until early 1970. Development and production were personally ordered by Jiang Qing (1914–1991), the fourth wife, and widow, of Chairman Mao and made by China's oldest camera maker, Seagull, as a demonstration of the capabilities of Chinese industry.

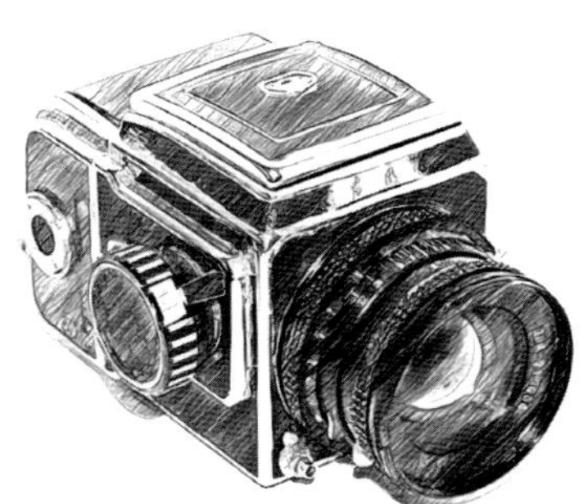

The cameras were blatant copies of the Hasselblad 500C, but with a few tweaks, as Jiang insisted their specs exceed those of the Hasselblad. So, a 1/1000 second shutter speed was added. But it only worked if the lens was wide open, at *f* 2.8. Although the build quality of the Dong Feng is not at the same level as the 500c, it was still considered one of the better Chinese film cameras. Just 97 cameras were produced.

**TRIVIA**

Mao's wife, Jiang Qing, was a keen photographer. When the then-Iranian king visited China, Jiang was presented with a Leica M3, which she adored. In the 1970s, China was pursuing an economic policy of absolute self-reliance, attempting to produce everything it needed. Against this background, Jiang ordered the production of a copy of Leica M3 and gave her M3 to Shanghai Camera Factory to dissemble. Each part of the original M3 was hand-copied and special glasses were imported from East Germany. The first batch of Red Flag 20 kits came out in 1973 with three lenses: 35mm *f* 1.4, 50mm *f* 1.4, and 90mm *f* 2, exact copies of the Summilux and Summicron. However, the quality of the Red Flag 20 was well behind that of the Leica, and production costs were unsustainably high, so only 187 Red Flag rangefinder cameras rolled off the production line.

**1970:** In a detailed, handwritten document which he writes to himself in his notebook, Olympus's legendary camera designer Yoshihisa Maitani sets out a philosophy of compactness, light weight and "ultimate reliability" for Olympus cameras. It is a direction both Olympus and its successors, OM Systems (See **2020**) will follow to this day.

**1971:** Employing patents purchased from Optical Coatings Laboratories Inc. of California, Asahi Optical Corp. (Pentax) introduces its SMC (Super Multi-Coat) Takumar lenses. This marks a turning point in the evolution of photographic optics, allowing the development of multi-element ultrawide-angle and wide-range zoom lenses. With the larger number of elements now standard in modern lenses, multi-coating becomes almost as necessary as glass in the crafting of quality optics.

A lens with six glass-to-air surfaces, such as the Tessar or Elmar, can transmit only about 70% of the light if left uncoated. Single layer coating increases the transmittance to 90%, but with multi-coating (three to 10 coatings, depending on the lens design) transmittance can go as high as 99.7%!

**1971:** Diane Arbus takes her own life. It is said that she "loves an eccentric like a salesman loves a sucker." During her career, she photographs outsiders of all shapes and sizes, the short, giant, obese, skinny, the people who have the courage and character to expose their vulnerability in front of her lens. She receives little recognition for her work until late in life but leaves a legacy that will influence photographers for generations (See Trivia entry under **1957**/Mamiya).

---

### TRIVIA

Late in Arbus's career, the Metropolitan Museum of Art indicated they would buy three of her photographs for $75 each, but citing a lack of funds, purchased only two. As she wrote to [ex-husband] Allan Arbus, "So I guess being poor is no disgrace."

---

**1971:** The Japanese government lifts import controls on colour film and Kodak become a huge competitor in Japan's domestic market. Fujicolor and Sakuracolor are reformulated for developing in Kodak's C-22 chemistry so they can compete in international markets.

---

### TRIVIA

Your scribe obtained some Sakuracolor film in 1966, shot it and sent it to Japan for development and printing, which took six-plus months. The returned prints were small, with vivid colours and high contrast. Results from Sakuracolor, after the reformulation for C-22 processing, were far superior to the original Sakuracolor.

---

**1971:** Nikon adapt a Nikon F for the Apollo 15 mission in July of the year that includes the historic space walk (EVA). The camera is equipped with a Photomic FTn finder with through-the-lens (TTL) metering. In 1973, a newer, specially modified version of the Nikon F with a motor drive will be delivered for use in Skylab. In 1980 and 1989, Nikon will deliver modified space-capable F3 and F4 cameras to NASA, which are used aboard the Space Shuttle. Modifications typically include matte black paint (to control reflections), larger controls (for use with space suit gloves), and every screw is glued in place (for launch vibrations).

**1971:** The Asahi Pentax Electro-Spotmatic is the first SLR with a focal-plane shutter that provides aperture-priority automatic exposure control (albeit with stop-down metering), and an innovative exposure compensation system. It is sold only in Japan.

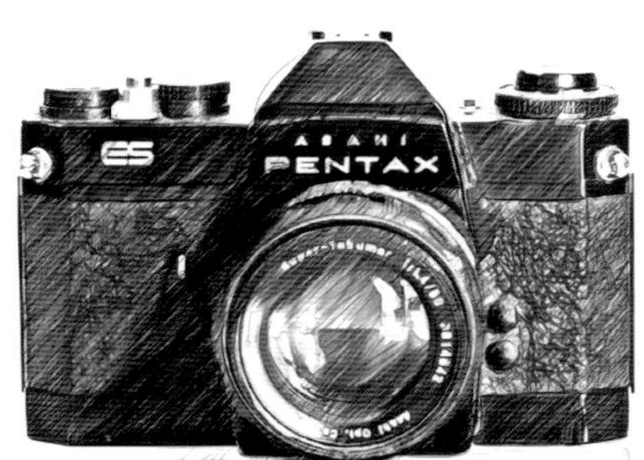

The Electro-Spotmatic was followed by the ES, which was sold internationally beginning in 1972. The ES had improved circuitry that addressed reliability issues in the original version. In 1974, it was followed by the ES II, which turned out to be the very last screw-mount camera made by Asahi Pentax before they switched to K-bayonet lenses.

---

### TRIVIA

These models were soon followed by automatic exposure (AE) models from Minolta, Nikon, Canon, and others. These Japanese AE SLRs very nearly ended the German camera industry when the Germans failed to keep up with their Japanese counterparts.

---

**1971:** Working for *LIFE* magazine, war photographer W. Eugene Smith travels to Minamata, Japan, and creates a long-term photo-essay on Minamata disease, the effects of mercury poisoning caused by a Chisso factory discharging heavy metals into the waters around Minamata. In January 1972, Smith accompanies activists who ask why union workers are used by the company as bodyguards and the group is attacked by Chisso Company employees and members of the union local who beat Smith up, permanently damaging his eyesight. He stays on until October of 1974 to complete his essay. His photographs are published first in *LIFE* in 1972 and then in the 1975 book *Minamata, Words and Photographs* by W. Eugene Smith and Aileen M. Smith, and draws worldwide attention to the effects of Minamata disease. It is Smith's last hurrah (see **1937** and **1948**).

**1971:** Canon unleash their F-1, a full-system 35mm single-lens reflex camera which features the new Canon FD breech-lock lens mount, though older Canon FL-mount lenses are also compatible (but without open-aperture metering). The F-1 is Canon's first truly professional-grade SLR system, supporting a huge variety of accessories and interchangeable parts so it could be adapted for different uses and preferences. The camera is built to endure 100,000 picture-taking cycles, in temperatures ranging from –30º C to +60° C and up to 90% humidity. The camera is sold for 10 years.

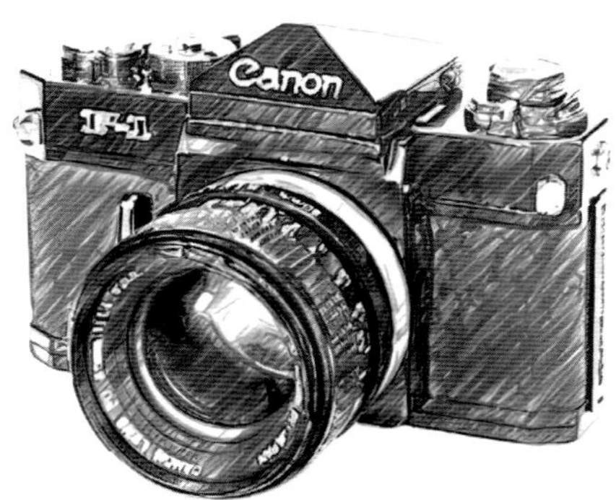

**1972:** Kodak introduce their Pocket Instamatic Cameras, using a new, smaller Kodak 110 film cartridge holding unperforated 16mm film. The line was so popular that more than 25 million cameras are produced in slightly under three years. Although the format is most closely associated with cheaply produced, low-cost cameras, Minolta (see **1975**) and Pentax (see **1978**), among others, offer sophisticated, expensive 110 cameras with excellent lenses.

---

### UPDATE

As of 2020, 110 film, though almost impossible to find in stores, is still available on-line through specialty suppliers, though commercial processing can be difficult, but not impossible, to find.

---

### ODDITIES

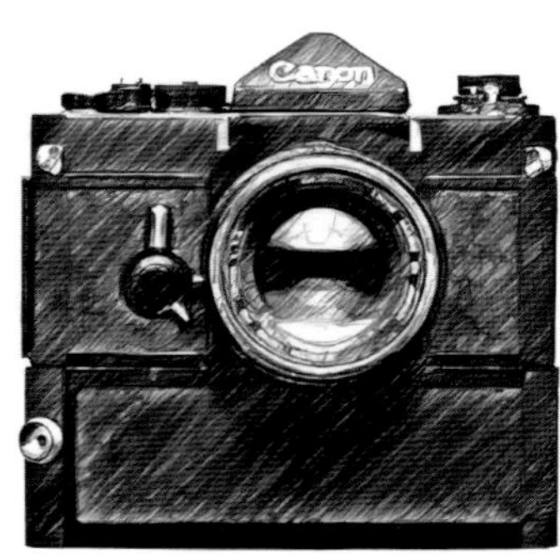

For the 1972 Olympics, Canon makes a special high-speed model of the F-1 with a fixed pellicle mirror, as used in the Pellix (see **1965**), which allows the user to always see the subject. But it is available only by special order to credentialled press photographers, and fewer than 100 are made. Equipped with a fixed motor drive (powered by an external battery pack taking 20 AA batteries), the camera is able to shoot up to nine frames per second, the highest speed of any motor-driven camera at the time.

Curiously, the camera will not operate unless the lens is stopped down (which is done by means of a front-mounted lever), and that same lever must be disengaged before the lens can be changed. The special model also has fabric shutter curtains instead of the F-1's normal titanium curtains. The camera does not have a self-timer.

---

**1972:** Leica purchase the remaining inventory of Zeiss Hologon 15mm *f* 8 lenses (see **1966**) and modify them for the Leica M-system, removing the need for custom lens modifications. Approximately 400 Hologons for Leica-M are produced, which makes the lens one of the most desirable collectible optics today.

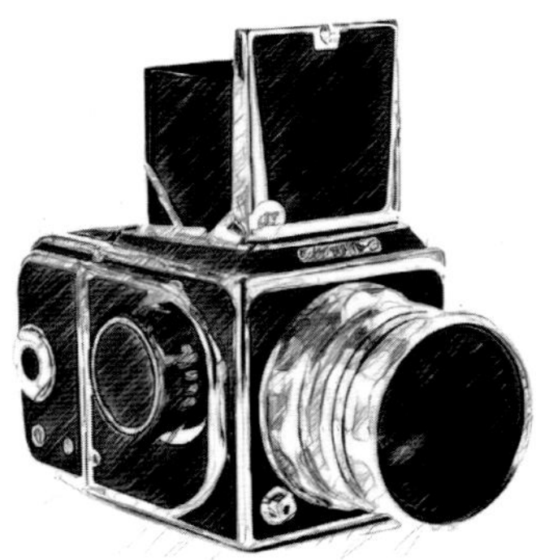

**1972:** The Arsenal plant in Kyiv starts making the Salyut-S 6 x 6cm SLR. This is an improved version of the original Salyut and now features a metal foil shutter and several internal improvements, and the lens mount is changed to the Pentacon Six mount. The Salyut-S name appears as Салют-C in Cyrillic, so the model is sometimes referred to as the Salyut-C. Around 1980 it is replaced by the Kiev 80, with the Salyut name being phased out by about 1981. The Kiev 88 follows and is essentially the same, but with a hot shoe for flash.

> **TRIVIA**
>
> Your scribe almost bought a Salyut-S in the fall of 1975, at an asking price of $100, including an 80mm lens and two 120 film backs. But, after trying one in Moscow's Beriozka store (a store that sells only for "hard" or foreign currencies), decided against it, as it was the only camera he'd ever seen that suffered from recoil, the fault of a large, very poorly damped mirror.

**1972:** A Canadian-born American physicist, chemist and engineer, Willis Adcock (1922–2003), working for Texas Instruments, patents an electronic camera that uses no film. His film-less camera (U.S. patent 4,057,830) is an analog rather than a digital design and no prototype is ever built.

**1972:** Polaroid introduce their flat-pack instant film and the SX-70 SLR camera that takes it. An incredibly complex and ingenious film, it contains 16 different emulsion layers and an opaque chemical layer which protects the developing image from light. After the developing action, this opaque layer gradually becomes transparent, revealing the developed colour image. Although the high cost of $180 for the camera and $6.90 for each film pack of 10 pictures limits demand, Polaroid sells 700,000 SX-70's by mid-1974.

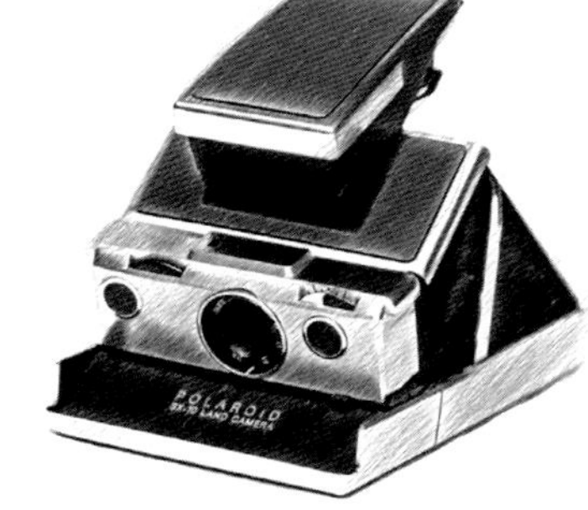

> **TRIVIA**
>
> Polaroid founder Edwin Land announces the SX-70 at the company's annual meeting in April 1972. On stage, he takes out a folded SX-70 from his suit coat pocket and in 10 seconds shoots five pictures, both actions impossible with previous Land Cameras. The company first sells the SX-70 in Miami in late 1972 and begins selling it nationally in the fall of 1973. It is said that the "S" stands for secret, while the "X" stands for Experimental. The number "70" is an arbitrary choice "that sounds good."

**1972:** A Korean company, Wako, is established as a lens maker in Masan, Korea, to manufacture CCTV lenses and inexpensive camera lenses. It will become the Samyang Optical Company in 1979. It builds both regular and reflex lenses in mounts for various cameras and also in mounts for the "T2" system of adapters. Its SLR lenses are branded under the Vivitar, Falcon, Rokinon, Walimex, Bower, Opteka, Bell & Howell, Polar, and Pro-Optic names. All can be readily identified as they are marked "Made in Korea."

**1972:** Fujica's ST801 is the first SLR with light-emitting diodes in the viewfinder. The camera has a scale with seven LED dots to indicate exposure: +1½ EV, +1 EV, +½ EV, 0 (correct exposure), -½ EV, -1 EV and -1½ EV readings of its silicon photo-diode light meter, instead of the traditional but delicate galvanometer needle pointer.

---

**TRIVIA**

In 1974, the Fujica ST901 will be the first SLR to use calculator-style LEDs to show the camera's aperture-priority shutter speeds from 20 to 1/1000 second in 14 steps. Although such displays were replaced by more energy-efficient and informative liquid crystal displays (LCDs) in the 1980s, the use of LEDs in the ST801/ST901 was a major step in the use of electronics in camera design.

These models were soon followed by automatic exposure (AE) models from Minolta, Nikon, Canon, and others. These Japanese AE SLRs very nearly ended the German camera industry when the Germans failed to keep up with their Japanese counterparts.

---

**1972:** Created by Olympus's chief designer Yoshihisa Maitani, the Olympus OM-1 is the smallest 35mm SLR to reach the market. Arriving up to a decade later than most of the established SLR brands, it succeeds because of its incredibly compact size, light weight, robust engineering, superb lenses, and excellent metering. A distinctive feature is the shutter-speed dial built around the lens mount. Compact but easy to use, it also boasts what is possibly the best viewfinder in any 35mm SLR camera. This combination, like that of the 1964 Pentax Spotmatic, makes it a runaway success.

---

**TRIVIA**

The OM-1 was originally called the M-1 (in honour of its designer, Maitani), but the model-name was changed after approximately a year, when Leica complained that the name was too close to their "M" series. (Early examples, with the M-1 markings, are highly sought after by collectors.)

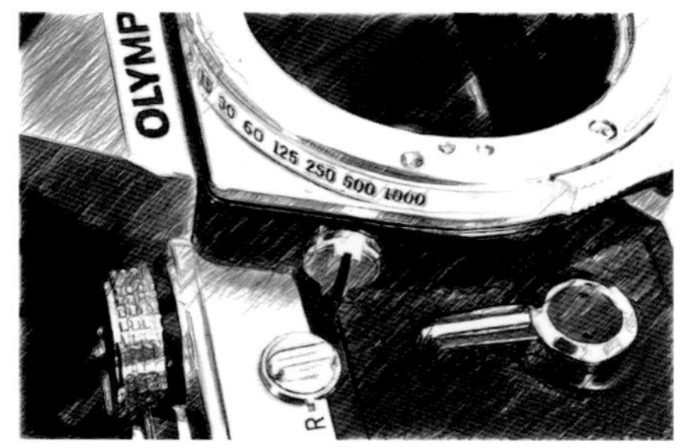

When Maitani was still a student, he designed and patented his first camera. Olympus were looking for talent and when the designer of Olympus's original camera, Eiichi Sakurai (1909–1998), came across the patent, he insisted the young Maitani work for Olympus. Years later, Maitani told his version of the story: "In those days a student who refused to work for the first company to offer him a position was regarded as a disgrace to his university. I had received a job offer from an automobile manufacturer, but I pretended that I hadn't and went to work for Olympus, instead."

Over a 40-year career, Maitani led design teams that created the Olympus PEN series, the Olympus AX and, of course the extensive OM series.

**1973:** Kodacolor II, Kodachrome 25, and the higher-speed Kodachrome 64 are all introduced.

**1973:** The E. Leitz Company buys a bankrupt precision watch factory in Vila Nova de Famalico (near Porto), Portugal. By doing so, it acquires not only a factory and precision tools, but also a workforce (mainly of women) who can do precision work. In 1976, they will assemble the Leica R3. In 2013, Leica Portugal will move to a new factory, where they continue to produce parts and sub-assemblies for various Leica products, which are then assembled in Wetzlar.

**1973:** Rollei take over Voigtländer and produce both lines in their own Singapore factory. The Braunschweig/Uelzen factories will be closed in 1975.

**1973:** Since leaving the Kodak fold in 1928, and going through a series of owners, the famous Graflex Camera company (by now part of the Singer Corp.) is closed, and the tooling sold to the Toyo Camera Co. of Japan.

**1973:** All film manufacturers standardize on Kodak's new C-41 chemistry, replacing the C-22 process for colour negative development.

**1973:** Fairchild Semiconductor lay the groundwork for the digital revolution when they release the first large image-forming CCD chip, a 100 x 100 pixel array, or 0.01 mega-pixels.

**1973:** Leica release their CL, a compact 35mm rangefinder camera jointly developed by Minolta and Leitz. Like the Leica M5 of 1971, it features match-needle TTL metering using a CdS cell on a stalk positioned behind the lens but in front of the shutter; the stalk is withdrawn moments prior to the exposure.

---

### TRIVIA

In Japan, the CL was marketed as the Leitz-Minolta CL. While the 40mm *f* 2 Summicron CL was built in Germany, the Minolta version featured a legally licensed copy, the Rokkor 40mm *f* 2 CL, manufactured by Minolta in Japan. However, when Leica discontinued the Summicron CL in 1977, Minolta continued manufacturing the Rokkor and even added multi-coating (the original CL lenses were both single coated). Even more interesting was the 90mm *f* 4 Elmar, which was made in Germany but marketed as the M-Rokkor 90/4 in Japan. This was the only time a German-made Leica lens has been branded as that of another company.

To avoid brand name and price dilution for the rest of the product line, Leica claimed that the lenses developed for the CL camera were not fully compatible with regular M cameras, allegedly because of different coupling cams on the C lenses. However, all M-series lenses worked on the CL and this claim has since been proven false.

Your scribe is still miffed that Leica charged him $75 to ensure his 90mm Elmar would work with his CL, when no work was required.

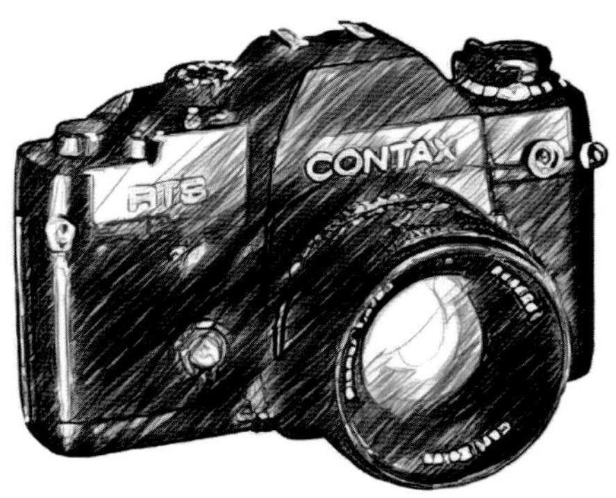

**1973:** Yashica begin a collaboration with Carl Zeiss AG (Oberkochen) called *Top Secret Project 130* to produce a new professional 35mm SLR with an electronically controlled shutter, bearing the Contax brand name. The Porsche design studio is hired to design an ergonomic yet stylish body shape. The new Contax RTS appears at the 1974 Photokina and proves an immediate hit. A new prestige line of Contax lenses, designed by Carl Zeiss, are introduced for the camera, with a new C/Y (Contax/Yashica) bayonet mount, which was also adopted on the regular Yashica SLR line, allowing lens interchangeability between all Contax and future Yashica SLR models. Yashica take the opportunity to upgrade and expand their regular line of 35mm SLR lenses, introducing improved optical designs and coatings. It proves to be a brilliant move for both companies.

---

### TRIVIA

At the time of Yashica's involvement with Zeiss, it was said that as part of the deal, Yashica offered to set aside one room, just off the production line, in which only German nationals would be permitted. Not even a Japanese cleaner could enter. There, the Germans could ensure quality control of Yashica's production without interruption or interference. Your author has been unable to confirm this rumour, but it makes a great story!

---

**1974:** Kenko Optical Co. is formed to specialize in the manufacture of tele-converters, both as OEM products and to be sold under their own Kenko brand. In 1998, they will acquire the Tasco binocular brand but will sell it to Bushnell in 2002. In 2001, they will buy the Slik tripod company. In 2011, they will merge with Tokina, making the Kenko-Tokina Co., which continues to operate to this day.

**1974:** The German DIN (logarithmic) and American ASA (linear) film sensitivity ratings are combined to create the new ISO system. For example, a film rated ISO 200/24° is twice as sensitive as one rated ISO 100/21°. In practice, the logarithmic scale has all but disappeared.

**1974:** Minox introduces a very compact 35mm camera with a glass-fiber-reinforced (Makrolon) body designed by Professor Fischer of Vienna. It is the Minox EL, which is the first of what will become a long series of Minox 35mm cameras. In fact, the Minox proves so popular that it is copied exactly, in Russia, as the Kiev 35A. It features a foldaway 35mm *f* 2.8 lens, aperture-priority exposure, and zone (i.e., guestimate) focusing. The orange shutter button on an otherwise all black body becomes a signature touch for all of the 30 models to be produced over next 22 years. They will remain the smallest cameras using standard 35mm film until the Minolta TC-1 is introduced in 1996.

**1974:** Italy's Manfrotto, a maker of lighting equipment, launches their first tripod. The innovative tripods find success in many markets. Such success, in fact, that by the mid '80s, Manfrotto has six production sites in Bassano, and expands to nearby Feltre, establishing another five plants in the space of just two years, in order to meet the demand. (See **1970**.)

**1974:** Vivitar's Series 1 70-210mm $f$3.5 (designed and manufactured by Kino—see **1959**) becomes the first professional-level close-focusing "macro" zoom lens for 35mm SLRs.

---

### BUSINESS TRIVIA

From the 1970s to 1990s, Vivitar was a very successful third-party photographic equipment supplier. Founded as Ponder & Best by German emigrants Max Ponder and John Best in 1938, the name was changed to the Vivitar Corporation in 1964. After a further two decades of very successful expansion, the owners sold the company to Hanimex in 1985. Further ownership changes followed. The trend towards auto-focus cameras and lenses during the late 1980s and the later switch to digital photography presented Vivitar with challenges it could not meet. In August 2008, Sakar International acquired the Vivitar brand out of bankruptcy, and now market a variety of products under the Vivitar name.

# 1975 to 1999

*Steve Sasson, a young engineer at Kodak, built the first digital camera in 1975. It was an eight-pound, 0.01-megapixel effort, but it worked! The mid-70s also saw a distinct shift in camera-making philosophy. Instead of making simpler, less-capable models for amateur shooters, manufacturers begin utilizing these models as testbeds for new technologies. This quickly turned the industry into a technology arms race, which produced electronic masterpieces such as Canon's A-1 and Minolta's XD-11, among others. This and the investments needed for auto-focus drove others from the business. By the early 1990s, the digital revolution is getting under way. It was a period of huge innovation.*

**1975:** Nippon Kogaku K.K. (now Nikon) introduce what will become the ultimate wide-angle lens: the 6mm *f* 2.8 Fisheye Nikkor, with a 5.2 kg (11.5 lbs) heft and a 220° field of view. Intended for scientific use, and loosely based on the Beck SKY (see **1923**), this lens can actually see behind itself. The lens is manufactured only to special order and just 56 will be made.

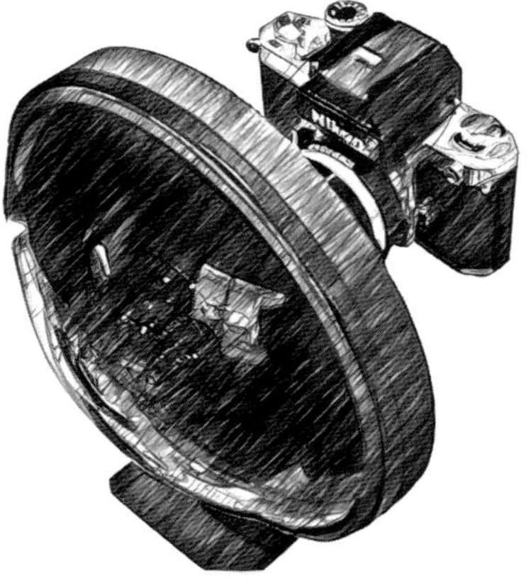

---

**AUCTION MADNESS**

When released, the 6mm *f* 2.8 fisheye Nikkor cost around $6,000 (about $27,000 today), a bargain by today's standards. In 2010, one appeared on eBay with an asking price of $34,000. In 2014, another (some say the 2010 lens being sold again) was sold by a U.K. auction house for an eye-watering £100,000, or approximately $160,000.

---

**1975:** Bryce Bayer (1929–2012) of Eastman Kodak designs what will become known as the "Bayer Pattern Filter." This filter is 50% green, 25% blue, and 25% red, to match the colour sensitivity of the human eye. It is the filter design that will allow almost every modern digital camera to "see" in colour. For this he is granted U.S. patent number 3,971,065, in 1976.

**1975:** Film manufacturers standardize on Kodak's new E-6 chemistry, replacing the E-4 process for colour transparency (slide) development.

**1975:** Leitz Canada introduce the ultra-high-resolution 180mm *f* 3.4 APO-Telyt-R. Developed for the U.S. military, it is the first apochromat lens for SLR use and is supposed to remain a "top secret" technology. However, the contract with Leitz Canada is poorly worded and fails to prevent Leitz from releasing a consumer version. Designed by the renowned Walter Mandler, resolution is said to be *"limited only by available film!"* It remains in production until 1998.

**1975:** Pentax replace their M-42 thread-mount with the newly designed (some say with the help of Leica, some say with the help of Zeiss) "K" bayonet lens mount. The new mount is met with some resistance by current Pentax owners, who fear obsolescence of the thread-mount lenses they already own. But it is a significant move, for Pentax had been the major promoter of thread-mount lenses. With the new mount they acknowledge that the more precise bayonet system is better suited to aligning the contacts needed for electronic cameras and lenses.

### BACKSTORY

Screw mount lenses had a problem. The threads didn't always stop the lens at exactly the same spot, making electrical connections tough to match up. So, when most of the major manufacturers changed to bayonet mounts, Mamiya felt they had a better idea. Starting with their DSX series cameras of 1974, they used a locking pin that engaged a slot on the back of the lens mount, much as a locking pin secures a bayonet mount, but with a M42 threaded lens mount. (The pin and slot are circled in the images at the right.) Mamiya lenses featured a mechanical pin which transmitted the *f*-stop information to the camera, eliminating the need to stop down for metering.

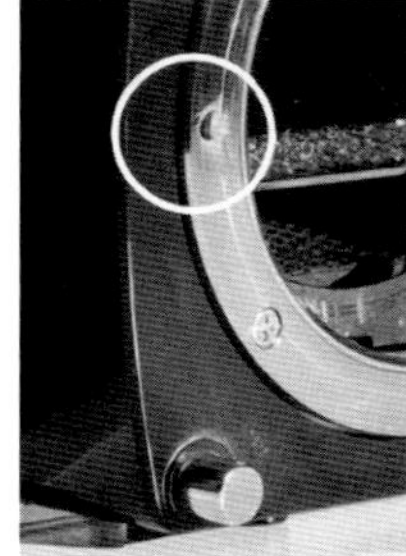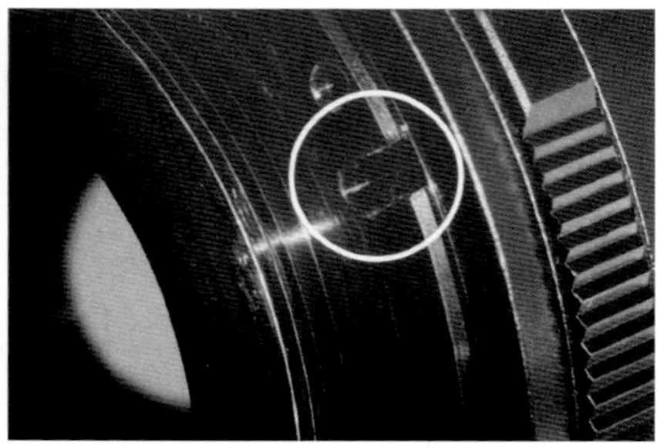

However, this arrangement could easily have been used to precisely align electrical contacts while maintaining compatibility with older thread-mount lenses.

The so-called M-42 thread used by Pentax lenses was originated by Carl Zeiss (Jena) in 1949 for their Contax-S and was used on many East German cameras marketed mainly under the Praktica name. Today, it is widely known as the Praktica/Pentax thread (after its two main proponents), but at the time was referred to, in the West, as simply the Pentax mount, in order not to give any credit or advertising to the Soviet bloc's Pentacon during the Cold War.

**1975:** After two years of development, the Rollei A110 is introduced and advertised as the world's smallest pocket camera. It is a small, well-built camera with nice clean lines. Unlike most 110 cameras, it is mostly metal with a few plastic parts. The camera body consists of two interlocking shells that pull apart (similar to the Minox subminiature cameras), which reveals the lens and viewfinder, cocks the shutter, turns on the

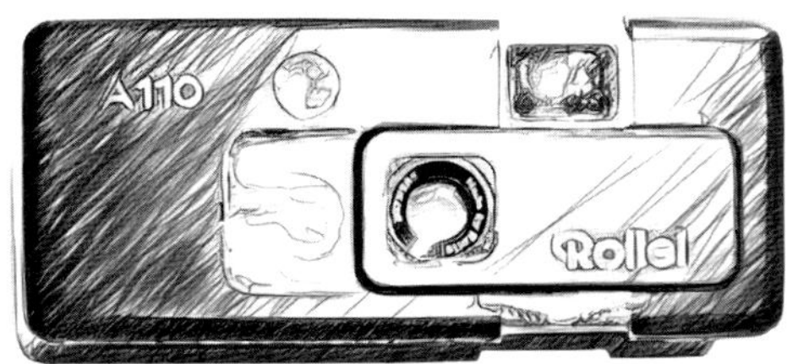

meter, *and* advances the film. Closed, it makes a tight, compact, and durable package. The lens is a Carl Zeiss 23mm Tessar with four elements in three groups, with automatic aperture control from $f2.8$ to $f16$. It is coupled to an electronically variable shutter from four seconds to 1/400 second.

---

### TRIVIA

With 260 parts, the Rollei A110 was complicated to make and, unlike other Rollei products, somewhat unreliable. In 1978, production was moved from Germany to Singapore, where the camera continued to be made until 1981, when production ceased.

---

**1975:** The Cyclops is introduced by Cromemco and is the first consumer, all-digital camera. It is not a standalone camera and must be connected to an "Altair" microcomputer to function. But it is a start. The camera's sensor is a modified 1K memory chip. The opaque cover on the chip is removed and replaced with a glass lid. Resolution is 32 x 32 pixels (0.001 megapixels). It is offered only as a kit, and few are sold. But—it is a sign of things to come.

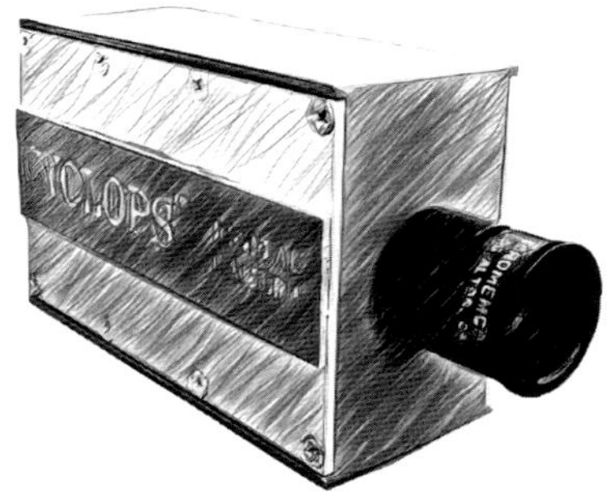

---

### TRIVIA

Note the use of the term "microcomputer." Early home computers were called microcomputers because they were smaller (and less capable) than the minicomputers made by Digital Equipment Corp., Data General, Wang Laboratories, and others, which were in turn smaller (and less capable) than the mainframe computers made at the time by the likes of IBM, Control Data and Univac. The term "Personal Computer" or " PC" only arrived with the introduction of the IBM "5150" in 1981.

The "Altair" was the first microcomputer, designed in 1974. The computer revolution started when it was featured on the cover of the January 1975 issue of *Popular Electronics* magazine.

---

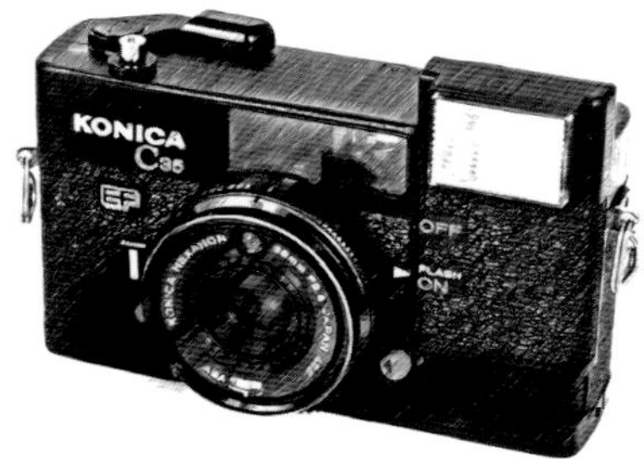

**1975:** Konica's C35 EF appears. It is a compact rangefinder camera that sports a very sharp 38mm *f* 2.8 lens and the world's very first pop-up flash.

> ### TRIVIA
> For what it's worth, the C35 EF was Andy Warhol's favourite camera.

**1975:** Researchers at Honeywell create one of the first successful autofocus systems around this time. They call it the "Visitronic" system, and they obtain four patents on it. They do not commercialize this technology in their own cameras but license it to Konica for their pioneering Konica C35 AF of 1977.

> ### BUSINESS TRIVIA
> In 1987, Honeywell sues several Japanese camera makers for infringing its autofocus patents. A 1991 court decision finds Minolta guilty, owing Honeywell $96.3 million in unpaid royalties. Ultimately Minolta pays Honeywell $127.5 million in back royalties, and for license rights to continue using Honeywell's autofocus technology. Collectively, the world's camera manufacturers pay in excess of $300 million to licence Honeywell's autofocus patents.

**1975:** GE introduce the "Flip-Flash" (called "Top-Flash" by Philips in Europe), a tall array of 10 AG-1 bulbs. The intention is to move the flash further from the lens of a 126 or 110 camera, thus avoiding the dreaded "red eye."

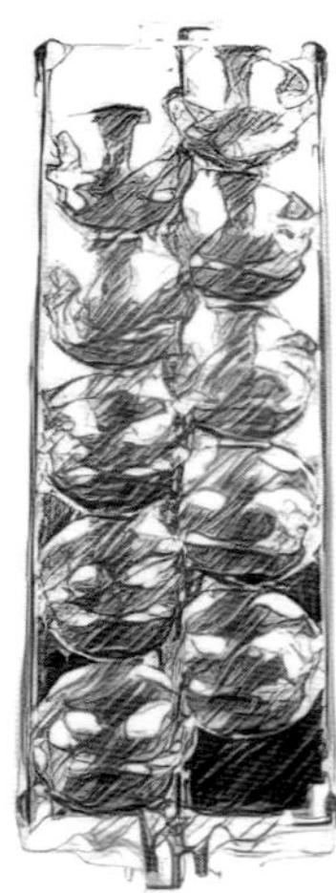

> ### TRIVIA
> How did they do it in the era before cheap integrated circuits? In several different very clever ways, all with a common theme: use the heat released by the flash to wire up the next bulb to fire (and/or disconnect the last one to fire). Sylvania used conductive plastic which shrank with the heat of the flash, thereby breaking the circuit and wiring up the next bulb.

**1975:** The Olympus OM-2 is the first camera to measure light during, rather than before, the exposure by measuring "off the film." It has two rearward-facing silicon photodiodes in the mirror box to meter light reflecting off the film. Its circuitry could detect when enough light was exposed and either close the shutter or even automatically quench a "dedicated" electronic flash.

> **TRIVIA**
>
> To develop the TTL direct-metering system, Olympus collected film from virtually every maker worldwide and measured the reflection ratios for each roll. They discovered that while film is made in many colours, their reflectivity varied by only 0.1 EV, which meant that measuring the light off the film was indeed possible. These results were also used to determine the density of printing on the shutter curtain.

**1975:** The Mamiya M645 becomes the first 645 medium-format-system SLR, taking fifteen 4.5 x 6cm exposures on a roll of 120 film.

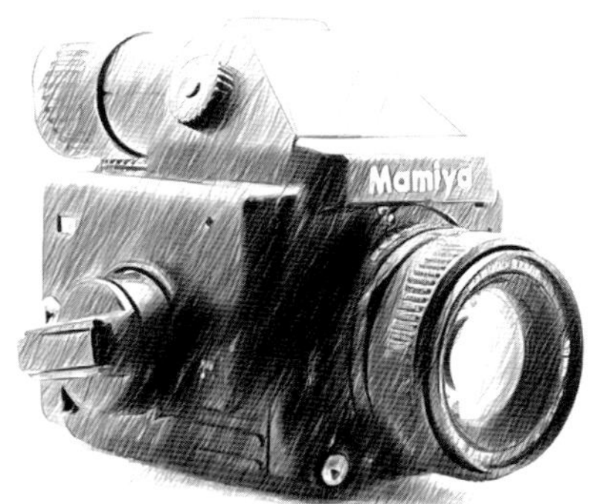

> **TRIVIA**
>
> Mamiya never finds success as a producer of 35mm SLRs, despite a half-dozen attempts between 1959 and 1980. However, it becomes a leader in medium-format photography, first with the Mamiya C series (see **1956**), the only successful interchangeable-lens twin-lens reflex (TLR) cameras ever made, and then with the RB67 (see **1970**) and the M645 series of SLRs.

**1975:** At Kodak, a 24-year-old electrical engineer, Steven Sasson (b. 1950), is asked to "see what he can do" with the newly developed CDD (Charge Coupled Device). The word "digital" is never mentioned. With the help of two very talented technicians, Bob DeYager and Jim Schueckler, in less than a year he designs and builds the world's first working, self-contained digital camera, using a CCD chip from Fairchild Semiconductor.

It is not the first camera to produce digital images, but it is the first self-contained, hand-held, digital camera. (Earlier examples of digital cameras included some cameras used for satellite photography, a few experimental devices, and the Cromemco Cyclops—see **1975**.)

The camera weighs 3.6 kg (eight pounds) and records its 0.01 megapixel (10,000 pixels) black-and-white images on a Philips-style data cassette in just 23 seconds. (A separate minicomputer is required to play back the image.) This prototype camera is a technical exercise, not intended for production, but it proves that digital photography is possible.

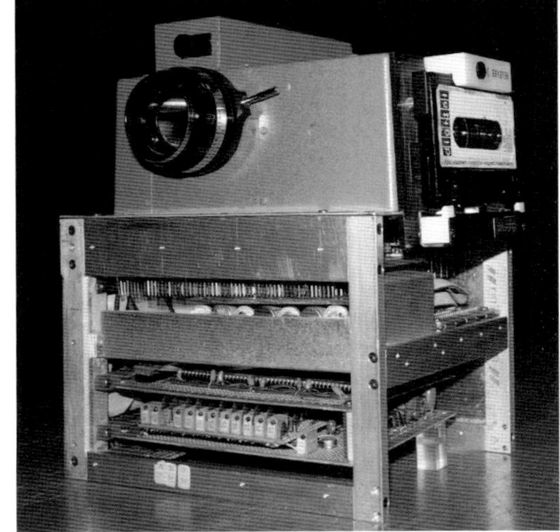

*World's first digital camera invented by Kodak's Steve Sasson.*

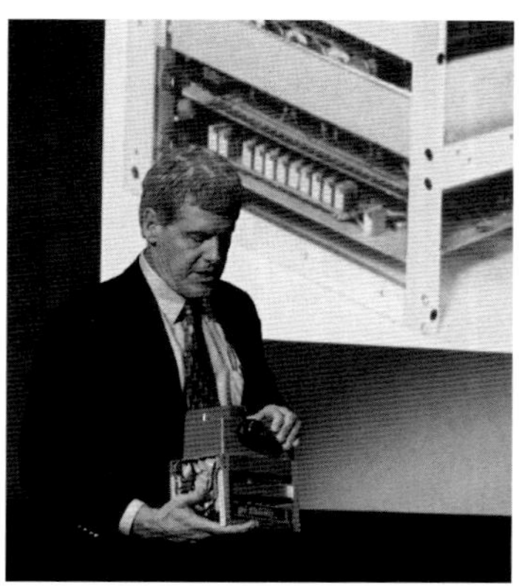

*Steve Sasson*

## TRIVIA

On 9 December 1975, Sasson persuaded a nearby technician, Joy Marshall, to pose for a photo. The camera had an electronic shutter, with just one speed (1/20th of a second or 50 milliseconds). The black-and-white image took just 150 milliseconds to be recorded to memory, but a further 23 seconds to be permanently stored on a digital cassette tape. It then had to be read into a microcomputer for playback on a television screen. When it popped up on the screen "you could see the silhouette of her hair," but her face was a mass of static. She was less than happy with the results and left saying, "*It needs work.*"

But Sasson quickly realized what the problem was and, after reversing a set of wires, the young lady's image was restored, and digital photography was born. Sadly, he did not save the photo, as the cassette was often reused.

Sasson set the capacity of the digital cassette to 30 photographs, a number chosen to be conveniently between 24 and 36—that is, the number of photos on a roll of 35mm film. He could have had it record just one or two, but he knew his bosses would say that wasn't practical. He could just as easily have chosen 100 or even 1,000, but he also knew that nobody would be able to wrap their head around such a concept at that time. When he first showed his creation to his superiors, in a presentation he called "Filmless Photography," they were less than impressed.

Sasson was forbidden to talk about the camera outside the company until 2001, when he wrote an article for the 16 October edition of the *Rochester Democrat and Chronicle*, which also contained the first public photo of the original prototype. When the news broke, Sasson was in for a treat: *For 10 minutes my kids actually thought I was cool.*

Only one prototype was built. It still exists, unchanged from when it took its last image sometime in 1976. It no longer functions, as the wire-wrap connections used for the digital circuitry were only meant for temporary prototyping use. The box on top, containing the optics, was painted, since leaving it unpainted would have shown all kinds of oil and stains from handling. Blue was chosen simply because that was the paint at hand.

The camera had no official name, although Sasson has said he called it some rather uncomplimentary things when it stopped working (which it did frequently.)

Sasson retired from Kodak in 2009 and, in 2010, he received the National Medal of Technology and Innovation from President Obama. Today, his creation is on display in the museum in George Eastman House, Rochester NY.

**1976:** In order to better compete with Hasselblad in the "studio" camera market, Bronica abandons the focal plane shutter. The new ETR model boasts lenses equipped with Seiko between-the-lens electronic leaf shutters. It maintains compatibility with the 120/220 interchangeable film magazines, inserts, Polaroid, 70mm backs, and interchangeable finders of the earlier models and offers auto/manual metering capability.

**1976:** FujiFilm introduce their Fujica Pocket 350 Zoom, the first 110 camera with a zoom lens. It's a seven element 25~42mm lens with manual focusing and has a zoom viewfinder. It has a three-position aperture setting on the top with weather symbols for exposure control, and a single speed (1/125) shutter.

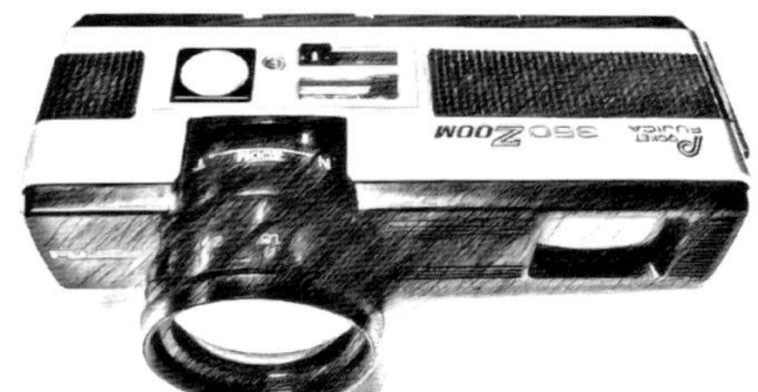

**1976:** The Canon AE-1 is introduced. A microprocessor (computer chip) is used in an SLR for the first time, which forever changes how cameras are designed. Although the exposure system is analog, the microprocessor controls almost everything else. Internally, the AE-1 is divided into five separate modules, which allows automated manufacturing. According to Canon, by incorporating electronics, combined with a highly automated manufacturing process, it is possible to eliminate 300 parts from the camera, thus enhancing both features and reliability, while lowering the cost.

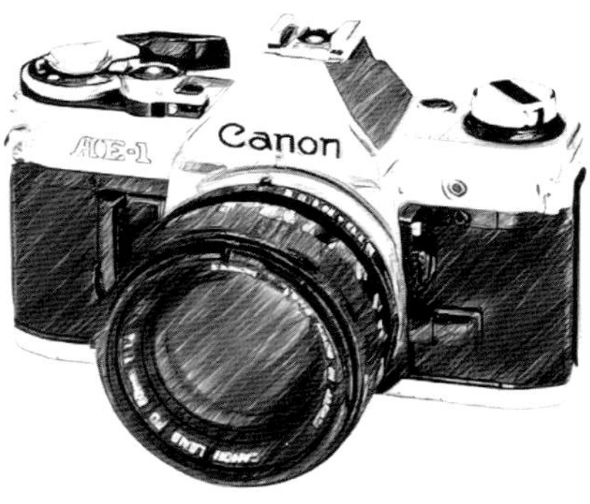

The AE-1 also incorporates features that will soon become standard in future SLRs, including a detachable power winder. It is advertised extensively, with the slogan "So advanced, it's simple," and becomes a best seller.

---

**TRIVIA**

Thanks to its new electronic innards, the AE-1 is also the first camera that limits the trigger voltage for electronic flash units to a maximum of six volts. Canon's contemporary flash units are all compatible, but most others of the day are not. (To learn more about this, see "Trigger Voltage" in the Glossary.)

---

**1976:** The Minolta 110 Zoom SLR is the first SLR with a zoom lens for 110 films. Priced at $249 (or roughly $800 today) it features a 25~50mm $f$4.5 zoom lens (roughly equivalent to 50~100mm in 35mm terms) that focuses down to 11.3 inches. The auto-exposure system is aperture priority, with shutter speeds from 10 full seconds to 1/1000. There is even a ± 2 EV exposure compensation slider.

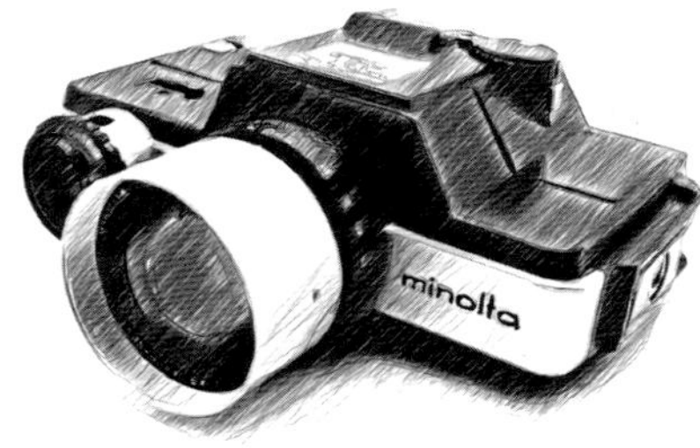

**TRIVIA**

The 110 Zoom was introduced to America with a TV ad showing a Minolta SR-T 101 appearing to explode and then, like magic, reassemble and become a Minolta 110 Zoom SLR. The exploding part of the commercial had been shot with a Hulcher high-speed camera (see **1953**) and baby powder was used to simulate the smoke. Some of the surviving small pieces of the demolished SR-T were cast in Lucite blocks and given to important dealers and journalists.

**1976:** A small firm called Yashima Kōgaku (Yashima Optical) is started in August 1975 by the brother of the founder of an earlier Yashima, which became the Yashica Camera Company. This new Yashima is a subsidiary of a firm making OEM parts for the audio industry. In early 1976, they introduce an SLR, the Yashima EMC750 (also sold as the Osanon Digital 750 and Rony EMC750).

It is the first camera with a continuously variable electronic shutter that is set by an automatic aperture-priority exposure system with speeds indicated by a digital readout in the viewfinder. Yashima does not have the resources to produce the cameras in quantity and only 2,000 are made. This new Yashima goes bust in 1980, but the camera is a precursor of things to come.

**TRIVIA**

There is today a manufacturer of microscopes called the Yashima Optical Company Ltd., based in Tokyo. Your scribe has been unable to determine if it is in any way related to either the Yashima Kogaku (above) or the earlier Yashima Kōgaku Seiki K.K., which became Yashica and later part of Kyocera.

**1976:** Leitz introduce the 50mm $f$ 1.0 Noctilux for the Leica-M rangefinder cameras. Designed by the legendary Walter Mandler and produced at the Leitz factory in Midland, Canada, it is said to capture more information on film than the photographer can see with the naked eye. This ultimate high-speed lens is only superseded by an $f$ 0.95 version in 2008.

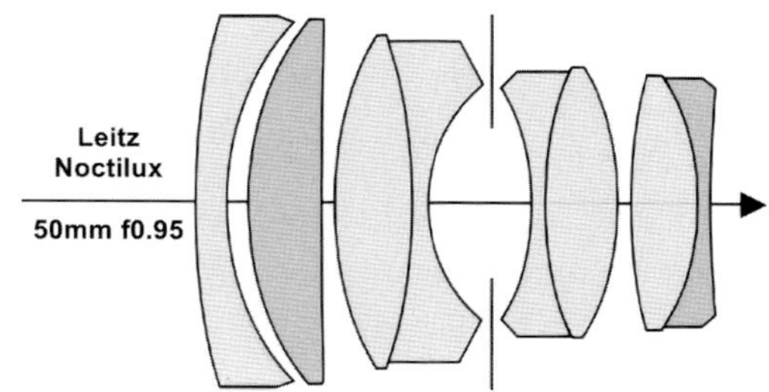


**TRIVIA**

The story is told that Mandler had worked on the $f$ 1.0 Noctilux for some time, without permission from the head office. On a trip to Wetzlar, he slipped the prototype into his pocket and flew to Germany. When he showed it to the German staff, they were amazed, and the lens was quickly approved for production in Canada.

**1976:** Unable to keep up with the increasing automation of the larger manufacturers and the increasingly sophisticated electronics of competing cameras, Miranda stop producing cameras and go bankrupt, along with its American owner, AIC Photo. The Miranda name will have a short revival in the 1980s when a British firm, Dixon's, buys the name and briefly sells rebadged cameras made by Cosina.

**1976:** At Photokina, Leica present a prototype auto-focus camera based on their numerous auto-focus patents from 1960 through 1973. It makes Leica the first company to develop a working assisted-focus system, built into the shell of a functioning Leica SL-2, but renamed the CK2. Focus is obtained by turning the focus ring towards one of two LEDs visible in the viewfinder. When both LEDs are out, the camera is focused. Leica refer to it as Correfot but is never produced.

---

### TRIVIA

CdS light meter cells were also sensitive to variations in contrast. And it was known that an image displays the highest contrast when in focus. By using two CdS cells it was possible to accurately determine the highest contrast level and thus accurate focus. The system was similar in concept to today's phase-detection systems . . . except that it required a vibrating diffraction grating (see Glossary) to work accurately.

---

**1976:** Japanese shutter maker Seiko build a vertical-run focal-plane shutter they call the MFC to compete with the Copal Square. The MFC is a metal shutter with five sections on the first curtain and six on the second. It is designed so that the first blade moves back after the exposure, creating a double baffle. The first camera to use the MFC is the Pentax ME.

**1976:** Asahi's Pentax ME is the first auto-exposure-only SLR. It has aperture-priority exposure control only (that is, the photographer could not manually select a shutter speed) for simple snapshot operation. Popular with the point-and-shoot crowd, those learning photography choose the K1000.

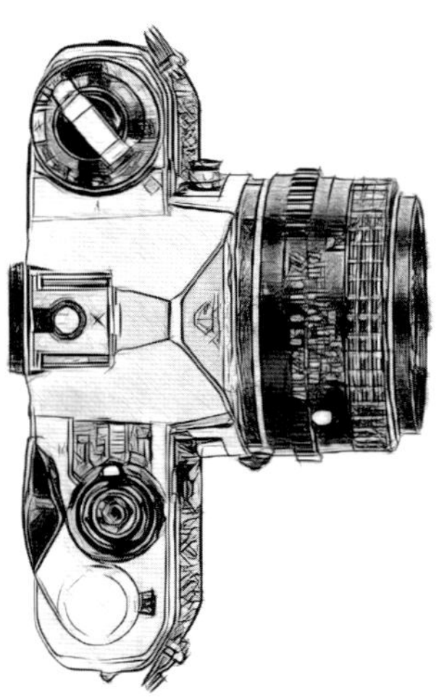

---

### TRIVIA

Interchangeable lens auto-exposure-only SLRs disappeared in the mid-1980s, because even snap-shooters demanded that SLRs (i.e., "good cameras") have a manual mode.

---

**1976:** Having gained much experience manufacturing Polaroid's instant film from 1963 to 1969, Kodak introduce their first instant camera, the EK4, also known as the "Colorburst 100." Kodak's instant film is different from Polaroid's in several ways.

Primarily, Kodak's film is exposed from the back without a mirror, the opposite of Polaroid's film, which was exposed from the front with a mirror to reverse the image. This means that both the cameras and film are simpler to manufacture, and the prints can use a matte surface to reduce glare on the face of the photo. The film path is also much simpler, allowing the use of a simple mechanical crank to spread the developer and eject the print, instead of an electric motor, as in Polaroid's cameras.

**1976:** Polaroid sue Kodak for patent infringement, claiming that Kodak have violated 12 of their patents in the making of their new instant films.

---

### UPDATE

Kodak had made several improvements to the Polaroid system and had hoped that these would qualify their film as a "new" product. In 1985, the judge does not agree and finds Kodak guilty on seven of the 12 patent infringements. Kodak are forced out of instant photography the following year.

---

**1976:** Victor Hasselblad retires and sells his firm to the Swedish investment firm of Säfveån AB.

---

### TRIVIA

Two years later, in 1978, Victor Hasselblad passed away at the age of 72. He left the majority of his sizable fortune to the Erna and Victor Hasselblad Foundation "to promote research and academic teaching in the natural sciences and photography." The foundation has, since 1980, distributed an annual prize, "The Hasselblad Award," to "a photographer recognized for major achievements." Currently the award comprises the sum of one million Swedish Krona (about $122,500), a gold medal, and a diploma. The winner of the award is usually announced around 8 March, Victor Hasselblad's birthday. Previous winners include Ansel Adams, Irving Penn, Ernst Haas, and Sophie Calle.

---

**1977:** Fujica's AZ-1 becomes the first interchangeable-lens camera to be offered with a zoom lens as its primary lens, rather than the usual 50 to 58mm "normal" lens. However, the regular Fujinon-Z 55mm $f$ 1.8 lens remains a popular option. The AZ-1 is also one of the last Japanese-made M42 screw mount cameras released.

---

### TRIVIA

The purchase of a zoom instead of a prime lens as the first lens will become normal with virtually all amateur 35mm SLRs in the latter 1980s.

---

**1976:** The Asahi Optical Co. presents its Pentax K1000, an interchangeable lens 35mm SLR. Other than its "K" bayonet lens mount, it is based on, and is almost identical to, the earlier Pentax Spotmatic F; the only changes are the self-timer, depth-of-field preview, and a few other features that have been removed to save cost. The K1000's inexpensive yet reliable simplicity earns it an unrivalled popularity as a basic but sturdy workhorse, particularly among students of photography. The K1000 is an almost-all-metal, mechanically 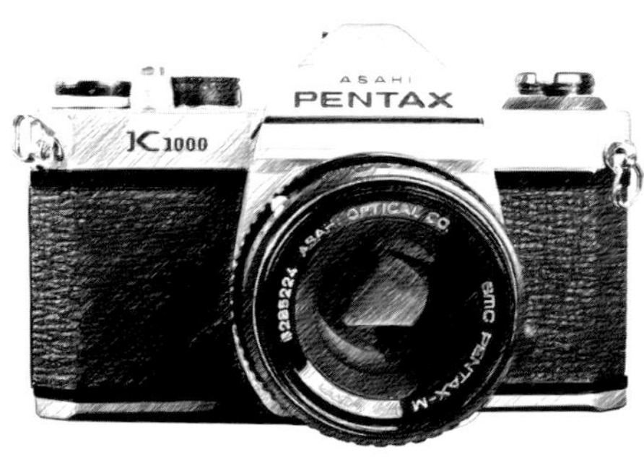 controlled (i.e., with springs, gears, and levers), manual-focus SLR with manual-exposure control, and is completely operable without batteries (needed only for the TTL light meter).

The Pentax K1000 eventually will sell more than three million units over a 21-year run. Made first in Japan (1976–1978), then Hong Kong (1978–1990), and finally in mainland China (1990–1997), production ends when manufacturing costs of its older design become unsustainable and when obtaining its precision analogue micro-galvanometers (for the light meter) finally becomes near impossible.

The MZ-M is supposed to be the next K1000, but the all-plastic M does not have the solid "feel" of its predecessor, and photo students prefer a second, third, or even fourth-hand K1000 to learn the craft.

**1977:** Konica's C35 AF is the world's first production auto-focus still camera. The C35 AF uses Honeywell's "Visitronic" AF system employing infrared light beams invisible to the human eye to 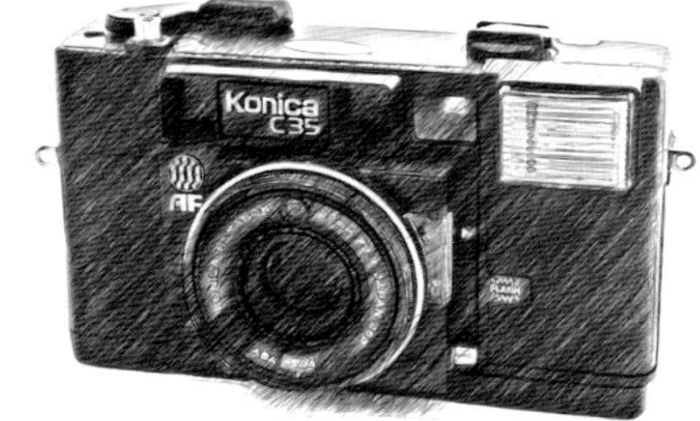 determine focusing distances. The camera is produced under patents licensed from Honeywell, and Konica sells one million units.

### TRIVIA

In the early 1980s, BeLomo (Belarus) released a rather blatant copy of the Konica C35AF, the Elikon Autofocus. It had both autofocus and a built-in flash, two features that rarely appear in a Soviet camera. It has only been seen with Cyrillic lettering and was never sold outside the USSR. The original price was 139 rubles.

**1977:** George Eastman and Edwin Land are inducted into the National Inventors Hall of Fame.

**1977:** Pentax establish their own distribution in the U.S., squeezing Heiland/Honeywell out of the business. Their cameras now appear in the U.S., as they have all along in the rest of the world, as Asahi Pentax.

### ODDITIES

In 1977, Carl Zeiss (Oberkochen) introduced their N-Mirotar. At a price of $16,500 (or roughly $70,500 today), this highly sophisticated lens is not intended for the average amateur. But it can do incredible things.

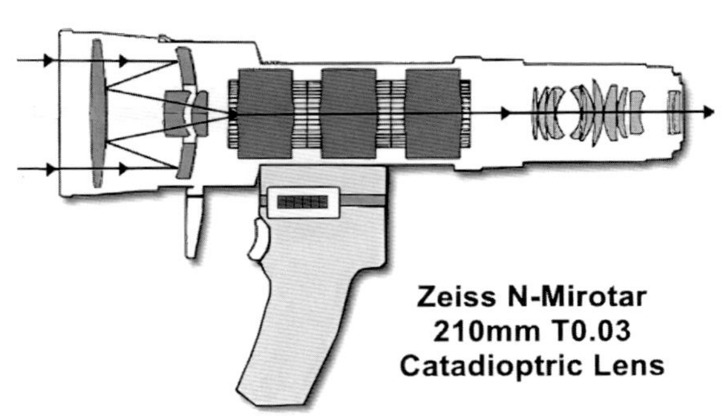



Designed for hand-held night photography, it features a Zeiss 210mm catadioptric lens positioned in front of three cascaded photo-multiplier tubes connected by optical fibers. When the picture is taken, the image passes through the lens and is then magnified in brightness some 80,000 times by the photo-multiplier tubes and projected onto a circular screen within the lens. An internal relay lens (consisting of two objectives, the first an inverted Planar in front of a second lens of Sonnar design) picks up the intensified image from the screen and focuses it on the focal plane of the camera.

The "catch-22" with this system is that the lens is only usable with black-and-white film, as the fluorescent screen emits a monochromatic, yellowish-white image. The final image is 30mm in diameter, with low resolution and low contrast, and looks much like the circular image of some fish-eye lenses. But it is highly effective for the intended purpose.

The resulting increase in lens speed is a phenomenal 2,500 times that of an $f$ 1.4 lens, or, to put it another way, it gives it an effective T-stop of 0.03, allowing shots using ASA/ISO 400 film, at 1/500 of a second under a full moon. Only 43 were made, nearly all for military or intelligence agencies and all in the Contax/Yashica mount.

**1977:** Ricoh introduce their XR-1. It is not a particularly innovative camera but rather than use a proprietary lens mount, the Ricoh uses a Pentax K bayonet mount. Saburo Matsumoto, president of Asahi Optical, is quoted as saying, "I agree to Ricoh's request of their using our K mount on their new SLR because I personally prefer not to be narrow minded and exclusive about this. I would rather have this mount become an international standard." Over time, that is just what will happen.

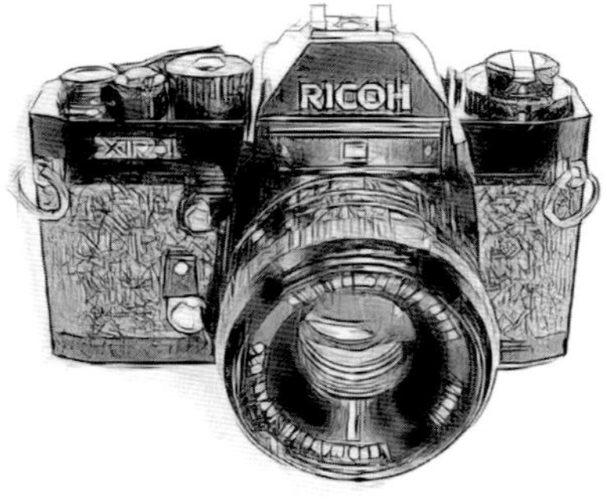

The Ricoh is the first camera, other than a Pentax, to use the K mount but, by 1978, K mount cameras will be introduced by Topcon, Cosina, Carena (Switzerland), and Bauer (Germany), all with the permission of Pentax. When, late in the year, VEB Pentacon (East Germany) introduce a Praktica with a mount (almost) compatible with the K mount, the 40-year-old M-42 threaded lens mount is effectively dead.

**1977:** The Minolta XD11 (called the XD7 in Europe and the XD in Japan) is the first camera to offer both aperture-priority and shutter-priority auto-exposure methods in an SLR. The camera is developed by Minolta in conjunction with Leica, and the body will be the basis for the R4, R5, R6, and R7 series of Leica cameras. Leica added a more advanced metering system into the body (including spot metering), but most of the other features of the camera are the same in both bodies.

<table>
<tr><td>TRIVIA<br>Previously, each AE SLR brand offered only one mode or the other, and aggressively advertised its choice as superior to the other. The XD11 offered both, thus ending the debate.</td></tr>
</table>

**1978:** At Photokina, Leitz again show the Leica Correfot SLR, this time built into a modified R4-MOT body with a fully operational autofocus system. It now uses a servomotor connected to a modified manual-focus lens through a gear that engages ridges engraved in the focusing ring of the lens. (In other words, it actually turns the conventional focusing ring to effect automatic focusing.) With other lenses, it can be focused manually with focus confirmation using two LEDs on top of the viewfinder, as was shown in the 1976 version. It is contrast-detection-based, no longer requiring the vibrating diffraction plate, and works more like modern phase-detection systems. It is never produced.

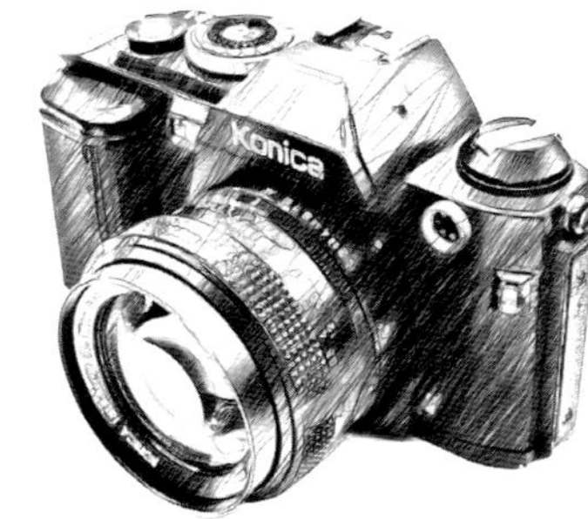

**1978:** At Photokina, both the Contax 137 and Konica FS-1 are shown, each featuring an integral motor drive. But the Konica passes JCII export inspections in December of the year, while the Contax does not do so until March 1980. Thus, the Konica FS-1 becomes the first SLR marketed with an integrated motor drive.

**1978:** Polaroid introduces "Polavision," an instant motion-picture film. It has an image format similar to Super-8 film but requires a special camera and tabletop viewer. Unfortunately, Polavision is introduced just as Betamax and VHS video recorders are entering the market. When Land shows it to his friend Akio Morita, president of Sony, Morita tells him, "It's a fantastic scientific innovation, but it's past its time." Polavision costs over $500 million to develop, yet Polaroid sells fewer than 60,000 systems—a fraction of what they had projected—and it is discontinued in less than a year.

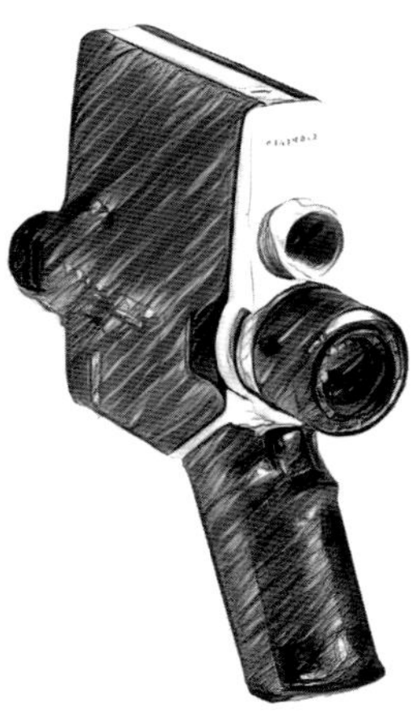

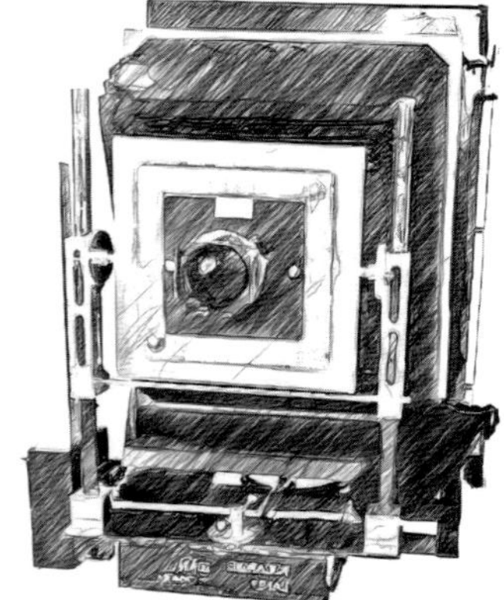

**ODDITIES**

In January of 1978, Edwin Land showed off the Giant Polaroid, a 235-pound camera which took 20 x 24-inch Polaroid photos in both colour and black and white. Three lenses in 600, 800, and 1200mm focal lengths were designed for it, but only five cameras were made. In 1997, a sixth "Hybrid" camera was assembled using parts from a prototype and a Wisner front.

Famous artists and photographers were invited to use the cameras at the Polaroid studios on the condition that Polaroid was allowed to keep some of the resulting images. The film was discontinued in 2008, with some 550 boxes in frozen storage at that time. As of late 2023, you could still shoot with a Giant Polaroid for about $2,000 per day plus $200 per shot.

There was also one experimental 40 x 80-inch Polaroid made. Its whereabouts today are unknown.

**1978:** Canon's A-1 is the first SLR with a digitally controlled, programmed auto-exposure mode. Instead of the photographer picking a shutter speed to freeze or blur motion and choosing a lens aperture *f*-stop to control depth of field (also called depth of focus), the A-1 has a microprocessor programmed to automatically select a compromise exposure based on input from the light meter. It is also the first camera to have all four of the now standard PASM (program/aperture-priority/shutter-priority/manual) exposure modes.

**1978:** Pentax introduce their 110 Auto, which accepts six bayonet mount interchangeable lenses. It is followed by the "110 Super" variant in 1982. They become the only system SLR cameras made for the 110 film format and are manufactured until 1985.

**1978:** Canon introduce their 500mm *f* 8 catadioptric (mirror) lens to compete with the Reflex Nikkor 500mm *f* 8 (see **1968**). Though small, lightweight, affordable, and totally free of chromatic aberrations, it suffers from the problems of all mirror lenses: fixed, small aperture, low contrast, and weird "donut" bokeh. The lens is made only a few years.

**1978:** The designer of the Wirgin Edixa and Rollei 35, among many other cameras, Heinz Waaske starts his own technical design office in Braunschweig, Germany. He will work not only with camera builders but also on other projects, such as loudspeakers for Blaupunkt. His work is characterized by a "technical minimalism," with just a few small parts providing as many functions as possible.

---

**TRIVIA**

Waaske is very critical of the "collectible" edition of the Rollei 35, with casing made of precious metals. He is also quick to reject all requests to design military equipment, arguing that after his experience in the Second World War, he'd had enough of war.

---

**TRIVIA**

In October of 2020, Canon will patent a series of five fast (at least by the standards of mirror lenses) catadioptric lenses, each with image stabilization, for all their newest mirrorless cameras. They are a 400/3.6 (!), 800/5, 1200/8, 1200/10.5, and a 2000/15. Rumours abound that these will appear as low-cost alternatives to Canon's normal tele-lenses. After all, not everyone can afford the five-figure price of pro-quality long glass. But, as of mid-2024, no such lenses have come to market.

---

**1978:** Glen Serbin starts *Photographer's Forum*, a quarterly magazine for emerging photographers. It will enjoy a 40-year run, ending in 2018.

**1978:** Polaroid update their SX-70, making it the first camera to use a small ultrasonic sound system to compute the distance to subjects, thus becoming the first auto-focus camera. The SX-70 Sonar is otherwise identical to the original SX-70 (see **1972**).

---

**TRIVIA**

The principle of self-developing "instant photography" came to Edwin Land in 1943. The first production instant camera was the non-SLR Polaroid Land Model 95 of 1948, which produced sepia-toned peel-apart pictures. The original SX-70 was the culmination of a camera-and-film project to create full-colour, self-contained, develop-before-your-eyes, "garbage-free" prints. The project took seven years and cost nearly a quarter-billion dollars.

---

**1979:** Canon introduce their AF35M "Sure Shot," the world's first true point-and-shoot camera. With this camera, Canon create the compact automated camera segment. Known as the Autoboy in Japan and the Sure Shot in the USA, Canon's AF35M immediately becomes a market success, for it is the first compact camera in which focus, film advance, film rewind and exposure are all handled by the camera.

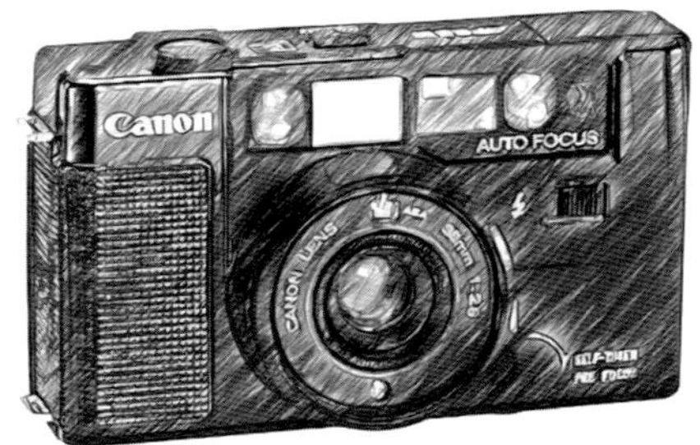

---

**TRIVIA**

The early auto-focus cameras used a passive system that worked well in good light but suffered in low light. Like Konica's C35AF (see **1977**), Canon's AF35M uses an active infrared beam. It focuses well up to 27 feet from the camera. Beyond that, it simply selects infinity focus.

---

**1979:** The Mamiya ZE is the first camera to use electrical contacts to transmit information from the body to the lens. All previous cameras use mechanical arms for this, even if some of them only trip switches within the camera body. It is interesting that the body has just three contacts, but the lenses have 10, for future models beyond the ZE. The lenses can transmit the maximum and minimum aperture, exposure correction values, and focal length. The ZE itself uses just the focal length information to set a minimum shutter speed. While most makers are reluctant to change their lens mounts for fear of making older lenses obsolete, Mamiya has few previous models and is thus able to aggressively promote their new bayonet mount.

---

**ODDITIES**

The 1979 Hanimex Reflex Flash 35 (made by Sedic of Japan) is notable for being the first SLR with built-in electronic flash. Otherwise, it is a cheaply made, eminently forgettable camera with a fixed Hanimar 41mm *f* 2.8 lens and a mirror that acts as the shutter.

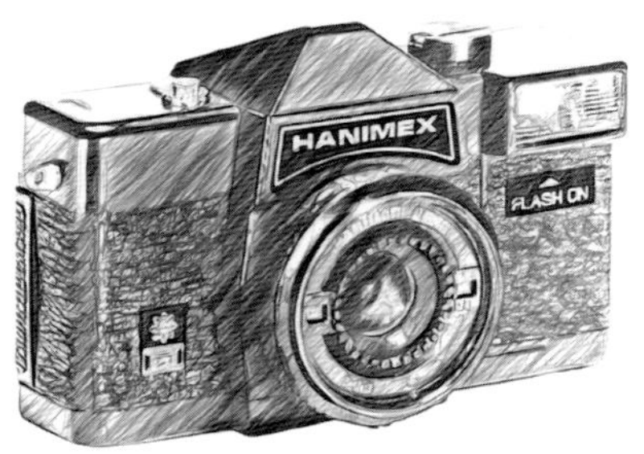

---

**1979:** After stints with photo agencies Sygma and the Paris-based Gamma, Sebastião Salgado (b. 1944) joins the international cooperative of photographers, Magnum Photos. But he will leave in 1994 and, with his wife Lélia, form his own agency, Amazonas Images, in Paris, to represent his work. In 2024, he will announce his retirement, at the age of 80.

**1979:** Olympus introduce their XA, with true range-finder focusing, an excellent, relatively fast 35mm *f* 2.8 lens, and aperture-priority metering. It is the first camera with neither lens cap nor case but features a sliding hard shell to protect the lens and yet still fit in a shirt pocket. It is another triumph for designer Yoshihisa Maitani.

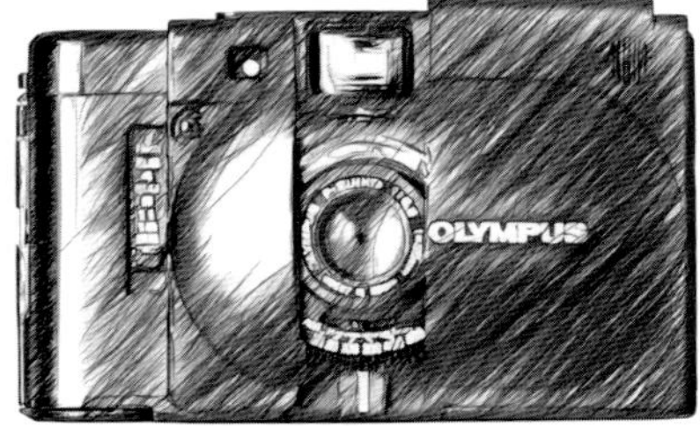

**1980:** Ilford develops the first chromogenic film. XP1 is a black-and-white film with colour dye technology and can be processed in conventional C-41 colour chemistry.

**1980:** In the fall, Leica show a further improved Correfot at the Minneapolis meeting of the Leica Historical Society of America (now known as the International Leica Society). The camera shown is based on Leica's new R4-Mot and equipped with a servo-motor-driven 50mm $f$1.4 Summilux-R lens, which provides true autofocus operation. Low-light performance is quite good, though focusing is slow by today's standards, as the servomotor must run through several gears to gain the torque needed to focus the lens. As a result, the camera suffers from high power consumption, with power supplied by a battery pack made from the housing of a Leica R3 motor drive unit and attached to the bottom of the camera. Its six batteries provide just one hour of operation. The Correfot, in any form, is never produced. In fact, despite their incredible lead in the field, Leica will not produce an auto-focus camera until their medium-format S2, in 2009!

---

### TRIVIA

Unfortunately, Leica never market their auto-focus cameras, thus missing the honour of being the first company to do so. The company feels that its customers know how to focus their cameras and want to do so. So, it abandons auto-focus development, and sells (or gives—it's not clear) its patents to Minolta, with whom it has a technology exchange agreement. The honour of building the first auto-focus SLR goes to Minolta, who introduce their Minolta 7000 in 1985. But, the Minolta 7000 would have never seen the light of day without the Leitz Correfot technology.

---

**1980:** Nikon's F3 is introduced. Successor to the Nikon F and F2 professional cameras, it is the first Nikon to have aperture priority automation. Although the F3 is superseded by the F4 in 1988 and the F5 in 1996, it remains in production through to 2001, with over 751,000 cameras in numerous variants produced. It is also the first Nikon to be styled by the Italian automobile designer Giorgetto Giugiaro, rather than by Nikon engineers.

---

### TRIVIA

Giugiaro has designed beautiful bodies for Lotus, Lamborghini, and Ferrari, among others. He even designed the DeLorean DMC-12 we know from "Back to the Future" movies. With the F3, he included a red accent stripe on the handgrip. The red accent has become (with variants of stripes and various other shapes) a signature feature of many Nikon cameras.

---

**1980:** During the summer, the last of the Nikkorex/Nikkormat series of cameras are built. Afterward, all cameras produced by Nippon Kogaku bear the Nikon name.

**1980:** Physicist, John Goodenough (1922–2023) invents a lithium-based battery in which the lithium can migrate from one electrode to the other as a lithium ion. This allows more electricity to be stored in a smaller, lighter battery. In 2019, Goodenough will be awarded the Nobel

Prize for Chemistry, alongside M. Stanley Whittingham (b. 1941) and Akira Yoshino (b. 1948). Goodenough becomes the oldest person to be awarded a Nobel Prize.

**1980:** Pentax honour their 60th anniversary with their LX, their first (and only) true 35mm system camera. (LX, incidentally, means 60 in Roman numerals.) The LX features an interchangeable viewfinder, interchangeable focusing screens, better sealing against water and dust, a 5 frames-per-second motor, battery packs, winders, an extra grip, and a variety of lenses. Production ends in 2001.

---

### TRIVIA

Though normally aiming at the amateur market, Pentax does produce cameras for professionals. In 1969, the company released its Pentax 6 x 7, a full system camera (known as Pentax 67 after some minor upgrades were made in 1990) for 120/220 film. It was discontinued in 2009 and a digital version produced. Pentax also released the 645 in 1982, also for the pros. A digital version, the 645D, was introduced in 2010, and won an award for "best professional camera" in 2011.

---

**1981:** Fuji start marketing their Instax cameras and instant film in Japan. Employing technology licensed from Polaroid, these cameras will see exponential growth over the next 40 years, after Polaroid leaves the business.

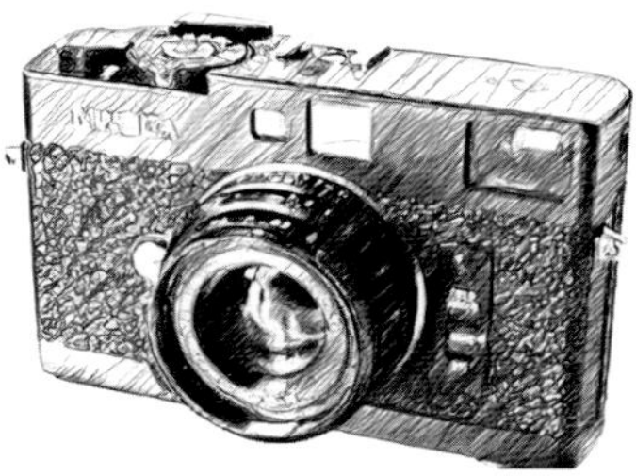

**1981:** Though Leica cease the production of the Minolta-made CL (see **1973**) in 1975, Minolta improves it to make their "CLE." Slightly larger than the original CL, it boasts TTL metering with rearward-facing silicon metering sensors that measure the light falling on the film, like the Olympus OM-2 (see **1975**). It also adds automatic exposure, although the shutter is now battery dependent. The camera is also able to offer TTL flash—an incredible breakthrough at the time.

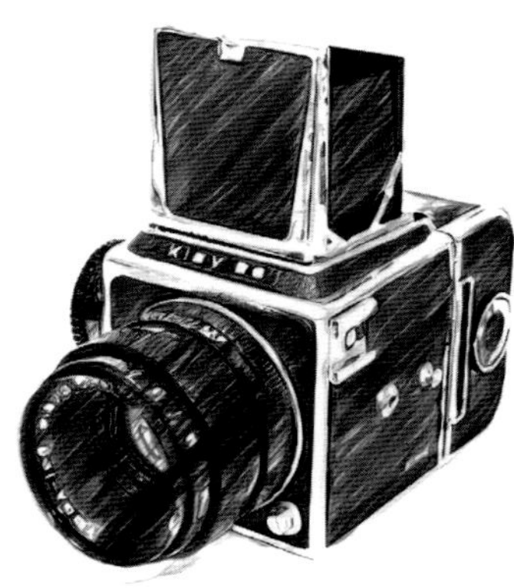

**1981:** The Sigma 21-35mm *f*3.5-4 becomes the first superwide-angle zoom lens for 35mm SLRs. For decades, combining the complexities of rectilinear superwide-angle lenses, retrofocus lenses and zoom lenses seemed impossibly difficult, yet Sigma does the impossible, reaching a 91° maximum field of view with a complex, all-moving 11-element formula.

**1981:** Still based on the 1948 Hasselblad 1600F, and sometimes referred to as the "Hasselbadski," the Salyut-S morphs into the Kiev 80 and later the Kiev 88, and begins to be sold overseas. (The only substantial differences are that the 80 has a cold flash shoe, the 88 a hot shoe.) Later, the 88 is offered with a large, if quirky, TTL metering prism. Production ends in 2005, but the factory continues to sell upgraded examples, based on new-old stock, under the ARAX name.

---

**TRIVIA**

The Kiev 80/88 models see a further redesign of the winding mechanism, introducing a small pin that takes the full load of winding the shutter curtains and is prone to wear or snapping. More importantly, they fail to redesign the "stacked gears," as Hasselblad did with their 1000F, and this remains the Kiev's Achilles heel.

---

**1981:** Pentax becomes the first camera manufacturer to produce 10 million SLR cameras, just 29 years after the Asahiflex hit the market, in 1952.

**1981:** Pentax release the ME-F. The first auto-focus SLR with auto-focus sensors in the camera body, the ME-F has a special motorized SMC Pentax AF 35mm~70mm $f$2.8 zoom lens. It also features a unique K-F bayonet lens mount with five electric contact pins to pass focus-control information between the body and the lens; auto-focus performance, however, was poor. While not a great marketing success, it does have reasonable sales and sets the basic design for AF-SLRs from all makers.

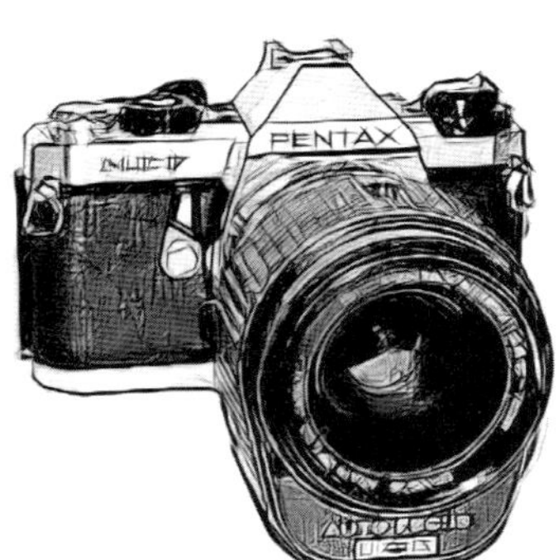

---

**TRIVIA**

In 1981, Ilford introduced Ilford HP-5 Power Winder Film (ISO 400) coated on a very thin polyester base. This allowed enough film for 72 exposures to be packaged in a standard 35mm cassette and was intended for the motor-drive cameras of the day. Also offered was a special high-capacity developing tank and loader (made by Kindermann in Germany but marked Ilford).

The film was not a success and was short-lived for several reasons. Film counters on most cameras only went to 36 exposures and some cameras, equipped with auto-rewind, would rewind the film as soon as they reached 38 exposures. Polyester is a much stronger film base than the normal tri-acetate and would not tear, sometimes damaging the motor-drive-equipped cameras if something went wrong. As well, the polyester base "pipes" light, reducing contrast in the images. Finally, the thin base made it difficult to load into the special stainless steel film reels and tanks. Some said that it was "like trying to load wet toilet paper!"

By 1984, the tanks and loaders were being advertised at clear-out prices "while stocks last," though it seems that the 72 exposure loads lived on for a while, as a specialized surveillance film. That too was gone by 1987.

**1981:** Kodak introduce their Ektaflex PCT (Photo Colour Transfer) system with special films, papers, and a mechanical processor. (Two processors are available; the more expensive one is motorized.) You expose your negative or transparency on to the appropriate film with your enlarger, as you would in any printing process, soak it in "activator" for 20 seconds, then run it through a series of rollers to laminate it to a receptor sheet. After about six minutes you peel the film from the receptor sheet and reveal your colour print. A wonderful idea, but the materials are expensive, the results are mediocre, and the system disappears within five years.

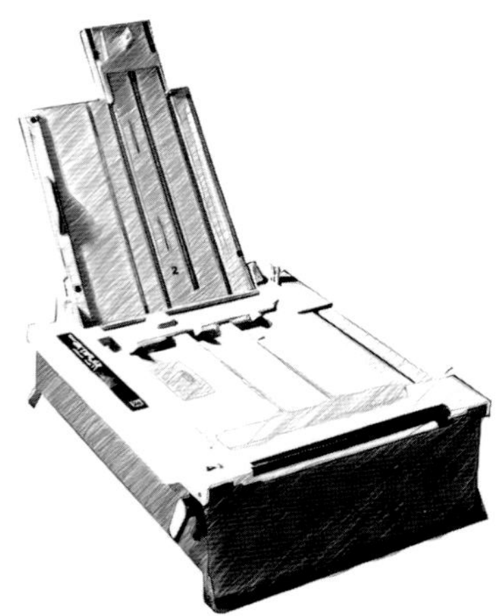

*Kodak Ektaflex Processor*

**1982:** Electronics giant Sony demonstrate their "Mavica," a hand-held electronic camera. It is an analog (not digital) camera that records television-like signals to a 2 x 2-inch "video floppy." In essence, it is an analog video camera that records single (freeze) frames, 50 per disk. The pictures are viewed on a television, and image quality is considered equal to that of televisions of the day. This prototype is never produced, but a few later models are. Finally, in 1997 a true digital Mavica will be produced: the MVC-FD-5.

---

### ODDITIES

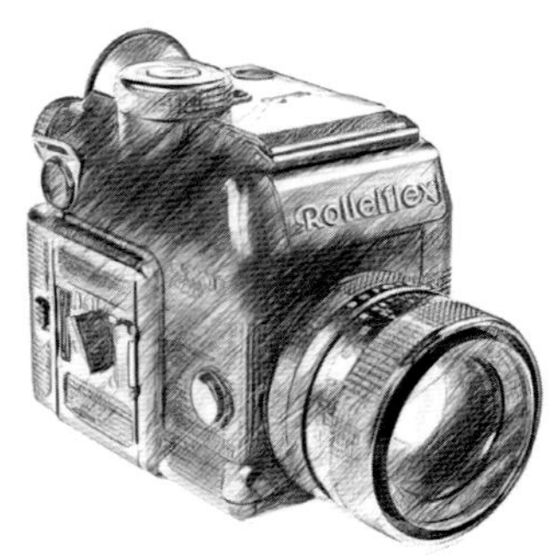

The Rolleiflex SL 2000F is first shown at Photokina in 1976 but (possibly due to financial restraints at Rollei) it does not reach the market until 1981. Reminiscent of the Olympus MDN prototype (see **1967**), it is a 35mm camera of modular design, with both eye-level and waist-level finders, interchangeable dark slide film magazines, and a motorized film advance powered by five AA-size rechargeable batteries. The camera has an electronically controlled focal-plane shutter with speeds from 16 seconds to 1/1000 second and flash sync at 1/100 second. It features aperture-priority automatic exposure, with ±2 stops of exposure compensation. Zeiss lenses, from 16 to 200mm are offered, as well as 500 and 1000mm mirror lenses. There is also a range of somewhat cheaper Rolleinar lenses, made by Mamiya.

Designed by Zeiss (Oberkochen) and built to Rollei's high standards, it proves to be a reliable camera. However, most people weaned on traditional SLRs find it "different" and sales are slow. An updated Sl-3003 (1/2000 shutter) and a simplified SL-3001 (no waist-level finder) soon follow, but it all ends when Rollei goes bankrupt in 1982. Had Rollei survived, the 2000F, 3001 and 3003 would have been prime candidates for digital backs.

**1982:** Designed by T. M. Lee, the Holga is a plastic camera using 120 roll film and is intended for low-income Chinese families. As 35mm takes over in China, the factory turns to export sales, starting in 1989. The Holga then gains a worldwide, almost cult-like following, for its low-tech approach and artfully flawed optics, light leaks, and other idiosyncrasies. In the coming years, many variants will be produced under the Holga name and sales will reach 200,000 units per year (see **2015**).

**1982:** Kodak introduce T-grain technology in Kodacolor VR1000 colour negative film. This technology will be widely used in other films, including their T-Max films.

**1982:** Ricoh's XR-S becomes the first and, perhaps only, solar-powered SLR. Essentially it is a Ricoh XR-7 (introduced in 1981), modified with two silicon photovoltaic cells in the sides of the pentaprism housing that charge a unique three-volt 2G13R "5-year" silver oxide battery. This battery could be replaced with two regular 1.5-volt S76 (SR44) silver oxide batteries if necessary.

**1982:** Production of Voigtländer and Rollei cameras ceases. Rollei is bankrupt.

---

### ODDITIES

During the early 1980s, a small number of little-known camera repairmen in Russia started making copies of the Leica I (see **1925**) called the Aciel. However, these were left-handed cameras, being assembled completely backwards, with the film-winding knob on the left and the rewind on the right. Lens says it's an Elmar 3.5/50, but the coated lens elements are from an Industar 95 enlarging lens! Many parts had to be individually made by hand and very few were produced.

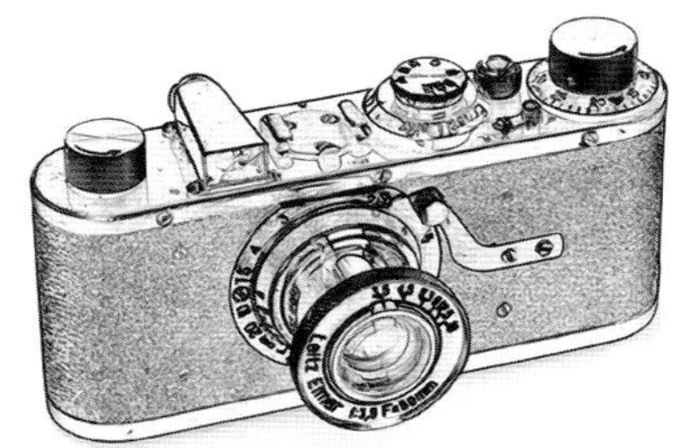

*The "Aciel"*

---

**1982:** The world's first low-cost moulded glass aspherical lens elements are used in the unnamed 12.5mm *f* 2.8 lenses found in Kodak's Disc 4000 cameras. Within 10 or so years, other lens makers will master the art of moulding glass aspherical elements, dramatically lowering the cost of such elements and increasing the performance of the lenses that use them.

**1982:** Japanese production of interchangeable zoom lenses surpasses that of prime (single focal length) lenses for the first time.

---

**TRIVIA**

Many, if not most, of today's zoom lenses are not "parfocal" (that is, they are not true zooms), but in fact are "varifocal"—that is, the focus point shifts when the focal length changes. These are easier to design and cheaper to manufacture and so can sell at a lower price point. The focus shift usually goes unnoticed as they are most often used with auto-focus cameras that will automatically refocus faster than you can notice the problem. You can readily tell the difference, however. Varifocal lenses have an aperture that changes as they are zoomed. True (i.e., parfocal) zooms have one constant aperture throughout their zoom range. These days, true zooms are advertised as "constant aperture" zooms.

In the October 1993 issue of *Popular Photography*, Herbert Keppler explained it all rather simply: "Here's how you can tell if your 'zoom' is actually varifocal. Zoom to maximum focal length and focus on an object manually about 10 feet away. Now zoom back to the shortest focal length. If the viewfinder is still sharp, you have a true zoom. If it's hopelessly out of focus, it's varifocal." Of course, this test only works with older, manual focus zoom lenses, or if you turn autofocus off.

---

**1982:** Eastman Kodak announce the Disc System, which includes three new cameras. The 8.2 x 10.6mm negative is less than half the size of the already small 110 format. Sales begin well, but the small negative requires a 13-times enlargement to make a standard print (compared to less than four times for a standard 35mm negative); the prints are grainy and, in Japan, processing is twice the price of the much-higher-quality 35mm prints. In a bid to improve picture quality, the DISC 4000 features the world's first low-cost aspherical glass lens—albeit in a rather basic fixed-focus, four element 12.5mm *f* 2.8 four-element lens with one aspheric element. But this molded glass lens is the precursor of things to come.

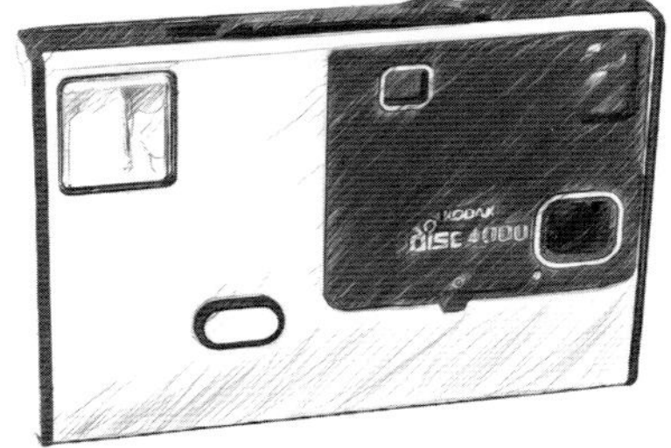

In 1983, several more disc cameras are introduced, by Fuji, Konica, and Minolta, but in the format's second year, sales drop drastically. Although small numbers of cameras are produced through 1990, the format is effectively dead within a couple of years. Disc film is discontinued in 1998.

---

**TRIVIA**

Although disc-film cameras were marketed by several companies, nearly all were OEM products of Haking Industries of Hong Kong. The sole exception was one made for Germany's Osram by Japan's Fuji Koeki (Osram's long time supplier of electronic flash units)—a firm not connected to Fuji Photo Film.

**1982:** The Nimslo-3D camera, designed in the U.S. but made in the U.K., is brought to market. It features four (rather than the usual two) lenses and makes four simultaneous images which are then printed in register on a lenticular paper to create the 3D effect without needing special glasses. Although the idea of a consumer-level camera that can make lenticular 3D prints similar to those that have existed for many years on book covers and other novelty items certainly has appeal, the Nimslo does not receive substantial sales, partially due to the high costs of processing and longer wait times than for traditional cameras. The Nimslo company goes bankrupt in 1989, though the patents are purchased by the Nashika company, who make several successor cameras before quitting the business.

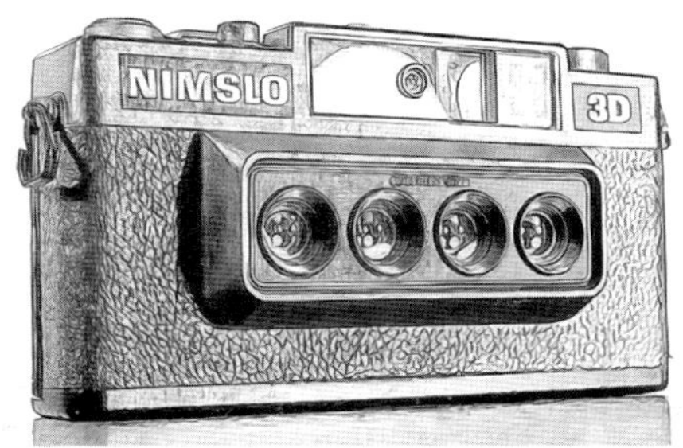

**1983:** Polaroid brings Polachrome to market. Derived from Polavision (see **1978**) it is an easy-to-develop 35mm slide film. Each roll of film comes with a cartridge containing developing chemicals which were pressed between the film and a developing strip by a hand-cranked machine called the Auto Processor. Although the Auto Processor is inexpensive and does not require a darkroom, the results are somewhat variable (to be polite) and the resolution is not as good as conventional film. Film sensitivity is low (ISO 40), even for a slide film. It remains in production for nearly 20 years but is never a real commercial success.

**1983:** Nikon's FA is the first camera with a multi-segmented (or "matrix" or "evaluative") automatic multi-pattern exposure meter. The FA had a built-in microprocessor programmed to analyze light levels in five different segments of the field of view for convenient exposure control in difficult lighting situations.

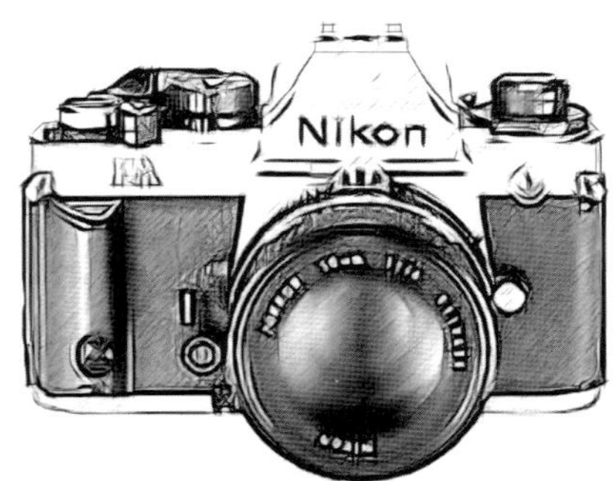

---

**TRIVIA**

At the same time, Nikon present an evolution of their flagship camera, the Nikon F3-AF with its DX-1 viewfinder and two AF lenses, the AF 80mm *f* 2.8 and AF 200mm *f* 3.5 ED. Although never officially confirmed, it is rumoured that Nikon purchased the technology for the Correfot system from Leitz to develop the F3-AF.

---

**1983:** The Olympus OM-4 becomes the first camera with built-in multiple-spot meter (2% of view, or 3.3° with a 50mm lens). It can measure eight individual spots and average them for precise exposure.

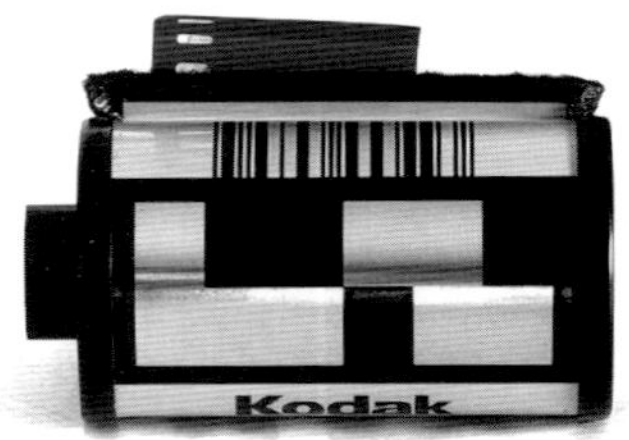

**1983:** Kodak introduce their DX encoding system for 35mm film canisters. It is not unlike an earlier Fuji system, using a series of insulating or conducting blocks which allow sensors in the camera to distinguish which film it holds. It can set the ISO film speed in 24 steps from 25 to 5000. There is a barcode for film processors, and the film itself has bar coding along the edge to allow automated processing. Within a year, all film makers adopt the system.

---

### TRIVIA

Your scribe has found references to an earlier, though short-lived system, by FujiFilm, which would allow Fujica cameras to detect whether the film in them was either ASA 100 or 400. The Fujica Auto-7 (1981) could use these special cassettes, or the film speed could be set manually if regular films were used. Details on how these special cassettes worked remain elusive.

---

**1983:** The Yashica Company Ltd. is acquired by ceramics giant Kyocera. Initially, the merger results in few outward changes, but in 2005, Kyocera will halt production on all Contax, Yashica, and other Kyocera-branded film and digital cameras in order to concentrate on the burgeoning market for camera modules to be built into mobile telephones.

**1983:** The Vivitar Tec-35 (made for Vivitar by the West Electric subsidiary of Matsushita Electric), a point-and-shoot camera, is the first camera to be fitted with a top-mounted liquid crystal display to show the film speed and exposure count. Such displays will later become commonplace on digital cameras.

---

### TRIVIA

The Vivitar *TEC-35* (sold in Japan as the National Chance C-700), had an ingenious active auto-focus system. It discharged a tiny electronic flash set behind an infrared filter, then measured the intensity of the reflected light.

---

**1983:** The Pentax Super A (called Super Program in USA) is the first SLR with top-mounted LCD data display. It shows the selected shutter speed, while both speed and aperture are visible on LCD displays inside the viewfinder.

**1983:** General Igor Kornitzky, right-hand man to the USSR Minister of Defense and Industry, shows a little Japanese compact camera (the Cosina CX-2) to his comrade, Michail Panfiloff, who is the Director of Lomo (the Leningrad Optical Mechanical Association), the powerful Russian arms and optical factory. Panfiloff

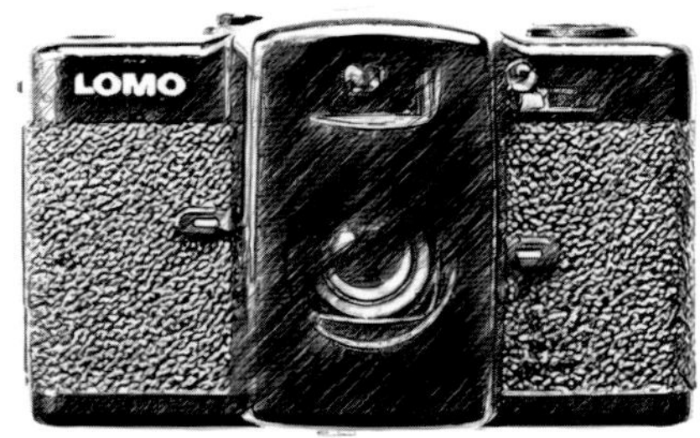

carefully examines the item, observing its sharp glass lens, sensitive CdS meter, and robust casing. Realizing its potential, the two gentlemen order the Leningrad (now St. Petersburg) factory to create an improved version of the Cosina CX-2. Sadly, the Lomo factory is not up to the challenge.

**1984:** The Pentax PC35AF-M, a point-and-shoot camera, is the first camera equipped to read the new DX films (see **1983**).

**1984:** Renowned photographer Garry Winogrand (1928–1984) dies just six weeks after being diagnosed with cancer. Winogrand is one of the first practitioners of "street photography," a style that is very popular the 1960s and later. He becomes known for his portrayal of American life, and many of his photographs depict the social issues of his time. He is just 56.

---

**TRIVIA**

When he dies, Winogrand leaves behind over 300,000 images and more than 2,500 undeveloped rolls of film.

---

**1984:** America's Grand Old Man of Photography, Ansel Adams, dies at the age of 82.

---

**TRIVIA**

In response to years of increasing regulations prohibiting photography in federal buildings and public parks, the United States Congress restored First Amendment rights to photographers on all public lands with "The Ansel Adams Act" of 2015.

---

**1984:** Mamiya's main international distributor, Osawa (formerly Bell & Howell Japan) declares bankruptcy. It is the largest financial failure in modern Japanese history and creates severe financial difficulties for Mamiya. Mamiya continue to manufacture their profitable medium-format SLRs, but by June, 35mm camera production stops. Mamiya will eventually recover and, in 2006, become Mamiya Digital Imaging.

---

**BUSINESS TRIVIA**

Over time, Mamiya entered other business markets by purchasing other companies. Until 2000, it made fishing rods and reels. In 2006, the Mamiya Op Co., Ltd., transferred the camera and optical business to Mamiya Digital Imaging Co., Ltd. (see **2009**). The original company, now doing business as Mamiya-OP, continues to exist and makes a variety of industrial and electronics products. It also makes golf clubs, golf club shafts and grips, and golf balls through various subsidiaries.

---

**1984:** The Lomo LC-A begins mass-production, with 1,200 people building 1,100 units per month for the Russian market. The camera's popularity quickly spreads to other Communist countries such as Poland, Czechoslovakia, and Cuba, primarily due to a lack of decent alternatives.

### ODDITIES

Canon again produce a limited set of high-speed F-1 cameras, this time for photographers accredited to the 1984 Los Angeles Olympics. Based on the newest version of the F-1 with an electromagnetically controlled titanium shutter, it uses the pellicle mirror, as did the earlier version (see **1972**), but is capable of 14 frames per second—and the automatic diaphragm works. Fewer than 100 are made.

**1984:** Canon introduce the longest (and most expensive) auto-focus lens ever made: the EF 1200mm *f* 5.6L USM. Originally developed with an FD mount for the 1984 Los Angeles Olympics, five lenses were made available for newspaper, magazine, and wire service coverage of the games. All five FD-mount lenses were then shipped back to Canon Japan and converted into EF-mount optics. They went on sale in mid-1993, priced at ¥9,800,000 apiece (or $82,080, which, allowing for inflation, works out to roughly $135,000 today).

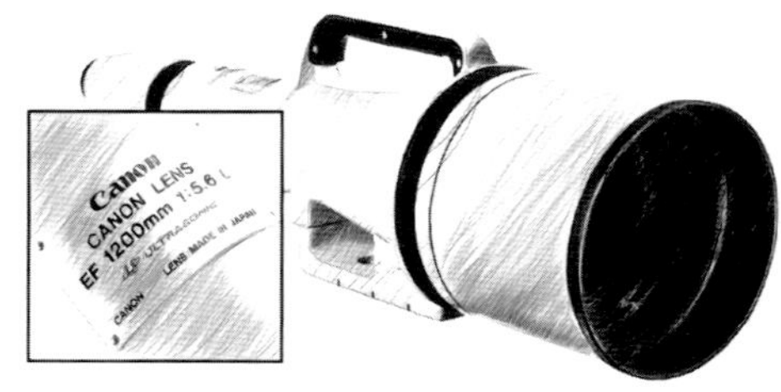

### TRIVIA

Only a dozen or so were made to special order, through 2005. A $10,000 deposit was required, and manufacturing would only start when several lenses were put on order, so delivery times averaged 18 months. Two of the lens elements are constructed from enormous fluorite crystals that, according to legend, took more than a year to grow. The lens weighs just over 36 pounds, is nearly three feet (0.9 metres) long, and the front opening is nine inches (23cm) across. Who bought them? *National Geographic* magazine and *Sports Illustrated* were known to own a couple. Otherwise, various spy agencies and a small number of well-heeled photo enthusiasts probably round out the pack.

In 2015, B&H Photo (New York) will offer one of these lenses, described as showing "little or no signs of wear" for a mere $180,000. In the fall of 2021, Wetzlar Camera Auctions (Wetzlar, Germany) will sell one for €500,000 (about $580,000), the highest price ever paid for a camera lens up to that point.

**1985:** Chinon begin manufacturing cameras for the Eastman Kodak Company. In 1995, Kodak will take a majority stake in the firm and, in 2004, will buy the rest. Between 1998 and 2002, five million units will be produced.

---

**UPDATE**

Curiously, Chinon build cameras only for export and never sell a single camera in Japan. Following Kodak's withdrawal from the camera market in 2004, Chinon now specialize in optical display film for electronic display devices.

---

**1985:** Kiron's 28~210mm $f$ 4-5.6 is the first large-ratio "super zoom" lens for 35mm still cameras, covering from reasonably wide-angle to telephoto, albeit with a small variable maximum aperture to keep size, weight, and cost within reason.

---

**TRIVIA**

Although the 10-to-1 ratio Angénieux 12~120mm $f$ 2.2 zoom had been introduced for 16mm movie cameras in 1961, and consumer Super-8 movie and Betamax/VHS video cameras had long had super-zooms, early 35mm SLR zoom focal length ratios rarely exceeded 3-to-1 because of 35mm film's larger negative and more demanding image standards.

---

**1985:** The Soviet Union's *"perestroika"* results in a drastic drop in military orders, and the Arsenal factory falls into a financial crisis still being felt today. In an effort to increase sales of consumer goods, the section making Salut-S cameras is expanded and starts producing what will become 37 different 35mm, subminiature, and medium-format cameras, copying designs from Nikon, Zeiss, Hasselblad, and even the East German powerhouse, Pentacon. They use the Salyut, Kiev, and Arax brands. Initially the lenses come from KMZ (Moscow) but, later, Arsenal will build their own lenses under the Jupiter and Industar brand, in Kyiv. Production of both lenses and will end around 2005.

---

**TRIVIA**

Jupiter lenses are essentially Sonnar designs, while the Industar line are Tessar derivatives. You can't quite call them copies because Soviets did serious work on those formulas to adapt them to the types of glass they had on hand at any given time. In many cases, their lenses were a match for the originals, in others, not. However, quality control remained, shall we be polite and say, "problematic."

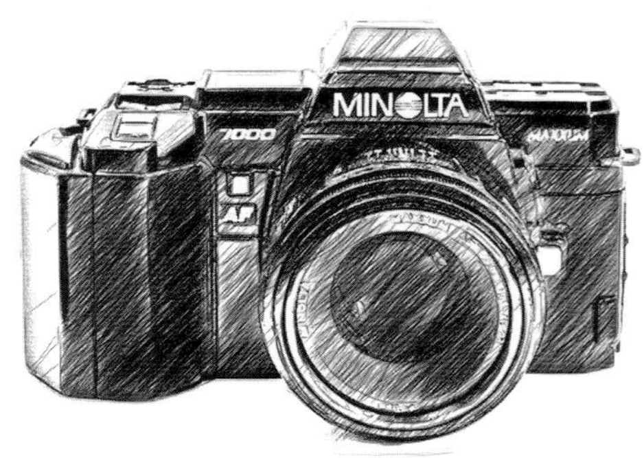

**1985:** Minolta market the Minolta 7000 (called the "Maxxum" in the U.S.). It is the world's first SLR with an integrated autofocus system, meaning both the AF sensors and the AF drive motor are housed in the camera body. It is also the first 35mm with automated film handling, as it loads the film, senses the film speed, advances the film, and then rewinds it, all under motor control. Power is supplied by four AAA batteries housed in the large grip. The Maxxum 7000 is also the first SLR to have the body made entirely of plastic.

---

### TRIVIA

Curiously, the Maxxum 7000 was considered "advanced" because it placed the focus motor in the camera body. Earlier efforts by Leica, Pentax, and others all used motors built into or attached to the lenses, making them bulky (for example, the Pentax ME-F of 1981). Ironically, the best modern AF cameras have the motors built into the lenses—but then these newer motors are much, much smaller.

The Maxxum 7000 has a light plastic body, but it doesn't feel cheap—its tough, almost unbreakable ABS gives it the advantage of reduced weight while avoiding any feel of flimsiness. But, almost 35 years on, that old ABS plastic (made from bromine) can turn yellow from UV exposure (something you're guaranteed to encounter in photography). The result is that Minolta's white often appears beige.

---

**1985:** A research team led by Akira Yoshino at Asahi Chemical, Japan, develops the first practical lithium-ion battery prototype, a more stable version of John Goodenough's lithium battery (see **1980**). Sony will be the first to commercialize this lithium-ion battery, in 1991, and it will go on to power the digital camera revolution.

---

### TRIVIA

Depending on the transition metal used in the lithium-ion battery, the cell can have a higher capacity but can be more reactive and susceptible to a phenomenon known as "thermal runaway." In the case of lithium-cobalt-oxide batteries for Sony laptop computers made in the 1990s, this led to many such batteries catching fire. In the 1990s, Goodenough will discover a stable lithium-ion cathode based on lithium, iron, and phosphate. This cathode is thermally stable but results in somewhat less capacity. Today such batteries are used in electric vehicles where safety is of paramount importance, while the original lithium-cobalt-oxide cells power most consumer devices.

**1986:** Fuji introduce their Utsurun-Desu ("It takes pictures") or QuickSnap line, employing 35mm film. The QuickSnap is the first "disposable" camera, although the name is quickly changed from "disposable" to "single use," both for environmental and marketing reasons. Kodak follow with their own single-use cameras two years later.

**1986:** At Photokina, Nikon show an operational prototype of the first SLR-type digital camera, manufactured for them by Panasonic. The Nikon SVC (Still Video Camera) was built around a two-thirds-inch charge-coupled device of 300,000 pixels. Storage media is a magnetic floppy inside the camera that can record 25 or 50 black-and-white images, depending on the image size (in pixels) of the photographs. The camera is never produced.

**1986:** Kodak engineers invent the world's first megapixel sensor. It has 1.4 megapixels and can produce a 5 x 7-inch photo-quality print.

**1986:** Having been caught out violating Polaroid's patents (see **1976**), Kodak end production of its instant cameras and matching films.

**1986:** The Aqua-Snappy by Canon is a fully automatic, compact, and lightweight 35mm underwater camera that can withstand depths down to 10 metres. It has an $f4.5$ fixed-focus lens and motorized film transport. If it is not the first low-cost underwater camera it is certainly the first successful one and gains a bit of a cult following.

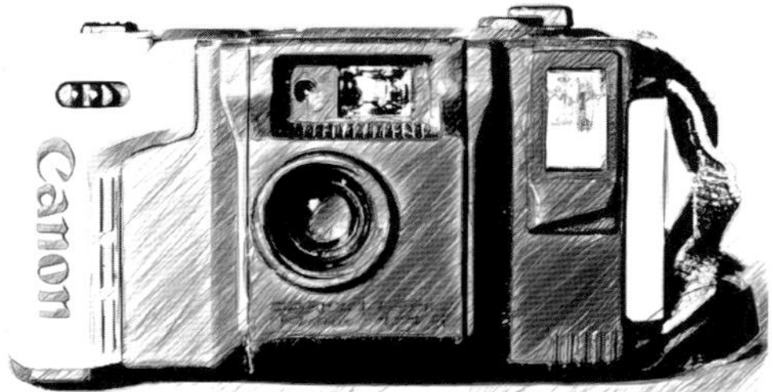

**1987:** Arsenal starts production of the Kiev 90, an ambitious electronic version of the Kiev 88. Unfortunately, the Kiev 90 is just beyond the capabilities of the factory and the vast majority of these cameras do not work properly. Production stops in 1990.

**1987:** The Pentax SF-1 (called the SFX in Japan) is the first interchangeable-lens SLR with built-in electronic flash and the first built-in flash with TTL auto-exposure in any camera.

---

### TRIVIA

Built-in electronic flashes first appeared on the non-SLR Voigtländer Vitrona (see **1964**) and had been common on point-and-shoot cameras since the mid-1970s. Built-in TTL auto-flash became standard on all but the most expensive 35mm SLRs cameras by the early 1990s.

---

**1987:** Konishiroku Photo Industry changes its name to Konica, in honour of their very successful line of cameras. They simultaneously introduce the world's fastest colour print film, SRG 3200.

---

**TRIVIA**

The "S" in "SRG 3200" is a homage to the Sakura brand used for Konishiroku's films since 1929. The Sakura name is dropped, and the Konica brand used after the introduction of SRG3200.

---

**1987:** Thomas Knoll (b. 1960), a PhD student at the University of Michigan, starts working on a program to show grey-scale images on a monochrome display. The program catches the attention of Thomas' brother, John (b. 1962), and the two work on the program, now called ImagePro, for six months. After the program was finished, Thomas works out a short-term deal with a scanner manufacturer to distribute copies of the program, now renamed "Photoshop," along with their scanners, and about 200 copies are shipped.

Later in the year, John Knoll demonstrates Photoshop to Apple and Adobe engineers. Eventually Adobe purchase the Photoshop license in 1988 and two years later, Photoshop 1.0 is released for Macintosh. The rest, as they say, is history.

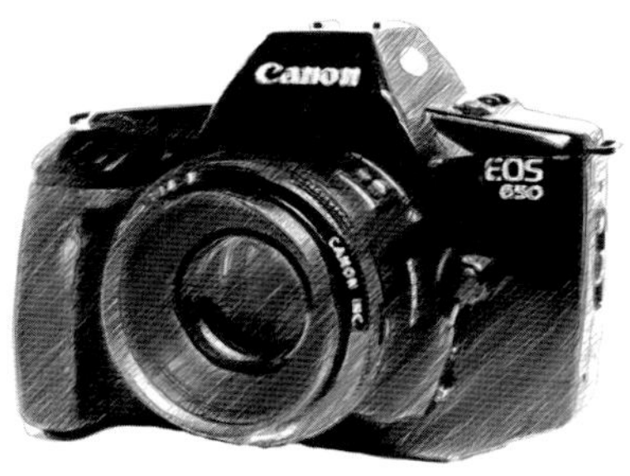

**1987:** Canon introduce two new cameras, the Canon EOS 650 and the EOS 620, the first cameras equipped with their new EF all-electronic-contact camera lens mount. The lens mount becomes, in essence, a computer data port. Mechanical camera-to-lens linkages can trigger automatic diaphragms, instant-return mirrors, and focal-plane shutters, but electronic autofocus requires additional electronic data exchange between a camera and its lens. With the EF, Canon decides to place everything under electronic control, even though it means that earlier Canon lenses will not be usable with the new bodies. It is a big gamble, but it succeeds.

**1987:** After three years of development, Canadian engineer Tom Abrahamsson (1943–2017) releases his Rapidwinder for Leica cameras. With just 10 parts, it is a simpler and more reliable version of the Leicavit trigger winder. Over time, models are made for both LTM and M-mount Leica film cameras. They allow a photographer to shoot at two to 2.5 frames per second—exceptional for a non-motorized camera. The Rapidwinder is produced until Abrahamsson's death, in 2017.

---

**UNOBTANIUM**

It is rumoured that some time in the early 2000s, one (and only one) Rapidwinder was made from "unobtanium." It is said that a worker at Boeing, Seattle, "liberated" a small block of a (then, and possibly still) top-secret alloy used to make the hinges for the cargo-bay doors on the Space Shuttles. The material made its way into Abrahamsson's hands and was made into a unique Rapidwinder. Your scribe has no idea if this is true, but it makes a great story!

---

**TRIVIA**

A few "Super-Deluxe Rapidwinders" were made with stainless steel drives and teflon bearings, for an even smoother advance. These took six times as long to manufacture and have never been listed for sale. A half-dozen were made, on special order, for *National Geographic* magazine. Another two dozen or so were made but never sold. Instead, Abrahamsson bartered them for prints by photographers whose work he admired.

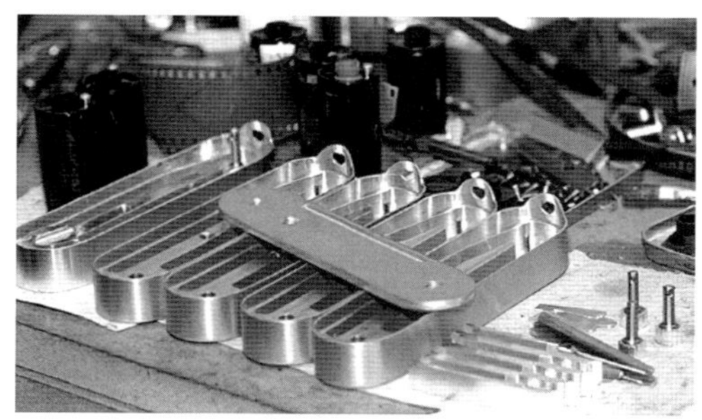

*Rapidwinders during manufacture, 2004*

---

**1988:** Hewlett-Packard's DeskJet is the first mass-market inkjet printer. It sells for $1,000, but by 1993 the price drops to $365. Colour versions, which will create a revolution in the home printing of digital photographs, will arrive in 1994.

**1988:** Kodak introduce T-Max 3200, the world's fastest black-and-white film. It can be rated at speeds up to ISO 50,000.

**1988:** At the Photokina trade fair in Germany, FujiFilm show a working model of their FUJIX DS-1P, the world's first true consumer-oriented digital camera. It is developed jointly with Toshiba and contains a 400 kilo-pixel CCD, saving the images to a removable Toshiba SRAM card. Card capacity is a mere five to 10 photographs and the camera is never marketed. Fuji will not enter the digital camera market for another 10 years, when, in 1998, they introduce their FujiFilm FinePix MX-700.

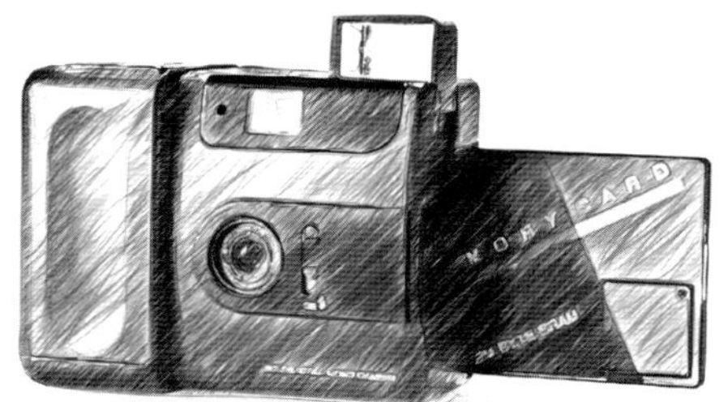

---

**TRIVIA**

Until the late 1970s, cameras made by FujiFilm were called "Fujica," a contraction of FUJI and CAmera (similar to Leica, Yashica, etc.). Later, film cameras were simply called "Fuji," whereas all of their digital cameras (other than the experimental FUJIX camera noted above) are branded as FujiFilm. Go figure.

---

**1988:** In August, Epson (Japan) show off their EVF liquid crystal module, the first commercially produced ultra-compact full-colour liquid crystal display module for video camera viewfinders. Prior to this, video camera viewfinders were all monochrome and used tiny cathode-ray tubes. This causes a revolution in video camera design and later models will go on, in the early 2000s, to make the mirrorless camera revolution possible.

**1988:** Nippon Kogaku K.K. change their name to Nikon Corporation.

**TRIVIA**

In the May 1988 issue of *Popular Photography*, Herbert Keppler offers what your scribe considers the best-ever photographic advice: "The older I get, the less inclined I am to overload my camera bag and then stagger out to take pictures. I try to pick and choose equipment thoughtfully, with a view to low bulkiness and light weight. The last type of case I think of using is a giant hold-everything bag."

**1988:** Leica's camera division moves its factory from Wetzlar to Oskar Barnackstrasse in Solms, a roughly 10-minute drive from Wetzlar, as one of the preparations for spinning off Leica Camera from the other Leitz divisions. The factory will remain in Solms until it moves into a new purpose-built factory at Leitz Park, in Wetzlar, April 2014.

**1989:** The JDMC/JCII testing program ends and its famous, gold "PASSED" sticker passes into history.

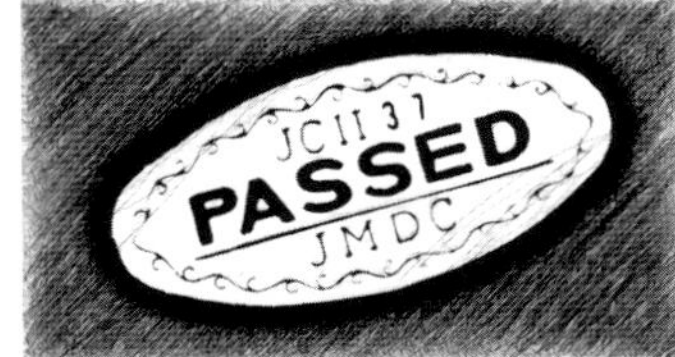


**ODDITIES**

Yashica's Samurai Z-L (1989) is the first (and perhaps only) SLR designed for left-handed operation. It takes 72 half-frame exposures with a horizontal orientation that runs the film vertically. It has a unique vertical body with a fixed auto-focus 25~75mm f 4-5.6 zoom lens, an inter-lens leaf shutter, programmed auto-exposure, built-in motor drive (claimed to reach 4.5 frames per second), and a built-in electronic flash. In essence, it is a mirror copy of their Samurai Z auto-everything point-and-shoot camera. Despite the addition of two lesser-featured models, in 1990, that year was also the end of the Samurai series.

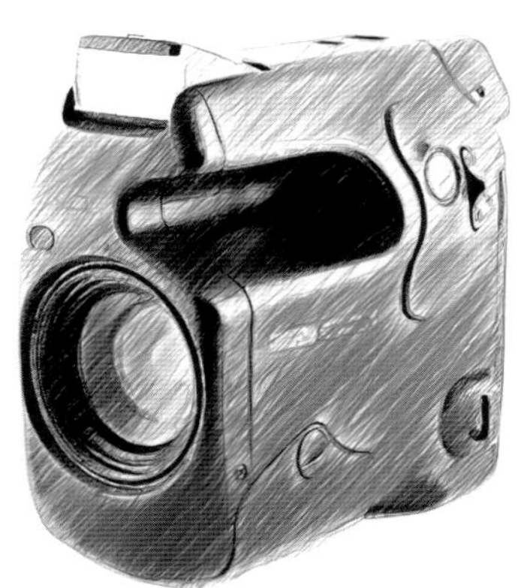

*Yashica ZL, one of the few cameras designed for left-handed people.*

**1989:** Steve Sasson, the inventor of the digital camera (see **1975**) and a colleague, Robert Hills, create and patent the first modern digital single-lens reflex (dSLR) camera that looks and functions like today's professional models. It has a 1.2-megapixel sensor and uses image compression and memory cards. But Kodak's marketing department tells Sasson that while they could sell it, they won't, because they fear it will eat away at film sales. Still, until the patent expires in 2007, it helps Kodak earn millions (if not billions) of dollars, since they, not Sasson and Hill, own the patent and make other digital camera manufacturers pay for the use of the technology.

### BUSINESS TRIVIA

Patents on inventions made by someone working on "company time" are normally assigned to the employer, as a condition of employment. Patents for inventions made entirely on that same employee's private time are hers alone.

**1989:** The U.K. investment firm Vitec buys Italy's Manfrotto, a top-line tripod maker.

### ODDITIES

In 1989, Konica released their "Kanpai," the world's first sound-activated camera. It would swivel on its built-in tripod (which wore tennis shoes!) to take a snapshot wherever it heard someone yell *"Kamlai!"* or other loud burst of sound. Sold only in Japan, it was interesting, but not a huge commercial success.

In 2021, Canon will promote their PowerShot "Pick" through crowdfunding. It is supposedly an AI-enabled camera that will swivel and follow you, taking photos on command or on its own. Will it be a crowd pleaser or another dead-end, like the Kampai? Well, in 2023, one reviewer will write: "If it truly was our 'own personal photographer,' we probably wouldn't hire it again."

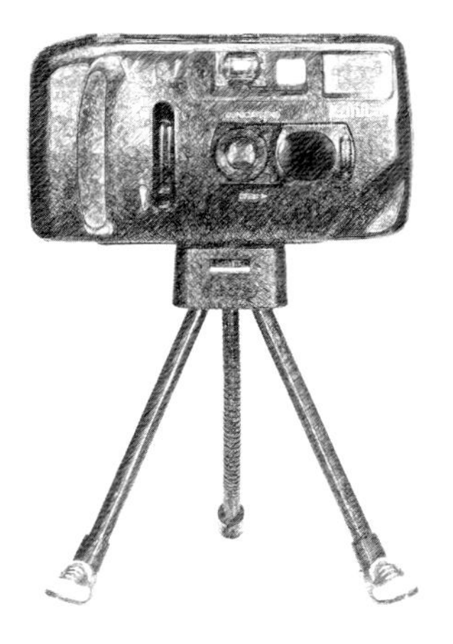

**1989:** *Modern Photography* magazine comes to the end of its road. Not long after Capital Cities-ABC sells the magazine to Diamandis Communications, Diamandis announces that it is shutting *Modern* down. After all, they already own *Popular Photography*, *Modern Photography*'s larger competitor, so the move has a certain business logic. *Pop Photo* will soldier on until 2017.

### TRIVIA

How did this happen? Few people know for sure, but the legend goes something like this: Herbert Keppler, who ran *Modern* during its heyday (1960s through the mid-80s) felt changes, not for the better, were coming, due to a switch of ownership. *Popular* was struggling and, in 1987, offered him the opportunity to come aboard and turn the publication around. Keppler accepted. Thus, *Modern* ended up losing of a lot of old hands, stumbled on a couple of years and was then sold again before it could go under. If you read *Pop Photo* in the 1990s, you'd be forgiven for thinking that *Modern* had survived and *Popular* had not.

**1990:** The Hughes Aircraft Company, California, buys Ernst Leitz Canada Ltd., and changes the name to Hughes Leitz Optical Technologies Ltd. In a $5.5m transfer, Hughes Aircraft moves both the equipment and technology of a sister operation in Des Plaines, Illinois, to Midland.

---

**UPDATE**

In 1997, the Raytheon company will acquire the Hughes Midland factory and the optical department of Texas Instruments, renaming them ELCAN Optical Technologies, and later will add the Raytheon name at the front. Though now primarily military and space contractors, both Hughes and Raytheon will continue to manufacture lenses and sub-assemblies for Leica, under contract, for many years. They also make rifle scopes, for the retail market, under the ELCAN name.

---

**1990:** The Swiss firm of Pignons SA, makers of the famed Alpa Reflex cameras, goes broke.

**1990:** After German reunification, VEB Pentacon is controlled by a German government board concerned with the privatization of East German corporations. It decides to close the firm as the company is grossly inefficient, employing 6,000 when it could have sufficed with 1,000, and selling its cameras at a loss. Production ceases on 30 June 1991.

---

**TRIVIA**

In 1990, investor Heinrich Manderman (1923–2002) purchased the Pentacon brands and several portions of its assets, including the former military production building in Dresden. The company was re-established as Pentacon GmbH, a member of the Jos. Schneider group, but production of cameras and lenses is now outsourced to South Korea. In Germany, the new Pentacon does precision moulding of plastics and makes metal parts for various industries, including the German camera industry.

---

**1990:** After German reunification, the East German firm of VEB Carl Zeiss (Jena) is purchased by the Carl Zeiss Foundation. The name is changed to Jenoptik Carl Zeiss Jena GmbH and, in 1992, to a simpler Jenoptik GmbH. In 1995, Jenoptik will be absorbed into Carl Zeiss AG (Oberkochen), leaving only that firm, its subsidiaries, and their overarching Foundation using the Carl Zeiss name.

**1990:** Fuji launches Velvia, a 17-layer slide film which is the first serious competition to Kodachrome and has the advantage of E-6 processing.

**1991:** While visiting Prague, a group of students from Vienna discover the Lomo LC-A and are inspired by its "unique, colourful, and sometimes blurry" images. The International Lomography Society is started the next year and Lomography is born!

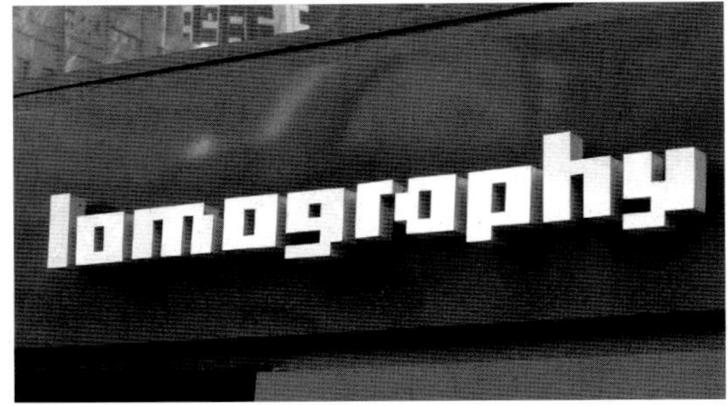


*The Lomography Store, San Francisco, in 2013.*

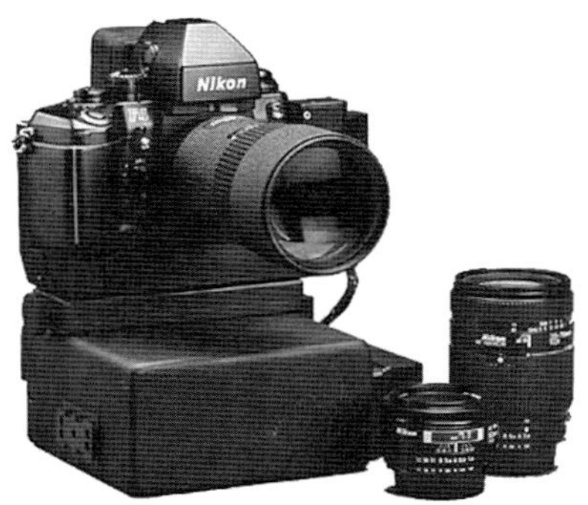

**1991:** Based on the Nikon F4, NASA's "Electronic Still Camera" is one of the first and the rarest of all digital SLRs. Nikon supplies NASA with 14 modified Nikon F4 bodies for prototyping use, but most of the electronics and housings for the digital camera are designed and built by NASA at the Johnson Space Center. The camera first sees service in September, on the Space Shuttle Discovery. In the end, only three such cameras are made.

---

### TRIVIA

NASA's "Electronic Still Camera" has a one-megapixel monochrome CCD image sensor (1024 x 1024 pixels) developed by Ford Aerospace and has a fixed sensitivity of 200 ISO (or 400 ISO if the infrared filter is removed). Removable IDE hard disks are used, each of which stores 40 digital images. Later upgrades include a four megapixel (2048 x 2048) CCD sensor, a colour CCD and various architecture changes. However, by 1995 the project is abandoned, and the cameras are replaced by the 6.3 megapixel Kodak DCS 460—at a cost of just $35,000 each. They are a bargain, compared with the cost of developing the "Electronic Still Camera" from scratch.

---

**1991:** After a 14-year legal battle, Kodak are finally ordered to pay Polaroid a total of $909 million ($925 million with interest) for patent infringement. They are also ordered to give 4.2 million U.S. customers between $50 and $70 in cash and coupons, for "bricking" their cameras.

---

### TRIVIA

In August of 2015, Apple will be awarded $1.05 billion in its patent fight with Samsung. But Polaroid's $925 million came in 1991, which means that when adjusted for inflation, Polaroid's outcome was far greater . . . it won today's equivalent of $1.56 billion!

---

**1991:** Kodak introduce their DCS-100, the first commercially available digital SLR. It has a 1.3 megapixel cropped CCD sensor in a modified Nikon F3HP body. Although it has the excellent optical viewfinder of the Nikon F3, the DCS100 does not have an LCD on the rear panel. Instead, it is tethered to a Digital Storage Unit (DSU) plus a hard drive, battery, and display, all of which are carried in a shoulder pack—all for the modest price of $20,000. Appearance is much like the NASA unit illustrated above.

**TRIVIA**

Kodak chose the Nikon F3HP SLR because it was the most widely used professional camera at the time. But, they had to solve many problems, including how to accurately position the sensor in the film plane and how to synchronize the mechanical shutter with the electronic sensor. Fortunately, the F3 had motor-drive contacts that could be utilized for electronic synchronization. A prototype system was tested by Associated Press photographers in 1987 and 1988, and there was sufficient enthusiasm that the unit was publicly shown at the 1990 Photokina and made available in 1991.

The Institute of Electrical and Electronics Engineers has called the DCS's Kodak KAF-1300 image sensor one of "25 Microchips That Shook the World" because the DCS series of cameras started the digital revolution in SLRs.

**1991:** Although their SLRs are largely based on Leica's "Correphot" technologies, parts of Minolta's auto-focus designs for point-and-shoot models are found to infringe Honeywell's patents. After protracted litigation, Minolta are ordered to pay Honeywell damages, penalties, trial costs, and other expenses in a final amount of $127,600,000. The firms settle out of court for an undisclosed amount in 1992.

**1992:** Kamera Werk (Dresden) release their Noblex series of panoramic cameras. The cameras are well made, with an aircraft aluminum frame and plastic body panels. Models are made for both 35mm and 120 film and, as in many panoramic cameras, the lens rotates during exposure to cover the wide format, with a slit at the back of the drum acting as a focal plane shutter as it travels across a curved film plane. The slit does not vary, so shutter speed is controlled by the rotational speed of the lens/slit drum. However, the Noblex has two major differences from other panoramic cameras. The first is that the lens/shutter drum is driven by an electric motor (powered by four AA cells) rather than a spring-driven mechanism. The second is that while most panoramic cameras have a lens that swings through little more than the angle required to cover the picture, the lens in the Noblex rotates through a full 360°—twice. The first rotation serves to accelerate the lens so that its speed is constant during the exposure, which is made during the second rotation. This results in a more even exposure across the frame.

**UPDATE**

It appears that Kamera Werk is still in business, making CCTV cameras for industrial control, but the Noblex Panorama cameras are gone. In 2015, the website of their Canadian distributor shows some "demo" cameras as being available but notes that new cameras are no longer available from the factory. As of 2022, Noblex repairs are still being offered by precisioncameraworks.com.

**1992:** An organization called the Joint Photographic Experts Group creates the now-universal JPEG (often abbreviated to JPG), a method of compressing files in digital form to make them smaller and thus easier to store and transmit.

**1992:** Leaf introduce the first digital back for medium and large-format cameras. It is nicknamed "The Brick" because of its shape and its two-pound (907 gram) weight. It features a 4 x 4cm, 4 megapixel black-and-white CCD. With no screen, it only works tethered to a computer, so it's restricted to studio work. It captures black-and-white images or works with a motorized filter wheel mounted in front of the lens to take separate exposures through red, green, and blue filters, which are then assembled into a single full-colour photo.

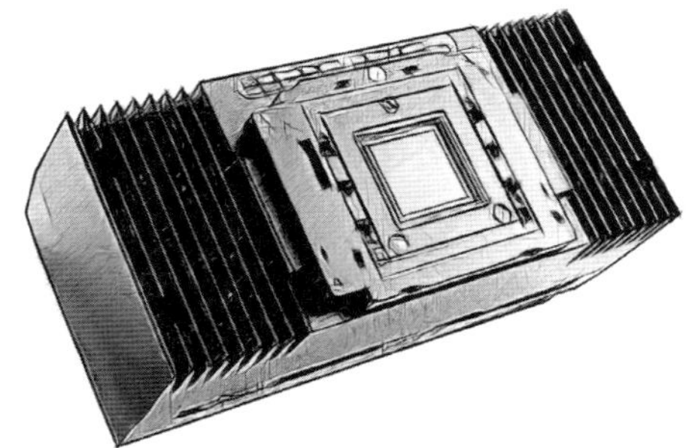

### TRIVIA

In 1992, this first digital back sells for $35,000. In 2017, a pair of these backs are offered, along with an adapter for a Fuji camera, for $125. For both!

**1992:** Italy's Manfrotto (well, its parent company, the U.K.'s Vitec Group) buy the French firm Gitzo, another top-line tripod maker.

### TRIVIA

Gitzo will continue to make tripods in Paris until Vitec shifts production to Italy. That process is started in 2001 but not completed until 2005. The transfer is done slowly to ensure continuity of both production and quality.

**1992:** Nikon's Nikonos RS is the first (and perhaps only) waterproof 35mm system SLR. Certified for a maximum depth of 100 metres, it features auto-focus, auto-exposure, TTL auto-flash, and a number of top-quality interchangeable lenses.

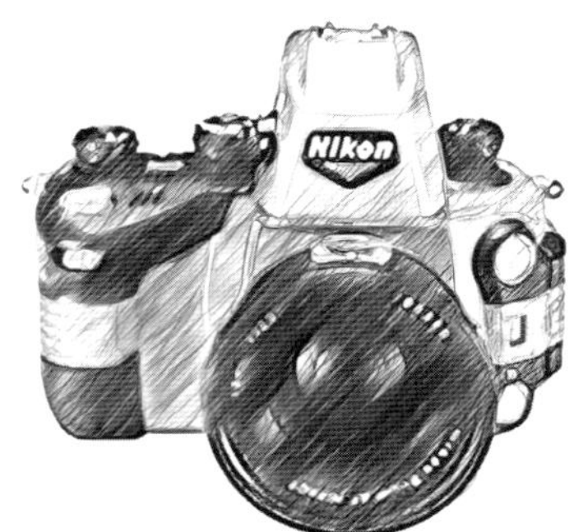

**1993:** The U.K.'s Vitec Brands, already the owner of tripod makers Gitzo and Manfrotto, buys Bogen, Manfrotto's American distributor and, in 2010, will drop the Bogen name entirely.

**1993:** Mere shadows of their former selves, Germany's two remaining makers of exposure-meters, Gossen and Metrawatt, merge. The new firm continues to make a variety of exposure meters under the Gossen name, as well as industrial light measurement systems (including, with partners, some in the medical field).

**1994:** Sandisk produce their Compact Flash (CF) card for digital cameras. This becomes the dominant memory card for digital cameras until the introduction of the smaller Secure Digital (SD) card, in 2000. However, it remains popular in top-of-the line cameras, which are often compatible with both CF and the newer XQD version (introduced in 2011).

**1994:** Angénieux (now owned by the Thales group) end the production of lenses for consumer still cameras but continue to this day producing lenses for the movie and video industry, as well as military and other specialized applications.

**1994:** Nikon introduce the Zoom-Touch 105VR. The "VR" is the first camera with Vibration Reduction, but the camera does not catch on, possibly because consumers do not see the need for the technology in a compact camera equipped only with a short telephoto.

**1994:** Nikon offer their Nikon E2, developed in collaboration with Fuji, which features a 2/3-inch CCD sensor with 1.3 million pixels. It is the first SLR-type digital camera to sell for under $20,000. Fuji's equivalent model is called the DS505.

---

### TRIVIA

In 1996, the E2 is improved slightly and becomes the Nikon E2n. In 1998, Nikon will present their Nikon E3 and Nikon E3s. All are developed in cooperation with Fuji and are priced lower than their predecessors.

---

**1994:** In a move that predates the camera-phone by almost a decade, the Olympus Deltis VC-1100 is a 442,368-pixel model and the first digital camera with the ability to transmit images over a phone line without the intermediary of a computer or other device.

**1994:** The computer company Apple releases what is believed to be the first "consumer" digital camera (that is to say, priced under $1,000) that can take colour photos. The QuickTake 100 sells for the remarkably low price of $750. Designed by Kodak and built in Japan by Chinon, it looks very similar to the Kodak DCS-50 (see **1996**). However, its internal memory fills up after just eight 640 x 480 pixel images, taken on a 0.3 megapixel sensor. Like all consumer digital cameras at the time, it lacks a preview screen, though it has a small black-and-white LCD screen that shows text, indicating the camera's settings. An RS-232C port is used to transfer photos (in QuickTake or PICT format) to a Mac computer.

---

### TRIVIA

A successor, the QuickTake 150, comes about 15 months later and is priced a bit lower, at $700. It looks identical to the QT-100 but offers twice the storage (16 photos!), comes with a macro conversion lens, and now supports Windows PCs. Not wanting to leave original QT 100 owners out in the cold, Apple releases a firmware update that allows the 100 to act like a QT 150, using better compression algorithms to increase the photo storage capabilities.

---

**1995:** Leica introduce their 70–180 *f* 2.8 Vario Apo-Elmarit zoom lens. Though expensive, it is the first zoom lens to match or outperform the finest fixed focal length lenses throughout its range. The zoom lens finally comes of age.

**1995:** Heinz Waaske, designer of the Wirgin Edixa and Rollei 35, dies.

**1995:** Canon unveil their EF 75–300 *f* 4-5.6 USM lens, the world's first commercially successful zoom lens with optical image stabilization. As with Nikon's later VR system, it works by feeding the signals from two shake-detection sensors (which are in fact tiny solid-state gyroscopes) to a microprocessor and then moving (de-centering) a lens element or group, using electro-magnets to alter the optical path and keep the image stationary on the film or sensor. Nikon will follow, but not until 2001.

### BACKSTORY

Centering the optical elements has always been critical to the performance of any lens, something that the better lens makers pay great attention to. So, intentionally decentering a lens element, as is done in optical image stabilization systems, seems not such a good idea. But the argument is that a photo that is slightly less "crisp" but without blur from camera movement is preferable. And they are right.

**1995:** Casio introduce their QV-10, the world's first consumer-grade digital camera to come with a rear LCD for previewing and reviewing images. The 250-kilopixel camera features a 1.8 inch (diagonal) rear screen and costs ¥65,000 or nearly $1,000 today.

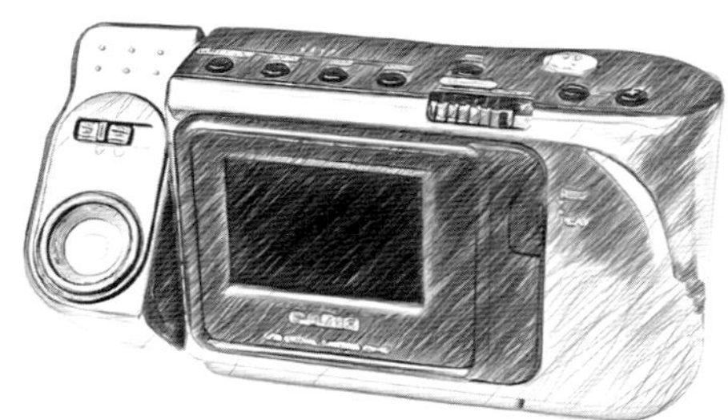

**1995:** The Ricoh RDC-1 gets the photo-video convergence going by being the first digital still camera to also record video, albeit only in five-second chunks. These are recorded at 30 frames per second and saved in the new MPEG format, and can be played back, in colour, on the camera's 2.5 inch (diagonal) rear screen or on a TV.

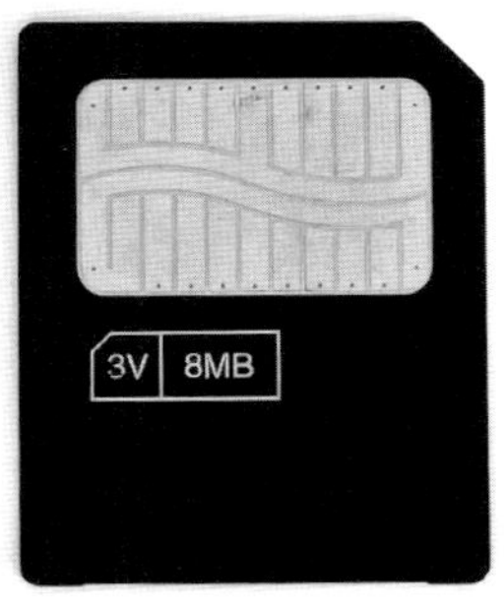


**1995:** Toshiba introduce their SmartMedia memory cards. Originally intended as a replacement for the floppy disk in computers, they are quickly picked up by both Olympus and FujiFilm for use in digital cameras. The cards are large, at 36 x 45mm, but ultra-thin and thus easily damaged. The format exhibits problems as camera resolutions increase, since SmartMedia cards were limited to 128MB. As another drawback, SmartMedia cards frequently become corrupt and unusable when the cards are read or written to in a card-reading device. These problems, combined with the introduction of the SD card in 2000, will spell the end of the SmartMedia card.

**1996:** Leica introduce their S1 studio camera. It is a scanning camera, producing 26mp images with 11 stops of dynamic range, on a 36 x 36mm sensor, while connected to a matching computer. It takes 185 seconds to produce one photo, but the quality exceeds anything available at the time. It is designed for Leica-R series lenses, but with adapters can accept lenses from many other makers. Just 160 cameras are produced, nearly all being sold to museums and research institutions.

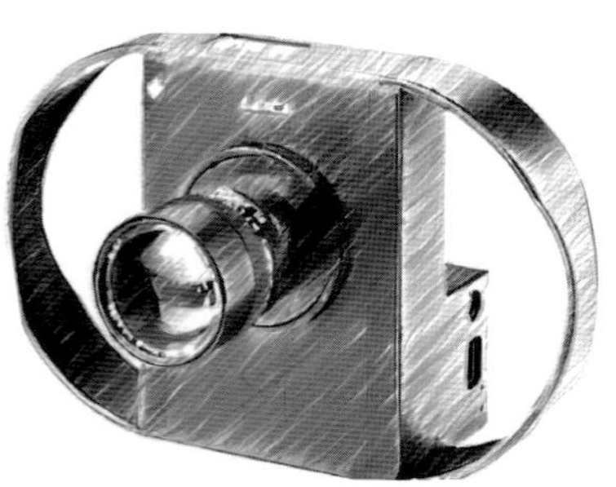

**1996:** The Kodak DC-120 features a 1280 x 960 pixel CCD with a fixed ISO of 120. An electronic shutter offers speeds from 16 seconds to 1/500 second, and there is a 38~114mm autofocus $f$2.5 zoom lens. More importantly, it is the first 1-megapixel camera to break the $1,000 price barrier, with a manufacturer's suggested retail price of just $799.

**1996:** The Ernst Leitz company changes its name to Leica Group, capitalizing on their famous brand.

**1996:** Kodak introduce their DC-50, which is quite advanced for a budget digital camera. It features a slide-out flash, a 3x zoom lens with an optical zooming viewfinder, and a 0.38 megapixel CCD colour sensor. The picture format is 756 by 508 resolution, which is rather unusual, as most cameras of the day take pictures at a maximum of

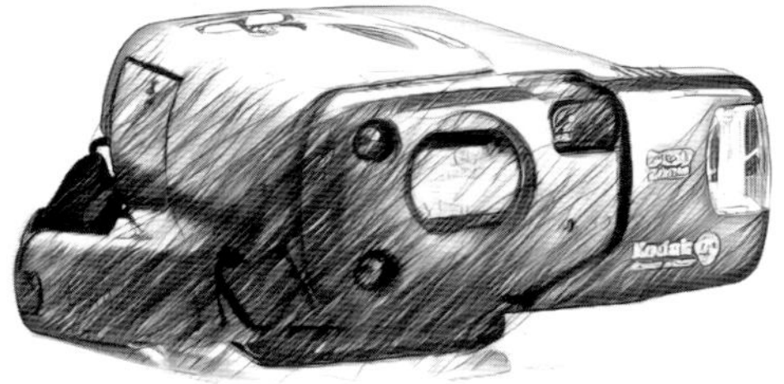

640 x 480. It has no preview screen but uses a Compact Flash card for memory (SD cards will not be marketed for another year). It is powered by four AA batteries.

---

### TRIVIA

The use of a Compact Flash card is remarkable, for at the time most consumer cameras use only internal memory, which limits the number of shots you can take. Unsurprisingly, 18 years on, your scribe's DC-50 (above) still turns on when given fresh batteries but will no longer zoom or take photos.

---

**1996:** After six years of negotiating, a new firm, Capaul & Weber, buys the Alpa name from Pignons' receivers and sets about marketing Alpa as a top-quality modular medium-format camera. In 2022, Ursula Capaul and Thomas Weber sell their business and Alpa remain in operational today.

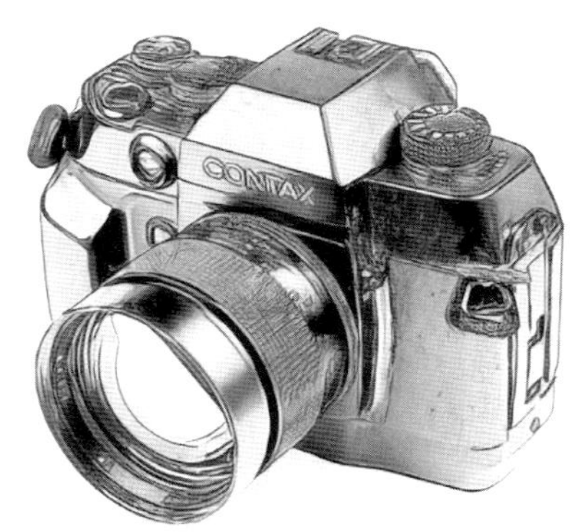

### ODDITIES

In 1996, Carl Zeiss introduce the Yashica/Kyocera-made Contax AX. Zeiss engineers create a unique auto-focus camera, which will work with older manual focus lenses. It moves the film track, mirror box, focusing screen, and primary viewing optics (including the pentaprism) on a track. Auto-focus is achieved by a backwards shunt of up to 10mm from the infinity position. This makes the entire body noticeably thicker and requires a strong motor in the base. The Contax AX is well-made with impressive specifications, including a titanium top cover, die-cast main unit, shutter speeds to 1/6000, full automation, auto-bracketing, a five-frames-per-second motor wind, and 1/200 flash synchronization. The AX proves to be a robust, reliable camera, but the AF is very slow and battery drain is high. It is made until 2005, but the Contax AX is not a success and the focusing system is never seen again.

**1996:** Minolta's Vectis S-1 becomes the first APS (Advanced Photo System) SLR. It features a flat-topped Porro-prism-style viewfinder in a compact design with good lenses and a large accessory system, but never proves popular.

**1996:** A new firm, Leica Camera AG, is spun off from the Leica Group of companies and becomes fully independent in 1998. This is done because the cameras division is slowly losing market share (and money), while the other divisions are doing well. Management wishes to prevent the others going down with the camera division. Thus, the strongest member of the group, Leica Microsystems, owns the Leica name so that should Leica Camera fail, the brand name will not be lost. The Leica name is licensed to the other two firms.

### BUSINESS TRIVIA

Ownership of the Leitz/Leica company is convoluted, but in 2004, Andreas Kaufmann's holding company, ACM, started buying up Leica's suppliers, as well as stock in Leica. By the end of 2006, Kaufmann owned 97% of Leica, having invested some $85 million. Over time, Kaufmann slowly acquired the remaining shares and took the company private in 2012.

**1997:** Film camera production reaches its all-time peak of 36.7 million units. However, as consumers rush to purchase digital cameras, film camera production declines. By 2008, it will be so low that industry associations will no longer bother to compile film camera statistics!

**1997:** Foveon Inc. is started in Santa Clara, California. The Foveon sensor is the first commercial image sensor that does not require colour filters to create a colour image. Instead, it has three transparent layers of pixels, each one sensitive to blue, green, and red respectively, which are analogous to the layers of chemical emulsion used in colour film. Foveon sensors will be used in cameras sold under the Sigma, Polaroid, and Toshiba brands. Sigma is the biggest and best-known user and, in 2008, will buy Foveon Inc.

**TRIVIA**

The Foveon name (originally called Foveonics) is derived from the fovea of the human eye, which enables sharp imaging while reading or watching television.

**1997:** Although the Mavica debuted as an analog camera (see **1982**), Sony go fully digital with the FD5 and its 10x zoom-equipped twin, the FD7. The two quickly garner nearly 40% of the still-small digital consumer camera market and get millions of people into the habit of popping the digital memory out of their cameras and into their computers. Of course, in the case of the Mavica, that memory is still a floppy disk.

**1997:** The Toyo Company of Japan, a maker of large-format field and studio cameras, announces an auto-focus 4 x 5 film Graflex camera, but there is no record of it ever being produced.

**TRIVIA**

Cameras for Kodak's APS film are introduced by Kodak, Canon, Fuji, Minolta, and Nikon, as part of Kodak's last attempt (of many) at drop-in film loading. APS was moderately popular but faded quickly and the system was almost dead by 2002, partly because its smaller negative yielded poorer results than 35mm film, but also due to the advent of the digital revolution.

**1998:** After stints of ownership by various firms since 1982, the Rollei management buys out the company, and production is again started in Germany.

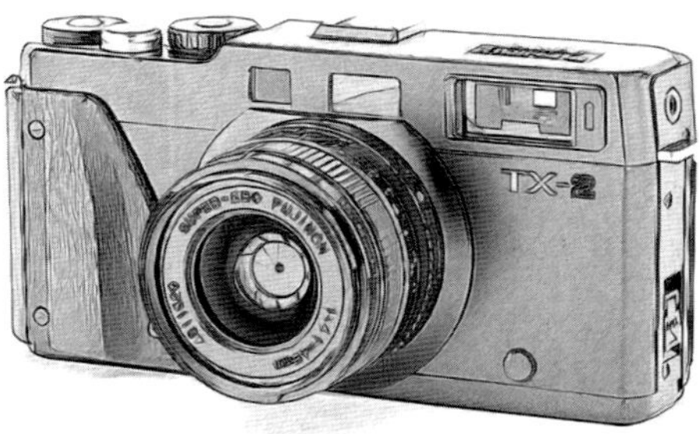


**1998:** First shown at Photokina and available early in 1999, the Fuji TX-2 is sold in Europe and America as the Hasselblad X-Pan. It is a dual-format camera that can be changed at will from 24 x 36mm normal size to 24 x 65mm in panoramic mode. In panoramic mode you get 21 shots from a 36 exposure roll or 13 shots from a 24 exposure film. Three lenses are produced: an $f$5.6 30mm and $f$4 lenses in 45 and 90mm. It is replaced by the X-Pan II in 2004, which is produced until 2006.

**1998:** The first consumer cameras with full, one megapixel sensors are introduced by various makers. Less than a year later, they are producing cameras with up to 2.3 megapixels.

---

### ODDITIES

Shin Yasuhara had been a camera engineer in Kyocera but dreamed of building his own cameras. In 1998, he introduced his T-981 rangefinder camera. His claim was to be "the world's smallest camera maker," producing cameras with a "classic, 1950s feel." Production was around 100 per month, but they inspired a revival of manual rangefinder cameras by bigger companies like Konica, Nikon, and Voigtländer.

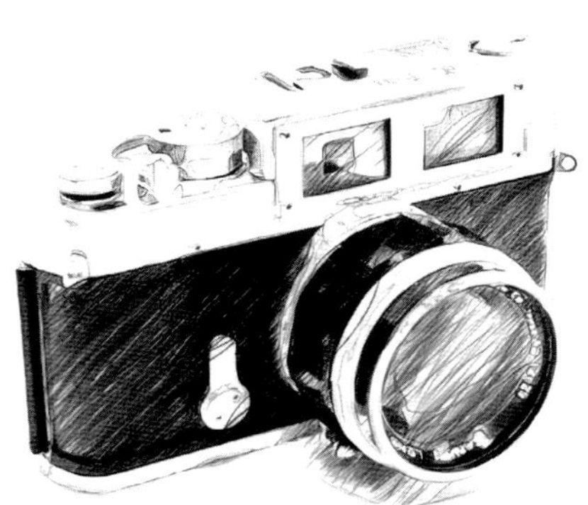

Unfortunately, the Chinese-made cameras had several problems, including shutter light leaks. The finish, while adequate, was not up to modern standards and the company went out of business in 2004. However, the Yasuhara Co. was re-started in 2011, and presently make a series of unusual niche lenses for modern mirrorless cameras. In 2019, they introduced their Anthy series of manual focus lenses for mirrorless dSLRs, and in 2020 brought out a 5x macro lens with built-in LED ring lighting. They are well priced and well reviewed.

---

**1998:** In partnership with Germany's Ringfoto, Cosina (see **1959**) reintroduce the venerable Voigtländer name to the photographic marketplace with a new line of Voigtländer cameras and lenses manufactured in Japan.

They start with their "Snap-Shot Skopar" 25mm $f$4 lens in Leica thread mount. The first lens to bear the Voigtländer name in 16 years, it is followed by a series of high-quality lenses and cameras that spark a modern revival in rangefinder cameras.

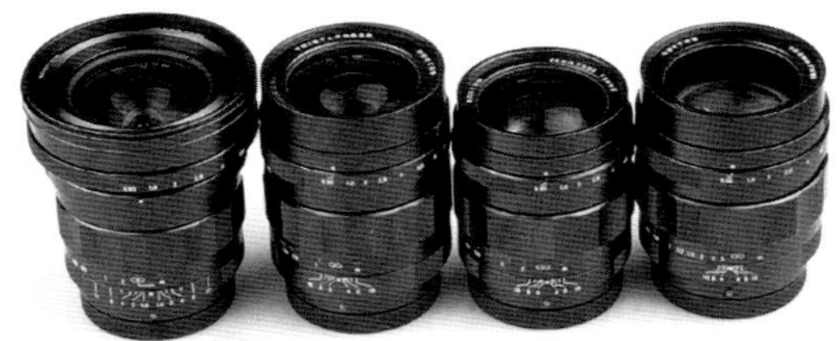

*Voigtländer f0.95 lenses. Image courtesy: CameraQuest.com*

**1998:** After the merger of East and West Germany, the Orwo film company is privatised in 1990. After two bankruptcies, it fails. A new company, FilmoTec GmbH, is formed, which continues to manufacture a reduced range of Orwo black-and-white films to this day.

---

### TRIVIA

Orwo films prove so good that they are selected for archival reproductions by the U.S. Library of Congress, the Smithsonian Institution, and the Museum of Modern Art (MOMA).

**1998:** Following the death of founder Zenzaburo Yoshino, Zenza Bronica Ltd. is acquired by the lens manufacturer Tamron, who continue to make Bronica cameras until 2005.

**1998:** Silicon Film's electronic film system (EFS-1) promises a cassette that will enable photographers to take digital photos with their film cameras. This is done by using a film cartridge that has a digital sensor in a "tongue" that slides into the film gate, with the electronics built into the "film" canister. There is certainly plenty of appeal (and demand!) for such a system, but in an era where even the most affordable digital SLRs cost upwards of $3,000, Silicon Film's promise seems too good to be true. It is. The product is never released and becomes increasingly obsolete due to improvements in digital camera technology and affordability. Silicon Film will be bankrupt by 2001.

---

**TRIVIA**

In 2017, the RE-35 project will promise the same dream, with a website pledging pics and specs as "coming soon." But by 2018, a disclaimer is added to the site: "Some things are too good to be true! RE-35 does not really exist. We (the design company Rogge & Pott) created RE-35 as an exercise in identity-design. We invented the "product" because it was something that we had wished for a long time (as many others). We launched the website and sent out "press releases" on April first . . . thinking that the date would make clear, that RE-35 is just wishful thinking . . . a classic April Fools Prank!"

---

**1998:** Fuji release their Instax instant film, along with the matching cameras in the U.S. market. Unlike Kodak, the Fuji films are introduced with Polaroid's blessings and will become Fuji's biggest selling product line.

The Instax films and cameras are based upon the improvements Kodak made to Polaroid's SX-70 instant film system for the instant film cameras Kodak sold in the 1970s and 1980s, namely the ability to expose the film through the rear of the photograph, and the reversal of the order of the dye layers so that development in the blue layer is visible first. As a result of these changes the photograph does not need to be taken using a reflex mirror in order to reverse the image (as all Polaroid SX-70 style cameras do), and colour balance and tonal range are improved over Polaroid flat-pack instant films.

**1998:** The business divisions of the Leica Group become three independent companies; Leica Camera, Leica Microsystems, and Leica Geosystems (see **1996**).

**1999:** Nikon introduce their D1, a 2.74-megapixel camera, the first SLR by a major manufacturer designed exclusively for digital. It is relatively cheap, at just $6,000 (about $10,450 in 2014 dollars).

**1999:** Kyocera release their VP-210, the first mobile telephone with a 110,000-pixel camera built in. Released only in Japan, the camera faces the user, so that video calls can be placed, rather than on the back for general photography. Capable of both still and video capture, it starts the trend of replacing small point-and-shoot cameras with telephones, a revolution that has not yet seen its end.

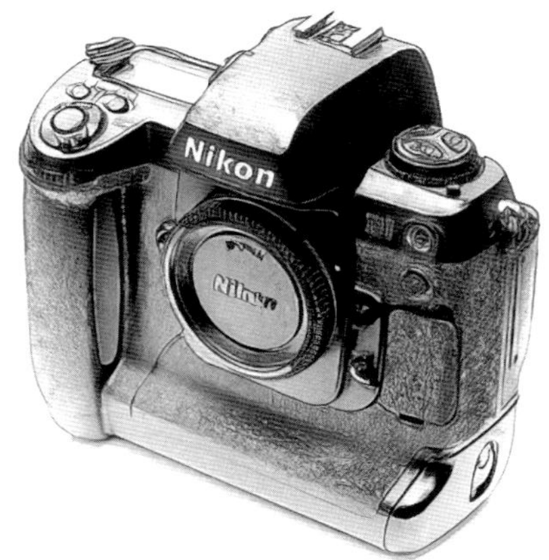

# 2000 to Now

*The pace of camera development has vastly increased compared to the 20th century. Film cameras typically had a model life (the time until a replacement model was introduced) of four to five years (or even more than 12 years, in some instances). Digital cameras have a product cycle of six to 12 months at the low-price end, and 18 to 36 months as we move towards the top professional models.*

*This discrepancy between low-end cameras and high-end ones is because professionals invest many thousands in equipment and simply will not purchase new cameras more frequently. If manufacturers make their cameras "obsolete" too quickly, they risk losing their customers.*

*But improvements in digital performance continue at a staggering pace. The first consumer-oriented one-megapixel cameras became available in 1998. By later that same year, the pixel count was up to 2.3 megapixels. Now, just 23 years later, ultra-resolution cameras are available, cameras with an astonishing 150 megapixels are being introduced, and 30 to 50 megapixel models are readily available, if not yet commonplace.*

*It was said, in years gone by, that one of the sharpest of films, Kodachrome 25, was the informational equivalent to a 24-megapixel sensor. For a long time, that number of pixels on a sensor was the holy grail. Today, many cameras exceed the resolution of most films.*

*Some will say that film has a better "look," but that is akin to vinyl record fans who insist that vinyl records and tube amplifiers "sound better." It may be true, but it's hard to prove.*

*Still, much development goes into new sensors, new filters, and ever-improving software. As the number of pixels increases, the likelihood of moiré patterns appearing in images goes down. Thus, makers have been removing the low pass (AA) filters, bringing digital imaging nearer to or even surpassing film in virtually all aspects.*

*That being said, it seems there is a huge revival of film. Just as there has been a recent revival of turntables and vinyl records, boutique firms like ADOX (Germany), Bergger (France), Ferrania (Italy), Forma (Czechia), Ilford (England), and Indus (India) are making high quality black-and-white films in small batches. Even Kodak are reintroducing Ektachrome colour transparency film and may bring back Kodachrome!*

*In a way, these small film-making firms are like the small vacuum tube makers who (back in the 1960s and 1970s) bought up entire factories of machinery from the likes of RCA, GE, and Philips and installed them in Belarus, Cambodia, Vietnam, and other low-labour-cost countries. There, they continue manufacturing tubes in small batches. Thus, even though they became obsolete some 60 years ago, you can still buy almost any tube ever made. Film looks as if it is going to be the same. Hard, but not impossible, to find—if you're interested in shooting with it.*

**2000:** Agfa files patents for an advanced film technology which may produce photographic film up to 10 times more sensitive to light. Published in the journal *Nature*, researchers say they have captured every particle of available light on film by employing a chemical called formate. This means true-to-life photographs of even dimly lit subjects can be captured without using a flash or any artificial lighting. Agfa says that more research is needed in colour reproduction.

**2000:** The *Chicago Tribune* reports that scientists at Eastman Kodak are researching other chemicals that would allow nearly all freed electrons to combine with silver crystals, stating they think it will be too difficult to produce commercial film using formate. Agfa does not say if, or when, they will manufacture formate-enhanced films. Neither of these new Agfa or Kodak films are ever produced.

**2000:** SD cards, a joint effort between SanDisk, Panasonic, and Toshiba, go on sale. The SD (Secure Digital) cards will become the dominant format for digital storage in cameras. The original cards hold up to 2 gigabytes (GB) of data, but later versions such as the SDHC (2006) can hold up to 32GB, and the SDXC (2009) cards can hold up to 2 Terrabytes (TB).

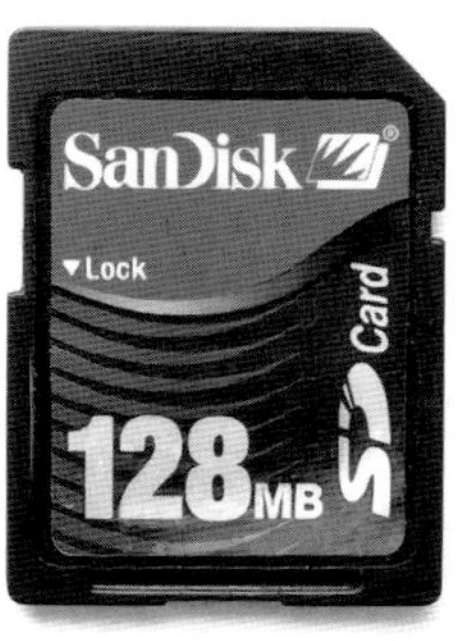

---

**TRIVIA**

For a while, the SD card is king in consumer cameras, while Compact Flash (CF) cards hold sway in the professional end, due to their wider data path, which gives them faster transfer (write) speeds. But as SD cards improve in both capacity and speed, they become ubiquitous, and CF cards fade away.

The "×" rating that you see on the packaging is a multiple of the standard CD-ROM drive speed of 150 kilobits per second. Basic cards transfer data at up to six times (6x) the CD-ROM speed, whereas some of the latest ones can be 1,000 times the base rate, or even faster. The "times" rating is still seen, but has been officially replaced by classes 2, 4, 6, and 10 (meaning minimum write speeds of 2, 4, 6, and 10 MBs). The higher the class, the faster the card. A newer standard, UHS (I, II, and III), denotes still faster operation (30MB/s or more for U3), rather than more capacity.

Manufacturers nearly always advertise their best-case (the famous "up-to") read speed, which is typically much faster than the card's write speed. However, it is the write speed (how fast the camera can move your photos from the buffer to the card) that counts in photography. So be sure to read the specifications very carefully before you buy. If only one speed is listed, always assume it is the read speed. The write speed will always be slower. The packaging usually won't lie, but it can be very misleading.

---

**2000:** Canon's EOS D30 is the first digital camera to use an 8.2 megapixel complementary metal-oxide semiconductor (CMOS) sensor rather than the more power-hungry CCD sensors. It is also the first relatively affordable digital SLR intended for the advanced amateur. Using the cheaper (but lower quality) CMOS sensor allows a (body only) price of just $3,499, about half the price of CCD-based professional-level cameras.

**2000:** Despite selling some four million slide projectors over the years, the Braun Camera-Werke in Nuremberg, Germany, ceases operations.

**2000:** The Olympus Camedia E-10 (shown at right) is the first digital SLR to offer a live LCD view. It replaces the standard SLR mirror with a beam-splitter that channels incoming light to both the optical viewfinder and the sensor. This design allows the image feed from the CCD to be displayed live on a rear-panel LCD.

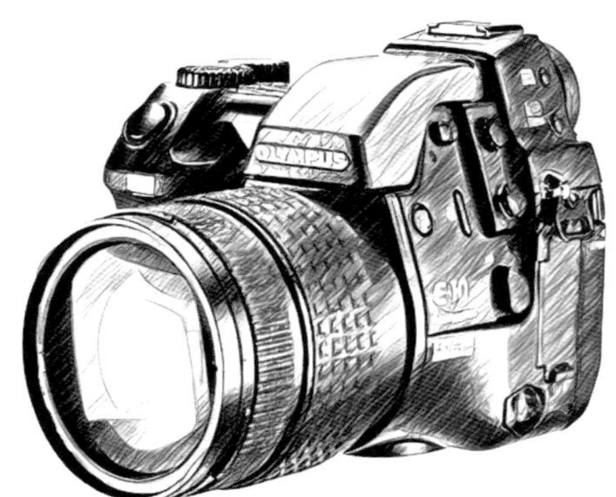

**2000:** Olympus offer their Camedia C-211Z, a 2.1 megapixel camera with a 3x optical zoom lens. It can print the photos it takes directly on to Polaroid 500 instant film. The price is price $799, with the film coming in at an additional $9.99 for 10 shots.

---

**TRIVIA**

The Olympus C211Z is billed as "North America's first printing camera." They word it that way because FujiFilm produced the first digital printing camera (the PR-21) a year earlier but didn't release it in the U.S. market. If you can find a C-221Z camera today, you will not be able to print anything as the Polaroid 500 series film it used is no longer made . . . by anyone.

---

**2001:** The Braun Camera-Werke is reorganized to sell camera accessories from Asia, as well as projectors and scanners of its own manufacture, for business use. In 2004, it will change its name again, to Braun Photo Technik GmbH, which remains in business to this day.

**2001:** The FujiFilm Finepix S1 Pro is based on the Nikon N60 and is the first interchangeable lens dSLR to break the $3,500 barrier, making it accessible to serious amateur photographers. Later in the year, it is joined by the Canon EOS D30 (not to be confused with the 30D), and the "prosumer" dSLR market is born.

**2001:** FujiFilm introduce Reala 500D motion picture colour negative film; it has the world's highest sensitivity among daylight-type films.

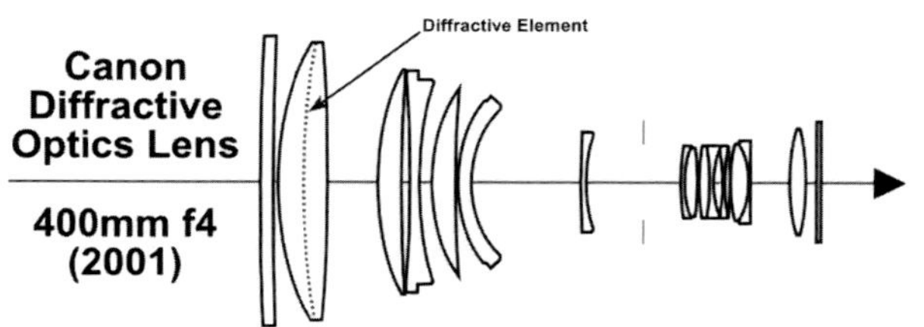


**2001:** Canon's EF 400mm $f$4 DO IS USM is the first diffractive-optics lens for consumer cameras. Normally, photographic cameras use refractive lenses (with the occasional reflective mirror) as their image-forming optical system. Diffractive optics employ a Fresnel lens, taking advantage of its opposite colour dispersion to correct chromatic and spherical aberrations with less low-dispersion glass and fewer aspheric surfaces, resulting in smaller, more compact lenses with (supposedly) lower costs. To date, only a small handful of such lenses have been offered and the technology seems dead, amid user complaints that while size and weight are reduced, optical performance has not been up to expectations.

---

**UPDATE**

In 2015, Nikon will introduce a 300mm $f$4 "Phased Fresnel" lens . . . essentially the same technology with a different name. They also patent 400, 500, and 600mm variants, all at $f$5.6. In 2020, Canon will introduce two new but very slow ($f$11), collapsible, DO lenses at 600 and 800mm. Will any of these lenses be photographic powerhouses and/or financial successes? The jury is still out.

---

**2001:** A management group led by Thorsten Kortemeier (b. 1967) buys 51% of Minox from its long-time owner, Leica. They will later purchase the remaining 49%, and make Minox fully independent of Leica, in 2005. Minox no longer build cameras but remain successfully in business making binoculars and other optical products in Wetzlar, Germany.

**2001:** Poorly financed and suffering from a string of new but unsuccessful products, Polaroid is unprepared for the digital revolution and declares bankruptcy.

**2002:** *"Mama Don't Take my Kodachrome away . . ." (Paul Simon).* Introduced in 1961 as Kodachrome II, Kodak discontinue Kodachrome 25 in March of the year. Kodachrome 200 is discontinued a short time later.

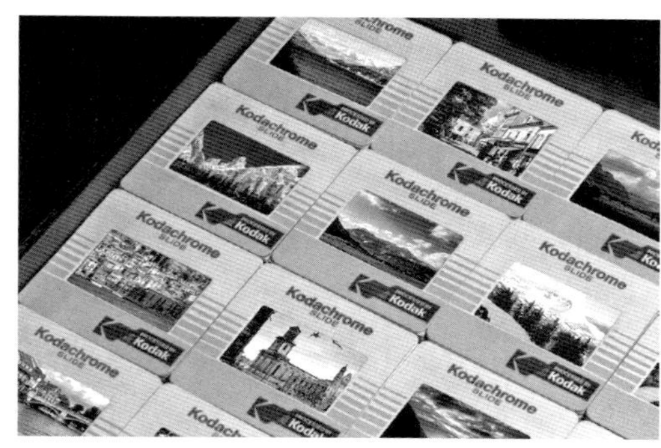

**2002:** Sigma launch their SD-9, the first dSLR to use the Foveon X-3 sensor.

### TRIVIA

Sigma's Foveon sensor becomes famous for having incredibly good low-ISO performance, but also has many shortcomings, such as unfortunate mid-ISO and hideous high-ISO performance. Over time, the Foveon sensor will improve but, while it will remain a cult classic among some photographers, it fails to be a force in the photographic market.

**2002:** Contax launch what will be their final camera, the 6 MP "N" Digital. It is the first full frame dSLR (meaning the sensor is the same size as a frame of 35mm film) to be unveiled. While capable of capturing high-quality images, it suffers performance flaws that cause it to be outshone, and outlasted, by two other full-frame dSLRs that are introduced later the same year: the Kodak DCS Pro 14n and Canon EOS-1Ds.

**2002:** Fuji and Olympus launch their short-lived XD-Picture card for digital cameras. (For more, see the "XD Card" entry in the Glossary.)

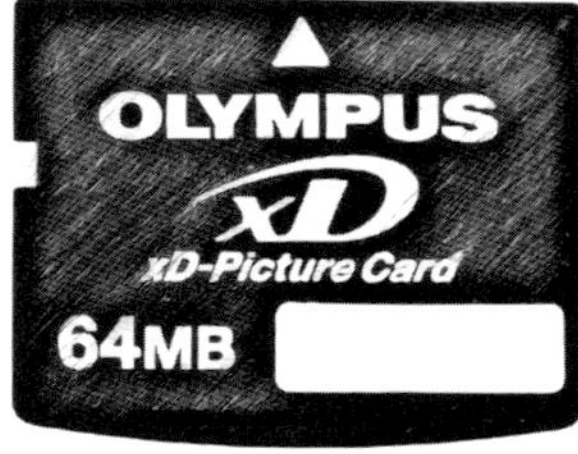

**2003:** The "FourThirds" sensor standard for dSLRs is introduced with the Olympus E-1. It is the first dSLR camera system designed from the start to be digital, and includes new lenses, also designed specifically for digital sensors. This contrasts with its contemporaries, which offer cameras based on re-used parts and lenses from previous 135 film systems. It is only moderately successful, but leads to the introduction, in 2008, of the *micro*-FourThirds (mFT) system, which will be wildly successful.

**2003:** Eight-megapixel consumer digital cameras are produced by numerous makers.

**2003:** Walter Zapp, inventor of the Minox subminiature camera, dies in Switzerland.

**2003:** Minolta introduce their 5 megapixel Dimage A1, a compact digital camera with a fixed 7x zoom lens. It is the first to use in-body image stabilization (IBIS) technology, which moves the sensor, rather than de-centering optical elements in the lens. It will be followed by the series of dSLRs in 2004, where the IBIS system will prove a ground-breaking technology.

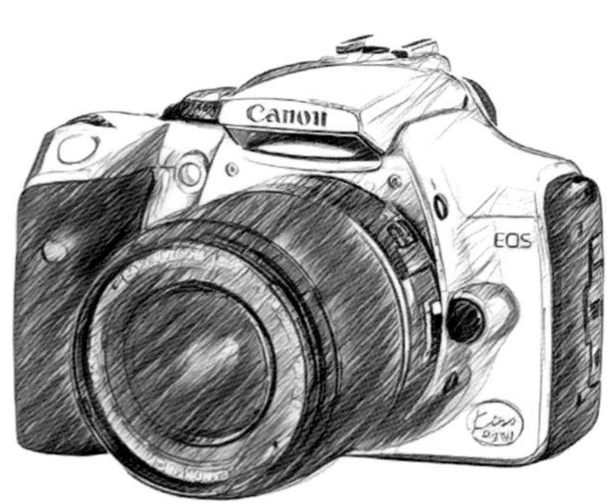

**2003:** In August, Canon introduce their 6.3 megapixel Digital Rebel (also known as the 300D in Europe and the Kiss Digital in Japan), the first consumer digital camera under $1,000 (original list price: $899 body only, or $999 with an 18-55mm f 3.5-5.6 Canon EF-S zoom lens).

---

### TRIVIA

Canon's Digital Rebel sold 1.2 million units around the world in just 16 months and was probably the biggest reason for digital SLR sales vaulting past film SLR sales worldwide in 2004.

---

**2004:** Epson introduce the R-D1, the first digital rangefinder camera ever made. Built by Cosina and based on Cosina's Voigtländer Bessa body, it has a 6.3 megapixel APS-C sensor, a body of magnesium alloy, and accepts Leica M (bayonet mount) lenses. A unique design choice is a shutter charge lever, which resembles a typical film rapid advance lever and is used to cock the shutter. A few follow-on models (RD-1s and RD-1x) are produced with the same sensor; after a few years, all are discontinued.

---

### TRIVIA

In a rare display of dedication to its customers, Epson will announce that they will finally end repairs and support for their RD-1 series in April of 2024, 20 full years after introduction!

---

**2004:** Minolta and Konica, two well-respected long-time camera makers, merge to form Konica-Minolta.

**2004:** Kodak discontinue production of slide projectors and all reloadable film cameras. Single-use film cameras continue.

**2004:** The Sigma 12-24mm $f$ 4.5-5.6 EX DG Aspherical HSM is the first zoom lens to reach a 122° field of view, wider than any SLR prime lens to date. They do it by taking advantage of aspherical elements and low dispersion glasses.

**2004:** Having purchased Hasselblad the year before, the Shriro Group acquires the Danish high-end scanner and digital-camera-back manufacturer Imacon, to respond to the trend away from film to digital and prepare for the H2 line of digital cameras, introduced in 2005.

---

### TRIVIA

Acquiring Imacon secures Hasselblad's market position, with nearly all their medium-format film-camera competitors having been sold (Mamiya and Pentax), or closing (Contax, Bronica, Exakta 66, Kiev). Despite this, Hasselblad struggles to turn a profit in the digital age and in 2011 will be purchased by the Swiss/German firm Ventizz. In late 2015, a Chinese aerial photography and drone maker, DJI, buys a minority interest and in 2017 takes full control of Hasselblad.

---

**2004:** The market for black-and-white photo papers, Ilford's main product, falls 26% in one year. Ilford Ltd. (founded in 1879) files for bankruptcy protection. Harman Technology, a group of Ilford managers, will buy the firm in 2005 and use the tradename "Ilford Photo."

---

### TRIVIA

The "Harman" in the Harman Technologies name comes not from any member of the group of managers, but from Alfred Hugh Harman, the original founder of Ilford, in 1879.

---

**2004:** The Belgian firm Agfa-Gevaert withdraws from the consumer market, including photographic film, cameras, and other photographic equipment. The consumer imaging division (AgfaPhoto) is sold through a management buyout, but the new firm, AgfaPhoto GmbH, files for bankruptcy after just one year.

---

### TRIVIA

Because Agfa-Gevaert still produced photographic films for the aerial photography market, it was still possible to buy fresh Agfa-produced photographic films for use in consumer cameras. The Lomography Society and Rollei purchased the aerial photography film from Agfa-Gevaert and then cut and packaged it into consumer photographic formats. As of 2012, such products carry a small Agfa logo discreetly on their packaging but are not sold as Agfa branded products. By contrast, AgfaPhoto-branded photographic films were made by Italy's Ferrania until that plant closed in 2009. Current Agfa-branded films are produced by FujiFilm in Japan.

---

**2004:** Fashion photographer Richard Avedon dies. An obituary, published in *The New York Times*, reads, "His fashion and portrait photographs helped define America's image of style, beauty and culture for the last half-century."

**2004:** Konica-Minolta introduce their Maxxum 5D and 7D cameras (sold as the "Dynax" outside the USA and the "a-7" in Japan), the first SLRs with sensor-shifting in-body image stabilization (IBIS), which they call "anti-shake." This has the advantage that the purchaser buys the system once, with the body, rather than re-buying the IS system with each lens. Pentax will follow suit in 2006 and Olympus in 2007. All three firms adopt the IBIS system, in part because they have the engineering know-how, but to a greater degree because they do not have any image-stabilized lenses and thus have no reason not to. However, the 5D and 7D are the first and only dSLRs to bear the Konica-Minolta name before K/M depart the camera business in 2006.

---

**TRIVIA**

The biggest reason why both Nikon and Canon use in-lens image stabilization rather than in-body stabilization is that in-camera stabilization was extremely difficult to incorporate into film cameras. It is one thing to re-position a sensor inside the camera body, quite another to try to re-position an entire roll of 35mm film. When Canon and Nikon started offering image stabilization, the vast majority of photographers were still using film. With such an investment in lens stabilization technology, they were reluctant to give it up, leaving in-body image stabilization (IBIS) to smaller and more agile players who did not have a huge investment in film products.

---

**2004:** In the Winter issue of the American quarterly *Photographer's Forum* (see **1978**), photographer Ted Grant (1929–2020) is described as "Canada's Greatest Living Photographer." It is a phrase he hates, but it fits.

---

**TRIVIA**

In 2015, Ted is awarded the Order of Canada "for his achievements as a premier photojournalist who captures Canadian culture and social history through his lens. He has contributed close to 300,000 photographs to Canada's national archives—the largest [individual] collection in Canadian history." In fact, the total is closer to 400,000 images.

---

**2004:** Memory cards remain expensive, so most photographers only own one. Small battery powered hard-drives with card readers and dedicated software, collectively known as Photo-Banks, start to appear to provide extra photo storage, on the go. Such units are still available today, though without the name. But, with memory cards a fraction of the price they were, most photographers simply use more cards, and that market becomes restricted to professionals and a few advance amateurs.

**2004:** Hit hard by the digital revolution, Tamron discontinue all of Bronica's SLR models in October of the year. The last Bronica model, the RF645 rangefinder camera, will be discontinued exactly one year later.

**2004:** Henri Cartier-Bresson dies.

**2005:** Canon introduce their EOS-5D, the first consumer-priced full frame (24 x 36mm, the same as 35mm film) digital SLR. It sells for just $3,000.

**2005:** The Arsenal Factory (maker of Kiev, Salyut, and Arax cameras and various Jupiter lenses) in Kyiv, Ukraine, reorganizes as a much smaller firm, making medical and banking equipment, gauges for the natural gas industry and LED-based traffic lights, as well as military optics (most of the military production is purchased by Russia). Camera production ceases but some say small-scale production of camera lenses continues until 2009. Their fate after the Russian invasion of 2022 remains unknown.

---

### BUSINESS TRIVIA

When the Soviet Union collapsed (1991), most state factories had their problems switching over to a competition-driven capitalist system. Camera maker KMZ was no exception. Suddenly, companies needed to make profits. The markets opened for foreign products and the ruble deflated rapidly. For KMZ's workers, it meant either seeking another job or be content with a lower wage. KMZ was not used to producing economically, while the market was flooded with better and cheaper cameras from Asia. Moreover, their product lineup was a hardly competitive line of Zenit-E descendants. The other state-owned optical houses faced similar challenges, and most did not survive. KMZ struggled until 2005 but could not keep up with the digital revolution and closed.

---

**2005:** Kyocera leave the camera business, stopping production of both Contax and Yashica cameras and lenses to concentrate on manufacturing camera modules for tablet computers and mobile telephones. This causes problems for both Leica and Zeiss, for whom Kyocera make lenses under contract.

**2005:** Polaroid, now owned by Petters Group, cease the manufacture of professional Polaroid cameras. They will stop making consumer cameras the next year.

**2005:** Rollei, under new owners since 2002, is split into two companies: "Rollei GmbH" in Berlin, which licenses the brand, and "Franke & Heidecke GmbH," to actually make products.

**2005:** Kodak discontinue production of black-and-white photographic printing paper, leaving Ilford Photo the largest player in the remaining black-and-white business.

**2005:** Gitzo's French manufacturing is discontinued as Gitzo completes the transfer of production from France to Italy, a process which had begun in 2001.

**2005:** Pentax partner with Samsung to share development costs on camera technology and recapture lost market share. Pentax and Samsung subsequently release new dSLR siblings. The

Pentax *istDS2 and *istDL2 also appear as the Samsung GX-1S and GX-1L, while the jointly developed (90% Pentax and 10% Samsung) Pentax K10D and K20D are also marketed as the Samsung GX-10 and GX-20 respectively. Some Pentax lenses are also re-branded as Samsung Schneider Kreuznach D-Xenon and D-Xenogon lenses for the Samsung dSLRs.

**2005:** Leica introduce their Digital-Modul-R, a 10.2 megapixel digital back for the Leica R8/R9 film-based SLRs. Designed by Leica, it is built by Imacon. The pair become the only cameras able to capture images digitally or by using 35mm film, which is done simply by changing the camera back. The DM-R is a unique unit, with "quirky" firmware, but is the first 35mm-size dSLR to do away with the low-pass (or AA) filter. Just 2,200 of these somewhat behind-the-times, expensive but superb image makers are produced. It will be discontinued after just two years.

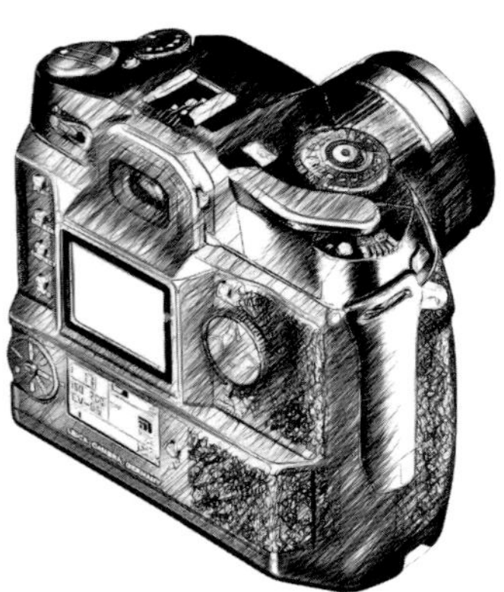

---

### RUMOUR

The following is not fully substantiated, but it seems that Leica contracted a Danish scanner maker, Imacon, to build its DM-R in late 2003, as Leica was suffering financially at the time. Leica did not realize that Imacon had their own financial difficulties, which caused the DM-R to be delivered much later than planned. So, while the contracted units were delivered in 2005, it seems that service manuals and an adequate supply of repair parts were not. Thus, Leica was unable to repair broken or damaged DM-Rs except by robbing working bits from other defective units. This method of repair is both very expensive and seldom successful. (Your scribe's DM-R suffered through two such replacement units, neither of which lasted for more than 48 hours.) These problems led to the rapid demise of an otherwise superb image cutter.

---

**2005:** Astrum Ltd. (formed in 1995 in Shostka, Sumy Oblast, Ukraine) starts producing both black-and-white and colour films under the Astrum brand, utilizing much of the equipment from the old Svema factory. While the company primarily makes aerial films, other companies import, slit, and package the film under various brands, for retail sale. They also produce a few specialized for Kodak.

---

### TRIVIA

At the time of writing, the Film Photography Project (USA) offers Svema branded film in numerous formats, including the long unavailable 620 and 110 sizes.

---

**2006:** A group of six artists creates the world's largest print (31 x 107 feet or 9.5 x 32.6 metres) in the world's largest camera. They turn an F-18 fighter jet hanger at the U.S. Marine Corps Air Station in El Toro, California, into a pinhole camera and make their image on a roll of muslin, coated with 21 gallons (80 litres) of gelatin silver halide solution, which they hang from the ceiling at a distance of about 80 feet (24 metres) from a pinhole, just under six millimetres (0.24 inches) in diameter and situated 15 feet (4.6 metres) above ground level on the hangar's metal door. The distance between the pinhole and the cloth was 55 feet (17 metres) and the exposure time is 35 minutes, in broad daylight. Because the muslin is simply hung, it is not particularly flat, and the image quality is low. But it *is* big!

**2006:** The Lomo LC-A+ is introduced to the world, offering the same endearing qualities of the original Lomo camera: sharp(ish) lens, high contrast, rich saturation, and the Lomo's trademark vignetting.

---

**TRIVIA**

Lomo's LC-A+ was first shown at the 2006 Photokina by the Lomographic Society, under a huge banner that proclaimed, "The Future Is Analog!"

---

**2006:** Nikon discontinue all film cameras except their entry level FM-10 and flagship F6 SLRs.

---

**TRIVIA**

The FM-10 is kept because it has a steady market among those seriously learning photography, as it is relatively inexpensive and has the full gamut of manual options. The F6 (introduced in 2004) has proven remarkably successful for a relatively expensive ($2,000+) film camera. F6 production ends in the fall of 2020, an amazing 16-year run for an analog camera in the digital age.

---

**2006:** Even though they were a major players in the 1980s and 1990s, Konica/Minolta are not able to keep up when the market goes digital. Konica-Minolta leave the photo business, selling their camera designs and patents, as well as their camera manufacturing plant, to the electronics giant Sony. Already a maker of both point-and-shoot digital cameras and video cameras, Sony re-brand the Minolta line of cameras as its Alpha series. Overnight, Sony becomes the world's third-largest manufacturer of the cameras, behind Canon and Nikon.

---

**UPDATE**

Minolta may be gone, but they are not forgotten. Although they no longer manufacture cameras, Konica-Minolta are still in the optical business, creating lenses for the copiers, projectors, planetariums, and medical equipment that K-M build. They also make both lens assemblies and complete lenses for other manufacturers on an OEM basis. They are said to have designed several lenses sold under the Sony, Panasonic, and Leica brands.

---

**2006:** Carl Zeiss resume camera and lens production under the Zeiss Ikon name, as rights to the Contax name are still held by Kyocera. The rangefinder cameras and most lenses are made by Cosina for Zeiss, and use the Leica M mount, now long out of patent protection. However, a few of the top tier lenses are made in Germany. Later, several Zeiss lenses will be introduced in mounts for Nikon and, in 2014, for Fuji X-mount and Sony E-mount cameras as well.

**2006:** Dai Nippon Printing (DNP) acquire Konica's photo paper plant in Odawara. Konica's film plant is transferred to DNP a year later and, in 2007, DNP relaunches Konica's Centuria film line. However, that is discontinued two years later, when DNP consolidate their photo business. DNP continue to produce photo papers under their own brand but sell the Konica chemical factory.

**2006:** Leica introduce their M8. It is not the first digital rangefinder—that honour goes to Epson's RD-1 (see **2004**). However, it can be honestly said that is the first successful digital rangefinder camera and is followed by a series of models that continue in production.

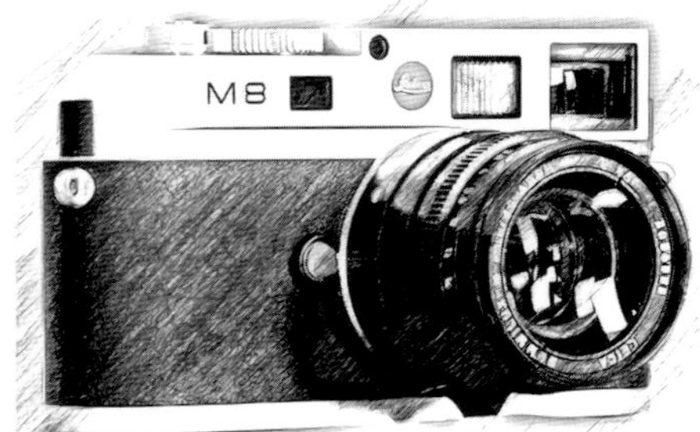

Your scribe had the privilege of being a pre-production tester for Leica's M8 and it was a magnificent image maker, despite its lack of IR filter. His review of the M8 was published in *Viewfinder* magazine.

### TRIVIA

The Leica M8 was rushed to market before it has gained its infrared (IR) filter. So, although most colours are reproduced faithfully, certain black tones have a distinct magenta cast because of the sensor's innate IR sensitivity. Leica were forced to offer each buyer several IR filters that fit their various lenses in order to cure the problem. It was a costly fix, that also cost Leica some customer loyalty, but many credit the move with saving the company, which was then struggling financially.

**2006:** At Photokina, Zeiss show their new "monster lens," a one-off built-to-order Zeiss Apo Sonnar T* 1700mm *f* 4 lens. Made in Germany and designed to be used with a Hasselblad 6 x 6 medium-format camera (that's the Hassy, at the right of the lens), this monster lens weighs in at 256 kg (564 pounds) and uses servo-controlled aiming and focusing systems

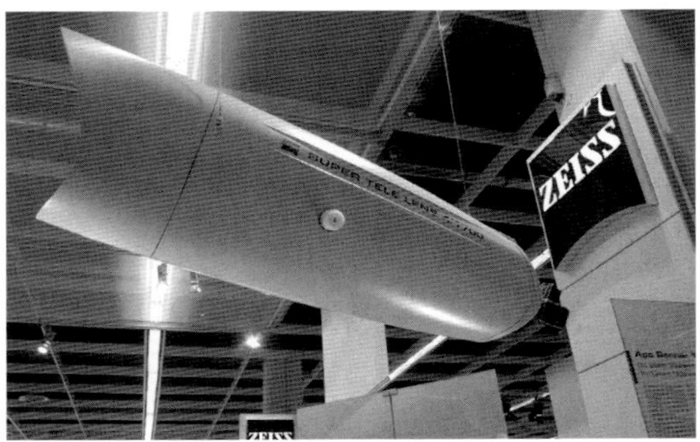

modelled after those used in large telescopes and satellite optical instruments. The resulting lens consists of 15 optical elements in 13 groups. It is the largest telephoto lens ever produced for civilian photographic purposes.

---

### TRIVIA

Zeiss never divulge the price or the name of the buyer, but some of the text on the lens is in Arabic, and it carries a "State of Qatar" emblem. Although it is supposed to be a one-off, Zeiss build two. One for the customer and one for themselves.

---

### ODDITIES

In 2006, what is said to be the world's most expensive lens, a Leica APO-Telyt-R 1600mm *f* 5.6 (for Leica's "R" series cameras), is delivered to Qatar's former Minister of Culture, Sheikh Saud Bin Mohammed Al-Thani (1966–2014), at a price reported to be just over $2 million. The lens is a unique one-off design, but the prototype is on display at Leica's factory.

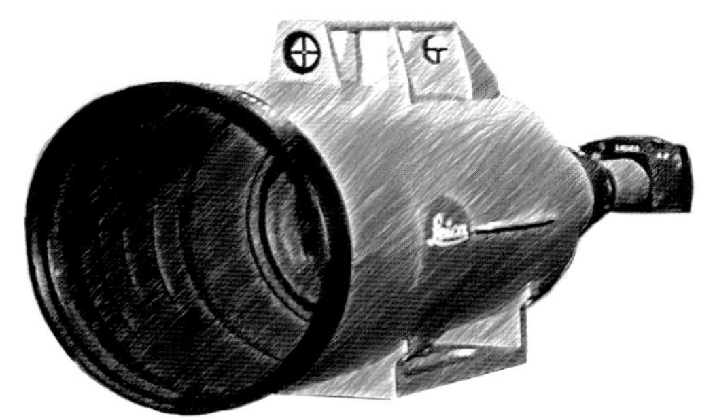

At 1.2 metres long without the lens-hood, 42cm in diameter, and weighing in at over 60kg, getting sharp images from such a large lens requires a very solid tripod. It is reported that Sheikh Al-Thani commissioned a specially equipped Mercedes four-wheel drive to move his expensive lens about. Whether this setup has been successful in sufficiently steadying the lens is unknown since no images taken with the lens have ever been released.

It may, or may not, not be the world's most expensive lens, as neither the price nor the buyer for the Zeiss Apo Sonnar T* 1700mm *f* 4 lens have ever been revealed.

---

**2006:** Kodak are the first to put dual lenses and sensors under the same roof, long before they appear on smartphones. The EasyShare V-570 has both a 23mm (equivalent) prime lens and a 37-117mm (equivalent) folded-optic zoom lens, coupled with two 5MP CCD sensors, in order to give a wider range of picture-taking options.

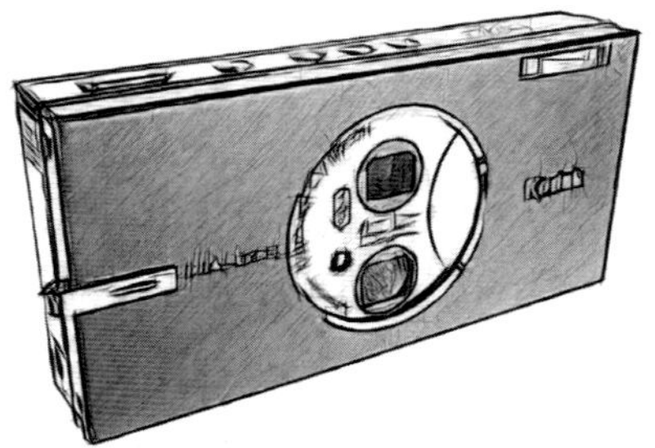

---

**TRIVIA**

Kodak's advertising was a wee bit misleading, for they advertised the V-570 as having a 5x zoom lens, when it was really a wide-angle prime and a 3x zoom that you could switch between. Still, it was the first dual-lens implementation—an idea that did not catch on with camera manufacturers at the time, but one that has caught on with camera-phone makers, a decade later.

---

**2007:** Kodak announce new colour filter technology for digital sensors which will double a sensor's sensitivity to light in digital cameras. These RGBW (red, green, blue, and transparent or white) patterns have one or more clear (unfiltered) pixels, to increase light sensitivity. However, none of the patterns shown are as small as the 2 x 2 pixel Bayer pattern. Despite these improvements, the Bayer filter remains dominant. In fact, other than Fujifilm's X-Trans sensor (see **2012**), it remains almost universal.

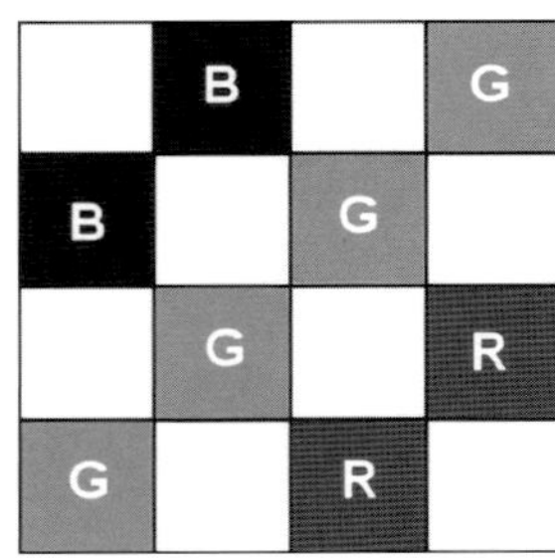


**2007:** First introduced in 2005 as a 35mm film camera, GoPro's Digital Hero sparks a revolution. This go-anywhere camera with a rugged case is suddenly found strapped to the helmet of almost every motocross rider, skate boarder, skier, and snow boarder around. It records 640 x 460 pixel images and shoots VGA-definition 320 x 240 video at 10 frames per second, for a maximum of 10 seconds. It features 32 megabytes of internal memory, but no SD card slot. It goes on to create an entirely new genre of "action cameras" and spawns a host of rivals, as well as cheaper knockoffs.

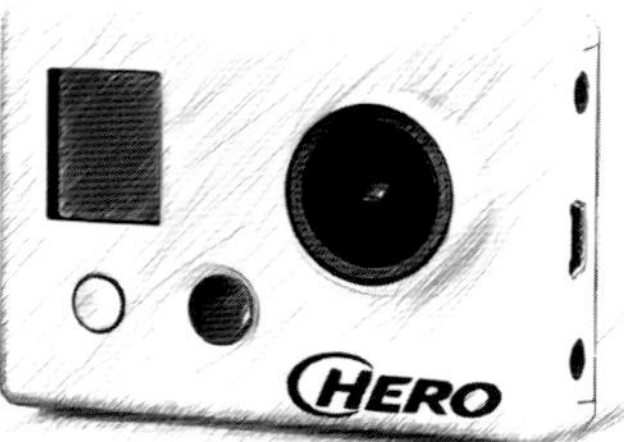


**2007:** David Llado (Barcelona, Spain), a 30-year Pentax user, wants to use a Leica "R" series lens on his Pentax. Instead of employing an adapter (which will not work, as there is insufficient space for an adapter while still maintaining infinity focus) he machines a new mount for the Leica lens with a "K" bayonet instead of the Leica bayonet. It works perfectly and he starts Leitax (formed from Leica and Pentax) to make and market his adapters. He moves to CNC (Computer Numerical Control) machining to assure consistent quality, and Leitax quickly gains a reputation as the best in the business.

When Leica discontinue their "R" (reflex) series of cameras and lenses later in the year, his operation booms as "R" users look for ways to use their beloved lenses on their new digital cameras. In the following years, he expands his product lines to include new mounts for many different brand combinations, and Leitax remains a successful business.

**2007:** In a desperate attempt to downsize and fit into the digital world, Kodak "implode" two buildings totalling 1.2 million square feet (~111,500 square metres) of film and paper manufacturing space in two days. Just 104 of 212 buildings in Kodak Park remain standing and in use. The digital revolution means that Kodak film, previously made in several factories around the world, is now all manufactured on just two coating machines, in Rochester.

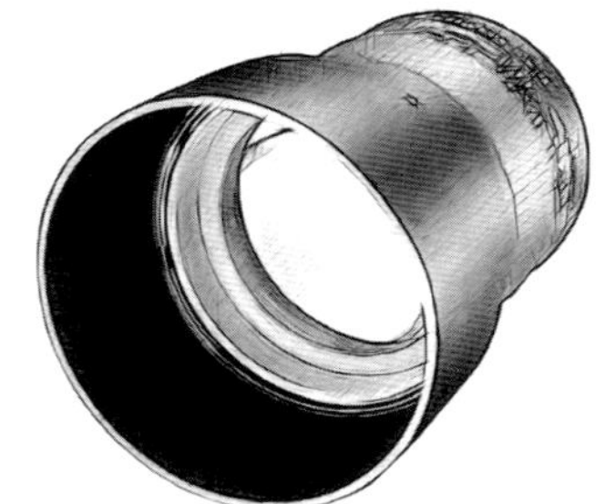

**2007:** Apple introduce the iPhone. It becomes one of the most massive successes in modern technological history, as thousands of people line up to buy the first units. Apple sell one million iPhones in the first 74 days and photography is changed forever.

**2008:** Pentax merges with optical glass and photo-filter maker Hoya. Hoya close the Pentax-owned factory in Tokyo and move most Pentax operations to southeast Asia, with lenses being produced in Vietnam and cameras in the Philippines. In 2011, Hoya will sell the Pentax camera operations to Ricoh, but keep Pentax's medical-related business, patents, and expertise.

**2008:** Korea's budget lens maker, Samyang, moves up-market, building higher-quality manual focus prime lenses in various camera mounts. Their first offering is an 85mm $f1.4$ portrait lens under its own name. Reviewers indicate that while not quite up to the top brand lenses in performance, it comes close and represents good value if you're willing to manually focus. It will be the first of many.

**2008:** Photographic publisher and columnist Herbert Keppler dies at the age of 82.

---

**TRIVIA**

*The New York Times* obituary for Keppler quoted from *Modern Photography*'s January 1966 issue. Writing about single-lens reflex cameras, Keppler had said: "It seems impossible to turn out a camera free of all idiosyncrasies. Cameras are obviously like people which is, I suppose, one reason why they make such a good combination."

---

**2008:** CFast cards are introduced as an updated variant of the now 14-year-old Compact Flash. CFast (also known as CompactFast) cards are based on the Serial ATA interface rather than the Parallel interface used by the original Compact Flash cards. They will be largely replaced, three years later, by the still faster XQD cards. None of these designs will fare well against the by-now ubiquitous SD cards (see **1994**).

**2008:** Gone in an instant. Polaroid stops manufacturing all forms of the instant film that made it famous. On 18 December, the "new" Polaroid Corporation files for bankruptcy.

**TRIVIA**

Polaroid's departure is directly related to the bankruptcy of its then owners, the Petters Group (see **2005**). In September of 2008, the FBI raided the Petters Group offices over suspicions they were running a Ponzi scheme. On 13 October 2008, Petters Group Worldwide filed for bankruptcy. On 2 December 2009, Thomas J. Petters (b. 1957) and several co-conspirators were convicted on counts related to the theft of $2 billion through this Ponzi scheme. On 8 April 2010, Petters (then age 53), was sentenced to 50 years in federal prison.

**2008:** The Impossible Project is started when its three founders meet at the Polaroid factory's closing event and decide to form a company to produce films for the 200 million existing Polaroid cameras. In October, Impossible buys the production machinery from Polaroid and leases the Polaroid production plant in Enschede, Netherlands. They develop new instant film formulas and will, in 2010, begin deliveries of several types of instant film. In their first full year they sell more than a half million rolls and become profitable.

**TRIVIA**

The main reasons that the Impossible Project developed new film formulas was that first, they now owned the machinery but did not have rights to the original film patents; and second, the newer formulas lowered the risk of pollution during their manufacture.

**2008:** On 5 August, at the urging of Four-Thirds partner Panasonic, the micro-FourThirds system standard is introduced. It brings with it dramatic reductions in the size and weight of digital interchangeable-lens camera bodies and lenses.

Micro-FourThirds camera systems are introduced by both Olympus and Panasonic. Unlike the original FourThirds SLR cameras, the mFT system does not provide space for a mirror box or a pentaprism, allowing smaller, lighter bodies and a shorter "registration" (i.e., the distance from lens-flange to sensor-plane), which allows smaller lenses to be designed.

Better models have an electronic viewfinder, or EVF, essentially a small flat-screen TV, while lower-priced models use only the back-panel display as a viewfinder. Although it takes a half-dozen more years of camera and EVF development, mFT cameras eventually become a great market success story, forcing larger rivals such as Nikon and Canon to produce their own mirrorless cameras in order to compete. By 2022, the switch from dSLRs to mirrorless designs will be virtually complete.

**2008:** Leica replace their 1976 Canadian-made $f$1.0 Noctilux with a new 50mm $f$0.95 ASPH (aspherical) lens, both designed and made in Germany. The practical difference in light gathering between $f$1 and $f$0.95 is insignificant. The designation really serves only to tell the two versions apart.

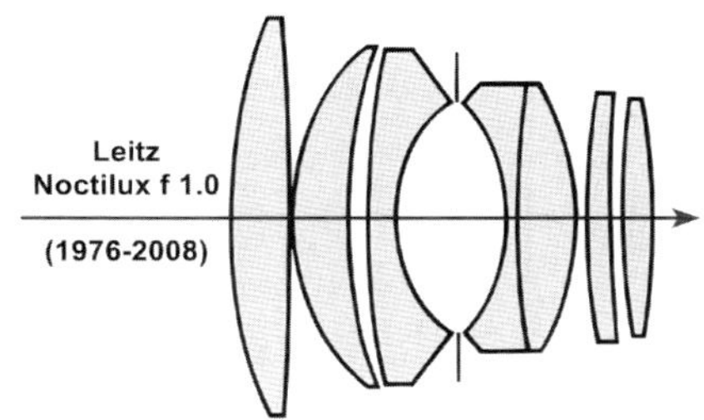


---

**TRIVIA**

By the end of the production run for the 1976 Noctilux, Leica had already sold their Canadian factory in which it was designed and manufactured. However, they had an arrangement whereby the new owners (first Hughes, then Raytheon) continued to make the Noctilux for Leica. But, when the last guy who knew how to make them retired, it was the end of the $f$1.0 Noctilux. As Peter Karbe, Leica's current lens designer, said, "it needed a redesign anyway," and thus the German-designed and built $f$0.95 Noctilux came to be.

---

**2008:** Nikon's D90 becomes the first digital SLR with high-definition video-recording capability. It features a 12.3 MP APS-size CMOS sensor with secondary 1280 x 720 pixel (720p) 24 frames-per-second HD video capture with monaural sound, but recording time is limited to five minutes per clip.

---

**TRIVIA**

Just two months later, the Canon EOS 5D Mark II will boast a 21.1MP full-frame sensor and be capable of recording a 1920 × 1080 pixel (1080p) 30 frame/s HD video with monaural sound (stereo with external microphone) for up to 12-minute clips.

---

**2008:** Hong Kong based, MF Jebsen Group buys the Yashica trademark from Kyocera (see **1983**) and markets inexpensive, digital camcorders, digital photo frames, etc. under the Yashica brand. In 2018, they bring out their Y35 digiFilm camera. Poorly built and with multiple problems, it is not a success.

**2009:** Kodachrome 64 colour slide film is retired, concluding its 74-year run. Legendary photographer Steve McCurry is given the last 36 exposure roll.

**2009:** Production of film at Italy's Ferrania ceases and the factory is shuttered.

**2009:** ADOX Fotowerke GmbH opens the "worlds smallest photochemical factory" in Bad Saarow, Germany, to make ADOX black-and-white films and papers using the original recipes and methods. Working with a low level of automation and a large degree of manual labour allows them to be very flexible and manufacture many different types of films and papers with little overhead or fixed costs. Today, their website reads: "Doktor C. Schleussner Fotowerke . . . also used similar machines in their times, but we are now much smaller."

**2009:** After many changes of ownership, the Fisher-Price division of toymaker Mattel announce that they have stopped making scenic View-Master reels depicting tourist attractions but say they will continue to produce reels of animated characters. In late 2009, Alpha-Cine announce they will take up the scenic reel production under an agreement with Fisher-Price. In 2015, View-Master will introduce a "Virtual Reality" viewer based on Google's cardboard VR software and phone, using scanned View-Master reels.

**2009:** Franke & Heidecke go bankrupt, but production carries on, in Braunschweig, Germany, at DHW Fototechnik, a company founded by three former Franke & Heidecke employees. DHW will go on to present two new Rolleiflex cameras and a new electronic shutter at Photokina, in 2012.

---

### BUSINESS UPDATE

DHW Fototechnik filed for insolvency in 2014 and the factory was liquidated at auction in August of 2015 ending any further production of cameras, lenses, and accessories.

In later 2015, a smaller company was created by two former DHW Fototechnik employees, under the name DW Photo, at the same location. DW Photo focus on producing the Rolleiflex Hy6 mod2 medium-format SLR camera (digital and film), servicing existing cameras, and providing firmware and hardware upgrades. As of late 2023, their website was still in operation. Rollei GmbH & Co. KG. (Hamburg) now own the rights to the Rollei brand in Europe, and market Rollei and Rolleiflex-branded accessories as well as basic digital cameras made by others.

---

**2009:** Based in Saint Petersburg, Russia, FotoApteka produce developers and other photographic chemicals and resell films made by Agfa and Kodak. In 2017, they will adopt the Silberra brand and introduce three new black-and-white films of their own manufacture. Two orthochromatic films will be added in 2018, as well as three C-41 colour negative films in 2021.

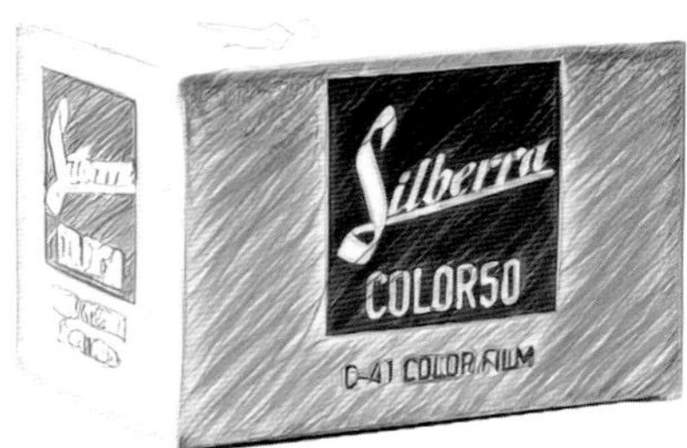


---

### TRIVIA

Silberra's black-and-white formulations are of their own design and are coated for them by Micron (Moscow), a firm with more than 80 years of experience in synthesis and coating of emulsions. In 2017, Silberra launched a IndieGoGo campaign to raise funds to buy or upgrade equipment so they can mass manufacture their films. It reached just 30% of its goal, so they continue to hand-roll their film.

**2009:** Phase One, the Danish builder of medium-format digital camera backs, purchase a major stake in Mamiya. In 2012, they will combine Mamiya with another subsidiary, Leaf Imaging, creating the Mamiya Leaf brand, and integrate both companies' product lines. The firm continues today.

**2009:** Patriarch Partners LLC win an auction for Polaroid Corporation's assets, including the company name, patents, and photography collection. (The price paid varies from $52.7 million to $59.1 million, depending on the information source.)

**2010:** Sony release their SLT a33 and SLT a55, the first dSLRs without an optical viewfinder. What looks to be a conventional pentaprism houses a high-resolution electronic viewfinder (EVF)—essentially, a tiny, flat-screen TV which displays the image on the sensor. The SLT in the name stands for "Single Lens Translucent," a reference to the first use of a fixed pellicle mirror since the Canon Pellix (see **1965**). The mirror lets most of the light pass straight through to the sensor, while always reflecting a portion of the light onto a phase-detection auto-focus array housed in the top of the camera.

**2010:** In Japan, 40% of camera sales are the new mirrorless type. It is a sign of things to come.

**2010:** Peter Gowland, who photographed ravishing women at a time when "the pinup girl" was a nearly ubiquitous fixture of American life, dies. Over his career, Gowland's photographs appear on more than 1,000 magazine covers.

**2010:** The Impossible Project market their type 600, 700, and SX-70 films for Polaroid cameras. (Film type 100, discontinued by Polaroid in 2008, is still produced by FujiFilm until 2016.)

**2010:** New55 Film is a start-up filmmaker formed after Polaroid Type 55 P/N was discontinued. After four years of development, they create an instant 4 x 5-inch film that produces both a negative and positive instant print. A Kickstarter funding project is launched in March of 2014 to acquire additional equipment and materials. Unfortunately, they suffer quality-control problems, particularly with the uneven spread of chemicals when the film is developed. After two further, unsuccessful Kickstarter campaigns to raise funds, New55 Film will go out of business at the end of December 2017.

---

### TRIVIA

In the 1930s, the dye transfer reversal process was invented by Edith Weyde (1901–1989) while working at Agfa. This is the basis for all instant print films. Once the Second World War was over, captured German technology was offered to American companies, with Polaroid being an interested party. Though Edwin Land is the father of modern instant print films, he simply perfected Weyde's system and built a practical camera for it.

**2011:** Nikon's CoolPix S1000pj becomes the world's first digital camera with a built-in projector. The 12MP camera can project either images it takes, or those from a computer, up to 40" wide, at up to 5.5 feet. Photo quality is average, but projection is no match for 35mm slides and does not prove popular.

**2011:** Designed as a replacement for the older (1994) CF cards, the XQD card uses PCI Express as a data transfer interface, allowing both read and write speeds from 1 GB per second (125 Mbytes/second) to about 4 Gb/s (500 Mbytes/second) and storage capabilities beyond 2 Terabytes. It is aimed at high-definition camcorders and high-resolution digital cameras. While they have a similar form factor to CF cards, they are not backward compatible with either CompactFlash or the short-lived CFast cards (see **1994** and **2008**).

---

### UPDATE

In June 2012, version 2.0 of the XQD specification is announced. The cards now feature support for PCI Express 3.0 with transfer rates up to 8 Gbit/s (1000 Mbyte/s).

---

**2011:** In October, British-born Michael Woodford (b. 1960) is suddenly ousted as chief executive of the Olympus Corporation, after holding the position for just over six months. The former CEO turned whistleblower is fired for exposing "one of the biggest and longest-running loss-hiding arrangements in Japanese corporate history"—117.7 billion yen ($1.5 billion) of investment losses and other dubious fees and payments, dating back to the late 1980s, according to the *Wall Street Journal*. It becomes a huge scandal in Japan and worldwide.

---

### TRIVIA

Between 2000 and 2011, the average price of a point-and-shoot digital camera drops from $393 to $78.

---

**2012:** The digital revolution drives interchangeable lens production to its peak: 30 million lenses, more than four times the lens production in 2005 and an increase of 58,677% over 1955 production, when records were first kept.

**2012:** The Finnish wireless phone maker Nokia introduces its Pureview 808 mobile phone with an immense 41-megapixel sensor, once again bringing telephones closer to cameras.

**2012:** In January, unable to post a profit since 2007, Kodak file for bankruptcy protection, with debts of $6.75 billion. Film production continues while Kodak work out a settlement with their creditors.

**2012:** Cinestill Film (USA) begin Beta testing of film for still cameras made from Kodak's "Vision 3" motion picture film balanced for tungsten light. They remove the separate anti-halation layer used to protect the film in motion picture cameras; this allows the film to be rated at ISO 800, rather than the 500 rating of the original Kodak film, and also allows the use of the standard C-41 chemistry.

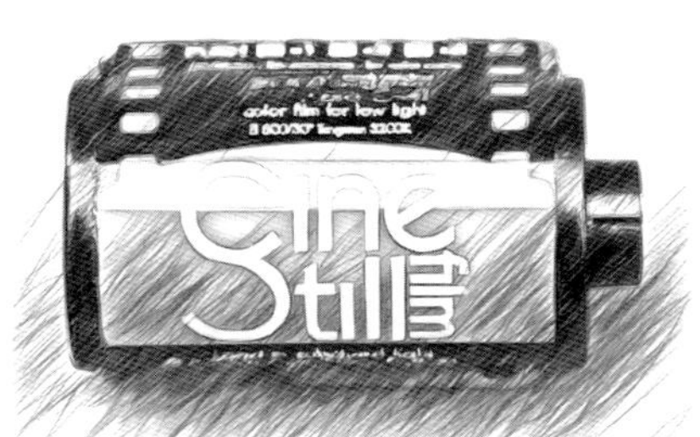

However, without the anti-halation backing, the film exhibits a glowing effect on the image in areas with strong highlights. The company will go on to make "50Daylight Xpro C-41" from Kodak's "Vision3 50D" motion picture film and repackage Kodak's Double X black-and-white film.

**2012:** Michael Woodford, ex-CEO of Olympus, publishes *Exposure*, a scathing indictment of past business practices at Olympus. He is named Businessperson of the Year by four major newspapers and receives numerous other awards. Reading like a well-written thriller, the book becomes required reading for all students of both business and photography.

---

**TRIVIA**

Woodford's publisher hired a ghostwriter to write *Exposure* after interviewing Woodford. Woodford was so unhappy with the results that he fired the ghostwriter and wrote the book himself. Despite not being a trained writer, the result is a riveting exposé that is hard to put down!

In 2012, Woodford was awarded $16 million in damages from Olympus for defamation and wrongful dismissal.

In July 2013, the former Olympus board chairman and the former executive vice-president were both sentenced to three years in prison, with an additional five years suspended sentence. The auditor who had been party to the fraud was sentenced to 2.5 years in prison, four years suspended. Olympus was fined 700 million yen ($7 million). In April 2014, six banks file a civil suit against Olympus over the fraud, seeking an additional 28 billion yen in damages. At the time of writing, the results of that case are unknown.

The financial strain of the scandal will result in Olympus selling their camera division in 2020 and, in 2022, offering their Scientific Device unit for sale.

---

**2012:** Nikon celebrate the shipment of the 75 millionth Nikkor lens.

**2012:** At age 46, Kazuto Yamaki (b. 1966) becomes the second CEO of Sigma, the family-owned 1,600-employee lens maker. He realizes that if Sigma is to remain in business while still keeping production in Japan, it is not possible to continue making low-end lenses. He orders their engineers to create top-quality optics that can be sold at a price which will support

Japanese manufacturing. The result is the "ART" series, which radically improves the reputation and financial fortunes of Sigma.

**2012:** Mexican reporter/photographer Regina Martinez (1963–2012) is killed while investigating links between organized crime and politicians. The bodies of two more news photographers, Gabriel Huge Córdova and his nephew, Guillermo Luna Varela, are found, along with that of Esteban Rodríguez, a former news photographer, and Irasema Becerra, an acquaintance of Córdova and Varela, just two days later. Their deaths mark the beginning of a series of journalists' murders that make Mexico the most dangerous country in the world to be a photographer.

**2012:** In February, Kodak announce they will cease making digital cameras, pocket (mini) video cameras, and digital picture frames in order to focus on the corporate digital imaging market.

**2012:** Using light-field technology based on his PhD thesis, Yi-Ren Ng, CEO of the U.S. firm Lytro (founded in 2006), introduces the first light-field camera available to the general public. The camera opens an entire world of new possibilities for photographers. The technology captures information from a subject being photographed in a way that enables the resulting image to be refocused after it's been taken. Unfortunately, the technology also significantly lowers the camera's resolution. The camera itself is very basic and is not a big market success.

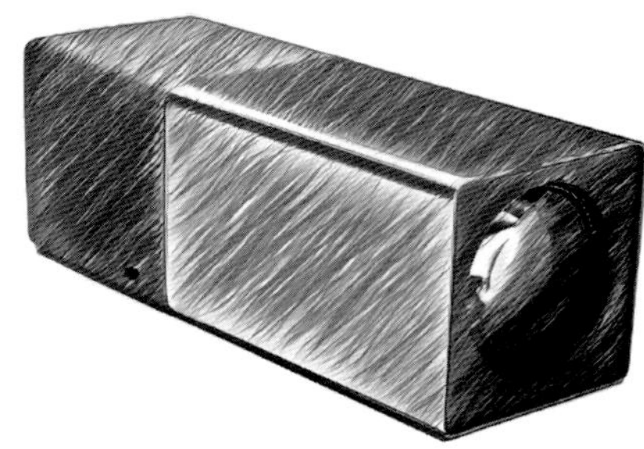

**2012:** Fuji introduce their X-Trans CMOS sensor. The sensor is claimed to provide better resistance to colour moiré than the Bayer filter, and thus can be made without an anti-aliasing filter. This in turn allows cameras to achieve a higher resolution with the same megapixel count and to have a more "film like" look.

**2012:** Samsung deliver their Galaxy camera, which features a 4.8-inch touchscreen and uses Google's Android OS—a first. A year later, the company will launch the Galaxy NX—the first mirrorless camera to use Android as its operating system.

**2013:** Worldwide camera shipments drop 49% from the previous year, with just 62 million units shipped, as mobile telephone/cameras continue to replace the formerly ubiquitous point-and-shoot cameras. Shipments of higher priced dSLR and mirrorless cameras also drop, but only by a few percent, while prices rise, keeping their makers profitable.

In spite of this massive drop in sales, digital camera production is still close to double the peak of film camera production (see **1997**).

**2013:** Despite being a successful maker of precision cameras for the aerospace industry during the 1990s, by 2010, Korean industrial giant Samsung fails to make much of a dent in the consumer camera market. But, with the 2014 launch of their brilliant NX-1 mirrorless system camera, Samsung shows that it can be a leading camera manufacturer. While several mFT cameras have already come to market, the field is much less crowded than other segments, which gives Samsung a much greater chance to stand apart. The NX series cameras win praise, and their lenses build an excellent reputation.

---

**UPDATE**

In late 2015, just one year after its introduction, Samsung will discontinue its flagship NX-1 in Europe, the U.K., Hong Kong, and Australia. By 2017, it becomes apparent that despite no public announcement, Samsung has stopped all consumer camera manufacturing. Some say it is due to lack of sales, others maintain that it is due to the violation of patents belonging to other camera makers. Nobody outside Samsung knows for sure.

---

**2013:** Frenchman Lomig Perrotin starts "The Smallest Film Company in the World" in the closet of his Parisian apartment, eventually moving to a somewhat larger premises (a family garage) in Saint-Nazaire. Still a "one man band," the company is today located in a set of decommissioned French Army containers in Brittany. Film Washi produce handcrafted black-and-white films and papers. They also re-size and repackage other manufacturers' films originally made for technical, motion picture, industrial, or aerial applications, even X-ray films, and remain in business today.

---

**TRIVIA**

Film Washi's unusual name comes from their first product: a black-and-white handcrafted film that was hand-coated on a traditional Japanese paper known as Washi. It was inspired by the paper negatives of Henry Fox Talbot.

---

**2013:** Olympus introduce their OM-D / E-M1, a professional-level micro-Four-Thirds (mFT) camera, with the world's first five-axis sensor-shifting image-stabilization system. The model name is a mouthful, but the camera proves to be excellent, reliable, and popular.

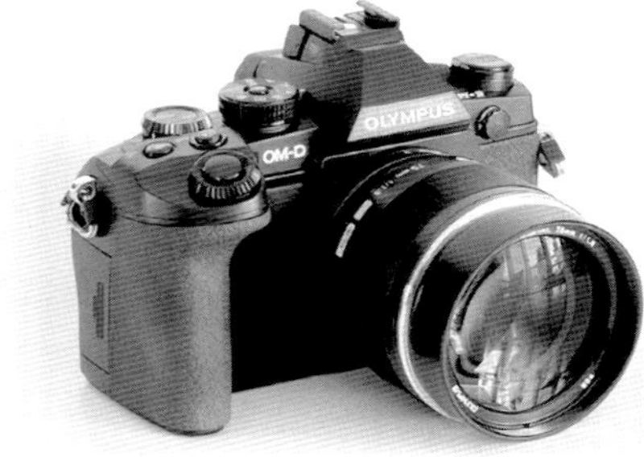

**2013:** Kodak emerges from bankruptcy. The new Kodak focuses on commercial products, such as high-speed digital printing technology and printing on flexible packaging for consumer goods. The Kodak name still appears on digital cameras and other consumer goods, but they are made by others, with the brand-name used under license.

**2013:** Ferrania's photographic film production line is acquired by a new company, Film Ferrania s.r.l. Funds to restart the factory are raised through crowdfunding and the requisite goal of $250,000 is surpassed. Ferrania encounters many problems with recalcitrant equipment and with asbestos found in the buildings. The first production of black-and-white film is not expected until the spring of 2017, while production of the promised colour reversal films seems a long way off (see **2017**).

---

### TRIVIA

In 2013, photographer Ed Drew takes a tintype photograph in Afghanistan, becoming the first to take a tintype photograph of a war zone since the American Civil War.

---

**2013:** Alaris is spun off from Eastman Kodak to settle a $2.8 billion claim by the U.K.'s Kodak Pension Plan. Alaris takes over the manufacture of scanners, photographic paper, printing kiosks and such, and becomes the global distributor for Eastman Kodak's consumer films. In this arrangement, Kodak Alaris shares the Kodak brand with the Eastman Kodak Co. of Rochester.

---

### BUSINESS TRIVIA

Prior to its bankruptcy, Kodak had tried to sell its profitable document and personal imaging divisions, but due to its unfavourable bargaining position did not find a buyer at the right price. A deal was reached between the British KPP (Kodak Pension Plan) and Eastman Kodak that enabled the sale of both divisions for $325 million. It was considerably less than Eastman Kodak wanted, but in return, the sale released the company from KPP's $2.8 billion claim. The result was Kodak Alaris, which took over the manufacture of scanners, photographic paper, printing kiosks, and such, while Eastman Kodak continued to produce all the film. However, Kodak Alaris became the exclusive worldwide distributor for Kodak's still films, such as Portra, Ektachrome E100, Gold, Colorplus, Tri-X, and T-Max, but not their manufacture.

In April of 2016, Kodak Alaris announced they would shutter a U.K. manufacturing plant, one of five they operate, due to lack of demand. In 2020, Kodak Alaris sold its photochemical and photo paper operation to their largest distributor, Sino Promise Holdings of Hong Kong. Established in 1993, Sino Promise had been making the photo chemicals and paper for Kodak Alaris in their Xiamen and Wuxi factories for several years. While the paper and chemical division was profitable, the KPP (Alaris' only shareholder) needed the money to fund a $1.9 billion obligation to former Kodak employees.

Sino Promise also sells photopaper and chemicals under its own "Honor" brand.

---

**2013:** With its existence rumoured since 2010, or even before, the Nolab digital replacement for Super-8 cameras is finally introduced. It makes sense, for unlike the "digital film" for 35mm cameras, the Super-8 cartridge allows the sensor to be placed easily in the film plane, providing space for a battery, SD card, and circuitry. As well, the film pawl provides an easy way to synchronize the sensor scans with the camera's shutter. It is claimed to have a 5 megapixel sensor and record video in 720p HD.

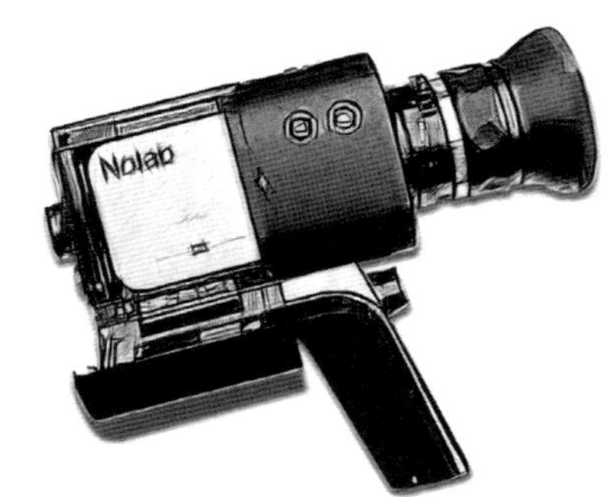

The Nolab Super-8 cartridge seems like a wonderful idea, but the potential market is small, and the product is never heard from again.

**2013:** The firm behind Ilford opens Harman Labs, to combat the rapidly shrinking film develop and print business, by providing the service by mail, in the U.K. as well as the USA and Canada. The strategy works.

---

### AUCTION MADNESS

A one-off prototype Leica camera, designed by famed industrial designer Marc Newson (b. 1963) and Apple's former Chief Design Officer Jony Ive (b. 1967), was built around the innards of the 24-megapixel Leica M Type 240 and fitted with a matching 50mm *f* 2 APO-Summicron ASPH lens. It sold at auction for $1.8 million in 2013. The actual limited-edition versions looked a bit different and sold for much, much less, though still far from pocket-change.

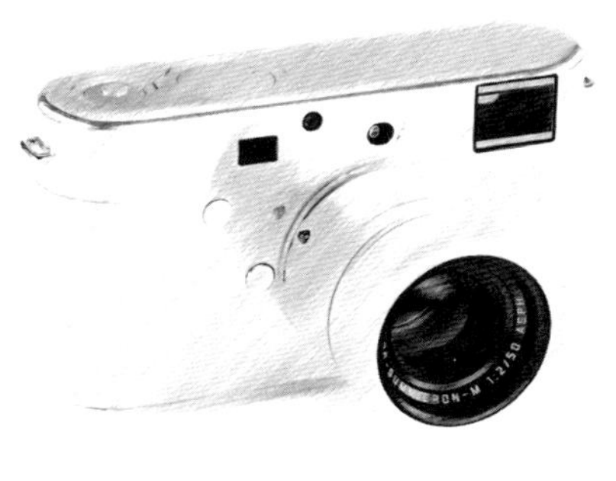

---

**2014:** Hasselblad introduce the 200C back for their H5D camera. Designed for studio, product, and still-life photographers, the H5D 200c can produce spectacular 200 megapixel images, but at a cost just north of $30,000.

---

### TRIVIA

Hasselblad's multi-shot technology uses a 50-megapixel sensor mounted on piezo-electric actuators (similar to those used in the in-body image stabilization systems of consumer cameras) and then captures four or six shots by moving the sensor 1½ pixels at the time, taking multiple shots which are then blended, in the camera, to create a 200-megapixel capture. The system works well, but only for stationary subjects with the camera on a tripod.

---

**2014:** Lytro introduce their second (and last) consumer light-field camera. The very futuristic-looking Illum features a much better sensor to try to overcome the resolution problem.

Its ability to refocus an image after it has been taken seems to be a solution in search of a problem, and fails to capture the imagination of the public, though it does develop a small, devoted customer base.

**2014:** Sony introduce three Alpha 7 series cameras. They are the first with "full frame" (24 x 36mm) sensors in a compact mirrorless body.

**2014:** Sony produce the first experimental curved CMOS sensor. It features a curvature similar to that of the human eye, which should help fix optical distortions normally created by flat sensors. Sony say it will, in theory, provide better image quality and pave the way to simpler lenses. It is not put into production.

**TRIVIA**

While curved sensors are wonderful in theory, they work only with specially designed lenses. Sony admit that it will be difficult to design high-power zoom lenses to work with a curved sensor. In early 2018, Sigma's CEO, Kazuto Yamaki, will say: "The curved sensors would be an interesting solution for smartphones but too restrictive for a conventional camera." Despite many patents on both curved sensor designs and the lenses to work with them, from Microsoft, Nikon, Sony, and others, to date no camera with a curved sensor has been released.

**2014:** Metz continue to build high-end LCD televisions in Germany but cannot compete with lower-cost Asian producers. In November, they file for bankruptcy.

**UPDATE**

In March of 2015, new investors are found and two new companies are formed. The TV business is taken over by the Chinese manufacturer Skyworth, while the plastics technology and flash business become Metz mecatech GmbH. Nearly 300 former Metz employees are hired, and production of Metz electronic flash units continues in Solms, Germany.

**2014:** Sony, building on their QX camera introduced the previous year, announce their QX-1/QX-30. The QX-1 is a 20.1MP camera that is physically attached to a smartphone and communicates with it via Bluetooth, using the phone's screen as the viewfinder and accepting Sony E-Mount lenses. The QX-30 is similar but has a built-in 30x zoom lens.

**2014:** In Japan, Olympus introduce their "Air," a competing device to Sony's QX series, which accepts the smaller, lighter mFT lenses. It will appear in the USA in 2015. Although a tad awkward to use, both systems bring telephones still closer to cameras in terms of photographic capability.

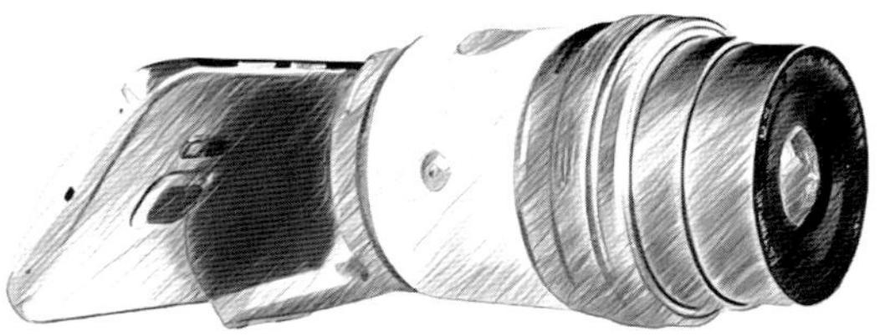

### UPDATE

Unfortunately, the Sony models are reportedly plagued with buggy software. The QX1/30 transfers photos extremely slowly and a majority of the phone's camera features (especially for users of Apple's iOS software) were not accessible through Sony's software. By late 2016, the QX-1 is gone. The Olympus "Air" gets better reviews, and, at the end of 2018, it and Sony's QX-30 are still available, though at heavily discounted prices, suggesting that neither has been particularly successful.

**2014:** It is reported that Fuji make more money on their Instax cameras and film than with their digital cameras. They constantly top camera sales rankings. Combine this fact with New55 and the Impossible Project's successes and you wonder where Polaroid went wrong!

### TRIVIA

Fuji's Instax films and cameras are based upon the improvements Kodak made to Polaroid's SX-70 instant film in the Kodak instant film cameras of the 1970s and 1980s, namely the ability to expose the film through the rear of the photograph and the reversal of the order of the dye layers so that development in the blue layer is visible first. Thus, unlike Polaroid cameras, the image does not need to be taken by means of a reflex mirror. Colour balance and tonal range are also improved. Fuji's decision to integrate the pressure plate springs and electrical power sources into the camera bodies rather than the disposable film pack also helps make the Instax system more economical per exposure.

Although Kodak itself ceased production of instant film cameras when it was successfully sued by Polaroid for patent infringement, the Instax cameras were made and marketed under an agreement with Polaroid that specified they could not be officially distributed in certain territories, such as the USA, until the original Polaroid patents expired in the mid-1990s.

Fuji sells 100,000 Instax cameras in 2004 but will sell five million Instax cameras in 2015. In 2018, FujiFilm will sell a staggering 8.5 million Instax cameras in just nine months. By comparison, Fuji sold just 700,000 of their highly rated (though much higher priced) X-series digital cameras between 2011 and 2013.

**2014:** A new firm, net SE-Globell Deutschland (Koblenz), acquires the Meyer-Optik brand and introduces five new lenses, in a variety of mounts, under the "Meyer-Optik-Görlitz" name. This includes two lenses at $f$ 0.95 in 35 and 50mm focal lengths.

---

**UPDATE**

Although the Meyer Optik $f$ 0.95 "Nocturnus" lenses are advertised as "Made in Germany," several sources claim that they are simply re-branded "Mitagon Speedmaster" lenses of Chinese manufacture. Meyer-Optic admit they purchase their components "internationally," but claim to do the assembly and quality control testing in Germany, saying adjustment for each lens takes up to 3½ hours and that their close tolerances lead to a reject rate of 50% for core components. This additional work qualifies the lenses for the "Made in Germany" status. Whether the additional price is warranted is a decision the author will leave to prospective purchasers.

---

**2014:** Late in the year, a team of photographers spends two weeks at 3,500 metres altitude, in -10C weather, using a Canon 70D dSLR, a Canon 400mm $f$ 2.8 lens and a Canon 2x extender on a special robotic mount. They capture 70,000 photographs over 35 hours of shooting to create a gigantic panoramic photograph of Mont Blanc, Europe's highest mountain. This new record-holding image weighs in at a staggering 365 gigapixels. Post-processing and computer stitching the 46 terabytes afterwards takes two months, resulting in a 365-gigapixel photo.

---

**TRIVIA**

If this image were printed (an unlikely prospect) at 300 dpi, the photo would just fit in a soccer field.

---

**2015:** In September, Canon announce the development of a 250 megapixel APS-H sensor. Canon consider the application of this technology in specialized surveillance and crime-prevention tools, ultra-high-resolution measuring instruments, etc., but do not expect it to appear in consumer cameras.

**2015:** Canon announce two new cameras with full-frame 50.6 megapixel sensors that begin to rival the resolution of their medium-format competitors such as the Pentax 645Z, Phase One, and Hasselblad models. Because the sensors are smaller in the new Canons as compared to the sensors in the medium-format models, their pixels are smaller, resulting in somewhat more sensor "noise" under equivalent conditions. But they come remarkably close, at a fraction of the cost, shaking up the top end of the market once again.

**2015:** *American Photo* magazine's print edition ceases publication, and the magazine is combined with *Popular Photography,* effectively ending a decades-long run. The combined publication will run only another two years, but its website continues to operate today.

**2015:** Olympus introduce an upgraded version of their E-M5, the EM-5-II. It is the first consumer-priced camera to use a technology like Hasselblad's "Multi-shot," to take 40 MP images with a 16MP sensor. As with the Hasselblad, it works only on a tripod, with perfectly still subjects. Although of limited use to most photographers, reviewers say that it provides superior results to several of the better full-frame cameras equipped with 30+ megapixel sensors and costs about $29,000 less than the Hasselblad!

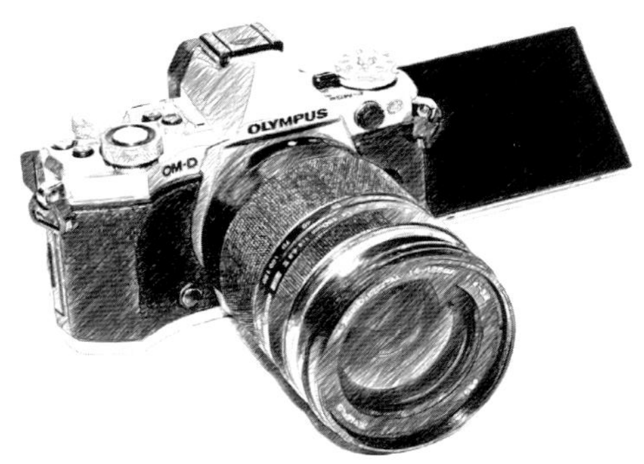

---

**UPDATE**

In 2017, the Olympus E-M1 Mk II, will receive an updated version of this feature, capable of taking a 50mp JPEG, or an 80 MP RAW file, with its 20 MP sensor. By 2022, the OM-1 will be able to do this, hand held.

---

**2015:** In October, Canon deliver their new HD video camera for low-light shooting. Capable of filming in just 0.00005 Lux, it has the equivalent of four million ISO—but at a cost of roughly $15,000. It is intended for industrial use, and while not practical for photographers or videographers, it shows the changing limits of technology.

**2015:** Epson deliver the first 4.4 megadot electronic viewfinder module in the limited-production Leica SL. They announce full production (meaning it will appear in coming mFT and other mirrorless cameras, probably in 2016 or 2017) in December. By 2022, resolutions will increase to 5.76 megadots in the OM-Systems OM-1, among others.

---

**TRIVIA**

"Megadot" and "megapixel" are the same thing. But makers use "megadot" to describe electronic viewfinder (EVF) and rear camera panels, so as not to confuse the general public with the megapixels used to describe sensors.

---

**2015:** Nikon announces their new 300mm *f*4 Nikkor; weighing just 1.66 pounds, it is the world's lightest 300mm full frame prime autofocus lens to date. It employs their "Phase Fresnel" technology, which, like Canon's "Diffractive Optics," is based on the Fresnel lens originally developed by French physicist Augustin-Jean Fresnel for lighthouses (see **1822**). The principal downside of the technology is that it can cause colourful ring-shaped flares when strong light sources are inside or just outside a frame.

**2015:** Absent since 1978, Kowa return to the consumer camera market, producing three lenses for the micro-FourThirds (mFT) cameras: an 8.5mm *f* 2.8, a 12mm *f* 1.8, and a 25mm *f* 1.8—all under the Prominar name. Unusually, they are offered in black, silver, and green finishes.

### ODDITIES

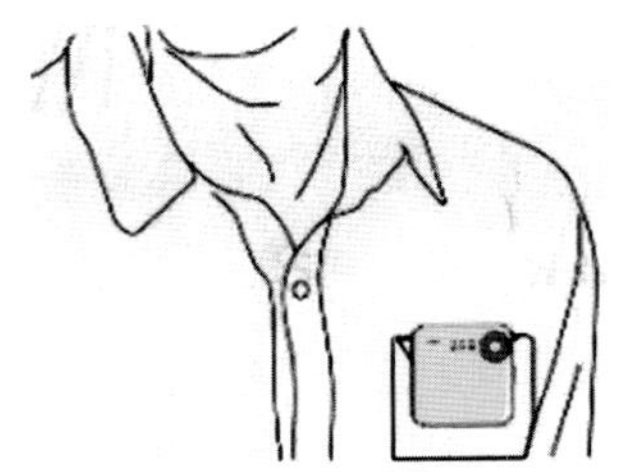

ION's SnapCam was a tiny (1.6 x 1.6 x 0.5), 1 oz. (30 g) camera that was intended to be worn, held on your clothing by a clip or magnet. You simply tapped it to take a photo. With no view-finder the problems began with that tap, which often moved the camera away from where you thought it was aimed and/or gave blurry images. Picture quality, from the 8 MP camera was acceptable, if not great. A wi-fi connection was needed, to com-municate with an Android-only App to control the camera. However, while the company is still with us, it seems the app is not. When it was available, one reviewer gave the SnapCam one star out of five, noting that it "doesn't work." Originally $149, in late 2023, it can be found new, in factory sealed packaging, on various auction sites for under $10. Caveat Emptor.

**2015:** In November, Lytro confirms they will no longer make "classic" cameras. In a complete change of direction, they will focus on their new "Immerge," a light-field camera and special server, aimed at the cinematographer who wishes to combine light-field photography with CGI (Computer Generated Images) footage for both the cinema and "virtual reality" markets. But, after burning through some $200 million in funding, Lytro will close its doors in March of 2018.

**2015:** Introduced in 1981, the plastic low-cost 120 roll-film Holga camera is no more. Like the Lomo, the Holga had gained a cult following for its unusually soft ren-derings, vignetting images, and "creative" light leaks. However, the tooling is worn out and sales do not warrant replacing it. All tools and dies are discarded and the Holga fades into history.

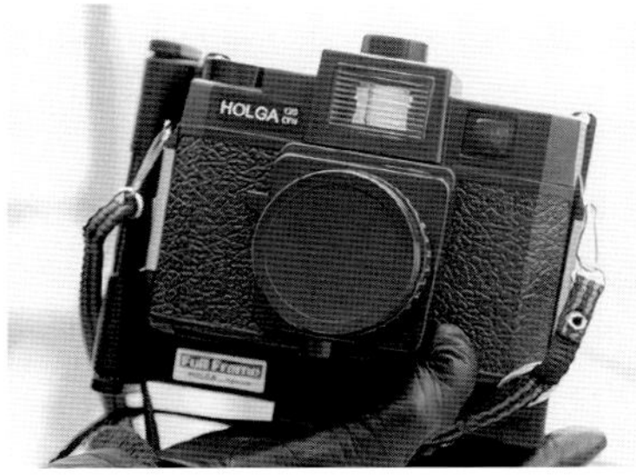

### JUST PLAIN WEIRD . . .

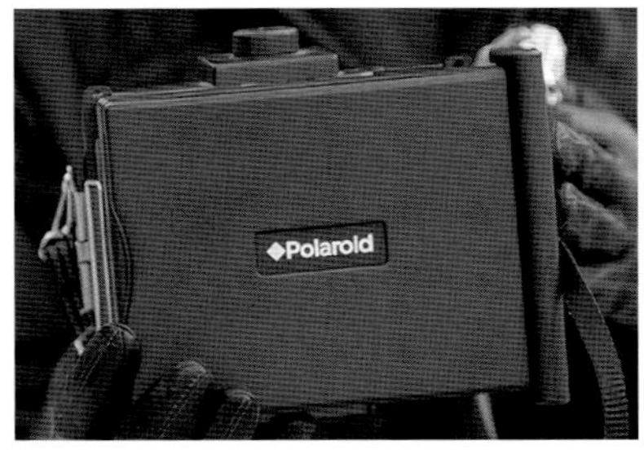

The Holga, shown above and to the right, was most unusual in that it had been modified to use a Polaroid back and is probably the only one like it, anywhere. It was photographed in 2007, by your scribe, on an Alberta ski slope—which explains the gloves on the owner's hands.

**2016:** Switzerland's Alpa and Phase One (Denmark) introduce their A-Series IQ3, the first medium-format camera equipped with a 100 megapixel sensor. It seems the megapixel race is not yet over!

**2016:** Looking much like Polaroid 2.0, the Impossible Project (see **2008**) introduce the first camera in 20 years to take Polaroid Film Packs. The I-1 works like the classic Polaroids of yore, but with an app for your phone which uses blue-tooth communications to give the camera full manual controls.

**2016:** Citing falling sales, FujiFilm discontinue production of its FP100C, the last peel-apart film it (or anyone) makes for the original Polaroid cameras of the 1960s and 1970s.

---

### ODDITIES

In 2015, a start-up company, Light, made a splash by announcing a pocketable point-and-shoot camera called the L16. It looked like a smart phone but housed 16 separate cameras that computationally created high-quality, 52 megapixel photos from 16 small low-resolution sensors. The idea was good, but the execution poor. Finally released in 2017, the $2,000 Light L16 delivered too little, too late, for too much money. One reviewer simply said: *"Brilliant . . . and braindead".*

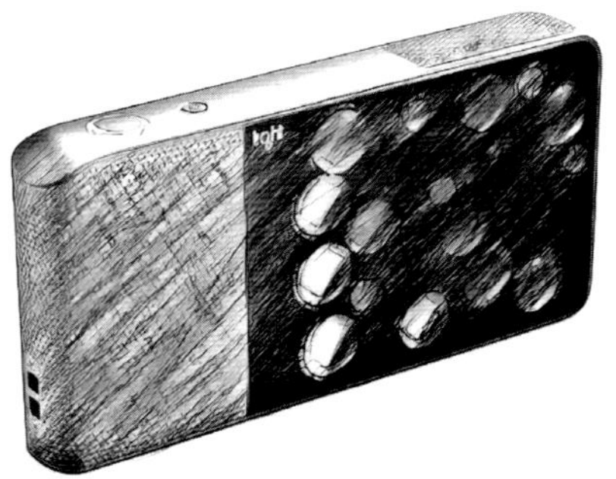

In 2020, Light abandoned the consumer market to focus on autonomous vehicle vision. Despite having raised a staggering $185.7 million in venture funding, the company closed its doors in May of 2022, when tractor maker John Deere acquired parts of the firm and some of its staff.

In late 2023, Light's L16s were still being offered as "new, old stock", still factory sealed, on various online platforms, for as little as $180.

---

**2016:** Guy Gerard, a chemical engineer at Guilleminot (see **1858**) for 30 years, starts Bergger, becoming a successful boutique maker in the high-silver-halide content photo-film market, offering black-and-white films, papers, and photo-chemicals.

---

### TRIVIA

Claimed by some to be "the best film company that you have never heard of," Bergger is one of the very few independent film makers actively developing new films, in-house. Their Pancro400 receives rave reviews when it is introduced at Photokina in 2016.

---

**2016:** In February, the Russian state corporation Rostec (which develops, builds, and exports high-tech products in both the defence and civilian sectors), announces that it will bring the Zenit (Зенит) camera brand back to life. Last made in 2005 as a basic low cost SLR for the masses, they say that the new Zenit cameras will be of much higher quality, made in limited quantities, and will compete at the top-end of the market.

---

### TRIVIA

The first new Zenit products to see the light of day are not cameras, but three very fast lenses: the Zenitar 50mm *f* 0.95, 50mm *f* 1.2, and 85mm *f* 1.2. All fit the Leica M mount, but other mounts soon become available. Despite Rostec's assertion that they will compete in the luxury end of the market, prices are rumoured to be no more than $600 each.

In May of 2022, the American distributor for Zenit lenses, Zenit-U.S., will write on their website: "The Russian invasion of Ukraine is distressing. We do not support this war and attack on democracy itself. We can no longer do business with Russia."

---

**2016:** In June, Hasselblad (the market leader in medium-format cameras) stuns the photographic world by announcing their X1D, a Swedish-made mirrorless medium-format 50-megapixel camera that is smaller than many dSLRs. But what really stirs things up is the price: it is less than one-third the price of previous Hasselblad digital bodies and significantly lower priced than almost all its competition. By September, the company receives orders for more X1D cameras than they expect to sell in their first year—which leads to somewhat delayed deliveries as they sort out how to ramp up production.

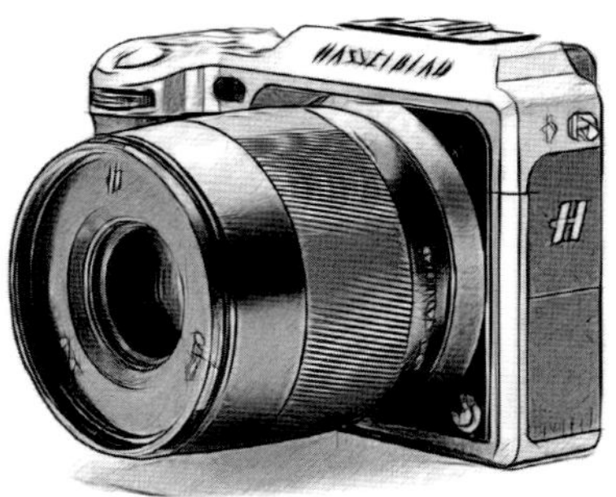

**2016:** In 2016, Chinese drone maker DJI takes a minority stake in Hasselblad and in early 2017 will purchase a controlling interest.

---

### BUSINESS TRIVIA

Whether Hasselblad like to admit it or not, their strategy of focusing only on ultra-high-end cameras hasn't exactly paid off. The company has floundered in the digital era and ownership has changed, multiple times. Now they have a formidable parent company in DJI that is a powerhouse both in China and the United States. Hasselblad gains solid financial backing, while DJI gain both design skills and the respected brand that they've been lacking on their drone cameras.

---

**2017:** Korean budget lens-maker Samyang move up-market again (see **2008**), adding their first auto-focus lenses, a 35mm *f* 2.8 and a 35mm *f* 1.4, for various mirrorless cameras.

**2017:** In January, the inventor/builder of the Rapidwinders (see **1987**) for film-era Leica cameras, Tom Abrahamsson, dies after a long struggle with cancer. Abrahamsson was an internationally respected authority on the cameras and lenses of Leica, Nikon, and Cosina/Voigtländer (see the dedication at the front of this book).

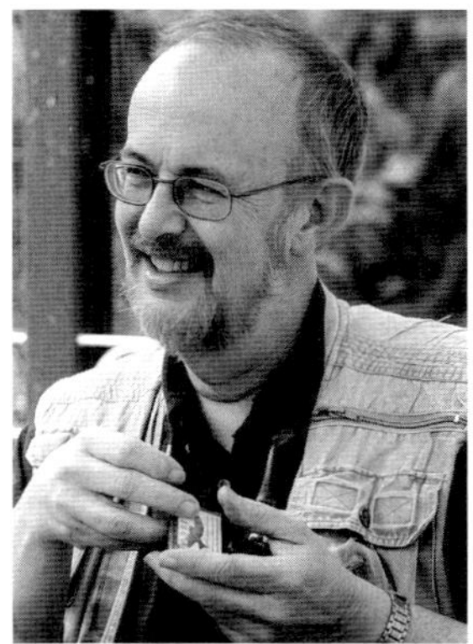

---

### TRIVIA

Abrahamsson once told your scribe: "All my Rapidwinders have a lifetime warranty. My lifetime."

---

**2017:** A resurgence in the popularity of analog photography creates a demand for new and old film products alike. At the January Consumer Electronics Show (CES), Kodak announce they will make Ektachrome and Professional Ektachrome available once again in both Super-8 and 35mm formats (for both still and motion picture use). After being discontinued in 2012, the film will again be manufactured in Rochester. Though availability is promised for the fourth quarter of 2017, Ektachrome in 35mm finally becomes available in October of 2019, with the 16mm versions offered later in the year.

Late in the year, Kodak announce they will use "all new equipment" to make the film, bringing costs down for smaller manufacturing runs. Continuing to produce the film in large production runs had been cost-prohibitive, which is why it was discontinued. Now, Kodak are behaving like the many small, but successful, boutique film producers.

---

### RUMOURS

Kodachrome, beloved for its fine grain and vibrant colours, met its demise back in 2009. However, at the CES, Kodak drop hints that if the return of Ektachrome is a success, then Kodachrome may follow, though the time to ramp up production will be longer than for Ektachrome. As of publication, Kodachrome is still waiting in the wings.

---

**2017:** In July, Nikon (or Cosina, who make the camera for Nikon) finally discontinue the Nikon FM-10, leaving the Nikon F6 and the Leica M7 the only film cameras in series (albeit limited) production.

**2017:** In May of 2017, the Impossible Project's largest shareholder acquires the brand and intellectual property of the original Polaroid Corporation. The Impossible Project is renamed "Polaroid Originals" on 13 September, the 80th anniversary of Edwin Land's original Polaroid company, and the Polaroid brand is, once again, used on the film. The name will be simplified to "Polaroid" in 2020.

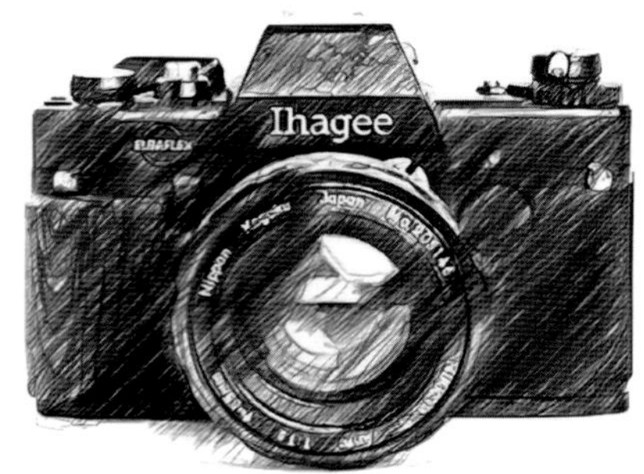

**2017:** A new firm, called Ihagee GmbH, is formed in Dresden, Germany, and designs a new Elbaflex. (The Exakta name is owned by another firm.) It is a fully manual meter-less 35mm film camera in the Exakta spirit, but accepts Nikkor lenses, probably because the lenses are good and the patent on the lens mount has expired. The universal M42 (Pentax/Praktica) thread mount is offered as an option. A Kickstarter campaign garners just 60% of the required funds. At the time of writing, the future of the camera is uncertain (see **1969** for details of the original Elbaflex).

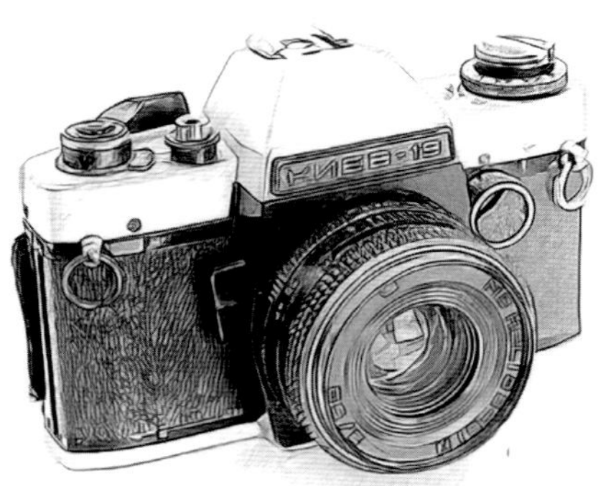

### TRIVIA

This new Elbaflex was to be made in the Arsenal factory in Kyiv. The company planned to save money by basing the Elbaflex on the Kiev 19M SLR (at right), made during the 1970s, but with an all-new shutter and mirror that are claimed to be smoother, quieter, and much more reliable. However, shutter speeds are 1/2 second to just 1/500 of a second, and the Elbaflex website makes no mention of any form of built-in exposure meter. Your writer suspects that the fund-raising campaign failed, because used Japanese-made cameras, with better specifications and in top condition, are readily available on the used market for considerably less than the $300 to $500 Kickstarter price for the Elbaflex. The camera is never heard from again.

**2017:** *Popular Photography*, America's largest photo-enthusiast magazine, ends an 80-year run (see **1937**) due to the drop in advertising caused by the shift from mail-order to online purchasing and the general decline of the consumer camera market. The March/April 2017 issue is its last. The magazine will be revived in 2021 as an online only publication but will shutter its doors once again, in late 2023.

### TRIVIA

Around 2002, the magazine had changed its name to *Popular Photography and Imaging*, reflecting the changes as digital cameras changed photography forever. Within five years it had become clear that photography had gone digital, so the title was, once again, just *Popular Photography*.

**2017:** In June, Micron Technologies announce they will leave the memory-card market due to a lack of profitability. This signals the end of their Lexar brand.

---

### TRIVIA

In 2018, Longsys (China) will buy the Lexar trademark from Micron and re-introduce the name. Longsys is a maker of flash memory products, from SD cards to solid-state computer drives, and will use the Lexar brand to sell Lexar's traditional devices: memory cards and USB flash drives.

---

**2017:** A successful Kickstarter campaign promises to create a new analog camera—"the first new 35mm film SLR design in 25 years." The Reflex-1 camera features TTL metering (ISO: 25–6400), daylight changeable film backs ("so you can swap films mid-roll, without losing a shot") and interchangeable lens mounts for M42, Nikon F, Canon FD, Olympus OM, and Pentax K lenses (so you can mount glass from various makers without needing adapters); there is, however, no exposure automation. It also features an LED modelling light and an electronic flash. First deliveries are promised for the summer of 2018, but as of October of the year, their Kickstarter page is still saying "soon."

---

### UPDATE

It seems that the Reflex team quickly ran into problems, including the need to design their own shutter rather than buy one "off the shelf," as originally planned. It is a costly endeavour. In July 2020, they admit "that if we don't start making revenue before the end of the year, we won't make it." In October 2020, they admit negotiations with a potential financial backer have failed. By November, the money is gone, and the project is dead. Those who backed the project lost their money.

---

### UPDATE

In April of 2017, Film Ferrania (see **2013**) start shipping Ferrania P30, an 80 ISO panchromatic black-and-white film which, like ADOX, has a high silver content. Production is just 1,000 rolls per week, while demand is said to be 10 times that. By August of the year, production rises to 3,000 rolls per week. In 2023, they announce that their supply and production problems are behind them and all 35mm film is now made and packaged fully in-house. They also announce a new orthochromatic film, Orto, with an ISO rating of 50. Production of the colour reversal film promised back in in 2013, however, still seems a very long way off.

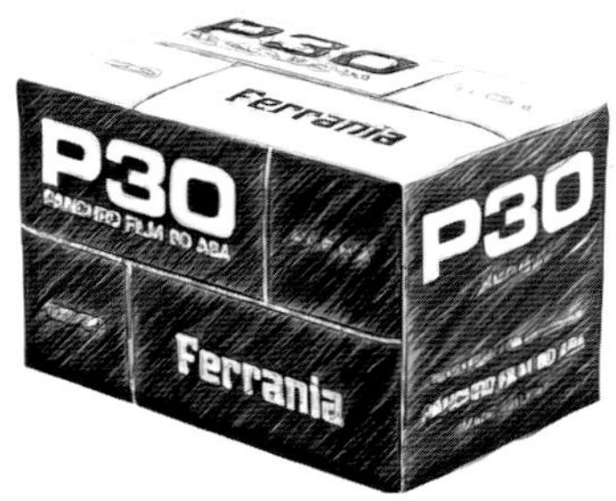

**2018:** Hasselblad improve on their multi-shot technology (see **2014**) by offering a new back that has an effective resolution of 400MP by means of a six-shot image capture. It still works only in a studio while the camera is tethered to a computer and requires a completely stationary subject. The image is saved as a 2.3GB 16-bit TIFF (23,200 x 17,400 pixels) and the price is just shy of $48,000. For those who want one but don't have the coin, Hasselblad plans to rent the camera for roughly $400 per day.

**THOUGHT BUBBLE**

Your scribe has had 27-foot-wide billboards made from his 10-megapixel images. Given that the reproduction limit of a good quality magazine page is typically around 70mb, just where you would use a 400mb image to its fullest advantage is unclear.

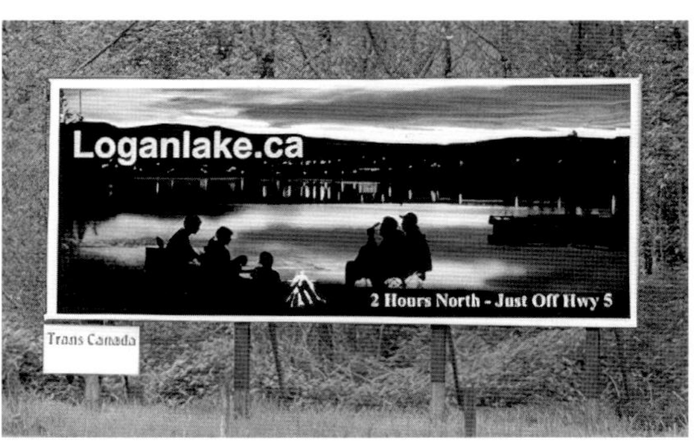


**2018:** In September, Nikon, Canon, and Panasonic all announce full-frame mirrorless cameras to compete with the Sony models. They are all successful and serve to accelerate the mirrorless revolution.

**2018:** Famed photojournalist David Douglas Duncan dies at 102 years of age.

**2018:** Wet plate collodion photographer Ian Ruhter, with the help of a few friends, installs a lens into a board placed over a window of an abandoned building in a forgotten town called Bombay Beach, located on the edge of California's Salton Sea. They turn the room into a giant camera obscura and, using a 200-pound (roughly 91kg) glass plate, create the world's largest wet-plate collodion photograph, an ambrotype, measuring 66 x 90 inches, or 1.68 x 2.29 metres.

**2018:** In October, Tetenal Europe GmbH, one of the world's largest photographic chemical manufacturers (see **1847**), files for creditor protection. Tetenal is a major maker of chemicals for Ilford and Kodak, as well as the manufacturer of most Epson printer inks for the European market. The search for a buyer is unsuccessful and the following January, courts declare the firm insolvent after 173 years.

**2018:** Kodak announce their own crypto currency, the KodakCoin. It shows a crypto "mining" computer (made by someone else). There is a lot of hype around crypto currencies, and investors latch on to Kodak's plan, but in the end the plan goes nowhere.

**2018:** In October, Net SE-Globell Deutschland (Koblenz, Germany), who were founded in 2014 to sell lenses under the old Meyer Optik Görlitz, C.P. Goerz, and Oprema Jena brands, go bankrupt and close their doors, stranding many customers who have paid for lenses through crowd-funding sites, without product or refunds.

**UPDATE**

In December, OPC Optical Precision Components Europe GmbH, based in Bad Kreuznach, acquire the trademark rights to Meyer Optik Görlitz, but not the Net SE company behind it all. A specialist firm in both spherical and aspherical industrial lenses, OPS see the Meyer Optik brand as an entry to the consumer market but promise to use only classic retail distribution—not the crowd-funding and pre-sales that got Net SE-Globell Deutschland into such trouble.

**2018:** In December, a new firm, Pixii SAS, starts shipping its first digital rangefinder camera, made in Besançon, France. The camera is designed without a rear screen in order to reproduce the film-shooting experience; however, the user can review the photos on a smart-phone app. The camera has no memory card slots—instead, you get eight or 32 GB of internal storage and the ability to share data with smart-phones. Photos are transferred from internal memory to a computer or "thumb-drive," and the battery is charged, all by means of a USB cable. It is the first consumer camera to feature a silent, global shutter and a 12 megapixel, APS-C sized CMOS sensor designed in Belgium.

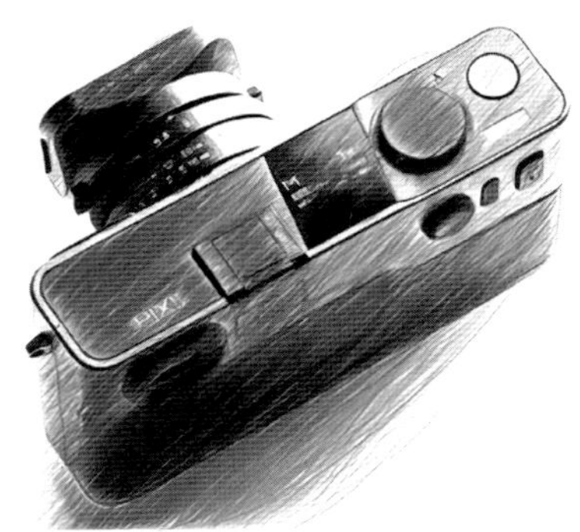

Pixii SAS offers no lenses, but its camera uses the Leica M mount, meaning lenses from Zeiss, Leica, Voigtländer, and others are all compatible. Only time will tell if it will be successful in the marketplace.

**UPDATE**

By late 2022, Pixii had updated its cameras several times, first with a new, 26mp, BSI sensor, and then the world's first 64-bit processor in a camera. However, these models do not have a global shutter. Older versions can be upgraded by the factory. They appear to be doing very well indeed.

**2018:** CIPA (the Camera & Imaging Products Association) reports that camera production of all types drops from 121 million units in 2010 to a mere 19 million in 2018—an 84% decline. In 2018, for the first time, more dSLR and mirrorless cameras are made than point-and-shoot cameras—an indication of just how far telephones have come in replacing inexpensive cameras for the bulk of the world's population. (By 2022, worldwide camera production will drop to 8.3 million units.)

**2019:** After five years of work, Ball Aerospace (Boulder, Colorado) and Arizona Optical Systems (Tucson) complete the world's largest high-performance lens. Destined for the Vera C. Rubin Observatory in Chile, the lens is 1.55 metres (5.1 feet) in diameter. When combined with its smaller companion lens that is only 1.9 metres (3.9 feet) across and paired with the world's first 3,200 megapixel sensor (see 2020), they will create the world's largest digital camera.

**2019:** Erwin Puts, a Dutch writer with a worldwide reputation for expertise on all matters concerning Leica cameras and lenses, has a public falling out with the firm that shakes the photographic world. Believing that the soul of Leica is gone, Puts loses interest in covering the company's products, writing: "The company has sketched a future and follows a path that I am no longer willing to go." He will die in 2021.

**2019:** Some 45 former Tetenal employees form Tetenal 1847 GmbH, in February of 2019, purchase Tetenal from its administrators. Tetenal is back in business by April of the year and quickly develops tablet forms of the famous Neofin Blue developer and other chemicals. This extends product shelf-life and lowers shipping costs, helping return the firm to profitability (See **2018**).

**2019:** Though promised when SDXC cards were first introduced in 2009, and shown first by SanDisk (see **2016**), Lexar finally introduce the first one-terabyte (1-TB) SD card.

**THOUGHT BUBBLE**

Your scribe wonders about the wisdom of the 1-TB card. Yes, it's convenient, but sadly, SD (and all memory) cards can fail. Thus, the common wisdom is to have more cards of lower capacity, so that should a card fail, you will lose fewer of your precious photos. The 1-TB card probably makes more sense for those recording 4k or 8k video.

**2019:** After OPC Optical Precision Components Europe GmbH acquire the Meyer Optik brand (see **2018**), they announce on their website (translated from the German): "We became aware that internally the Somnium was actually a modified Russian lens and the Nocturnus was a modified Chinese lens. That is an absolute no go. As a German manufacturer using the 'Made in Germany' quality seal, this is a shameful indictment. These lenses may be perfectly good in their own right, but their production methods and marketing go against all our principles . . . with us, nothing of this nature will occur. At the same time, we are not ruling out launching lenses with similar characteristics in the future. But if we did decide to do so, they would, of course, be our own designs and produced by us, in order to genuinely earn the 'Made in Germany' label." The decision is made to drop the Somnium and Nocturnus lines, at least for the time being (see **2014**).

---

**UPDATE**

In February of 2020, OPC Optics' Managing Director Timo Heinze reveals that the company will have six lenses on display at the 2020 edition of Photokina: the Trioplan 100, Trioplan 50, Trioplan 35, Primoplan 75, Primoplan 58, and the Lydith 30—all 100% German made, with availability promised by the time Photokina opens in late May. Despite the cancellation of Photokina, the new owners of Meyer Optic release their Meyer Optik Trioplan 100mm *f* 2.8 II and Trioplan 50mm *f* 2.8 for various reflex cameras. The lenses are in stock, in stores, by April 2020, with three more lenses promised by summer. Production is entirely in-house, in Bad Kreuznach, with other components coming entirely from German partner companies, so the "Made in Germany" label is true, once again. In the fall of 2021, OPC Optics will open a new dedicated lens manufacturing facility in Hamburg.

---

**2019:** Though the number of units is smaller, the value of mirrorless cameras surpasses that of SLRs for the first time.

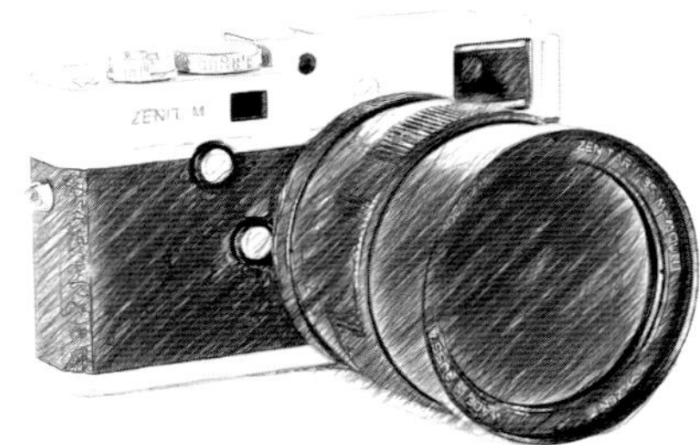

**2019:** In December, Zenit announce their long-promised "luxury" rangefinder camera (see **2016**). Called the Zenit-M, it turns out to be a version of Leica's Type 240 (made in Germany, by Leica), without the 6-bit lens code reader and with Russian-coded firmware. Thus, the only lens profiles built into this camera are for three Zenit-made lenses: the 35mm *f* 1.0 "kit" lens, a 50mm *f* 1.0, and a 21mm *f* 2.8. Only 500 cameras are to be made and the price is on par with a "real" Leica but includes a Russian-built 35mm *f* 1.0 Zenitar lens. By late 2021, its website will list the Zenit-M as "sold out." Several new Russian-made lenses are introduced at the same time, all under the Zenitar brand.

---

**TRIVIA**

The extent to which Zenit has altered the Leica is debatable. Zenit says the camera was "designed in Russia" and is only "assembled in Wetzlar," while the 35mm *f* 1.0 Zenitar lens that comes with it is designed and assembled in Russia.

As one wag said, "I'm tempted, but I need to save my money for the inevitable Ferrari/Trabant collaboration."

---

**2020:** In April, the 2020 edition of Photokina, the world's largest photographic exhibition, is cancelled, due to the Covid-19 pandemic. Most major photo exhibitions and shows follow suit, with many moving their 2021 editions to online-only events. The next Photokina is expected in May of 2022, but in November of 2020, Koelnmesse (the owners of the fair) announce that Photokina is to be suspended "until further notice." At the end of 2023, this has not changed.

**2020:** Having been involved in KPP's retiree payments since the beginning (see **2013**) the U.K.'s Pension Protection Fund buys Kodak Alaris. In 2023, after losing money in 2021 and 2022, they will put it up for sale in 2023. No word of the asking price or when a sale might take place.

**2020:** Using a large-format photo printer placed at the highest point on the ski jump in Oberstdorf, Germany, Canon produce the world's longest photograph, at 357.7 feet or 109.4 metres. Printed on a roll of special weatherproof paper provided by Ilford and helped along by the force of the printer and gravity, the photo simply slid down the ramp as it was printed.

**2020:** Scientists at the U.S. Department of Energy's SLAC National Accelerator Laboratory (Menlo Park, California) capture their first test images with a 3,200 megapixel digital composite sensor, which is comprised of 189 16MP CCD individual sensors in a perfectly flat 0.6 metre (~2 foot) diameter array. When combined with two of the world's largest precision lenses (see **2019**) and cooled to -100C (-148F), it will become the core of the world's largest camera, to be installed in the LSST telescope at the Vera C. Rubin Observatory in the Andean foothills of Chile. As designed, it will be capable of spotting objects 100 million times dimmer than can be seen with the naked eye or, on a different scale, detecting objects the size of a golf ball at a distance of 24 kilometres.

---

**TRIVIA**

Using a pinhole camera (no lens) to test the sensor arrray, scientists photograph a head of broccoli (chosen for its highly detailed surface texture).

---

**2020:** "The times they are A-changin'." (Bob Dylan) This year marks the first time that more mirrorless, interchangeable lens cameras (MILCs) are shipped than dSLRs. More importantly, while the value of MILCs shipped surpassed that of dSLRs in 2019, the gap widens further in 2020.

**2020:** After 84 years, Olympus, once one of the world's oldest camera brands, sell their camera division to Japan Industrial Partners (JIP). JIP forms a subsidiary called OM Digital Solutions Corporation (OMDS), which takes over production of cameras and lenses, now under the OM Systems brand. OMDS keep the Zuiko, OM-D, and Pen brands and license the Olympus name for their first camera, the OM-1, which will be released in 2022.

It is hard to tell if Olympus, like all camera makers, are suffering from the shrinking camera market, or if they are under-financed due to their ¥117.7 billion ($1.5 billion) investment loss and its resulting scandal (see **2011**). Or a combination of both.

**2020:** Press reports about the Metalens start appearing. It's a paper thin, flat, silicon structure with multiple waveguides—each measuring roughly 600 nanometers long (less than the length of 10 hydrogen atoms). Though it seems they may eventually find use in chip manufacturing, medicine, and even mobile phone cameras, they don't transmit light as efficiently as traditional lenses and are too small to capture large amounts of light, meaning they are not, and may never be, suitable for top-quality photography. In October of the 2023, Canon will announce they will make both Metalenses and the equipment to manufacture them.

**2020:** Kodak launch Kodak Pharmaceuticals and move towards drug-making after securing a 25-year $765 million loan from the U.S. government. The fallen giant of the photography industry is to make ultra-pure ingredients used in generic drugs to reduce the USA's dependency on foreign countries for medical supplies. However, this loan is on hold, due to accusations of insider trading by Kodak executives. What could be a lifesaver for Kodak may, or may not, come to pass.

---

### BUSINESS UPDATE

In May of 2021, the Attorney General of New York announced insider trading charges and the whole idea remains in doubt. In 2022, top Kodak officials say the company still plans to move ahead with its pharmaceutical enterprise, even if it doesn't get a government loan. As of early 2023, Kodak is still "exploring" the drug business, the loan has not been reinstated and the legal issues regarding insider trading remain unresolved.

Also in 2022, Kodak will buy a stake in Wildcat Discovery Technologies, who make batteries for electric vehicles. It turns out that rechargeable battery manufacturing requires coating technologies akin to making film. Film coating machines worth $70 million (which Kodak were trying to sell for $2 million) can be inexpensively converted to making EV battery components and, in Wildcat, Kodak have a built-in buyer. Kodak may yet again find success!

---

**2020:** Rounding out the year, Cosina introduce their Voigtländer Super-Nokton 29mm *f* 0.8 Aspherical lens designed specifically for micro-Four-Thirds (mirrorless) cameras. It is the fastest production lens ever made for still photography.

**2020:** The man the U.S. magazine *Photographer's Forum* called "Canada's Greatest Living Photographer," Ted Grant, dies, bringing a brilliant 60+ year career to a close.

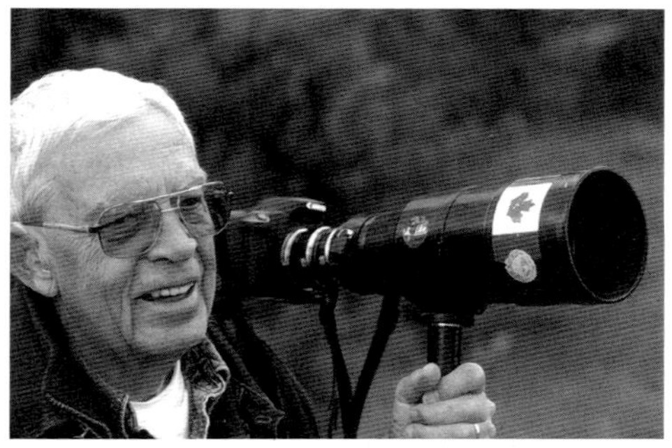

He leaves a legacy of five published books of his photographs, an hour-long TV documentary, a biography (written by Thelma Fayle—see **Further Reading**), and a collection of some 380,000 photographs, split between Canada's National Archives and Canada's National Gallery.

Grant was also a close friend and mentor to your scribe, which will explain the dedication at the beginning of this book.

# Further Reading

*For those who wish to learn more about the history of photography, many fine books are available. Below are a few I can recommend from personal experience, shown in the order of their publication.*


*L. J. M. Daguerre*, Helmut and Alison Gernsheim; Dover Publications, 1968
ISBN 10: 048622290X / ISBN 13: 9780486222905

*The History of Photography*, Helmut and Alison Gernsheim; McGraw-Hill, 1969
ISBN 10: 0500010609 / ISBN 13: 9780500010600

*A Century of Cameras*, Eaton S. Lothrop, Jr.; Morgan & Morgan, Inc., 1970
ISBN 10: 087100044X / ISBN 13: 9780871000446

*The Birth of Photography*, Brian Coe; Taplinger Publishing Co., 1976
ISBN 10: 0600562964 / ISBN 13: 9780600562962

*The Camera and its Images*, Arthur Goldsmith; Ridge Press/Newsweek Books, 1979
ISBN 10: 0882252720 / ISBN 13: 9780882252728

*History of Photography*, Peter Turner; Brompton Books, 1987
ISBN 10: 0861243129 / ISBN 13: 9780861243129

*The History of the Japanese Camera*, Gordon Lewis, Editor;
The International Museum of Photography at George Eastman House, 1991
ISBN 0-935398-16-3

*Cameras*, Prince R. De Croy Roeulx; Chronicle Books, 1993
ISBN 10: 0811814718 / ISBN 13: 9780811814713

*The History of Photography: As Seen Through the Spira Collection*,
S. F. Spira, Eaton S. Lothrop Jr., Jonathan B. Spira; Aperture Press, 2001
ISBN 10: 0893819530 / ISBN 13: 9780893819538

*Selecting and Using Classic Cameras*, Michael Levy; Amhurst Media, 2002
ISBN 10: 1584280549 / ISBN 13: 9781584280545

*Ted Grant, 60 Years of Legendary Photojournalism*; T. Fayle, Heritage House, 2014
ISBN 10: 1927527341 / ISBN 13: 9781927527344

# Glossary

*Photography is filled with acronyms and other technical terms that mean something—but only if you already know what they mean. If you don't, they can form a bewildering array of bafflegab. So, let's see if we can shed some light on the situation.*

**120:** A popular medium format film with a paper backing, originally introduced by Eastman Kodak for their Brownie No. 2 in 1901 and still widely available today.

**135:** The term "135" (meaning one roll of 35mm film) was introduced by Kodak in 1934 as a designation for the cassette for 35mm film, specifically for still photography. It quickly grew in popularity, surpassing 120 film by the late 1960s to become the most popular photographic film size. Despite competition from formats such as 110, 126, 127, 828, and APS, it remains so today. The 135 film format is defined as being a 24 by 36mm frame, eight perforations wide with a 2mm gap between images. Over the years it has been commonly produced in 12, 20, 24, 27, and 36 exposure rolls.

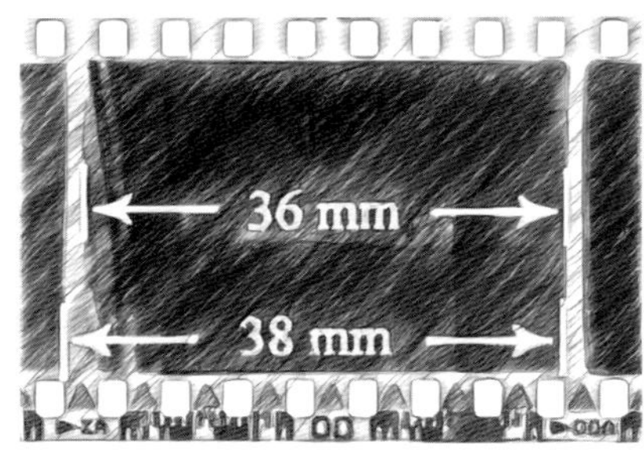


**220:** Introduced in 1965 in the same width as 120 film but with double length (144cm) and thus twice the number of exposures per roll. Unlike 120, there is no backing paper behind the film itself, just a leader and a trailer. This allows a longer film on the same spool, but as a result there are no printed frame numbers for old cameras that have a red window as frame indicator. Some cameras capable of using both 120 and 220 film will have a two-position adjustment of the pressure plate (as well as a switch elsewhere to adjust winding), while others will require different film backs.

**620:** A medium format film, identical in size, length, and backing to 120 film but on a spool with a thinner core and an end flange different from the more standard 120 film. Though long discontinued, users can transfer 120 film to a 620 spool in a dark-bag or darkroom.

**Aberrations:** In optics, aberrations are the blurring and distorting properties of an optical system. A high-quality lens will produce a smaller number of aberrations. All lens design is a compromise between numerous factors, not excluding cost. Using a smaller aperture can reduce most, but not all, aberrations. They can also be reduced dramatically by using an aspherical lens element, but these are more complex to grind than spherical or cylindrical lenses. However, with modern manufacturing techniques, the extra cost of manufacturing aspherical lenses is decreasing, and small aspherical lenses can now be made by moulding, allowing inexpensive lenses with fewer aberrations.

**Accessory Shoe:** A mounting point on the top of a camera for attaching a flash unit, rangefinder, or other accessories. It takes the form of a short, squared-off u-shaped metal bracket, with a front barrier (often just a post, as shown) to prevent the accessory from sliding in too far (see also **Hot Shoe**).

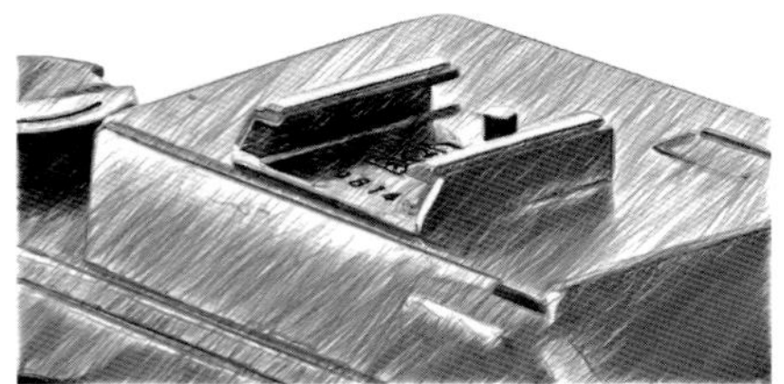

**Achromat:** A style of lens invented (or, at least, patented) in 1758, which greatly controls chromatic aberrations by using a minimum of two elements, each of glass with a different index of refraction, to bring both the red and blue rays of light into the same plane of focus. In general, an achromat consists of one negative (or concave) element made out of flint glass, which has relatively high dispersion, while the other is a positive (convex) element made of crown glass, which has lower dispersion. The lens elements are mounted next to each other, often cemented together, and shaped so that the chromatic aberration of one element is counterbalanced by that of the other.

**Additive Colour:** Colour created by mixing red, green, and blue light. This is the system used in photography, as opposed to subtractive colour, used in printing (see also **Subtractive Colour**).

**AEL (Automatic Exposure Lock):** A button on a camera you press to hold the current exposure settings until you release the shutter. Some cameras lock the exposure when you press the button, others require that you continuously hold the button to hold the exposure.

**AF:** See **Automatic Focus**.

**AF Assist:** A feature built into a camera to enable focusing in dim light, using infrared or visible LED lights to illuminate the subject.

**AF-C (Continuous Auto-focus):** Used for tracking the focus on moving subjects.

**AG:** See **GmbH**.

**Albedo:** The reflection coefficient or reflecting power of a surface.

**Albumen:** In photography, an emulsion made of egg-white and alcohol.

**Aliasing:** The effect that occurs when an optical or digital image is sampled or re-sampled at a rate which is too low for its resolution. This can produce moiré patterns in the image. Most digital cameras have anti-aliasing filters (sometimes called "low pass" filters) to reduce aliasing by intentionally blurring the image to match the sampling rate. The image is then re-sharpened electronically within the camera. This technique does reduce the chances of moiré patters in your images, but also reduces the amount of fine detail in the photographs (see also **Anti-Aliasing Filter** and **Moiré**).

**Ambrotype:** An image produced by backing a thin (under-exposed) wet-collodion glass plate with black cloth, paper, or similar material. Like a paper print, it is viewed by reflected light and appears as a positive. Also known as a "collodion positive" in the U.K.

**Amorphous Silicon:** The non-crystalline form of silicon used for industrial solar cells and the metering cells in some exposure meters.

**Anti-Halation:** See **Halation**.

**Aperture:** The (usually adjustable) opening through which light is admitted to a camera.

**Angle-of-View:** See **Field-of-View.**

**Anti-Aliasing Filter:** A low pass filter used in cameras to reduce or prevent moiré patterns in digital images, when a geometric (repeating) pattern in the scene interferes with the geometric pattern of the sensor. Such filters work by slightly blurring the image, which is then re-sharpened electronically. However, in this process some of the fine detail in the image is lost, depending on the strength of the AA filter used—the higher the resolution of a sensor, the less likely that moiré patterns will occur. Thus, with the ever-increasing number of pixels on sensors, more and more modern digital cameras are doing without such filters (see also **Aliasing** and **Moiré**).

**Apochromat:** A lens of superior design which brings all three primary colours of light into focus on the same plane; often abbreviated to simply **APO**.

**APS-C:** A digital sensor similar in size to the film used in Kodak's Advanced Photo System (APS) cameras—hence the name. APS cameras were multi-format, so the "C" refers to the "Classic" format, which maintained the 3:2 aspect ratio of 35mm film, but in a smaller 25.1 x 16.7mm frame. Though smaller than a 35mm frame, such sensors are still larger than the sensors in a micro-FourThirds (mFT) camera. Crop factors are typically 1.5 (most Nikon) and 1.6 (most Canon). Other so-called "APS-C" format digital cameras have crop factors varying from 1.3 to 1.7, though most are right around 1.5 (see also **Crop Factor**).

**ASA:** An acronym which stands for the **A**merican **S**tandards **A**ssociation, a body which set, among other things, standards for measuring film speed. The ASA standard for film speed or sensor sensitivity is arithmetic, where each doubling of the number indicates a doubling of the sensitivity to light. Now replaced by the ISO system.

**Aspheric Lens:** A camera lens specifically designed to correct common lens aberrations to improve optical quality. Its surface is not spherical (see also **Aspherical Lens**).

**Aspherical Lens:** A lens design with aspherically curved surfaces—that is to say, it does not follow the curve of a sphere—created to avoid the spherical aberration caused when off-axis light is focused closer to the lens than axial rays, an effect that degrades image sharpness, especially in very wide angle or wide aperture lenses. Although this concept has been understood since the 17th century, the grinding of aspheric glass surfaces was extremely difficult and prevented their use in consumer lenses until 1966, when the E. Leitz company introduced their 50mm $f$1.2 Noctilux for their Leica M-series of 35mm rangefinder cameras. The use of modern precision moulded plastic or glass aspheric lens elements has now made aspheric lenses relatively common. Often abbreviated ASPH.

**Automatic Focus:** The ability of a camera to find the focus point of a subject automatically without input from the photographer.

**Automatic White Balance (AWB):** A system in a digital camera that senses the colour of the ambient light and adjusts the imaging algorithms accordingly—an improvement over the days of film, when we had to be concerned with daylight and tungsten balanced films.

**B:** Abbreviation for "Bulb," a shutter speed setting which holds the shutter open for as long as the shutter release button is depressed. The term originates from early shutters which used an air bulb and flexible air-tight tubing to hold the shutter open if the photographer continued to squeeze the bulb (see also **Packard Shutter**).

**Barlow Lens:** A negative achromat magnifier, used with both astronomical telescope eyepieces and camera lenses, to increase magnification. Barlow lenses work by magnifying the central part of the image, so while the effective focal length is increased, resolution is decreased (see also **Teleconverters**).

**Bayonet Lens Mount:** A system of mounting a lens onto a camera. The lens has three to four tabs at its rear, which can be aligned with the lens mount using marks on the camera and the lens (typically coloured dots). Often the tabs are "keyed" by uneven spacing, or by making one tab larger, so that misalignment is impossible. After aligning the lens with the body, the lens is twisted either in a clockwise or counterclockwise direction (depending on the manufacturer) until it locks into place. Each mount is proprietary, and the mounts of competing manufacturers are almost always incompatible (see also **Breech Lock**, **K-Mount**, **M-Mount** and **Thread Mount**).

**Bellows (1):** The pleated, expandable, accordion-like component in a camera which allows the lens to move further from or closer to the film or sensor plane and thus focus the lens.

**Bellows (2):** As an accessory for a camera that accepts interchangeable lenses, a bellows allows the lens to move much further from the focal plane than would be possible with extension tubes or even the double-helicoid mount of a specialized macro-lens; this allows closer focusing and thus greater magnification.

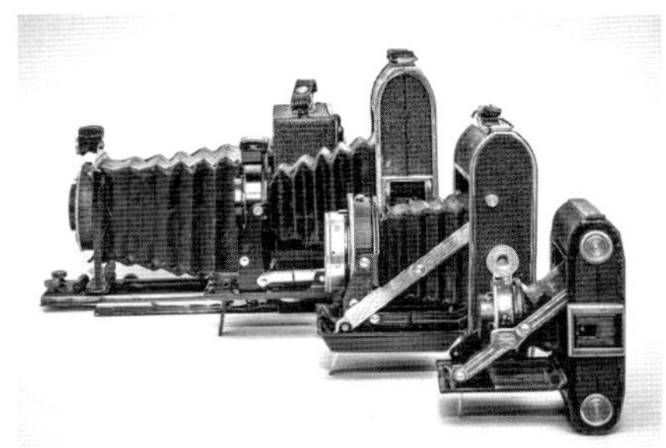
*Bellows (1)*

**Bellows Mount Lens:** A lens made without a helicoid focusing mount, intended to be permanently used with a bellows and designed for close-up (macro) photography. Most such lenses, when used on a bellows manufactured by the lens maker, will allow infinity focus while still enabling extreme close-ups to be made (see also **Focusing Helicoid**).

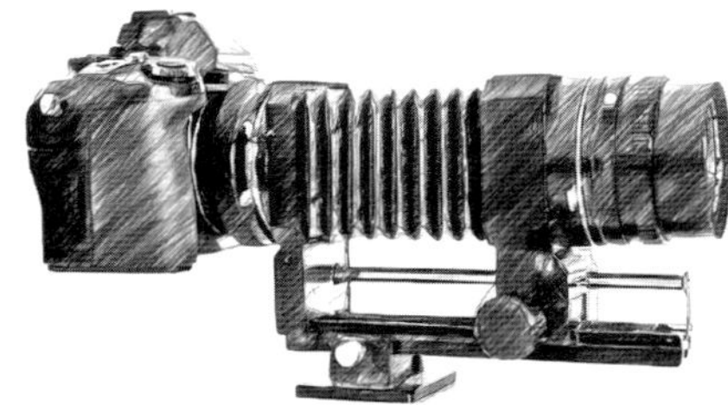
*Bellows (2)*

**Between-the-lens shutter:** See **Leaf Shutter**.

**Bit Rot:** The loss of data, over time, in record-able CDs and DVDs caused by light turning the clear bits black, as well as the memory loss in flash memory cards (CF, SD, XD cards, and also "thumb-drives") caused over time by cosmic rays.

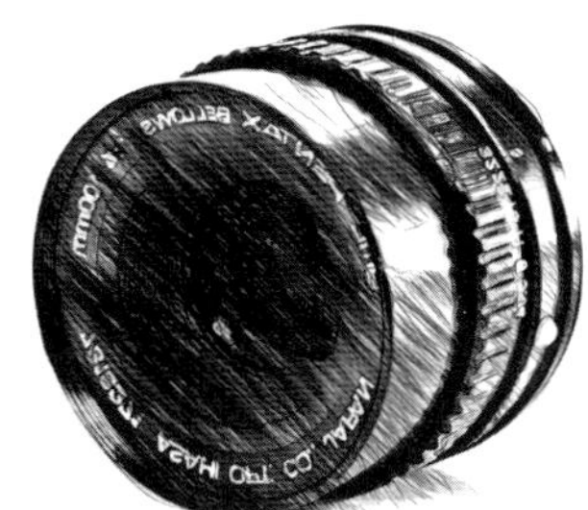

**Bitumen of Judea:** A naturally occurring tar found in large deposits around the Dead Sea area. It was used by the Egyptians to preserve mummies, by the Romans to caulk their ships, and by Niépce to make the first photograph (see also **1827**). Although it hardens in sunlight, the unhardened portion is easily dissolved with solvents and washed away.

*Bellows Mount Lens*

**Bounce Flash:** The technique of reflecting the light from a flash gun off the ceiling or walls, to soften the shadows.

**Breech Lock:** A system for mounting camera lenses to camera bodies. The lens is attached to the camera by means of a rotating collar which fits over tabs on the camera's lens mount. When the ring is rotated it tightens the lens to the camera by friction (see also **Bayonet Lens Mount** and **Thread Mount**).

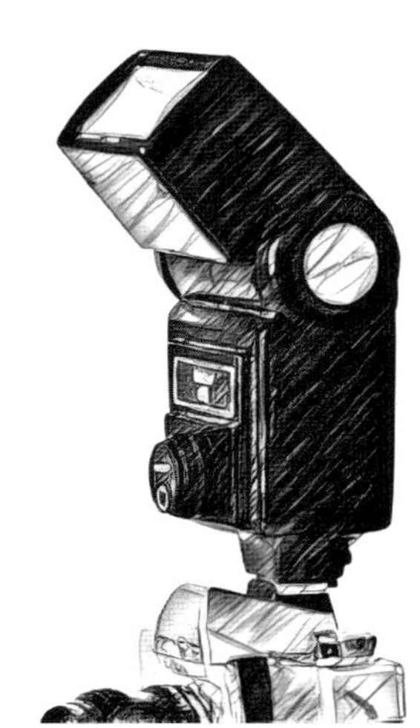

**Bridge Camera:** A type of camera that is either an dSLR or mirrorless design, with a permanently mounted (non-interchangeable) zoom lens, sometimes referred to as an "All-in-One" camera or ZLR (for **Z**oom **L**ens **R**eflex).

**Bright:** The new term for a "fast" lens (see also **Fast Lens**).

**BSI (Back Side Illuminated):** A term referring to a digital sensor from which the silicon substrate has been shaved off. In effect, this allows the sensor to be turned around and the "back side" to be used for light collection. This means that all the connection wiring is positioned behind the light-sensitive part of the pixel, rather than getting in the way. This allows more light to reach the photosites, thus delivering higher sensitivity, less noise and better all-round image quality (see also **Stacked Sensor**).

**Buffer:** All digital cameras contain a small amount of high-speed memory referred to as the"buffer." The image is written from the sensor to the buffer very quickly, so that the camera can then shoot another photo. Images are moved from the buffer to the card for storage, at a slower rate. The faster a card can accept data from the buffer (its "write speed") the more images a camera can take before it bogs down in digital transfers and can no longer take photos because the buffer is full.

**C-Mount:** A lens mount for 8 and 16mm film cameras, as well as a variety of smaller video formats including CCTV cameras. It has a nominal 1 inch (25.4mm) diameter, with 32 threads per inch (0.794mm pitch), and a flange-to-focal plane distance of 0.69 inch (17.526 millimetres).

**Cable Release:** A flexible cable that usually screws into (or, in the case of Leica or early Nikon cameras, over) the shutter release. Many modern digital cameras use an electric release, though some newer models are going back to the older flexible mechanical cable release. Either type allows the photographer to trip the shutter without actually pressing the shutter release, thus reducing vibrations. Commonly used for longer (night and macro) exposures.

**Calotype:** The Calotype or Talbotype is an early photographic process introduced in 1841 by William Henry Fox Talbot, using paper coated with silver iodide to produce a translucent negative image. The latent image was then chemically developed using a gallo-nitrate of silver solution while gently warming the paper. The image was then "fixed" using sodium thiosulphate.

**Camera Obscura:** A darkened room or box, with a pinhole opening (or a convex lens) for projecting the image of an external object onto a screen inside. This image is upside down and laterally reversed. Known since at least 300 BC, the Camera Obscura was important in the development of photography.

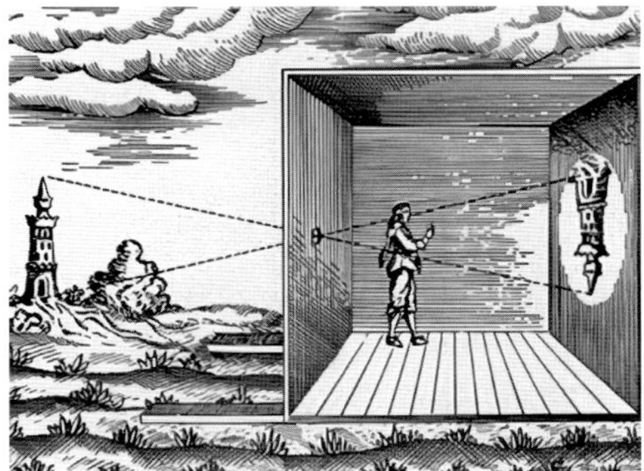

**Catadioptric:** Catadioptric (or simply "CAT") lenses use a combination of mirrors and lenses to "fold" the light path, making shorter, if somewhat fatter, lenses. They are the only practical way to make lenses of a 1000mm focal length or longer. The main drawback of the design is that it is impossible to add an adjustable diaphragm. Thus, CAT lenses are always used at their maximum (if somewhat slow) aperture. Other than the Minolta Reflex 500/8 of 1989, all CAT lenses are manual focus.

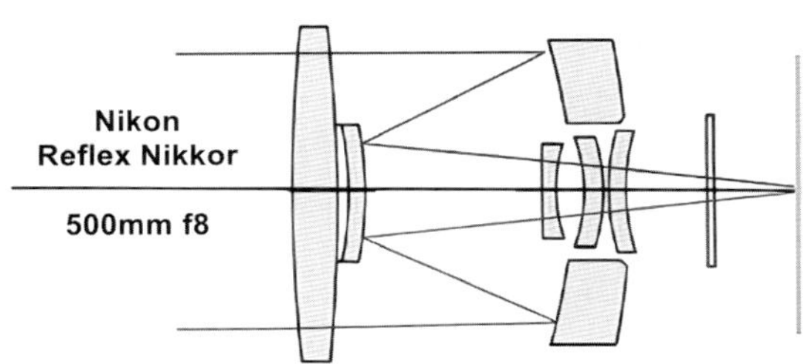


**Catchlight:** Reflected light in the eye(s) of a subject, be it bird, beast, or human, causing the eyes to seem to "sparkle." Outdoors, this can be a reflection of the sun; indoors, a reflection from a flash unit.

**CCD:** The original sensors for digital cameras, the CCD or **C**harged **C**oupled **D**evice is said to deliver the best image quality but consumes much more power than the newer CMOS sensors.

**CdS:** Unlike a selenium cell, which creates a current, cadmium sulphide (CdS) cells are resistors that vary their resistance with the amount of light that illuminates them. Using a battery to provide the power allows a CdS meter to be much more sensitive than the older selenium meter cells. However, they are a bit slower to react to widely varying lighting conditions. As well, CdS meters are sufficiently power-hungry that most cameras have some form of switch to turn off the meter circuit to conserve battery life. (In a few cases, the photographer is simply expected to cap the lens; in darkness the current flow drops to a minimum.) Still, makers quickly replaced the older selenium cells in cameras with built-in light meters, starting around 1962 with Minolta's SR-7.

**Celsius:** A scale of temperatures used world-wide except in the United States, the Bahamas, the Cayman Islands, Liberia, Palau, the Federated States of Micronesia, and the Marshall Islands. Sometimes referred to by its older name, Centigrade, and noted as °C, or just C.

**CES:** The CES (**C**onsumer **E**lectronics **S**how) is the largest electronics fair in the world and is held each January in Las Vegas. In recent years, more and more photography-related announcements have been made there, as modern digital cameras are more akin to electronics than photography, and the CES is beginning to rival some of the main photo fairs.

**CF (or Compact Flash):** An earlier memory card format, with a 16-bit data path for faster transfers to the storage device. Still used in some pro-level cameras, but slowly dying out as smaller, lighter SD memory cards become faster and faster.

**CFast:** Introduced in 2008, CFast cards are a later variant of CompactFlash. CFast (also known as CompactFast) cards are a faster card employing a newer, internal interface than the one used by the original CompactFlash cards. They were replaced, three years later, by the XQD cards (see also **XQD card**).

**CFexpress:** Announced in 2016, the CFexpress card is intended to replace the XQD card. It uses the same form-factor and interface but employs a new protocol for higher speeds and lower power consumption. By 2022, a small number of top-line cameras use these cards (see also **XQD card**).

**Chromatic Aberration:** A form of distortion caused by a lens having a different
refractive index for different wavelengths of
light, so that the three primary colours (red,
green, and blue) come into focus at different points, making it impossible for the lens
to make a truly sharp image. Blue light, for
example, will generally bend more than red

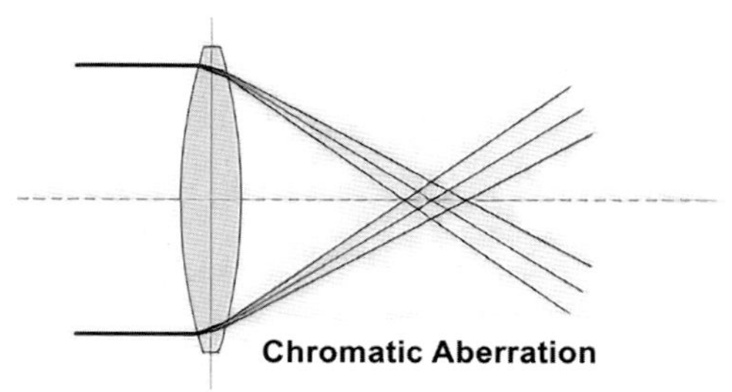


light. Chromatic aberration is compensated by using lenses made out of glasses with different refractive indexes, so two (achromat) or all three (apochromat) light beams can be brought into the same plane of focus and thus cancel out the chromatic aberrations.

**Chrome:** A common suffix in the brand names of films to indicate a colour transparency. Examples would be Kodachrome, Ektachrome, Fujichrome, Ilfochrome, etc. (see also **Colour**).

**CIPA:** The **C**amera & **I**maging **P**roducts **A**ssociation is a trade group which collects and disseminates sales statistics for the photographic industry and promotes the industry through their CP+ show, held each February in Yokahama.

**Circle of Confusion:** If you draw ever-smaller circles, eventually the circle will be so small that the human eye cannot tell the difference between the circle and a dot. That is the circle of confusion. A lens can precisely focus objects at only one distance. But, for an area before and behind the plane of focus, the error is so small that the human eye cannot tell the difference. This area is referred to as the "Depth of Field" or "Range of Focus."

**Close-up Lens:** A supplementary lens that attaches to a lens in the manner of a filter, but which modifies the close focus distance.

**CMOS:** **C**omplementary **M**etal **O**xide on **S**ilicone. CMOS sensors used to be considered inferior to CCD sensors for photographic use, but this is no longer the case. The advantages of the CMOS sensor are lower cost to produce and lower power consumption, so that batteries last longer. Also, CMOS sensors are less prone to "noise" than their CCD cousins.

**Coating:** See **Lens Coating**.

**Cold Shoe:** See **Accessory Shoe** and **Hot Shoe**.

**Collodion:** A flammable, syrupy solution of pyroxylin (also known as "nitrocellulose," "cellulose nitrate," "flash paper," and "gun cotton") in ether and alcohol. Collodion could be used as an alternative to albumen on glass photographic plates to reduce the exposure time necessary for making an image. This method became known as the "wet-plate" method. Collodion is relatively grain free and colourless, although it tends to yellow over time. It made possible one of the first high-quality duplication processes, also known as negatives.

**Color:** A common suffix in the brand names of films, used to denote colour negative films such as Kodacolor, Anscocolor, Sakuracolor, etc. (The "chrome" suffix, in contrast is used to denote colour transparency films, such as Agfachrome, Ektachrome, Orwochrome, etc. (see also **Chrome**).

**Colour:** The spectral composition of visible light—specifically, red, orange, yellow, green, blue, indigo, and violet.

**Compact Camera:** Generally, a small digital or film camera that includes automatic exposure, automatic focusing, and automatic flash (if required). Commonly called point-and-shoot or point-and-pray cameras. Generally considered below a "Bridge Camera" in capabilities and price (see also **Point-and-Shoot**).

**Contact Sheet:** A contact print of a group of negatives, used for filing and as a reference when selecting negatives to print. In modern use, a printed page of thumbnail images from a digital camera, used for filing and locating images.

**Contrast Detection:** A simpler form of auto-focus used in lower priced cameras.

**Converging Verticals:** The effect when two parallel lines in an image (such as the two sides of a building) seem to get closer (converge) as if they were leaning in towards one another at the top. The effect is readily seen when you angle your camera up when taking an image of a tall structure in an attempt to fit it all in. The more pronounced the tilt, the more pronounced the lean. It is more noticeable when using wide-angle lenses. (See also **Keystoning**.)

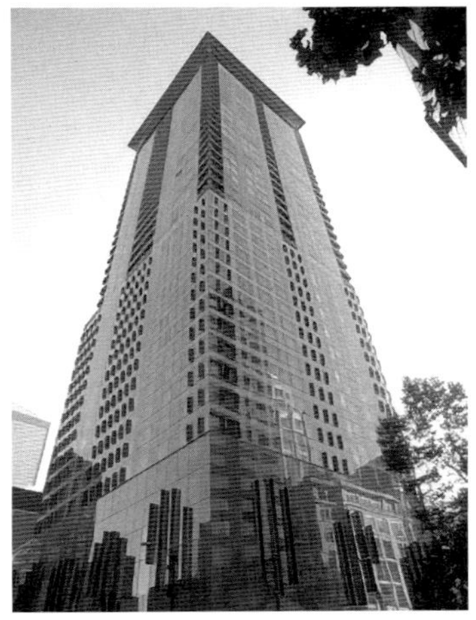

**Converter:** See **Teleconverter**.

**Copal Square:** A focal plane shutter design which runs vertically, rather than horizontally. The shorter distance allows higher effective shutter speeds without needing the mechanism to work faster. The Copal Square, its descendants, and its competitors now dominate the Japanese market for interchangeable lens cameras.

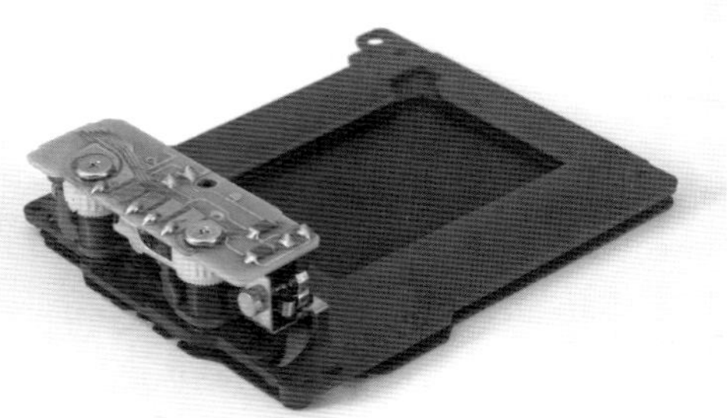

*A descendent of the Copal Square shutter. A vertical run, electronically controlled, focal-place shutter.*

**Crop Factor:** The ratio of a digital camera's sensor size compared to the size of a standard frame of 35mm film. If, for instance, a digital camera has a crop factor of 1.5, it means that because of its smaller sensor, a lens will have a field of view equivalent to a lens that has a focal length 1.5 times that of its real focal length. In other words, a 50mm lens will have the field of view equal to that of a 75mm lens, simply because the smaller sensor captures only the light from a smaller part of the image. If the crop factor were 2 times (as in an mFT camera) then the 50mm lens would have a field of view equivalent to that of a 100mm lens on a 35mm camera. In all other respects (depth of field, *f*-stop, etc.) the 50mm lens is still a 50mm lens.

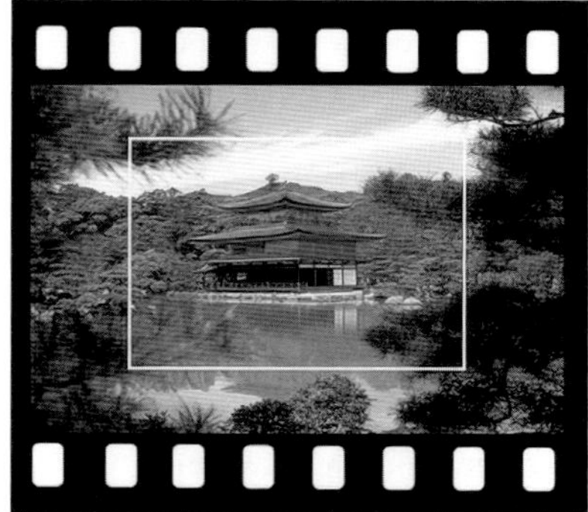

**Cyanotype:** A photographic printing process that produces a cyan-blue print. The image darkens in daylight and is "fixed" by simply washing away the unexposed emulsion with water. Never popular for photography, it becomes the basis for modern engineering blueprints.

**Daguerreotype:** The first form of practical photography. A polished silver-plated copper sheet is treated with chemicals that make its surface light-sensitive; exposed in a camera for as long as was judged to be necessary (which could be as little as a few minutes for brightly sunlit subjects or much longer with less intense lighting), the resulting latent image is made visible by exposing it to mercury vapour fumes. The image is then made permanent (fixed) by bathing it in a strong salt solution, rinsed and dried. The delicate surface is then placed behind glass in a protective enclosure.

**Dandelion Chip:** A Dandelion Chip is an electronic device glued onto the bayonet mount of a non-electronic lens or T-adapter which enables the lens to "talk" to a digital camera. The device consists of a

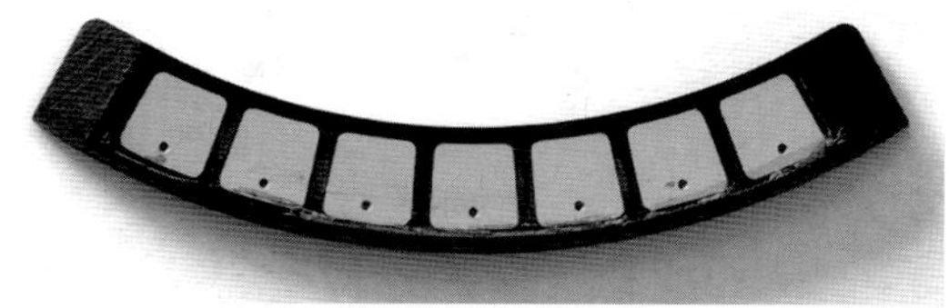

programmable integrated circuit connected to a series of exposed electrical contacts, in a curved package which matches the lens mount. It is designed to be affixed in a particular position on the mount, in order to mate with matching contacts on the camera body.

Originally developed in Russia, such chips are now available from several makers around the world. Camera functions enabled by the chip may include exposure metering, aperture display and control, focus confirmation and fine-tuning, and EXIF metadata recording (see also **EXIF**).

The chip gets its name from the French "dent de lion" (tooth of a lion) referring to the pattern of the contacts on the chip.

**Decisive Moment:** That split second where the frozen slice of time tells the entire story. Coined by the French photographer Henri Cartier-Bresson.

**Depth of Field:** A lens can precisely focus objects at only one distance. But there is an area before and behind the plane of focus where the difference between those areas in focus and those out of focus is so small the human eye cannot tell the difference. Thus, it sees everything within this range as if it were in focus. This range is not equal, but roughly one-third is before the plane of focus and two-thirds behind it (see also **Circle of Confusion**).

**Depth of Field Preview:** A lever or button on some SLR, dSLR, or mirrorless cameras which will close the diaphragm to the shooting aperture (or stop), so that the precise depth of field can be seen in the viewfinder.

**Diffraction:** The modification which light undergoes when passing through narrow openings such as small *f*-stops in lenses. The rays appear to be deflected, causing small details of your photographs to blur.

**Diffraction Grating:** An optical component that diffracts light into several beams travelling in different directions (i.e., different diffraction angles). Reflective gratings have fine ridges or rulings on the surface, while transmissive gratings have hollow slits on the surface.

**Diffraction Limit:** An optical system with resolution performance at the instrument's theoretical limit is said to be diffraction limited (see also **Diffraction**).

**Digital:** Refers to any method of storing images in a binary (zeros and ones) format.

**Digital Focus Accuracy:** Digital sensors are more demanding of a lens, as the sensor is virtually perfectly flat, whereas it is always a struggle to keep film flat. Thus, digital sensors are almost always at the "ideal" film plane. In general, if a lens works well with a digital camera, it works well on film. The reverse is not necessarily true.

**Digital ICE (or Digital Image Correction and Enhancement):** Developed around 1989, ICE uses an infrared layer to detect scratches and dust in transparent media (photographic slides) and correct them from within the scanner, so unlike the software-only solutions it does not alter any underlying details of the image.

**Digital Rot:** The rapid reduction in monetary value of a digital camera, caused by the rapid introduction of newer, better models.

**DIN:** An acronym which stands for **D**eutsches **I**nstitut für **N**ormung (in English, the German Institute for Standardization). The DIN standard for film speed or sensor sensitivity is a logarithmic scale in which each 3° indicates a doubling of the sensitivity to light. Now supplanted by the ISO system.

**Diopter:** A diopter (USA) or dioptre (U.K.) is a unit of measurement of the optical power of a lens or curved mirror. Commonly used to describe the optical power of close-up lenses.

**Diopter adjustment:** A small control on better dSLR and SLR cameras allowing adjustment of the optical system in a viewfinder so that the user's eye can focus clearly on the viewfinder image. Usually located next to the viewfinder.

**Double Exposure:** Originally, two separate exposures made upon one frame of film (a result that was usually unintended and occurred mostly in entry-level cameras that lacked double-prevention mechanisms; now possible as a deliberate technique with a limited number of digital cameras).

**dSLR:** An SLR-style camera that takes digital images rather than using film (see also **SLR**).

**Dynamic Range:** The difference between the lightest and darkest parts of a photograph. Once an image exceeds the camera's dynamic range, the highlights wash out to pure white, losing all detail, or the dark parts become black blobs, again lacking in detail.

**ED:** **E**xtra **L**ow **D**ispersion (sometimes called **LD**, for **L**ow **D**ispersion) glass made by Shott in Germany and Hoya in Japan. Such types of glass help the lens designer achieve optical excellence, though this is due more to the designer than the glass. The ED or LD designation simply mean that such glass was used in one or more of the elements.

**Effective Focal Length:** The apparent focal length of a lens when the "crop factor" of a particular camera is considered. For instance, a lens of 50mm has an effective focal length of 80mm when used on a camera with a 1.6 crop factor.

**Effective *f*-stop:** The actual *f*-stop value of the aperture in a camera's lens when the lens is used in conjunction with extension tubes, a bellows, or tele-extender.

**Electronic Flash:** A flash lamp, usually attached to a camera or housed within the camera body, that produces brilliant flashes of light by the discharge of current through (typically) a xenon-gas-filled tube. Sometimes referred to as a "Strobe" or "Speedlight" in the USA. Typical flash durations can be 1/2,000 to 1/50,000 of a second, with specialized unit generating much shorter flashes (see also **Trigger Voltage**).

**Element:** An individual lens within a more complex photographic lens. If two or more elements are cemented together with optically clear glue, they are referred to as a "group."

**Ever-Set Shutter:** A simple shutter on rudimentary film cameras in which the photographer's finger loads a spring while opening the shutter. The spring then closes the shutter. Only one speed, typically around 1/25 of a second, is available.

**eVF:** The **e**lectronic **V**iew**F**inder found in newer mirrorless cameras. Such devices are essentially tiny LED or OLED displays (similar to those used in flat screen TV sets) housed behind the viewfinder lens group. Also sometimes referred to as **EV** (see also **LED** and **OLED**).

**EXIF:** The **EX**changeable **I**mage **F**ile which holds the meta-data for your photos: shutter speed, aperture, ISO setting, date, location (if GPS-enabled), photographer's name, whether the camera was on automatic or manual control, whether the flash fired or not, and other details. Used with all digital photos, whether from cameras, video cameras, smart-phones, or scanners.

**Existing Light:** Any light there is, other than that provided artificially by the photographer.

**Expiry Date:** All undeveloped films deteriorate over time, losing contrast and colour balance. This is a gradual chemical reaction. The rate at which it takes place is a function primarily of storage conditions. Since most film is sold in retail stores which do not use refrigeration, film makers print "process before" dates on their packages, typically two or three years from the month in which the film is packaged. This "process before" date of film is many months before any deterioration is likely to be visible. Expired films can continue to give excellent images for many years, if sealed in moisture-proof containers (for example, Tupperware or zip-lock type bags) and stored in a refrigerator. Storing film, especially black-and-white film, in a freezer can extend the life of film for decades.

**Extender:** A common short form of TeleXtender (see also **Teleconverter**).

**Exposure:** Light is most easily controlled using the camera's aperture (measured in *f*-stops), but it can also be regulated by adjusting the shutter speed. The proper exposure is obtained by adjusting these two factors (and the ISO setting in a digital camera) to get an acceptable image on the film or digital sensor.

**Exposure Meter:** An instrument for measuring the intensity of light, used chiefly to show the correct exposure when taking a photograph. Typically, an exposure meter will include either a digital or an analog electronic circuit, which allows the photographer to determine which shutter speed and *f*-number should be selected for an optimum exposure, given a certain lighting situation and film or sensor speed. 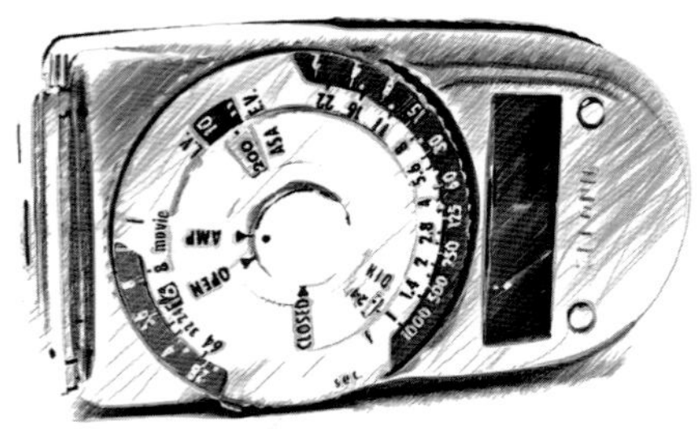 Early units used photovoltaic (selenium) cells, which generated their own power and needed no battery, while later versions used cadmium sulphide or silicon photoresistors, which do need battery power. An exposure meter can be either a hand-held unit, or a miniaturized version built into a camera.

**Extension Tubes:** A non-optical rigid set of tubes of various lengths, inserted between the lens and the camera to increase the lens-to-sensor distance, thus allowing closer focus and an increased subject size.

**F-stop:** A method of measuring a consistent amount of light admitted by an adjustable aperture, calculated by dividing the aperture into the focal length. Thus, an aperture of 25mm and a focal length of 50mm results in a ratio of 1:2, or more simply, an *f*2 lens (see also **T-Stop**).

**Faraday Cell:** See **Rapatronic Shutter**.

**Fast Lens:** A lens which gathers a lot of light. Such lenses usually have a maximum aperture of *f*2, *f*1.8 or even *f*1.4. Such lenses are called "fast" as their light gathering abilities allow the use of faster shutter speeds in a given light. Lenses with a maximum aperture of *f*1.2 or wider are usually called "ultra-fast" (see also **Bright**).

**Ferrotype:** Also known as a tintype or a melainotype, this is a photograph made by creating a direct positive on a thin sheet of metal coated with a dark lacquer or enamel and used as the support for the photographic emulsion. It is like the ambrotype but removes the need for a black backing and can be produced at a much lower cost than the ambrotype's glass plate. The term can also refer to "Ferrotype Plates," used in a darkroom, to impart the glossy surface to chemically processed prints.

**Field-of-View:** The area included in an image by a given lens, measured in degrees (°).

**Film Plane:** See **Focal Plane**.

**Film Scanner:** A specialized scanner for scanning film, both negatives and transparencies (slides) in high quality and at high resolution; now difficult units to find, at least new.

**Film Speed:** Film speed is the measure of a photographic film's sensitivity to light, determined by sensitometry and measured on various numerical scales, the most recent being the ISO system. A closely related ISO system is used to measure the sensitivity of digital imaging systems.

Relatively insensitive film, with a correspondingly lower speed index, requires more exposure to light to produce the same image density as a more sensitive film, and is thus commonly termed a "slow" film. Highly sensitive films are correspondingly termed "fast." In both digital and film photography, the reduction of exposure corresponding to use of higher sensitivities generally leads to reduced image quality (due to coarser film grain or higher levels of noise in a digital image). In short, the higher the sensitivity, the grainier (or noisier) the image will be.

**Filter:** A camera accessory that can be inserted into the optical path. The filter can be a square or oblong shape and mounted in a holder accessory or, more commonly, a glass or plastic disk in a metal or plastic ring frame, which can be screwed into the front of or clipped onto the camera lens. Filters of various types are used to remove distant haze (UV), remove reflections (polarizing), or change contrast (various coloured filters, when used with black-and-white film).

**Flange Distance:** The distance between the mounting flange (which is the outer part of the lens mount when viewed from the side) and the film/sensor (or focal) plane. Also known as the "flange focal distance," "flange back distance," or the "register" or "registration," this is the distance required for the lens to focus from its closest focusing point to infinity. Every camera system has its own flange distance and it's the flange distance that determines which lenses can be adapted to which cameras bodies.

**Flash Bulb:** Flashbulbs are expendable, high intensity light sources of brief duration. They are hermetically sealed glass bulbs filled with crumpled or shredded thin strips of metal (aluminum, zirconium, magnesium, or halfnium) in a nearly pure oxygen atmosphere. Ignited by an electric current, the strips rapidly burn, providing an intense white light. While once manufactured in many forms from the tiny AG-1 to flashcubes to bulbs the size of a 100W household light bulb, flash bulbs are now virtually obsolete, having been replaced by the electronic (strobe) flash, and have all but disappeared from stores; they are, however, still available from a few websites on the Internet.

**Flash Memory:** A form of non-volatile computer memory that does not lose its content when the power is turned off, it is used in CF and SD cards as well as so-called "thumb drives," among other storage systems (see also **Memory Card**).

**Focal Length:** The distance (usually measured in millimetres or centimetres) from the optical centre of a lens to the imaging sensor (or film) when the lens is focused at infinity. (Contrary to common belief, focal length is not a measure of how long or short a lens is physically; telephoto designs, for example, can be much shorter than their focal length, while retrofocus wide-angle designs are often much longer than their actual focal length.)

**Focal Plane:** The position at which the image is formed and at which the sensor or film is placed. It is sometimes, but not always, marked on the top of a camera and usually denoted by a circle with a line through it, as shown. Film cameras will have the mark near the rear of the camera while digital cameras have it closer to the middle of the body, as they need more space behind the sensor for the rear panel display, circuitry, and other elements.

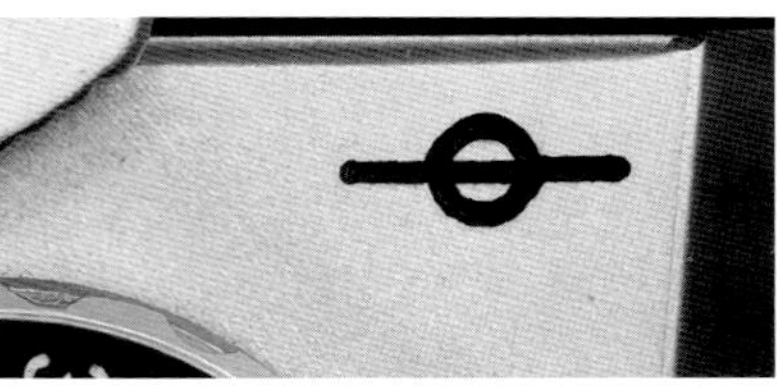

**Focal Plane Shutter:** The traditional type of focal-plane shutter in 35mm cameras, pioneered by Leitz for use in its Leica cameras, uses two shutter curtains, made of opaque rubberized fabric, that run horizontally across the film plane. For slower shutter speeds, the first curtain opens (usually) from right to left, and after the required time with the shutter open, the second curtain moves in the same direction to close the shutter. When the shutter is cocked again the shutter curtains are moved back to their starting positions, ready to be released.

For faster shutter speeds, the second curtain is released before the first one reaches the end of its travel. This forms a moving "slit" across the film or sensor, resulting in an effective shutter speeds of up to 1/1000 second. In modern cameras, focal plane shutters move vertically, to reduce the distance which needs to be travelled. Thus, they can achieve speeds of up to 1/8000 of a second.

**Focus:** The propensity for light rays to reach the same place on the image sensor or film, independent of where they pass through the lens. For clear pictures, the focus is adjusted for distance, because at a different object distance the rays reach different parts of the lens with different angles. In modern photography, focusing is often accomplished automatically.

**Focusing Helicoid:** A helicoid is the internal non-rotating threaded tube enabling the photographer to rotate the barrel of a lens to achieve focus. Most manual-focus lenses use this method of focusing. The rotating motion of the barrel is converted, using a thread, into linear movements of the lens elements, moving them nearer to, or further from, the focal plane.

Alternative systems include rack-and-pinion focusing (commonly used on TLRs and view cameras) and trombone focusing (for a few very long lenses), or simple threads which allow the front of the lens to rotate when focused (see also **Rack-and-Pinion Focusing** and **Trombone Focusing**).

**FourThirds:** The FourThirds system is a standard created by Olympus and Panasonic for both digital single-lens reflex camera (dSLR) and mirrorless cameras that makes possible the interchange of lenses and bodies from different manufacturers. The sensor is standardized at 18 x 13.5mm (22.5mm diagonal), with an imaging area of 17.3 x 13.0mm (21.63mm diagonal), making the sensor's area about 30–40% smaller than APS-C sensors used in most other dSLRs, but still around nine times larger than the 1/2.5 inch sensors typically used in compact digital cameras. This smaller sensor allows for more compact cameras and more compact lenses. This has been realized to its full potential in the micro-FourThirds (mFT) cameras that have eliminated the need for a mirror box.

Members of the FourThirds group include Olympus, Kodak, Panasonic, Zeiss, Cosina, Fuji, Schneider, Kenko/Tokina, Leica, Kowa, and Tamron, among others.

**FPS:** Frames per second—the number of photos that film cameras (especially when equipped with rapid-winders or motor-drives) or that digital cameras can take per second.

**Fresnel Lens:** A compact lens which reduces the amount of material required compared to a conventional lens by dividing the lens into a set of concentric 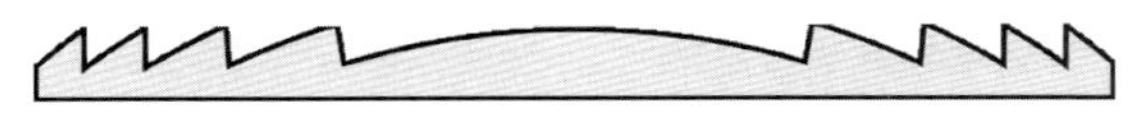 annular sections. First used in lighthouses, in photography it finds use as a light (usually plastic) condenser lens in the viewfinders of SLR and dSLR cameras. More recently, Fresnel lenses have appeared as elements in a few photographic lenses. (For more, see Wikipedia.)

**Full Frame:** A format whose sensor is essentially the same size as a frame of 35mm film (24 x 36mm); this format—which is larger than APS-C and FourThirds—is often abbreviated to **FF**.

**F-Sync:** A now-obsolete setting where the camera would fire a flash a few milliseconds earlier than M-sync, so that special Type-F flashbulbs could ignite and be at full brilliance by the time the shutter was starting its travel. Such bulbs were relatively long burning, so that they would continue to burn as the slit of a focal plane shutter travelled across the film. This allowed flash photography at higher-than-normal shutter speeds (see also **M-Sync** and **X-Sync**.).

**GB:** 1024 Megabytes (see also **MB** and **KB**).

**Global Shutter:** All the sensor's pixels are read out simultaneously. This eliminates the curved lines which can occur in rapidly rotating objects, such as airplane propellers, when the sensor is read out line by line. Global shutters are normally found only in a few, specialized cinema and astrophotography cameras. The Pixii (see **2018**), is the first consumer camera with a global sensor, but 2023 will see both the Sony Alpha 9 III and the Nikon Z9 full-frame cameras introduced with global shutters. The Nikon is also the first without a mechanical shutter (see also **Rolling Shutter**).

**GmbH:** An abbreviation of the German phrase "Gesellschaft mit beschränkter Haftung," which means "company with limited liability." It's a suffix used after a private limited company's name in Germany (versus AG—for Aktiengesellschaft—which is used to indicate a public limited company). Similar to an LLC, LLP, or Ltd. entity in the U.K. or North America.

**Grain:** All films have a "shiny" side and a "dull" side. The dull side is the emulsion, a gelatin that suspends an array of silver halide crystals. These crystals contain silver grains that determine how sensitive the film is to light exposure, and how fine or grainy the negative the print will look. Larger grains mean more sensitivity to light, allowing for a faster exposure but a grainier appearance; smaller grains are finer looking but take more exposure to activate. The graininess of film is represented by its ISO factor. Lower numbers generally indicate finer grain but slower film, and vice versa.

**Grey Card:** Grey-coloured cardboard that reflects precisely 18% of the light it receives; used to make exposure readings to represent a medium tone.

**Group:** Either a cemented pair of optical elements within a photographic lens, or a set of elements (cemented or not) which move as a group within a zoom lens.

**Halation:** The reflection of bright points of light off the film base and pressure plate, that causes a glow in the strong highlights on some images. This effect is most evident when light sources are in focus in the photograph. In modern films, this is prevented by an anti-halation backing put on the film during manufacturing.

**Half Plate:** See **Plate Sizes**.

**Half-Frame:** A format using half the standard 35mm frame to double the number of exposures in a vertical format. Thus a 24 exposure roll yields 48 shots.

**Helicoid:** See **Focusing Helicoid**.

**High Dynamic Range (HDR):** All films and digital sensors have a limit to the range they can cover from the blacks to whites. In both slide films and digital sensors, the easiest

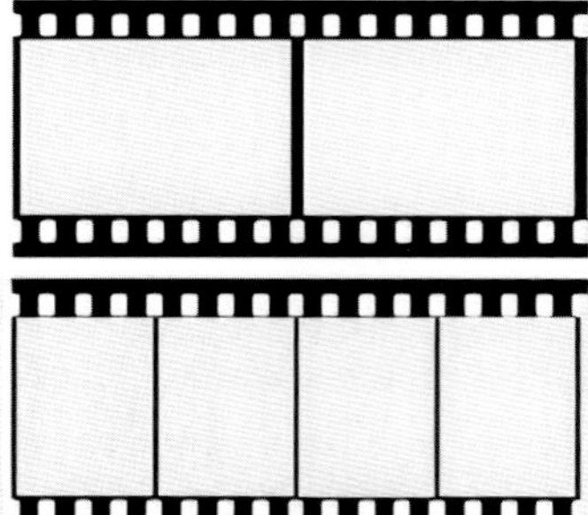

evidence of this is "blown" highlights, where the white tones lose all detail. HDR photography works by taking several images, from somewhat underexposed to somewhat overexposed, and then blending them, usually with special software that takes the best exposed bits of each to make one image with extended dynamic range. In some modern high-end cameras, the blending is done automatically.

**High Refractive Glass:** See **Index of Refraction**.

**High-Speed Camera:** A camera capable of capturing photographs at a rate in excess of 250 frames per second, although there is no "official" standard for the term; other, slower speed models like the 50fps Hulcher (see also **1953**) models are often considered high-speed cameras.

**Hot Shoe:** A development from the original "cold shoe" used to attach a rangefinder, flash, or other accessory that originated with Oskar Barnack and the original UR Leica in 1913. After the Second World War, many 35mm cameras featured a Leica-type accessory shoe that had added a single, central electrical contact (the

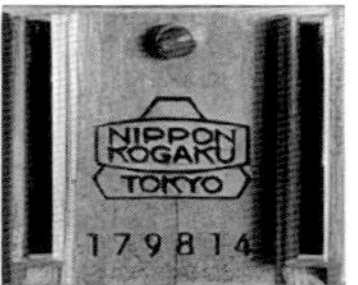 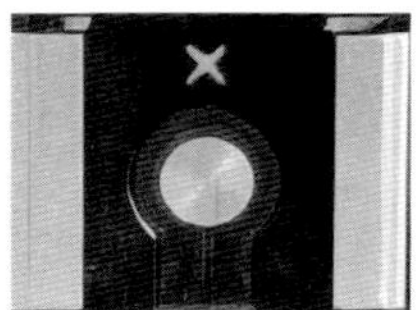 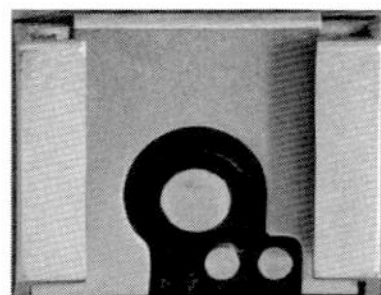

Cold shoe          ISO hot shoe          Hot shoe Canon FTb

present-day ISO hot shoe) that could synchronize a flash attachment. Sometimes the contact was switchable, but more often was simply set to X sync, for electronic flash.

However, in 1971, "dedicated" shoes for electronic flashes with automatic flash exposure control began appearing, starting with the Canon FTb. They use ISO-style shoes with extra proprietary electrical contacts. Each SLR brand uses contacts that are incompatible with other makers—a practice that continues to this day (see also **Accessory Shoe**).

**Hunting:** A term that describes the actions of a lens or camera when it fails to determine the proper focus (usually in poor light) and the lens goes back and forth as it "hunts" for the point of perfect focus, which it may or may not find.

**Hyperfocal Distance:** The point of focus at which subjects from half that distance to infinity seem in focus. Hyperfocal distance varies with the focal length of the lens and the *f*-stop. This effect is used to make "focus free" or fixed-focus cameras (see also **Circle of Confusion**).

**IBIS:** An acronym which stands for **I**n **B**ody **I**mage **S**tabilization and refers to the "sensor shift" style of image stabilization using piezoelectric gyroscopes to detect motion and then shift the sensor to compensate for it (see also **Piezoelectric Gyroscopes** and **Sensor Shift**).

**Ideal Format:** Any format that closely matches the ratio of a traditional 8 x 10, 11 x 14, or 16 x 20 print with little cropping. Typically, today, the term refers to 2¼ x 2¾ inch or 6 x 7cm images shot on 120 or 220 roll film, the 24 x 32mm format on 35mm film, or the FourThirds format in digital cameras.

**ILC:** A term becoming popular in the last few years to denote a camera that accepts interchangeable lenses . . . an **I**nterchangeable **L**ens **C**amera.

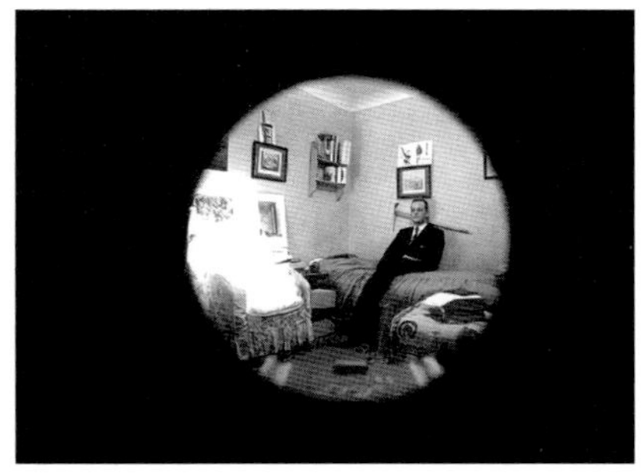

**Image Circle:** The diameter of the round image projected by a lens on a monitor or photo paper. If the image circle is smaller than the diagonal of the sensor, the image will have dark corners. If the image circle is *much* smaller than the format of the film or sensor used, we will see a round image on a black background, as seen in extreme fisheye photos, although without that distortion. To illustrate the point, the photo shown was taken with a 50mm Nikkor lens (for a 35mm camera) mounted on a Linhoff Technica camera, using 4 x 5 Polaroid film.

**Image Stabilization:** The mechanism(s) used to reduce blurring caused by the motion of a camera during exposure. Motion sensors (tiny solid-state gyroscopes) detect camera shake, and then either move one or more elements in the lens, or shift the sensor to compensate for camera movement or "shake."

It is important to note that image stabilization systems cannot prevent motion blur caused by the movement of the subject or by extreme movements of the camera. Image stabilization is capable only of reducing blur that results from the normal, minute shaking of a lens due to hand-held shooting (see also **O.I.S.**, **Piezoelectric Gyroscope**, and **Sensor Shift**).

**Index of Refraction:** A measure of how light propagates through a material. The higher the refractive index the slower the light travels, which causes a correspondingly increased change in the direction of the light. A lens that has a higher refractive index can bend the light more and allow the profile of the lens to be lower, meaning that the lens can be thinner and thus lighter (always a good thing). The index of refraction is not measured in any unit but is expressed as a ratio. To obtain the index of refraction, simply divide the speed of light in a vacuum (299,792.5 km/s) by the speed of light through the glass you are testing. *(Easier said than done!)*

**Infinity:** In photography, the point or distance beyond which everything will appear to be in focus. For a standard 50mm lens on a 35mm camera, it is usually anything further than 30 to 35 feet (9 to 10 metres) away from the camera, though this is affected by the *f*-stop. Often indicated by the ∞ symbol.

**Instant Camera:** A self-processing type of camera which produces its own colour or black-and-white prints in a matter of minutes. Often called a Polaroid camera, after the company that was the major developer of instant cameras.

**Instant Return Mirror:** The mirror in an SLR or dSLR camera that reflects the image into the viewfinder. This mirror must flip out of the way before the shutter can open. If it automatically returns immediately after the exposure is complete, it is an "instant return" mirror.

**Inter-lens shutter:** See **Leaf Shutter**.

**Internal Focus:** A system of focusing a lens by moving one or more elements within the lens to achieve focus, rather than simply moving the entire lens closer to or further away from the sensor or film plane. In auto-focus systems, this often results in faster auto-focus performance and also facilitates making the lens more weather resistant.

**Intervalometer:** An electronic device that counts intervals of time and is used to signal the operation of some other device at accurate time intervals. In photography, intervalometers are used to trigger exposures in a time-lapse series. Historically, intervalometers have been rare and expensive accessories for cameras, but in recent years, with the advent of newer, less expensive computer chips, they are becoming common as built-in features in better dSLR and mirrorless cameras. They are also becoming readily available as inexpensive accessories for those cameras without one (see also **Time Lapse Photography**).

**ISO:** The short form for the **I**nternational **O**rganization for **S**tandardization. Because the Organization would have different acronyms in different languages (IOS in English, OIN in French), it was decided to give it the short form ISO, which is derived from the Greek word *isos* (meaning "equal"). In photography, its main standard is for rating the sensitivity to light for both film and digital sensors. The higher the ISO rating, whether on film or the setting on a digital camera, the less light is needed to make an image. The earlier ASA and DIN film speed standards have been combined into the ISO standards since 1974. For example, a film rated ISO 200/24° is twice as sensitive as one rated ISO 100/21°, though in common use (at least in North America) the second number (21°) is generally ignored.

**JPEG:** Acronym for the **J**oint **P**hoto **E**xperts **G**roup—the chaps who set the standard. It is the one format all digital cameras, regardless of size or cost, will shoot and virtually every piece of software will reproduce.

**JPEG 2000:** A newer standard with a modest increase in compression performance compared to the original JPEG. The main difference is a superior representation of the image in terms of visual artifacts. However, JPEG 2000 requires encoders/decoders that are complex and computationally demanding. Thus, it is not supported by all web browsers and has struggled to become popular, in any form.

**KB:** Kilobyte or 1024 Bytes. A unit of storage memory (see also **MB**, **GB**, and **TB**).

**Kelvin:** A unit of measurement in degrees Celsius or Centigrade above absolute zero (−273.15°) that indicates the relative colour temperature of a light source; usually expressed with the abbreviation "°K".

**Keystoning:** A type of unwanted distortion. When a camera is tilted up, vertical parallel lines appear to converge at the top. When a slide projector is tilted up, the image widens at the top (see also **Converging Verticals**).

**Kickstarter.com:** The self-proclaimed "World's largest funding platform for creative projects. A home for film, music, art, theater, games, comics, design, photography, and more." Projects are presented and if the project gains enough supporters to reach their goal, they receive the money. In return, supporters usually get a bonus, either as a discounted price on the item, or additional gear. If the project fails to garner enough supporters, it fails, and the backers do not pay. However, backing a project is not without risks, as successful projects take supporters' money and can then sometimes fail, leaving them with nothing.

**K.K.:** Abbreviation for "Kabushiki Kaisha," a type of Japanese business corporation. In Japanese, "K.K." is the equivalent of "Co.," Ltd.," or the rough equivalent of "Inc." in the USA. In English, *kabushiki kaisha* is usually used, but the original Japanese pronunciation is closer to *kabushiki gaisha*.

**K-Mount:** A proprietary bayonet lens mount design belonging to Pentax, which Pentax have allowed other companies to use for free, making it the de-facto bayonet mount for SLR and dSRL cameras (see also **Bayonet Lens Mount**).

**L-39:** See **M-39 Lens Mount**.

**LD:** See **ED**.

**Leaf Shutter:** A series of light metal "leafs" that open to allow the exposure on film or a digital sensor; also called an interlens or between-the-lens shutter.

**Leaning In:** Photographers' slang for converging verticals (see also **Converging Verticals**).

**LED:** Abbreviation for **L**ight **E**mitting **D**iode—a solid state light source with incredibly long life.

**Leica Thread Mount:** See **M39 Lens Mount**.

**Lens:** A photographic lens is usually composed of several individual lenses to focus light on the film or sensor in a camera. The various lens elements are designed to reduce the effects of chromatic aberration, coma, spherical aberration, and other aberrations. A simple example is the three-element Cooke triplet, still in use over a century after it was

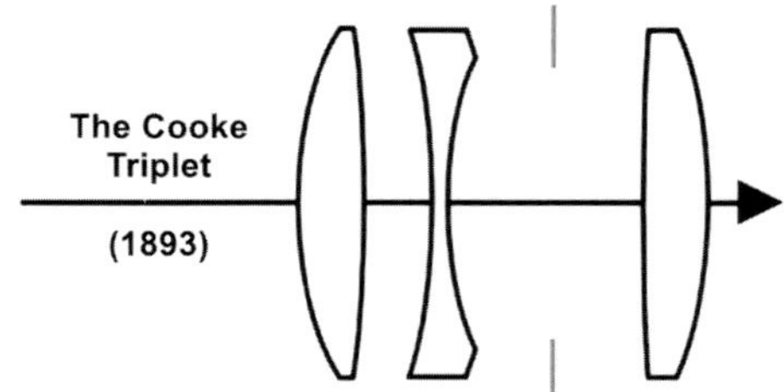


first designed, but many current photographic lenses are much more complex. All lens design is a compromise between numerous factors, not excluding cost.

**Lens Adapter:** A device that allows a lens from one camera mount to be used on a camera with a different mount. While some manufacturers provide lens mount adapters with full compatibility and autofocus features, most adapters are "dumb," and cannot transmit electronic data.

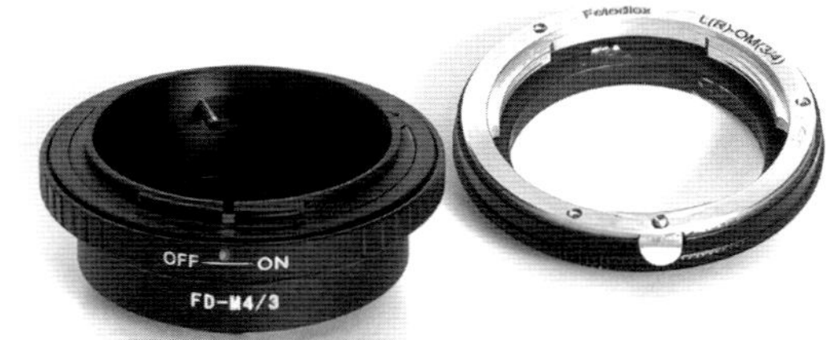

To use an adapter to mount a lens from one brand on a camera of another, the thickness of the adapter has to be equal to the difference between the lens's register and the camera's register, so that the camera's register plus the adapter's thickness put the lens at the exact distance from the film or sensor plane the lens has been designed for. Obviously, therefore, adapters are not possible for some camera/lens combinations.

The Nikon F mount has one of the longest registers of all 35mm SLR mounts: 46.5mm. Only the Leica R (47mm), Contax N (48mm), Icarex (48mm), and Praktina (50mm) mounts have a longer register. Contax N lenses can't be adapted since their aperture is electrically commanded. Lenses in Icarex and Praktina mounts are few in number. Otherwise, if the registration of the lens is longer than the registration of the camera body to be adapted, an adapter is—at least theoretically—possible.

Because micro-FourThirds cameras do not have to allow for a mirror, their registration is mere 19.25mm, which means that virtually any lens made in the last 80 years can be adapted to those cameras. In fact, the only mount adapter your scribe has been unable to find is from the short-lived Exakta Real to mFT. Just about anything else, no matter how obscure, can be found. This has led to a rise in the value of older top-quality lenses (see also **Flange Distance**).

**Lens Coating:** A coating applied to the surface of a lens element to reduce light reflection and increase light transmission within the lens. Coatings can be comprised of one to 14 (or even more) layers in modern lenses. An uncoated lens will lose roughly 4% of its light to reflections at every air/glass surface. So, a typical six-element lens (incorporating two cemented pairs) might have eight glass/air surfaces. But eight surfaces would mean a 32% loss of light. This reflected light lowers contrast and increases flare in the final image, and also causes a sizable increase in the needed exposure. Modern multi-coating can reduce these losses to around 0.2% for each glass/air surface, meaning the total loss in our hypothetical six-element lens would be reduced from 32% to 1.6%.

**Lens Hood:** A metal, rubber, or plastic extension in front of a lens that shields it from direct rays of light, to prevent or reduce fare; also called a lens shade. Think of it as a ball cap for your lens!

**Lens Mount:** A lens mount may be screw-threaded, bayonet, or a breech-lock (friction lock) type. Modern still camera lens use bayonet mount because the bayonet mechanism precisely aligns mechanical and electrical features between lens and body (see also **Bayonet Lens Mount**, **Breech Lock**, **M-39 Lens Mount**, and **M42 Lens Mount**).

**Live View:** The view seen on the back of a camera when the image is received directly from the sensor. Common in small point-and-shoot cameras and with the more advanced mFT system cameras, now becoming possible with some dSLR-style cameras as well.

**Light Meter:** See **Exposure Meter**.

**LOMO:** The Leningrad Optical Mechanical Association, a camera manufacturer in Leningrad/ St. Petersburg, Russia, known for making cameras of "modest" quality.

**Long Focus Lens:** A lens design with a physical length from the optical centre to the film or sensor (the focal plane) that is the same as its focal length. Note that the actual physical length will be slightly

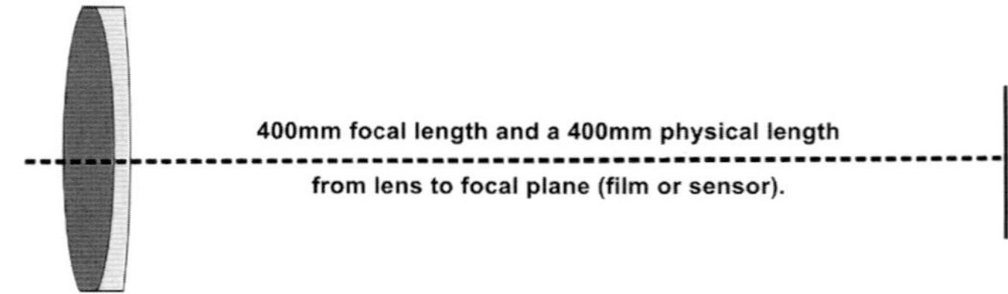


shorter than the focal length, to allow for the depth of the camera body, but will be noticeably longer than a comparable lens of telephoto design (see also **Telephoto Lens**).

**Lux:** A unit of illumination equal to one lumen per square metre, or the amount of light measured at one metre from a one-candlepower source.

**M-39 Lens Mount:** A screw mount, primarily used to attach lenses to the bodies of pre-1954 Leica and Canon rangefinder cameras up to 1961 (commonly known as the Leica Thread Mount or LTM). The threads are 39mm in diameter with a pitch of 26 threads per inch (tpi), which is the pitch of the Whitworth thread form. This odd combination of metric and imperial measurements came about because, when the mount was developed, Whitworth threads were the norm in microscope manufacturing and Leitz was a major microscope manufacturer, so that tooling for Whitworth threads was already in place. Leica introduced the LTM with its Leica II rangefinder camera in 1932. The high cost of quality lenses led to the use of camera lenses on enlargers; as a result, almost all enlargers accept LTM lenses, even today.

**M-42 Lens Mount:** Also called the Pentax, Pentax/Praktica, or Universal Screw Mount, the M-42 is a mount for SLR and dSLR cameras. It is more accurately known as the "M42 x 1mm" standard, which means that it is a metric screw thread of 42mm diameter and 1mm thread pitch. Since there were no proprietary elements to the M42 mount, many other manufacturers used it; this has led many to call it the Universal Thread Mount or Universal Screw Mount.

The M42 mount cameras fell out of general production during the late 1970s and early 1980s, with the exception of the Russian Zenit range. Pentax moved to the Pentax K mount from 1975 onwards, whilst Praktica adopted their (mostly compatible) electronic bayonet (B-Mount) in 1979. Note: The M42 lens mount should not be confused with the T-mount, which shares the 42mm throat diameter, but uses a different thread pitch (see also **M-39 Mount**, **C-Mount**, and **T-Mount**).

**Macro Lens:** A specialized lens that has been optimized for close-focus work, but which will still focus to infinity. Most macro lenses will focus to a 1:2 image ratio and, with a matched extension tube, go to 1:1, at which setting an object 2cm across would be rendered 2cm across on the negative or sensor. A few such lenses will focus to 1:1 without an extension tube and a very few specialized ones will focus to 2:1 without extension tubes (see **Reproduction Ratio**).

**Macro Mode:** A setting on some zoom lenses or compact cameras which allows close-focusing, though not to the extent that a true macro lens does.

**MB:** A megabyte, or 1024 kilobytes. That equals 1,048,576 bytes, but manufacturers typically use 1,000,000 as a megabyte in advertising (see also **KB**, **GB**, and **TB**).

**M-Bayonet:** The lens mount introduced with the Leica M3 rangefinder camera in 1954 that has been used on all subsequent Leica M series cameras. Now long out of patent protection, the M-mount (as it is also referred to) has been used on the Minolta CLE, Konica Hexar RF, Voigtländer Bessa, Rollei 35RF, Pixi, and the latest series of Zeiss Ikon cameras, among others. It has become the de-facto standard for 35mm rangefinder cameras (see also **Bayonet Mount**).

**Medium Format:** Traditionally, a camera that uses film that produces a negative larger than 35mm film, but smaller than a 4 x 5 field camera. Normally, this would a negative of 2¼ x 2¼ inches, or 6 x 6cm in size. More recent usage refers to any digital camera with a sensor larger than the "full frame" or 24 by 36mm size.

**Megadot:** A term used by manufacturers to describe Electronic Viewfinder (eVF) panels. ("Megadot" and "Megapixel" are the same thing, but makers use the former term so as not to confuse the general public with the megapixels used to describe sensors.)

**Megapixel:** A megapixel (that is, a million pixels) is a unit of image-sensing capacity in a digital camera. In general, the more megapixels in a camera, the better the resolution when printing an image in a given size—for instance, a digital camera with a 1.3 megapixel resolution will print a good quality 4 x 3-inch print at 300 dpi (dots per inch). If a higher quality is required or a larger print at the same quality, a camera with a higher megapixel value will be needed.

**Melainotype:** See also **Ferrotype**.

**Memory Card:** A convenient form of non-volatile memory (usually "flash" memory, which will retain its data without power being applied) for photographs in digital cameras. The primary types used in photography are: **CF**, **CFexpress**, **C-Fast**, **Flash Memory**, **Memory Stick**, **SD-Card**, **SmartMedia**, and **XD Card**.

**Memory Stick:** Introduced in 1998, the "memory stick" is a proprietary Flash Memory card, used only in Sony products. With the increasing popularity of SD cards, in 2010 Sony switched to that format for their cameras and most of their other products, though Sony continue to support Memory Sticks on certain devices.

**Micro-Four-Thirds (mFT):** A four-thirds type sensor which measures 18 × 13.5mm (22.5mm diagonal), comparable to the frame size of 110 film. Such cameras are mirrorless and thus have a shorter flange-focal distance (registration), allowing smaller bodies and smaller lighter lenses, while maintaining excellent image quality. The format also allows old lenses from other brands to be readily fitted using inexpensive adapters.

**Minipod:** A very small tripod that can be easily carried. Often called a "table tripod" or "travel tripod."

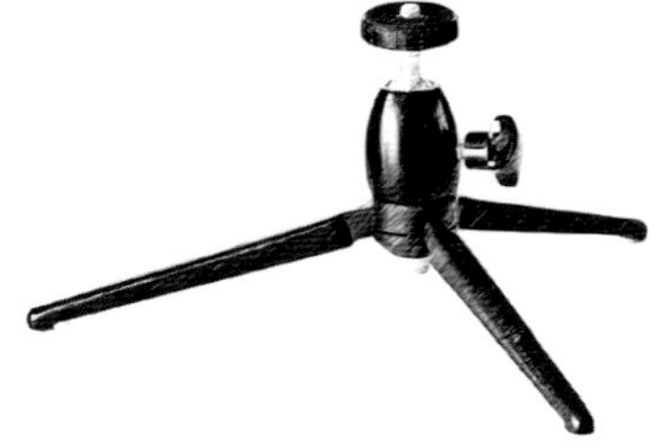

**Mirror Lock-Up (MLU):** Sometimes called "Mirror Pre-release" or "Mirror Pre-fire," the MLU is a mechanism on better dSLR and SLR cameras that will either raise the mirror at will or bring it up shortly before an exposure, so the vibration from raising the mirror can be damped down for best stability. The MLU is only really usable when the camera is on a tripod.

**Mirrorless Camera:** A camera in which the reflex mirror box has been eliminated in favour of a "live view" feed from the sensor to an electronic viewfinder (eVF), which is essentially a tiny TV set you view through an eyepiece. Mirrorless cameras are smaller and lighter than the typical dSLR.

**Moiré:** A pattern that occurs when a scene or object being digitally photographed contains repetitive details (such as lines, dots, etc.) that exceed the sensor resolution. As a result, the camera produces a strange-looking wavy pattern as seen in the blinds in the photo at right.

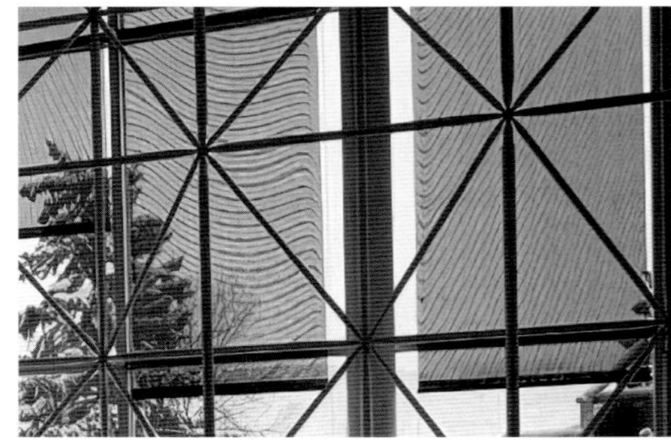

**M-Mount:** See **M-Bayonet**.

**Monopod:** A single-legged camera support, sometimes called a Unipod.

**Mooney 11:** A useful rule of thumb: just as the "Sunny 16 Rule" says to use $f$16 in full daylight with the shutter speed equal to the inverse of the ISO, the "Mooney 11 Rule" says to use $f$11 when photographing the moon with the shutter speed equal to the inverse of the ISO. Thus, ISO 400 would mean an exposure of $f$11 at 1/400th of a second. The moon is an object lit by full sunlight, but the moon's albedo reduces exposure by one stop.

**Motion Blur:** The effect caused when either the camera or the subject moves during the exposure, resulting in a distinctive streaky appearance to the moving object or, in the case of camera shake, the entire picture. Motion blur due to subject movement can usually be prevented by using a faster shutter speed. The exact shutter speed will depend on the speed at which the subject is moving and the angle in which it is moving in relation to the camera. For example, a very fast shutter speed will be needed to "freeze" the rotors of a helicopter, whereas a slower shutter speed will be sufficient to freeze a runner. A commonly cited rule of thumb is that the shutter speed in seconds should be about the reciprocal of the 35mm equivalent focal length of the lens in millimetres. For example, a 50mm lens should be used with a minimum speed of 1/50 second, and a 300mm lens at a minimum of 1/300 of a second. Motion blur caused by camera shake can be reduced (but never totally prevented) by the use of the Image Stabilization systems in modern cameras. A good IS system can reduce camera shake by between two and 4.5 stops, thus allowing lower shutter speeds. These systems, however, will do nothing to prevent motion blur if the subject moves (see also **Image Stabilization**).

**Motion Sensor:** See **Piezoelectric Gyroscope**.

**Mount Adapter:** See **Lens Adapter**.

**Movable Group:** A group of lenses within a zoom lens, that may contain a cemented pair(s) or sets of individual elements, but which moves as a unit within the lens.

**M-Sync:** A method for firing a flash bulb a few milliseconds prior to the shutter fully opening, so that the bulb has time to ignite and be burning at full intensity by the time the shutter is fully open. If used with an electronic flash, the flash will be over before the shutter is open (see also **F-Sync** and **X-Sync**).

**Ninety-degree Finder:** See **Right-angle Finder**.

**Normal Lens:** A normal lens is one that has a focal length roughly equal to the diagonal of the format. Such lenses produce a field of view comparable to that of the human eye (excluding peripheral vision). For 35mm film, this is a diagonal of 43.3mm—thus a 45mm lens would be considered "normal" for the format. In reality, lenses from 40 through 58mm have long been considered "normal" for 35mm cameras, with 50mm being by far the most common.

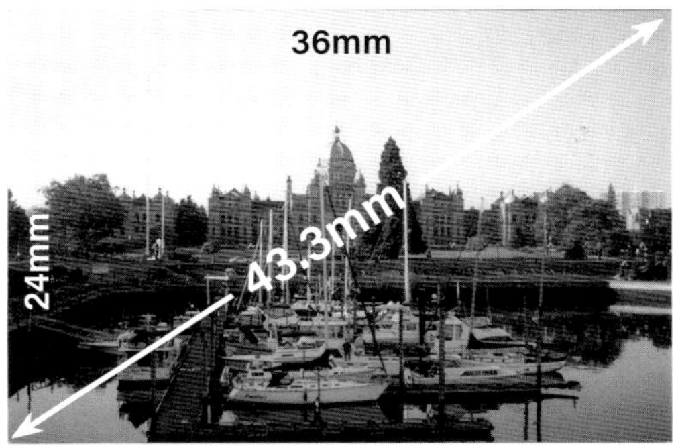


*A "normal" lens has a field of view roughly equal to that of the human eye (excluding periperal vision).*

Lenses with a shorter focal length than the "normal" lens for the film or sensor format will show a wider field of view and are referred to as "wide-angle" lenses. Lenses with a longer focal length will show a more restricted field of view and are referred to as "long focus" or "telephoto" lenses, depending on their optical design.

**O.E.M:** Abbreviation for **O**riginal **E**quipment **M**anufacturer—the primary maker of a product or a firm which builds parts or even complete units, under another company's brand, for that company, under contract.

**O.I.S:** An optical image stabilizer (often abbreviated as OIS, IS, or OS) which uses tiny motion sensors to detect camera movement and thus control the movement of a floating lens element, in order to alter the light path and thus compensate for any vibrations detected. There are both advantages and disadvantages to this technology. The main disadvantage is that each lens requires its own image stabilization system, thereby increasing both lens size, weight, and cost. As well, lens makers go to great effort to "centre" each element in a lens system to achieve the highest optical quality; shifting a lens element de-centres it and thus slightly reduces optical performance. However, proponents of OIS correctly point out that this loss is far less than the quality-reduction to the entire image that would result from blur. Also, a major advantage of OIS systems is that image-stabilized lenses can also be used with film cameras which are equipped to use them (see also **Piezoelectric Gyroscope**, **Sensor Shift**, and **Image Stabilization**).

**One Touch Zoom:** A zoom lens with a single control collar, which you turn for focus and push or pull for zoom adjustment; common in older, manual focus zoom lenses (see also **Two Touch Zoom**).

**Orthochromatic:** An emulsion sensitive to blue and green light, but not red.

**Oxymel:** One of the first "dry" photographic processes, which modified the earlier collodion process by adding a further treatment of exposed plates in a bath of oxymel (a honey/vinegar solution). The resulting product was much less sensitive than the collodion process, but it meant that negatives could be prepared in advance and later developed at leisure.

**Packard Shutter:** The best-known brand of air or bulb shutters, Packard shutters stay open as long as the air bulb is squeezed by the photographer. They are the reason that the position on the shutter dial on modern cameras, which holds the shutter open if the shutter release is held down, is labelled "B," for "Bulb."

**Panchromatic:** An emulsion sensitive to all three primary colours of light: red, green, and blue.

**Panorama (Digital):** A super-wide-angle shot, made by combining two, three, or more individual overlapping shots in a computer using specialized stitching software, to gain a view not otherwise possible. (The panorama shown is made of five vertical overlapping shots of Canada's Salmon 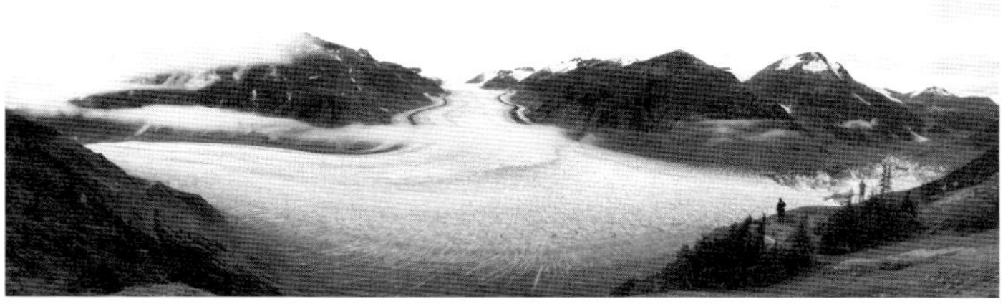 Glacier and stitched using HugIn.) Such shots can also be made by scanning photos from film cameras, and then stitching them together in a computer (see also **Swishy-Pan**).

**Panorama (Film):** A super-wide angle shot created with specialized cameras, such as the Fuji TX-1 (also sold as the Hasselblad X-Pan), Horizon, Widelux, Linhof Techknorama, Cirkut, Noblex, and other similar, specialized cameras (see also **Swishy-Pan**).

**Parfocal:** The proper name for a true zoom lens, usually advertised today as a "constant aperture zoom." A parfocal lens has a constant aperture at any focal length and holds its focus point as it is zoomed. Such lenses are normally considered optically superior to varifocal zooms, as befits their higher price (see also **Varifocal Lens** and **Zoom Lens**).

**PASM:** An abbreviation referring to the common exposure modes of a modern camera: **P**rogram/**A**perture-priority/**S**hutter-priority/**M**anual.

**Pellix:** Technically "a thin skin, cuticle, membrane, or film," in photography the term is used to describe a thin semi-transparent fixed mirror which allows most of the light to pass through to the film or sensor, while a percentage is directed to the viewfinder.

**Pentaprism:** A camera lens reverses images both vertically and laterally. While an SLR's reflex mirror *re-inverts* the image *vertically*, that image still remains reversed *laterally* on the camera's focusing screen. This can be corrected by replacing one of the reflective faces of a normal pentaprism with a "roof" section with two additional surfaces angled towards each other and meeting at 90°. This reverses the image back to normal. (The more accurate name for this type of prism is "roof pentaprism.") 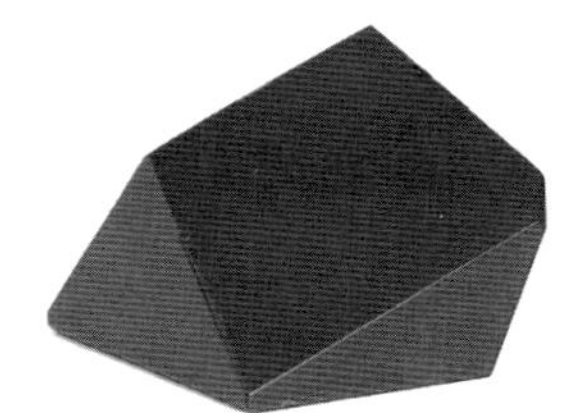

**Pentax Screw Mount:** See **M-42 Lens Mount**.

**Perspective Control Lens:** Lenses with a large image circle that make it possible to displace the optical axis horizontally and/or vertically to prevent converging verticals in architectural photographs. Often referred to simply as PC lenses, these special purpose lenses have been both expensive and rare, though they are becoming more readily available as they are slowly being replaced by combination Tilt-Shift lenses (see also **Tilt-Shift**). 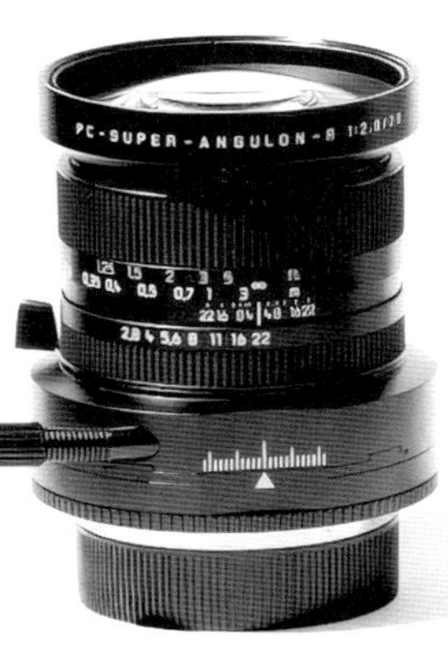

**Phase Detection:** A sophisticated and highly effective implementation of auto-focus in cameras.

**Photokina:** The largest photographic exhibition in the world, comprising 14 enormous exhibition halls, that was held every second year (on even numbered years) in Cologne, Germany, from 1950 to 2020. Now "suspended" indefinitely.

**Piezoelectric Gyroscope:** A material that can be made to vibrate with a tiny electric current, much the same as the crystal in a quartz watch. Due to the Coriolis force, lateral motion can be measured to produce a signal related to the rate of rotation. This signal is then used to direct the movement of a lens element or sensor to compensate for the motion of the camera. Often thought of as "tiny gyroscopes," they have no moving parts in the normal sense of the term (see also **Image Stabilization**, **O.I.S.** and **Sensor Shift**).

**Pixel:** A word coined by Fred Billingsley of Jet Propulsion Laboratories in 1965, derived from **PIC**ture **EL**ement and pronounced "Picsel or Pixel," to describe the basic unit of an image on a computer display or digital photograph.

**Plastic Glass:** The use of plastic as an element in inexpensive camera lenses has been around since 1959 (see also **1952** and **1959**). However, in high-quality optical systems, plastics suffer from significant problems: In the words of Sigma CEO Kazuto Yamaki, "A major problem: they [expand] when it is hot and shrink just as much when it is cold. These variations are detrimental to optical performance."

**Plate Sizes:** For glass plates, a "full plate" is 6½ x 8½ inches, a "half plate" is 4¼ x 6½ inches, and a "quarter plate" is 3¼ x 4¼ inches. Tintypes were just slightly smaller in each size.

**Point-and-Shoot:** A term which usually refers to inexpensive cameras with limited controls but fully automatic operation. Ideal for non-photographers who wish the occasional memory photo, but now being replaced more and more by the cameras built into mobile telephones (see also **Compact Camera**).

**Polaroid:** A brand name for both polarizing films and Edwin Land's Picture-in-a-Minute cameras.

**Porro-Prism:** A system of (usually) plastic front-surface mirrors which accomplishes the same function as a roof prism in an SLR camera, but which is lighter and less expensive to make. Named for its inventor, Ignazio Porro (1801–1875), an Italian optical

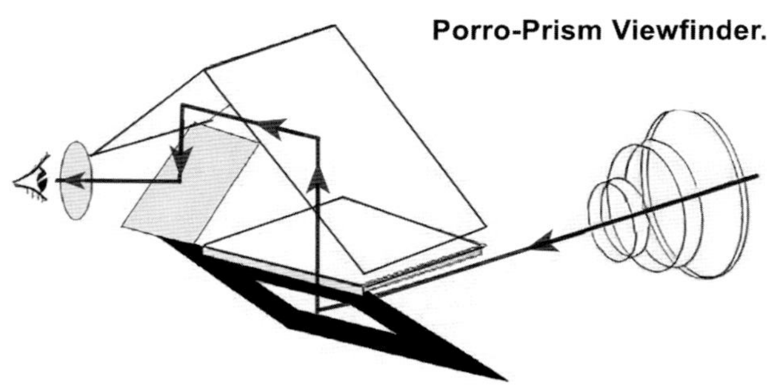


*The use of plastic, front surface mirrors results in a lighter, lower cost viewfinder but with a somewhat dimmer view.*

engineer, it is also advertised as a "penta-mirror." Today it is frequently found in lower priced dSLRs. It has the drawback of a slightly larger "footprint" and a smaller, dimmer viewfinder image, as compared to a camera equipped with a true roof pentaprism.

**Portrait Lens:** See **Short Tele**.

**Pre-Set Diaphragm:** An improvement over the manual diaphragm just for SLRs. One ring selects the desired shooting aperture and a second—the control ring, usually without click-stops—controls the actual diaphragm. Thus, the photographer can focus and compose with the iris fully open for the brightest image; then (without taking her eye from the viewfinder) quickly close down to the chosen *f*-stop just before exposure by rotating the control ring. Popular in the 1940s, '50s and '60s, and still found in very low-cost lenses, even today.

**Prime Lens:** A lens that has only one focal length, as opposed to a zoom lens, which can vary its focal length.

**OLED:** **O**rganic **L**ight **E**mitting **D**iodes, a newer form of LEDs that offer a brighter display (see also **LED**).

**Quarter Plate:** See **Plate Sizes**.

**QR (or Quick Release):** A style of mounting plate that allows you to attach or remove your camera or lens from a tripod or monopod head with the flip of a lever or the twist of a knob.

**Quench Tube:** In early TTL and auto-flash systems prior to the use of thyristors, a flash burst would be terminated by dumping the remaining charge in the flash capacitor into a second small xenon arc tube, known as a "quench tube," which was connected in parallel with the main tube but hidden inside the case. The quench-tube method for automatic flash exposure became immediately obsolete when Vivitar introduced their 283 electronic flash, manufactured by Panasonic (see also **1970**).

The reason, of course, is that the quench tube dumps all the available energy in the capacitor, whereas a thyristor flash circuit simply turns off the flash when needed, saving the rest of the power for the next flash. This means many more flashes for a set of batteries.

**Rack & Pinion Focusing:** A method of varying the distance between a lens and the focal plane to achieve focus. Turning a knob on the end of a pinion gear moves the lens board along a toothed rail (the "rack"), thus varying the distance; commonly used in TLRs and view cameras (see also **Trombone Focusing** and **Focusing Helicoid**).

**Rangefinder:** An optical focusing aid in cameras for manually focusing a lens by triangulation; the rangefinder may show twin or split images which, when lined up, indicate focus.

**Rapatronic Shutter:** A shutter mechanism developed by "Doc" Edgerton in the late 1940s, based on the Faraday Rotation effect (i.e., the rotation of polarization in dense glass when a magnetic field is applied). Essentially, a coil is wrapped around a special glass cylinder made with three pieces of Polaroid Corp. HN-23 polarizing material sandwiched between extra thick discs of flint glass, with the central disk at right angles to the outer two, thus blocking the light. When the coil is energized, the magnetic field created by the coils changes the polarization of the central disc, thus opening the shutter only for the duration of the pulse. Shutter speeds of 10-billionths of a second can be achieved without moving parts, thus allowing recording rates of up to 10 million frames per second. The Rapatronic Shutter was first used to record above-ground nuclear tests.

**RAW:** "Shooting raw" means capturing the raw data from the imaging sensor in its most basic form on to your camera's memory card, rather than first converting that data to the JPEG format. Conversion to JPEG or other human-viewable formats can then be done after the fact, using special software on a computer. Think of the raw file as a digital negative from which you make viewable prints.

**Read Speed:** The speed at which data can be read from a CF or SD memory card.

**Rear Curtain Sync:** See **Second Curtain Sync**.

**Recycle Time:** The time it takes for an electronic flash to recharge its capacitors and be ready to fire again.

**Red Eye:** The undesirable effect that results when a flash reaches and photographs the retina inside a subject's eyes. This effect occurs because the light of the flash occurs too quickly for the pupil to close, and much of the very bright light from the flash passes into the eye. The light then reflects off the back of the eyeball and out again, via the pupil. Since the light goes through the blood in the choroid which nourishes the back of the eye, the colour of the eye is red, hence this annoying effect.

Some flash systems in camera or accessory units are designed to reduce red eye by emitting a brief series of lower power pre-flashes or a steady LED beam prior to the actual firing of the flash, causing the pupils of the eyes to constrict.

Red eye can also be removed by a variety of software programs that detect the tell-tale redness and replace it with black. This can sometimes give the subject a "blank" look, but that is still considered preferable to the "red eye" effect. The technique can be effective on digital images, or on the digital files of film that has been scanned.

**Reflex Camera:** A camera that uses a mirror or other optical device to present the scene to the photographer exactly as the camera's film or sensor will record it. A single-lens reflex (SLR) uses one lens both to view and photograph the scene, while a twin lens reflex (TLR) uses one lens for viewing and another for filming (see also **dSLR**, **SLR**, and **TLR**).

**Refractive Index:** See **Index of Refraction**.

**Register or Registration:** The distance between the lens mount and the focal plane (see also **Flange Distance**).

**Reproduction Ratio:** A calculation used in close-up photography to indicate the size of a subject reproduced on the film or sensor in relation to the actual size of the subject. When both sizes are the same, the image is said to be "life sized," and the reproduction ratio is one-to-one, expressed as 1:1. A reproduction ratio of 1:2 indicates the subject appears at one-half life-size, while a ratio of 2:1 means the image is twice the size of the real-life subject.

**Retrofocus:** An inverted telephoto design that gives wide-angle lenses sufficient distance between the rear element and the film or sensor plane to allow space for the mirror box in SLR and dSLR cameras.

**Reverse Ring:** An adapter with a filter thread on one side and a camera mount on the other that makes it possible to install a lens in a camera in reverse position. Useful for making close-up shots, this is also called a "reverse macro adapter."

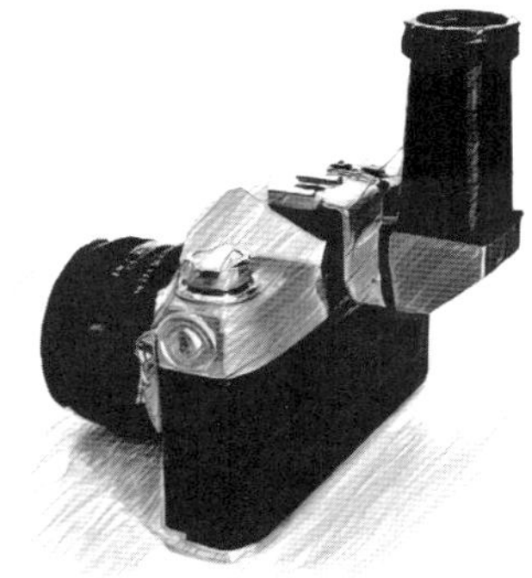

**Right-Angle Finder:** An accessory that (usually) clips onto a camera's hot or cold shoe directly above the eyepiece that allows the user to view through the finder of an SLR while looking down, as one would with a TLR. Optical quality varies with price, but is irrelevant, as flaws show only in the viewfinder, not in the final image.

**Rolling Shutter:** The effect of straight lines becoming curved when pixels are read line by line if the subject moves during exposure (see also **Global Shutter**). A more common result of rolling shutter is an oval wheel on a fastmoving motorcycle (see also **Swishy-Pan**).

**Roof Pentaprism:** See **Pentaprism**.

**Rule of Thirds:** A concept of composition that positions the subject of a photograph for the most appealing image.

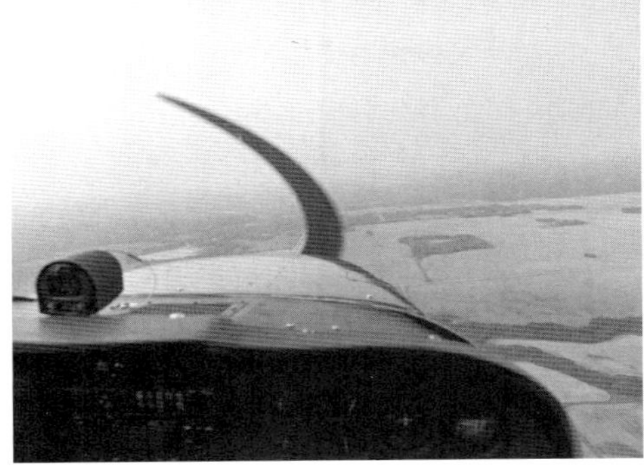

*Rolling shutter effect*

**Scheimpflug Principle:** The technique of tilting the lens up or down or from side to side (swing) to effectively tilt the plane of focus, thus gaining a considerable apparent increase in depth of field (see also **Tilt-Shift Lens**).

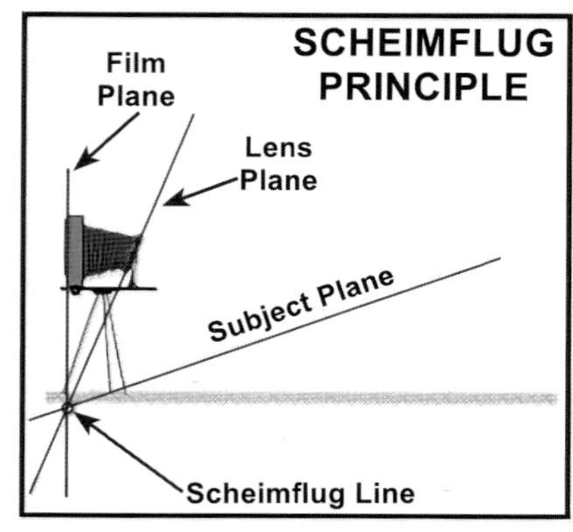


**Screw Mount:** See **C-Mount, M-39 Lens Mount** and **M-42 Lens Mount**.

**SD Card:** A secure digital flash card memory that is the predominant method of storing images in digital cameras today. The card has an (almost never used) switch which prevents it from being overwritten or erased. Smaller and lighter than the older CF cards, it can hold up to 4 GB of data. An SDHC—a **H**igh-**C**apacity **SD** card, capable of holding up to 32 GB—is widely used by photographers. A further improved, e**X**tended **C**apacity SD card, capable of holding up to 2 TB (2048 GB) of information, is also available.

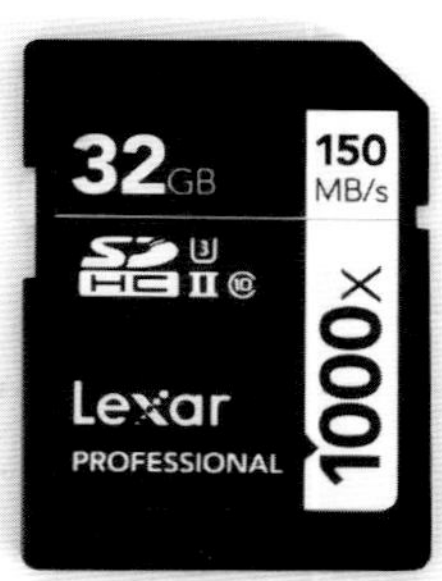


The capacity of SD cards is measured in multiples of 1,000 bytes, with each named unit having 1,000 times the capacity of the one before. From the smallest on up, they are kilobyte (KB); megabyte (MB); gigabyte (GB); terabyte (TB); petabyte (PB); exabyte (EB); zettabyte (ZE); and yottabyte (YB). Beyond those there are two or three proposed prefixes that are becoming recognized in the measurement community: the brontobyte (BB, a reference to the Brontosaurus, the biggest dinosaur) and the helabyte (HB, derived from having "a hell of a lot of bytes"). Both are equal to 1000 yottabytes or a 1 followed by 27 zeros.

The class of an SD card is shown by a number inside a larger letter "C." You will see Classes 2, 4, 6, or 10 on SD Cards. This is the speed rating which measures maximum transfer speed for reading and writing images to and from a memory card, expressed as megabytes per second. Cards faster than Class 10 are common (see also UHS).

**Second Curtain Sync:** A feature where the flash is fired just prior to the second curtain of a focal plane shutter closing, rather than firing when the first curtain has just opened. This allows the portrayal of moving objects with a blurred light trail behind them. Also called Rear-curtain sync and Trailing Sync.

**Selenium Meter:** Introduced in the 1930s, selenium cells were the most common early type of photoelectric light meter. Multiple "insect eye" lenses covering the photocell are characteristic of a selenium

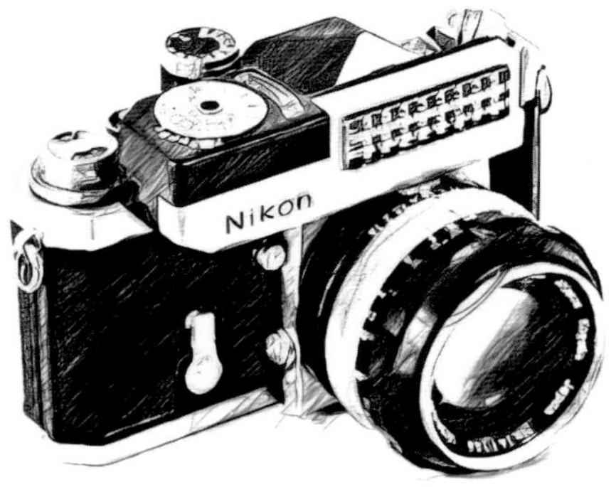

*Nikon "F" with selenium meter*

meter. Essentially a small solar panel, the selenium cell generates its own electric current, which deflects an indicator needle by varying amounts proportionate to the level of illumination.

**Sensor Shift:** An image stabilization system for digital cameras that uses tiny motion sensors to detect camera movement and then shift the sensor to counteract the motion of the camera. The advantage of moving the image sensor, instead of a lens element, is that it does not de-centre the lens; it also allows the manufacture of smaller, lighter, and lower-cost lenses, as the system need be bought only once, in the camera body. In many cases, it also allows older lenses made long before image stabilization was even a dream, to become image-stabilized (see also **Image Stabilization**, **O.I.S.**, and **Piezoelectric Gyroscopes**).

**Series Filters:** Glass (or gelatin) disks mounted in a non-threaded metal rim and attached to the lens with the help of an adapter and a retaining ring. Series filters were widely used from the 1930s to the 1970s, but since then have largely been replaced by threaded filters.

**Short Tele:** A telephoto or long-focus lens that has a focal length longer than that of a "normal" lens, but not by a lot. In 35mm photography, such lenses would be in the 75 to 105mm range and are ideal for making portraits of people, as the added "shooting distance" they allow, while still filling the frame, keeps the subject's facial features in proper perspective.

**Shoulder Brace:** An attachment similar to a gun stock, which is fastened to the camera's tripod socket and used to provide additional support for the camera, especially when using long telephoto lenses.

**Shutter:** A device for controlling the length of time the film or digital sensor is exposed to light. A shutter can be located either between the lens elements (a leaf shutter), behind the lens, or placed in front of the focal plane (where the film or sensor sits).

**Shutter Lag:** The time it takes from the moment you press the shutter until the camera fires the shutter. In a top-line camera it can be on the order of 35 to 50 milliseconds, whereas in a low-priced P&S camera it can be a full second, or even more.

**Silicon Blue:** Silicon (Si) cells combine the best of both selenium and cadmium sulphide metering cells. Like cadmium sulphide cells they are small, offer good performance in low light conditions, and are driven by batteries. Like selenium they rapidly adapt to intensity changes and react to a wider range of wavelengths. They require a blue filter to cut down that end of the spectral sensitivity, so they're often advertised as "silicon blue" cells.

**Six by Six (or 6 by 6):** Meaning 6 x 6cm, or 2¼ inches square, being the square format using 120 or 220 roll-film. Typically used in Rollei (and other) TLRs as well as the Bronica and Hasselblad medium-format SLRs and older folding cameras such as the Zeiss Ikonta or the Beauty Six (on the cover of this book).

**Skylight Filter:** Essentially a UV filter with a subtle, light-salmon-coloured tint to it. This provides a slightly warmer image and is often used with lenses that produce a "cooler" blueish image, such as various Nikon or Zeiss optics. As with a UV filter, it is normally left on a lens to provide mechanical protection for the front element (see also **UV Filter**).

**SLR (or Single-Lens Reflex):** An expression that some would call a misnomer, as these cameras accept multiple lenses, the term actually distinguishes this form of camera from a film camera now rarely seen: the twin lens reflex, which has a viewing lens directly above the taking lens. In an SLR, a mirror diverts light to an optical finder and, at the moment of exposure, swings out of the way to allow the light to reach the film or sensor (the term dSLR simply denotes a digital version of the SLR design (see also **Reflex Camera**).

**SmartMedia:** Launched in the summer of 1995, SmartMedia is a flash memory card standard owned by Toshiba, with capacities ranging from 2MB to 128MB. SmartMedia was popular in digital cameras and reached its peak in about 2001, when it garnered nearly half of the digital-camera market. But, as camera resolutions increased and cameras reached a size where even SmartMedia cards were too big to be convenient, the format fell from favour. Manufacturing ended in 2006, though such cards still seem readily available both new (Amazon) and used (e-Bay), even today.

**Speedlight:** See **Electronic Flash**.

**Spherical Aberration:** An optical problem that occurs when parallel light rays of incoming light do not converge at the same point after passing through the lens. Because of this, Spherical Aberration can affect resolution and clarity, making it hard to obtain sharp images (see also **Aspherical Lens**).

**Spot Metering:** An exposure metering system built into some SLR, dSLR, and mirrorless cameras that reads only a very limited area, allowing more precise exposure control.

**Stacked Sensor:** A term referring to a digital sensor from which the silicon substrate has been shaved off. This allows chips to have random access memory built directly in the sensor, providing super-fast readouts, which make more frames per second or higher video resolutions possible (see also **BSI**).

**Strobe:** See **Electronic Flash**.

**Stop-down Metering:** A system in which the lens closes its diaphragm to the shooting aperture (*f* stop) when the exposure measurement is made.

**Stops:** A term derived from the early days of photography, when metal plates with various sized holes were placed in front of a lens to "stop" excess light from entering, in order to control the exposure. Because shutter speeds also affect exposure, in modern usage the term "stop" defines the relationship between shutter speed and aperture for a given total exposure. Changes to either of these controls are often measured in units known as "stops," with a stop being equal to a factor of two.

**Subtractive Colour:** The mixing of a limited set of dyes, inks, paint pigments, or natural colourants to create a wider range of colours, each the result of partially or completely subtracting (that is, absorbing) some wavelengths of light and not others. The colour seen on the surface depends on which parts of the visible spectrum are not absorbed and therefore remain visible. The primary colours for this process are cyan, magenta, and yellow. In printing, pure black is also used; the customary abbreviation is "CMYK" with the K meaning black.

**Sunny 16:** The Sunny 16 rule says that you can get a decent exposure, on a bright sunny day, if you set your lens for $f$16, and the shutter speed to the number "1" divided by the ISO. So, if you've got ISO 400 film, on a sunny day you'd get a good exposure at $f$16 and 1/400 of a second. After that, you'd open up a stop on an overcast day, another stop for rain, etc. It worked for film if your light meter failed; these days, however, if the meter in a digital camera fails, chances are the rest of the camera is dead, too. Still, it's a rule to remember, for one day it just may bail you out (see also **Mooney 11**).

**Swishy-Pan:** A shot made by moving the camera in perfect sync with your subject, while shooting with a slow shutter speed. This yields a blurred background and a sharp subject, giving a better impression of motion. The name is said to have originated with Ted Grant, to distinguish the style from panoramas made by combining multiple images or by moving the camera with the subject but using high shutter speeds to "freeze" the action.

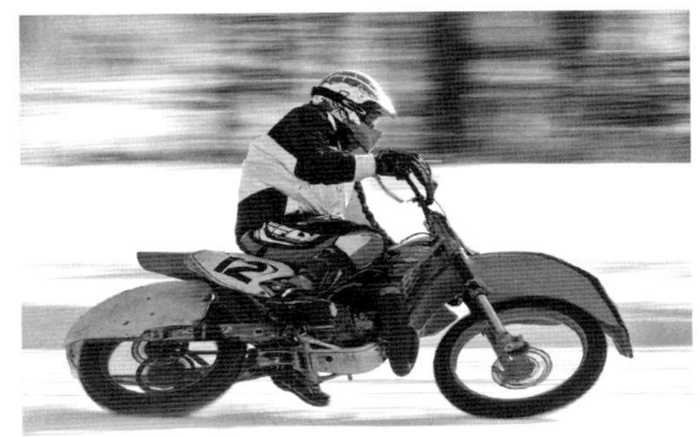

**Table Tripod:** See **Travel Tripod** and **MiniPod**.

**TB:** A unit of digital memory equal to 1024 megabytes, or 1.0995 x 10¹² bytes (see **KB**, **MB**, and **GB**).

**T-stop:** Also known as a Transmission-stop, this is very similar to the $f$-stop. The major difference is that rather than being a purely mechanical (calculated) ratio, the light coming through the lens is measured with sophisticated instruments, so that going from, say, T-2.8 to T-2 yields exactly twice the light. This is important in movies and videos, where exposure must balance, scene to scene—something not as important in still photography. Using T-stops allows for the losses in the various elements of a lens. In early years, before lens coating, the difference between the $f$-stop and a T-stop was significant. Lens coating made the differences much smaller. In the modern era of multi-coated lenses, the differences are usually very small indeed (see also **$f$-stop**).

**Teleconverter:** Teleconverters fit between the lens and body of a camera to increase the effective focal length of the lens by magnifying the central portion of the image. They are commonly available in 1.4x and 2x magnifications. Rarely, they have been made in 1.7x and 3x units. Teleconverters affect both exposure and image quality. A 1.4x teleconverter in effect changes the effective lens setting by one *f*-stop—if the lens had been set at *f*4, for example, with a 1.4 teleconverter that setting in effect becomes *f*5.6; similarly, a 2x teleconverter changes the setting by two *f*-stops, making our *f*4 lens an *f*8 one, and so on. If a top quality converter is used with a good prime lens or a top-quality zoom, there is very little loss of image quality. With lesser quality optics the loss will be greater. Prices can vary from $30 to $700, and you get what you pay for (see also **Barlow Lens**).

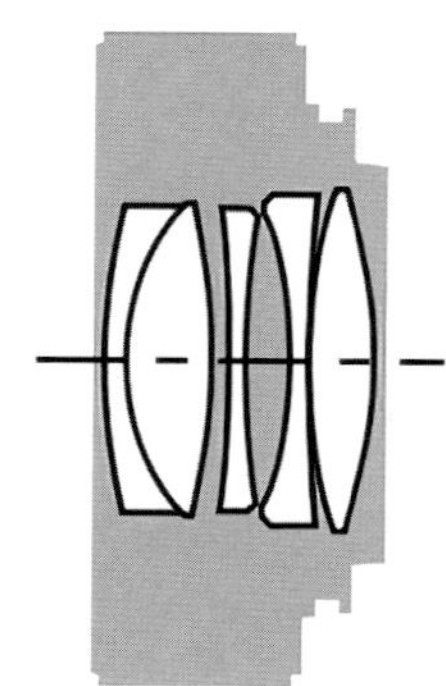

**Telephoto Lens:** A lens which has an effective focal length longer than its physical length. A telephoto lens is made physically shorter than its nominal focal length by pairing a front positive imaging cell with a rear magnifying negative cell. The powerful front group forms the image, the rear restores the focal plane, thereby greatly shortening the physical length of the lens (see also **Long Focus Lens** and **Normal Lens**).

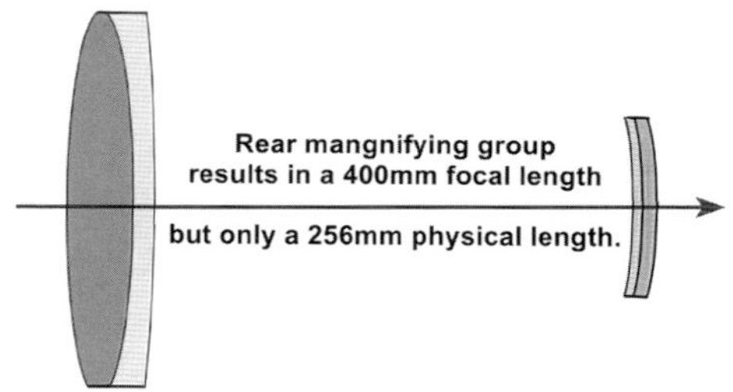


**TeleXtender:** A brand-name for teleconverters, used by Spiratone Incorporated of the USA (see also **Teleconverter**).

**Thread Mount:** A method of attaching a lens to a camera body with a screw thread (see also **C-Mount**, **M-39 Lens Mount**, and **M-42 Lens Mount**).

**Thyristor:** First made commercially available in 1956, the thyristor is a bi-stable, solid-state switch that can control large amounts of power. It was first used photographically in the Vivitar 283 electronic flash. By eliminating the quench-tube in auto-flash units, it delivered many more flashes per set of batteries, thus making the 283 the most successful electronic photoflash in history (see **1970**). By 1975, thyristors were used by virtually every maker to control auto-flash (see also **Trigger Voltage**).

**Tilt-Shift:** A tilt-shift lens changes its position in relation to a camera's film or image sensor. When the lens tilts so that it is no longer parallel to the camera's image sensor, it shifts the plane of focus and alters the depth of field (see also **PC Lens** and **Scheimpflug Principle**).

**Time Exposure:** An exposure of longer than one second usually require setting the shutter speed to "B" or "T" to hold the shutter open, though a few cameras do have markings for speeds in excess of one second.

**Time Lapse Photography:** A series of photographs of the same subject, taken over a period of time without moving the camera (see also **Intervalometer**).

**Tintype:** See **Ferrotype**.

**TLR** **T**win **L**ens **R**eflex**:** A style of camera that features a viewing lens above the taking lens. The image in the viewfinder is laterally reversed, as it is reflected to the top viewing screen by a mirror set at 45° (see also **Reflex Camera**).

**T-Mount:** The T-mount and adapter system was released in 1957 by Tamron, an independent lens maker. The original model was an M37 x 0.75 thread; Tamron's revolutionary M42 x 0.75 T-thread didn't appear on the market until about 1962. The usual T-mount is a screw mount using a male 42 x 0.75 metric thread on the lens, with a flange focal distance of 55mm. (This should not be confused with the M42 lens mount, which is also 42mm diameter, but has a 1mm thread pitch.) Because the T-mount lenses have a long flange distance of 55mm and most 35mm cameras have shorter flange distances, a simple mechanical adapter called a T-Ring is needed to adapt a T-mount lens to almost any camera body to achieve infinity focus. Thus, a retailer could stock a small number of expensive lenses and a variety of T-rings, that would fit a large number of camera brands. The system is commonly referred to as the T-mount, T-thread, T-ring or most commonly as a T or T-2 adapter, though T-2 was the trade name that Soligor used for its version of the T-adapter. The T-mount is a solely mechanical specification—electrical or mechanical connections (such as for autofocus) are generally not provided. Since some dSLRs won't meter without electronic lens data, some adapters are now sold fitted with a Dandelion Chip, which can be programmed to identify the focal length and aperture limits and enable metering and, in some cases, focus confirmation (see also **Dandelion Chip**).

**T-Stop:** Unlike *f*-stops, which are calculated ratios, T-stops (Transmission stops) are a measurement of how much light is actually getting through the lens at any given opening. T-stops take into account the amount of light lost thorough glass-air surfaces and other factors in a lens system. Thus, while an aperture of *f*2 theoretically admits twice the light as *f*4, T2 admits precisely twice the light as T4. The differences used to be significant, but with modern, multi-coated lenses the differences are small, but still important when matching scenes in video.

**Travel Tripod:** A compact, lightweight tripod often made of carbon fibre and a bit shorter than standard tripods to save space and weigh (see also **Minipod**, **Table Tripod**, and **Tripod**).

**Trigger Voltage:** The voltage presented on the pins of an electronic flash. In older flash units, this voltage is often 250 volts or more. Older film cameras have mechanical contacts that can withstand this voltage, but the electronic circuits in modern digital cameras and some of the more recent computerized film cameras, such as Canon's AE-1 (see **1976**) can handle no more than eight to 12 volts, with a few being rated as low as five volts. If given higher voltage, major damage to the camera will occur. If in doubt, without connecting the flash unit to a camera, fully charge the flash and measure the voltage across the contacts with a voltmeter. *If it is more than 12 volts, or, if you're simply unsure, do not use the unit with a modern camera.*

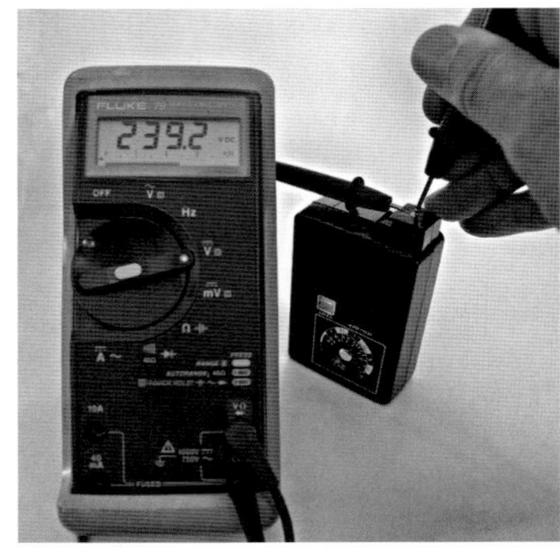

*Older electronic flash showing 239.2 volts.*

**Tripod:** A tripod is a three-legged device used to hold the camera steady and thus avoid motion blur due to camera shake. A tripod is recommended for exposure times longer than the reciprocal of the focal length of the lens. In other words, a 50mm lens should be used on a tripod for exposures longer than 1/50 of a second. Similarly, with a long 400mm telephoto lens, a tripod should be used for exposures longer than 1/400 of a second, for maximum sharpness, as the longer focal length magnifies not only the image but the amount of camera shake. (Modern image stabilization methods, however, will improve this performance—see also **IBIS**, **Image Stabilization**, **O.I.S.** and **Sensor Shift**).

**Trombone Focusing:** The trombone focusing system was the fastest way to focus a long lens before the advent of auto-focus, and was intended for sports and wildlife photography. Typically, makers replaced the normal helicoid focusing threads with three polished stainless-steel rails. To focus, you press a button and push or pull on the front tube (which rides on the rails) as you would push or pull the slide in a trombone. Releasing the button locks the lens in place. Unusual, but fast, remarkably easy to use and accurate. To your scribe's knowledge, Leica used this method only with their Leitz Telyt 400 and 560mm *f* 6.8 lenses from the late 1960s. Novoflex had a similar system using a pistol grip with trigger to focus the lens. Their lenses were available in 240, 400 and 640mm focal lengths with adapters to fit various lens mounts.

**TTL:** In the 1930s, TTL (meaning **T**hrough **T**he **L**ens) originally referred to the an SLR's ability to let you view your photo right through the taking lens. Since the 1960s, it has more commonly referred to the ability of a camera to meter the scene through the taking lens for greater accuracy. Since the Olympus OM-2 (see **1975**) the term can also refer to the ability to measure a flash exposure this way.

**TTL Flash:** Refers to the ability of a sensor somewhere behind the lens to measure the exposure and turn off the flash, when appropriate.

**Two Touch Zoom:** A zoom lens with separate rings or collars: one for focus, the other for zooming. Almost universal in zoom lenses with automatic focus (see also **One Touch Zoom**).

**UHS:** A designation (short for **U**ltra **H**igh **S**peed) for some super-fast SDHC and SDXC cards which allow higher speed transfers from a camera's buffer to the card. All UHS cards are faster than the earlier Class 10 cards, though they are all marked Class 10, as they meet that standard too.

**UHS-1 and UHS-3:** Further improved standards for SD cards, resulting in still faster writes to the memory card. Aside from the labels, UHS-3 cards can be readily identified by a second row of pins on the back. UHS-2 and -3 cards come in both HC and XC capacities. UHS utilizes a new data bus that will not work in non-UHS host devices. If you use a UHS memory card in a non-UHS camera, it will default to the standard data bus and use the "Speed Class" rating instead of the "UHS Speed Class" rating. But at least it will work.

**Unipod:** See **Monopod**.

**Universal Thread Mount:** See **M-42 Lens Mount**.

**UV Filter:** A filter to remove the ultra-violet wavelengths from the light entering the camera, to reduce haze. More commonly used to prevent mechanical damage to the front element of a lens.

**Varifocal Lens:** A zoom lens that changes its focus and maximum aperture as it is zoomed. Such lenses have become popular since the advent of auto-focus cameras because they are easier to design and less costly to manufacture yet retain good optical quality. 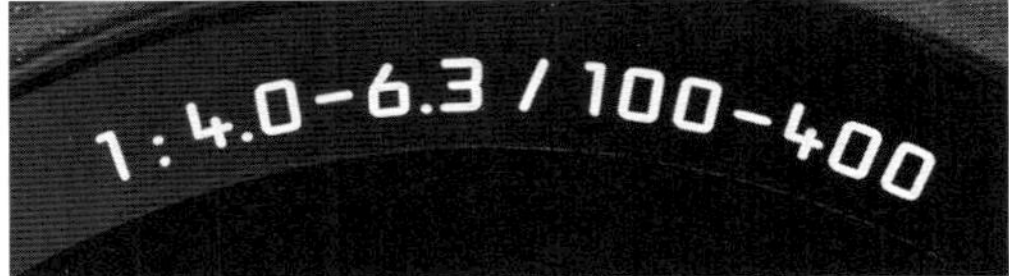 This change of focus is not a major drawback, as a modern autofocus camera will refocus the lens so fast the photographer rarely notices it happening. The major "tell" that a lens is a varifocal design, rather than parfocal, is that as you zoom the lens to a longer focal length, its maximum aperture is reduced, often by two stops or more (see also **Parfocal** and **Zoom Lens**).

**Vibration Reduction:** The term used by Nikon to indicate their in-lens image stabilization feature (see also **Image Stabilization**).

**Vignetting:** An undesirable effect that darkens the corners of an image. Often caused by a lens shade or filter ring that extends into the field of view, it can also be caused by a lens of simple design, which cannot adequately cover the film or sensor used.

**Wide-Angle Lens:** A lens with a focal length shorter than the diagonal of a given film or sensor, which will produce an image with a wider field of view than the "normal lens." (See also **Normal Lens**.)

**Write Speed:** The speed at which data can be written to a CF or SD memory card. The faster the write speed, the better performance of your camera, especially when shooting in "burst" or "motor drive" mode. One note of caution: Purchasing memory cards with write speeds greater than those that are supported by your camera wastes money and provides no benefit. Check your manual before purchasing.

**XD Card:** A memory card that was proprietary to FujiFilm and Olympus, just as the Memory Stick format is to Sony. Made by Samsung and Toshiba, the XD (or XD Picture Card) was introduced in 2002 as a competitor to the SD card. But development of the technology (notably in both capacity and write speeds) did not keep up with the more robust SD cards. It did not help that as of September 2009, 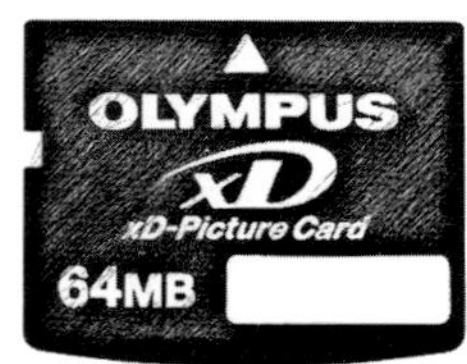 2GB XD cards retail price was roughly three times that of same-capacity SD cards. By 2010, the card was no longer used by any camera maker.

**XD Card Adapter:** New "old stock" XD cards up to 2 GB can still be purchased at very high prices. Adapters can be found which will accept a Micro SD card, which then slips into the XD card slot of the camera—a possible way to salvage an older camera that needs an XD card.

**XQD Card:** The modern replacement for the now dated (1994) CF card. Employing the PCI Express 3.0 with transfer rates up to 8 GB per second (1000 Mbyte/s), and with capacities to 2 TB, the card is suitable for top-tier digital cameras and 4K digital camcorders. As of early 2019, only Sony, Nikon, and Phase One support XQD cards in their newest cameras. Because of this relatively small number of participating manufacturers, production is limited and prices remain high.

The XQD card is already obsolescent, as the CFexpress card has the same form-factor and interface but uses a new protocol for higher speeds and lower power consumption.

**X-Sync:** Fires the flash the moment the shutter is fully open (see also **F-Sync** and **M-Sync**).

**ZLR:** Zoom Lens Reflex camera (see also **Bridge Camera**).

**Zoom Lens:** A lens which can vary its apparent focal length in order to adjust the subject's image size. The design of zoom lenses involves many elements, which often move in varying directions and distances, and thus additional compromises must be made by the designer. While a handful of expensive zoom lenses can match the finest primes, most zooms do not. Today, modern zoom lenses can offer excellent performance—something that could not be said of early zooms. (See also **Parfocal** and **Varifocal**.)

# Image Credits



1545—Camera Obscura

1727—Johann Heinrich Schulze, engraving

1777—Carl W. Scheele

1795—Thomas Wedgewood

1816—J.N. Niépce, Daguerreotypist unknown

1819—Sir John Herschel, by Julia Cameron

1822—Louis Daguerre, photographer unknown

1827—The first permanent photograph, by J.N. Niépce

1834—Fox Talbot, photographer unknown.

1838—Daguerreotype showing people

1839—Daguerreotype of Hippolyte Bayard

1840—Joseph Petzval—1854 drawing by Adolf Duathage

1840—Patent diagram

1843—Photogram of algae, by Anna Atkins, *c.*1843

1853—Felix Nadar, photographer unknown

1853—Mother & son, by Mary Dillwyn

1856—Woodcut, *c.* 1874

1860—Image of tartan ribbon

1861—Mathew Brady, photographer unknown

1867—Anasuma ad, *c.* 1922

1872—Horse photos, by E. Muybridge

1872—E. Muybridge, photographer unknown

1873—Ernst Abbe, photographer unknown

1874—Photographer with equipment. Woodcut from Les Mervieilles de la Photographie, by Gaston Tissandiere

1880—Walker & Co. ad

1884—Smith & Co. ad

1886—Snowflake photographs by W.A. Bentley [2]

1888—Louis La Prince, photographer unknown

1888—Kodak ad

1889—Connon camera patent

1900—Kodak ad [9]

1900—Train camera by J. Anderson

1900—Photos from a multiple camera, by H. Magnum

1902—Wright Bros. first powered flight, John T. Daniels, photographer

1902—Penny Pictures, photographer unknown

1902—Plaubel Instruction-book cover [9]

1907—Autochrome of the Taj Mahal, photographer unknown [9]

1922—Asanuma ad [9]

1926—*Asahi Camera* magazine [9]

1930—Dufaycolor ad [8]

1935—Noviflex ad [8]

1936—Mikut Color ad, from June 1936 *The Camera* magazine [8]

1937—First issue cover of *Popular Photography*
  magazine [1]

1935—WeeGee rubber stamp [9]

1938—Mercury ad from 1948 [8]

1939—Sun Optical ad from 1955 *Asahi
  Camera* [8]

1940—U.S. Patent #2,214,283

1941—Spiratone ad, *c.* 1965 [8]

1946—Earth from space, White Sands
  Missile Range/APL [2]

1946—Haneel Trivision ad [8]

1947—Japanese language Minolta ad [8]

1948—Japanese language Nikon ad [8]

1949—PhotoPac Camera ad [8]

1952—Ad for Big Bertha cameras by
  unknown advertiser or source [9]

1957—Calypso Camera [1]

1957—Mamiya C222 and 330 TLRs [2]

1957—First scanned photo [9] Image credit:
  R. Kirsch/NIST

1964—Orwochrome slide [1]

1966—Earth from Lunar Orbit image
  courtesy NASA [2]

1969—Hasselblad 500EL/M Moon
  Camera [9] Image courtesy NASA.

1991—Modified Nikon F4 camera image
  courtesy NASA [2]

2002—Kodachrome slides courtesy Nathan
  Anderson [5]

Early Years—Camera Obscura [9]

Glossary—Bellows cameras image courtesy
  R. & P. Skitterians [10]

Glossary—17C Camera Obscura drawing [9]

Glossary—Fresnel lens [1]

**NOTES:**

[1] via Wikipedia.org (either Public Domain
  or CC0)

[2] via Wikimedia.org (either Public Domain
  or CC0)

[3] via pixabay.com (All CC0)

[5] via unsplash.com (All CC0)

[6] via ISOrepublic.com (All CC0)

[7] via flickr (CC0)

[8] Copyright expired or not renewed.

[9] Public Domain

[10] via skitterphoto.com (All CCo)

***The following images are not covered by the
author's copyright, as they are used under a
Creative Commons license (as noted).***

**1614**—Angelo Sala (engraving), courtesy
  of the Wellcome Library, London.
  http://creativecommons.org/licenses/by/4.0/

**1899**—Victor Electric Flash,
  courtesy Race Gently.
  https://creativecommons.org/licenses/
  by-sa/2.0/

***The following images are not covered by the
author's copyright and are used courtesy of:***

**Camera Quest**—www.cameraquest.com
  **1998**—Four *f* 0.95 Voigtländer lenses.

**Charles A. Hulcher Co. Inc.**, Hampton, VA.
  **1953**—Hulcher 70 ad.

**Gore, Tom**—http://tomgore.1x.com/
  **Glossary**—Image Circle.

**Merklinger, Harold. M.**—www.trenholm.
  org/hmmerk/
  **Glossary**—Sheimpflug Principle drawing

**R. Kirsch/National Institute of Standards
and Technology,**
  **1957**—First scanned photo

# Index

Note: This index refers to the year of entries, not the page numbers.

3M: 1902, 1964
8mm film (movie): 1924, 1932
16mm film (movie): 1923, 1932
17.5mm film (movie): 1923
35mm film: 1892, 1902, 1905, 1907, 1924, 1925, 1927, 1934, 1935, 1936, 1938, 1941, 1947, 1949, 1951, 1952, 1953, 1957, 1964, 1968, 1973, 1975, 1983, 1986, 1996, 2004, 2005, 2009, 2017
110 cartridge film: 1972
120 roll film: 1901
126 cartridge film: 1963
127 roll film: 1912
135 film: 1934, 1936, 1953, 1964, 2003

Abbe, Ernst: 1866, 1873, 1884
   *See also: Zeiss (Jena)*
Abrahamsson, Tom: 1987, 2017
   *See also: Rapidwinder*
Achromat lens: 1758, 1839
   *See also: Hall, Chester Moore*
Actinograph, The: 1888
ACM, *Salzburg*: 1990
   *See also: Leica Camera AG*
Adams, Ansel: 1932, 1933, 1936, 1952, 1984
Adcock, Willis: 1961, 1972
Adox: 1860, 1888, 1947, 2009
Adonal: 1888
Aerial photographs: 1915
Aeronautical Research Institute: 1923
   *See also: Nippon Kogaku KK*
Agfa (Germany): 1867, 1880, 1888, 1914, 1928
   *See also: Agfa-Ansco*
   *See also: Anthony & Co.,*
   *See also: Scovill Mfg. Co.*
Agfa (West Germany): 1953, 1959, 1964, 1965, 2000, 2004

   *See also: AgfaPhoto GmbH*
Agfa-Ansco Corporation: 1928, 1939
   *See also: Anthony & Company,*
   *See also: GAF Corp.*
   *See also: Scovill Mfg. Company*
Agfacolor: 1914, 1939, 1945, 1947
Agfa-Gavaert: 1964
   *See also: Agfa (West Germany)*
   *See also: Gavaert, Lieven*
AgfaPhoto GmbH: 2004
Akira, Ogihara: 1946, 1947
Albumen emulsion: 1844, 1847, 1851, 1853
Allied Impex Corporation: 1956
   *See also: Miranda*
Alpa cameras: 1918, 1923, 1936, 1942, 1948, 1949, 1950, 1990, 1996, 2016
Alpha-Cine film: 2009
Ambrotype: 1853, 1854, 1856, 2018
*American Photo* magazine: 2015
Ampex Corp: 1951
Anastigmat lens: 1890, 1950
   *See also: Carl Zeiss (Jena)*
   *See also: Rudolph, Paul*
Asanuma Shōkai lens makers: 1867, 1974
Anderson, J.: 1900
Android: 2012
Angénieux, Pierre: 1936, 1950, 1994
   *See also: Retrofocus*
Anschütz, Ottomar: 1886
Ansco: 1842, 1914, 1927, 1928, 1939, 1940, 1941, 1962, 1965
Anscochrome film: 1941
Ansco colour film: 1941
Anthony, Edward: 1842
Anthony, Henry T.: 1842

Anthony & Company, E. & H.T.: 1879, 1902, 1907
Anti-aliasing filter: 2012
Anytar lens: 1917, 1930
   *See also: Nippon Kogaku KK*
Aoco: 1919
Aperture Foundation: 1952
*Aperture* magazine: 1952
Aplanat lens: 1866
Apple: 1987, 1994
Apochromat lens: 1763, 1975
   *See also: Dolland, Peter*
APS *(Advanced Photo System)*: 1996
Arbus, Diane: 1957, 1971
Archer, Frederick Scott: 1851, 1857
   *See also: Collodion*
Argentina (cameras): 1941
Argus camera: 1936, 1938, 1939
Arizona Optical Systems: 2019
Armstrong, Neil: 1969
Arnold & Richter Cine Technik: 1917
Arriflex Cine cameras: 1917
Arsenal factory: 1764, 1945, 1972, 1987, 2005
*Asahi Camera* magazine (Japan): 1926
Asahiflex camera: 1952, 1954, 1957
   *See also: Asahi Optical Co.*
   *See also: Pentax*
Asahi Kōgaku Kōgyō G.K.: 1919, 1931
   *See also: Asahi Optical Co.*
   *See also: Pentax*
Asahi Optical Co.: 1954, 1960, 1961, 1969, 1971, 1977
   *See also: Pentax*
Asahi Pentar: 1957
Aspherical lens: 1901, 1952, 1956, 1966, 2004
   *See also: Von Rohr,*
   *See also: Zeiss (Jena)*

# About the Writer

Canadian photographer David Young has been behind a camera since the early 1960s, capturing images in 34 countries. His articles and photographs have appeared in numerous newspapers and magazines, in both Canada and the USA, while his photographs grace walls from the Ukraine to Abu Dhabi to Tasmania.

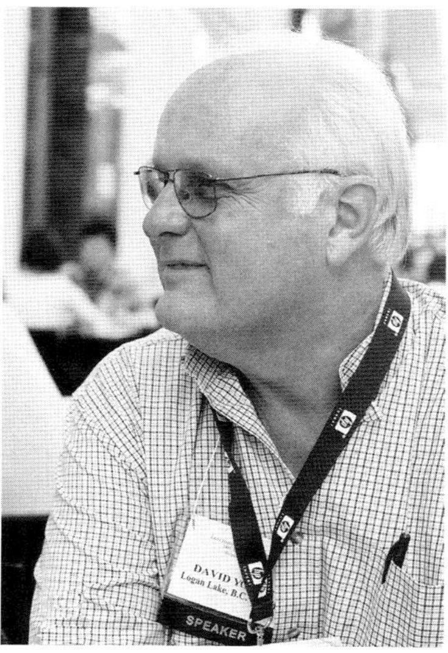

David has been a guest speaker and presenter at photographer's conventions in Germany, across the USA, and, of course, his native Canada. He has judged the National Nature and National Open competitions for CAPA *(The Canadian Assoc. for Photographic Art)* and has served on the board of the International Leica Society.

Now retired, he has found time to write and lives with his wife, dog, and two cats in Logan Lake, B.C., Canada

*Photo courtesy of Alex Hurst (Ireland)*